T0394976

Saints' Lives for
Medieval English Nuns, I

MEDIEVAL WOMEN: TEXTS AND CONTEXTS

Editorial Board under the auspices of the School of Philosophical,
Historical & International Studies, Monash University

General Editors

Constant J. Mews, *Monash University*

Editorial Board

Renate Blumenfeld-Kosinski, *University of Pittsburgh*
Miri Rubin, *Queen Mary University of London*
Gabriela Signori, *Universität Konstanz*
Claire M. Waters, *University of California, Davis*
Nicholas Watson, *Harvard University*
Barbara Zimbalist, *University of Texas at El Paso*

Previously published volumes in this series are listed at the back of the book.

VOLUME 18

Saints' Lives for Medieval English Nuns, I

A Study of the 'Lyves and Dethes' in Cambridge University Library, MS Additional 2604

Veronica O'Mara and Virginia Blanton

BREPOLS

British Library Cataloguing in Publication Data

A catalogue record for this book is available from the British Library.

© 2023, Brepols Publishers n.v., Turnhout, Belgium

All rights reserved. No part of this publication may be reproduced,
stored in a retrieval system, or transmitted, in any form or by any means,
electronic, mechanical, photocopying, recording, or otherwise,
without the prior permission of the publisher.

D/2023/0095/243
ISBN: 978-2-503-54551-6
e-ISBN: 978-2-503-56282-7
DOI: 10.1484/M.MWTC-EB.5.106988
ISSN: 1782-3366
e-ISSN: 2294-8406
Printed in the EU on acid-free paper

Dedicated to the memory
of our beloved mothers

Mary O'Mara
(née Tynan)

and

Bonnie Scott Blanton

Contents

List of Illustrations	viii
Acknowledgements	xiii
Abbreviations and References	xvii
Colour Plates	xix
Preface	xxvii
I. The Manuscript	1
II. Language and Dialectal Provenance	69
III. Convent and Geographical Location	107
IV. Hagiographical Context and the Selection of Saints	159
V. Latin Sources and Analogues	213
VI. Reading the 'Lyves and Dethes'	271
Conclusion	309
Appendix 1. Universal Latin Saints' Lives: Sources and Analogues	311
Appendix 2. Latin and Middle English Versions of Æthelthryth	323
Appendix 3. Middle English Translations of John the Evangelist	337
Bibliography	343
Index	385

List of Illustrations

Colour Plates

Plate 1. John the Baptist, with cadel head and title 'The lyves and dethes of the martyres' glued in fol. 1r, Cambridge, Cambridge University Library, MS Additional 2604. Reproduced by kind permission of the Syndics of Cambridge University Library. xix

Plate 2. Cecilia and Barbara, fol. 47v, Cambridge, Cambridge University Library, MS Additional 2604. Reproduced by kind permission of the Syndics of Cambridge University Library. xx

Plate 3. Barbara and Æthelthryth, fol. 52v, Cambridge, Cambridge University Library, MS Additional 2604. Reproduced by kind permission of the Syndics of Cambridge University Library. xxi

Plate 4. Eormenhild and Wærburh, with cadel head, fol. 62v, Cambridge, Cambridge University Library, MS Additional 2604. Reproduced by kind permission of the Syndics of Cambridge University Library. xxii

Plate 5. Eorcengota and Wihtburh, with cadel head and strapwork, fol. 66v, Cambridge, Cambridge University Library, MS Additional 2604. Reproduced by kind permission of the Syndics of Cambridge University Library. xxiii

Plate 6. Martha, fol. 93v, Cambridge, Cambridge University Library, MS Additional 2604. Reproduced by kind permission of the Syndics of Cambridge University Library. xxiv

Plate 7. Martha and Domitilla, fol. 97v, Cambridge, Cambridge University Library, MS Additional 2604. Reproduced by kind permission of the Syndics of Cambridge University Library. xxv

Plate 8. Leonard, with cadel head and strapwork, fol. 137r, Cambridge, Cambridge University Library, MS Additional 2604. Reproduced by kind permission of the Syndics of Cambridge University Library. xxvi

LIST OF ILLUSTRATIONS

Figures

Figure 1. John the Evangelist, fol. 12r, Cambridge, Cambridge University Library, MS Additional 2604. Reproduced by kind permission of the Syndics of Cambridge University Library. 46

Figure 2. Columba, with an unusual daisy flower, fol. 22r, Cambridge, Cambridge University Library, MS Additional 2604. Reproduced by kind permission of the Syndics of Cambridge University Library. 47

Figure 3. Columba and Agatha, fol. 25v, Cambridge, Cambridge University Library, MS Additional 2604. Reproduced by kind permission of the Syndics of Cambridge University Library. 48

Figure 4. Wærburh and Eorcengota, fol. 65r, Cambridge, Cambridge University Library, MS Additional 2604. Reproduced by kind permission of the Syndics of Cambridge University Library. 49

Figure 5. Eadburh, with pen flourishing in the left margin, fol. 78v, Cambridge, Cambridge University Library, MS Additional 2604. Reproduced by kind permission of the Syndics of Cambridge University Library. 50

Figure 6. Eadburh and Eanswith, with contracted spraywork and marginal annotation of 'vanitas', fol. 79r, Cambridge, Cambridge University Library, MS Additional 2604. Reproduced by kind permission of the Syndics of Cambridge University Library. 51

Figure 7. Martha, Domitilla, and Justina, with full spraywork in the left margin of fol. 97v and compressed spraywork in the left margin of fol. 98r, fols 97v–98r, Cambridge, Cambridge University Library, MS Additional 2604. Reproduced by kind permission of the Syndics of Cambridge University Library. 52–53

Figure 8. Modwenna, without spraywork, fol. 113r, Cambridge, Cambridge University Library, MS Additional 2604. Reproduced by kind permission of the Syndics of Cambridge University Library. 54

Figure 9. Section summaries written in textura in Modwenna, fol. 124v, Cambridge, Cambridge University Library, MS Additional 2604. Reproduced by kind permission of the Syndics of Cambridge University Library. 55

Figure 10. Catchword 'fraunce' in Leonard on fol. 139v, which is only fully visible under ultraviolet light, Cambridge, Cambridge University Library, MS Additional 2604. Reproduced by kind permission of the Syndics of Cambridge University Library. 56

Figure 11. Script of London, British Library, MS Harley 5272, fol. 137v. © The British Library Board and reproduced by kind permission. 57

Figure 12. Script of Cambridge, Trinity College, MS. R. 3. 21, fol. 257r. Reproduced by kind permission of The Master and Fellows of Trinity College, Cambridge.. 58

Figure 13. Fragment of an antiphoner bound in at the opening of the manuscript, fol. ii recto, Cambridge, Cambridge University Library, MS Additional 2604. Reproduced by kind permission of the Syndics of Cambridge University Library. 59

Figure 14. 'Condemne no man' pasted in on paper towards the beginning of the manuscript, fol. vi recto, Cambridge, Cambridge University Library, MS Additional 2604. Reproduced by kind permission of the Syndics of Cambridge University Library. 60

Figure 15. List of saints' lives added by Reverend George Burton at the beginning of the manuscript, fol. xxx recto, Cambridge, Cambridge University Library, MS Additional 2604. Reproduced by kind permission of the Syndics of Cambridge University Library.. . . . 60

Figure 16. Note about the handwriting of Reverend George Burton, with a stamp of 'BURY', written on the back of the list of saints' lives, fol. xxx verso, Cambridge, Cambridge University Library, MS Additional 2604. Reproduced by kind permission of the Syndics of Cambridge University Library. 61

LIST OF ILLUSTRATIONS

Figure 17. 'Life of St Christopher' in verse at the end of the manuscript, fol. xxxi recto, Cambridge, Cambridge University Library, MS Additional 2604. Reproduced by kind permission of the Syndics of Cambridge University Library........................ 62

Figure 18. 'On St Benedict and the Benedictines' in prose at the end of the manuscript, fol. xxxiv recto, Cambridge, Cambridge University Library, MS Additional 2604. Reproduced by kind permission of the Syndics of Cambridge University Library............ 63

Figure 19. Ownership inscription by G. B. Burrell, noting its acquisition from George Tasburgh in 1788, fol. 75v, Cambridge, Cambridge University Library, MS Additional 2604. Reproduced by kind permission of the Syndics of Cambridge University Library..... 64

Figure 20. Signed inscription by George Bird Burrell, London, British Library, MS Additional 39177, fol. 9r. © The British Library Board and reproduced by kind permission. 65

Figure 21. Countermark of James Whatman of the Whatman firm, fols viii recto, Cambridge, Cambridge University Library, MS Additional 2604. Reproduced by kind permission of the Syndics of Cambridge University Library.................................. 66

Figure 22. St Peter's Hall, St Peter South Elmham, Suffolk, the home of the Flixton Tasburghs in the sixteenth century and later. Photo by the Authors... 67

Figure 23. St Mary's Church, Flixton, Suffolk, where many of the early Tasburghs are interred. Photo by the Authors................... 67

Figure 24. Part of the remains of the Church of St George's Nunnery, Thetford, Norfolk. Photo by Mike Toms. Reproduced by kind permission of the British Trust for Ornithology...................... 68

Tables

Table 1. List of Medieval Saints' Lives in Add. 2604 3

Table 2. Female Communities in East Anglia and Beyond.................... 112

Table 3. The Add. 2604 Universal Lives in Early Continental
Latin Legendaries.. 173

Table 4. The Add. 2604 Lives in Late Medieval Continental
Latin Legendaries.. 174

Table 5. The Add. 2604 Universal Saints in a Selection of
Early Printed Sermons.. 175

ACKNOWLEDGEMENTS

Our first debt of gratitude is to the inestimable Godfrey Waller, the former superintendent of the Manuscripts Reading Room in Cambridge University Library, to whom we owe our initial acquaintance; we are very grateful to him for indirectly initiating what has been an enduring collaboration from which we have both greatly profited. It is always a pleasure and a privilege to work in the Manuscripts Reading Room in Cambridge; this is due to the range of facilities available but particularly to the efficiency and kindness of the staff, to all of whom we are deeply thankful, especially to Frank Bowles, Louise Clarke, and Suzanne Paul. We are indebted to the Syndics of Cambridge University Library for granting permission for the reproduction of the images from MS Additional 2604 on the cover and in the body of the book and for the publication of an edition of it in our companion volume, *Saints' Lives for Medieval English Nuns, II: An Edition of the 'Lyves and Dethes' in Cambridge University Library, MS Additional 2604*. Gratitude is also extended to the following for permission to reproduce material in their care: the Board of the British Library; the British Trust for Ornithology (BTO) and the Archivist, Lesley Hindley for facilitating the images; and the Master and Fellows of Trinity College, Cambridge.

Particular thanks is due to the archivists, keepers of manuscripts, and librarians at the various institutions where we have consulted material in person: Advocates Library, Edinburgh; Alnwick Castle, The Archives of the Duke of Northumberland, Alnwick; Badische Landesbibliothek, Karlsruhe; Bibliotheek van het Ruusbroecgenootschap, Antwerp; Bibliothèque royale de Belgique/ Koninklijke Bibliotheek van België (KBR), Brussels; Bodleian Library, the University of Oxford; the Bollandist Research Institute and Library, Brussels; British Library, London; Cambridge University Library, Cambridge; Christ's College, Cambridge; Durham University Library, Palace Green, Durham; East Riding Archives, Beverley; Edinburgh University Library, Edinburgh; Folger Shakespeare Library, Washington, D.C.; Glasgow University Library,

Glasgow; Gray's Inn Library, London; Huntington Library, San Marino, California; Institute of Historical Research, London; John Rylands University Library, Manchester; King's College, Cambridge; Lambeth Palace Library; Library of Congress, Washington; Liverpool University Library, Liverpool; The National Archives (TNA), London; National Library of Scotland, Edinburgh; Norfolk Public Record Office, Norwich; Queen's College, Oxford; Sheffield City Archives and Local Studies Library, Sheffield; Sidney Sussex College, Cambridge; Special Collections, Leeds University Library, Leeds; Suffolk Archives, Bury St Edmunds, Ipswich, and Lowestoft; Thetford Library, Thetford; Trinity College, Cambridge; Trinity College, Dublin; Ushaw College, Durham; Warburg Institute, London; Wellcome Collection, London; Westminster Abbey Library, London; York Minster Library, York. In addition, our research would not have been possible on a day-to-day basis without access to the excellent holdings of Leeds University Library and Miller Nichols Library, University of Missouri-Kansas City. The staff at the above institutions were very helpful and we are so grateful to them, but we should particularly like to thank those who went beyond the call of duty: Christopher Hunwick, The Archives of the Duke of Northumberland, Alnwick Castle, Alnwick; Patricia De Bruyn and Joke De Wilde, Bibliotheek van het Ruusbroecgenootschap; Pietro d'Agostino, François de Vriendt, and Robert Gooding, the Bollandist Research Institute and Library; Tamsyn Chadwick, British Library (Boston Spa); Lucy Hughes, Christ's College, Cambridge; Carlotta Barranu, Eton College Library; Andrew Parry, Gloucestershire Archives; Jérôme Beck, Mickey Redant, and Pascal Trousse, KBR; Grace Watson, Suffolk Archives (Ipswich); Ivan Bunn, Neil Coles, and Chloe Pearson, Suffolk Archives (Lowestoft); and Kaleigh Garrod, Thetford Library.

This book has been a long time in production, addressing as it does a unique set of texts whose complicated context and history had to be investigated *ab initio* and which are edited for the first time in our companion volume. We have done our utmost to cast light on the subject but wish to apologise in advance for any errors that remain in the volume. As with any scholarly endeavour, at various points we have received advice and/or answers to queries from a range of experts and to all of them we are deeply thankful: David Bagchi, Richard Beadle, Caroline Bowden, Margaret Connolly, Pietro Delcorno, Mathilde van Dijk, Clarck Drieshen, Martha Driver, Brenda Dunn-Lardeau, Andrew Dunning, Tony Edwards, Vincent Gillespie, the late Richard Hamer, Ralph Hanna, Simon Horobin, Holly James-Maddocks, Michael Kuczynski, Jason Lawrence, Julian Luxford, Mary Beth Long, Paolo Maggioni, William Marx, Linne Mooney, Nigel Morgan, Suzanne Paul, the late Richard Pfaff, Oliver

ACKNOWLEDGEMENTS

Pickering, Kari Anne Rand, Sherry Reames, Laurie Ringer, Olivia Robinson, Nicholas Rogers, Courtney Rydel, Selene Scarsi, Kathleen Scott, Jeremy Smith, Mike Toms, and Daniel Wakelin. Above all we are grateful to Susan Powell and Patricia Stoop for all their encouragement and scholarly assistance. We are especially indebted to the work of the late Nesta Evans and that of Francis Young; without their invaluable historical research on the Tasburgh family, our work would be the poorer. We are grateful to the organisers of the various conferences for inviting one or other of us (and sometimes both), and the audiences for their valuable comments, at the venues where we gave papers: Auckland; Bochum; Cambridge; Columbia (Missouri); Dublin; Exeter; Hull; Kalamazoo; Leeds; London; Poughkeepsie; and Sydney. We are immensely grateful to the Institute for Medieval Studies at the University of Leeds and Women's, Gender, and Sexualities and the Faculty Research Grant programs at the University of Missouri-Kansas City, for supporting our work.

Our research have been greatly helped by two site visits: one to Flixton and St Peter's Hall, St Peter South Elmham, in Suffolk and one to Thetford in Norfolk. Jill Hall, the former owner of St Peter's Hall, provided a guided tour in September 2018 and in July 2020 Lesley Hindley introduced us to what remains of St George's Convent at the headquarters of the BTO at Nunnery Place, Thetford. To both of them we extend our gratitude. Kindly companionship and enthusiastic help for the first visit were provided by the late Maria Morgan (d. 30 December 2020); in the second visit we were greatly aided by Nathan Oyler and Scout Blanton Oyler. We are inestimably thankful to them and to all the other members of our families.

We are indebted to the Editorial Board of Medieval Women: Texts and Contexts and to the series editor, Constant Mews, for accepting this volume into its series and for helpful comments at the peer review stage. Above all our gratitude goes to the wonderful Guy Carney, Publications Manager at Brepols, who has rendered us every assistance over many years and to our superlative typesetter, Martine Maguire-Weltecke.

We gratefully acknowledge financial support from the Marc Fitch Fund towards publication costs.

Finally, we lovingly dedicate this book to our dear mothers, our first educators, the late Mary O'Mara (d. 16 March 2020) and Bonnie Scott Blanton (d. 22 September 2023).

Veronica O'Mara and Virginia Blanton
8 October 2023

ABBREVIATIONS AND REFERENCES

Acta sanctorum   *Acta Sanctorum [...]*, ed. by the Société des Bollandistes, 67 vols (Anvers & Bruxelles, and other places: Société des Bollandistes, 1643–1940); reproduced in an 'Impression anastaltique' by the Éditions 'Culture et Civilisation' (Bruxelles, 1966–71) and online in 1999 by Chadwyck Healey (http://acta.chadwyck.co.uk); 3rd edn (Paris and other places: Victor Palmé, 1863–71)

Bede   *Bede's Ecclesiastical History of the English People*, ed. and trans. by Bertram Colgrave and R. A. B. Mynors (Oxford: Oxford University Press, 1969; repr. 1992)

BHL   *Bibliotheca Hagiographica Latina Antiquae et Mediae Aetatis*, ed. by the Société des Bollandistes, 2 vols (Bruxelles: Société des Bollandistes, 1898–1901)

BHL *Supplementum*   *Bibliotheca Hagiographica Latina Antiquae et Mediae Aetatis Novum Supplementum*, ed. by Henricus Fros (Bruxelles: Société des Bollandistes, 1986)

BHO   British History Online (www.british-history.ac.uk)

Cantus   'Cantus: A Database for Latin Ecclesiastical Chant — Inventories of Chant Sources' (https://cantus.uwaterloo.ca)

EEBO   Early English Books Online (www.proquest.com/eebo)

EETS   Early English Text Society

eLALME   *e-LALME: A Linguistic Atlas of Late Mediaeval English* (www.amc.lel.ed.ac.uk)

Historie plurimorum sanctorum   Jacobus de Voragine, *Legenda aurea sanctorum, sive Lombardica historia* [and] *Incipiu[n]t historie pl[ur]imor[um] s[an]c[t]or[um] novit[er] addite laboriose collecte [et] p[ro]lo[n]gate* (Köln: [Ulrich Zel], 1483); *Historie plurimorum sanctorum* (Louvain: Johannes de Westfalia, October 1485)

KBR   Bibliothèque royale de Belgique/Koninklijke Bibliotheek van België

LALME   Angus McIntosh, M. L. Samuels, and Michael Benskin, *A Linguistic Atlas of Late Mediaeval English*, 4 vols (Aberdeen: Aberdeen University Press, 1986)

Legenda aurea	Iacopo da Varazze, *Legenda aurea con le miniature del codice Ambrosiano C 240 inf.*, ed. by Giovanni Paolo Maggioni, Edizione nazionale dei testi mediolatini, 20, 2 vols (Firenze: Sismel & Milano: Biblioteca Ambrosiana, 2007)
Liber Eliensis	*Liber Eliensis*, ed. by E. O. Blake, Camden Society, Third Series, 92 (London: Royal Historical Society, 1962)
MED	*Middle English Dictionary*, ed. by Hans Kurath, Sherman M. Kuhn, and Robert E. Lewis, 115 fascicles (Michigan, MI: University of Michigan Press, 1952–2001) (https://quod.lib.umich.edu/m/middle-english-dictionary/dictionary)
Nova Legenda Anglie	John of Tynemouth, *Nova legenda Anglie* (London: Wynkyn de Worde, 1516) (STC 4601); *Nova Legenda Anglie*, ed. by Carl Horstman, 2 vols (Oxford: Clarendon Press, 1901)
ODNB	*Oxford Dictionary of National Biography*, ed. by Brian Harrison (Oxford: Oxford University Press, 2004) (www.oxforddnb.com)
Sanctilogium	John of Tynemouth, *Sanctilogium Angliae Walliae Scotiae et Hiberniae*
Sanctuarium	Boninus Mombritius, *Sanctuarium sive Vitae Sanctorum* ([Milano: Printer for Boninus Mombritius, *c.* 1477); Boninus Mombritius, *Sanctuarium seu Vitae Sanctorum*, ed. by Two Monks of Solesmes, 2 vols (Paris: Albertus Fontemoing, 1910)
STC	A. W. Pollard, and G. R. Redgrave, *A Short-Title Catalogue of Books Printed in England, Scotland, and Ireland, and of English Books Printed Abroad*, second edition, revised and enlarged by W. A. Jackson, F. S. Ferguson, and Katherine F. Pantzer, 3 vols (London: The Bibliographical Society, 1976–1991); revised at estc.bl.uk
TNA	The National Archives
USTC	Universal Short Title Catalogue (www.ustc.ac.uk)
Vincent de Beauvais	www.vincentiusbelvacensis.eu
'Who were the Nuns?'	'Who were the Nuns?: A Prosopographical Study of the English Convents in Exile 1600 1800', directed by Caroline Bowden (https://wwtn.history.qmul.ac.uk/search/howto.html)

Colour Plates

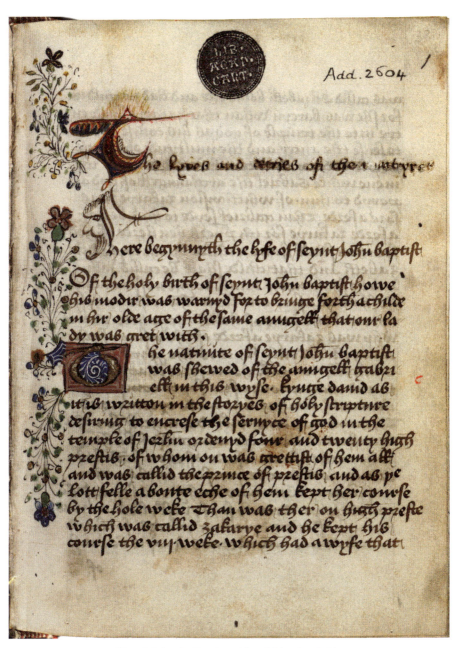

Plate 1. John the Baptist, with cadel head and title
'The lyves and dethes of the martyres' glued in, fol. 1r.

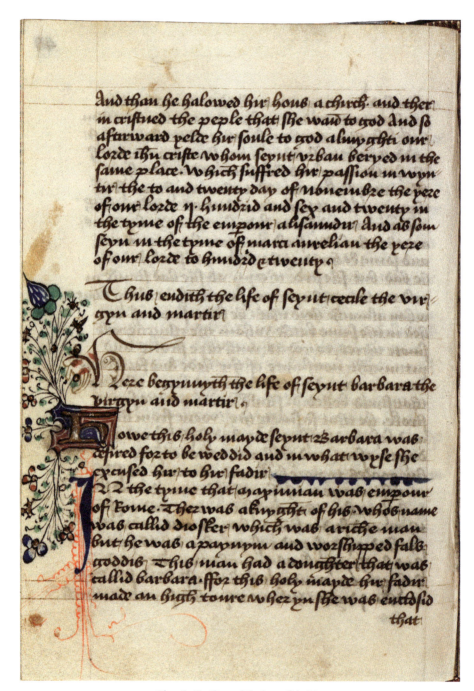

Plate 2. Cecilia and Barbara, fol. 47v.

COLOUR PLATES

body of this holy mayde and beried it in a place that
was callid soledite whereupon he bilded a litell
chapell and ther in to this day many myracles
ben wrought and many folke ben made hole
from their sekues This holy mayde seynt barbara
suffred hir passion in the empours dayes ayayu
nyau and his iustice was callid ayarcyaue
Regnynge with us our saviour ihu criste to who
be glorye roy and honour with outen eude Amē

Thus endith the martirdome of seynt barbara

The life of seynt Audry of hely

Of seynt Audre howe she was weddid to twayu
hosboudes on aftir an other and attway she was
a mayde and aftirward made nonne

he blessid virgyu seynt Audre was
the doughter of kynge Anne that
was kynge of estengloude which
had foure doughters On was clepid sey burgh
an other dilburgh the third Audre and ye fourt
witburgh This mayden seynt Audre whan
she came to age was weddid a yenst hir
with

613

Plate 3. Barbara and Æthelthryth, fol. 52v.

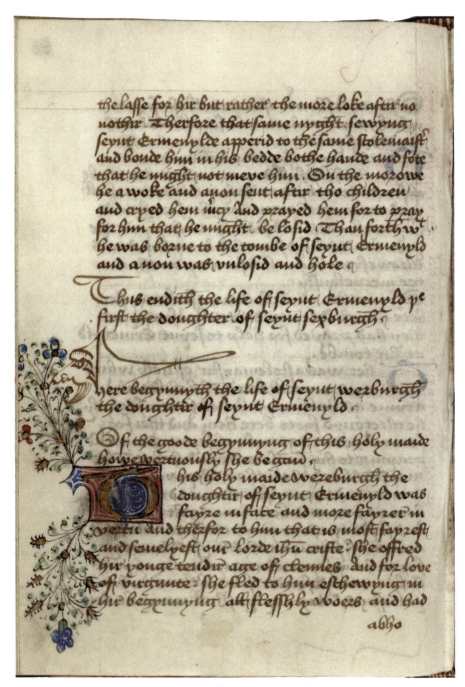

Plate 4. Eormenhild and Wærburh, with cadel head, fol. 62v.

COLOUR PLATES   xxiii

in the same monastery of brige and was an abbes
of the same She lyved also in grete abstinens and
wakyng and pyers And so passid the seventh day
Jenle that is vp on the tyslacion of seynt thomas
of Caunthery Seven yere aftir hir body was
founde vncorrupt and vnrotid ffor like as she lyved
vndefoulid and vncorrupt from all flesshly lustis
right so she was founde vncorrupt aftir hir deth
blessid be maydenhode

Thus endith shortly the lyves of seynt Erkengode
and of seynt Alburgh not the abbes of berkyng
but the abbes of brige in fraunce

[Here] begynnyth the life of seynt whitburge

howe this mayde lyved in hir monastery and aftir
howe holily she passid and of a miracle showed by
hir lyve

Seynt whitburth was the sister of
seynt awdre of hely and seynt Sex-   of
burgh and of seynt Alburgh of brige
The holines of lyving of this virgyne whitburgh and hir clennes shewith well by the
holy body of hir that lay in the grounde aftir
hir passing the hundreth yere and almost four
and fourty vncorrupte This holy mayde whi-
                                              ¶ this

Plate 5. Eorcengota and Wihtburh, with cadel head and strapwork, fol. 66v.

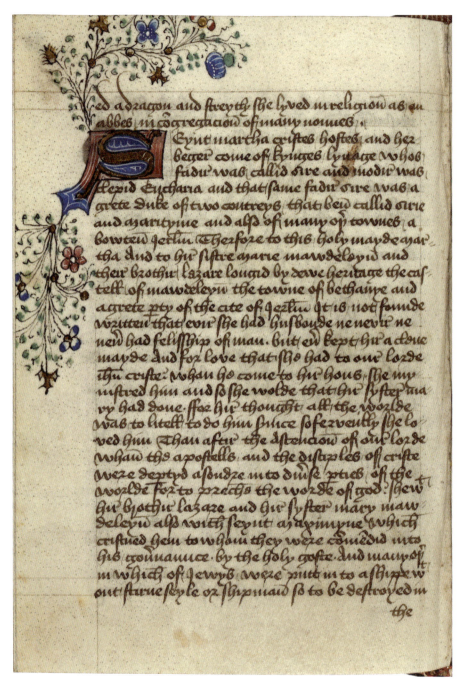

...ed a dragon and streyth she lyved in religion as an
abbes in cōgregacioū of many nonnes.

Eynt martha cristes hostes and her
better come of kynges lynage whos
fadir was callid sire and modir was
clepid Eucharia and that same fadir sire was a
grete duke of two cuntreys that beu callid sire
and azarityne and also of many of townes a-
bowten jerlm. Therfore to this holy mayde martha and to hir sistre marie mawdeleyn and
their brothir lazare longid by dowe heritage the cas-
tell of mawdeleyn the towne of bethanye and
a grete pty of the cite of jerlm. It is not founde
written that evir she hed husbonde ne nevir ne
neu had felisship of man. but eu kept hir a clene
mayde and for love that she had to our lorde
ihu criste. whan he come to hir hous she my-
nistred him and so she wolde that hir syster mary had done. ffor hir thought all the worlde
was to litell to do him sithe so ferveutly she loved him. than after the ascencion of our lorde
whan the apostells and the disciples of criste
were deptyd asondre into diuse ptyes of the
worlde for to preche the worde of god. shew
hir brothir lazare and hir syster mary mawdeleyn also with seynt azymyne which
cristened hem to whom they were cōmedid into
his gouuaunce by the holy goste. and many of
in which of Jewys were putt in to a shippe w'out
sturne syle or shipmaid so to be destroyed in
the

Plate 6. Martha, fol. 93v.

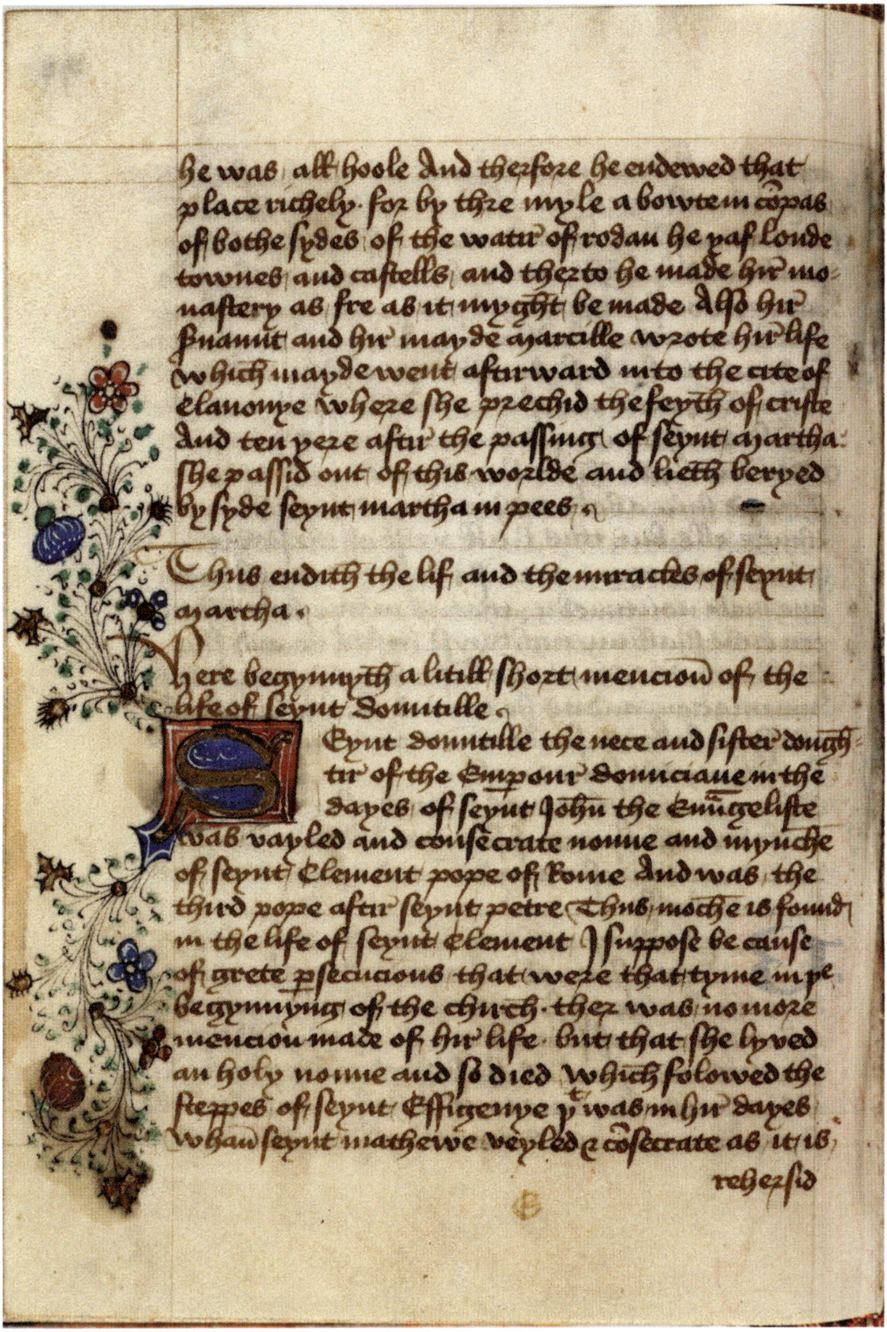

COLOUR PLATES   XXV

he was all hoole And therfore he endewed that
place rychely for by thre myle a bowt in compas
off bothe sydes off the watur off rodan he pas loude
townes and castells and therto he made hir mo
nastery as fre as it myght be made Also hir
frunnit and hir mayde ajarcille wrote hir life
which mayde went afturward into the cite of
elanonye where she prechid the feyth off cryste
And ten yere aftir the passing of seynt ajartha
she passid out off this worlde and lieth beryed
by syde seynt martha in pees

Thus endith the lif and the miracles of seynt
ajartha

Here begynnyth a litill short mencion off the
life of seynt Domitille

Seynt Domitille the nece and sister daugh
tir of the Emperour Domiciaue in the
dayes off seynt John the Euntgeliste
was vayled and consecrate nonne and in such
of seynt Clement pope off Rome And was the
third pope aftir seynt petre Thus moche is found
in the life of seynt Clement I suppose be cause
off grete psecucions that were that tyme in þe
begynnyng off the church ther was no more
menciou made off hir life but that she lyved
an holy nonne and so died Which folowed the
steppes off seynt Effigenye þ was in hir dayes
whau seynt mathewe veyled & cosecrate as it is
                                                rehersid

Plate 7. Martha and Domitilla, fol. 97v.

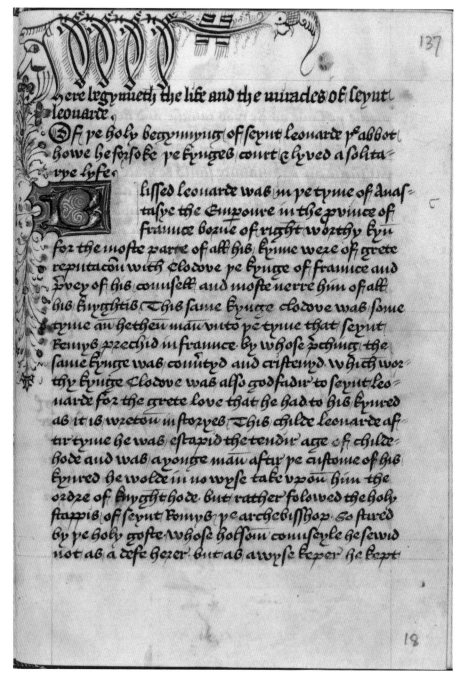

Plate 8. Leonard, with cadel head and strapwork, fol. 137r.

PREFACE

Cambridge University Library MS Additional 2604 (hereafter Add. 2604) contains a unique (anonymous) legendary almost entirely of female saints, all of whom are virgins, martyrs, or nuns, and all rendered in Middle English prose. The (imperfect) manuscript, which has until now been unedited and virtually unstudied, is written in one hand of the last quarter of the fifteenth century or a little later (probably *c.* 1480–1510).[1] It is consistent linguistically and clearly dependent on a mixture of Latin sources and analogues by Jacobus de Voragine, John of Tynemouth, and much else besides. The lives of three male saints, John the Baptist and John the Evangelist at the opening and Leonard at the end, frame a very eclectic collection. The grouping of universal and native saints begins with the virgin martyrs: Columba of Sens, Agatha, Cecilia, and Barbara, followed by ten lives of English saints, some

---

[1] From information first provided by Veronica O'Mara and Jayne Ringrose, Oliver Pickering provided a very brief listing of the lives in Add. 2604 in his survey of 'Saints' Lives', in *A Companion to Middle English Prose*, ed. by A. S. G. Edwards (Cambridge: Brewer, 2004), pp. 249–70 (p. 258). Virginia Blanton discussed part of the manuscript in *Signs of Devotion: The Cult of St. Æthelthryth in Medieval England, 695–1615* (University Park, PA: The Pennsylvania State University Press, 2007), pp. 257–73. The manuscript was catalogued in 2009: Jayne Ringrose, *Summary Catalogue of the Additional Medieval Manuscripts in Cambridge University Library Acquired before 1940* (Woodbridge: Boydell, 2009), pp. 16–17. The first essay to discuss this manuscript as a whole is Veronica O'Mara and Virginia Blanton, 'Cambridge University Library, Additional MS 2604: Repackaging Female Saints' Lives for the Fifteenth-Century English Nun', *Journal of the Early Book Society*, 13 (2010), 237–47, followed by Virginia Blanton, 'The Devotional Reading of Nuns: Three Legendaries of Native Saints in Late Medieval England', in *Nuns' Literacies in Medieval Europe: The Hull Dialogue*, ed. by Virginia Blanton, Veronica O'Mara, and Patricia Stoop, Medieval Women: Texts and Contexts, 26 (Turnhout: Brepols, 2013), pp. 185–206. In addition, a few other scholars have referred briefly to Add. 2604: Cynthia Turner Camp, *Anglo-Saxon Saints' Lives as History Writing in Late Medieval England* (Cambridge: Brewer, 2015), pp. 91–101; Catherine Sanok, *New Legends of England: Forms of Community in Late Medieval Saints' Lives* (Philadelphia, PA: University of Pennsylvania Press, 2018), passim; and Jessica C. Brown, 'The Birthplace of Saint Wulfthryth: An Unexamined Reference in Cambridge University Library Additional 2604', *Quidditas*, 42 (2021), 220–25.

of whom have familial ties and geographical associations: Æthelthryth of Ely (Cambridgeshire); her sisters, Seaxburh and Wihtburh; Seaxburh's daughters, Eormenhild and Eorcengota; and Eormenhild's daughter, Wærburh of Chester (Cheshire).[2] There is also a brief account of Æthelburh, another of Æthelthryth's sisters, appended to the end of the life of Eorcengota and a comment about a half-sister, Sæthryth, included in the account of Eorcengota.[3] In addition to the Ely saints, there are several luminaries of the early English Church: Edith of Wilton (Wiltshire); Eanswith of Folkestone (Kent); Eadburh of Minster-in-Thanet (Kent); and Hild of Whitby (Northumberland). These English saints are followed by another mixture of universal lives, starting with the biblical Martha, complemented by the martyrs Domitilla, Justina, and Benedicta, and ending with the insular Modwenna, and the French Leonard.

With the exception of Eormenhild (as presented in John of Tynemouth and thus Add. 2604), the Ely women were all abbesses and they comprise more than a quarter of the saints represented in the codex.[4] This emphasis suggests that the manuscript was produced near the cult centre at Ely, where four of the women were buried, or in some locale in East Anglia, where medieval devotion to Æthelthryth and her family is most densely attested, and which is also a suitable linguistic fit for the dialect in the manuscript. The legendary, currently comprising eleven universal and eleven native saints, is a welcome addition to other col-

---

[2] In all quotations from the manuscript in this *Study* we cite our own *Edition*; for example, a quotation from line 5 of the first life (John the Baptist) will be given as 1/5.

[3] By universal saints are meant those celebrated across the Christian Church, such as John the Baptist and Cecilia, as opposed to native English saints such as Edith of Wilton; some saints, such as the hermit Leonard, are counted as universal saints but also have local (or native) significance, in this case particularly in the area of Noblac (now Saint-Léonard) near Limoges in France. In referring to the native or insular saints (with their historic localisations) we use some standard nomenclature, and if possible, the native language forms to signify their historic origins. It should be noted, however, that in the scholarly tradition these saints are also commonly referred to as follows, depending on whether a Latinised, semi-Latinised, or later English version of the name is being provided: Etheldreda, Audrée, or Audrey (Awdry); Sexburga; Withburga; Ermenhilda; Earcengota; Ethelburga; Saethryd; Eanswida, Edburga or Eadburga, and Hilda. Edith (not Eadgyth) and Osith (not Osyth or Osgyth) have been retained, as they are the most usual forms. We recognise the inconsistency of this approach. Honouring native spellings in nomenclature is the ideal, but even this remains difficult where little consistency can be found in the manuscript or scholarly traditions. Furthermore, as far as possible references to locations ignore the 1974 local government boundary changes; for example, we cite Whitby in Northumbria rather than in North Yorkshire.

[4] In the Ely tradition, however, Eormenhild is abbess, first of Minster-in-Sheppey and second at Ely. The other figure who is not represented as an abbess in Add. 2604 is Eanswith.

PREFACE   xxix

lections that often feature only universal saints or just native saints but not both. This collection of Middle English prose, clearly made available for a readership of women religious, offers a new and particularly significant avenue of research for those interested in female reading and piety. It demonstrates important insights into the production and transmission of hagiographical texts in late medieval England especially when set against European developments in Latin and the vernaculars. Coming at the end of the Middle Ages, the manuscript has an involved transmission history, with the saints' lives being supplemented by various post-medieval material. At one point it was owned by the brother of the reigning English monarch and its fractured ownership history also provides important evidence for links between the medieval past and post-Reformation Catholic recusant England. We present our findings, all based on primary research,[5] in an effort to reveal fully what we have discovered over many years of intensive study of the fascinating complexities of the saints' lives in Add. 2604 that are published for the first time in our companion volume, *Saints' Lives for Medieval English Nuns, II: An Edition of the 'Lyves and Dethes' in Cambridge University Library, MS Additional 2604* (hereafter *Edition*).[6]

[5] The list of manuscripts and archival material consulted in the course of this *Study* is too lengthy to detail here so we refer readers to the relevant sections of our Bibliography.

[6] Edited by Veronica O'Mara and Virginia Blanton, Medieval Women: Texts and Contexts, 32 (Turnhout: Brepols, 2024). We also note here some of the significant work we have used in our wider research on female piety and devotional reading in medieval England; this list (which does not include editions of texts) is by no means complete as other contributions will be noted elsewhere in the volume: Gail McMurray Gibson, *The Theater of Devotion: East Anglian Drama and Society in the Late Middle Ages* (Chicago, IL: University of Chicago Press, 1989); Eamon Duffy, 'Holy Maydens, Holy Wyves: The Cult of Women Saints in Fifteenth- and Sixteenth-Century England', *Studies in Church History*, 27 (1990), 175–96; Jocelyn Wogan-Browne, 'Saints' Lives and the Female Reader', *Forum for Modern Language Studies*, 27 (1991), 314–32; Stephanie Hollis, *Anglo-Saxon Women and the Church: Sharing a Common Fate* (Woodbridge: Boydell and Brewer, 1992); Jocelyn Wogan-Browne, 'Chaste Bodies: Frames and Experiences', in *Framing Medieval Bodies*, ed. by Sarah Kay and Miri Rubin (Manchester: Manchester University Press, 1994), pp. 24–42; Jocelyn Wogan-Browne, 'The Virgin's Tale', in *Feminist Readings in Middle English Literature: The Wife of Bath and All Her Sect*, ed. by Ruth Evans and Lesley Johnson (London: Routledge, 1994), pp. 165–94; David N. Bell, *What Nuns Read: Books and Libraries in Medieval English Nunneries*, Cistercian Studies Series, 158 (Kalamazoo, MI: Cistercian Publications, 1995); Karen A. Winstead, *Virgin Martyrs: Legends of Sainthood in Late Medieval England* (Ithaca, NY: Cornell University Press, 1997); Marilyn Oliva, *The Convent and the Community in Late Medieval England: Female Monasteries in the Diocese of Norwich, 1350–1540*, Studies in the History of Medieval Religion, 12 (Woodbridge: Boydell, 1998); Mary Erler, 'Devotional Literature' and Carol M. Meale and Julia Boffey, 'Gentlewomen's Reading', in *The Cambridge History of the Book in Britain*, III: *1400–*

1557, ed. by Lotte Hellinga and J. B. Trapp (Cambridge: Cambridge University Press, 1999), pp. 495–525 and pp. 526–40 respectively; Patricia Cullum and Jeremy Goldberg, 'How Margaret Blackburn Taught Her Daughters: Reading Devotional Instruction in a Book of Hours', and Jocelyn Wogan-Browne, 'Outdoing the Daughters of Syon?: Edith of Wilton and the Representations of Female Community in Fifteenth-Century England', in *Medieval Women: Texts and Contexts in Late Medieval Britain, Essays for Felicity Riddy*, ed. by Jocelyn Wogan-Browne, and others, Medieval Women: Texts and Contexts, 3 (Turnhout: Brepols, 2000), pp. 217–36 and 393–409 respectively; Jocelyn Wogan-Browne, *Saints' Lives and Women's Literary Culture, c. 1150–1300: Virginity and its Authorizations* (Oxford: Oxford University Press, 2001); Nancy Bradley Warren, *Spiritual Economies: Female Monasticism in Later Medieval England* (Philadelphia, PA: University of Pennsylvania Press, 2001); Mary C. Erler, *Women, Reading, and Piety in Late Medieval England*, Cambridge Studies in Medieval Literature (Cambridge: Cambridge University Press, 2002); Rebecca Krug, *Reading Families: Women's Literate Practice in Late Medieval England* (Ithaca, NY: Cornell University Press, 2002); A. S. G. Edwards, 'Fifteenth-Century English Collections of Female Saints' Lives', *The Yearbook of English Studies*, 33 (2003), 131–41; Theresa Coletti, *Mary Magdalene and the Drama of Saints: Theater, Gender, and Religion in Late Medieval England*, The Middle Ages Series (Philadelphia, PA: University of Pennsylvania Press, 2004); Pickering, 'Saints' Lives'; John Scahill, with Margaret Rogerson, *Annotated Bibliographies of Old and Middle English*, VIII: *Middle English Saints' Legends* (Cambridge: Brewer, 2005); *A Companion to Middle English Hagiography*, ed. by Sarah Salih (Cambridge: Brewer, 2006); David N. Bell, 'What Nuns Read: The State of the Question' and Mary Erler, 'Private Reading in the Fifteenth- and Sixteenth-Century English Nunnery', in *The Culture of Medieval English Monasticism*, ed. by James G. Clark (Woodbridge: Boydell, 2007), pp. 113–33 and 134–46 respectively; Jessica Brantley, *Reading in the Wilderness: Private Devotion and Public Performance in Late Medieval England* (Chicago, IL: University of Chicago Press, 2007); Catherine Sanok, *Her Life Historical: Exemplarity and Female Saints' Lives in Late Medieval England*, The Middle Ages Series (Philadelphia, PA: University of Pennsylvania Press, 2007); Nicole R. Rice, *Lay Piety and Religious Discipline in Middle English Literature*, Cambridge Studies in Medieval Literature (Cambridge: Cambridge University Press, 2008); Carole Hill, *Women and Religion in Late Medieval Norwich*, Royal Historical Society Studies in History (Woodbridge: Boydell, 2010); *Barking Abbey and Medieval Literary Culture: Authorship and Authority in a Female Community*, ed. by Jennifer N. Brown and Donna Alfano Bussell (Woodbridge: York Medieval Press, 2012); Mary C. Erler, *Reading and Writing During the Dissolution: Monks, Friars, and Nuns 1530–1558* (New York: Cambridge University Press, 2013); Camp, *Anglo-Saxon Saints' Lives as History Writing in Late Medieval England*; *Sanctity as Literature in Late Medieval Britain*, ed. by Eva Von Contzen and Anke Bernau (Manchester: Manchester University Press, 2015); *Devotional Literature and Practice in Medieval England: Readers, Reading, and Reception*, ed. by Kathryn Vulić, Susan Uselmann, and C. Annette Grisé, Disputatio, 29 (Turnhout: Brepols, 2017); *Saints and Cults in Medieval England: Proceedings of the 2015 Harlaxton Symposium*, ed. by Susan Powell, Harlaxton Medieval Studies, 27 (Donington: Shaun Tyas, 2017); Sanok, *New Legends of England*; Katie Ann-Marie Bugyis, *The Care of Nuns: The Ministries of Benedictine Women in England During the Central Middle Ages* (Oxford: Oxford University Press, 2019); Laura Saetveit Miles, *The Virgin Mary's Book at the Annunciation: Reading, Interpretation, and Devotion in Medieval England* (Cambridge: Brewer, 2020); Karen A. Winstead, *Fifteenth-Century Lives: Writing Sainthood in England*, ReFormations: Medieval and Early Modern (Notre Dame, IN: Notre Dame University Press,

PREFACE   xxxi

2020); *Manuscript Culture and Medieval Devotional Traditions: Essays in Honour of Michael G. Sargent*, ed. by Jennifer N. Brown and Nicole R. Rice, York Manuscript and Early Print Studies, 1 (Woodbridge: York Medieval Press, 2021); and *Late Medieval Devotion to Saints from the North of England: New Directions*, ed. by Christiania Whitehead, Hazel J. Hunter Blair, and Denis Renevey, Medieval Church Studies, 48 (Turnhout: Brepols, 2022). Valuable European perspectives have been provided in particular by the essays in the three volumes: *Nuns' Literacies in Medieval Europe: The Hull Dialogue*, ed. by Blanton, O'Mara, and Stoop; *Nuns' Literacies in Medieval Europe: The Kansas City Dialogue*, ed. by Virginia Blanton, Veronica O'Mara, and Patricia Stoop, Medieval Women Texts and Contexts, 27 (Turnhout: Brepols, 2015); and *Nuns' Literacies in Medieval Europe: The Antwerp Dialogue*, ed. by Virginia Blanton, Veronica O'Mara, and Patricia Stoop, Medieval Women Texts and Contexts, 28 (Turnhout: Brepols, 2017).

I. THE MANUSCRIPT

The Saints' Lives

Cambridge University Library, MS Additional 2604 consists of the medieval saints' lives that are the focus of this *Study*, together with additional material in different formats. Two parchment folios from medieval liturgical Offices are found at the beginning. The saints' lives are preceded and followed by a varied range of items from the sixteenth, seventeenth, and late eighteenth centuries (or possibly early nineteenth century). These are either written or pasted in on late eighteenth- or early nineteenth-century paper. The saints' lives are therefore surrounded by an amalgam of material. For the sake of clarity, we have divided the manuscript description into two parts. The first deals with the medieval core text of saints' lives and the second takes account of the added items alongside ownership and compilation. This latter material provides contextual clues to the possible provenance and readership of this unusual legendary. Plates 1–8 and Figures 1–21 are offered to substantiate our discussion and will be referred to in the relevant sections below (with Figures 22–24 in III. Convent and Geographical Location). Most of these images present whole leaves or particular details of Add. 2604; unless otherwise indicated, all Plates and Figures are of Add. 2604.

Physical Description

This parchment manuscript, measuring approximately 186 mm x 137 mm, currently comprises 121 leaves (with 31 missing).[1] These are paginated in pencil as 1 to 152 in a modern hand; this same hand notes when pages have been cut out or gone missing. In addition, fols 1r to 26r are paginated as 1 to 49 in a hand of the late eighteenth or early nineteenth century. As noted below in Additional Contents, Ownership, and Compilation, the dimensions of the additional material, like the items themselves, are hugely varied. There is definite evidence on fols 75v, 104r, and 130r that, either before or more likely for the present

---

[1] The manuscript is described in Ringrose, *Summary Catalogue of the Additional Medieval Manuscripts in Cambridge University Library Acquired before 1940*, pp. 16–17; we are very grateful to her for showing us a draft copy in advance of her publication.

binding, the manuscript was trimmed at the top and bottom, and to a lesser extent at the sides. The partial excision of some eighteenth-century writing in the lower left-hand corner of fol. 75v demonstrates that the manuscript had to have been trimmed by at least a centimetre at the bottom and there is also some slight trimming at the side. Trimming is also supported by the evidence from the spraywork throughout the manuscript as parts of it are often cut off at the sides (and sometimes at the top or bottom). A drawing of a flower in the top margin of fol. 104r and an apparent Janus-faced type of cadel head in the top margin of fol. 130r each lack at least a centimetre. Folios 113–28 (the first two quires) of the life of Modwenna would seem to have been inserted with little trimming at the bottom margin and all the trimming at the top; this gives added weight to the evidence that as it stands the manuscript is now somewhat smaller than it once was; at one point it would have been at least a centimetre bigger all round, if not considerably more at the top and bottom.

Dating

This is discussed under Hands and Decoration.

Contents

On fol. 1r the title is given as 'The lyves and dethes of the martyres' (see Plate 1). Only the 'Th' is original and the 'T' has been coloured in during the late eighteenth- or early nineteenth- century; the other letter-forms have been cut out and pasted on. The cut-outs are in the manuscript hand and so must have been included somewhere at the outset, while the 'T' (without colour) is virtually identical with that on fol. 75v 'Thus endith [...]'). It is not known whether this would have been the original title of the manuscript or if it was devised in the late eighteenth or early nineteenth century; considering that not all of these saints are martyrs in the usual meaning of the term, this might well have been the case.[2] Evidence in favour of its being part of an original title, even if not the current one, is the spraywork emerging from the outer middle of the 'T'. Conversely, the opening 'Th' may have signalled (as in the life of Edith on fol. 75v) the end of a (now missing) life rather than the beginning of an overall title, albeit that it would have been unusual to find it at the top of a page.

The saints' lives (with their usual feast dates supplied) are as follows in Table 1.

---

[2] It is for this reason that we have given an abbreviated version of this title in our *Study* and *Edition*.

THE SAINTS' LIVES

Table 1. List of Medieval Saints' Lives in Add. 2604

Item	Folios	Missing Folios	Saint	Feast	Universal or Native	Role
1	1r–11v		John the Baptist	24 June	U	Apostle
2	11v–21v	fol. 14 cut out	John the Evangelist	27 Dec.	U	Apostle
3	22r–25v		Columba of Sens	31 Dec.	U	Virgin
4	25v–32v		Agatha (atelous)	5 Feb.	U	Virgin
	(33r–40v)	Quire 5 missing				
5	41r–47v	fol. 44 cut out	Cecilia (acephalous)	22 Nov.	U	Virgin
6	47v–52v		Barbara	16 Dec.	U	Virgin
7	52v–59r	fol. 58 cut out	Æthelthryth (incomplete)	23 June	N	Abbess
8	59v–61r		Seaxburh	6 July	N	Abbess
9	61r–62v		Eormenhild	6 July (13 Feb.)	N	Nun
10	62v–65r		Wærburh	6 July (3 Feb.)	N	Abbess
11	65r–66v		Eorcengota (and Æthelburh, with a comment about Sæthryth)	7 July (26 Feb.)	N	Abbesses
12	66v–69r		Wihtburh	8 July (17 Mar.)	N	Abbess
13	69v–75v		Edith of Wilton	16 Sept.	N	Abbess
14	76r–79r		Eadburh	13 Dec.	N	Abbess
15	79r–80v		Eanswith (atelous)	31 Aug. or 12 Sept.	N	Nun
	(81r–88v)	Quire 11 missing				
16	89r–93r		Hild (acephalous)	17 Nov.	N	Abbess
17	93r–97v		Martha	29 July	U	Abbess
18	97v–98r		Domitilla	12 May?	U	Nun
19	98r–105v	fols 106–107 cut out	Justina (atelous)	26 Sept.	U	Abbess
20	108r–112v	fols 106–107 cut out	Benedicta (acephalous)	8 Oct.	U	Abbess
21	113r–136v	fol. 126 cut out	Modwenna (incomplete)	5 July	N	Abbess
22	137r–152v	fols 138, 140, 143 cut out; fols 146–151 missing	Leonard (incomplete)	6 Nov.	U	Hermit

Collation

The manuscript is tightly bound but string is visible in most quires, marked below with an asterisk (*). Evidence for the quiring structure is also provided by the list of quire numbers in modern pencil in the lower right-hand margin (catchwords are no help as they occur virtually after every verso, with the exceptions given below): 1 ⁸ (fols 1–8)*; 2 ⁸ lacking 6 (fols 9–16, with fol. 14 cut out)*; 3 ⁸ (fols 17–24)*; 4 ⁸ (fols 25–32)*; 5 ⁸ lacking 1–8 (fols 33–40 lost); 6 ⁸ (fols 41–48, with fol. 44 cut out); 7 ⁸ (fols 49–56)*; 8 ⁸ lacking 2 (fols 57–64, with fol. 58 cut out)*; 9 ⁸ (fols 65–72)*; 10 ⁸ (fols 73–80)*; 11 ⁸ lacking 1–8 (fols 81–88 lost); 12 ⁸ (fols 89–96)*; 13 ⁸ (fols 97–104)*; 14 ⁸ lacking 2–3 (fols 105–112, with 106–107 cut out)*; 15 ⁸ (fols 113–120)*; 16 ⁸ lacking 6 (fols 121–128, with fol. 126 cut out)*; 17 ⁸ (fols 129–136), 18 ⁸ lacking 2, 4, 7 (fols 137–144, with fols 138, 140, and 143 cut out); 19 ⁸ lacking 2–7 (fols 145–152, with fols 146–151 missing). In the main text the centres of quires (that is, the fifth folio) have been marked with a cross in pencil as follows: fols 5, 13, 21, 29, 45, 53, 61, 69, 77, 93, 101, 109, 117, 125, 133, 141. (For the collation of the added material see Additional Contents, Ownership, and Compilation).

Catchwords

The catchwords (which are in the hand of the main scribe), their absence, or their partial visibility under ultraviolet light reveal some detective clues about the compilation of the manuscript over time.

Visible catchwords occur at the end of every verso (see Plates 2, 3, 4, 5, 6, and 7), apart from the following (for reasons explained in brackets below): 4v (a heading occurs on fol. 5r); 21v (a new life, Columba, begins on fol. 22r); 32v (the following quire 5 is missing); 43v (fol. 44 has been cut out); 61v (a heading follows on fol. 62r); 75v (a new life, Eadburh, begins on fol. 76r); 80v (the following quire is missing); 112v (a new life, Modwenna, begins on fol. 113r); 125v (fol. 126 has been cut out); 133v and 134v (there is no obvious explanation for the last two omissions); 136v (a new life, Leonard, begins on fol. 137r; see Plate 8); 137v (fol. 138r has been cut out); 139v (fol. 140 has been cut out); 145v (a catchword 'shewed' occurs here but does not match the following text; see below); and 152v (the end of the manuscript).

Where there *are* catchwords, these *appear* to reveal when quires or folios were cut out or lost, that is, in medieval or post-medieval times. Two folios have catchwords that do not link up with the text following: fol. 13v after which fol. 14 is cut out and fol. 105v after which fols 106–107 are cut out. This demon-

THE SAINTS' LIVES

strates that the relevant folios were cut out *after* the catchwords were added (we presume in post-medieval times, as discussed below). In the case of the missing fols 146–51, they are in the middle of a quire and so prone to loss, which could have happened at any point.

Where catchwords do not exist (or do not *seem* to exist which is a different matter that will be dealt with below) and material is lost afterwards, the reasonable presumption is that such material was lost in the medieval period *before* the catchwords were added. There are far more examples of this. These are as follows: fol. 32v with the fifth quire containing fols 33–40 missing; fol. 43v with fol. 44 cut out; fol. 57v with fol. 58 cut out (however, the word 'commit/ tyd' is written over two lines making it look as if a catchword is present); fol. 80v with the eleventh quire containing fols 81–88 missing; fol. 125v with fol. 126 cut out; fol. 137v with fol. 138 cut out; fol. 139v with fol. 140 cut out; and fol. 145v which is a complicated case in that a repair has been made to the manuscript and so a catchword is present but is not the original catchword (see below). In two cases, even though folios have been cut out afterwards, catchwords exist. In both instances (fols 57v and 142v) these are written as hyphenated words 'commit/tyd' and 'ora/tory'; such hyphenations are also found elsewhere (fols 96v and 124v) as bone fide catchwords.

This last example opens up a new set of intriguing complications. Although catchwords do not *seem* to exist on the examples above, very faint traces (partially visible under ultraviolet light) of catchwords are revealed in most cases. These words or parts of words have been so well excised that much is indecipherable, but catchwords once existed on the following folios: 32v, 43v, 80v, 125v, 133v, 136v (where no material is apparently lost and where there is a patch on the manuscript on which an indecipherable catchword or word is written), 137v, 139v, and 145v. In all of these only one word is immediately visible to the naked eye: 'fraunce' (fol. 139v; Figure 10); the only others that can be made out clearly with the aid of ultraviolet light are 'that' (fol. 125v); 'wenne' (fol. 133v); 'go' (fol. 137v); and 'blysse' (fol. 145v). All the others can only be vague guess-work. The catchwords are in the same hand as the main one and, where decipherable, they match up grammatically with the text: fol. 125v: 'west end of Inglond' [catchword: 'that']; fol. 133v: 'seynt mode' [catchword: 'wenne']; fol. 137v: 'thedir he wolde' [catchword: 'go']; fol. 139v: 'kynge of' [catchword: fraunce]; and fol. 145v: 'to rewarde hym in [catchword: 'blysse'].

It is patently obvious that someone set about 'tidying up' a manuscript that was mutilated at some point. Our painstaking medieval scribe would hardly have cut out pages or tried later to give the appearance of completeness to a volume that by then did not make full sense owing to missing text, more especially since he himself would have had to erase catchwords that he had so methodically added in the first place. Neither would it seem plausible for a later medieval compiler to have damaged the book or perhaps sought to have given a better impression of it. At any rate, knowing that pages had been cut out at some point in history and that quires had gone missing, someone at a later stage must have tried to disguise this fact by eliminating the catchwords that would have given the game away. Or perhaps the manuscript was already in such a poor state before it was bound that someone decided to cut out certain pages in order to render the manuscript more presentable and so eliminated the giveaway catchwords; we note below the repair to fol. 69 which might indicate ill treatment to the volume earlier on. One way or another, we witness a tidying-up exercise that saw the erasure of the catchwords, alongside the additional material in the manuscript (for which see Annotation below and Additional Contents, Ownership, and Compilation for a discussion of the identity of the person who must have been responsible for much of the form and the content of Add. 2604 as it currently stands).

Wear and Repair

The ink has faded on various pages throughout; see in particular fols 18v, 19v–20r, 21v, 25r–26v, 31v, 32r, 52v, 108r, 122v, 129r–130v, 132v, 133v, and 134v–136v, with the most obvious fading being in the quires containing Modwenna (fols 113r–136v). Given that the life of Modwenna may be somewhat set apart from the rest (see Decoration below), this could be yet another sign that this life was produced at a different point. Likewise, the opening of Æthelthryth on fol. 52v is especially noticeable for its faded ink and the apparent vicissitudes of use, something that is not obvious in the life of Barbara in the upper half of the page (see Plate 3).

At various points manuscript pages have been patched with parchment clearly from elsewhere in the same manuscript (these are noted below as recto or verso, depending on where the patch is more obvious). This was no doubt done as part of the post-medieval clean up referred to above. On fol. 67v the corner has been patched. At fol. 69r a strip from the outer margin of the same folio has been cut away and replaced by a piece from another leaf. On the added strip various letter-forms and parts of words are visible; these are clearly in the same hand as the rest of the manuscript. The reverse of this strip partially obscures a cadel head (see Decoration below). Fol. 99r has been patched at the top and bottom and fol. 133r at the bottom (with a trace of the descender of a letter-form visible). Fol. 136v has a patch at the lower left-hand corner with

THE SAINTS' LIVES

an indecipherable word; this was presumably one of the erased catchwords (see Catchwords above). On fol. 145v there is a patch on which is visible the trace of a letter-form in the extreme left-hand corner plus an apparent catchword 'shewed' (clearly in the manuscript hand), which does not match the following text (see Catchwords).

Hands

The manuscript is written by one scribe (capable of writing more than one script) in a stylish hand of the second half of the fifteenth century or later. A difficult hand to date, it may be towards the end of the last quarter of the fifteenth century or the early years of the sixteenth-century, that is, at some point between *c.* 1480 and *c.* 1510. The scribe lays out the text block carefully, writing an average of about twenty-seven lines per page (veering at least between twenty-five and at most thirty lines), with each leaf being carefully presented with frame ruling in ink (with a double frame on the horizontal). For the saints' lives the scribe uses a consistent secretary hand that is marked by secretary's distinctive single-lobed 'a', the unlooped 'd' (albeit with the occasional looped variety), single compartment 'g', short 'r' (both the right-shouldered and 'z' or '2' forms), a 'B' form of final 's', and a simplified 'w' that looks like two conjoined forms of 'v'. The hand has the characteristic flat-topped 'g' (though without any horns) that normally indicates manuscripts produced around 1500.[3] This 'g' also has a distinctive trailing lower loop (see, for example, Plate 3). The scribe takes a minimalist attitude to punctuation; it is so sparse throughout the manuscript as to be barely noticeable. He occasionally makes use of the *punctum* either on the line or in a raised position. In general there is no obvious logic to its use, apart from indicating some sort of pause, though the scribe is relatively consistent in putting the *punctum* on the line after his section headings, presumably to mark a full stop. His only other mark of punctuation is the *punctus elevatus* that again occurs occasionally without any regular significance except that it too marks a type of pause.

Taken as a whole, the hand bears comparison with some fine French hands of the period not in terms of the letter-forms but in the clarity of execution, elegance of the script, and overall proportions. In this respect a resemblance may be seen with the traditions of *lettre bourguignonne* or *bâtarde*, a hand named

---

[3] See, for instance, Plates 14–16 in Anthony G. Petti, *English Literary Hands from Chaucer to Dryden* (London: Arnold, 1977), p. 64, with discussion on p. 65.

8 I. THE MANUSCRIPT

for its use in the Burgundian court for the production of deluxe manuscripts commissioned by Philip the Good (1419–67) and his son, Charles the Bold (1467–77), and which came from the Low Countries to England in the second half of the fifteenth century.[4] It is quite feasible that a fairly high-grade manuscript such as the current one might betray a little of its influence (even if it is not as marked as in some other examples) and that this influence might serve to help date the manuscript later in the second half of the fifteenth century rather than earlier.[5] Our scribe is clearly not using the *lettre bourguionne* script *per se* but one particularly marked feature, albeit in a less pronounced fashion. The secretary hand in Add. 2604 demonstrates the characteristic left-leaning sloping qualities of the descenders in some letter-forms in *lettre bourguionne*, namely 'f', 'p', and initial and medial 's', while 'f' and 's' also have its usual tapered descenders. In addition, capital 'I' in Add. 2604 also has a slope. There is likewise a pronounced tendency to include a hairline downward flourish (either like a backwards elongated 'S' or a straight line) after final 'r', 's', and 't', with less obvious examples after final 'f', 'g', and double 'l'. This feature, combined with the absolute uniformity of layout (where letter-forms are regular in execution and size, and the space between lines even), serves to elevate the script overall so that one gets the impression of a scribe who has his own distinctive style. Given the current almost complete lack of evidence for late medieval English nuns as scribes, translators, or writers and conversely the overwhelming degree of evidence for male clerics acting for female religious in various capacities (as pastors, administrators, preachers, translators, and composers of literary and theological works), we may assume that the scribe of Add. 2604 is male.[6] We

---

[4] For further information, see Albert Derolez, *The Palaeography of Gothic Manuscript Books from the Twelfth to the Early Sixteenth Century* (Cambridge: Cambridge University Press, 2003), pp. 157–60 and passim.

[5] An example of a very marked use of *lettre bourguionne* may be seen in Oxford, Bodleian Library, MS Arch. Selden B. 10, a manuscript copy of excerpts from John Lydgate printed in 1519 and copied in *c.* 1520; fol. 205r is reproduced as Plate 15 (ii) in M. B. Parkes, *English Cursive Book Hands, 1250–1500* (Oxford: Oxford University Press, 1969), p. 15.

[6] This issue is too complicated for discussion here but entails a multiplicity of factors ranging from a dearth of female educational opportunities, the small size of the majority of English convents, poor Latinity, and the importance of commercial book production to the overwhelming lack of evidence of female scribal ability especially when set in a European context. This discussion need not be re-iterated at this point as it has been extensively explored through a detailed analysis of archives, manuscripts, and printed books from thirty English and one Scottish convent (that is, virtually the entire known corpus) from the fourteenth to the sixteenth centuries; see the following by Veronica O'Mara (and references therein), 'The

THE SAINTS' LIVES

9

have therefore deduced this book to be one made for a convent of nuns in East Anglia by a trained scribe who may or may not have been a scribe by profession. He could have functioned as the nuns' spiritual guide (either remote or near at hand) or their convent chaplain or have been acting under his direction (or indeed under that of the abbess or prioress of the relevant convent). This same man may also have been responsible for the translation of the saints' lives and their subsequent compilation in Add. 2604. (For this reason we use the terms 'scribe', 'writer', 'translator', and 'compiler' interchangeably in this *Study* and associated *Edition*.)

This is a scribe too who is capable of producing other sorts of script. In the life of Modwenna (fols 113r–136v) there is a section running from fols 124v (Figure 9) to 129v where he uses a textura script for his section or chapter headings. He clearly tries this out before in the heading on fol. 113v, 'Howe this holy mayde modewenne beganne to lyve vertuously' (21/19), but it ends up, either wittingly or unwittingly, as a mixture of styles with 'mayde modewenne beganne' looking more like textura and the rest like his normal secretary. But between fols 124v and 129v he shows that he is capable of proper textura, even if it is not of the highest quality at this point. It is not clear whether he is wandering into textura because he is getting bored with secretary or if his heart is not quite in textura. For instance, on fol. 128v he slips up when writing 'Of the miracles that she did by the way' (21/468) and uses a secretary 'a' in 'that' for the usual two-compartment 'a' of textura. Conversely, like linguists with perfect fluency, it could be that he is such an adept scribe that he is just writing without necessarily being aware of which script he is producing. Then after fol. 129v he reverts to his normal secretary form, only using textura on one other occasion, on fol. 137r in the title for Leonard (see Plate 8). It is interesting that textura only appears in the last two lives which are the only ones in self-contained quires and from which several folios are missing. As noted below, there are also some unusual features in the decoration in these lives so the use of

---

Late Medieval English Nun and her Scribal Activity: A Complicated Quest', in *Nuns' Literacies in Medieval Europe: The Hull Dialogue*, ed. by Blanton, O'Mara, and Stoop, pp. 69–93; 'Nuns and Writing in Late Medieval England: The Quest Continues', in *Nuns' Literacies in Medieval Europe: The Kansas City Dialogue*, ed. by Blanton, O'Mara, and Stoop, pp. 123–47; 'Scribal Engagement and the Late Medieval English Nun: The Quest Concludes?', in *Nuns' Literacies in Medieval Europe: The Antwerp Dialogue*, ed. by Blanton, O'Mara, and Stoop, pp. 187–208; and 'A Syon Scribe Revealed by Her Signature: Mary Nevel and Her Manuscripts', in *Continuity and Change: Papers from the Birgitta Conference at Dartington 2015*, ed. by Elin Andersson and others, Kungliga Vitterhets Historie och Antikvitets Akademien, Konferenser, 93 (Stockholm: Kungliga Vitterhets Historie och Antikvitets Akademien, 2017), pp. 283–308.

textura here may be further confirmation that these lives were produced at a different period from the rest of the manuscript. Given the length of Modwenna and relative length of Leonard (and their self-contained quires), it is also possible that the scribe copied these lives first, before determining a plan for the chapter or section headings in the collection (or conversely that they were copied later). If so, it would make sense that he was experimenting with the use of textura as a distinguishing script for these headings, but then had a change of mind. Yet the presence of textura in the manuscript also has other significance. Throughout, the scribe produces a meticulously formalised version of secretary, but with what may be described as 'a textura sheen'; in other words, the whole manuscript has the regularity and precision expected in a textura hand, the very features that elevate such hands and make them so difficult to date precisely.[7]

It is clear from the layout of the text, the general appearance of the secretary script, and the inclusion of an obvious very occasional textura hand that this is the work of a very proficient scribe who rarely makes mistakes apart from some eye-skip and very occasional blank spaces (dealt with in the Textual Apparatus in the *Edition*). This is someone who, even if not a professional scribe in the accepted sense of writing for payment, is nevertheless highly skilled. A particular clue to this lies in his frequent use of cadel heads (discussed in Decoration below), a sign of a scribe used to producing liturgical manuscripts or calligraphic work.[8] Given the complexities of liturgical manuscript production (with the inclusion of music and so forth), we can posit that the scribe of Add. 2604 is someone used to producing high-grade manuscripts, something that is also obvious in his use of some elaborate penwork. Under such circumstances one might have expected to have been able to identify him, but this is not currently the case as we have been unable to source his hand in the many manuscripts of

---

[7] We are very grateful to Ralph Hanna for giving us the benefit of his expert opinion on the scribe of Add. 2604.

[8] See Kathleen L. Scott, *Later Gothic Manuscripts, 1390–1490*, A Survey of Manuscripts Illuminated in the British Isles, ed. by J. J. G. Alexander, 2 vols (London: Harvey Miller, 1996), II, 370, who notes that cadel heads are 'often found with musical notation in liturgical manuscripts'. Examples of cadel heads in very professional looking productions include a manuscript of Bishop Richard Fox's 1517 translation of the Benedictine Rule in Cambridge, Cambridge University Library, MS Mm.3.13 and the Chester Processional in San Marino, Huntington Library, MS EL 34 B7 (both of which have music). See also Anne Bagnall Yardley and Jesse D. Mann, 'Facing the Music: The Whimsical Cadels in a Late Medieval English Book of Hours', *Peregrinations: Journal of Medieval Art and Architecture*, 7. 2 (2020), 52–85. Examples from devotional collections (without music) include London, British Library, MS Harley 4012, owned by the Suffolk heiress Anne Harling (d. 1500).

THE SAINTS' LIVES

the period that we have examined.[9] There are a couple of manuscripts where the initial appearance of the script is closer to Add. 2604 but, when the relevant hands are carefully studied, our scribe cannot be identified with either of them. These two examples are found in London, British Library, MS Harley 5272 and Cambridge, Trinity College, MS R.3.21 (Figures 11 and 12). MS Harley 5272 comprises three texts: Lydgate's *Life of Our Lady* in verse (fols 1r–98v); the verse life of St Dorothy (fols 99r–104v); and the *Abbey of the Holy Ghost* in prose (fols 105r–137v). The scribe of the Lydgate finishes the text by noting 'Here endith þe life of oure lady. Quod Johannes fforster' (fol. 98v), and he appears to have been responsible for the three texts. Whoever John Forster was, he was not the scribe of Add. 2604. While this hand demonstrates some overall superficial likeness to Add. 2604, it can easily be distinguished from the scribe of Add. 2604 by its use of an Anglicana 'a' and 'g' unlike the secretary 'a' and flat-topped 'g' routinely found in Add. 2604. The scribe of Trinity MS R.3.21 is referred to as the 'Trinity Anthologies' scribe by Linne Mooney and Simon Horobin in their 'Late Medieval English Scribes' online repository, the other manuscripts listed being Cambridge, Trinity College, MS R.3.19, Oxford, Bodleian Library, MS Douce 322, and Oxford, Bodleian Library, MS Eng. e. 18.[10] The text of Trinity R.3.21 contains over thirty-two items, with one of the most interesting for present purposes being the life of St Antony (divided into

---

[9] In the preparation of this *Study* we have investigated a wide variety of manuscripts in an effort to track down the scribe (and the decoration) of Add. 2604. We began with a selection of *Gilte Legende* manuscripts: London, British Library, MS Additional 11565; London, British Library, MS Additional 35298; London, British Library, MS Egerton 876; London, British Library, MS Harley 630; and London, British Library; MS Harley 4775, and then proceeded to examine all those manuscripts that might bear any comparison in any way with the texts in Add. 2604. These included fifteenth-century manuscripts associated with English convents (especially those in East Anglia) and those incorporating fifteenth-century hagiographical material. Too numerous to list here, these manuscripts may be found in structured notes or sections (for instance, manuscripts associated with particular convents) throughout this volume and/ or cumulatively in the Bibliography. In addition to the various manuscripts listed throughout, we have tried to investigate various samples in the online survey of scribes by Linne Mooney and Simon Horobin, 'Late Medieval English Scribes' at (https://www.medievalscribes.com) (accessed 5 February 2023). We have also consulted a range of experts, Ralph Hanna, Holly James-Maddocks, Julian Luxford, Linne Mooney, Nicholas Rogers, and Kathleen Scott. Neither we nor they have encountered this precise hand or its decorative features elsewhere.

[10] See 'Late Medieval English Scribes' at https://www.medievalscribes.com/index. php?page=about&nav=off (accessed 5 February 2023). For the present purposes we do not enter into discussion about these four manuscripts being by the same scribe; we restrict ourselves to a comparison between the hand in Add. 2604 and that in Trinity, R.3.21.

12   I. THE MANUSCRIPT

three parts) on fols 257ra–273rb from where the present scribal comparison is taken.[11] It is interesting that, like Add. 2604, the manuscript is late (dating from the reign of Edward IV probably at some point between 1471 and 1483). The appearance of this script is closer to Add. 2604 than that in MS Harley 5272. Yet there are marked differences too, for instance, in its use of an Anglicana 'd' as opposed to Add. 2604's secretary 'd' and in its more upright duct. Even some of the similarities, such as the flat-topped 'g' it shares with Add. 2604, may be owing simply to dating. Yet overall it is a useful point of comparison, even if we are no closer to discovering the identity of the scribe of Add. 2604 or of finding any other manuscript in his hand.

Decoration

The level of decoration in Add. 2604 is quite ornate in the champ letters, feathering, and the flowers, but the tinting of green on the spraywork seems rushed or made using an overly large brush tip (see Plates 1 and 8). This hastiness is not unusual however in earlier manuscripts.[12] Overall the presentation of the major decoration is somewhat varied, as if the illuminator is trying out different styles of floral decoration. This adds considerably to the interest of the volume, but

---

[11] The Trinity manuscript is fully described in Linne R. Mooney, *The Index of Middle English Prose: Handlist XI, Manuscripts in the Library of Trinity College, Cambridge* (Cambridge: Brewer, 1995), pp. 23–28. This manuscript and associated ones have attracted various articles over a lengthy period; see in particular, Linne R. Mooney, 'Scribes and Booklets of Trinity College, Cambridge, Manuscripts R.3.19 and R.3.21', in *Middle English Poetry: Texts and Traditions, Essays in Honour of Derek Pearsall*, ed. by A. J. Minnis, York Manuscripts Conferences Proceedings Series, 5 (Woodbridge: York Medieval Press, 2001), pp. 241–66, and Holly James-Maddocks, 'Scribes and Booklets: The 'Trinity Anthologies' Reconsidered', in *Scribal Cultures in Late Medieval England: Essays in Honour of Linne R. Mooney*, ed. by Margaret Connolly, Holly James-Maddocks, and Derek Pearsall, York Manuscripts and Early Print Studies, 3 (Woodbridge: York Medieval Press, 2022), pp. 146–79 and references therein.

[12] Similar evidence of less attention to detail can be seen in some of the green tinting in later folios of London, British Library, MS Harley 2278, fols 96v, 97v, 105v, 106v, 107v, 108v, and 109v. This is John Lydgate's celebrated verse life of St Edmund, a royal gift to Henry VI. The spraywork in Harley 2278 is less ornate than the decorative work in Add. 2604 but as an East Anglian production of a slightly earlier date, it provides a useful point of comparison. A digitised copy is available at The British Library: (http://www.bl.uk/manuscripts/FullDisplay. aspx?ref=Harley_MS_2278) (accessed 5 February 2023) and a useful facsimile is *The Life of St Edmund King and Martyr: John Lydgate's Illustrated Verse Life Presented to Henry VI, a Facsimile of British Library MS Harley 2278*, introduced by A. S. G. Edwards (London: The British Library, 2004).

THE SAINTS' LIVES   13

also indicates that this illuminator, who may or may not be the same person as the scribe, was not the most accomplished as he does not show the absolute consistency of format that might be expected in work of the finest calibre. Yet where many miscellanies in prose rarely have such decoration, Add. 2604 stands out as one that features a unique presentation of saints' lives augmented by pleasing decorative touches. In the volume as a whole this comprises varied levels of initials, delicate spraywork, and some penwork.

(i) Initials

Five types of initials aid readers in locating particular sections of the manuscript: champ; two-line blue with red flourishing; one-line blue (or occasionally black with a blue paraph or a *nota*); chapter initials set in blocks with red flourishing; and large I/[J], which are set in the margin, often with red flourishing (see Plate 2). These are typical of English manuscript decoration of the period. The most elaborate are champ initials either red or blue with filigree surrounding an initial in gold leaf but are not uniformly quartered or halved red and blue but a mix of decorative approaches.[13] A small section of each champ letter extends into the margin. This section is coloured opposite to the main block colour (for example, blue for red or red for blue). The champ initials in this codex appear on fols 1r (Plate 1), 12r (Figure 1), 22r (Figure 2), 25v (Figure 3), 47v (Plate 2), 52v (Plate 3), 59v, 61r, 62v (Plate 4), 65r (Figure 4), 66v (Plate 5), 69v, 76r, 79r (Figure 6), 93v (Plate 6), 97v (Plate 7), 98r (Figure 7), and 137r (Plate 8). Spraywork extends from the outside corners of these champ letters and occasionally a sprig at the outer centre accentuates the extension. Most of these champ letters are three-line initials used to designate the opening of a saint's life, with the exception of Cecilia, where the opening is lost with the missing quire 5; Hild, where the opening is lost with the missing quire 11; Benedicta, which is incomplete at the beginning owing to fols 106–107 being cut out (albeit that there is a tiny trace of spraywork visible on the stub of fol. 106r); and Modwenna, which has a blank half-page before it, as though it was not completed. Irregularities in the three-line champ letter structure occur at fols 22r (Figure 2) and 47v (Plate 2), where the scribe left space only for a two-line initial, not a champ letter, and on fol. 25v (Figure 3), where the scribe blocked out only two lines for a champ letter.

---

[13] See, for example, Scott, *Later Gothic Manuscripts, 1390–1490*, i, Figure 437.

Within the lives of saints, one-line blue initials (or the equivalent) draw attention to the rubrics between sections or chapters within a life, where two-line blue initials, with red pen flourishing, mark the beginning of each chapter. Occasionally, these chapter initials are more elaborate and are set in square blocks of penwork with red flourishing and marginal scrolls (see (iii) below). When the initial 'I' or 'J' occurs, it is a four- to seven-line blue letter written in the margin, with red flourishing, such as on fols 3v, 19r, 31v, 127r, and 129v. The scribe makes no use whatsoever of paraph marks in the course of the texts (apart from the example above); he has been clear with his layout of titles, headings, and divisions and it would seem that he does not wish to delay the progress of the narrative in any way.

(ii) Spraywork

The spraywork in this manuscript, albeit presented somewhat idiosyncratically, is fairly typical of the period in that it features penwork vines of feathering (both straight and curling in form) with lobes tinted green and occasionally gold.[14] Coloured motifs include finials or lobes of balls, bryony leaves, and pine-cones in gold or finials of flowers (trefoil, quatrefoil, and cinquefoil as well as aroid and poppyheads) in rose and blue accented by gold or white. The quatre-foil and cinquefoil flowers, like those on fol. 1r (see Plate 1), are reminiscent of those in books produced in Bruges.[15] The trefoil or trilobe flowers, such as the ones on fol. 47v (see Plate 2), are much like the cinquefoils featured in what was probably a London production, Cambridge, Harvard University, Houghton Library, Widener MS 2, fol. 72v, which are half white with blue- or red-tipped

---

[14] Kathleen L. Scott, *Dated and Datable English Manuscript Borders c. 1395–1499* (London: The Bibliographical Society and The British Library, 2002), p. 10. A typical example of English spraywork appears on pp. 86–87 (Plate XXVIIb). Interestingly this manuscript, Oxford, Bodleian Library, MS Bodley 108, fol. 3v, which has a copy of John Bury's *Gladius Salomonis*, is probably from Suffolk and dates from *c.* 1457; John Bury was himself an Austin friar at Clare (see further II. Language and Dialectal Provenance below). For additional background on English spraywork in the fifteenth century, see Scott, *Later Gothic Manuscripts, 1390–1490*, I, 23–25.

[15] See Scot McKendrick, *Flemish Illuminated Manuscripts, 1400–1550* (London: The British Library, 2003), p. 33 (Figure 18) and pp. 116–17 (Figures 101–02), which are from London, British Library, MS Arundel 71, fol. 24r (dated between 1464 and 1467), and London, British Library, MS Additional 22567, fols 31v–32r (dated to the 1490s). See also Janet Backhouse, *The Illuminated Page: Ten Centuries of Manuscript Painting in the British Library* (Toronto: University of Toronto Press, 1997), p. 193 (Figure 171) and p. 203 (Figure 181).

THE SAINTS' LIVES   15

petals and gold balls in the centre, like viola,[16] but are particularly reminiscent of Bruges manuscripts.[17] Of interest here is that similar trilobe (albeit green) flowers adorn the spraywork extending from champ letters in Manchester, The John Rylands University Library, MS Eng. 1, fol. 25v, which is John Lydgate's *The Siege of Troy* (produced probably in London in the late 1440s). But as Kathleen Scott observes, these green flowers are customary in English decoration and also appear in the Chronicle of the Kings of England preserved in Oxford, Bodleian Library, MS e Musaeo 42, fol. 1v, dated after 1467 and before 1469.[18] The ones in Add. 2604 (see Plate 6) that are half coloured in red or blue and half in white, as Scott shows, are continental and occur later than the green ones, such as in the frontispiece and first text page of London, British Library, MS Additional 33736, which contains Pietro Carmeliano of Brescia's poem on the birth of Prince Arthur, *c.* 1486.[19] Gold balls are also used at times as segment points on the central stem of the spraywork from which sections of feathering extend (see Plate 4), like those in other London manuscripts of the period.[20] The poppyheads are quite detailed in their execution and compare favourably

[16] Scott, *Later Gothic Manuscripts, 1390–1490*, I, Figure 457.

[17] See Maurits Smeyers, *Flemish Miniatures from the 8th to the mid-16th Century: The Medieval World of Parchment* (Turnhout: Brepols, 1999) for various examples, for instance, in Plates 40–42 on pp. 262–63; this was first published as *Vlaamse miniaturen van de 8ste tot het midden van de 16de eeuw. De middeleeuwse wereld op perkament* (Leuven/Louvain: Davidsfonds, 1998). These half-blue, half-white trefoil flowers are especially obvious in the right-hand margin of fols 53v and 103r of the Llangattock Book of Hours, dating from *c.* 1450 and originating in Bruges, in Los Angeles, J. Paul Getty Museum, 83.ML.103 (MS Ludwig IX.7), (Plates 40 and 41, p. 262). For the understandable overlap in certain features found in manuscripts from Bruges, London, and Paris produced under the auspices of Bruges illuminators, see Smeyers, ch. 4, section 2, 'Flemish Illuminators in France and England', pp. 179–89.

[18] For Scott's discussion of *The Siege of Troy* manuscript, see *Later Gothic Manuscripts, 1390–1490*, II, 259–63. A colour image of this folio is available on the John Rylands website (https://www.digitalcollections.manchester.ac.uk/view/MS-ENGLISH-00001/64) (accessed 5 February 2023). For the Chronicle of the Kings of England manuscript, see Scott, *Dated and Datable English Manuscript Borders c. 1395–1499*, Plate XXVIII, pp. 88–89. See also the colour image on the Bodleian Library's website (https://iiif.bodleian.ox.ac.uk/iiif/viewer/c44571e0-8732-40ad-9e14-f272437fe3fb#?c=0&m=0&s=0&cv=13&r=0&xywh=-1953%2C1765%2C9030%2C4135) (accessed 5 February 2023).

[19] See Plates XXXVa and XXXVb in Scott, *Dated and Datable English Manuscript Borders c. 1395–1499*, pp. 106–07 and the discussion on p. 105.

[20] Camarillo, CA, St. John's Seminary, Edward L. Doheny Memorial Library, MS 3970 (*olim*), fol. 7r and Città del Vaticano, Biblioteca Apostolica, MS Rossiana 275, fol. 108v, which Scott illustrates as Figures 401 and 463 in *Later Gothic Manuscripts, 1390–1490*, I.

to work in Bruges manuscripts such as London, British Library, MS Cotton Vespasian B. i, fol. 15r.[21] The inclusion of poppyheads help date this decoration to the 1460s or after, when this element was introduced into English border decoration.[22] One distinctive aroid or flower of the alum family on fol. 47v (see Plate 2) is somewhat akin to those seen in Bruges manuscripts, such as London, British Library, MS Harley 1211, fol. 15r or Baltimore, Walters Art Gallery, W. 721, fol. 188r, but the segmented daisy on fol. 22r that adorns the spraywork for the life of Columba is unusual.[23] Another distinguishing feature is that the bryony leaves in the spraywork such as on fol. 97v are not like those of English spraywork of the period (with a straight edge to the lower palmate design) but feature a curved edge, like those seen in manuscripts from Bruges. Still, the petals of the bryony leaves are not like the Bruges decoration, so it seems this is an interesting conflation of continental and English practice (see Plate 5). A couple like those in Add. 2604 can be seen in the lower border of the Wingfield Psalter in New York, Public Library, MS Spencer 3, fol. 19r, which was likely produced in London before 1467.[24]

In addition to feathering used to decorate the manuscript's title 'The lyves and dethes of the martyres' on fol. 1r,[25] spraywork decorates the opening of each life, with the exception of Cecilia and Hild, whose lives are acephalous due to the loss of quires 5 and 11, Benedicta, which lacks fols 106–107 after the end of Justina, and Modwenna, whose life begins a new quire on fol. 113r and has a different rubric (Figure 8).[26] The previous leaf (fol. 112v) is partially blank, so there may have been an intention to include a champ initial and spraywork

---

[21] See McKendrick, *Flemish Illuminated Manuscripts*, p. 35 (Figure 20), which is a deluxe manuscript made by the Master of the Harley Froissart in Bruges, *c.* 1465–70.

[22] Scott, *Dated and Datable English Manuscript Borders c. 1395–1499*, Plate XXVI, p. 82.

[23] See The British Library website for images of Harley MS 1211 (https://www.bl.uk/catalogues/illuminatedmanuscripts/ILLUMIN.ASP?Size=mid&IllID=19180) (accessed 5 February 2023). For Baltimore, Walters Art Gallery, W. 721, fol. 188r see Smeyers, *Flemish Miniatures from the 8th to the mid-16th Century*, Plate 42, p. 263.

[24] Scott, *Later Gothic Manuscripts, 1390–1490*, I, Figure 398.

[25] Feathering adorns the letter 'T' of the title and features finials of yellow balls and blue trefoil similar to the rest of the spraywork but a blue cinquefoil is unique to the manuscript; the variation of green and yellow decoration on spraywork is also unique, as this yellow decoration does not appear in other spraywork in the codex. It may have been done later when the so-called title was pasted onto fol. 1r.

[26] As noted above, there is a hint of spraywork on the stub of the excised fol. 106r, which must have formed the opening of the now imperfect life of Benedicta.

THE SAINTS' LIVES   17

there. It may also indicate that the scribe (at this point) was working in a series of booklets and neglected the regular rubric 'Here begynnyth [...]' on fol. 112v with a champ letter and spraywork, so it was necessary to add 'Thus begynnyth the lyfe of seynt modewyne' at the top of the leaf. The size of this incipit indicates that this line was shoved in perhaps as an afterthought. The scribe had begun the text with the usual four-line letter 'I' but had apparently either neglected to put the heading (with the usual champ initial and spraywork) on fol. 112v or leave enough room for it on fol. 113r.

Overall the amount of space allocated for spraywork varies considerably: the spraywork on the verso leaves is generally more elaborate with more distinguished feathering and single motifs than that on the recto leaves, which feature quite modest single bursts of feathering that are squeezed into the left margin on each leaf; for example, see fols 97v (Plate 7), 98r (Figure 7) and 137r (Plate 8) for a comparison. As noted above, the pages have since been trimmed; to judge by fols 104r and 130r with the cropping of the flower and the cadel-type head, there is at least a centimetre missing in the top margin.

(iii) Flourishing

The red flourishing that accompanies the large blue two-line capitals at the beginning of new sections or paragraphs looks like a standard type found in English manuscripts. In each case the initial is filled in and squared off with lines and circles or semi-circles. Where a number of capitals occur on the same page (Figure 5) the flourishing, which comprises circles (sometimes with dots) and lines, runs down the page connecting one capital with another. At its more elaborate the flourishing then extends generously into the margin tied together with swags and decorated with what look like free-floating 'c' type squiggles that seem like bubbles in the air (these are unlikely to be annotated letter-forms as discussed below under Annotation). Where the long capital is a four- or six-line 'I' (that is 'J'), the initial is not squared off but is flourished as it stands in the margin outside the text area; in the manuscript there is just one example where a large capital 'I' ['J'] is not flourished; this is found on fol. 113r (Figure 8) at the beginning of the life of Modwenna (see (ii) above for other unique presentational features here).

18 I. THE MANUSCRIPT

(iv) Penwork

Calligraphic Decoration

Elongated ascenders, sometimes with calligraphic work, is a periodic feature on the first line of individual leaves. Two such ascenders feature cadel heads (fols 17v, whose first line is the most calligraphically pronounced in the manuscript, and 130r).[27] On fol. 16r there is a decorative zoomorphic (lizard-like) feature from the ascender 'd' in the first line; on fol. 73r there is a type of elongated leaf emerging from the ascender of the 'd' in the first line; on fol. 75v there is a leaf in the ascender of the 'I' in the first line. The scribe's most elaborate penwork occurs on fol. 66v (see Plate 5), beginning the life of Wihtburh, and fol. 137r at the opening of the life of Leonard (see Plate 8). Both feature cadel heads that emerge into interlaced strapwork. The strapwork preceding the life of Leonard is ciliated and ends in a tail, forming a kind of dragon's body for the cadel head. Less elaborate strapwork appears on fol. 69v at the opening of Edith, and there appears to have been another cadel head to accompany this calligraphic work (the remains of a pointed beard can be seen). One feature that occurs only in the last two lives, Leonard and Modwenna, which have some other idiosyncrasies, are elaborate descenders in pronounced backwards figures of eight at the bottom of the page on medial or final 'y' (fols 127v and 131r) and medial 'h' (fol. 137v).

Cadel Heads

The scribe included some eleven male cadel heads, although there may have been others on leaves now cut out or in the missing quires. As noted above, two appear on ascenders (fols 17r and 130r). Seven others mark the opening of a saint's life, where the rubric announces 'Here begynnyth [...]'. These faces on fols 1r (Plate 1), 47v, where it is very small and indistinct (Plate 2), 59v (also somewhat indistinct), 62v (Plate 4), 66v (Plate 5), 69v (only partly visible), and 137r (Plate 8) are similarly drawn, with a curled, pointed beard. Most have bulbous noses, but the figure in Leonard on fol. 137r has a thin nose. That on fol. 17v is more like a man-in-the-moon figure. A distorted smaller cadel head appears as part of the catchword 'fende' on fol. 99v. He has the usual bulbous

---

[27] For elaborate ascenders, see Scott, *Later Gothic Manuscripts, 1390–1490*, I, Figures 437 and 438. On calligraphic work plus cadel heads and their use in liturgical manuscripts, see Scott, *Later Gothic Manuscripts, 1390–1490*, II, 370 and II, Figures 23–29.

THE SAINTS' LIVES   19

nose but appears to be clean shaven; his ugly features are presumably meant to exemplify the word itself. On fol. 125v trailing down from an otiose descender in the second line on a capital 'A' in 'And' is a distorted drawing that may be a bug-eyed face. Another unusual type of cadel head, if indeed it is one, appears at the top margin of fol. 130r, in the middle of the life of Modwenna. It decorates the ascender of the letter 'L' and shows a large two-sided face with a pointed beard on the left and a clean-shaven chin on the right.

Other Features

Other decoration is rare, including only a partial, heart-shaped finial on fol. 71r, springing from the penwork on the initial (damaged when the leaf was trimmed), and an ornate, six-petaled barbed flower with spraywork and hatching on the stem drawn in the upper margin of fol. 104r. This flower has also been mutilated by trimming.

(v) Influences and Dating

The decoration of Add. 2604, with its lobed gold balls, pinecones, and feathering, was executed by an illuminator (or scribe) who was quite familiar with the English artistic traditions of the second half of the fifteenth century, particularly the 1460s and 1470s. There are also some continental features evident that might indicate a foreign artist copying English work. But more likely they demonstrate that an English illuminator was influenced by Flemish or French styles, something that would not be unexpected in a manuscript that in many other ways is associated with East Anglia. According to Kathleen Scott, the spraywork is 'probably of the late third to the fourth quarter' of the fifteenth century, although she also notes that the 'smudgy green on the lobes of the feathering was earlier (in the 1440s) typical of East Anglian borderwork, but at this later date might only be a trait of the limner'. In Scott's expert view the features that help date the spraywork to the later fifteenth century include 'the roundish, ball-like poppyhead motif and the gold balls with three lobes only half-painted in a colour' (see Plate 7). These lobes that are half coloured in blue or pink/red and half in white she elsewhere notes as a continental feature.[28] In addition, Scott notes that the 'blue motif at the top of the spray at St Barbara on fol. 47v (Plate 2) looks foreign'. As noted earlier, there is a slightly idiosyncratic

---

[28] Scott, *Dated and Datable English Manuscript Borders c. 1395–1499*, p. 105.

approach to the appearance of the different examples of spraywork. Indeed, there is also something unusual in the very existence of the spraywork itself. Scott comments that, although not unknown, 'Normally, champ letters do not have sprays with painted motifs but only gold motifs' and she speculates that the sprays may have been added later to pre-existing champ initials. Whether or not this is the case is impossible to say.

Our view of Add. 2604 being an example of East Anglian work from the later fifteenth century or beyond that is heavily influenced by Flemish style is firmly supported by Holly James-Maddocks and Julian Luxford. Nicholas Rogers comments particularly on the 'loose' penwork sprays which are indicators of East Anglian style. Most significantly, Rogers notes that 'the free way in which the green globules are applied are reminiscent of Bury work of the third quarter of the century such as Yates Thompson 47', a comment that is supported by Luxford, who notes that fifteenth-century East Anglian penwork tends to have 'a rapid, sometimes almost impressionistic, quality', as seen in various earlier non-illuminated examples in the registers of Abbot Curteys of Bury (d. 1446).[29] At any rate what we have in this decoration is a unique blend of decorative features produced by an unidentified limner (who may also have been the scribe) no doubt operating somewhere in East Anglia in the last decades of the fifteenth century.

Annotation

Apart from post-medieval annotation, which is dealt with in Additional Contents, Ownership, and Compilation, there is virtually nothing in the way of other medieval annotation, apart from the following. Periodically throughout the manuscript there occur random individual letters possibly in the main hand in the margins. They are found as follows. Folio 1r (Plate 1) in the right-hand margin (near 'dauid as'), fol. 12r (Figure 1) in the right-hand margin (near 'Salome'), and fol. 137r (Plate 8) in the right-hand margin between 'Anas/tayse' and 'of' have a red letter lower-case 'c'. It is conceivable that these carry instructions for the limner to produce a capital, that is, a champ initial, but unlikely

---

[29] Personal communications. We are very grateful to Kathleen Scott, Nicholas Rogers, Julian Luxford, and Holly James-Maddocks for their helpful advice and the interest taken in our work. See Scott, *Later Gothic Manuscripts, 1390–1490*, I, Figures 416–19 and II, Catalogue 112, pp. 307–09, for London, British Library, MS Yates Thompson 47, which contains a copy of Lydgate's lives of Edmund and Fremund and is dated after 1461; for the Curteys registers, see London, British Library, MSS Additional 7096 and 14848.

THE SAINTS' LIVES   21

as they occur in the right rather than the left margin.[30] On fol. 22r (Figure 2) is a repetition three times vertically in the right-hand margin of what looks like 'C', 'E', or 'e' (near from 'on a' to 'day'). On fol. 97v (Plate 7) in the bottom margin there is a sort of capitulum mark, that looks like a 'C', 'E' or 'e'. The lower margin of the final leaf, fol. 152v, has some random additional letter-forms in black. In addition, just after the explicit for Leonard there is a little decorative mark in red, while the explicit is highlighted lightly with red lines (features not found in the other lives so it presumably is a means of signalling the end of the collection visually). A more obvious annotation is found on fol. 75v after the explicit, although it is now only visible under ultraviolet light: 'O gloriyous kynge of'. On fol. 71v there is a red flower in the flourishing. There is an 'oracio' in the right-hand margin of fol. 141r that signals a prayer by Leonard.

Most importantly, at the end of Leonard in the lower margin of fol. 152v in a different medieval hand from the main one is written what *appears* to be 'Summa quaternorum xviij' in a heavily abbreviated form. If it is a calculation of the number of quires — as it seems to be — then this was written *after* the manuscript had lost quires 5 and 11. However, it is not quite accurate as there are currently nineteen quires in the manuscript. Yet, given that the life of Leonard is so imperfect with the eighteenth quire lacking 2, 4, 7 (fols 138, 140, and 143 are cut out) and the nineteenth quire lacking 2–7 (fols 146–151 are missing), it is quite conceivable for a miscalculation to have been made as quires eighteen and nineteen only comprise seven folios between them (fols 137, 139, 141, 142, 144, 145 and 152). In a manuscript routinely comprising quires of eight, it would not be so unusual for a leaf to go missing. If this speculation is correct, could this same scribe have been responsible for some of the tidying up that would have involved him in the deletion of the now inappropriate catchwords that do not match up owing to missing folios or quires, and *possibly* (though probably not) the addition of the pasted-on title on fol.1r? On fol. 145v a catchword from a now lost leaf of the manuscript has been added (as part of a repair); this may have matched up with what should have been fol. 146 that is now gone. Were this folio present when this scribe was counting quires, then it would have accounted for the missing folio in what he must have assumed

---

[30] Such instructions are fully described by Kathleen L. Scott, 'Limning and Book-Producing Terms and Signs *in situ* in Late-Medieval English Manuscripts: A First Listing', in *New Science out of Old Books: Studies in Manuscripts and Early Printed Books in Honour of A. I. Doyle*, ed. by Richard Beadle and A. J. Piper (Aldershot: Scolar Press, 1995), pp. 142–88; see also Kathleen L. Scott, 'Instructions to a Limner in Beinecke MS 223', *The Yale University Library Gazette*, 72 (1997), 13–16.

to have been the eighteenth quire. Yet this whole hypothesis about this scribe's interference is difficult to accept as it is questionable why a medieval scribe would have taken such trouble to obliterate catchwords and so 'improve' a text that in many ways he knew to be imperfect. On a practical level too, it is not feasible as any deletion of material could only have been done by scraping with an implement and, as noted above, the deleted catchwords are today only visible under ultraviolet light with no signs of damage to the manuscript. It therefore seems more plausible that this scribe simply counted the quires by eye, as it were, and that the tidying up and the adding to were the responsibility of a later owner, a matter that will be treated fully below under Compilation.

Ownership

This is discussed in Additional Contents, Ownership, and Compilation.

Binding

See Additional Contents, Ownership, and Compilation.

Additional Contents, Ownership, and Compilation

Further to the material described in The Saints' Lives above, there are also two vellum pages from fifteenth-century liturgical Offices inserted at the beginning, in addition to twenty-eight eighteenth- or early nineteenth-century paper pages, as well as twenty-eight such pages following the saints' lives. These pages contain a range of items from the sixteenth, seventeenth, and eighteenth — or in some cases possibly early nineteenth — centuries. This material is described below, alongside Ownership and Compilation.

Physical Description

Two pages from a fifteenth-century manuscript of liturgical Offices are now foliated as i and ii. The lower portion of each page is turned up to match the size of the leaves containing the medieval saints' lives; these leaves measure 167 mm (when folded back on themselves) and 205 mm (when opened) x 108 mm. The medieval saints' lives are preceded and followed by paper leaves (from the late eighteenth- or early nineteenth-century), which are numbered sequentially from fols iii to lviii, with fols iii to xxx inserted at the beginning of the manu-

ADDITIONAL CONTENTS, OWNERSHIP, AND COMPILATION   23

script and fols xxxi to lviii at the end; these pages have been trimmed to fit in with the size of the saints' lives. After the Offices, seventeen items from a sixteenth-century writing-master's book are pasted in horizontally on some of these pages. These have been cut out individually and vary greatly in size.

Dating

The additional material in the manuscript dates from the fifteenth to the late eighteenth or early nineteenth century. The exact dating for this late material hinges on which hand was responsible; though it all looks to be late eighteenth century, it is conceivable that any material that may have been added by owner George Bird Burrell could date between 1788 and 1823 (or 1811).

Contents and Hands

Endpaper verso: Pasted onto this endpaper is the cut-out title 'Prouncialis wilhelmi lyndewode'; beneath this and centred is mounted the word 'Liber', surrounded by the following individually mounted letters set out in a balanced fashion. There is a large initial capital 'F' on the extreme left and another on the extreme right of the page, with 'Liber' in the middle of them, surrounded by the following capitals: a 'Q' above an 'F' to the left of 'Liber' and to its right an 'I' above an 'A'. Beneath this is written in a late eighteenth- or early nineteenth-century hand 'A Specimen of some of the earliest printing in England: / Being some of Caxton's Type: A:D:1495:'; in pencil on this same folio there is the word 'Ancient' in a late eighteenth- or early nineteenth-century hand, plus what looks like an indecipherable shelf-mark or price.

These cut-outs were neither published by Caxton nor printed in 1495. Instead they are from a copy of William Lyndwood's *Prouinciale seu Constitutiones Anglie*, printed in Paris in 1501 by André Bocard.[31] The person responsible for the cut-outs was interested in symmetry as the layout described above makes clear. He takes a left-hand running-head for the title, a right-hand running head

---

[31] We owe the identification of the precise edition to Ringrose, *Summary Catalogue of the Additional Medieval Manuscripts in Cambridge University Library Acquired before 1940*, p. 17. This information has been confirmed by consulting the four copies of the text (STC 17107) in Cambridge University Library, respectively Sel. 2. 10, Sel. 2. 22, Syn. 3. 50. 2, and Ta. 54. 1; see n. 32.

24   I. THE MANUSCRIPT

for the word 'Liber' and then the various capitals, as noted above.[32] It is impossible to say whether or not the printed text was cut up for this purpose or was already mutilated. In view of the care with which the cut-outs are laid out, it may be suspected that much of the mutilation had already occurred and that little of this text was left, albeit enough to attribute it (mistakenly) to Caxton's period and provide a date. This view about prior mutilation may be re-inforced from the evidence of the proverbial statements pasted in.

Between the verso of the endpaper and fol. iii recto: There are two pages from a manuscript of fifteenth-century liturgical Offices that are folded in two and bound in before fol. iii recto (foliated in pencil). It has to be supposed that these folios, now consisting largely of non-sequential pages from Offices in mid-October, derive from a once complete antiphoner that may have had a connection with the convent in which the saints' lives were used.

The two vellum pages in Latin are written in a Textus Quadratus hand. Such hands are typically very hard to date precisely because of their extreme formal qualities. The fragments contain portions of Offices for the Translation of St Edward the Confessor (13 October), St Calixtus (14 October), and the Dedication of Mont-Saint-Michel or Michael *in Monte Tumba* (16 October), with an added reference to St Wulfran (15 October). As they stand, the pages are set into the manuscript in the wrong chronological order so that fol. i recto–verso contains Calixtus, fol. ii recto has Michael (with the added mention of Wulfran), and fol. ii verso has Edward the Confessor. They have been trimmed very near to the bottom of the pages which are blackened and difficult to read, and there is also text missing. They equate with the liturgical Offices as follows:

fol. i recto: This begins imperfectly 'gerentur ad immolandum ydolis'. This folio equates with 'Sancti Calixti papæ et martyris', in *Breviarium ad usum insignis ecclesiae Sarum*, ed. by Francis Procter and Christopher Wordsworth, 3 vols (Cambridge: Cambridge University Press, 1879–86), III (1886), cols 915–18, where there are three lessons. The Add. 2604 text is missing only a few words from the beginning of Lesson 1 but ends half-way through Lesson 2; the opening of Lesson 1 is 'Temporibus Macrini et Alexandri facta est inquisitio in urbe

---

[32] See, for example, the opening at fol. Clxvii (and the opposite verso) where there is also an example of a large initial capital 'F'; see William Lyndwood, *Prouinciale seu Constitutiones Anglie: Cum summariis atq[ue] justis annotationibus: honestis characteribus; summaq[ue] accuratione rursum impresse*, ed. by Josse Badius (Paris: André Bocard, 1501) (STC 17107) in Cambridge, Cambridge University Library, Ta. 54. 1.

ADDITIONAL CONTENTS, OWNERSHIP, AND COMPILATION

Roma de Christianis, ut cogerentur ad immolandum ydolis' (col. 915). The fragment in Add. 2604 ends very indistinctly and illegibly owing to its blackened state; it can be reconstructed from the end of the printed version, 'Dicit ei sanctus Calixtus episcopus, Noli errando deridere veritatem. Respondit Palmacius cum lachrymis, dicens, Domine meus non derideo: sed in veritate cognovi, quia Dominus Deus Christus est' (col. 915) where the last word in Add. 2604 is possibly 'sed'.

fol. i verso: This begins imperfectly towards the beginning of Lesson 3 of Calixtus, '[...] matibus et lintheaminibus eum recondidit'. This equates with '[...] Quem beatus Calixtus de flumine levavit: et cum aromatibus et lintheaminibus eum recondidit' (col. 916). Add. 2604 finishes very near the end of Lesson 3 with 'qui vivit et reg'; this equates with 'Cujus corpus presbiter Asterius cum clericis suis de puteo elevavit, et sepelivit: præstante Domino nostro Jesu Christo qui vivit et regnat cum Deo Patre [col. 918] in unitate Spiritus Sancti Deus, per omnia secula seculorum. Amen' (cols 917–18).

fol. ii recto: This folio is the only one with music (Figure 13). Beginning imperfectly, it contains two chants, a verse and response, with the first beginning imperfectly, 'domine deprecamur Ut quos honore prosequimur contingamus et mente' followed by 'Perpetuum nobis domine tue miseracionis presta subsidium quibus et angelica prestitisti suffragia non deese'. In full the first should be 'Archangeli Michaelis interventione suffulti te domine deprecamur [...]'. They are listed in 'Cantus: A Database for Latin Ecclesiastical Chant — Inventories of Chant Sources' (https://cantus.uwaterloo.ca; accessed 5 February 2023) under Cantus ID 006118 and 0066118a respectively. Of the thirty-one examples of the first, twenty-seven are for the feast of Michaelmas (29 September) with only one for the Dedication of Mont-Saint-Michel or Michael *in Monte Tumba*; for the second of the nineteen listed, eighteen are for Michaelmas and none for the Dedication. The one example of this first chant being used for the Dedication occurs in a mid-fourteenth-century antiphoner of Sarum Use (Aberystwyth, Llyfrgell Genedlaethol Cymru / National Library of Wales, MS 20541 E). In view of the other October feasts in Add. 2604, this one must have been for the Dedication of St Michael. This is supported by the rubric at the end of the musical section referring to the Magnificat and continuing 'cum oratio sicut in alio festo memoria de sancto wlfranno [...]' as Wulfran's feast took place on 15 October.

fol. ii verso: The final Office (and first chronologically, on 13 October) opens with much missing. The 'Translatio Sancti Edwardi Regis et Confessoris', which should have nine Lessons (cols 909–14), begins half-way through Lesson 8 with 'quinto in ipsa nocte qua virgo'. This equates with 'Anno Dominicæ incarnationis millesimo sexagesimo quinto, in ipsa nocte qua virgo puerpera sine dolore' [...]' (col. 913). Add. 2604 finishes indistinctly with the end of Lesson 9, followed by a few more concluding indistinct lines. The ending of Lesson 9 equates with 'Ad tumbam ejus diversa fiunt a Christo ipso intercedente miracula: et odoris ejus suavitas et fragrantia membra reddit invalida cælesti medicamine solidata' (col. 914).

fols iii verso–v verso: Blank, apart from the number '7959' in ink on at the bottom of fol. v verso.

fols vi recto–xxii recto: Pages are pasted in on the rectos (the versos are blank) from a writing-master's book; in pencil underneath the first image is written in modern pencil: cf LE. 34. 32 (no. 7684) (Figure 14). There is some scribbling on the pages as follows: at the bottom of fol. vi someone has written in ink what looks like 'the' which is then crossed out; on fol. viii there are a few letters/words scribbled in what looks like a sixteenth-century hand; on fol. xi someone has been trying to emulate the letter-forms and clearly were doing this before the plates were pasted on as some of the writing has been cropped; on fol. xxi there are a few early letter-forms and what looks like 'ffra-' in an eighteenth- or nineteenth-century hand (again this has been cropped). Because there are a further eight folios all blank (apart from the additions below), it may be supposed that it was intended to paste on additional material.

Thomas Vautrouillier, a Huguenot scholar-printer, settled in Blackfriars (London) in 1562 and published *A Booke Containing Divers Sortes of Handes [...]* in 1570 and in 1574 he published *A Newe Booke of Copies [...]*. It is from some edition of the latter work (with its different images) that the Plates here have been taken. Rather than follow the order of the original, where each set of letter-forms is accompanied by a proverbial comment beginning with a different letter of the alphabet, the text in Add. 2604 appears in a haphazard fashion. A comparison with *A Newe Booke of Copies, 1574: A Facsimile of a Unique Elizabethan Writing Book in the Bodleian Library, Oxford*, ed. by Berthold Wolpe (London: Oxford University Press, 1962) is as follows. Apart from the penultimate item on fol. xxi, the text here equates respectively with Plates 4 (fol. vi), 27 (fol. vii), 8 (fol. viii), 6 (fol. ix), 7 (fol. x), 2 (fol. xi), 26 (fol. xii), 5 (fol. xiii), 12 (fol. xiv), 3 (fol. xv), 22 (fol. xvi), 17 (fol. xvii), 15 (fol. xviii), 11 (fol. xix), 16 (fol. xx), and 30 (fol. xxii). The fact that the Plates are not in order and their frequently darkened state would suggest that the book from which

ADDITIONAL CONTENTS, OWNERSHIP, AND COMPILATION 27

they were taken was either unbound or in a state of severe disrepair when the pages were cut out. Apart from Plate 16, which is in Latin, and the last two Plates, the unidentified one (on fol. xxi) and Plate 30, which are in French, all the others are in English. The format of the English Plates follows the same pattern: an elaborate device normally appears at the top of the page (only the two French Plates and Plates 2, and 27 lack any device). There is a very decorative and historiated initial capital before the proverbial statement, followed by the relevant alphabet (to illustrate a particular hand). There is some slight variation in whether or not there are four dots in the device at the top of the plates; in a few cases the version in Add. 2604 either includes or lacks the dots, as follows: in Add. 2604's Plates 4, 5, and 17 the dots are added but not in Add. 2604's Plates 7, 3, 15, and 11. The text found in Add. 2604 is not therefore from the precise edition as that by Wolpe.

fol. xxiii recto: This contains a handwritten note from the late eighteenth or early nineteenth century about items referred to in the manuscript with the relevant page number, as follows: 'Bede mentioned page 9 / Bone Fire, on St John's day —10 / Dragons etc in the Air how expelled —11 / Verulane in Companye 26 / Edward the Confessor and his ring — 39 / Columbe Virgin 41'. Clearly this is the same person who was responsible for the pagination of the manuscript, which stops at 49, following the life of Columba; because this pagination takes no account of the missing fol. 14, this page was clearly missing before the pagination was carried out.

fols xxiii verso–xxx verso: This section is blank, except that pasted onto the left margin of fol. xxx recto is a list of the saints' lives, excluding John the Evangelist and listing only Erkengota (rather than Erkengota and Æthelburh) (Figure 15). Clearly the numbers were written down first, hence the error at Martha; it is also obvious that the transcriber was copying from the text in question. This demonstrates that at least by the late eighteenth century the manuscript did not have a contents list, if such ever existed. This list is written vertically on the back of the sheet or envelope addressed (horizontally) 'To / The rev'd Mr Burton / [o]f Elden Thetford / Norfolk'; in a different hand at the top of the now pasted-in page is written (vertically): 'The hand Writing of my much esteemed friend the Rev: Geo. Burton Rector of Eldon Suffolk' (Figure 16), that is, the parish of Elveden near Thetford. On this same page in the opposite corner and upside down there are some figures in the same ink, '28/288/1', underneath which is written '28' and underneath that either '8' or '-8'.

The lives are given as follows:

'1 — Lives in this M:s
2 — Lyfe of St John Baptist
3 — Life of St Colombe
4 — Life of Seynt Agate the virgyn
5 — Life of Seynt Cecile
6 — Life of Seynt Barbara
7 — Lyfe of St Awdry of Hely
8 — Lyfe of St Sexburgh sy<s>ter to St Awdry
9 — Lyfe of St Hermenylde 1st Doughter of St Sexburgh
[with 'h' superimposed on 'a']
10 — Lyfe of St Werburg doughter of St Ermenyld
11 — Lyfe of St Erkengoode 2d doughter of St Sexburgh
12 — Lyfe of St Whitburg Syster of St Awdry
[possibly with 'h' superimposed on 'a']
13 — Lyfe of St Edith of Wylton
14 — Lyfe of St Edburg abbes aft<i>r St Mildrede
15 — Lyfe of St Aswyde the nonne of Folkstone
16 — Lif of St Hilde Abbes of Streneshall
17 — Lyfe of St Martha abbes of many nonnes
and the syst[cut off at margin]
18 — of Mary Mawdelen
19— Lyf of St Domitille
20 — Life of St Justine abbes & Martyr
21 — Life of St Benett
22 — Lyfe of St Modewyne
23 — Lyf of Leonarde the abbot'

At the end of the medieval saints' lives there are three added texts.

fols xxxi recto–xxxii recto: 'A curious Legend of St Christopher' in a hand of the late eighteenth century (or a little later) that begins 'There was a man of stature bigge, and bigge withall in minde / For serue he would, yet one than whom he greater none might find' (Figure 17) and ends 'And of his Carriage,

ADDITIONAL CONTENTS, OWNERSHIP, AND COMPILATION 29

Christo-fer, should thence forth be his Name'; it is attributed at the end to 'William Warner'.

This verse text tells how a man (subsequently named Christopher) left the service of a king, who feared the devil, for the service of the devil, who feared the cross; in quest of Christ, Christopher eventually discovered him through unwittingly ferrying the Christ-Child across a river. Described in the online *Oxford Dictionary of National Biography* (ODNB) as 'an eclectic mixture of classical mythology and Christian legend, together with episodes from the English chronicles and theological debate', the poet William Warner's (1558/9–1609) *Albion's England, or, Historicall Map of the same Island* was first published in 1586 and in the editions that followed over the next twenty-six years (until 1612) it was expanded from four to sixteen books.[33] For instance, the fifth edition of 1602 (STC 25083) has thirteen books. The text in Add. 2604 — a very careful transcription albeit with the narrative shorn of its context — is part of chapter 50 as found in the ninth book of William Warner's *Albion's England* (London: *Edm[und] Bollifant* for *George Potter*, 1602), pp. 227–30 (pp. 228–29). At face value the choice of this source is rather odd in what is meant to be a Catholic volume. Instead of choosing a straightforward Catholic hagiographical text, someone has extracted the life of Christopher from a non-Catholic context involving 'papist' criticism. It is perhaps less of a mystery, given the identity of the compiler who is discussed below.[34]

fols xxxii verso–xxxiii verso: Notes in prose on St Christopher by the same hand as the preceding, beginning 'St Christopher was of the Linage of Cananees, great of stature, and terrible of Countenance, being twelve cubits long' and ending 'and amongst many other Passages of his Life was at last beheaded, and his Blood there spilt cured those that were blind'; the source is given as 'A Helpe to discourse / 1648'. The second St Christopher text narrates the story again of Christopher ferrying the Christ-Child but omits the part about the king and the devil found in the previous text and in the source, *A helpe to discourse: or, more merriment mixt with serious matters [...]*. In its original title this work is often attributed at least in part (no doubt incorrectly) to the poet William

---

[33] For William Warner, see the entry by Katherine A. Craik in the ODNB (https://doi.org/10.1093/ref:odnb/28770) (accessed 5 February 2023).

[34] It should also be noted that inevitably there was not always a firm demarcation in what was Catholic or what was Protestant material in the post-Reformation period; see, for example, John R. Yamamoto-Wilson, 'The Protestant Reception of Catholic Devotional Literature in England to 1700', *Recusant History*, 32 (2014), 67–89.

Basse (*c.* 1583–1653?).[35] *The New Helpe to Discourse*, which was first printed in 1669, was assigned to William Winstanley.[36] As noted above, the source title is provided and the date of 1648.[37] Apart from the abbreviation, the text follows its source carefully; see, for instance, *A helpe to discovrse: or, more merriment mixt with serious matters [...]*, 11th edition (London: *I*[ohn]. *B*[eale] Printed for *Nicolas Vavasour*, 1635), pp. 151–53 (STC 1552) (USTC 3018267). In some ways this text was an even stranger choice for our copyist than *Albion's England* because *A helpe to discovrse*, which is a digest of dialogues on matters religious, historical, and fanciful, was an example of one of the many useful manuals aimed at 'common readers' or in this case 'the commonest of readers' in the seventeenth and eighteenth centuries.[38] It is therefore an unexpected source from which to choose hagiographical texts, albeit that there is nothing strange about the immediate context as in *A helpe to discovrse* Christopher is preceded by the story of St George (pp. 148–56) and followed by that of the Seven Sleepers (pp. 153–56). Why Christopher was selected for addition to the manuscript on two occasions remains unclear, especially since it is effectively almost the same story told twice.

fols xxxiv recto–xxxvii recto: This final section comprises notes in prose on St Benedict, written in a different late eighteenth- or early nineteenth-century hand from the preceding, beginning 'Saint Benedict the founder of the Order of the Benedict Monks, was born in Italy about the year 480' (Figure 18). It is immediately followed by a piece on the Benedictines that begins 'Those Monks of his Order, were called Benedictines. Their Habit was a loose Black Gown with large wide sleeves and a capuche, or Cowl, on their heads ending in a point behind [...]'. The whole ends (rather in mid-air) with a note about the nuns: 'There are Nuns likewise who follow the Rule of S[t] Benedict, among whom,

---

[35] For William Basse, see the entry by David Kathman in the ODNB (https://doi.org/10.1093/ref:odnb/1633) (accessed 5 February 2023).

[36] Lawrence E. Klein, 'Politeness for Plebes: Consumption and Social Identity in Early Eighteenth-Century England', in *The Consumption of Culture 1600–1800: Image, Object, Text,* ed. by Ann Bermingham and John Brewer (London: Routledge, 1995), pp. 362–82 (p. 378 n. 9). Klein provides a computation of the numerous editions of both titles reckoning that 'If one counts only editions for which copies are extant, there were at least twenty-two editions between 1619 and 1799. If one accepts the numbering of editions on title pages, there were as many as twenty-six' (p. 378 n. 9).

[37] *A helpe to discourse: or, more merriment mixt with serious matters [...]*, 13th edn (London: Printed by M[oses]. B[ell]. for I. B.,1648).

[38] Klein, 'Politeness for Plebes', pp. 368 and 370.

ADDITIONAL CONTENTS, OWNERSHIP, AND COMPILATION   31

those who call themselves mitigated, eat Flesh 3 times a Week, on Sundays Tuesdays and Thursdays: The others observe the Rule of St Benedict in its rigour, & eat no Flesh unless they are sick:'.

The piece on St Benedict is followed straightaway as if it is part of the same text by the item on the Benedictines that outlines their habit, customs, and impact on England, ending with a couple of sentences about Benedictine nuns. No indication of the source is provided in Add. 2604, but the text is actually from the second edition of the *Encyclopaedia Britannica*; see *Encyclopaedia Britannica [...]*, ed. by James Tytler, 2nd edn, 10 vols (Edinburgh: Printed for [...], 1778–83), II (1778), 1101 col. 2–1102, col. 2.[39] The text in the manuscript is exactly the same as that in the printed version, with one item following directly on from the other, even with the apparent after-thought about the nuns.

fols xxxvii verso–lviii verso: Blank

Collation

The two parchment pages look like a bifolium but contain non-sequential material (see above). The added eighteenth-century (or early nineteenth-century) material, twenty-eight pages at the beginning and twenty-eight at the end, is all tightly bound. It is not possible to work out definitely the collation of the first eight folios (fols iii–x). The obvious solution would be a quire of eight but evidence of string (albeit late) suggests that it is a quire of six and a bifolium (that is, fols iii–viii, and fols ix–x), though it may originally have been a quire of ten like the following quires in this section; these problems are compounded by the fact that the watermarks are not particularly helpful. The following two quires, on the basis of string (indicated by *) and watermarks, are quires of ten (fols xi–xx)* and (fols xxi–xxx)*. The last twenty-eight folios fall into a quire of ten (fols xxxi–xl)*, on the basis of string, and another quire of ten (fols xli–l)*, also on the basis of string. We then have a mirror image of the opening of this added section; on the basis of watermarks, the last quire has to be one of six (fols liii–lviii) so again there may be a bifolium (fols li–lii) at the end as at the beginning.

---

[39] The first edition does not have this full text, only an entry on the Benedictines with no mention of the nuns; see *Encyclopaedia Britannica [...]*, ed. by William Smellie, 1st edn, 3 vols (Edinburgh: Printed for [...], 1771), I, 540 cols 1 and 2. We are grateful to Olivia Robinson for verifying the text in the second edition for us.

Watermarks

The watermark detected is a crown above a fleur-de-lis, though it is difficult to make out and it does not occur throughout (for example, there are no watermarks on fols iv–v, and xi). The presence of the crown watermark at the beginning and end of the manuscript demonstrates that the paper here is clearly from the same stock. Part of this image may be seen (upside down) in the left-hand top corner near the gutter from fols xii–xix, and xxi–xxx at the beginning of the manuscript and from fols liii–lviii at the end (for instance, on fol. xxiv at the beginning of the volume and on fol. liii at the end, where the pages are blank and the image may be more clearly seen). In the above folios only the top portion of the watermark on the left-hand side is visible; that is, the crown part and the top of where a fleur-de-lis would be expected. At the end of the manuscript fols xxxi–lii all contain the same image in the top left hand-margin near the gutter; this is the bottom right-hand portion (the right-way up) of the fleur-de-lis. In addition to this crown/fleur-de-lis watermark, at the beginning of the manuscript, fol. iii has a loop going off to the right in the top centre and what may be letter-forms; fols vi–x and xx, for example, also have letters in the top left-hand margin, most clearly visible on fol. viii recto (Figure 21) at the front of the manuscript where they look like 'ATMAN'. It has not been possible to identify the image fully, but close comparisons have been found. Initially, the nearest equivalent owing to the shape of the crown seems to be an image in Edward Heawood's collection that has been dated to 1767; further investigation demonstrates that 'ATMAN' is part of the name 'Whatman' and that the curling loop detected is the cipher of the famous Whatman Kentish firm of paper manufacturers as shown in an image in W. A. Churchill's collection.[40]

---

[40] See no. 1743 on Plate 235 (and its dating on p. 103) in the fleur-de-lis section of Edward Heawood, *Watermarks: Mainly of the 17th and 18th Centuries*, Monumenta Chartæ Papyraceæ Historiam Illustrantia, 1 (Hilversum: The Paper Publications Society, 1950) and Edward Heawood, *Watermarks: Addenda and Corrigenda*, Monumenta Chartæ Papyraceæ Historiam Illustrantia, 1 (Hilversum: The Paper Publications Society, 1970), p. v. More or less the same watermark but with the Whatman cipher and name 'JWHATMAN' is found as no. 324 in W. A. Churchill, *Watermarks in Paper in Holland, England, France, etc. in the XVII and XVIII Centuries and their Interconnection* (Amsterdam: Menno Herzberger & Co., 1935), p. CCLIV; Whatman's connection with paper manufacture in the Netherlands is briefly discussed on p. 40. James Whatman, the elder (1702–59), was responsible for high quality paper at Turkey Mill in Kent, being the first paper maker in Europe to produce wove or vellum paper; on his death, his son, James Whatman, the younger (1741–98), took over the firm, which in 1794 became the firm of Hollingworths and Balston and from 1806 that of W. and R. Balston; all continued to use the Whatman trademark, which makes precise dating of the watermark in Add.

ADDITIONAL CONTENTS, OWNERSHIP, AND COMPILATION 33

Annotation

Later annotations are found in the manuscript. These date from various periods (possibly seventeenth to the early nineteenth century) and are in different hands, with the most extensive being the faint pencil annotations almost exclusively in the native lives, which would appear to have been written by the same hand (which may also be identified with the hand that made the list on fol. xxiii recto); this may be the hand of George Bird Burrell, one of the owners. On fol. 19r there are a couple of indecipherable letter-forms or numbers in ink at the bottom of the page. On fol. 49r by the section where Barbara is about to explain the doctrine of the Trinity to her father, 'note' is written in ink in the right-hand margin and this section is lightly underlined in the manuscript. On various folios the same word is repeated in ink. On fol. 79r: 'vanitas vanitatis' is written at the top of the page and 'v [*sic*] vanitas vanitatis omnia vanitas' in the upper right-hand corner and into the right margin; this italic-type hand would appear to date possibly from the seventeenth century. In the same hand on fol. 90r 'vanitatis vanit' [*sic*] occurs at the top of the page; on fol. 103r in the upper margin is written 'vanitas v', and on fol. 110r 'vanitas vanitatis v vanitatis omnia vani [*sic*]'. On fol. 132r at the top of the page is written in ink 'O llorde [unidentified letter] Barlle [?]'. The following are all in pencil: fol. 52v: 'Anna was King of East Anglia 643:' fol. 53v: in the top margin 'Saint Wulfride was Archbishop of York Anno Dom. 728'; fol. 55r: 'AD 673' (marking the death of Æthelthryth) occurs in the top right-hand margin; fol. 59v: 'Ercombert King of Kent A.D. 641' is written at the bottom of the page; opposite the opening of Eanswith on fol. 79r is written 'Folkstone'; it also appears in what looks like palimpsest (in pencil) as 'Folkestone' below this; 'Kent' occurs in pencil at the very bottom of the page; fol. 79v: 'St Peter' occurs towards the top of the page; on fol. 89r 'St Hilda' occurs; on fol. 99r: there is a very faint word (on a patched folio at the top of the page) in pencil; it begins with an 'T' or 'I' and ends 'gche'; on fol. 123r 'wenyst' is found in the right-margin as a gloss on the text with 'n' underlined. In addition, on fol. 78v: 'Year 1085' is written in ink in the bottom left-hand margin; this merely gives in figures the date given in the

2604 difficult. See further J. N. Balston, *The Elder James Whatman, England's Greatest Paper Maker (1702–59): A Study of Eighteenth Century Paper Making Technology and its Effect on a Critical Phase in the History of English White Paper Manufacture*, 2 vols (West Farleigh, Kent: J. N. Balston, 1992), and Thomas Balston, *William Balston: Paper Maker, 1759–1849*, A Garland Series, Nineteenth-Century Book Arts & Printing History, ed. by John Bidwell (London: Methuen, 1954; repr. New York: Garland, 1979).

34   I. THE MANUSCRIPT

manuscript for when Lanfranc translated the relics of Mildrith and Eanswith to Canterbury; it would appear that this is the same hand who has written the number '5' (also in ink) in the right-hand margin of fol. 55r. Both these ink additions look to be in an earlier hand than the pencil annotation.

Ownership Inscriptions

Inside front cover: There is a bookplate of the Duke of Sussex, consisting of his coat of arms, bearing the words 'Honi soit qui mal y pense', flanked by a lion and a unicorn, with St George and the motto, 'Si deus pro nobis quis contra nos' underneath; written on the blank space on the plinth below this is the shelf-mark 'VI / H. g. 1'. This bookplate, available in two slightly varying forms, does not contain the Duke of Sussex's name; the shelf-mark here is in line with what is usually found in his books.[41] The bookplate also has the name of a former owner, 'R. C. Hussey' written in ink at the top in a nineteenth-century hand, to the left of which occurs '13 CCLXIII', also in ink. The latter is the number (13) and page reference (cclxvii) to the manuscript in the catalogue of the Duke of Sussex's books drawn up in 1826 by his surgeon and honorary librarian, Thomas Joseph Pettigrew, and published in 1827.[42] In addition, in pencil at the top

[41] See Brian North Lee, *British Royal Bookplates and Ex-Libris of Related Families* (Aldershot: Scolar Press, 1992), for a full description of the bookplate: 'Armorial: the Royal arms as borne 1801–37 without an inescutcheon in the Hanoverian inescutcheon and over all a label of three points argent charged on the centre point with two hearts in pale and on the others with a cross gules, the arms in the Garter ribbon and collar, the George depending; with coronet, Royal crest and supporters charged on the shoulder with a label as on the arms. The motto, in translation "If God is for us, who can be against us", is draped over a bracket below which has blank oval for the shelf-mark. There were two varieties used [...] a) The letters of the motto are shaded etc. Unsigned. [...] b) The motto lettering is open, the "sun's rays" shading is lighter, etc. Signed "Perkins and Heath Hardened Steel Plate" [...]'. (p. 41, Plate 24 Anonymous (Duke of Sussex), showing both varieties; that in Add. 2604 follows the b) variant.

[42] Thomas Joseph Pettigrew, *Bibliotheca Sussexiana: A Descriptive Catalogue, Accompanied by Historical and Biographical Notices, of the Manuscripts and Printed Books Contained in The Library of His Royal Highness The Duke of Sussex, K.G., D.C.L., &c &c &c &c in Kensington Palace*, 2 vols in eight parts (London: Printed for Longman and Co., Paternoster Row; Payne and Foss, Pall Mall; Harding and Co., Pall Mall East; H. Bohn, Henrietta Street; and Smith and Son, Glasgow, 1827; Longman and Co., 1839), I, Part 1 (1827). The catalogue only covers the theological portion of the library, with I, Part 1 being devoted to manuscripts, I, Part 2 to printed editions, and II (1839) to Bibles. Nothing more was published and the collection was sold in 1844–45 (see below). The number of English manuscripts is small — a mere fourteen — in comparison with the one hundred and forty-eight Latin or even the thirty-four French. Add. 2604 is

ADDITIONAL CONTENTS, OWNERSHIP, AND COMPILATION   35

right-hand corner of the label, there is a very faint note referring to the manuscript, '[illegible] Dethes of the Martyres', which is how it is described in the
sale catalogue. Beneath the page reference 'G' is written twice. At the bottom of
the label, to the left and the right, are found '7 x 5 In' and 'Sæc XV'. (clearly the
way in which it is referred to in the Duke's descriptive sale catalogues).[43] A later
hand has added 'Add. 2604' in between the two copies of 'G'.

Endpaper recto following inside front cover: An insertion is pasted onto the
marbled endpaper with the following inscription written in ink in a nineteenth-
century hand: 'This Ancient MSS was / purchased by a former owner / G. B.
Burrell at the Sale of the / Library of Geo. Tasburgh Esq / [the name is under-
lined] of Rodney [that is, Bodney] Hall in the County / of Norfolk in the Year
/ 1788 [underlined] – See a Memorandum / to that Effect in the Middle /
of this Volume'; a modern hand has added '(75[b])'. This memorandum on fol.
75v states, 'This ancient M:S: I purchased at the / Sale of George Tasburgh's
Esq of Bodney / hall in the County of Norfolk: 1788 / GBBurrell' (Figure
19).[44] This is followed by a curlicue underneath the signature. To the left of this
notice the same hand has written, again in ink, 'M[r] Tasburgh / [w]as a Roman
/'; the original word 'Catholic' has been cut away but has now been replaced
by 'catholic' in a different hand and ink. This shows that Add. 2604 can only
have been trimmed after it was bought by Burrell, for whom, see further below
under Ownership. In a list of his books and manuscripts compiled by Burrell
in 1811 Add. 2604 is not mentioned, unless it is the text referred to as 'Quarto
Roman Missal on Vellum Illuminated English'.[45] It seems unlikely that Burrell

---

listed as '13. THE LYVES AND DETHES OF THE MARTYRES. MS ON VELLUM. SÆC. XV, Quarto'
and then described as 'One hundred and twenty-one leaves. Seven inches by five. This Ms. is
written in a small but very legible gothic character, and the initials are illuminated in gold and
colours. The Lives contained in this volume are as follows' (p. cclxiii). The list of saints is then
accurately given, apart from 'Cecil' for Cecilia, the misspelling of Wærburh as 'Wexburgh' and
the reference to Domitille or Domitilla as 'Somitille' (p. cclxiv). For an account of the library
see Gabriel Moshenska, ' "The Finest Theological Library in the World": The Rise and Fall of
the *Bibliotheca Sussexiana*,' in *Book Collecting in Ireland and Britain, 1650–1850*, ed. by Elizabethanne Boran (Dublin: Four Courts Press, 2018), pp. 168–87 and the references therein.

   [43] See n. 46.

   [44] We have been unable to locate any catalogues for a book sale. We wish to thank Justin
Clegg in the British Library for help with this matter. A notice of the forthcoming auction of
household furniture from Bodney Hall is found in the *Bury and Norwich Post* for Wednesday,
16 April 1788 (p. 3), but without any mention of books.

   [45] Cambridge, Cambridge University Library, MS Additional 5906. This is bound with 'G.

as someone deeply knowledgeable about books would give such an inaccurate description, but the other explanation — that it was sold by 1811 — is more implausible given the evidence from Burrell's last will and testament discussed below. And it is true that while Add. 2604 may not be a Roman missal, it is a quarto, is in vellum, is decorated, and is in English.

fol. iii recto: The name 'John Egan' is written in ink at the top of the page; beneath this is the shelf-mark 'Add 2604' also in ink, and beneath are two ownership inscriptions in ink. The first reads 'Presented to His Royal Highness the / Duke of Sussex K.G. Etc Etc Etc Etc / by E. H. Barker Esq. M. A. / October 1826 / Sæc XV'. The second inscription beneath reads, 'Purchased at the Sale of the Library of the / late Duke of Sussex at Mr Evans in Pall / Mall the 3^d of August 1844' by Me / John Egan'; this signature is the same as that at the top of the page. The Cambridge Library stamp with the date of '3 JUL 87' (that is, 1887) occurs at the bottom of the page.

End leaf recto: There is the following nineteenth-century note in pencil, 'Bought of Bull & Auvache / 3 July 1887. Bibl. Sussex. vol. i, p. cclxiij.'

Ownership and History

Given the plethora of eighteenth- and nineteenth-century owners, we shall start with the latest one and work backwards sequentially. The manuscript was acquired by Cambridge University Library on 3 July 1887, as noted on fol. iii recto; it was bought from the London booksellers, Alfred Bull and Edward John Auvache, whose premises were at 35 Hart Street, Bloomsbury. Previously, as inscribed on the inside front cover, it had been owned by the architect Richard Charles Hussey (1806–87) of Harbledown near Canterbury before its sale on 20 May 1887. Before him, the owner was a John Egan (whose identity is not known), who noted on fol. iii recto that he had bought it on 3 August 1844, though this may actually have been 2 August. This was in the sale of one of the greatest libraries in the country that took place at the establishment of the auctioneer and bookseller, Richard Harding Evans (1778–1857) of Pall

---

B. Burrell / 1811' on the upper cover and his bookplate 'G. B. Burrell. / Thetfordiensis.' on the inside front cover. It is entitled 'A Catalogue. / of Manuscript's [*sic*], Books, Coins, / & / Miscellaneous Antiquities. in the possession of George Bird Burrell, / of / Thetford.' (p. 4). Apart from 'in the possession of', the rest of the script is set out in an elaborate fashion like a title plate. The handwritten catalogue itself is very systematic, listing Manuscripts, Ancient Deeds, Books (subdivided into Folio, Quarto, Octavo et cetera), and so forth.

ADDITIONAL CONTENTS, OWNERSHIP, AND COMPILATION

Mall in London, from 31 July to 3 August 1844.[46] From October 1826 until his death in 1843 our manuscript, as shown by his bookplate on the inside front cover, was in the care of the Duke of Sussex (1801 onwards), otherwise known as Prince Augustus Frederick (1773–1843), the sixth son and ninth child of George III and Queen Charlotte, and brother of the reigning monarchs George IV and then William IV. The prince was a supporter of social and political reform such as the abolition of the slave trade and Catholic Emancipation. He had an enlightened interest in the arts and was President of the Royal Society from 1830 to 1838. He was also a genuine bibliophile who was said to have built up a collection of more than 50,000 volumes, with particular strengths in editions of the Bible.[47] Add. 2604 was presented to him, as may be seen on fol. iii recto, possibly by someone trying to gain some sort of preferment, as he often did.[48] This person was the Yorkshire-born classicist, Edmund Henry Barker (1788–1839), a Cambridge scholar and author of several publications, who settled in Thetford after his marriage in 1814 and often had himself described as 'OTN' meaning 'of Thetford, Norfolk'. Aided by his wife's independent means, he built up a large library which included our manuscript, apparently acquired at some point after 1814. In 1835, before he moved to London and ended up bankrupt, he had been forced to sell his library.[49] However, he had presented Add. 2604 to Augustus Frederick years before, in 1826. He had acquired it from another inhabitant of Thetford, George Bird Burrell, who was a town clerk and, as we shall see, interested in antiquarian matters. We do not know when Barker acquired the manuscript, but it must have may have been after Burrell's death in 1823. Burrell himself is quite explicit on fol. 75v about the

[46] *Bibliotheca Sussexiana: The Extensive and Valuable Library of His Royal Highness The Late Duke of Sussex, K.G., &c. &c. [...] Which will be sold by Auction by Messrs. Evans, No. 93, Pall Mall on Monday, 1st July and twenty-three days following. (Sunday excepted)* (London: Evans, 1844). The sale catalogue was in six parts; the sale started on 1 July 1844 and the last items were being sold from 11 August 1845. The manuscripts were listed in Part 2 and the sale was said to have been on 31 July 1844 and the three days following. Add. 2604, described as 'Lyves and Dethes of the Martyres. MS. of the XVᴛʜ Century upon vellum. Size 7 inches by 5' (p. 26) was sold as Lot 294 on the Third Day of sale, which would make this 2 August and not 3 August as above.

[47] For Prince Augustus Frederick, see the entry in the ODNB by T. F. Henderson, revised by John Van der Kiste (https://doi.org/10.1093/ref:odnb/900) (accessed 5 February 2023).

[48] In the *Bibliotheca Sussexiana: A Descriptive Catalogue,* Pettigrew lists it as 'Presented to the library by my learned friend, E. H. Barker, Esq., of Thetford, Norfolk, 1826' (p. cclxiv).

[49] For Edmund Henry Barker, see the entry in the ODNB by Christopher Stray (https://doi.org/10.1093/ref:odnb/1393) (accessed 5 February 2023).

circumstances of his purchase in 1788, something that is repeated by another hand on the recto of the opening endpaper (albeit not entirely accurately). The binding of the manuscript, as noted in the manuscript description above, dates from the around the time of Burrell, as it bears the incised inscription 'T x BURREL' (with the 'x' in the middle of the line) on the upper cover (discussed further below). Finally we get to the earliest known and most important owner, George Tasburgh of Bodney Hall in Norfolk. The memorandum on fol. 75v confirms the sale of the manuscript to George Bird Burrell in 1788, five years after the death of George Tasburgh; it also records the important information that George Tasburgh was a Catholic. It is not known how or when Add. 2604 came into the Tasburgh family, though hints abound in the post-Dissolution period; this will be addressed in the section III. Convent and Geographical Location as it has a wider bearing on the history of the manuscript.

Compilation

As will be evident from the miscellaneous additional contents described above and the date of the paper, the volume as it currently stands had to have been compiled in the late eighteenth century or even into the early nineteenth century. Owing to the number of owners listed above and the different hands in the volume, there is a range of people to whom the compilation could be attributed. What follows here is a careful analysis of the post-medieval ownership to consider who may have been responsible for the current organisation of material in Add. 2604.

Given the reference to George Bird Burrell's former ownership, the writing on the recto of the first flyleaf, 'This ancient Mss ... volume', must surely be that of E. H. Barker, the next owner. On fol. iiii recto the presentation inscription to the Duke of Sussex must be by a member of his staff, possibly his surgeon-cum-librarian, Thomas Pettigrew (1791–1865), while the two signatures and ownership details of John Egan on the same page must obviously be in Egan's own hand. Likewise, we may assume that R. C. Hussey's signature on the inside front cover is his own. Yet there is no evidence that any of these later named owners had any part in compiling material in the manuscript not least because none of these hands occurs elsewhere in the volume. It would be tempting to believe that Barker might have tried to get the volume into a better state for presentation to the Duke of Sussex, but the argument for this is not forthcoming. Most importantly, the dating of the paper, and most probably the binding, would appear to signal a period at the end of the eighteenth century or the first

ADDITIONAL CONTENTS, OWNERSHIP, AND COMPILATION 39

decades of the nineteenth century that would rule out the active involvement of most of these later owners.

Although it would seem quite reasonable to suggest the involvement of the Catholic Tasburgh family in the additional items, it would seem that no member of the household (with one possible exception) played any part in the compilation of the manuscript. There is strong evidence of George Tasburgh's mother's writing style elsewhere. The former Mary D'Ewes (for whom see further under III. Convent and Geographical Location) can be completely ruled out for any of the three added eighteenth-century type items at the end of the manuscript or for any of the writing elsewhere.[50] Concerning George Tasburgh and his wives we have the following information. With regard to his first wife, Teresa Gage (d. 1773), there is a Declaration of Trust in 1756 and a Deed Appointing New Trustees of the Settlement in 1766; the former has both Teresa's and George's personal signatures. Teresa's hand is not identifiable with any of the added items in Add. 2604. In a Declaration of Trust dated 3 May 1782 we have both George's signature and that of his second wife, Barbara Fitzherbert (who outlived her husband).[51] Both hands are typical of the eighteenth century with a slanted duct and are quite similar to each other, except that George's signature is larger and more imposing with an elaborate curlicue beneath his surname (also found in the 1756 document). Barbara's hand does not occur in Add. 2604 and there is only a slim chance that it has any trace of George's hand, as discussed below.

After George's death, Bodney Hall was leased to a group of English Benedictine nuns from the French community of Montargis. Advertisements frequently appeared in *The Laity's Directory* noting that 'Bodney Hall is opened for

---

[50] Mary D'Ewes's markedly different hand from anything in Add. 2604 occurs in Cambridge University Library, MS Hengrave 88/3/90 in a letter to her sister, Delariviere Gage. The letter concerns a supposed supernatural event at the family's other home in Flixton (that is, in St Peter South Elmham) and is dated 23 February but without a year.

[51] For the documents associated with Teresa Gage, see respectively Gloucester, Gloucestershire Archives, D23/F18 and Sheffield, Sheffield City Archives, Arundel Castle Manuscripts, ACM/DD/153(19); the signatures in the latter are copied in the same hand. We are grateful to Andrew Parry for making available an image of the hands in the Gloucestershire document. Beverley, East Riding of Yorkshire Record Office, DDCC/135/63 is a document signed by the offspring of Thomas Fitzherbert of Swinnerton in Staffordshire: Basil Fitzherbert, Barbara Tasburgh, and Charlotte Gage, together with the daughters' husbands George Tasburgh of Bodney and Thomas Gage of Hengrave Hall (Suffolk). It concerns property sums settled for the provision of another sister Catherine Fitzherbert, under the will of her father. These five parties sign and seal their names at the bottom of the document.

40 I. THE MANUSCRIPT

the education of Young Ladies in every branch of useful knowledge becoming the delicacy of their sex'.[52] While the added hagiographical material would fit in well with a community of nuns or their pupils, their input can likewise be ruled out as the nuns did not take up residence in Bodney Hall until after the manuscript had been sold; some of the nuns arrived in December 1792 and the rest early in 1793.[53]

There is one other hand that has been implicitly identified: the list of saints' lives provided on the back of an envelope (which has the location of 'Bury' stamped on it), is attributed to 'my much esteemed friend the Rev: Geo. Burton'. This Anglican vicar and biblical scholar, George Burton, who was baptised in 1717 and who died in Bath in 1791, had scholarly interests and was a published author on biblical chronology.[54] He could have been a candidate for added material had it not been for their Catholic nature and most especially because his writing is very distinctive and bears no relation to any other in the volume.[55] But his presence in the manuscript may cast some light on what happened to it after it left the ownership of George Tasburgh.

George Bird Burrell added his ownership memorandum on fol. 75v so the identity of his hand is certain. The inscription on fol. 75v clearly demonstrates that after this time (1788) the manuscript pages were cropped, presumably for its current binding. This large and perfectly legible hand does not at first sight appear to occur elsewhere in the manuscript. But the convincing evidence comes from another manuscript owned by Burrell, London, British Library, MS

---

[52] A detailed example is available in *The Laity's Directory; For the Church Service on Sundays and Holy Days, for the Year of our Lord M DCC XCV [...]* (London: J. P. Coughlan, 1794), p. 6, which begins 'The BENEDICTINE DAMES of MONTARGIS. — *Bodney Hall* is opened for the education of Young Ladies in euery branch of useful knowledge becoming the delicacy of their sex [...]' and, after some outline of the nuns' reputation for education and their aim 'of being useful' to a country 'who received them in their distress', closes with information about where particulars may be sought. In later copies of *The Laity's Directory* the advertisement tends to concentrate only on the opening message and closing particulars.

[53] For a full account of these nuns at Bodney Hall, see Margaret J. Mason, 'Nuns of the Jerningham Letters: The Hon. Catherine Dillon (1752–1797) and Anne Nevill (1754–1824), Benedictines at Bodney Hall', *Recusant History*, 23 (1996), 34–78 (pp. 39–40).

[54] For George Burton, see the entry in the ODNB by Thompson Cooper, revised by Emma Major (https://doi.org/10.1093/ref:odnb/4128) (accessed 5 February 2023).

[55] For comparison's sake there are various examples elsewhere of Burton's rather inelegant hand. For instance, Norwich, Norfolk Record Office, Bradfer-Lawrence Collection, Miscellanea, BL/MC 39, which is dated 18 June 1739 when Burton became curate of Felstead in Essex, is described by Burton as 'Bishop of Norwich's Testimonial of my subscription to the 39 articles' (signed by him).

ADDITIONAL CONTENTS, OWNERSHIP, AND COMPILATION   41

Additional 39177. On fol. 9r (also numbered as 17) there is a signed inscription: 'George Bird Burrell, a sincere / lover and admirer of Antiquity:' (Figure 20) where it is also noted that the manuscript used to belong to George Ashby (the Suffolk antiquarian). This hand is identical to the handwriting of George Bird Burrell where he refers to 'his esteemed friend', the Reverend George Burton (Figure 16).[56] Through a careful analysis of duct and individual letter-forms it then becomes clear that George Bird Burrell was also responsible for the item on St Benedict and the Benedictines on fols xxxiv recto–xxxvii recto. He was also responsible for the comment underneath the cut-outs from Lyndewode's *Provinciale* on the reverse of the opening (marbled) flyleaf, 'A Specimen [...] of Caxton's types A. D. 1495' and the (now faint) notes about items in the manuscript on fol. xxiii recto. Admittedly, the reference to the saints' list by Burton is written in a different ink than any of these other items yet there is a remarkable similarity in the letter-forms (notably his very distinctive capital E, H, and T forms), most particularly in the section on Benedict and the Benedictines. It might also be assumed that he was responsible for the pagination and at least some of the other annotation in the manuscript. The address to Rev. Burton (which is now rather faint) on the front of the sheet on which the list is written, is probably also in Burrell's hand though there is an outside but unlikely chance that this might be by George Tasburgh.[57] Albeit of different generations (with Burton being born in 1717 and Burrell in *c.* 1756), it would seem entirely plausible that Burrell who lived in Thetford, with Burton nearby (as rector of the parishes of Elveden and Herringswell), were known to each other given their antiquarian interests.[58] The two items on St Christopher on fols xxxi–xxxiii,

[56] Cambridge, Cambridge University Library, MS Additional 5906, the list of Burrell's manuscripts and other antiquities is also written by Burrell but in a more careful hand that is not so immediately like his comment in Add. 2604 or his other inscriptions noted here.

[57] The writing is somewhat faint which makes comparison difficult. While it is most probably Burrell's more open hand as seen on fol. 75v rather than his spikier one on the reverse of the sheet, there are some general similarities with George Tasburgh's signature (see n. 51), but this may be no more than any similarity between one eighteenth-century hand and another.

[58] While Burton's published work had a theological focus (see n. 54), Burrell restricted himself to matters Thetfordian, as shown in George Burrell, Jun., *An Account of the Gifts and Legacies that have been Given and Bequeathed to Charitable and Public Uses in the Borough of Thetford, with their Present State and Management; Also, a Chronological Account of the Most Remarkable Events which have Occurred in Thetford, from the Earliest Period to the Present Time* (Thetford: Samuel Mills, 1809). Norwich, Norfolk Record Office, The Colman Manuscript Collection, Society of United Friars, Communications and related Papers, COL 9/110, is a presentation copy of this book with the following dedication by Burrell on the inside front

though with some similarities to Burrell's hand, would appear to be in a different and unidentified hand, not found elsewhere in the manuscript.[59] Taken as a whole, Burrell amassed a very amorphous collection of material to which he added wholesale the Benedictine item, and apparently annotated it here and there. That such procedure is typical of Burrell may be seen from another of his manuscripts, London, British Library, MS Additional 39177, as highlighted in an extract from a letter from E. H. Barker to Joseph Hunter (the new owner of the manuscript) on 10 June 1828, which is quoted on the verso of an opening flyleaf. Barker, who coincidentally also owned the present manuscript after Burrell, notes Burrell's added indexes (which are very extensive). At the end in a different ink (obviously by Hunter himself) is the acerbic comment: 'and I should have been as well pleased if they had not been there.'[60]

Add. 2604 was clearly bound under Burrell auspices as the binding has the name 'T x BURREL', yet the added items in the manuscript must date from

---

cover: 'Respectfully presented to the Society of United Friars by their sincere friend and Brother, the Author, Oct: 11. 1814'. The Society of United Friars was founded by eight Norwich citizens in 1785 with the purpose of promoting intellectual culture and fellowship, and with each member adopting the habit of a monastic order. The Society (which appears to have ended in 1828), formed a library and the members, who included John Sell Cotman and Humphrey Repton, read philosophical papers. In Norwich, Norfolk Record Office, Norfolk and Norwich Archaeological Society Collection, NNAS G6/10 (formerly G2), 'The Fraternity of United Friars, College of St Luke, of Norwich, with Descriptions of their Convent & Ceremonies and Notes of their Transactions compiled from their Minutes and Records (in the possession of J. J. Colman, M.P.), by Mark Knights (copy made by Ernest A. Kent)', it is noted that 'Burrell George, admitted in 1814 and made a Cistercian. He read papers on The History of Monarchism & the Reign of Henry VII' (p. 107). This handwritten copy was made in *c.* 1901.

[59] It is not clear whether or not Burrell had any part in the addition of the lives of Christopher, though it may not be insignificant that another manuscript owned by him, London, British Library, MS Additional 39177, has a piece from an unidentified printed text headed 'On the Castle of St George' pasted onto p. 16.

[60] Whatever Barker or Hunter may have thought, this manuscript, like Add. 2604, demonstrates Burrell's genuine enthusiasm for what he clearly regarded as the embellishment and expansion of his manuscripts. He was particularly keen on this manuscript as evidenced in his list in Cambridge, Cambridge University Library, MS Additional 5906, where it occurs as no. 14 and is described as 'A Beautiful Manuscript of that celebrated Herald and Antiquarian Sylvanus Morgan [...]' (fol. 5r). Another example of one of his decorative compilations is found in a manuscript in Thetford Library entitled 'The Charter Acts of Parliament; For the Foundation, of a School and Hospital, and Navigation of the River Ouse, with the Bye-Laws etc of the Corporation of Thetford, with Remarks of Occurrences, transacted by the Members of that Body, From the year 1680, carefully Collected By me Geo: B. Burrell, 1794' (shelf-mark L 352). We owe the discovery of this work to the kindness of Kayleigh Garrod of Thetford Library.

ADDITIONAL CONTENTS, OWNERSHIP, AND COMPILATION 43

before it was bound or re-bound. This is clear not only from the way that the cropping was done after Burrell's ownership inscription on fol. 75v but also how in the Benedictine piece the writing runs very close to the margin, in some cases unnaturally so. It is odd that Burrell chose to put his ownership inscription in the middle of the medieval manuscript rather than at the beginning or the end and that after compilation such severe cropping was permitted. The mixture of items in the volume is not perhaps such a mystery as Burrell had a tendency to compile disparate materials together. It is possible that many of the individual components were bought separately in the Tasburgh sale and then combined and/or added to later, or that they were already all in Burrell's ownership or acquired after the Tasburgh sale.

The addition of various materials, some of which *may* have lain about at Bodney Hall or in South Elmham (the location of the other Tasburgh ancestral family residence) over the years, is further complemented by a general 'tidying-up' of the medieval manuscript as outlined above.[61] As noted there, even the title that the manuscript now has 'The lyves and dethes of the martyres', is clearly an addition as the medieval letter-forms have been stuck onto the first page, with the colouring of the initial 'T' of the title looking like an eighteenth-century addition or later. As argued above in the Annotation section of the description of the saints' lives, it is highly likely too that as part of his tidying up and 'enhancement' of the manuscript by the addition of other material, that it was Burrell who was responsible for removing the catchwords that did not match up (presumably with some sort of solvent). This would fit in with his attention to the manuscript in general through what would seem to be his sporadic annotation, particularly in the native lives. Of course, it is also true that any of the later owners could have devoted themselves to such a clean-up opera-

---

[61] There is one intriguing potential link between the added contents and the Tasburgh family. William Basse, to whom *A helpe to discourse* is attributed (even if incorrectly) had earlier dedicated an example of Spenserian pastoral love poetry, *Three pastoral elegies; of Anander, Anetor, and Muridella* ([London]: Printed by V[alentine] S[immes] for I. B.[arnes], 1602) (STC 1556), to Jane (later Tasburgh), the mother of his patron, Sir Richard Wenman, by her first husband; see the entry by David Kathman for William Basse in the ODNB (n. 35). This Jane was in turn the mother, from another marriage, of Lettice Cressy, the Catholic matriarch of the Tasburgh Flixton line (see III. Convent and Geographical Location for the history of the Tasburgh family). There was then a direct link between the family and work by this poet and so it might be entirely plausible to think of a later eighteenth-century Tasburgh being interested in the St Christopher text, possibly by an author associated with Jane, a distant grandmother. On the other hand, this could just be random co-incidence and *A helpe to discourse* may have come from Burrell himself.

tion perhaps as part of preparing Add. 2604 for sale, but we think this unlikely. Of all the owners here, it is Burrell who has a definite track record of involving himself fully in his collection in a hands-on manner.

Burton became rector of Elveden in 1740 and rector of Herringswell (near the Suffolk border just south of Mildenhall) in 1751; he held both simultaneously and died in Bath on 3 November 1791. The list of saints' lives was made at some point in the period between 1788, when Burrell acquired Add. 2604 and before 3 November 1791. It seems odd that there are so many blank paper folios in the manuscript so the current enterprise *may* be an unfinished one begun during George Bird Burrell's lifetime. Perhaps the volume was not bound (or re-bound) until after his death in 1823; this would then explain why the inscription is 'T'. rather than 'G'. on the upper cover. It is not known precisely who this T. Burrell was, but an educated guess may be made. It is fortunate that George Bird Burrell left a detailed will, dated 12 September 1810, in which he writes tenderly of his wife, Elisabeth, 'who I well know is a devout and well disposed person'.[62] Evident too is his great care for his goods including books, coins, and manuscript collections. He makes bequests to Elisabeth 'who may take and have for her own use such books out of my collection as she shall wish and approve of' deeming that Elisabeth should make an inventory of the books, furniture, and other effects for their two sons, George and John, who will inherit after her death. One wonders if the list he drew up himself in 1811 was part of the same process.[63] Later in the will he bequeaths to his son George his 'cabinets of Coins and Medals and all other my Books (except as before excepted) and Manuscripts [...]'. In the event the son George predeceased his father and a codicil was drawn up on 12 November 1822 whereby the other son John became the beneficiary and sole executor (appointed on 11 November 1823). Most importantly for Add. 2604, in the course of the original will Elisabeth is requested to pay George Bird Burrell's brother, Thomas Burrell, 'one yearly annuity of three pounds'. Although Thomas is not bequeathed any books, it is not impossible to speculate that he was later given Add. 2604 by

---

[62] Norwich, Norfolk Record Office, Archdeaconry of Norwich: Marriage Licence Bonds and Affidavits, ANW 24/78/25 contains a marriage licence bond for Burrell and Elisabeth Esther Snare for 1 December 1803. Burrell's death is recorded in various local papers including the *Norfolk Chronicle* (p. 2) for Saturday, 28 June 1823; he is described as 'the well-known' antiquary in his sixty-seventh year whose death had occurred the previous week. For his will, see Norwich, Norfolk Record Office, Archdeaconry of Norwich Probate Records: Wills, ANW, Will Register, 1823–1825 (1823), fo. 123, no. 87, Burrell, George Bird, of Thetford.

[63] See n. 45.

ADDITIONAL CONTENTS, OWNERSHIP, AND COMPILATION

John after his father's death and that Thomas then had it bound or re-bound with his own name on the front.[64] This may go some way to solving a little more of the history of a manuscript that was at different times owned — among others — by a recusant, a town clerk, a bankrupt, and a prince.

Binding

The binding, which has the stamp of 'T x BURREL' on the upper cover, is described by Jayne Ringrose as 'xviii or xix cent. half roan, tree-calf sides'.[65] Given the later ownership, it has to date at some point between 1788 and *c.* 1823 or a few years later (see Compilation). There are dark blue, almost black, plain marbled endpapers at the beginning and end of the manuscript. On the spine there is the shelf-mark 'ADD / G / 60'.

The assembly of all the materials that make up Add. 2604 partly serves to demonstrate George Tasburgh's Catholic history melded together with the eclectic antiquarian interests of George Bird Burrell from the late eighteenth century. Effectively therefore there are two histories for the provenance of this manuscript, the late eighteenth-century one outlined here and an earlier post-Dissolution one. This history is interwoven with the history of the Tasburgh family down through the centuries; this will be traced in III. Convent and Geographical Location as it may be directly concerned with the medieval geographical provenance of Add. 2604. But before that, we shall turn to another sort of localisation in II. Language and Dialectal Provenance.

[64] From the evidence provided in a will by another George Burrell, who was a relative of George Bird Burrell, it appears to be extremely common in the family for sons to be named after their fathers; George Bird Burrell's brother, Thomas, seems to have been called after their father; see Norwich, Norfolk Record Office, Archdeaconry of Norwich Probate Records: Wills, ANW, Will Register, 1772–1773 (1773), fo. 156, no. 92, Burrell, George, of Thetford. It is very unlikely that George Bird Burrell would have had his deceased father's name inscribed on one of his manuscripts; that his brother did this at some point after 11 November 1823 (or possibly beforehand if he acquired the book during his brother's lifetime) seems plausible and so provides an approximate date for the binding, that is *c.* 1823.

[65] Ringrose, *Summary Catalogue of the Additional Medieval Manuscripts in Cambridge University Library Acquired before 1940*, p. 17; roan is a soft leather made from sheepskin, used in bookbinding as a cheaper substitute for morocco (sourced from goatskin); tree-calf is a highly polished calf binding with a distinctive tree-like pattern. For further information on book bindings of the period, see Stuart Bennett, *Trade Bookbinding in the British Isles, 1660–1800* (New Castle, DE: Oak Knoll Press; London: The British Library, 2004).

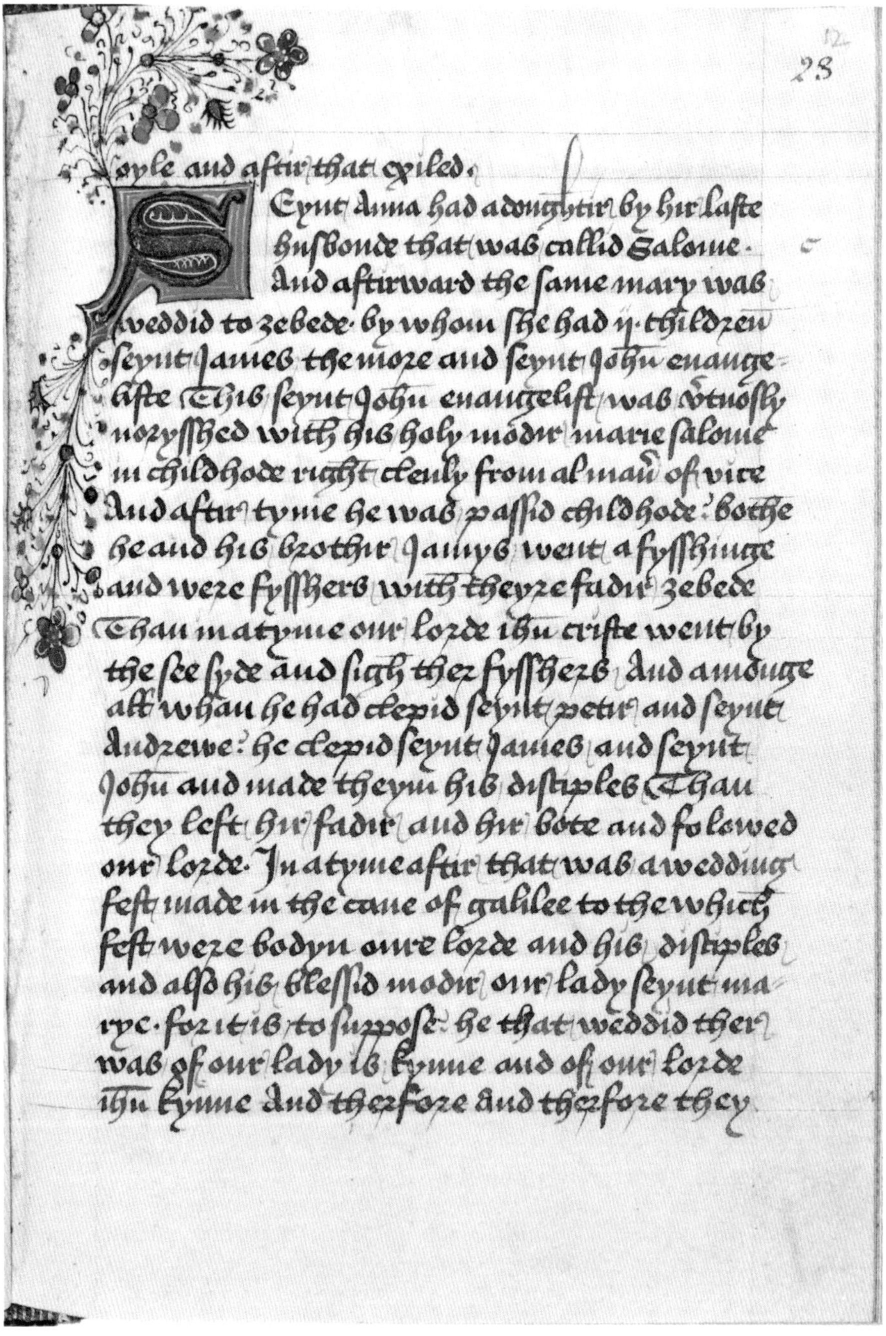

12
28

xyle and aftir that exiled.
Seynt Anna had a doughtir by hir laste
husbonde that was callid Salome.
And afturward the same mary was
weddid to zebede. by whom she had ij. children
seynt James the more and seynt John euangeliste. This seynt John euangelist was vertuosly
norysshed with his holy modir marie salome
in childhode right clenly from al man of vice
And aftir tyme he was passid childhode: bothe
he and his brothir James went a fysshinge
and were fysshers with theyre fadir zebede
Than in a tyme our lorde ihu criste went by
the see syde and sigh ther fyssherz And amonge
all whan he had clepid seynt petir and seynt
Andrewe: he clepid seynt James and seynt
John and made theym his disciples. Than
they left hir fadir and hir bote and folewed
our lorde. In a tyme aftir that was a wedding
fest made in the cane of galilee to the which
fest were bodyn oure lorde and his disciples
and also his blessid modir our lady seynt ma
rye. for it is to suppose: he that weddid ther
was of our lady is kynne and of our lorde
ihu kynne and therfore and therfore they

Figure 1. John the Evangelist, fol. 12r.

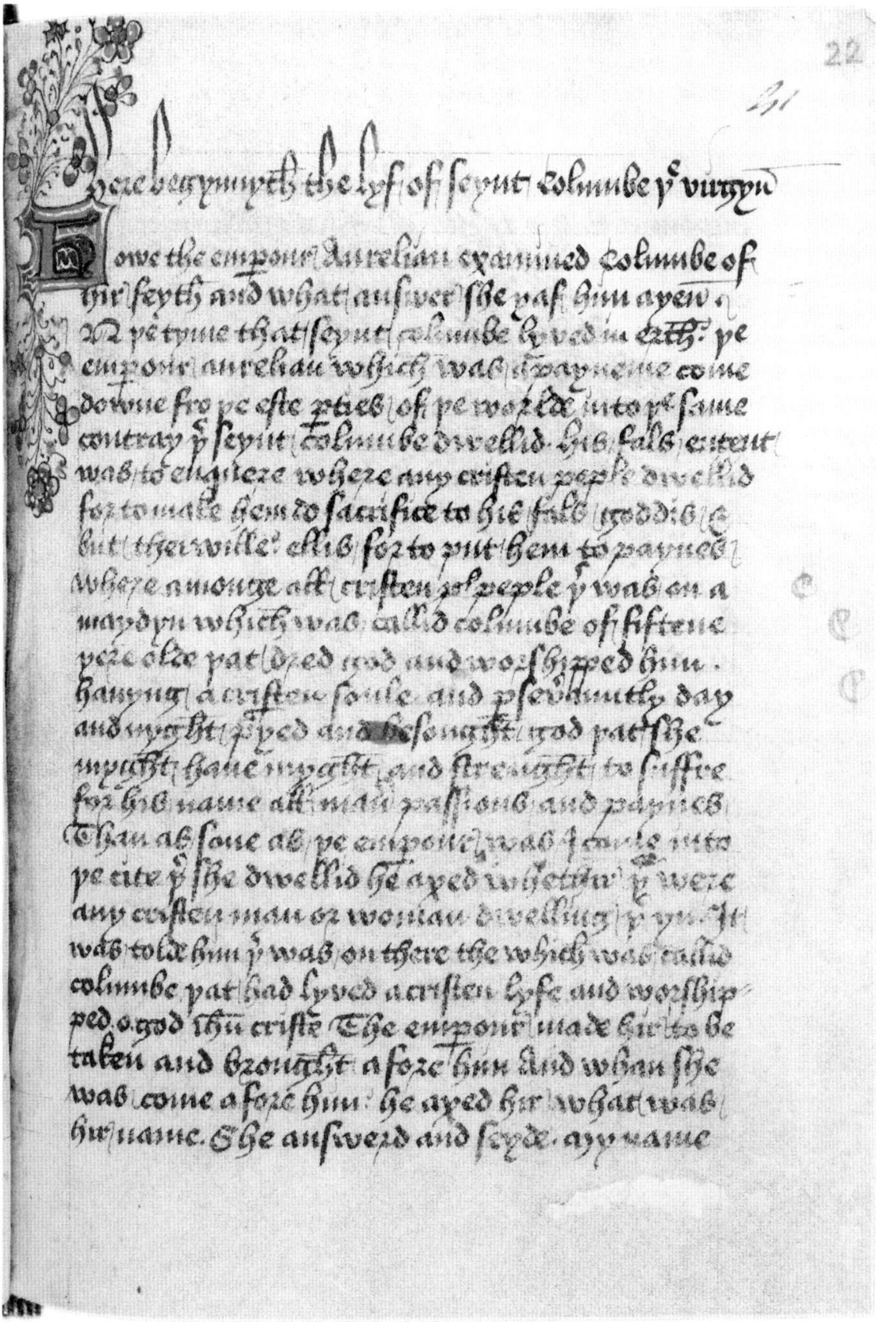

Here begynnyth the lyf of seynt columbe þe virgyn

Now the emperour Aurelian examined columbe of
hir seyth and what answer she gaf him ayew.
In þe tyme that seynt columbe lyved in erth þe
emperour aurelian whiche was a payneme come
downe fro þe este parties of þe worlde into þe same
contray þer seynt columbe dwellid his fals entent
was to enquere where any cristen peple dwellid
for to make hem to sacrifice to his fals goddis
but their wille ellis for to put hem to paynes
where amonge all cristen þe peple þer was on a
maydyn whiche was callid columbe of fiftene
yere olde þat loved god and worshypped hym
hauyng a cristen soule and prudently day
and nyght preyed and besought god þat she
myght haue myght and strenght to suffre
for his name all maner passions and paynes
Than as sone as þe emperour was entrid into
þe cite þat she dwellid he axed wheither þer were
any cristen man or woman dwelling þer yn It
was tolde him þer was on there the whiche was callid
columbe þat had lyved a cristen lyfe and worshypped o god Ihu criste The emperour made hir to be
taken and brought afore him And whan she
was come afore him he axed hir what was
hir name. She answerd and seyde my name

Figure 2. Columba, with an unusual daisy flower, fol. 22r.

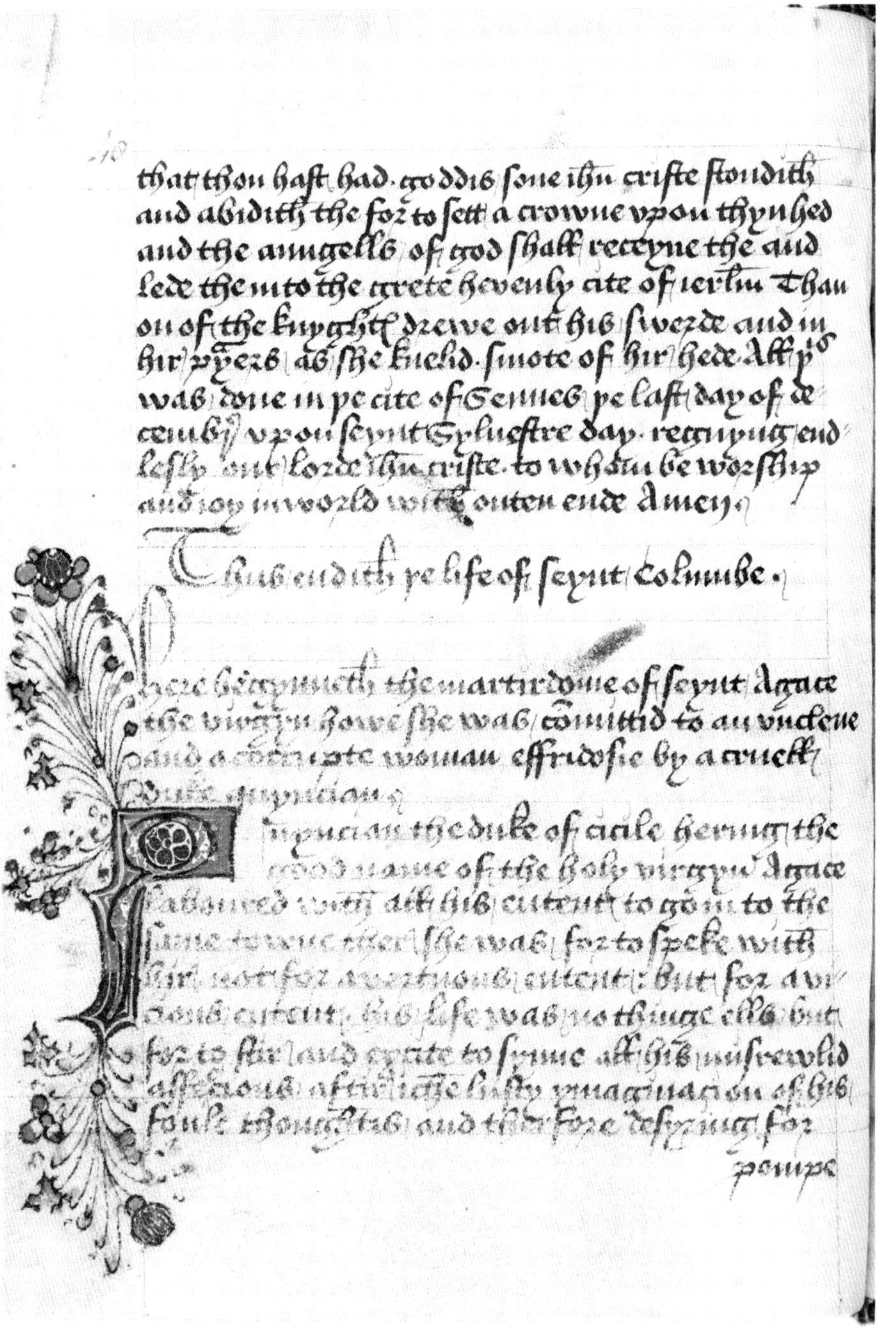

that thou haſt had. ço ddis ſone ihu criſte ſtondith
and abidith the for to ſett a crowne vpon thyn hed
and the aungells of god ſhaff receyue the and
lede the into the grete heuenly cite of ierlm Than
on of the knygḣtt dreue out his ſwerde and in
hir vyers as ſhe kneld. ſmote of hir hede. Aftp yis
was done in pe cite of Gennes pe laſt day of de
cembr vpon ſeynt Sylueſtre day. receyuyng end
leſly oure lorde ihu criſte. to whom be worſſhip
and ioy in world with outen ende Amen.

Thus endith pe life of ſeynt Columbe .

here begynneth the martirdome of ſeynt Agace
the virgyn howe ſhe was comittid to an vncleue
and a corrupte woman effridoſie by a cruell
Duke quyncian.

quyncian the duke of cicile heryng the
good name of the holy virgyn Agace
laboured with all his entent to gon to the
ſame toune ther ſhe was. for to ſpeke with
hir not for vertuous entent. but for a vi
ous entent. his life was no thinge ellis but
for to ſtir and egate to ſynne all his miſrewld
affecious after licite luſty ymaginacion of his
foule thoughtis and therfore deſyryng for
poumpe

Figure 3. Columba and Agatha, fol. 25v.

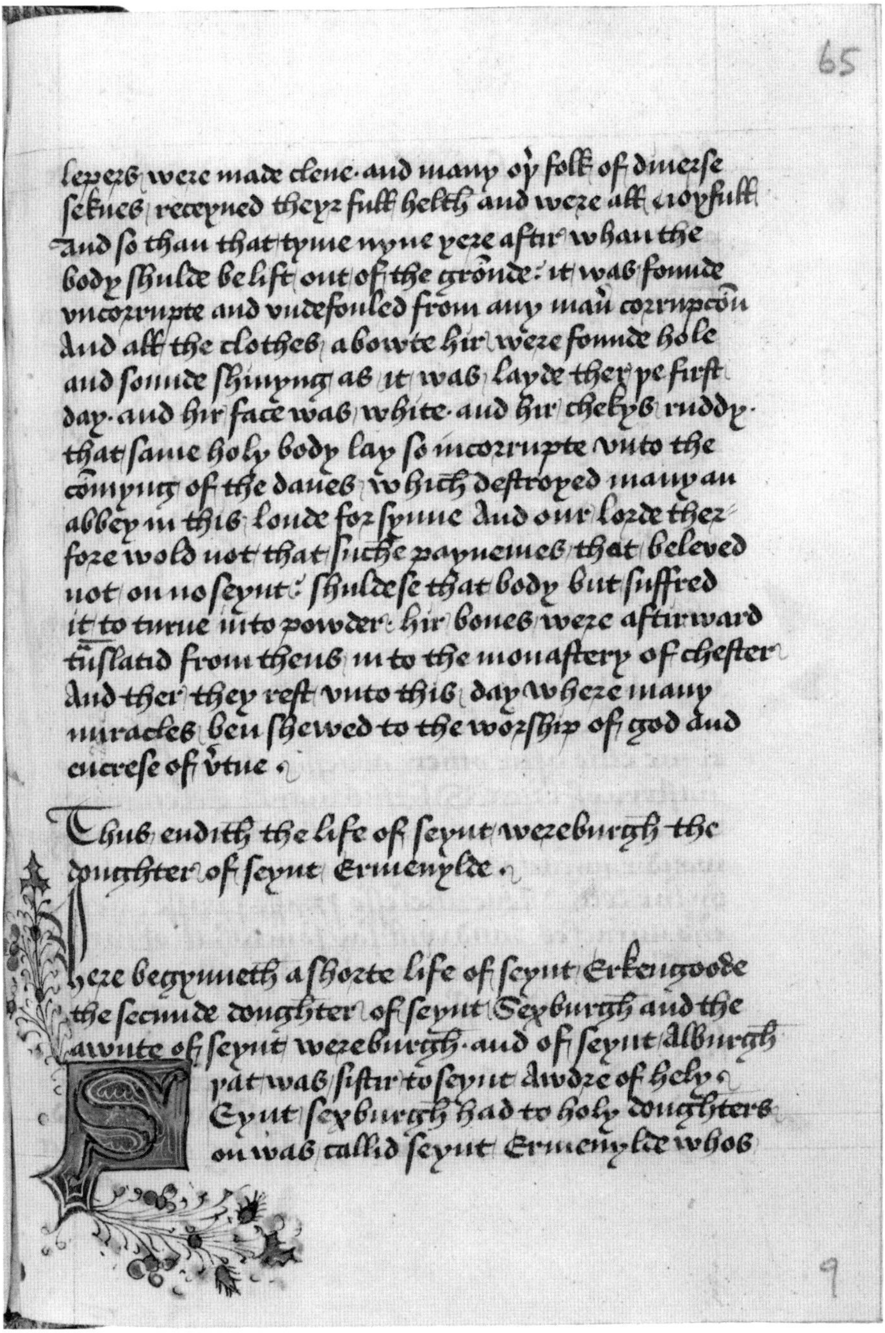

FIGURES 49

lepers were made clene. and many oþ folk of dmerse
seknes receyued theyr full helth and were all ioyfull
and so than that tyme nyne yere aftir whan the
body shulde be lift out of the gronde. it was fonnde
vncorrupte and vndefouled from any man corrupcon
And all the clothes abowte hir were founde hole
and founde shinyng as it was layde they þe first
day. and hir face was white. and hir chekys ruddy
that same holy body lay so mcorrupte vnto the
compmg of the danes which destroyed many an
abbey m this londe for synne And our lorde ther
fore wold not that suche paynemes that beleved
not on no seynt. shulde se that body but suffred
it to turne mto powder. hir bones were aftirward
trislatid from thens m to the monastery of chester
And ther they rest vnto this day where many
miracles ben shewed to the worship of god and
encrese of vtue.

Thus endith the life of seynt wereburgh the
doughter of seynt Ermenylde.

Here begynneth a shorte life of seynt Erkengode
the secunde doughter of seynt Sexburgh and the
awnte of seynt wereburgh. and of seynt Alburgh
þat was sistir to seynt Awdre of hely.
Seynt Sexburgh had to holy doughters
on was callid seynt Ermenylde whos

Figure 4. Wærburh and Eorcengota, fol. 65r.

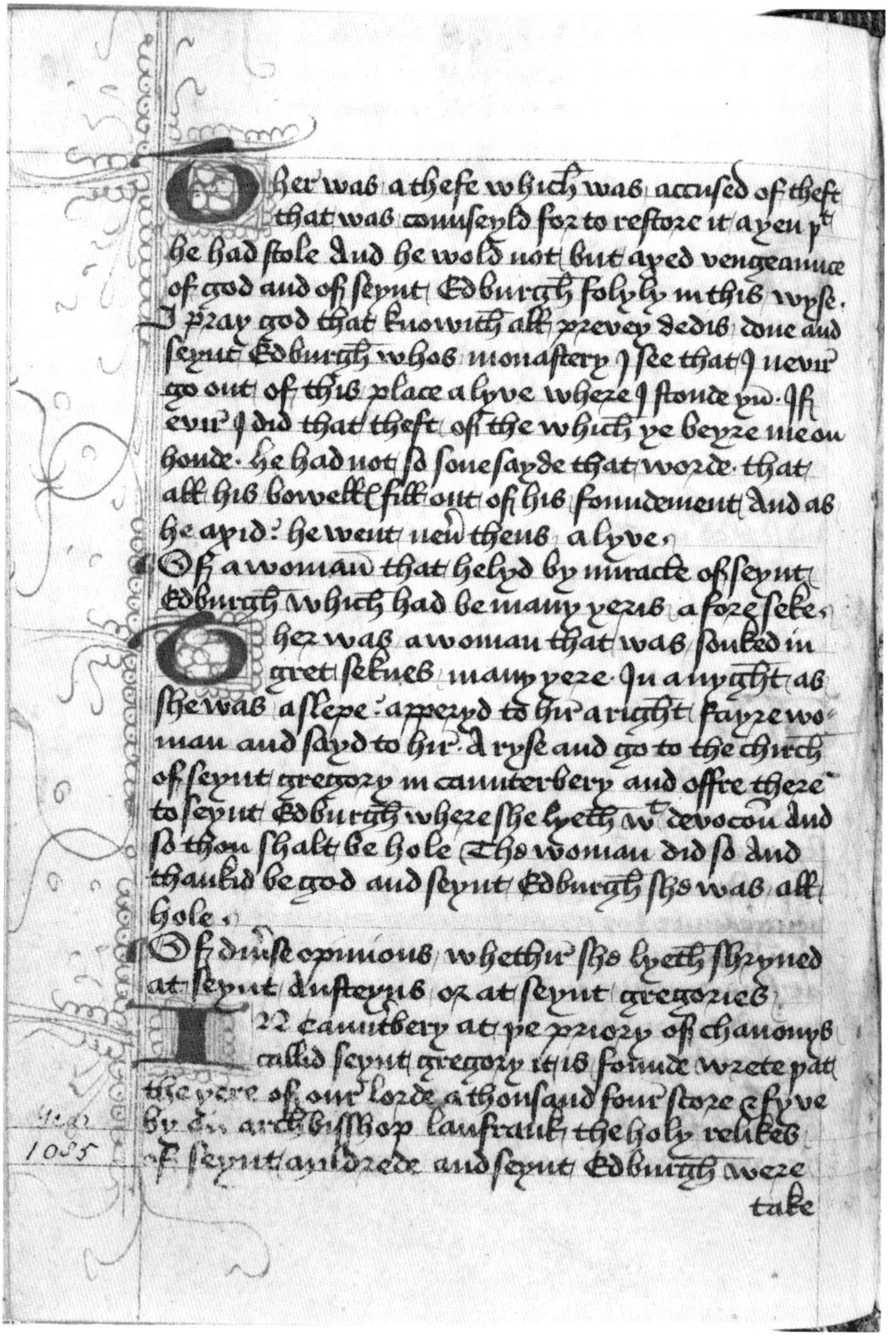
Ther was a thefe which was accused of theft
that was counseyld for to restore it ayen yt
he had stole and he wold not but ayed vengeaunce
of god and of seynt Edburgh folyly in this wyse.
I pray god that knowith all prevey dedis done and
seynt Edburgh whos monastery I see that I nevir
go out of this place alyve where I stonde ynne. If
evir I did that theft of the which ye beyre me on
honde. he had not so sone sayde that worde. that
all his bowellis fill out of his foundement and as
he ayid: he went new thens alyve.
Of a woman that helyd by miracle of seynt
Edburgh which had be many yeris afore seke.
Ther was a woman that was sonked in
gret seknes many yere. In a nyght as
she was aslepe: apperyd to hir a right fayre wo
man and sayd to hir. Aryse and go to the church
of seynt gregory in caunterbery and offre there
to seynt Edburgh where she lyeth wt devocon and
so thou shalt be hole. The woman did so and
thankid be god and seynt Edburgh she was all
hole.
Of diuers opinions whether she lyeth shryned
at seynt Austeyns or at seynt gregories.
In Cauntbery at the priory of chanouns
callid seynt gregory it is founde wrete that
the yere of our lorde a thousand four score and fyve
1085 by the archbisshop lanfrank the holy relikes
of seynt Mildrede and seynt Edburgh were
take

Figure 5. Eadburh, with pen flourishing in the left margin, fol. 78v.

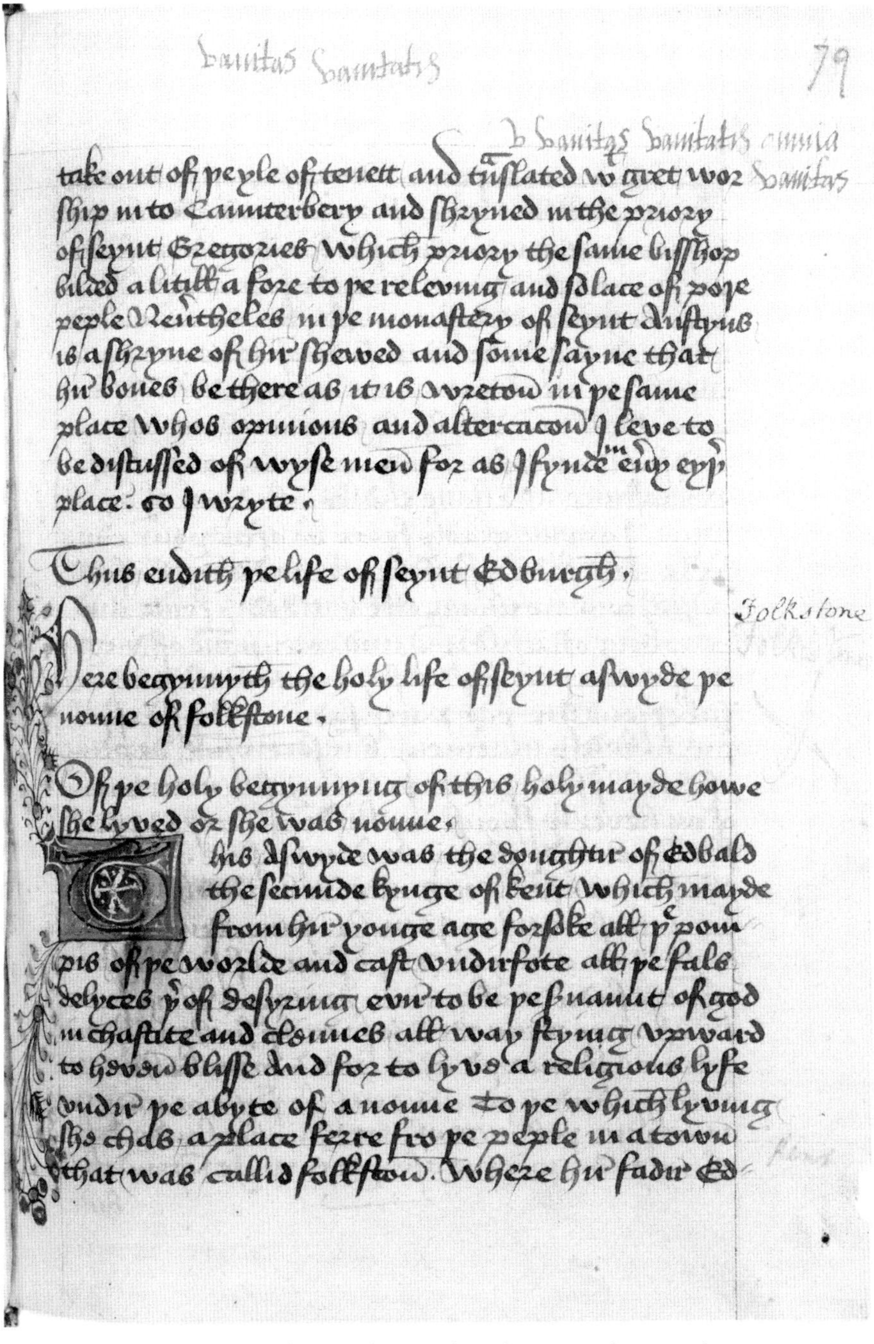

vanitas vanitatis

79

ɔ vanitas vanitatis omnia

take out of peyle of tenett and tislated w gret wor   vanitas
ship in to Caunterbery and shryned in the priory
of seynt Gregories Which priory the same bisshop
bilded a litill a fore to pe relevyng and solace of poie
peple Neutheles in pe monastery of seynt Austyns
is a shryne of hir shewed and some sayne that
hir bones be there as it is wretow in pe same
place Whos opinions and altercacow I leve to
be distussed of wyse men for as I fynde euy eyp
place: so I wryte

Thus endith pe life of seynt Edburgh.

Folkstone

Here begynnyth the holy life of seynt aswyde pe
nonne of folkstone.

Of pe holy begynnyng of this holy mayde howe
she lyved or she was nonne.
                    his Aswyde was the doughtir of Edbald
                    the secunde kynge of kent which mayde
                    from hir younge age forsoke all p pom
pis of pe worlde and cast vndirfote all pe fals
delytes p of desyring euer to be pe suaunt of god
in chastite and clennes all way stryng vpward
to heuen blisse and for to lyve a religious lyfe
vndir pe abyte of a nonne to pe which lyvyng
she chas a place ferre fro pe peple in a town
that was callid folkstow. Where hir fadir Ed

Figure 6. Eadburh and Eanswith, with contracted spraywork
and marginal annotation of 'vanitas', fol. 79r.

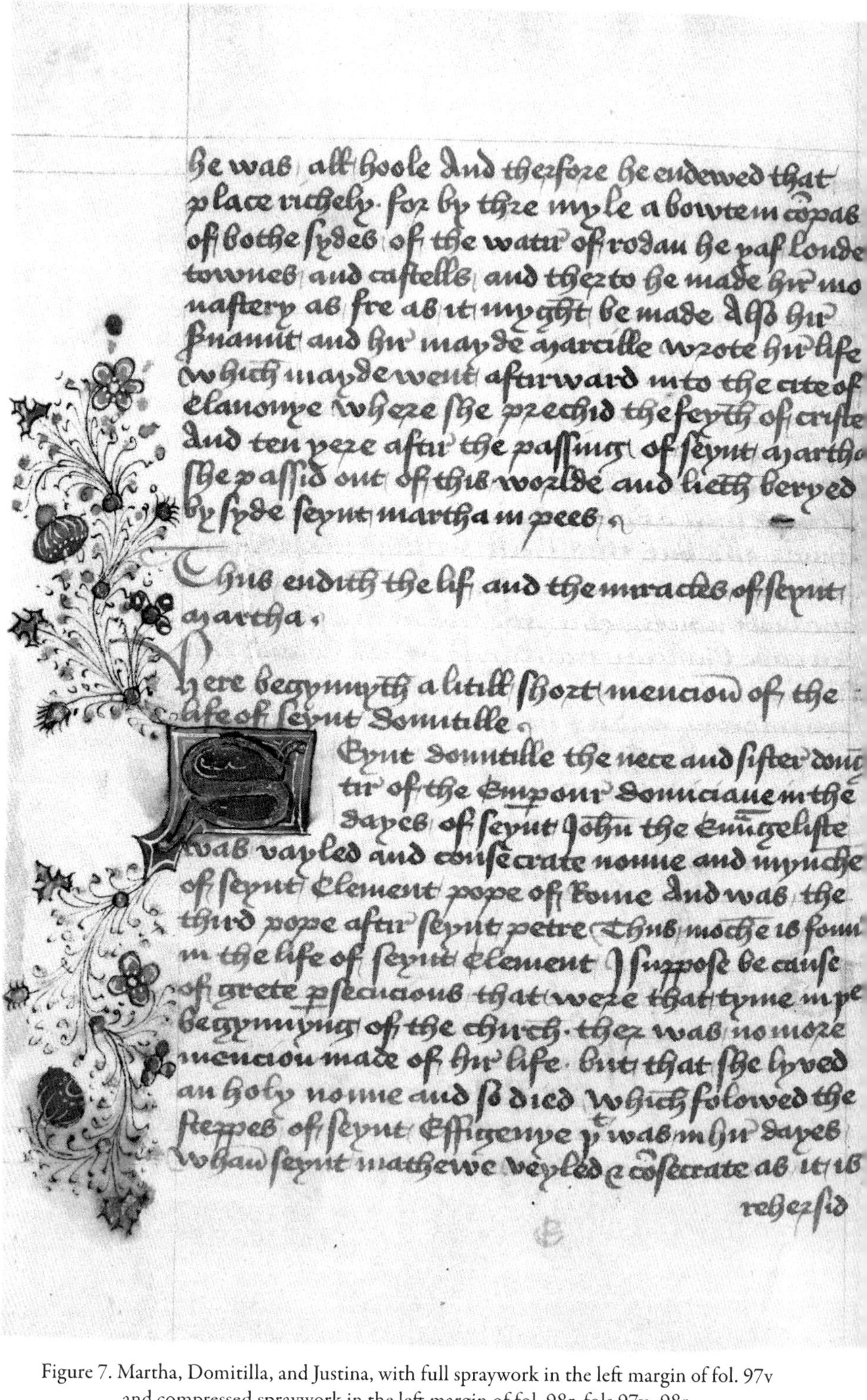

he was all hoole And therfore he endewed that
place richely for by thre myle abowte in copas
of bothe sydes of the watir of rodan he haf londe
townes and castells and therto he made hir mo
nastery as fre as it myght be made AĦ hir
snamit and hir mayde aymarille wrote hir life
which maydewent afturward into the cite of
elanowe where she prechid the feyth of criste
And ten yere aftir the passing of seynt ajartha
she passid out of this worlde and lieth beryed
by syde seynt martha in pees

This endith the lif and the miracles of seynt
ajartha

Here begynnyth a litill short mencion of the
life of seynt Domitille

Seynt Domitille the nece and sister doug
tir of the emperour Domiciane in the
dayes of seynt John the euangeliste
was vayled and consecrate nonne and mynche
of seynt clement pope of Rome And was the
third pope aftir seynt petre This moche is foun
in the life of seynt clement I suppose be cause
of grete psecucions that were that tyme in pe
begynnyng of the chirch ther was no more
mencion made of hir life but that she lyved
an holy nonne and so died which folowed the
steppes of seynt Effigenye y was in hir dayes
whan seynt mathewe veyled ¢ consecrate as it is
rehersid

Figure 7. Martha, Domitilla, and Justina, with full spraywork in the left margin of fol. 97v
and compressed spraywork in the left margin of fol. 98r, fols 97v–98r.

rehersid afore .

Thus endith the litull mension of seynt donutille nonne .

Of the life of seynt Justine abbes e martyr
howe she began for to growe e encrese in vertue
Seynt Justine the vgyne was doughtir
of a prestis of the temple which mayd
pryvely satt in a wyndowe and herde
howe a deken that was callid prelium pchid the
worthines of god and howe he toke vpon him
incarnacion And howe by the pphecye of holy p
phetis he was born off our lady seynt mary
that holy virgyn . and also of the ioy that ann
gells made in his birth and howe kynges wor
shippid him in bedlem w' golde mirre e encens
and of the bright sterre which shone afore he
and of toknes and of op wondir thingis that
were shewed and of grace and vtue of the crosse
in his holy passion and of his holy resurrecion
and of apperyng to his disciples . aftir his resu
rrecion and of his ascencion and howe nowe
he sittith on his fadir is right honde in his
reme of blis and this holy mayde herd all this
prevely in a wyndowe as she satt : she cowthe
no lenger suffre but in any wyse she wolde se
that deken which pchid so deuously for she
might no lenger hyde the byernyng hete of sp

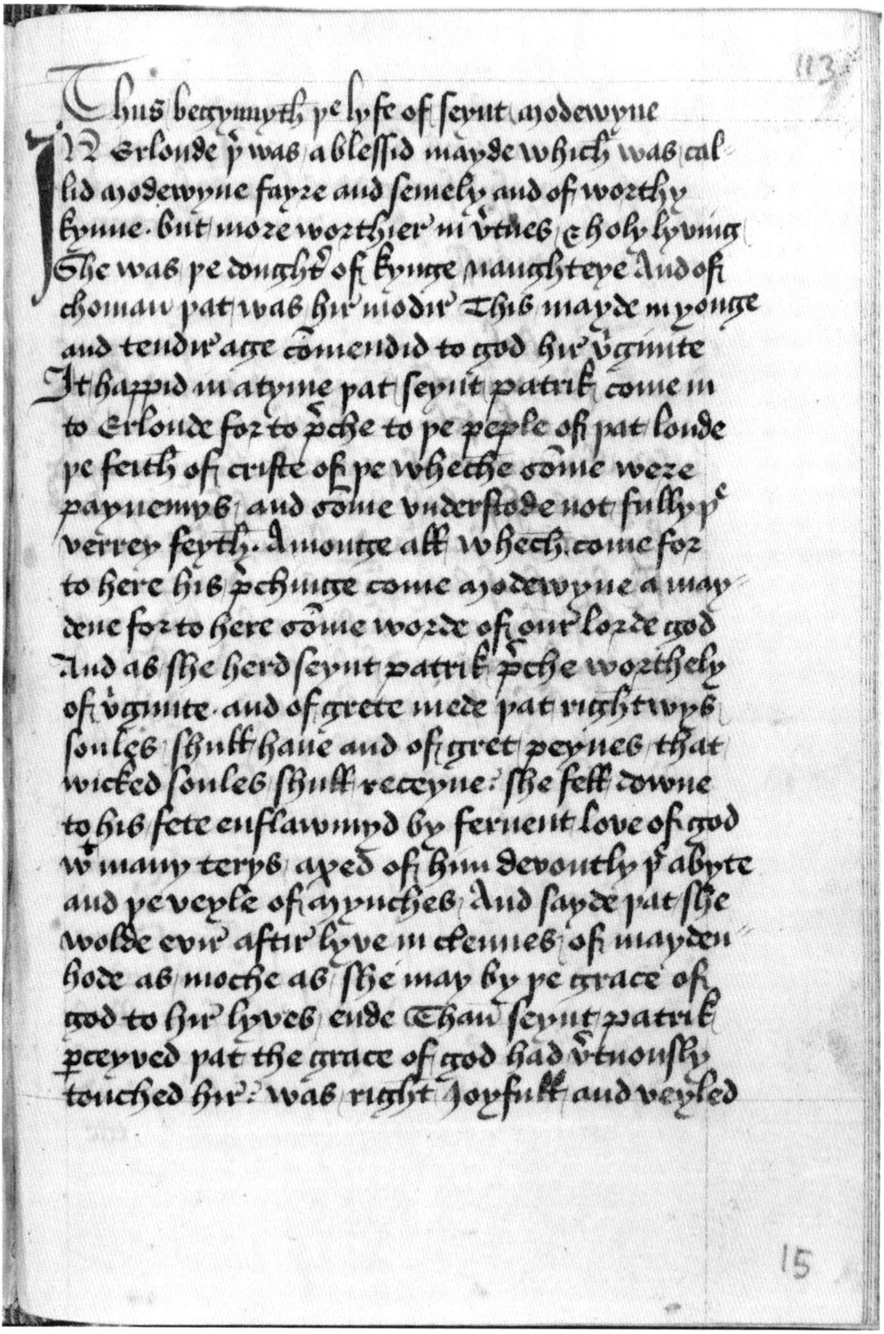

Thus begynnyth þe lyfe of seynt Modewynne

IN Erlonde þ[t] was a blessid mayde which was callid Modewynne fayre and semely and of worthy
kynne. but more worthier in vtues & holy lyvyng
She was þe doughter of kynge naughteye And of
a woman þat was hir modir This mayde in younge
and tendw' age comendid to god hir vgynite
It happid in a tyme þat seynt patrik come in
to Erlonde for to pche to þe peple of þat londe
þe feith of criste of þe wheche some were
paynemys and some vnderstode not fully þe
verrey feyth. Amoutge all wheche come for
to here his pchynge come Modewynne a may-
dene for to here some worde of our lorde god
And as she herd seynt patrik pche worthely
of vgynite and of grete mede þat rightwys
soules shull haue and of gret peynes that
wicked soules shull receyue. she fell downe
to his fete enflawmyd by feruent loue of god
w' many terys. axed of him deuoutly þ[e] abyte
and þe veyle of a ynches. And sayde þat she
wolde eur aftir lyve in clennes of maydenhode as moche as she may by þe grace of
god to hir lyves ende Than seynt patrik
preyved þat the grace of god had vtuously
touched hir. was right Joyfull and veyled

Figure 8. Modwenna, without spraywork, fol. 113r.

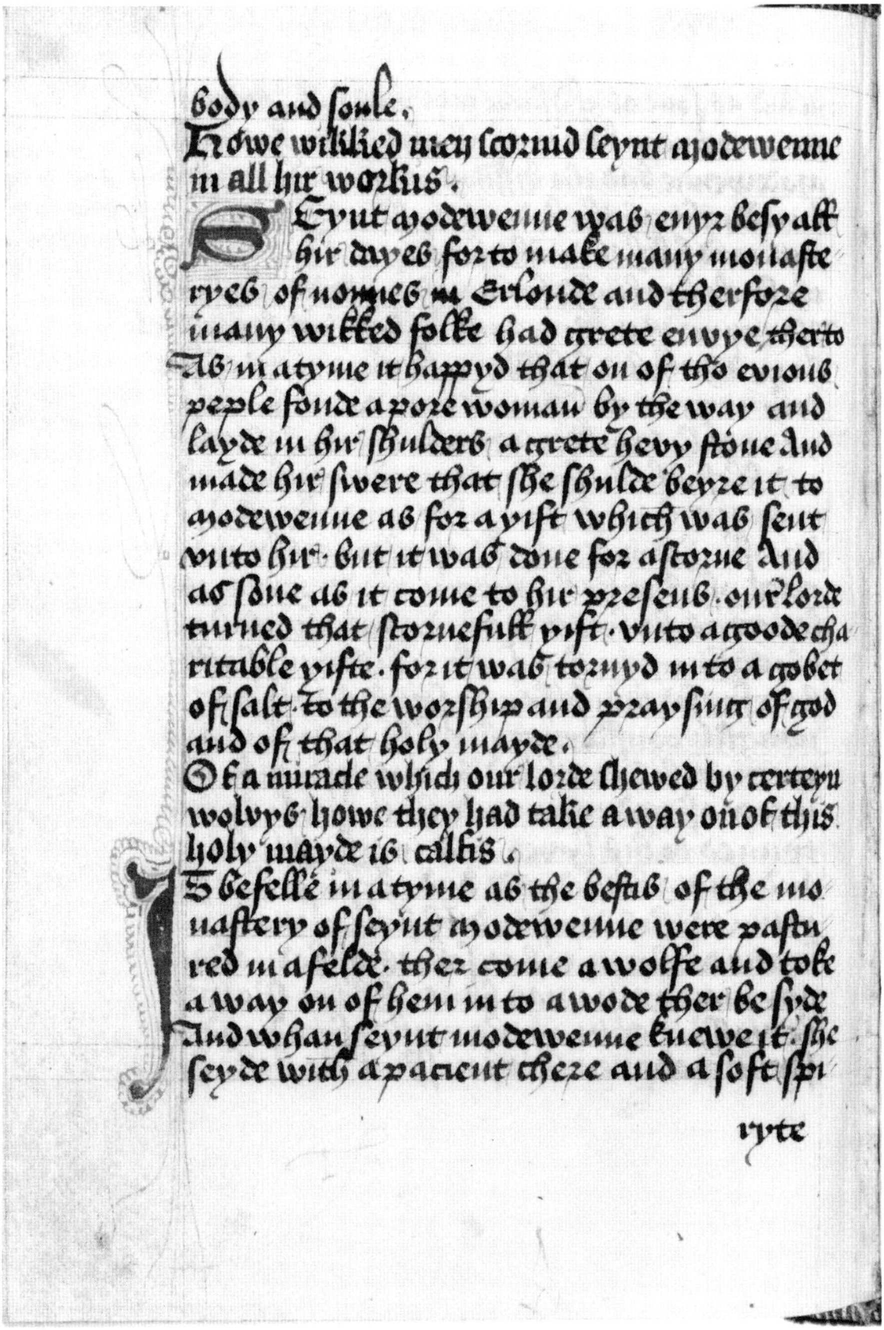

body and soule.

Howe wikkied men scornud seynt modewenne
in all hir workus.

Seynt modewenne was eny besyatt
hir dayes forto make many monaste
ryes of nonnes in Erlonde and therfore
many wikked folke had grete envye therto
As in a tyme it happyd that on of this evious
peple fonde a pore woman by the way and
layde in hir shulders a grete hevy stone And
made hir swere that she shulde beyre it to
modewenne as for a yift which was sent
onto hir but it was done for a storne And
as sone as it come to hir preseus our lord
turned that stornefull yift unto a goode cha
ritable yifte. for it was tornyd in to a gobet
of salt to the worship and praysing of god
and of that holy mayde.

Of a miracle which our lorde shewed by certeyn
wolvys howe they had take a way on of this
holy mayde is callis.

It befelle in a tyme as the bestus of the mo
uastery of seyut modewenne were pastu
red in a felde. ther come a wolffe and toke
a way on of hem in to a wode ther be syde
And whan seyut modewenne knewe it she
seyde with a pacient chere and a soft spi

ryte

Figure 9. Section summaries written in textura in Modwenna, fol. 124v.

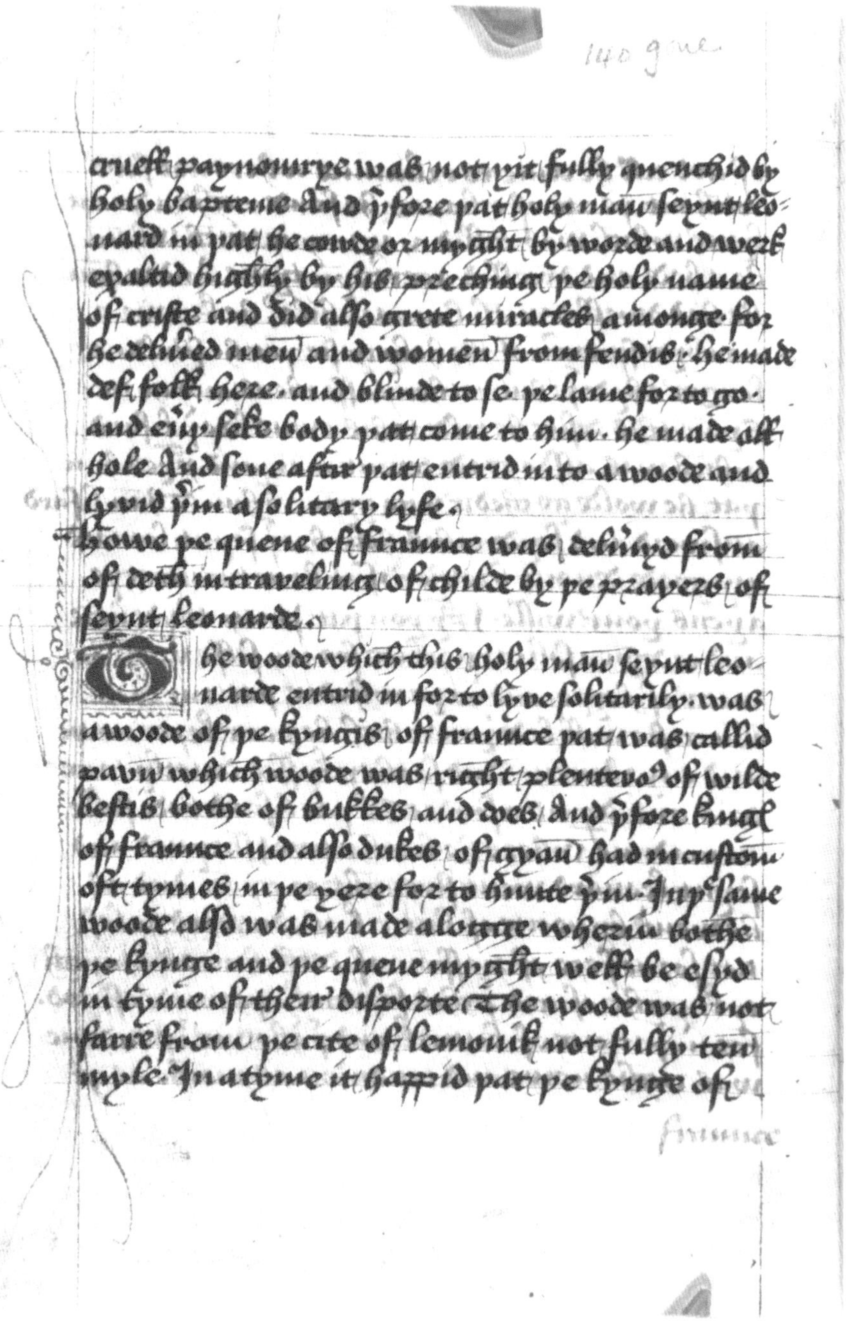

cruelt paynemrye was not yit fully quenchid by
holy baptem And þerfore þat holy man seynt leonard in þat he coude or myght by worde and werk
exaltid hiʒly by his preching þe holy name
of criste and did also grete miracles amonge for
he delivid men and women from fendis. he made
def folk here. and blinde to se. þe lame for to go.
and euy seke body þat come to him. he made all
hole And sone aftir þat entrid in to a woode and
lyvid þerin a solitary lyfe.
howe þe quene of fraunce was delivyd from
of deth in traveling of childe by þe prayers of
seynt leonarde.
The woode which this holy man seynt leonarde entrid in for to lyve solitarily. was
a woode of þe kyngis of fraunce þat was callid
pavn which woode was right plentevous of wilde
bestis bothe of bukkes and does And þerfore kyngs
of fraunce and also dukes of gyan had in custom
oft tymes in þe yere for to hunte þerin. In þe same
woode also was made a logge wherin bothe
þe kynge and þe quene myght well be esyd
in tyme of their disporte. The woode was not
farre from þe cite of lemouik not fully ten
myle. In a tyme it happid þat þe kynge of
fraunce

Figure 10. Catchword 'fraunce' in Leonard on fol. 139v, which is only fully visible under ultraviolet light

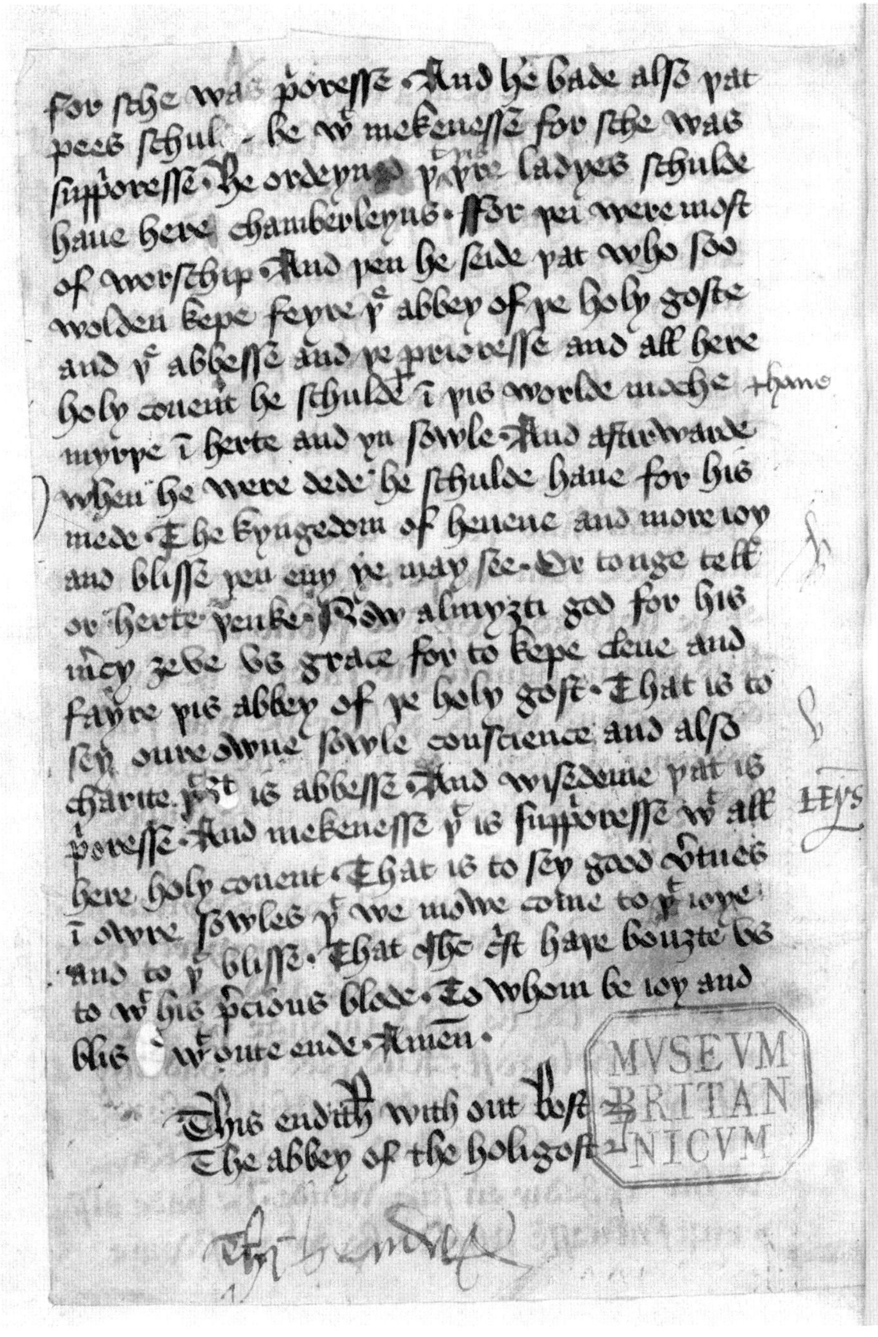
for sche was poueresse. And he bade also þat
þees schul[de] be wt mekenesse for sche was
supporesse. He ordeyned þt þre ladyes schulde
haue here chamberleyns. ffor þei were most
of worschip. And þen he seide þat who so
wolden kepe feyre þe abbey of þe holy goste
and þe abbesse and þe priouresse and all here
holy couent he schulde i þis worlde moche
myrþe i herte and yn sowle. And afturwarde
when he were dede he schulde haue for his
mede. The kyngedom of heuene and more ioy
and blisse þen eny ye may see. Or tonge tell
or herte þenke. Now almyzti god for his
mercy zeue vs grace for to kepe clene and
fayre þis abbey of þe holy gost. That is to
sey oure owne sowle consience. and also
charite. þat is abbesse. And wysedome þat is
priouresse. And mekenesse þat is supporesse wt all
here holy couent. That is to sey good vertues
i owre sowles þat we mowe come to þe ioye
and to þe blisse. That sche est haþe bouzte vs
to wt his precious blode. To whom be ioy and
blis wtoute ende. Amen.

This endith with out lese
The abbey of the holigost

Figure 11. Script of London, British Library, MS Harley 5272, fol. 137v.

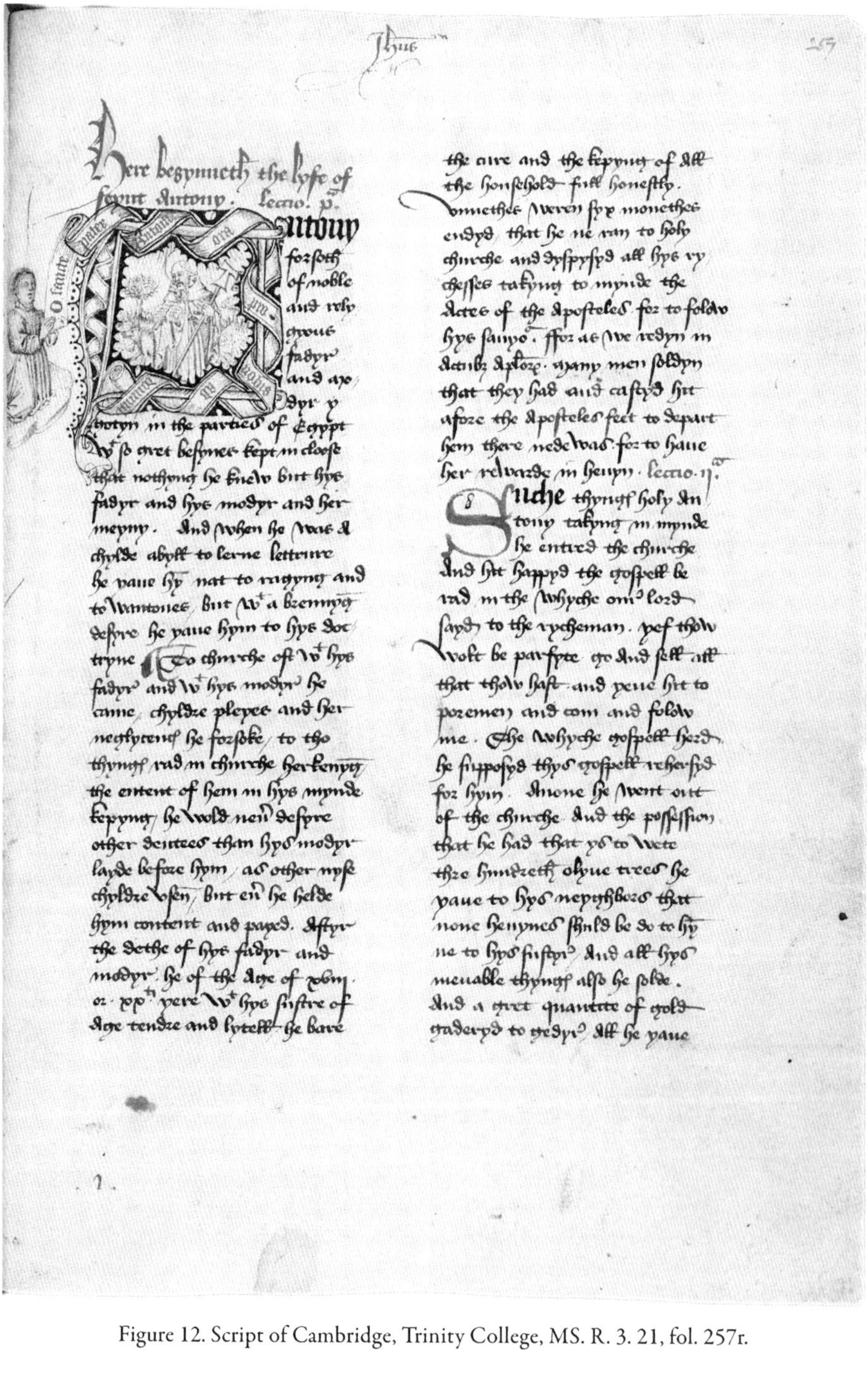

Figure 12. Script of Cambridge, Trinity College, MS. R. 3. 21, fol. 257r.

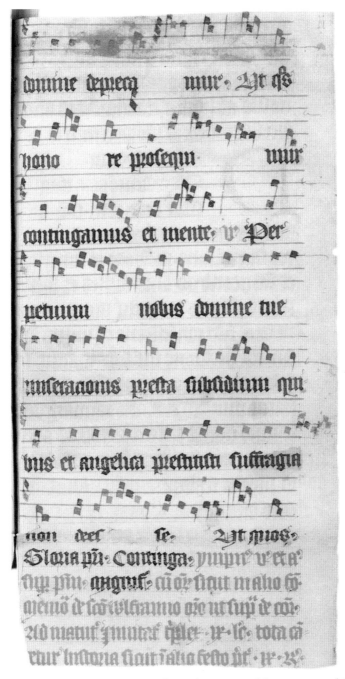

Figure 13. Fragment of an antiphoner bound in at the opening of the manuscript, fol. ii recto.

Condemne no man before thou haue tryed out the matter: and when thou hast made inquisition, then refourme righteously. geue no sentence before thou hast hearde the cause: but first let men tell our their tales:

a b c d e f ff g h i k l m n o p q r s ß t tt u v w.

Figure 14. 'Condemne no man' pasted in on paper towards the beginning of the manuscript, fol. vi recto.

xxix

1-Lives in this M:s
2-Lyfe of St John Baptist
3-Life of St Colombe
4-Life of seynt agate the virgyn
5-Life of seynt Cecile
6-Life of seynt Barbara
7-Lyfe of St Audrey of Ely
8-Lyfe of St Sexburga Syster to St awdry
9-Lyfe of St Ermenylde 1st Doughter of St Sexburgha
10-Lyfe of St Werburg doughter of St Ermenylde
11-Lyfe of St Orkengood (2) Doughter of St Sexburgh
12-Lyfe of St Whitburga Syster of St Awdrey
13-Lyfe of St Edith of wylton
14-Lyfe of St Edburg abbes after St Mildrede
15-Lyfe of St aswyde the nonne of Folkstone
16-Lif of St Hilde Abbes of Strenshale
17-Lif of St Martha abbes of many nonnes the Syst
18-of Mary Mawdelen
19-Lyf of St Domitille
20-Life of St Justine abbes & martyr
21-Lyfe of St Benett
22-Lyfe of St Modewyne
23-Lyfe of Leonarde the abbot

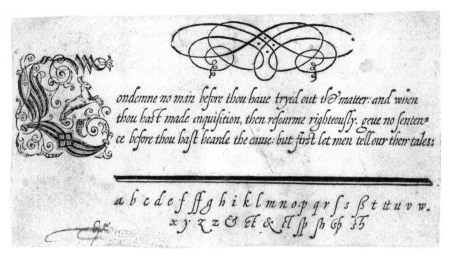

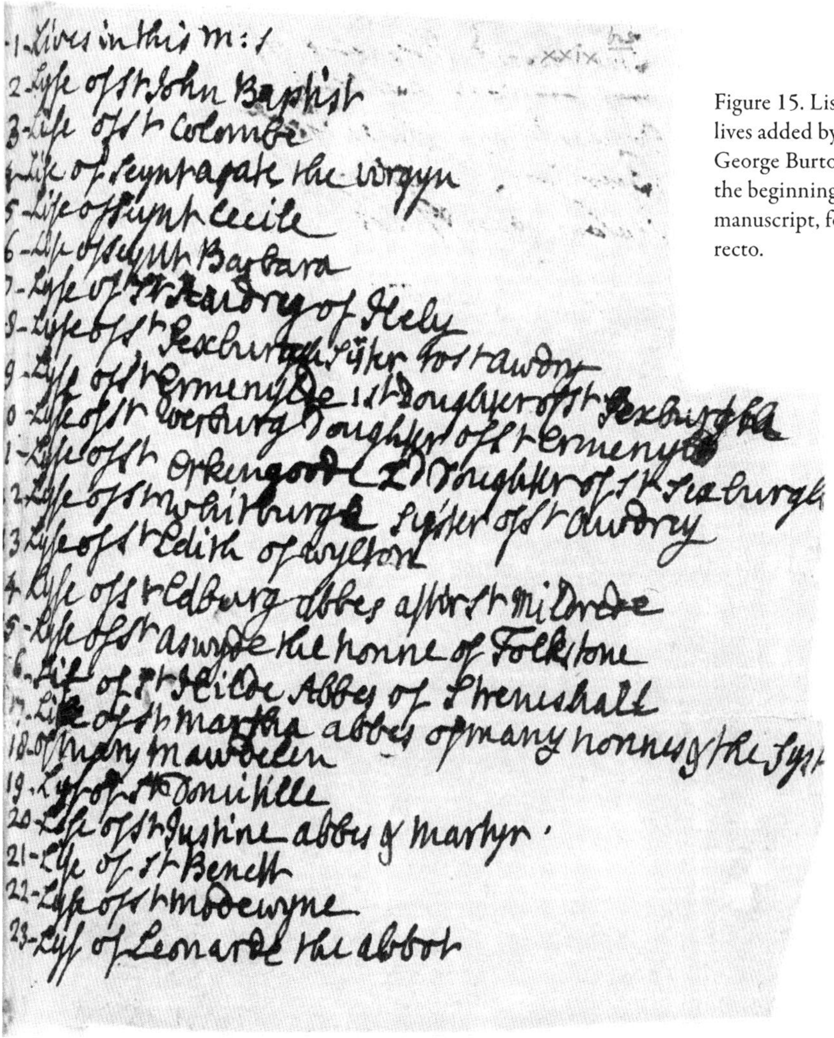

Figure 15. List of saints' lives added by Reverend George Burton at the beginning of the manuscript, fol. xxx recto.

Figure 16. Note about the handwriting of Reverend George Burton, with a stamp of 'BURY', written on the back of the list of saints' lives, fol. xxx verso.

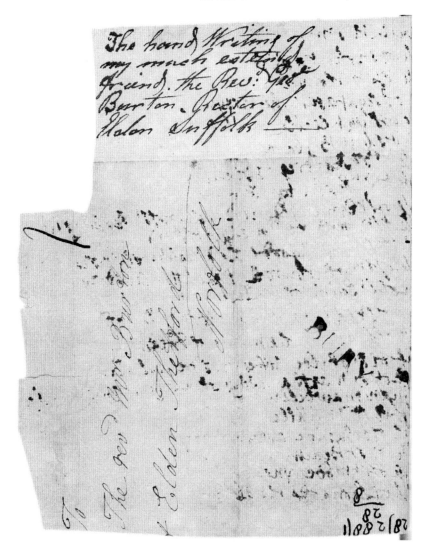

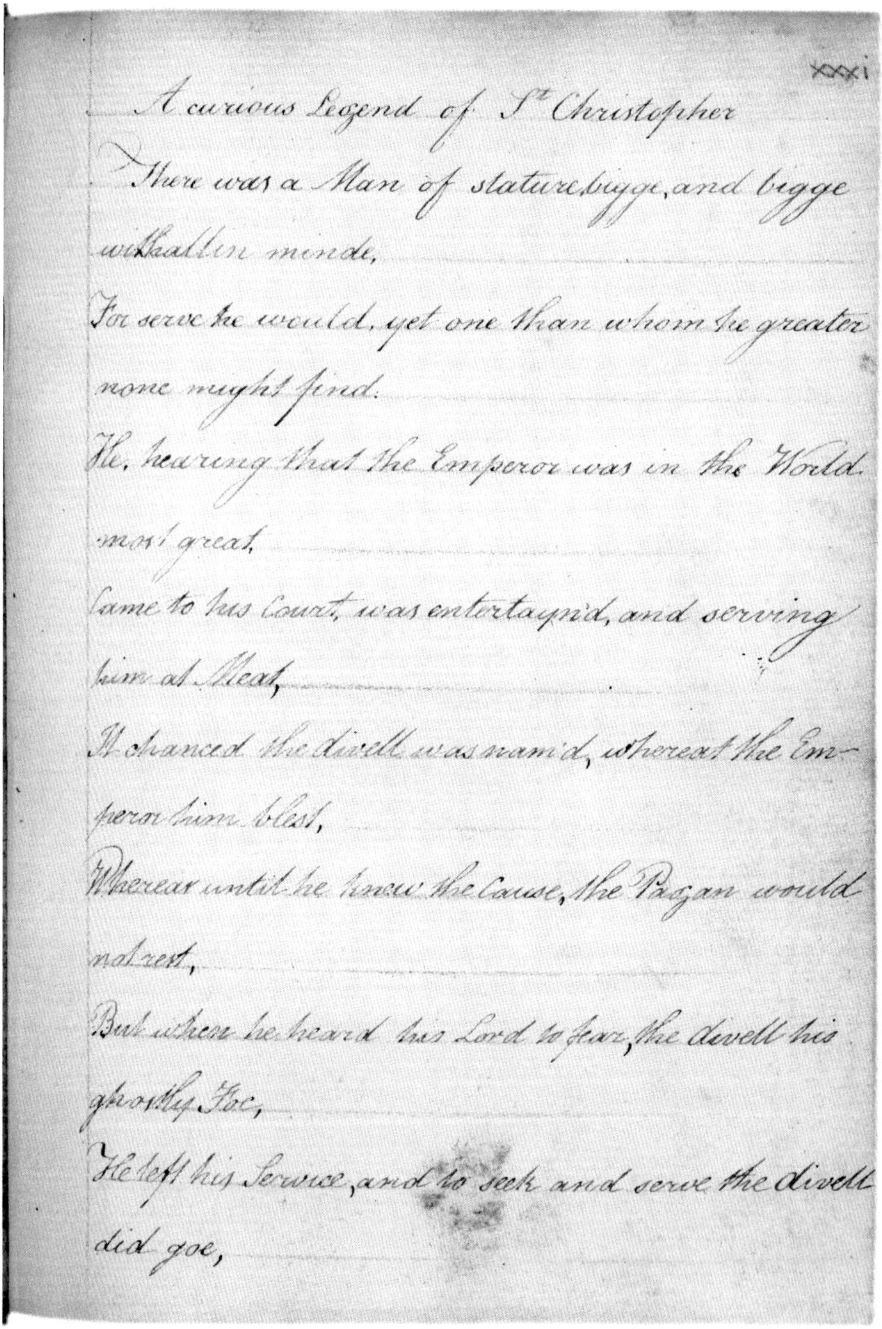

A curious Legend of St Christopher

There was a Man of stature bigge, and bigge
withallin minde,

For serve he would, yet one than whom he greater
none might find.

He, hearing that the Emperor was in the World
most great,

Came to his Court, was entertayn'd, and serving
him at Meat,

It chanced the divell was nam'd, whereat the Emperor him blest,

Whereas until he knew the Cause, the Pagan would
not rest,

But when he heard his Lord to fear, the divell his
ghostly Foe,

He left his Service, and to seek and serve the divell
did goe,

Figure 17. 'Life of St Christopher' in verse at the end of the manuscript, fol. xxxi recto.

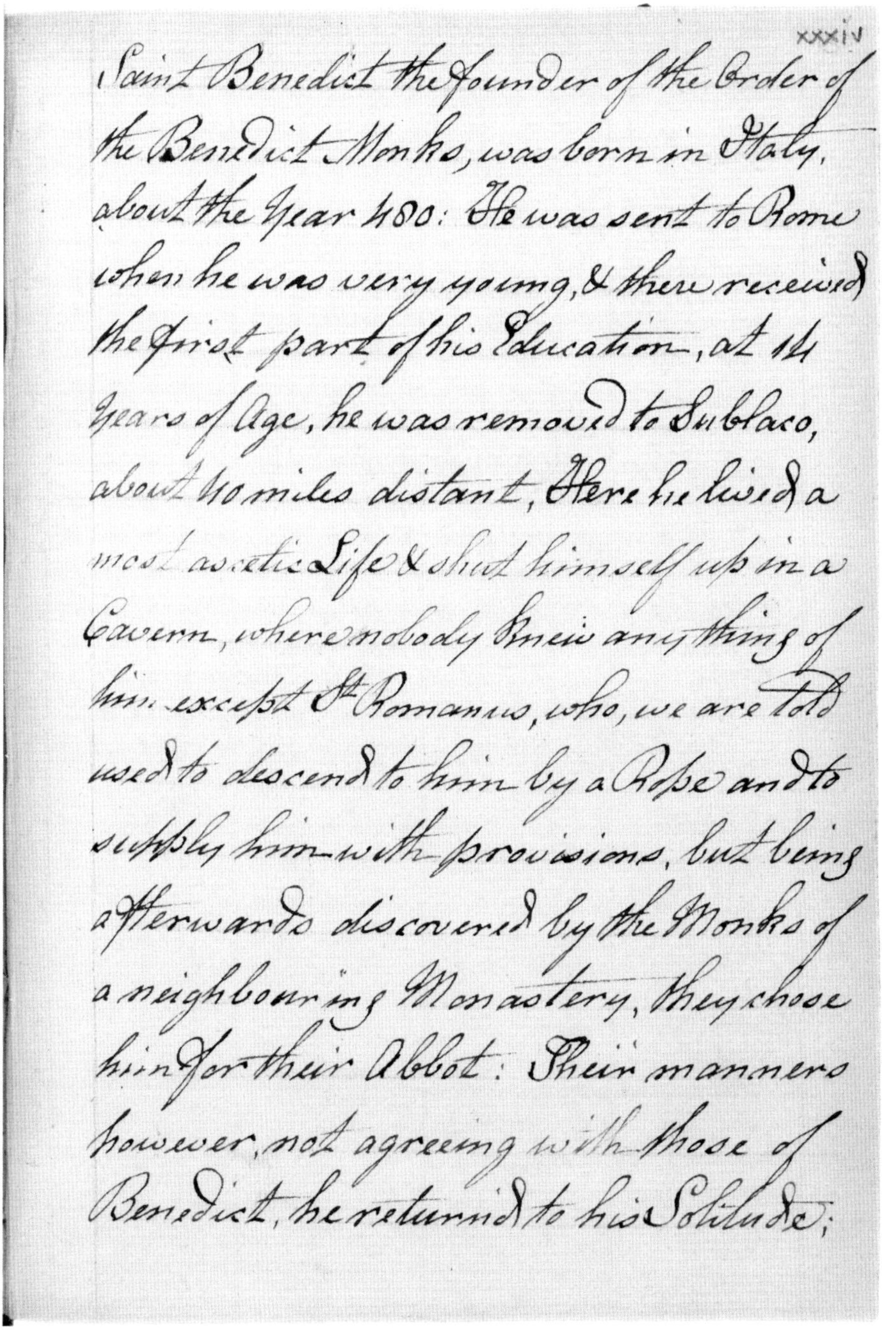

XXXIV

Saint Benedict the founder of the Order of
the Benedict Monks, was born in Italy,
about the Year 480: He was sent to Rome
when he was very young, & there received
the first part of his Education, at 14
Years of Age, he was removed to Sublaco,
about 40 miles distant, Here he lived a
most ascetic Life & shut himself up in a
Cavern, where nobody knew any thing of
him. except S.t Romanus, who, we are told
used to descend to him by a Rope and to
supply him with provisions, but being
afterwards discovered by the Monks of
a neighbouring Monastery, they chose
him for their Abbot: Their manners
however, not agreeing with those of
Benedict, he returnd to his Solitude;

Figure 18. 'On St Benedict and the Benedictines' in prose at the end of the manuscript, fol. xxxiv recto.

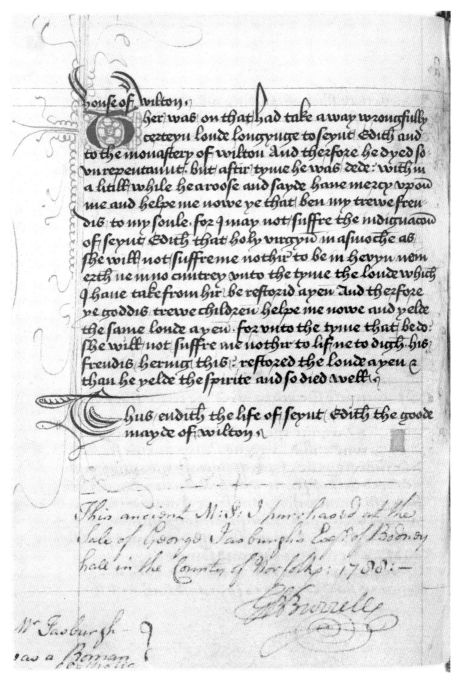

Figure 19. Ownership inscription by G. B. Burrell,
noting its acquisition from George Tasburgh in 1788, fol. 75v.

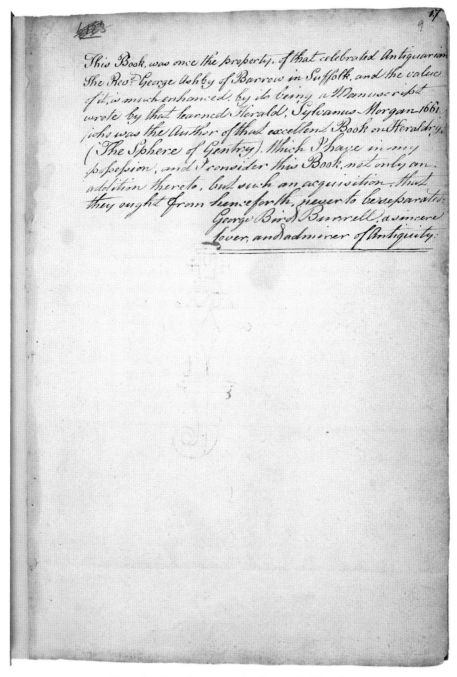

Figure 20. Signed inscription by George Bird Burrell, London, British Library, MS Additional 39177, fol. 9r.

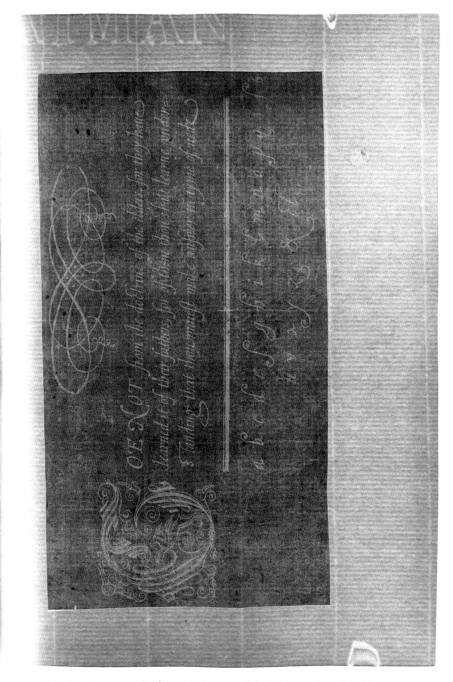

Figure 21. Countermark of James Whatman of the Whatman firm, fol. viii recto.

Figure 22. St Peter's Hall, St Peter South Elmham, Suffolk, the home of the Flixton Tasburghs in the sixteenth century and later.

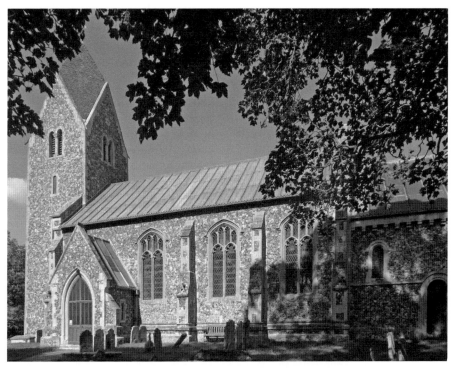

Figure 23. St Mary's Church, Flixton, Suffolk, where many of the early Tasburghs are interred.

Figure 24. Part of the remains of the Church of St George's Nunnery, Thetford, Norfolk.

II. Language and Dialectal Provenance

Overall there is remarkable consistency in the linguistic system of Add. 2604. This is in part an aspect of its late date (probably *c.* 1480–1510) but is also an indication that it has the hallmarks of a professional production by a trained single scribe that contains few of the linguistic vagaries or randomness of spelling found in more amateurish works. Most importantly, it was also produced at a time of increasing standardisation (or types of an incipient standard) in the written language, a process extending from about 1420 to 1550 that began at different points in the fifteenth century and proceeded at varying rates throughout the country.[1] In light of these factors it is difficult to

---

[1] See the various discussions about standardisation and the so-called 'Chancery Standard' (the language of London administrators) in Angus McIntosh, M. L. Samuels, and Michael Benskin, *A Linguistic Atlas of Late Mediaeval English*, 4 vols (Aberdeen: Aberdeen University Press, 1986), and the references therein, particularly I, 3 and 27. It is because of the growth of standardisation that LALME in general only includes literary material between *c.* 1325 and *c.* 1425 from the south, and between *c.* 1350 and *c.* 1450 from the north, and documentary material up to the end of Henry VI's reign (1460/1); later documentary non-standard material up to *c.* 1500 is included for northern counties and in the case of some Middle Scots and Hiberno-English texts (see LALME, particularly I, 40). This earlier cut-off in dating is one reason why the results from LALME have limitations for later texts. Apart from general language histories, the period between what is deemed the end of the Middle Ages and the beginning of the Early Modern period is much neglected, but see José Secundino Gómez Soliño, 'Variación y estandarización en el Inglés moderno temprano: 1470–1540' (unpublished doctoral dissertation, Universidad de Oviedo, 1984). The complexities of so-called standardised English (as against the importance of dialectal contact) is also the focus of Reiko Takeda, 'The Question of the "Standardisation" of Written English in the Fifteenth Century' (unpublished doctoral dissertation, University of Leeds, 2001). There are various discussions of LALME and some of the issues raised therein both before and after publication, for example, *So meny people, longages and tonges: Philological Essays in Scots and Mediaeval English Presented to Angus McIntosh*, ed. by Michael Benskin and M. L. Samuels (Edinburgh: Middle English Dialect Project, 1981); Angus McIntosh, M. L. Samuels, and Margaret Laing, *Middle English Dialectology: Essays on Some Principles and Problems*, ed. by Margaret Laing (Aberdeen: Aberdeen University Press, 1989); *Regionalism in Late Medieval Manuscripts and Texts: Essays Celebrating the Publication of 'A Linguistic Atlas of Late Mediaeval English'*, ed. by Felicity Riddy, York Manuscripts Conferences: Proceedings Series, 2 (Cambridge: Brewer, 1991); *Speaking in our Tongues: Proceedings of a Colloquium on Medieval Dialectology and Related Disciplines*, ed. by Margaret Laing and Keith Williamson (Cambridge: Brewer, 1994); John H. Fisher, *The Emergence of Standard*

II. LANGUAGE AND DIALECTAL PROVENANCE

provide a definite localisation for the language, but some indicators of possible provenance may be discovered.

Background to the Linguistic Analysis

In order to illustrate the language, we begin with a linguistic analysis on the basis of the original 280 diagnostic features in the *Linguistic Atlas of Late Mediaeval English* (hereafter LALME).[2] This LALME questionnaire is made up of four classes of evidence: graphological, phonological, morphological, and lexical. Because the collection comprises two traditions of saints' lives, univer-

---

English (Lexington, KY: The University Press of Kentucky, 1996); and Simon Horobin, *The Language of the Chaucer Tradition*, Chaucer Studies, 32 (Cambridge: Brewer, 2003). See also the essay by Jeremy Smith, 'On "Standard" Written English in the Later Middle Ages', in a cluster of essays entitled, 'Communities of Practice: New Methodological Approaches to Adam Pinkhurst and Chaucer's Earliest Scribes', in a forthcoming issue of *Speculum*; we are very grateful to Jeremy Smith for sharing this essay with us in advance of publication. There are also potential criticisms of LALME; see, for instance, T. L. Burton, 'On the Current State of Middle English Dialectology' and the firm rejoinder by Michael Benskin, 'In Reply to Dr Burton', in *Leeds Studies in English*, n.s. 22 (1991), 167–208 and 209–62, and references therein. However, LALME provides a large corpus gathered over an extended period and analysed by experts in the field. It is therefore the most important source of material currently available for dialectal analysis, albeit that the study of language is dynamic and so certain aspects of LALME may be subject to re-evaluation and re-interpretation over time as more information becomes available.

[2] This list combines both specific questions aimed at northern and southern texts and in between: 'The overlap is a belt across the Midlands, which broadens eastward to include all of Norfolk and the northern edge of Suffolk' (LALME, III, xii). See also e-LALME, M. Benskin, M. Laing, V. Karaiskos, and K. Williamson, 'An Electronic Version of A Linguistic Atlas of Late Mediaeval English' (http://www.lel.ed.ac.uk/ihd/elalme/elalme.html) (Edinburgh: © 2013- The Authors and The University of Edinburgh) (accessed 5 February 2023). In eLALME some of the Linguistic Profiles (hereafter LPs) are re-done and the Dot Maps and questionnaire list are expanded. There are 1,200 Dot Maps in LALME and over 1,700 in eLALME. There is currently a total of 424 items in the electronic questionnaire; some items in the original Southern Appendix form are interleaved with the 280 items bringing that number from 280 to 319; additionally there are extra items extending that number from 320 to 424. In the case of Add. 2604 it was felt to be counter-productive to include such a quantity of items and sub-items as it would have made the compilation of the questionnaire unnecessarily unwieldy, particularly with regard to the underlying five original questionnaires. However, full reference to all the expanded features of eLALME has been taken into account and the information gleaned from the printed version (see note 1) double checked against the electronic version as need be. Both northern and southern forms are taken into account in the survey below, even though all available evidence ruled out pronounced northern features from the start.

BACKGROUND TO THE LINGUISTIC ANALYSIS 71

sal and native, which are based on two kinds of sources, the survey here concentrates on five samples that cut across this universal/native divide and are spread throughout the manuscript:

1. John the Baptist (fols 1r–5v);

2. Barbara (fols 50r–52v) and Æthelthryth (fols 52v–54v);

3. Wihtburh (fols 66v–69r);

4. Hild (fols 91r–93r) and Martha (fols 93r–95v); and

5. Modwenna (fols 133r–136v) and Leonard (fols 137r–137v).[3]

Underlying the linguistic questionnaire below are five initial individual LALME questionnaires (not reproduced here) that were undertaken to highlight any linguistic or dialectal discrepancies between the universal and the native lives and/or between different parts of the manuscript. Care was taken to include samples that focused only on universal lives, native, or both combined to ascertain the best way of carrying out the final questionnaire. No linguistic differences emerged beyond the normal pattern of scribal variability (with distributive consistency across the range) so it can be confirmed that the language in Add. 2604 is the language of one scribe with no apparent consistent residual dialectal features from another copy.[4] This would support the view that, *if* the scribe is transcribing from something else, he is more than probably making a fair copy of his own work and/or (far less likely) translating from the Latin as he goes along, rather than copying wholesale the work of someone else.[5] Our view that he is not copying from another version of the same Middle English lives is supported by the somewhat idiosyncratic selection of the material in Add. 2604; quite simply, there were unlikely to have been two such manuscripts.

---

[3] This procedure is in line with that recommended in LALME I, 9 for large single texts in the same hand.

[4] While it is just possible that some of the few unusual forms or spellings noted below may be relicts from another copy, there is no discernible pattern here and so we consider them as part of the scribe's idiolect.

[5] There are some examples of eye-skip in the text that would point to the former, but also a few instances of blanks in the text that would seem to indicate that the scribe was engaging spontaneously with the Latin; for further details, see Textual Apparatus in the *Edition*.

LALME Questionnaire

These five sample texts have been combined into a single concordance that provides the material for the analysis below.[6] Rather than provide approximate ratios of occurrences in accordance with LALME practice, precise figures are given so that the degree of spelling variation between items and specific dialectal features may be illustrated numerically, apart from items 56 to 64 (where some entries are due to expansion of abbreviations and where otherwise the degree of computation involved would be excessive). In items 267–80 the actual forms rather than the numbers are provided as this is more meaningful. Entries are provided with the largest number of occurrences first and then broadly in alphabetical order thereafter; where a form is due to editorial emendation, the emendation is included separately in square brackets, for example: 'they (48); the[y] (2); thei (10)'. Where a form is given as 'herde (10 *pt*, 2 *ppl*)', this means that this spelling is used ten times in the past tense and twice as a past participle. Where *sg* or *pl* is specified, the contrasting form is also given, if available; if neither *sg* or *pl* is specified, the singular form only is supplied. Where a verbal form is asked for in a particular format in LALME, all forms of the verb are supplied where they occur (although not all of these may have dialectical significance). In some cases LALME's different entries are collapsed into one (for example, items 74 and 75). Where an entry is not found, it is labelled as n/a. The LALME questionnaire specifies whether or not an Item was originally collected for the north (NOR) or the south (SOU); where this is not specified, the Item was collected for both; these references are included below. The abbreviations follow those in LALME (with additional items in square brackets: *adj* = adjective; *adv* = adverb; *conj* = conjunction; *contr* = contracted; *cpv* = comparative; *def* = definite (article); [*gen* = genitive case]; [imp = imperative]; [*indef* = indefinite]; *inf* = infinitive; *intr* = intransitive; *ord* = ordinal number; *pl* = plural; *ppl* = participle; [*pres-ppl* = present participle]; *pr* = preposition; *pres* = present; [*pres-pl* = present tense plural; *pres-sg* = present tense singular]; *pron* = pronoun; *pt*: preterite; *pt-sg* = preterite singular; *pt-2sg* = preterite 2nd person singular; *pt-pl* = preterite plural; *pt-2pl* = preterite 2nd person plural; *rel* = relative; *sb* = substantive; *sg* = singular; *1sg* = 1st person singular; *2sg* = 2nd person singular; *3sg* = 3rd person singular; *sup* = superlative; *tr* = transitive; *vb sb* = verbal substantive; *wk-adj* = weak adjective

---

[6] We are very grateful to Laurie Ringer for so kindly and generously drawing up five full concordances that she then combined so that we could draw out and calibrate the material here. We also owe an inestimable debt of gratitude to Jeremy Smith for his expert opinion on the linguistic account that follows and to Susan Powell for reading it so scrupulously.

LALME QUESTIONNAIRE

1 THE NOR: the (498); þe (41)

2 THESE: these (2); thes (1)

3 THOSE NOR: tho (9)

4 SHE: she (152)

5 HER: hir (202); her (2); heris (1 *gen.*); hirres (1 *gen.*)

6 IT: it (80)

7 THEY: they (48); the[y] (2); thei (10)

8 THEM: hem (43); theym (11); them (3)

9 THEIR: their (16); theyr (4); theyre (3); theire (1); þer (1); her (2); hyr (1)

10 SUCH: suche (8); such (3)

11 WHICH: which (70); wheche (2); whech (1)

12 EACH: eche (3); iche (1)

13 MANY: many (17)

14 MAN: man (24)

15 ANY: any (11)

16 MUCH: meche (6); moche (4); mych (1)

17 ARE: ben (10)

18 WERE NOR: were (38); wer (1)

19 IS: is (64)

20 ART SOU: art (1)

21 WAS: was (231)

22 SHALL *sg pl*: shall (8 *sg*, 1 *pl*); shull (3 pl, 0 sg); shalt (1 sg, 0 pl)

23 SHOULD *sg* NOR & SOU: shuld (19 *sg*); shulde (9 sg); *pl* NOR: shuld (4 *pl*); shulde (2 *pl*)

24 WILL *sg, pl*: will (5 *sg*, 2 *pl*); wille (1 sg, 0 *pl*); woll (1 *sg*, 0 *pl*)

25 WOULD *sg* NOR & SOU: wolde (15 *sg*); wold (4 *sg*); *pl* NOR wolde (4 *pl*)

26 TO + *sb* NOR and 27 TO + *inf* NOR: to (265); [to] (1)

28 FROM: from (27); fro (10)

29 AFTER: aftir (55); aftyr (3); aftur (1)

30 THEN: than (67); then (2)

31 THAN: than (8); then (2)

32 THOUGH: though (4)

33 IF: if (2)

34 AS NOR and 35 AS + AS NOR: as (91)

36 AGAINST: ayenst (6); yenst (1)

37 AGAIN: ayene (7); ayen (5)

38 ERE *conj*: er (5)

39 SINCE *adv, conj*: n/a

40 YET: yit (17); yet (2)

41 WHILE: while (3); whiles (2)

42 STRENGTH *vb*: strenghthid (1 *ppl*)

43 LENGTH *vb*: n/a; lenght (1 *sb*)

44 WH-: WH-

45 NOT: not (47)

46 NOR: ne (10)

47 A, O NOR: o

48 WORLD *adj*: n/a; worlde (17 *sb*)

49 THINK: thenk (2); thenke (1)

50 WORK *sb, vb*: worke (2 *sb sg*); workis (1 *sb pl*); workys (1 *sb pl*); worching (1 *vb sb*)

51 THERE: ther (41); there (6); þer (4)

LALME QUESTIONNAIRE

52 WHERE: where (11)

53 MIGHT *vb, 2sg, pl*: might (5 *sg*, 0 *2sg*, 0 *2pl*)

54 THROUGH: thorowe (1)

55 WHEN: whan (36); whanne (1)

56 Substantive plural: -es [*vast majority*]; -is [*minority*]; -ys [*minority*]; -s [*in* 'angels']

57 Present participle: -ing [*slightly in the majority*]; -yng; -inge [*very rare*); -ynge (*very rare*)

58 Verbal substantive NOR: -ing [*majority*]; -yng; -inge [*very rare*); -ynge [*very rare*]

59 3sg present indicative NOR: -th

60 Present plural NOR: [*apart from* 'are', *examples are very rare, see:*] breke; foryete; rose

61 Weak preterite NOR: ed [*majority*]; id; ied (*rare*]

62 Strong preterite plural SOU: [*plural instances very rare:*] com; toke; yaf; [*strong preterite singular more plentiful; see for instance:*] arose; bare; becam; befille; bode; bonde; com/come; drewe; ete; fille [fell]; fonde; forsoke; sange; satt; sey/sigh [saw]; smote; sprange; sygh [saw]; toke; yaf

63 Weak past participle NOR: ed [*majority*]; id [*second most frequent*]; yd [*third most frequent*]; ied [*very rare*]; [*some examples minus final* 'd':] translate [*two occurrences, also* 'translatid' *and* 'translatyd']

64 Strong past participle NOR: en [*vast majority*]; on; yn [*very rare*]; [*some examples minus final* 'n':] overthrowe, take; unknowe

65 ABOUT *adv, pr* NOR: aboute (11); abowte (6); abowten (1)

66 ABOVE *adv, pr* NOR: aboue (3); above (2)

67 ADDER SOU: n/a

68 AFTERWARDS NOR: aftirward (12): aftirwarde (2)

69 AIR NOR: eyre (3)

70 ALL NOR: all (71); alle (2)

71 AMONG *adv, pr* NOR: amonge (10); amonges (2); among (1)

72 ANSWER *sb, vb* NOR: answerd (2 *pt*); answeryd (1 *pt*)

73 ASK: axe (3 *inf*); axid (3 *pt*, 2 *ppl*); axed (1 *pt*); axing (1 *vb sb*)

74 AT + *inf* NOR and 75 AT *rel* NOR: at (38)

76 AWAY NOR: away (5)

77 BE *ppl* NOR: beyng (2 *pres-ppl*); beth (1 *imp*)

78 BEFORE *adv, pr*: afore (16); before (1)

79 BEGAN TO *pl* NOR: began (1 *pl*, 3 *sg*); begynnyng (4 *vb sb*)

80 BEHOVES *pt* NOR: n/a

81 BENEATH *adv, pr* NOR: n/a

82 BETWEEN *pr* NOR: betwene (5)

83 BEYOND SOU: n/a

84 BLESSED NOR: blessid (8); blissed (3); blessyd (1)

85 BOTH: bothe (22); [bothe] (1)

86 BRIDGE SOU: brige (1 *sg*, 0 *pl*)

87 BROTHER *pl* NOR: brothers (4 *pl*); brethern (1 *pl*); brethirne (1 *pl*); brethreryn (1 *pl*); brothir (5 *sg*); brother (1 *sg*); broþer (1 *sg*)

88 BURN *pt, ppl* SOU: brenn (1 *inf*); brennyd (4 *pt*, 1 *ppl*); vnbrent (1 *ppl*); brennyng (I *pres-ppl*)

89 BURY *pt, ppl* SOU: beried (3 *pt*, 1 *ppl*); beryed (3 *ppl*); beryd (1 *ppl*); onberyed (1 *ppl*)

90 BUSY *adj, vb*: besy (2 *adj*, 0 *vb*)

91 BUT: but (45)

92 BY NOR: by (68)

93 CALL *pt, ppl*: callid (1 *pt*, 24 *ppl*); called (0 *pt*, 2 *ppl*); clepid (2 *pt*, 5 *ppl*); clepyd (1 *pt*, 0 *ppl*)

94 CAME *sg* NOR & SOU: cam (2 *pt*), *pl* NOR: n/a

95 CAN *pl* NOR: can (2 *sg*, 2 *pl*)

LALME QUESTIONNAIRE

96 CAST *pt, ppl* NOR: cast (4 *pt*, 0 *ppl*, 1 *imp*); castith (1 *sg*); casting (1 *pres-ppl*)

97 CHOOSE *pt, ppl* NOR: chese (1 *imp*)

98 CHURCH: chirch (8 *sg*, 0 *pl*)

99 COULD *sg, pl*: cowthe (4 *sg*, 0 *pl*); cowth (2 *sg*, 0 *pl*); cowd (1 *sg*, 0 *pl*)

100 DAUGHTER *pl* NOR: doughters (2 *pl*); doughter (3 *sg*); doughtir (1 *sg*)

101 DAY NOR: day (30 *sg*); *pl* NOR & SOU: dayes (8 *pl*)

102 DEATH NOR: deth (11 *sg*, 0 *pl*)

103 DIE *pt*: dye (2 *inf*); died (4 *pt*); dyed (2 *pt*, 1 *ppl*)

104 DO *2sg, 3sg* SOU: n/a; *pt-sg, pt-2sg, pt-pl* NOR & SOU: do (13 *inf*); did (10 *3pt-sg*); dyd (1 *3pt-pl*); done (11 *ppl*)

105 DOWN NOR: doun (4); downe (3)

106 DREAD, SPREAD SOU: drede (1 *imp*); dreding (1 *pres-ppl*); spred (1 *ppl*)

107 EARTH NOR: erth (5)

108 EAST NOR: est (1)

109 EIGHT *ord* NOR: n/a

110 EITHER *pron*: eyþer (1)

111 EITHER + OR: n/a

112 ELEVEN *ord* NOR: n/a

113 ENOUGH NOR: inogh (2); ynogh (1)

114 EVIL SOU: n/a

115 EYE NOR: n/a; *pl* NOR & SOU: eyghen (5 *pl*)

116 FAR *cpv* NOR: ferre (1 *not cpv*)

117 FATHER *pl* NOR: fadir (15 *sg*, 0 *pl*); fadirs (1 *sg gen*)

118 OE *fela* SOU: n/a

119 FELLOW NOR: n/a

120 FETCH SOU: fett (2 *inf*)

121 FIGHT NOR: n/a

122 FILL SOU: n/a

123 FILTH SOU: filth (1)

124 FIRE: fyre (5 *sg*, 0 *pl*)

125 FIRST NOR & SOU: first (8); *wk-adj* NOR: first (4 *adj*)

126 FIVE *ord* NOR: fyft (1); fyfte (1)

127 FLESH: flessh (3); flessh (1)

128 FOLLOW NOR: folowe (1 *inf*); folowed (2 *pt*)

129 OE *fon* SOU: n/a

130 FOUR *ord* NOR: fourt (3)

131 FOWL *pl* NOR: foule (2 *sg*, 0 *pl*)

132 FRIEND NOR: frendis (0 *sg*, 3 *pl*); frendes (0 *sg*, 1 *pl*)

133 FRUIT NOR: n/a

134 GAR *pt, ppl* NOR: n/a

135 GATE SOU: yates (0 *sg*, 2 *pl*)

136 GET *ppl* SOU: n/a

137 GIVE *pt-pl* NOR: yaf (2 *pt-pl*); yevon (1 *pt-pl*); *pt-sg, ppl* NOR & SOU: yaf (2 *pt-sg*); yafe (1 *pt-sg*); yevon (3 *ppl*); yif (2 *inf*, 1 *imp*); yeving (1 *pres-ppl*)

138 GO *2sg, 3 sg* SOU: go (6 *inf*)

139 GOOD *sb*: goodes (2 *pl*)

140 GROW NOR: grewe (1 *sg pt*, 1 *pt-pl*)

141 HANG *pt (tr and intr)* SOU: n/a

142 HAVE *inf* NOR & SOU: haue (10 *inf*); have (1 *inf*); *3sg, 2sg, pl* NOR: haue (3 *3pl*, 1 *1sg*, 2 *imp*); hast (4 *2sg*, 3 *3sg*); haste (1 *2sg*); hath (3 *3sg*); having (1 *pres-ppl*); *pt-sg, pt-pl* SOU: n/a

143 HEAD NOR: hede (4 *sg*, 0 *pl*); hed (1 *sg*, 0 *pl*)

LALME QUESTIONNAIRE

144 HEAR sou: herde (10 *pt*, 2 *ppl*); herd (6 *pt*); harde (1 *pt*);
hering (1 *pres-ppl*); hire (1 *inf*)

145 HEAVEN nor: hevyn (16 *sg*, 0 *pl*); heven (6 *sg*, 0 *pl*);
heuyn (1 *sg*, 0 *pl*); heyven (1 *sg*, 0 *pl*)

146 HEIGHT nor: n/a

147 HELL nor: hell (1 *sg*, 0 *pl*)

148 HENCE sou: hens (1)

149 HIGH *cpv, sup*: n/a

150 HIGHT sou: n/a

151 HILL: hille (6 *sg*); hilles (1 *pl*)

152 HIM nor: him (51); hym (12)

153 HITHER: n/a

154 HOLD *pt-pl, pt-sg* sou: holde (1 *ppl*, 0 *pt*); holding (1 *pres-ppl*)

155 HOLY nor: holy (76)

156 HOW nor: howe (34); how (3)

157 HUNDRED: hundrid (2); hundrith (2); hundreth (1)

158 I sou: I (24)

159 KIND *etc* sou: n/a

160 KNOW nor: knowe (1 *inf*); knewe (2 *pt*); knowest (1 *sg*); unknowe (1 *ppl*)

161 LADY nor: lady (10 *sg*, 0 *pl*)

162 LAND sou: n/a

163 LAUGH *pt* nor: n/a

164 LAW nor: lawe (3 *sg*, 0 *pl*)

165 LEAD *pt* sou: n/a

166 LESS: les (1)

167 LET *pt* sou: let (1 *imp*, 1 *inf*, 0 *pt*); lett (1 *imp*, 1 *inf*, 0 *pt*);
lettynge (1 *vb sb*)

80   II. LANGUAGE AND DIALECTAL PROVENANCE

168 LIE *vb* sou: lieth (2 *sg*)

169 LIFE *pl* NOR: lyfe (10 *sg*, 0 *pl*); life (4 *sg*, 0 *pl*); lif (2 *sg*, 0 *pl*); lyf (1 *sg*, 0 *pl*)

170 LITTLE: litell (4); litill (3); lytill (1)

171 LIVE *vb*: lyve (2 *inf*, 1 *pres sg*, 1 *imp*); lyved (14 *pt-sg*, 1 *ppl*); lyued (2 *pt-sg*)

172 LORD NOR: lorde (53); lordis (3 *sg gen*, 1 *pl*)

173 LOVE *sb, vb* NOR: love (8 *sb*, 1 *pres-pl*); loved (4 *pt-sg*); lovyd (1 *pt-sg*)

174 LOW NOR: n/a

175 MAKES *contr pres* NOR: make (15 *inf*, 1 *3pres-pl*, 1 *imp*)

176 MAY *pl* NOR: mowe (4 *pl*); may (1 *sg*)

177 MON NOR: n/a

178 MONTH NOR: moneth (1 *sg*); monethes (1 *pl*); month (1 *sg*); monthis (1 *pl*)

179 MOON NOR: n/a

180 MOTHER *pl* NOR: n/a

181 MY NOR: my (24)

182 NAME *sb* NOR: name (6 *sg*, 0 *pl*)

183 NE + BE sou, 184 NE + WILL *pt* sou, 185 NE + HAVE sou, and 186 NE + WITEN sou: ne (10)

187 NEITHER *pron* NOR: n/a

188 NEITHER + NOR: nother [...] ne (1)

189 NEVER NOR: nevir (12); never (1)

190 NEW NOR: newe (1)

191 NIGH *vb* NOR: n/a

192 NINE *ord* NOR: nyne (1)

193 NO MORE sou: more (7 *without no*)

194 NORTH NOR: n/a

195 NOW NOR: nowe (15)

LALME QUESTIONNAIRE

196 OLD NOR: olde (18)

197 ONE *adj, pron* NOR: on (13)

198 OR: or (14)

199 OTHER *indef, def* NOR: n/a

200 OUR NOR: our (56); oure (2)

201 OUT NOR: out (24); oute (1)

202 OWN *adj*: owne (6)

203 PEOPLE NOR: peple (18)

204 POOR NOR: n/a

205 PRAY NOR: pray (3 *inf*; 5 *sg*); prayed (13 *pt*; 3 *ppl*); prayde (1 *ppl*)

206 PRIDE *etc* SOU: n/a

207 READ *pt* SOU: n/a

208 RUN NOR & SOU: rennyth (1 *sg*); rennyng (1 *pres-ppl*); *pt* SOU: n/a

209 THE SAME SOU: same (44); that same (5); this same (2); tho same (1)

210 SAY NOR & SOU: say (4 *inf*); *3sg, pl, pt-sg, pt-pl, ppl* NOR: say (2 *ppl*)
   sey (1 *imp*); sayde (10 *pt-sg*, 1 *pt-pl*); sayth (1 *pres-sg*); seyd (5 *pt-sg*);
   seyde (10 *pt-sg*, 1 *pt-pl*); [seyde] (1 *pt-sg*)

211 SEE *3sg, pl* NOR: n/a; *pt-sg, pt-pl, ppl* NOR & SOU: se (4 *inf*); sey (1 *pt-sg*); sene (1 *ppl*); seyn (2 *ppl*); sigh (13 *pt-sg*, 2 *pt-pl*);
   sygh (1 *pt-sg*)

212 SEEK NOR: n/a

213 SELF *pl*: n/a

214 SEVEN *ord* NOR: n/a

215 SILVER SOU: n/a

216 SIN *sb, vb*: synne (2 *sb sg*, 0 *vb*); synnes (2 *sb pl*, 0 *vb*);

217 SISTER *pl* NOR: systers (5 *pl*); sisters (3 *pl*); systres (1 *pl*); sister (2 *sg*);
   sistir (1 *sg*); sistre (1 *sg*)

218 SIX *ord* NOR: sext (1)

219 SLAIN sou: n/a

220 SOME nor: some (9); somme (3); som (1)

221 SON nor: son (1); sone (1)

222 SORROW *sb, vb* nor: sorowe (1 sb, 0 vb)

223 SOUL *pl* nor: soule (7 *sg*, 0 *pl*)

224 SOUTH nor: n/a

225 SPAKE, BRAKE sou: speke (2 *inf*); brake (2 *pt-sg*)

226 STAR *pl* nor: sterre (1 *sg*)

227 STEAD: stede (1)

228 SUN nor: n/a

229 TAKES *contr, ppl* nor: take (6 *inf*, 3 *ppl*, 1 *imp*)

230 TEN *ord* nor: n/a

231 THEE nor: n/a

232 THOU nor: thou (13)

233 THY nor: thi (15); thy (2)

234 THENCE sou: thens (5); thense (1)

235 THITHER: thedir (8)

236 THOUSAND: thousande (1)

237 THREE *ord* nor: third (2); thirde (2)

238 TOGETHER: togedir (6); togedirs (1)

239 TRUE nor: trewe (3)

240 TWELVE *ord* nor: n/a

241 TWENTY nor: twenty (4)

242 TWO: two (11); twayn (2); twayne (2); twey (1); tweyn (1)

243 UNTIL sou: til (3); till (2)

244 UPON nor: vpon (15)

LALME QUESTIONNAIRE

245 WAY NOR: way (7); waye (1)

246 WEEK *pl*: weke (2 *sg*); wekys (1 *sg gen*)

247 WELL *adv* NOR: well (17)

248 WENT NOR & SOU: went (20 *pt-sg*); wentist (1 *pt-sg*);
pl NOR: went (8 *pt-pl*)

249 WHAT SOU: what (18)

250 WHENCE SOU: n/a

251 WHETHER: whethir (1)

252 WHITHER: whither (2)

253 WHO SOU: who (1)

254 WHOM SOU: whom (13); whome (3)

255 WHOSE SOU: whos (4); whose (3)

256 WHY NOR: why (3); whi (1)

257 WITEN NOR & SOU: n/a; *sg* NOR: wost (1 *2pres-sg*); wott (1 *1pres-sg*);
wottest (1 *2pres-sg*); *pl, pt-sg, pt-pl* NOR & SOU: wist (1 *3pt-sg*)

258 WITHOUT *pr, adv*: without (5 *pr*); withouten (3 *pr*);
withoute (1 *adv*); withowten (1 *pr*)

259 WORSE NOR & SOU: n/a; *sup* NOR: n/a

260 WORSHIP *sb, vb, adj*: worship (7); worchip (1); worshipped (1 *pt-sg*)

261 YE NOR: ye (7)

262 YOU NOR: you (5)

263 YOUR NOR: your (4)

264 YEAR NOR: yere (16 *sg*); yeres (1 *pl*, 1 *sg gen*); yeris (1 *pl*)

265 YIELD SOU: n/a

266 YOUNG NOR: yonge (8)

267 -ALD NOR: beholde (1); holde (1); olde (18)

268 -AMB NOR: lambe (1); wombe (1)

269 -AND NOR: and (567); bande (1); Northumberlande (1); thousande (1); bonde (1); bronde (1); Englonde (1); Erlonde (3); honde (2); husbond (1); husbonde (7); londe (7); Ynglonde (3)

270 -ANG NOR: longe (7); songe (2); stronge (5); wronge (1)

271 -ANK NOR: thanke (1)

272 -DOM NOR: kyngdome (2); kyngedome (1); martirdome (4); wysdome (1)

273 -ER: alder (1); depper)1); gretter (1); lenger (1)

274 -EST *sup* NOR: fayrest (1); grettist (1); strengest (1); swettist (2)

275 -FUL NOR: dredfull (1); ioyfull (4); vnlefull (1); worshipfull (2)

276 -HOOD NOR: childehode (1); knyghthode (1)

277 -LESS NOR: endles (2)

278 -LY: apertly (1); blessidly (1); blissidly (1); bodely (2); boldly (1); continuelly (1); cruelly (2); dedely (1); deuotly (1); deuoutly (2); devoutly (3); endlesly (1); erly (1); fervently (1); flesshly (1); gladly (3); gostly (3); graciously (1); gretly (1); hertely (1); hevenly (2); holily (3); homely (1); horribly (1); inwardly (1); ioyfully (1); lighthly (1); maydenly (1); mervelously (2); mischevously (1); myghtely (1); namely (1); namly (1); nycely (1); paciently (2); perfitly (1); prevely (4); purely (1); rially (1); sharply (1); sodenly (3); specially (2); streytly (3); strongly (1); sufficiently (1); symplely (1); trewly (2); truly (3); verely (1); violently (1); worshipfully (1); wrongfully (1)

279 -NESS NOR: clennes (1); dompnes (1); fatnes (1); feyrnes (1); gladnes (1); goodnes (1); holines (1); meknes (1); myldnes (1); seknes (1); swetnes (1); wildernes (2); wyldernes (1)

280 –SHIP NOR: felisship (1); worship (7); worchip (1)

Diagnostic Features

Working on the basis of the questionnaire above and with a full account taken of the rest of the language in the manuscript as need be, various Linguistic Profiles (LPs), Dot Maps, Item Maps, and other information in LALME and eLALME were examined to see if there were any broad diagnostic features that

DIAGNOSTIC FEATURES

would help to isolate linguistic provenance. It is immediately clear from this research that Add. 2604's general aspects rule out broad areas of the country from the North to the West Midlands and the South West, even though inevitably in such a late text there will be certain features that it shares with many of these dialectal areas. It is therefore of little value to spend time itemising the usual linguistic features that would rule out these regions, what in previous times were known as isoglossic tests as devised by Oakden or Moore, Meech, and Whitehall.[7] These take into account many specific features of spelling (and morphology) that broadly divide England into certain dialectal areas: for example, with 'a' spellings for Old English long 'a' regarded as a marker of northern dialects as in 'stane' for 'stone', while 'o spellings for Old English 'a' when followed by a nasal indicate the West Midlands, for example 'mon' for 'man', or the ways in which 'z' spellings highlight a Kentish text such as 'zenne' for 'sin', and so on. In its essentials such distinctions — among others — are what underlie the linguistic analysis in LALME, although it is now widely accepted that language change works in terms of continua rather than boundaries.[8]

Broadly speaking, given the content of the volume with its pronounced emphasis on East Anglian saints focusing on native saints from their cult centre at Ely, it is unsurprising that what dialectal evidence there is points generally to the eastern/south-eastern part of the country, that is, roughly from Middlesex to East Anglia.[9] The main linguistic basis for this argument is an examination of a total of two hundred and thirty-six LPs in LALME in the following counties that comprise East Anglia and surrounding areas (with the number of LPs provided in brackets): Bedfordshire (8), Cambridge (16), Essex (37), Hertfordshire (11), Huntingdon (12), Isle of Ely (15), Kent (14), London (6),

---

[7] J. P. Oakden, *Alliterative Poetry in Middle English: The Dialectal and Metrical Survey* (Manchester: Manchester University Press, 1930–35; reprinted by Archon Books, 1968) and Samuel Moore, Sanford Brown Meech, and Harold Whitehall, 'Middle English Dialect Characteristics and Dialect Boundaries: Preliminary Report of an Investigation Based exclusively on Localized Texts and Documents', in *Essays and Studies in English and Comparative Literature,* University of Michigan Publications in Language and Literature, 13 (Ann Arbor, MI: University of Michigan Press, 1935), 1–60.

[8] Likewise, as a non-northern text Add. 2604 does not possess the graphological feature whereby the letter 'y' can be written for 'þ' (in fact 'þ' is very rare in Add. 2604, another feature of its late date); see Michael Benskin, 'The Letters <þ> and <y> in Later Middle English and Some Related Matters', *Journal of the Society of Archivists,* 7 (1982), 13–30.

[9] In other circumstances the geographical locale of the content might have no bearing on that of the scribe.

Middlesex (9), Norfolk (64), Suffolk (29), and Surrey (15).[10] (And in the LPs from these counties, to which we shall return, all those containing saints' lives or definitely associated with nuns or nunneries were especially noted as well as those LPs that were near county boundaries.)

Yet there is no point in working comparatively here through this plethora of LPs in LALME picking out shared features, because it is not possible to plot accurately and consistently the relative overlap of forms between Add. 2604 and these particular LPs in LALME.[11] This is not to say that forms are not shared, but rather that they cannot be accounted for across the board in a meaningful fashion.[12] A comparison between the linguistic survey above from Add. 2604 and these individual LPs demonstrates the patchy levels of agreement both with our text and within and across counties, something that is inevitable in any system where absolute standardisation does not exist. This situation is exacerbated by the late date and thus relatively colourless language of Add. 2604 in dialectal terms.[13] We use 'colourless' in the sense defined by Michael Samuels when he notes how scribes could replace their own forms with others in widespread use so that 'The result [...] is a "colourless" regional language which may present almost as great an obstacle to exact

---

[10] All the LPs are in LALME III. As noted in LALME, 'The counties are the modern descendants of the mediaeval ones, substantially as they were just before the local government reforms of 1974 (England and Wales) and 1975 (Scotland); but Ely, the Soke of Peterborough, Middlesex and London are separately treated', LALME, I, 51.

[11] Part of the general difficulty is with LALME itself; because of the date restrictions (see n. 1), any comparison will be hampered by the uncertainties of chronological variables.

[12] This is not to invalidate this sort of comparison as it can be done to very good effect in particular circumstances, for instance, in *The Middle English 'Liber Aureus' and 'Gospel of Nicodemus'*, ed. by William Marx, Middle English Texts, 48 (Heidelberg: Winter, 2013), pp. xxvii–xl.

[13] This means inevitably that the language of Add. 2604 is never going to conform to any of the four broad Types of Middle English outlined in M. L. Samuels, 'Some Applications of Middle English Dialectology', *English Studies*, 44 (1963), 81–94, reprinted in McIntosh, Samuels, and Laing, *Middle English Dialectology*, ed. by Laing, pp. 64–80. Add. 2604 is hardly alone in this: in *The Language of the Chaucer Tradition*, Horobin illustrates how the same Chaucerian manuscripts often have features of the different Types (I: Central Midlands Standard; II: Fourteenth-century language of the greater London area; III: London English of *c.* 1400; and IV: Chancery Standard); see particularly 'Appendix 1: Notes on the Language of *Canterbury Tales* Manuscripts', pp. 146–63. These 'Types' and their interpretation are fully discussed in Smith, 'On "Standard" Written English in the Later Middle Ages'; see also the useful references in Smith's essay.

localization as standardization proper'.[14] We do not mean that Add. 2604 has no distinctive features, but that it does not have a set of forms that when combined would link incontrovertibly to a precise geographical area, albeit that some pointers may be found, as we shall see. There are therefore various possible explanations for the sort of language found in Add. 2604. Perhaps the most plausible — and in line with what is known about the communicative pressures that emerged in the late medieval period — is that the scribe was, in place of locally diagnostic features, increasingly deploying forms in widespread use in Middle English, either those that were emerging in the capital or elsewhere. Although there are definite elements in the text that can be associated with East Anglia, which is suggestive of the language's regional basis, the direction was largely towards this 'colourless' usage where more diagnostic regional forms are replaced by more commonplace ones, not necessarily those found in the various types of the 'incipient Standard' traditionally identified. And we realise that scribes, even late scribes, do not always write in a perfectly consistent manner and that they can move locales, but we postulate (for reasons that will become clear) that our scribe may well have been writing in the area of the country from which he originally hailed.[15]

[14] M. L. Samuels, 'Spelling and Dialect in the Late and Post-Middle English Periods', in *So meny people, longages and tonges*, ed. by Benskin and Samuels, pp. 43–54 (p. 43); see also the useful study by Goméz Soliño (see n. 1). This 'colourless' phenomenon is not to be confused with the concept of 'Mischsprachen' as discussed in Michael Benskin and Margaret Laing, 'Translations and *Mischsprachen* in Middle English Manuscripts', in *So meny people, longages and tonges*, ed. by Benskin and Samuels, pp. 55–106. There are, of course, numerous examples of Middle English texts whose precise linguistic parameters can not be easily ascertained; a very informative analysis of a broadly East Anglian manuscript (London, British Library, MS Additional 10304) is available in *On Famous Women: The Middle English Translation of Boccaccio's 'De Mulieribus Claris'*, ed. by Janet Cowen, Middle English Texts, 52 (Heidelberg: Winter, 2015), pp. xxvii–xxxviii; Cowen refers to 'a significant admixture of standardized forms which act to neutralize the indications of scribal dialect' (p. xxxiv). Important here too is one of the overall conclusions in Takeda, 'The Question of the "Standardisation" of Written English in the Fifteenth Century', about the greater variability in spelling and inflectional suffixes of East Anglian English (especially that of Norfolk), when compared, for instance, with the Yorkshire dialect.

[15] '[...] the *Atlas* tells us, in essence, *where the scribe of a manuscript learned to write*; the question of where he actually worked and produced the manuscript is a matter of extrapolation and assumption' (LALME, i, 23).

Norfolk and Suffolk Dialects

To demonstrate how we have reached these conclusions, we provide our methodology and rationale below. In order to work out how matters may be taken further, a close examination of LALME's and eLALME's Dot Maps and/ or Item Maps was undertaken.[16] Particular attention was paid to a range of Add. 2604's forms that are relatively noteworthy: 73 ASK; 86 BRIDGE; 99 COULD; 103 DIE; 113 ENOUGH; 115 EYE; 120 FETCH; 135 GATE; 137 GIVE; 176 MAY; 211 SEE; 226 STAR; 242 TWO; and 257 WITEN. The results of this search are largely inconclusive. To illustrate this, we shall cite just one example here (returning to this feature below), 73 ASK, where the forms used in Add. 2604 are: axe (3 *inf*); axid (3 *pt*, 2 *ppl*); axed (1 *pt*); and axing (1 *vb sb*). When forms with 'ax/ax-/axe' are respectively investigated in LALME, the results are as follows: 'ax' is located in one LP in Huntingdon; 'ax-' is found in LPs in Bedfordshire, Berkshire, Buckinghamshire, Cambridge, Derbyshire, Devon, Dorset, Ely, Essex, Gloucestershire, Hampshire, Herefordshire, Hertfordshire, Huntingdon, Kent, Leicestershire, London, Middlesex, Norfolk, Northern, Nottinghamshire, Oxfordshire, Shropshire, Somerset, Staffordshire, Suffolk, Surrey, Sussex, Warwickshire, Wiltshire, and Worcestershire. In turn 'axe' spellings occur in Bedfordshire, Berkshire, Buckinghamshire, Cambridge, Ely, Essex, Gloucestershire, Hampshire, Herefordshire, Hertfordshire, Huntingdon, Leicestershire, London, Middlesex, Northern, Nottinghamshire, Rutland, Shropshire, Soke of Peterborough, Somerset, Staffordshire, Suffolk, Surrey, Sussex, Warwickshire, Wiltshire, Worcestershire, and Monmouthshire.[17] All told, forms of this apparently distinctive 'ax/ax-/axe' spelling occur from Huntingdon to Devon. Indeed, when the LALME forms are examined, it soon becomes clear that this form is not at all unusual, particularly when compared with unique forms like 'hasch-' from Worcestershire or 'yask-' from Hampshire. Even statistics do not really help: for example, forms in 'ax-' are recorded in ten LPs in Herefordshire, but in eight each in Huntingdon and Suffolk. Admittedly, texts may not be localised on the basis of single items, but rather on a range of overlapping features and concentrated forms. Yet this one instance shows that it is difficult to pin down scribal provenance even with a methodical examination of the language at the micro

---

[16] For Dot Maps, see LALME, I (with the index on pp. 559–67) and for Item Maps, see LALME, II (with the index on pp. 375–80); see also eLALME for both.

[17] LALME, IV, 122–23.

NORFOLK AND SUFFOLK DIALECTS

as well as the macro level. Yet given the pronounced East Anglian emphasis of the manuscript's content and leaving aside the fact that both scribes and manuscripts can shift their locales, one might still expect a greater affinity between the language of Add. 2604 and that of the two main counties in East Anglia proper: Norfolk and Suffolk. Yet even here there are initial difficulties.

Classic markers for Norfolk and Suffolk dialects are the use of 'x' for 'sh' in 'shall' and 'should' (characteristic of Norfolk); 'q' for words with initial 'wh' (more prevalent in Norfolk); 't' or 'th' for 'ght'; and the use of 't' for 'th' in the third person present indicative singular. In addition, there are various other features such as the routine appearance of Old English 'y' as 'e' in words such as 'kende' or 'mende' for 'kind' and 'mind', forms for 'much' like 'mech/e' (more predominant in Suffolk) and 'mekyl' (more predominant in Norfolk), as well as distinctive spellings such as 'hefne' for 'heaven', 'werd' for 'world', and 'cure' for 'cover', plus the use of 'w' for consonantal 'v'.[18] Taken at face value, Add. 2604 lacks most of the well known marked features that would link it incontrovertibly only to East Anglia and nowhere else. For instance, in Add. 2604 there is no use of 'x' spellings in 'shall' and 'should' that are the absolute diagnostic of Norfolk dialects (albeit that they can also occur in parts of Suffolk).[19] Likewise, there is nothing obviously 'regional' about many of the forms. For instance, the scribe never makes use of the common 'qu/qw/qwh' East Anglian forms in words like 'where' and 'when'. In Add. 2604 as a whole there is a routine use of the 'ght' form (for example, 'strenght' and 'lenght') rather than the East Anglian 'th' or 't' forms. There is just one example of 't' for 'th' in the third person present tense: 'wrougt' [perpetrated]. In the manuscript the scribe misses off the final 'h' in 'fourt' on each of the four occasions it is mentioned, as well as writing 'fyft'; and there is one instance of the name 'Witburgh' alongside ten examples of 'Whitburgh' and one of 'Whithburgh'; the scribe also writes 'witter' for the comparative of the colour 'white'. The more typical East Anglian (particularly Suffolk) spelling of 'meche' is found, albeit alongside other spellings of the word. There are no examples in the survey here or in the manuscript

[18] For a very useful profile of the notable features of the Norfolk and Suffolk dialects isolated on the basis of localised documents, see Hilton Richard Leslie Beadle, 'The Medieval Drama of East Anglia: Studies in Dialect, Documentary Records and Stagecraft' (unpublished doctoral dissertation, University of York, 1977), especially ch. 3, 'Later Middle English in East Anglia — Some Distinctive Characteristics of its Written Form' (pp. 48–78). See also Richard Beadle, 'Prolegomena to a Literary Geography of Later Medieval Norfolk', in *Regionalism in Late Medieval Manuscripts and Texts*, ed. by Riddy, pp. 89–108.

[19] See Items 22 and 23 in LALME, IV, 37–43.

as a whole of 'world' spelt as 'werd' or of 'kind' (and related words) spelt as 'kende', of 'heaven' spelt as 'hefne' (a word we shall return to below) or of 'cover' spelt as 'cure'; instead we have the imperative form 'kever' and the past participle form 'coverid'. But there is one case of 'w' being used for consonantal 'v' in the manuscript: 'weyle' [veil], with the three other examples of this word all written with a 'v'.

Furthermore, in his study of East Anglian dialect Richard Beadle highlights two other important features: the relative distribution of 'th' and 'h' forms in East Anglia for the spellings of 'their' and 'them' and the use of either 'g' or 'y' spellings in 'give'. His notes that:

> By a fairly clearly defined date in the mid-fifteenth century many copyists and writers were beginning to use the initial <u>th</u> forms of the incipient 'Standard' language in preference to the regular south-east midland forms in <u>h, them</u> and <u>their</u> etc. rather than <u>hem</u> and <u>her(e</u>.[20]

He goes on to argue that before the mid-fifteenth century such northern 'th' forms 'are not found further south than southern Lincolnshire'.[21] In the questionnaire sample above the results are mixed, with the 'th' for 'their' well established and the 'th' for 'them' less so:

8 THEM: hem (43); theym (11); them (3)

9 THEIR: their (16); theyr (4); theyre (3); theire (1); þer (1); her (2); hyr (1).

But this result is not so different from many of the examples found in the two-hundred and thirty-six LPs from the Middlesex to East Anglian region. And LALME's cut-off point for such texts pre-dates 1450 which calls Beadle's cast-iron dating somewhat into question. With regard to 'g' and 'y', his argument is similarly clear cut: 'It is not until after 1450 that the forms with initial g become at all frequent in East Anglian work'.[22] The sample here is as follows:

137 GIVE *pt-pl* NOR: yaf (2 *pt-pl*); yevon (1 *pt-pl*); *pt-sg, ppl* NOR & SOU: yaf (2 *pt-sg*); yafe (1 *pt-sg*); yevon (3 *ppl*); yif (2 *inf*, 1 *imp*); yeving (1 *pres-ppl*)

This gives a clear sweep for the 'y' form; in fact in Add. 2604 as a whole there are only three examples of 'gif' in the infinitive and one of 'gaf' as a past tense,

---

[20] For the discussion, see Beadle, 'The Medieval Drama of East Anglia', pp. 73–75 (p. 73).

[21] Beadle, 'The Medieval Drama of East Anglia', p. 73.

[22] Beadle, 'The Medieval Drama of East Anglia', p. 75.

NORFOLK AND SUFFOLK DIALECTS

whereas by Beadle's reckoning 'g' should be more prevalent at this stage in the later fifteenth century. Yet here again in the two hundred and thirty-six LPs above there are mixed results. The most frequent spellings for 'give' and related forms are with yogh or 'g', with 'y' being very much in the minority. Marginally more incidences of 'y' are found in the LPs from Kent, London, Middlesex, Suffolk, and Surrey, with Suffolk having the largest number, which may be significant.

Otherwise, as may be seen in full above and from the examples below, there is nothing in the forms found to contradict a broad East Anglian or indeed south-eastern provenance.[23] Infinitives such as 'brenn' [burn] and related forms, normally associated with the eastern side of the country, are invariable, as are forms like 'bery' [bury] and 'besy' [bury]. Interesting infinitives in Add. 2604 as a whole include: 'denygh' [deny], 'digh/dighe/dygh' [die]; fett [fetch]; 'lese' [lose]; and 'shete' [shoot].[24] Distinctive past tenses are: 'bare' [bore]; 'brake' [broke]; 'breddist' [spread]; 'chase' [chose]; 'crape' [crept]; 'dalfe' [dug]; 'dighed' [died]; 'fett' [fetched]; 'foryeve' [forgave]; 'gedrid' [gathered]; 'halp' [helped]; 'hilde' [grasped]; 'hynge' [hung]; 'lad' [led]; 'lift/lifte' [lifted]; 'malt/malte' [melted]; 'picched' [pitched]; 'rad/radde' [read]; 'shove' [shaved]; 'seigh/sey/sigh/sygh' [saw]; 'soke' [sucked]; 'spett/spitt' [spat]; 'stale' [stole]; 'sware' [swore]; 'trade' [vanquished]; 'wanne' [gained]; 'wax/waxe/waxed/ waxid/wex' [waxed, grew]; and 'wysshe' [washed]. Noteworthy past participles are: 'fett' [fetched]; 'rad'/'radde' [read]; 'satelid' [settled]; 'shitt' [shut]; 'sey/ sighe' [seen]; 'smete of' [cut off]; 'sonked' [enveloped]; and 'spreyngid' [sprinkled]. Examples of the present tense end consistently in 'th' (rather than the northern 's') and the present participle ends in '-ing' (slightly in the majority); 'yng'; 'inge' (very rare); 'ynge' (very rare), while the verbal substantive has: 'ing' (majority); 'yng'; 'inge' (very rare); and 'ynge' (very rare). The weak past tense ends in the majority of cases as 'ed', much less frequently as 'id' and rarely as 'ied'. The weak past participle endings are as follows: 'ed' (majority); 'id' (second most frequent); 'yd' (third most frequent); 'ied' (very rare); with a few examples minus final 'd', for instance, 'translate'. In a few cases (though not in the sample above) the scribe makes use of the Old English 'ge' suffix in past par-

---

[23] Earlier in the period the East Anglian dialect would have been more differentiated from that in the south-east, for instance, by distinctive markers for East Anglian (such as the use of 'x for 'shall' or 'should' or 'q' for 'wh' words).

[24] The terms 'interesting', 'distinctive', and 'noteworthy' are used here from the limited viewpoint of modern readers; many of the forms below would have been commonplace or at least expected in certain Middle English regions.

ticiples, here spelt as 'i' or 'y', for instance in 'ibrende', and 'ybounde'. The strong past participle has 'en' (vast majority); 'on'; 'yn' (very rare), with a few examples in the manuscript minus final 'n': 'stole'; 'take'; 'unknowe'; and 'wrete'.

Overall the scribe is very consistent in his use of particular forms and spellings. It is especially noticeable throughout that he tends not to mix different spelling systems. And he has a liking for spellings in which 'e' replaces 'i', often associated with East Anglian texts. In Add. 2604 there are plenty of such cases: 'cetesens' [citizens]; 'defors/devorse' [divorce]; 'gebett' [gibbett]; 'lekyn' [liken]; 'levyd' [lived]; 'melke' [milk]; 'prevely' [privately]; and 'wekkedist' [most wicked]. These may be of dialectal significance, but some may also be a feature of the manuscript's late date. This is part of the problem — and the interest — in the language of Add. 2604: to what extent can potentially important dialectal and lexical features be extrapolated from what at first appears to be simply a late and somewhat linguistically anodyne text?

Dialectal and Lexical Features in Add. 2604

There are indeed a few unusual spellings or vocabulary usages. These include: 'abbeys' [abbess]; 'axesse'/'axisse' [attack of illness characterised by fever]; 'beresse' [female bear]; 'boluyng' [inflammation]; 'brist' [breast]; 'brokkes' [the young of locusts]; 'cacchepollis/chachepolle/chaccespolle/chacchepollis' [catchpole/s]; 'devlett' [little devil]; 'dayles' [ineffectual]; 'eyren' [eggs]; 'houches/owches' [bracelets, brooches, necklaces]; 'kene' [cows]; 'mastres' [mistress]; 'mynches' [nuns]; 'pament' [paved or tiled floor]; 'shrowes/strowes' [charters/documents]; 'swenysye' [swelling of the throat]; 'thristlewe' [thirsty]; 'wayle' [veil]; and 'yothe' [youth]. (Of these the most important are the words for 'eggs' and 'thirsty', discussed further below.) In the manuscript there is one example of the dropping and one of the addition of 'h': 'abyte' [habit] and 'hoke' [oak], with the latter also being the spelling for the word 'hook'. As may be seen from the Select Glossary in the *Edition*, most of these words do not occur more than once.[25] But there is one case where the scribe has a definitive alternative alongside a more common word: he uses 'nonne/s' sixty-two times to the five instances of the more noticeably rare and presumably old-fashioned 'mynche/s' [nuns]. The texts that use the word 'mynche', the lives of Martha

---

[25] For the spellings 'abbeys', 'mastres', 'wayle', and 'yothe', there are also the following: 'abbes/s' (routine spelling), 'maystres' (one occurrence), 'vayle' (one occurrence), 'veyle' (two occurrences), and 'youth/e' (usual spelling).

DIALECTAL AND LEXICAL FEATURES IN ADD. 2604

and Domitilla, also have the other term. No text of this period could have been written without some dependence on French vocabulary, hence 'avise' [advice or recommendation], 'delicates' [fine foods or luxuries], and so on. But particularly noteworthy is some decidedly Old English vocabulary in 'eme' [uncle] and 'syster son' [nephew] in Modwenna; and 'sister doughtir' [niece] in Domitilla. In addition, the scribe uses the common Old English word 'winter' for 'year'; for instance, in John the Baptist he is described as being in the wilderness until 'he was more than thirty wynter olde' (1/81).[26]

The volume is therefore, both in content and language, a somewhat unique mixture of the old-fashioned and the modern, though it is not always obvious which is which. For example, there is the use of the 'a'-gerund (one occurrence each of 'afysshynge' and 'amakyng' and two of 'areding'), a form ultimately deriving from an Old English construction, but lasting well into the early modern period.[27] Far more obvious throughout the lives is the scribe's very common use of what to modern eyes is the peculiar 'his' genitive (found alongside the usual form of the genitive). It is always spelt here as 'is' (for example, 'Seynt Blase is day' in Wærburh, 10/70). The 'is' form is customarily found after a name, though very occasionally it occurs in Add. 2604 after a common noun as in 'fadir is voyce' in John the Baptist (1/79).[28] Like the preceding a-gerund, the 'his' form, to which we shall return, is not so common in Middle English but is found as late as the seventeenth century.

Such forms encourage the discovery of what else may be unique to or idiosyncratic in Add. 2604. It has already been noted that the scribe is very con-

---

[26] There is one other instance in John the Evangelist (2/268) and in Hild (16/145).

[27] See Tauno F. Mustanoja, *A Middle English Syntax: Part I, Parts of Speech*, Mémoires de la Société Néophilologique de Helsinki, 23 (Helsinki: Société Néophilologique, 1960), pp. 577–78, 587–89, and 592, for a full discussion of this form; he points out that the formulation '*to be a-doing* enjoys its greatest popularity between 1500 and 1700' (p. 578).

[28] Mustanoja, *A Middle English Syntax*, pp. 159–62, provides an explanation for the development of this genitive, noting that it remains popular into the seventeenth century. However, see especially the detailed discussion, 'The Separated Genitive in English', in Cynthia L. Allen, *Genitives in Early English: Typology and Evidence* (Oxford: Oxford University Press, 2008), pp. 223–73. She traces the history and genesis of the form and in doing so thoroughly re-appraises other scholarship on the matter. She notes that 'The ME separated genitives are an entirely new phenomenon, with no chain linking them to the OE examples which have been adduced' (p. 227), that 'It is not until the late fourteenth century that separated genitives become more widespread' (p. 240), and that 'it does not appear to be true that the separated genitives were at any period found only in Southwestern texts' (p. 244). We are grateful to John Scahill for drawing our attention to Allen's informative study.

sistent in his use of particular forms and spellings (for instance, there is only one instance of 'whanne' above to thirty-six of 'whan'), albeit not as rigorous as someone like John Capgrave.[29] This also draws attention to the few cases that are especially variable. The main examples in the manuscript as a whole are the following (with numbers of occurrences provided in brackets):

CATCHPOLE: chachepolle (1); chacchespolle (1);
CATCHPOLES: cachepollis (1); chacchepollis (1);

DIE: die (0), digh (2), dighe (1), dye (14), dygh (1), dyghe (2);

DIED: died (22), dighed (1), dyed (6);

HEAVEN: hevyn (52), heven (43), heuyn (3), heyven (1);

MUCH: mech (0); meche (10), mich (2), miche (0), moch (0), moche (37), mych (4), myche (1);

SAW (past tense of the verb): seigh (1), sey (3), sigh (73), sighest (1); sygh (2)

SISTER: syster (46), sister (33), sistre (3), systre (2), sistir (2);
SISTERS (plural): sisterin (1); sistern (3); sistres (1); susters (1); systern (1); these are the only variant spellings as elsewhere in the manuscript the plural of 'sister' is 'systers' or 'sisters' in a ratio of two to one;

WHICH: whech (12), wheche (7), which (345), whiche (3), whych (0), whyche (0).[30]

It has been noted that the scribe does not make use of the East Anglian 'hefne' spelling for 'heaven', and yet there seems to be a little hesitancy with this word as he deviates between one major spelling and another, with a couple of variants for good measure. He seems to have particular trouble with the French loan-word, 'catchpole', a relatively unusual word, to which we shall return. Even greater inconsistency is obvious with 'sister' and 'sisters'; on balance the scribe favours a 'y' rather than an 'i' spelling, but in the plural in particular there is a

---

[29] Peter J. Lucas, 'Consistency and Correctness in the Orthographic Usage of John Capgrave's *Chronicle*', *Studia Neophilologica*, 45 (1973), pp. 323–55, carefully demonstrates the remarkable consistency of Capgrave's orthography in the autograph Cambridge, Cambridge University Library, MS Gg.4.12 of his *Chronicle*. This essay is reprinted in Peter J. Lucas, *From Author to Audience: John Capgrave and Medieval Publication* (Dublin: University College Dublin Press/Preas Choláiste Ollscoile Bhaile Átha Cliath, 1997), pp. 203–35.

[30] These forms are fully explained in the Select Glossary in the *Edition*.

DIALECTAL AND LEXICAL FEATURES IN ADD. 2604

definite uncertainty. Noticeable here is the inclusion of three examples of the outdated 'n-plural', or weak declension inherited from Old English, in 'sisterin/ sistern/systern'. The scribe also has the 'n-' spelling' for one of the three neuter nouns in the weak declension: 'eyghen/eyghyn/eyghyne'.[31] In addition, as we have seen above, he uses the 'n' spelling for the plural of 'eggs' in 'eyren', a form made famous by William Caxton, as a means of distinguishing between northern and southern dialects.[32] Some of the forms here *could* be relicts from an earlier version, though as argued throughout this volume, we think it highly unlikely that another copy of this somewhat specialised work existed.[33]

The increasing use of the 'Standard' may be seen particularly in the examples of 'much' and 'which' from Add. 2604 as a whole:

MUCH: mech (0); meche (10), mich (2), miche (0), moch (0), moche (37), mych (4), myche (1);

WHICH: whech (12), wheche (7), which (345), whiche (3), whych (0), whyche (0).

In the former amongst all the variant spellings the most prominent one is the more commonplace 'moche'; likewise in the latter, it is the increasingly common 'which' that is by far the most popular form. Similarly, the letter yogh is very rare in Add. 2604 (see 'broȝt' (15/54)) and the usage of 'þ' rather than 'th'

[31] The other neuter 'n' nouns in the plural for 'ear' ('eare') and 'cheek' ('wange') do not occur in Add. 2604.

[32] Caxton tells the story in his prologue to the printed translation of the *Eneydos* (*c.* 1490) of the merchant called 'Sheffelde' (presumably a Yorkshire man) stranded in a ship on the Thames who could not set sail for the Continent owing to the lack of wind at sea. Going to a house and asking for 'eggys', he is told by the woman of the house 'that she coude speke no Frenshe'. Eventually someone else explains 'that he wolde have eyren'. Caxton concludes with 'Loo! what sholde a man in thyse dayes now wryte, "egges" or "eyren"? Certaynly it is harde to playse every man bycause of dyversite and chaunge of langage'; for the whole account, see N. F. Blake, *Caxton's Own Prose* (London: Deutsch, 1973), pp. 78–81 (p. 79, l. 45 to p. 80, l. 59). This narrative (possibly told with a large measure of dramatic licence) has given rise to the belief in the Old Norse 'egg' and its 's' plural being solely a Northern Middle English word and the Old English 'ei' and its plural 'eyren' being a solidly Southern Middle English form (particularly Kentish). It would not be unexpected to have 'eyren' in a text that would appear to derive from the southern reaches of East Anglia; as noted in the MED under eg(ge n.(1), 'This ON word appears first in the N and the nEM dialects beside the (historically corresponding) native ei, which predominates elsewhere throughout the ME period.'

[33] See the discussion especially in IV. Hagiographical Context and the Selection of Saints.

throughout the manuscript is sporadic (for example, 498 instances of 'the' to forty-one of 'þe' in the questionnaire sample above) and may be the result of some similar sort of 'modernisation'. Yet in the midst of the examples above are the spellings for 'die/died' and 'see' that do not reflect the forms that were ultimately to become 'standard'.

Indeed, these are two of the forms that really stand out in the manuscript. While 'die' occurs as above in item 103 as 'dye (2 *inf*); died (4 *pt*); dyed (2 *pt*, 1 *ppl*)', the 'gh' form is also found in the manuscript as a whole, as follows: 'die': 'die (0), digh (2), dighe (1), dye (14), dygh (1), dyghe (2); died (22), dighed (1), dyed (6)'. This form with 'gh' rather than yogh is especially rare: 'dighe' occurs in LPs 2 (Nottinghamshire), 610 (North-West Yorkshire), and 468 (North Riding of Yorkshire); 'dygh-' is found in 8480 (Suffolk), 525, and 599 (both Northern Middle English); 'dyghe' occurs in 510 (Lincolnshire), 610 (North-West Yorkshire), 4 (West Riding of Yorkshire), 525, and 599 (both Northern Middle English); finally 'dyghed' is found in LP 510 (Lincolnshire).[34] Item 211 SEE above has quite a range: 'se (4 *inf*); sey (1 *pt-sg*); seyn (2 *ppl*); sigh (13 *pt-sg*, 2 *pt-pl*); sygh (1 *pt-sg*)'. Of these the most unusual form is 'sigh' and 'sygh' for the past tense. In the singular 'sigh' is only recorded in LPs 5101 (Devon), 302 (Leicestershire), 6410 (Middlesex), and 5820 (Surrey); in the plural it is found only in LP 6480 (Middlesex). The form 'sygh' in the singular occurs in LPs 193 (Staffordshire), 5730 (Surrey), 4685 (Warwickshire), and 7600 (Worcestershire); 'syghe' is noted only in LPs 6410 (Middlesex) and 5171 (Somerset); neither 'sygh' nor 'syghe' occur in the plural.[35] For two comparatively unusual spellings this is quite a geographical spread.

Add. 2604: Localisation in Suffolk?

Yet, when the results of the sample questionnaire above and particularly the language in the rest of the manuscript are taken into account, some conclusions may be drawn, albeit tentative. There would *seem* to be very few features in Add. 2604 that would help isolate precisely one dialectal area rather than another. Yet even though it has been noted more than once that the language of Add. 2604 as a whole can only be described as being in keeping with that in the eastern part of the country from East Anglia to Middlesex, there are, as we have seen, aspects that help narrow the focus.

[34] See Item 103 in LALME, IV, 150–52.

[35] See Item 211 in LALME, IV, 244–48.

ADD. 2604: LOCALISATION IN SUFFOLK?

Presumably as a result of its late date, the manuscript lacks many of the obvious regionalisms of the East Anglian dialect (the use of 'x' for 'sh' in 'shall' and 'should'; 'q' for words with initial 'wh', and so forth), as demonstrated above. Yet there is enough to point in the general direction of East Anglia, and possibly Suffolk, as we shall see, rather than Norfolk. Some of these features are shared with other dialects (for instance, the use of 'ng/e' for present participles); some are especially part of the East Anglian norm (such as a preference for 'e' rather than 'i' spellings), and some are very incidental details that may help prove the case. For example, the use of 'w' for 'v', found in 'wayle', mentioned above is rare testimony in Add. 2604 to a notable East Anglian feature. Another example, not previously mentioned, is the confusion of 'c' and 'g'. This happens with two names, normally spelt 'Agladius' and 'Glunelach', in Agatha and Modwenna respectively, where there is one example of 'Acladius' (albeit also found in a Latin analogue) and one of 'Clunelach'. These appear to be slips of the pen, but it is noted in an essay on the scribes of the Paston letters that Richard Calle, the head bailiff of the Paston family between 1450 and about 1475, had a similar tendency to confuse the two, writing 'cladde', 'classe', and 'goude' for 'glad', 'glass', and 'could'.[36] Calle apparently hailed originally from Framlingham in east central Suffolk which *may* indicate that the confusion of 'c' and 'g' was a Suffolk feature.[37] Likewise, although the Dot Map (under 115) for Item List 420 in eLALME confines examples of the 'his' genitive (what they call the 'detached genitive') regularly found in Add. 2604 mostly to the south west, this is also a feature that can be found in East Anglia. For instance, John Wykes, who also wrote for the Paston family in 1465–66, usually writes 'ys' separately, as in 'Arundell ys', 'Parker ys', and 'the Quyne ys', and there are examples from Capgrave in London, British Library, MS Additional 36704 in 'Valerie is desir was fulfillid' and 'fro Adam his synne'.[38] It also occurs in the sermon for the Nativity of the Virgin Mary in Dublin, Trinity College Dublin, MS 428, a revision of John Mirk's *Festial* localised in Norfolk: 'Joseph his hed' (fol. 41v). When some specific examples are found elsewhere, it is not always possible to tell whether such sporadic features are more customary in one dialectal

---

[36] See Norman Davis, 'Scribal Variation in Late Fifteenth Century English', in *Mélanges de linguistique et de philologie: Fernand Mossé in memoriam*, ed. by Fernand Mossé (Paris: Didier, 1959), pp. 95–103 (p. 102).

[37] Davis, 'Scribal Variation in Late Fifteenth Century English', p. 97.

[38] Davis, 'Scribal Variation in Late Fifteenth Century English', p. 100; Allen, 'The Separated Genitive in English', p. 244, where further East Midlands examples are also provided.

area or another or whether a shared item is mere coincidence.[39] In some other cases it is quite clear. More support for a Suffolk localisation may be found in Add. 2604's usage of the very rare word 'thristlewe' for 'thirsty', noted above.[40] There are only nine examples of this word recorded in the MED and the current spelling is only shared with one, the Middle English translation of the *Orologium sapientiae* as found in Oxford, Bodleian Library, MS Douce 114 (which is localised in Oxfordshire). Importantly, of the nine examples cited, four of them belong to the Suffolk writer John Lydgate.

It would seem then that in Add. 2604 we have a scribe who originates in East Anglia and who may hail from Suffolk, albeit perhaps with some Middlesex connections in his make-up. It would also seem that it is a scribe who, if not actively trying to censure his language like John Capgrave or some of the Pastons, he was effectively writing a relatively colourless language where occasionally some earlier linguistic habits came to the surface.[41]

With this in mind, we may return to the previous analysis of the two hundred and thirty-six LPs in LALME examined above. It has been noted that none of these provide a 'match' for the language in Add. 2604, something that

---

[39] An example of this is Add. 2604's single spelling of 'scilens' in Modwenna (21/711) besides two of 'sylens' (21/709, 21/710). The spelling with 'sc' is also found in John Capgrave, another East Anglian writer, 'Besides *silens* (2), *scilens* occurs once only'; see Lucas, 'Consistency and Correctness in the Orthographic Usage of John Capgrave's *Chronicle*' (p. 331 n. 4). Rather than being an East Anglian trait, this 'sc' spelling used by both scribes may just as easily derive from one of the Old French variants 'silence/silense/scilence'. See the Select Glossary in the *Edition* for 'scilens'.

[40] We are very grateful to Jeremy Smith for help with this point.

[41] With regard to Capgrave, Lucas demonstrates in 'Consistency and Correctness in the Orthographic Usage of John Capgrave's *Chronicle*', 'the extent to which there is conformity to some kind of "standard", at the expense of distinctively regional usages' (p. 325). For references to Paston examples, see Beadle, 'The Medieval Drama of East Anglia', I, 57 and II, 35 n. 47. One of the most obvious examples is that of Edmund Paston. There is dateable evidence between *c.* 1469 and *c.* 1479 linked to his time in Norfolk, London, or Calais of how he sought to rid himself of his Norfolk regionalisms; see Norman Davis, 'A Paston Hand', *The Review of English Studies*, n.s. 3 (1952), 209–21, who notes, 'These differences, then, are not scattered at random among the letters, but are seen to be a series of similar changes, without relapse into earlier practice, all tending in the same direction — away from old-fashioned and provincial spellings towards a more usual, presumably a more orthodox or "metropolitan", practice' (p. 219). Takeda's researches in 'The Question of the "Standardisation" of Written English in the Fifteenth Century' support Davis's point; she notes that educated and socially mobile East Anglian men used a language that 'was not a strict imitation of London forms in the prescriptive sense, but it displayed a gradual reduction of marked regional forms' (p. 246).

ADD. 2604: LOCALISATION IN SUFFOLK? 99

would be unexpected in any case given the late date of the manuscript, the fact that the bulk of LALME's LPs are pre-1450, and the other comments here. Yet the following LPs: 5820 (Surrey), 6410 (Middlesex), 6480 (Middlesex), and 8460, 8470, and 8480 (Suffolk) stand out. The first three texts consist of a copy of *Partonope of Blois* in Oxford, Bodleian Library, MS Rawlinson Poet. 14 (5820); a copy of the *Orchard of Syon* in Cambridge, St John's College, MS 75 (6410), a copy of the *Scale of Perfection* and other texts in Oxford, Bodleian Library, MS Rawlinson C. 894 (6480). The second three are the will of John Baret from Liber Hawlee in the Registers of the Commissary of Bury St Edmunds (8460); Lydgate's life of Edmund and Fremund in London, MS Harley 2278 (8470), and *A lettre sent to a relygyous woman of þe twelue frutys of the hooly goost* in Durham, University Library, MS Cosin V.iii.24, fols 92v–150v (8480).[42] These LPs stand out not because any one particularly matches up with the language of Add. 2604 but that overall the degree of similarity is perhaps greatest between the current manuscript and these LPs. A list of forms, chosen for what they highlight in Add. 2604, will illustrate this in these LPs (with LP 8470 now changed to LPs 4470 and 4471 via eLALME): 5820 (Surrey); 6410 (Middlesex); 6480 (Middlesex); 8460 (Suffolk); 8470 [4470/4471] (Suffolk); 8480 (Suffolk), and Add. 2604 (from the questionnaire list above, with added information from the manuscript as a whole where necessary):[43]

8 THEM: 5820: hem ((hym)); 6410: hem; 6480: hem; 8460: hem (heem, them); 4470: hem (them); 8480: hem, them, heem (theym) ((hom)); Add. 2604: hem (43); theym (11); them (3)

9 THEIR: 5820: here (hir, þer,); 6410: her (þeire); 6480: hyr, her; 8460: her, here, there, ther; 4470: ther ((there, her, here)); 8480: here; Add. 2604: their (16); theyr (4); theyre (3); theire (1); þer (1); her (2); hyr (1)

---

[42] The other texts are *The Doctrine of the Hert* (fols 1r–69v) and *A lettre of relygyous gouernaunce sent to a relygyous woman* (fols 72v–91v). An online description is available (https://reed.dur.ac.uk/xtf/view?docId=ark:/32150_s1sq87bt74j.xml) (accessed 5 February 2023); see further nn. 47 and 50.

[43] In eLALME LP 8470 has been re-done and re-numbered as LP 4470 (minus the rhyme forms) and LP 4471 (the rhyme forms only). These two new LPs have been thoroughly checked against LP 8470; there are some very minor changes to a few of the forms, but no change in the localisation. In the list above the analysis is taken from LPs 4470 and 4471. In the other LPs above there are very occasional minute changes between the printed text and the electronic text; where this happens, the forms here follow the electronic text.

11 WHICH: 5820: wheche, whiche; 6410: whiche; 6480: which, the-which, whiche; 8460: wiche, wich (þe-wiche); 4470: which ((whiche, the-which, whych)); 8480: the-whych, whych, wheche; Add. 2604: which (70); wheche (2); whech (1)

16 MUCH: 5820: moche (meche); 6410: miche (michel, mochil); 6480: much, moch (mych); 8460: moche ((mekyl)); 4470: moche, moch; 8480: moche (meche, muche); Add. 2604: meche (6); moche (4); mych (1)

30 THEN: 5820: þen, then; 6410: þan; 6480: þan (þen); 8460: thanne, than; 4470: than, thannne, tho; 8480: thanne, than, tho; Add. 2604: than (67); then (2)

36 AGAINST: 5820: ayenste, ayen (agan); 6410: aȝenste, aȝenst, aȝen; 6480: ayenst, aȝens, ayence; 8460: ageyn; 4470: ageyn (a-geyn, geyn) ((ageyns)); 4471: a-geyn, ageyn; 8480: aȝens, aȝenst; Add. 2604: ayenst (6); yenst (1)

73 ASK: 5820: aske, ax-; 6410: aske, axe; 6480: ask-; 8460: ask-; 4771: ax-; 8480: ax- (asch-); Add. 2604: axe (*inf*), axid (3 *pt*, 2 *ppl*); axed (1 *pt*); axing (1 *vb sb*)

103 DIED: 5820: n/a; 6410: n/a; 6480: died; 8460: n/a; 4470: n/a; 4471: n/a; deied; 8480: n/a; Add. 2604: died (4); dyed (2, plus 1 *ppl*)

115 EYE *pl.*: 5820: eyen; 6410: eyȝen, eyghen; 6480: yeȝ, yȝe, ȝien; 8460: n/a; 4470: eyen; 8480: eyghen; Add. 2604: eyghen (0 *sg*, 5 *pl*)

120 FETCH: 5820: feche; 6410: n/a; 6480: n/a; 8460: fetche; 4470: fette [pt.-ppl.]; 8480: n/a; Add. 2604: fett (2 *inf*)

135 GATE: 5820: yate; 6410: gate (ȝate); 6480: yate; 8460: gate; 4470: gate; 8480: ȝatys, ȝaatys (gates); Add. 2604: yates (0 *sg*, 2 *pl*)

137 GAVE: 5820: gafe, yaf, yafe; 6410: ȝaf; 6480: ȝafe; 8460: gaf; 4470: gaff ((gaf)); 8480: n/a; Add. 2604: yaf (4); yafe (1); yevon (1, plus 3 *ppl*)

211 SAW: 5820: sawe, sigh; 6410: seyh, saye, sigh, syghe; 6480: sigh; 8460: n/a; 4470: sauh, sawh ((saw)); 8480: seye; Add. 2604: sigh (15), sygh (1)

ADD. 2604: LOCALISATION IN SUFFOLK? 101

Taken as a whole (and not just from the examples above), it is possible to see various overlaps between and among the different LPs but none that provides a consistent pattern.[44] But overall the language of Add. 2604 is perhaps marginally closest to the LPs from Suffolk, with one important exception. Of the three, the Lydgate (8470 [4470/4471]) is the earliest, with the date of 1434–39 being posited for the manuscript's completion.[45] The will that makes up LP 8460 is dated to 1463.[46] And *A lettre sent to a relygyous woman of þe twelue frutys of the hooly goost* in LP 8480 is dated to *c.* 1460.[47] Apart from some features (shared in a patchy manner), most noteworthy in all three is the preference for 'th' over 'þ' (obvious in forms of 'then'). Also found in the three Suffolk texts is the alternation between 'hem' and 'them' forms as in Add. 2604 (discussed above). Whereas the Surrey and Middlesex texts in LPs 5820, 6410, and 6480 still show a decided preference for the 'h' form in 'them' and 'their', the Suffolk texts in LPs 8460 and 8470 [4470/4471], like Add. 2604, use the 'th' form. While only the Cosin manuscript in LP 8480 has the unusual 'gh' spelling for 'die' in the infinitive that is found a fifth of the time in Add. 2604 for the infinitive or the past tense (see above for details), both the Lydgate text and the Cosin MS have the 'ax-' spelling so popular in Add. 2604 (although the Cosin manuscript also makes use less regularly of the 'asch-' form). In addition, the Lydgate in 4470/4471 shares Add. 2604's usage of 'fett' for 'fetch'; it is found in Add. 2604 for the infinitive, past tense, and past participle forms.[48] There are, of course, minor differences throughout, for instance, in the will in LP 8460 there is the use of 'g' (as in 'gate' and 'gave') and in the Cosin manuscript in LP 8480 there is a pronouncd fondness throughout for 'yogh' not found in Add. 2604. Yet overall — even with the caveats above — it might be said that the language

---

[44] In many cases we are hindered by the non-occurrence of a particular word; 'hynge' (and 'henge') for 'hung' is found in the Surrey text (5820) similarly to the 'hynge' in Add. 2604, but is not found in any of the other LPs.

[45] *The Life of St Edmund King and Martyr*, introduction by Edwards, p. 14.

[46] *Wills and Inventories from the Registers of the Commissary of Bury St Edmund's and the Archdeacon of Sudbury*, ed. by Samuel Tymms, Camden Society, 49 (London: J. B. Nichols and Son, 1850), pp. 15–44. The will was drawn up in September 1463 and probate granted in May 1467.

[47] *A deuout treatyse called the tree & xii. frutes of the holy goost*, ed. by J. J. Vaissier (Groningen: J. B. Wolters, 1960), p. xvii.

[48] This is not to say that 'fett' is never found in a Middlesex text. For example, in one of the Middlesex LPs 'fet' occurs in the imperative alongside the usual 'ch' forms; see LP 6510 in LALME, III, 305–06 (p. 305).

of Add. 2604 is nearest to these three LPs, especially to 8470 [4470/4471] and 8480, than to any others in LALME, albeit that 'closest' is a very relative term here. The stumbling block to this is the non-appearance of Add. 2604's distinctive 'sigh' (and variants) for 'saw' in any of these Suffolk texts. Yet it does occur in the texts from Surrey (5820) and Middlesex (6410) and 6480), and, as we have seen above, in another Surrey text (5730), which is also a copy of *Partonope of Blois* (in Oxford, University College, MS C.188). It is not clear what to make of this. The 'sigh' form is an intrinsic part of the scribe's system (as noted above) so it may be postulated that he picked the habit up from his work in the southern area around Middlesex, that it highlights his origins in this area rather than in East Anglia, or that it simply means that we do not have any LALME or eLALME evidence for this form being used in Suffolk, but that is not to imply that they do not exist. We may recall that there are examples from LPs in the northern midland areas of Leicestershire (302) and Staffordshsire (193) so it is not inconceivable that this 'sigh' form was found in the eastern midland regions as well. More significantly, the form is found in the Norfolk Paston Letters; see, for instance, 'sygh' for 'saw' in a letter written in 1448 by James Gresham (from Holt in northern Norfolk) for Margaret Paston and 'seygh' for 'saw' in a letter penned by an unidentified hand probably in 1451 for Agnes Paston.[49] And there is an overlap between another rare 'see' form in Add. 2604: elsewhere in the manscript it makes use of 'seigh' for the past plural and 'sey' for past singular and plural and also for the past participle (see above for details), which are similar to the 'seye' spelling in the Cosin manuscript in 8480; and 'sey' for the past tense is also attested in *St Patrick's Purgatory* in the Book of Brome (New Haven, Yale University Library, Beinecke Rare Book and Manuscript Library, MS 365), from Brome Hall near Bury St Edmunds. One way or another such examples highlight the pull between East Anglia and the Middlesex area that has been characteristic of this investigation into the language of Add. 2604. On balance all the evidence explored here tends more towards arguing for a scribe who originated in East Anglia, specifically Suffolk, rather than elsewhere, but we recognise that there are factors that likewise give some credence to a more southern origin, for instance, around Middlesex.

---

[49] *Paston Letters and Papers of the Fifteenth Century*, ed. by Norman Davis, Richard Beadle, and Colin Richmond, EETS, s.s. 20, 21, 22, 3 parts (Oxford: Oxford University Press, 2004–05), I, 223–25 (p. 224, l. 36) and 33–34 (p. 34, l. 13).

The Provenance of the Add. 2604 Scribe?

These three LPs have been localised in LALME in Bury St Edmunds (Grid 585 264) where the will maker, John Baret, lived and his will was copied (8460) and the place in which Lydgate produced his work (8480 [4470 and 4471]). Significantly too the three texts in the Cosin manuscript were aimed at nuns in an unnamed East Anglian convent.[50] It is impossible to be categorical about the linguistic provenance of the scribe of Add. 2604 for all the reasons outlined above. Although it cannot be at all proved or even definitely asserted, nothing obviously seems to conflict with a localisation around Bury St Edmunds and there are incidental factors — linguistic and otherwise — that could help make this a plausble localisation. Some of these involve a closer comparison with the only document that has been incontrovertibly localised in Bury, John Baret's will.[51] Others are more incidental still, but perhaps even more telling.

---

[50] The three texts in Durham, Durham University Library, MS Cosin V.iii.24 (see nn. 42 and 47) are written in total by four scribes, with three hands overlapping in complicated ways in the writing of the first and third texts (*The Doctrine of the Hert* and *A lettre sent to a relygyous woman of þe twelue frutys of the hooly goost*). It is the work of Scribe III in the third text that has been localised in LP 8480 above; the work of Scribe IV, who is entirely responsible for the second text (*A lettre of relygyous gouernaunce sent to a relygyous* woman), has also been localised to the south of Bury St Edmunds in LP 8310 in LALME, ii, 482. The latter LP is not as close to the language in Add. 2604 as that in LP 8480. The hands are described on the Durham website (see n. 42) and in *The Doctrine of the Hert: A Critical Edition with Introduction and Commentary*, ed. by Christiania Whitehead, Denis Renevey, and Anne Mouron, Exeter Medieval Texts and Studies (Exeter: University of Exeter Press, 2010), pp. xlix–li (p. xlix), an analysis with which we agree.

[51] The language of John Baret's testament, the only document here that can be securely localised in Bury St Edmunds, is understandably formulaic; see *Wills and Inventories from the Registers of the Commissary of Bury St Edmund's and the Archdeacon of Sudbury*, ed. by Tymms (to which references are provided below). While it may share some of its essentials (in verbal endings, the non-use of 'x' forms, the preference for 'y' rather than 'þ', and so on), the expressions and vocabulary do not map readily on to a literary text like those in Add. 2604 (a problem with documentary material in LALME). But noticeable throughout is the particular East Anglian feature — also found in Add. 2604 and indeed in many of the Bury wills in the volume — of a fondness for 'e' spellings, for example: 'pet' [pit] (p. 15); 'messe' (Mass) (p. 17), 'peler (p. 19), 'prevy' (p. 20), 'kechene' (p. 22), and so forth. In Baret's will there is an alteration throughout between the 'g' and the 'y' form of 'give', whereas the Add. 2604 scribe restricts himself almost entirely to 'y'. But they do share one striking East Anglian feature in the use of 'w' for consonantal 'v'. This only occurs once in Add. 2604 in 'wayle' but is frequent in Baret's will where 'w' is also used for 'v'; examples include 'revardyd' [rewarded] (p. 16); 'vex' and vexe' [wax] (p. 17); 'awaylle' [avail] (p. 21); 'vagys' [wages] (p. 29); 'woyde' [void] (p. 39); 'knywes'

104   II. LANGUAGE AND DIALECTAL PROVENANCE

For example, already noted is the use of 'thristlewe' in Add. 2604, a rare word so favoured by Lydgate who hailed from Lidgate (six miles from Bury), and who lived and wrote in the abbey of Bury St Edmunds and so one might argue, a customary local word,[52] even if the extent of Lydgate's local idiolect (given the lack of a holograph) is not entirely clear.[53] In truth, the language would not prohibit origins elsewhere in Suffolk, but if the scribe hailed originally from the environs of Bury St Edmunds or was trained there, this would fit in well with wider factors.[54]

As noted by Michael Benskin, 'independent and extra-linguistic associations with the area in question' means that 'the reconconstruction will gain in its historical as well as its formal coherence'.[55] A scribe or translator based in the vicinity of Bury St Edmunds (or indeed in the Abbey itself) and thus within sight of the cult centre of the native saints in Ely might help account for some of the sources used in the compilation of the volume. Indeed, Bury monks celebrated Æthelthryth's feast, even if hers were a competitor to that of their own saint Edmund king and martyr (d. 869). Founded in 1020, the great Benedictine Abbey of Bury St Edmunds had a reputation for the production of books. Its celebrated writers include Denis Pyramus of the late twelfth century, Jocelin

---

[knives] (p. 41). One other notable shared form is that of 'kever' for 'cover' (as noted above) in Add. 2604 and 'keverid' (p. 20), 'keveryng' (p. 22), and 'kevvryd' (p. 41) in Baret's will, although here the typical East Anglian form also occurs in 'curyd' (pp. 19 and 42). For the original will, see Suffolk Archives, Bury St Edmunds, IC/500/2/2/95b.

[52] Noted earlier too is the trouble the Add. 2604 scribe had with spelling 'catchpole(s)'. The scribe of Bokenham's *Legendys of Hooly Wummen* in London, British Library, MS Arundel 327 appears to have had similar difficulty; in the MED (cacche-pōl n.) it is noted that the reading of this word in the manuscript is 'hacchepolles'. Such difficulties may be pure co-incidence or a clue that this word was not a common one in the area of Suffolk between Bury St Edmunds and Stoke by Clare.

[53] In *The Language of the Chaucer Tradition*, pp. 125–30, Horobin pays special attention to what may be extrapolated about Lydgate's own language as distinct from that of his scribes, noting that 'Despite the signs of increasing standardisation in Lydgate's language over that of Chaucer, there is evidence of dialect features which appear to derive from the poet's own idiolect' (p. 128).

[54] In personal correspondence Jeremy Smith notes the wide currency of individual forms in Add. 2604 but also the clustering of forms such as 'whech(e)', 'eche/iche', 'meche/moche/mych', 'eyghen', and 'hundrith' that could be convincingly associated with Bury St Edmunds. Albeit surrounded by the sort of caveats discussed above, he would therefore support us in our very tentative conclusions about provenance here. We are very grateful for these comments.

[55] Benskin, 'In Reply to Dr Burton, p. 247.

THE PROVENANCE OF THE ADD. 2604 SCRIBE? 105

of Brakelond of the early thirteenth century, and, of course, John Lydgate in the fifteenth century. Monks in the Abbey would not only have had scribal training but also the wider educational opportunities afforded by attendance at Gloucester College in Oxford (the national college for Benedictine monks), as well profiting from the oversight of formidably enterprising abbots such as William Curteys (d. 1446).[56] The extent of the Abbey's library is well attested, with its some two thousand volumes making it larger than Christ Church or St Augustine's in Canterbury in the later Middle Ages.[57] Significantly too the monks of the Abbey copied part of Oxford, Bodleian Library, MS Bodley 240, associated with John of Tynemouth who is essential for the sources of the native lives in Add. 2604. As one of the most consistently important towns in Suffolk, Bury St Edmunds had the necessary infrastructure and the literary and dramatic associations for manuscript production be it lay or clerical.[58] The East Anglian area was likewise a fruitful one for hagiographical enterprise if we take John Capgrave's work in Lynn into account and more locally that of Osbern Bokenham who was writing about fifteen miles just south of Bury St Edmunds in the Augustinian priory in Stoke by Clare almost on the Suffolk/Essex border. Clare Priory was a centre for literary activity with other writers like John Bury in addition to various male clerics who engaged in scribal activity (and who could also function as chaplains).[59] It has even been plausibly proposed that the clustering of important *Canterbury Tales* manuscripts in Suffolk may indicate the significance of Clare Priory as part of a network of London-East Anglian relationships facilitated by the friars who may have been involved in the dissemination or even copying of some of these manuscripts.[60] Such cos-

[56] For an overview, see Derek Pearsall, *John Lydgate*, Poets of the Later Middle Ages (London: Routledge and Kegan Paul, 1970), ch. 2, 'The Monastic Backgrouond', pp. 22–48.

[57] For the library at Bury St Edmunds, see *English Benedictine Libraries: The Shorter Catalogues*, ed. by R. Sharpe and others, Corpus of British Medieval Library Catalogues, 4 (London: The British Library in association with the British Academy, 1996), pp. 43–98.

[58] For the latter, see Gibson, *The Theater of Devotion*, pp. 107–35 and passim. For Suffolk more generally, see Mark Bailey, *Medieval Suffolk: An Economic and Social History, 1200–1500*, The History of Suffolk, 1 (Woodbridge: Boydell, 2007).

[59] See n. 14 in I. The Manuscript.

[60] Estelle Stubbs, 'Clare Priory: The London Austin Friars and Manuscripts of Chaucer's *Canterbury Tales*', in *Middle English Poetry: Texts and Traditions, Essays in Honour of Derek Pearsall*, ed. by A. J. Minnis, York Manuscripts Conferences Proceedings Series, 5 (Woodbridge: York Medieval Press, 2001), pp. 17–26. These Suffolk *Canterbury Tales* manuscripts are discussed in Horobin, *The Language of the Chaucer Tradition*, pp. 64–74, where he comments

mopolitan networks would also help to address linguistic and decorative influences in texts such as those in Add. 2604.[61] Most importantly of all, the art historical evidence from an examination of the spray and penwork of Add. 2604 (discussed in I. The Manuscript) supports some direct comparisons with other manuscripts produced in Bury St Edmunds.

In sum, even if there is no irrefutable evidence for the localisation of Add. 2604, the broader context does nothing to contradict — and much to support — a home somewhere around the Bury St Edmunds area. Moreover, as will be explained further below, the convents that may be most relevant to this study were localised geographically in East Anglia and its environs. With this in mind, it would make sense to have a locally based scribe or writer producing saints' lives for nuns in the region.[62] There is quite a choice for the location of the convent to which these saints' lives may have been addressed. Which area and which convents may be the best contenders will be discussed in III. Convent and Geographical Location where we shall see whether the evidence confirms or contradicts the tentative linguistic provenance above.

'The evident clustering of these manuscripts of high textual authority in the Suffolk area is striking and is certainly suggestive of local connections with a single collection of exemplars' (p. 66); he further notes that all these manuscripts were copied after 1450 (p. 66), while also alluding to research that links the Ellesmere manuscript with an earlier network focused on Bury St Edmunds (p. 67).

[61] One might expect similar evidence from Ely but what proof there is of hagiographical endeavours comes from a slightly later period and from a writer who is clearly more interested in humanistic concerns than the translator of Add. 2604. The poet and clergyman, Alexander Barclay (who may or may not have been Scottish), in a wide-ranging life (c. 1484–1552) during which he was alternatively a priest, a Benedictine monk, a Franciscan friar, and a secular priest in the new Church of England, produced many varied works of literature. While he was a Benedictine at Ely by 1513 (and possibly from c. 1509) up to 1521–28, he wrote most of his literary output, including a verse life of George published in 1515? (STC 22992.1), and it was said by John Bale that he also wrote lives of Katherine and Margaret; for an account of his life, see Nicholas Orme in the ODNB (https://doi.org/10.1093/ref:odnb/1337) (accessed 5 February 2023).

[62] For instance, two manuscripts owned by nuns in Campsey Ash, London, British Library, MS Arundel 327 that contains Bokenham's *Legendys of Hooly Wummen* and a copy of the *Scale of Perfection* and other texts in Cambridge, Corpus Christi College, MS 268, are both localised near Campsey Ash in LPs 6161 and 8390; see LALME, iii, 481 and 486–87.

III. Convent and Geographical Location

Add. 2604 provides no evidence that would allow us to specify a translator/scribe, patron, dedicatee or audience for this decorated collection of saints' lives. Nor is there an *ex libris* or other identifying mark of medieval ownership or any mention of provenance in the Middle Ages. Evidence from the few physical remains of English convents, unlike many in continental Europe, is very scarce and archaeological reports usually of limited value overall.[1] Post-Dissolution monastic reports can likewise be vague. Anything that may emerge about the potential provenance of this manuscript is therefore gleaned only after a great deal of detective work. But, as we shall see, there are always clues to be found. These range far and wide through the fields of book history and convent history, from the content to the dialect to the later provenance. Significant is the ownership in the late eighteenth century by George Tasburgh, a member of a prominent recusant Catholic family in Norfolk and Suffolk. And the clues found here about potential medieval and actual post-medieval provenance help to illuminate not only Add. 2604 but also the saintly literary landscape in East Anglia as a whole.

Our supposition about Add. 2604's use in a religious community of women is based on a variety of contextual material.[2] Our contention that it was produced in East Anglia and intended for nuns in this area is founded on explicit

---

[1] See Claude J. W. Messent, *The Monastic Remains of Norfolk & Suffolk* (Norwich: H. W. Hunt, 1934); Roberta Gilchrist, *Gender and Material Culture: The Archaeology of Religious Women* (London: Routledge, 1994); and James Bond, 'Medieval Nunneries in England and Wales: Buildings, Precincts, and Estates', *in Women and Religion in Medieval England*, ed. by Diana Wood (Oxford: Oxbow Books, 2003), pp. 46–90, and references therein. Gilchrist supplies plans for Barking (p. 114), Cambridge: St Radegund (p. 118), Campsey Ash (p. 58), Denney (p. 54), and Ickleton (p. 106).

[2] There is plenty of evidence for the interest of male religious in hagiography and for lay women who commissioned or read saints' lives, particularly in the vernacular. But in Add. 2604 the emphasis in the lives is so focused on nuns as to make a cloistered female audience or readership almost certain. Moreover, unless the folios from the antiphoner bound into Add. 2604 are merely the result of a later owner's random addition (which they may be), their presence would support a medieval religious rather than a lay context. While the text of the antiphoner is from another manuscript, it may still have derived from the same convent; for a description of the leaves from the antiphoner, see I. The Manuscript.

clues in the manuscript itself (fully discussed elsewhere in this volume), including the dialect and the focus of its medieval content on saintly women, many of whom were nuns and abbesses. Together, these elements hint at the first audience for Add. 2604, even as the manuscript itself provides particulars about its later ownership. Both medieval and post-medieval evidence pinpoints East Anglia, broadly conceived, as the region in which the manuscript was produced and in which it continued to circulate.[3] Foremost, the grouping of Ely saints — Æthelthryth; her sisters Seaxburh and Wihtburh; her nieces Eormenhild and Eorcengota (with a reference to another of Æthelthryth's sisters, Æthelburh); and a great niece Wærburh — form a significant core at the centre of the manuscript, and they comprise more than a quarter of the saints represented in the codex. This hagiographical focus, especially one that includes the lesser known Ely saints, Eorcengota and Æthelburh (who were rarely culted locally as they had left England for the Continent), suggests that the manuscript was produced or at least conceived somewhere in the environs of Ely in Cambridgeshire, the cult centre where four of the women were buried. We are looking therefore for some locale in East Anglia where medieval devotion to Æthelthryth and her family might be most clearly attested.[4] A collection of female saints' lives is not out of line with other contemporary hagiographical productions from East Anglia (as discussed in IV. Hagiographical Context and the Selection of Saints), but determining a specific home for the Add. 2604 collection remains difficult. In fact, there are a number of competing claimants for the nunnery in question and a range of complicated and sometimes contradictory evidence to consider in our search for a convent or convents that most clearly encapsulates the strongest evidence. We offer first a detailed discussion of the convents in this region (extending mainly for dialectal and source reasons as far as London and Middlesex, and with one Devonshire exception, as will be explained below), in an effort to rule in or out any particular location for the manuscript's first audience. We shall then turn to a consideration of the manuscript's ownership in a family of Catholic recusants in East Anglia; George Tasburgh's possession of the manuscript in the last decades of the eighteenth century opens up a

---

[3] While bearing in mind that scribes may move from their native areas and manuscripts be used for purposes other than originally intended, given the weight of evidence here in favour of East Anglia, it would seem foolhardy to start speculating about other areas of the country. An exception has been made for convents in London and Middlesex, as explained below.

[4] See Blanton, *Signs of Devotion* and Ian David Styler, 'The Story of an English Saint's Cult: An Analysis of the Influence of St Æthelthryth of Ely, c. 670–c. 1540 (unpublished doctoral dissertation, University of Birmingham, 2019).

new range of insights into the potential medieval and later provenance for the saints' lives in Add. 2604.

East Anglian Convents and Beyond

The boundaries of what constitutes East Anglia mainly consists of the counties of Norfolk and Suffolk, comprising the medieval diocese of Norwich (including a few Cambridgeshire parishes), but the definition of the region may be described more expansively. Using the pre-1974 county boundaries and employing the broadest interpretation, East Anglia can also be understood to incorporate the Isle of Ely and Cambridgeshire, which more or less made up the pre-Reformation diocese of Ely, and sometimes parts of Essex, which was mostly covered at the time by the diocese of London.[5] While Kent lay outside of the medieval imaginary of East Anglia, the inclusion of several Kentish saints in the manuscript indicates that it cannot be dismissed from consideration as a possible home for Add. 2604. If neighbouring Kent (mostly in the medieval diocese of Rochester) is added to our geographical consideration, this brings the total number of late-medieval nunneries in eastern and south-east England to twenty-six, of which late-medieval Norfolk and Suffolk together had eleven (see Table 2).

It is fairly certain that Add. 2604 has an East Anglian provenance (where convents mostly date from the twelfth and thirteenth centuries) on the strength of the centrality of the Ely saints in the manuscript, though for reasons to do with the difficulties of linguistic localisation, the search is broadened to include Middlesex. As fully discussed in II. Language and Dialectal Provenance, the linguistic analysis points to localisation in Suffolk (possibly to the area around Bury St Edmunds), but the language as a whole shares features with what would be expected in a broad swathe running from East Anglia to Middlesex. For this reason it is prudent to consider convents in this latter area alongside those in East Anglia and Kent that are the main locales of the native saints in Add. 2604. If the areas of London and Middlesex (in the diocese of London) are added for consideration, that makes for another seven potential homes for Add. 2604.[6]

---

[5] David M. Smith, *Guide to Bishops' Registers of England and Wales: A Survey from the Middle Ages to the Abolition of the Episcopacy in 1646* (London: Royal Historical Society, 1981).

[6] The information here derives from David Knowles and R. Neville Hadcock, *Medieval Religious Houses: England and Wales* (London: Longman, 1971; first published in 1953); see the relevant entries on pp. 194–96 and 251–89. Also drawn upon are the *Victoria County History* volumes where in each case religious houses are dealt with in the second volumes: *The Vic-*

More particularly, there is also one other factor with regard to shared sources (noted below) that makes a consideration of Syon necessary.

In Norfolk there were the priories of Blackborough, Carrow, Crabhouse, and Shouldham, and Thetford, as well as the abbey of Marham. Suffolk boasted the priories of Bungay, Campsey Ash, Flixton, and Redlingfield, along with the abbey of Bruisyard. Most of these convents were Benedictine: Blackborough, Bungay, Carrow, and Redlingfield. Three were Augustinian: Campsey Ash, Crabhouse, and Flixton, while Bruisyard was Franciscan; Marham, Cistercian; and Shouldham, Gilbertine. Cambridgeshire had five convents in the later medieval period: the abbeys of Chatteris and Denney (comprising Franciscan minoresses who had relocated from Waterbeach), and the priories of Ickleton, St Radegund in Cambridge, and Swaffham Bulbeck; all of these were Benedictine apart from Denney, which was Franciscan. In Essex there were three Benedictine convents: the seventh-century abbey of Barking, and the priories of Castle Hedingham and Wix. In Kent, which had seven female houses, there was the abbey of Malling and the priories of Canterbury St Sepulchre, Dartford, Davington, Higham, Minster-in-Sheppey, and Thanington (originally a hospital); all were Benedictine apart from Dartford, which was the only Dominican convent in the country. (Two other Benedictine convents had a limited history: Minster-in-Thanet on the Isle of Thanet in east Kent was absorbed into Christ Church, Canterbury in the eleventh century; Newington situated between Higham and Minster-in-Sheppey did not exist after *c.* 1087.)

toria History of the County of Cambridgeshire and The Isle of Ely, ed. by L. F. Salzman and others, 10 vols plus an index to vols I–IV (London: Oxford University Press, 1938–2002); *The Victoria History of the County of Essex*, ed. by H. Arthur Doubleday, William Page, and others, 10 vols, bibliography, and two bibliographical supplements (London: The St Catherine Press and other publishers, 1903–2000); *The Victoria History of the County of Kent*, ed. by William Page, 3 vols (London: Archibald Constable and Co., and other publishers, 1908–32; with the 1908 vol. reprinted in 1974); *The Victoria History of the County of Norfolk*, ed. by H. Arthur Doubleday and William Page, 2 vols (London: Archibald Constable and Co. Ltd, 1901–06); and *The Victoria History of the County of Suffolk*, ed. by William Page, 2 vols (London: Archibald Constable and Co. Ltd, 1907–11). These volumes are accessible at British History Online (https:// www.british-history.ac.uk/) (accessed 1 April 2023). For the London and Middlesex houses, we have used *The Religious Houses of London and Middlesex*, ed. by Caroline M. Barron and Matthew Davies (London: Institute of Historical Research, School of Advanced Study, University of London, 2007), which contains the *Victoria County History* entries duly updated. For East Anglia, see Roberta Gilchrist and Marilyn Oliva, *Religious Women in Medieval East Anglia: History and Archaeology c. 1100 to 1540*, Studies in East Anglian History, 1 (Norwich: Centre of East Anglian Studies, University of East Anglia, 1993) and Oliva, *The Convent and Community in Late Medieval England*.

EAST ANGLIAN CONVENTS AND BEYOND

The eleven houses in Norfolk and Suffolk were scattered around East Anglia. The convents of Blackborough, Crabhouse, Marham, and Shouldham could be found in a little group almost equidistant from each other in west-central Norfolk south of King's Lynn. Carrow was based in east-central Norfolk in the city of Norwich, opposite those above. The convent at Thetford (a town in Norfolk) is complicated, as the house lay south of the town and so was actually in Suffolk, directly north of Bury St Edmunds. At the other end of this line from Thetford along the Waveney Valley were Bungay and Flixton very close together in the extreme north-east of Suffolk in the places of the same name (south of Beccles, a few miles south of the Norfolk border). Redlingfield in north-east/central Suffolk was more or less midway between Thetford and Bungay and Flixton, albeit further away from the Norfolk border. Further south still was Campsey Ash near Wickham Market and west of Aldeburgh, with Bruisyard north-east of Framlingham and so mid-way between Redlingfield and Campsey Ash.

Cambridgeshire's five convents were located as follows. St Radegund, which became in 1496 the basis for Jesus College founded by John Alcock, bishop of Ely, was in the centre of Cambridge itself and thus some fifteen miles from Ely as the crow flies. The two convents in closest proximity to Ely were Chatteris (which lay ten miles north-west of Ely), and Denney, in north-central Cambridgeshire, near Waterbeach (which was some six miles south of Ely). Swaffham Bulbeck was east of Newmarket and also south of Ely, but nearer to the Suffolk border, with Ickleton in the extreme south-central area of the county barely north of the Essex border.

In Essex, Barking was at the very southern tip of the county quite near London; Castle Hedingham was in the north-central area below the Suffolk border, and Wix in the extreme north-east of the county near the Suffolk border.

Of the seven late medieval female houses in Kent, apart from Malling (which was in the west-central part of the county), all the other convents were located in the extreme north immediately south of Essex in a line from Dartford near London in the west to Canterbury in the east. In between (from west to east) were positioned Higham, Minster-in-Sheppey, Davington, and Thanington.

The London and Middlesex convents (all priories apart from Aldgate and Syon) include the Benedictine house of St Helen's Bishopgate in London; and in Middlesex the Augustinians of Holywell (or Haliwel) in Shoreditch; Kilburn situated in the parish of Hampstead; and St Mary Clerkenwell in the area around the Charterhouse; the Benedictines in Stratford at Bow; the

112   III. CONVENT AND GEOGRAPHICAL LOCATION

Franciscans in Aldgate; and the Birgittines of Syon (first at Twickenham and later in Isleworth).[7]

Finally, there is the one house in the country that was devoted to both John the Evangelist and Æthelthryth of Ely, which is the Austin community of Canonsleigh in Devon, noted here for the sake of completeness.

Table 2. Female Communities in East Anglia and Beyond

Community	Foundation	Dedication (beyond BVM)	Order
CAMBRIDGESHIRE			
Cambridge, St Radegund	before 1138	Radegund	Benedictine
Chatteris	1006x1016	All Saints?	Benedictine
Denney	1327	James, Leonard, Clare?	Franciscan
Ickleton	before 1174x1181	Mary Magdalene	Benedictine
Swaffham Bulbeck	1150x1200		Benedictine
DEVON			
Canonsleigh	1282	John Evangelist, Æthelthryth	Augustinian
ESSEX			
Barking	c. 666	Æthelburh	Benedictine
Castle Hedingham	1150x1200	James, Holy Cross	Benedictine
Wix	c. 1125		Benedictine
KENT			
Canterbury, St Sepulchre	c. 1100	Sepulchre	Benedictine
Dartford	1321	Margaret	Dominican
Davington	1153	Mary Magdalene	Benedictine
Higham	1148		Benedictine
Malling	c. 1200	Andrew?	Benedictine
Minster-in-Sheppey	c. 670	Seaxburh	Benedictine
Thanington	before 1343	James	Benedictine

---

[7] *The Religious Houses of London and Middlesex*, ed. by Barron and Davies, provides maps of these convents on pp. 26 and 240.

EAST ANGLIAN CONVENTS AND BEYOND

Community	Foundation	Dedication (beyond BVM)	Order
NORFOLK			
Blackborough	*c.* 1200	Katherine	Benedictine
Carrow	*c.* 1146	John Evangelist?	Benedictine
Crabhouse	1181	John Evangelist	Augustinian
Marham	1249	Barbara, Edmund	Cistercian
Shouldham	1148	Holy Cross	Gilbertine
Thetford [Suffolk]	1016x1035	George	Benedictine
LONDON/MIDDLESEX			
Aldgate	*c.* 1293	Francis	Franciscan
Holywell	before 1127	John the Baptist	Augustinian
Kilburn	*c.* 1130	John the Baptist	Augustinian
St Helen's Bishopgate	*c.* 1210	Helen	Benedictine
St Mary Clerkenwell	*c.* 1144		Augustinian
Stratford at Bow	before 1122	Leonard	Benedictine
Syon	1415	Saviour, Birgitta of Sweden	Birgittine
SUFFOLK			
Bruisyard	1366	Annunciation	Franciscan
Bungay	1160	Holy Cross	Benedictine
Campsey Ash	*c.* 1195		Augustinian
Flixton	1258	Katherine	Augustinian
Redlingfield	*c.* 1120	Andrew	Benedictine

We begin our survey of possible homes for Add. 2604 by acknowledging that some communities — on the available facts — have a lesser claim and others a more probable one. The arguments that may be invoked about a given convent focus on specific details: monastic order; house dedications; visitation reports; and library facilities, book bequests, and Dissolution inventories. Many of these factors incorporate issues of wealth and status albeit that there is not always an exact correlation between expectations and reality. These features are considered alongside the list of saints in Add. 2604 and dialectal evidence, as well as post-medieval history.

Monastic Order

The Benedictines had the greatest number of convents in eastern England, not surprising given the strength of the Benedictines in the country as a whole from the eighth century and long before new orders came into being from the twelfth century.[8] Among those under consideration, there are also six Augustinian houses, three Franciscan, and one each of Birgittine, Cistercian, Dominican, and Gilbertine, plus one former hospital. In Add. 2604 the focus on native abbesses and royal service to early monastic communities (many of which become Benedictine in an early incarnation) might imply a Benedictine convent of high status as the home of this collection of saints' lives. Yet, because most of these noble women date from the early English period when Benedictinism was on the rise and long before the advent of other orders, what precise weight should be given to this factor is uncertain. If the convent in question were Benedictine, then there are twenty from which to choose. But few of these were high-status (if high-status signifies a royal foundation): only Barking and Carrow. The latter had the advantage of being in a major urban centre with all its ecclesiastical and literary advantages for manuscript production. Being centred in Norfolk, the East Anglian county with the highest density of public devotion to Æthelthryth (the main English saint in Add. 2604), would also have lent certain advantages.[9] But there is no evidence of devotion to the saint by Carrow nuns, except for her inclusion in a thirteenth-century litany.[10] Dialectally the manuscript has far more in common with the southern

[8] Sally Thompson, *Women Religious: The Founding of English Nunneries after the Norman Conquest* (Oxford: Clarendon Press, 1991).

[9] For a list of church dedications and examples of material culture (including rood-screen paintings, guild lights, and other images of personal saints), calendars, and litanies, see Blanton, *Signs of Devotion*, pp. 295–306; Ann Eljenholm Nichols, *The Early Art of Norfolk: A Subject List of Extant and Lost Art including Items relevant to Early Drama*, Early Drama, Art, and Music Reference Series, 7 (Kalamazoo, MI: Medieval Institute Publications, 2002); and Styler, 'The Story of an English Saint's Cult', pp. 309–15. Norman Tanner notes that in Norwich wills there were no bequests for lights before images of the East Anglian saints Felix, Wulstan, Æthelthryth, or Wihtburh; Norman P. Tanner, *The Church in Late Medieval Norwich 1370–1530*, Studies and Texts, 66 (Toronto: Pontifical Institute of Mediaeval Studies, 1984), p. 84. There were, however, at least three altar lights (probably guild lights) in Norfolk in honour of Æthelthryth; see Blanton, *Signs of Devotion*, p. 305.

[10] Madrid, Biblioteca Nacional de España, MS 6422; see *English Monastic Litanies of the Saints after 1100*, ed. by Nigel J. Morgan, Henry Bradshaw Society, 119, 120, 123, 3 vols (Woodbridge: Boydell, 2012–18), I (2012), 91–92.

MONASTIC ORDER

parts of the East Anglian region; if judged by this criterion (even bearing in mind that scribes and manuscripts move about), Carrow would not appear to be the obvious home for Add. 2604.

If we seek a high-status foundation for the manuscript, size and wealth at the time of the Dissolution are other markers of status. Regarded as one of the 'Big Five' (that is, Amesbury, Barking, Shaftesbury, Syon, and Wilton), in terms of having an income over £500 per annum at the Dissolution, Barking would be an ideal candidate. As an early foundation with a secure pedigree for historical longevity, it was well connected socially and had a tradition of learning.[11] It also had a large library; Barking ranks second (after Syon) in the number of surviving books associated with a female religious house. Yet ironically with the highest pedigree in the convents under consideration here, Barking has a major strike against it. It would be highly unusual for a collection of native saints' lives to be intended for Barking and not include Æthelburh, the convent's patron and first abbess. That the translator was aware of the Barking saint is clearly demonstrated in Add. 2604. The life of Eorcengota closes with a brief account of another Æthelburh, one of the Ely sister saints who went to the Continent to lead a religious life. The rubric following this account makes it clear that this Æthelburh is the abbess of Brige (Faremoutiers-en-Brie) and not the abbess of Barking: 'Thus endith shortly the lyves of Seynt Erkengoode and of Seynt Alburgh (not the abbes of Berkyng but the abbes of Brige in Fraunce)' (11/47–48). Obviously, the translator was aware of the cult of Æthelburh of Barking and took pains to ensure that his audience would not mistake an Ely sister saint for the better known patron saint of Barking. That there is no other reference in Add. 2604 to a life of Barking's patron might suggest that she was not included in this manuscript. There is, however, more than one lacuna in the collection, and the one that would be most fitting for the Barking abbess to fill is in the now missing quire 11, which is between the lives of Eanswith (31 August or 12 September) and Hild (17 November). Æthelburh of Barking whose feast is 11 October would fit well into this gap (though there are other possibilities). Still, a litany from Barking dated *c.* 1450, just before the production of Add. 2604, does not include any of the Ely saints. The lack of attention in a Barking litany to Ely saints, especially when Æthelthryth appears more than any other native female saint in late medieval litanies, argues against Add. 2604 being intended for Barking (albeit it could have ended up at Barking or

---

[11] Bell, *What Nuns Read*, pp. 107–20, and *Barking Abbey and Medieval Literary Culture*, ed. by Brown and Bussell.

any of the female communities under consideration as a secondary or tertiary home).[12] This evidence against Barking suggests it will be more fruitful to look further afield.

Among other Benedictine houses, consideration might be given to four that had close associations with the cult centre at Ely: Chatteris, Ickleton, Swaffham Bulbeck, and Thetford. The first three were located within the diocese of Ely and were under the patronage of the Bishop of Ely. Of the three, Chatteris perhaps has the foremost claim, given its size and that it was a pre-Conquest foundation. The community was reasonably provided for, at least prior to the destruction of the barn, convent, and church by fire in the early fourteenth century. The nuns rebuilt and by 1535 the house was valued at £97 3s. 4d.[13] The close proximity to Ely Cathedral and the patronage by the Ely bishops indicate that Chatteris could have been the intended home for Add. 2604. A Latin cartulary survives, a relatively rare occurrence in medieval convents.[14] The Chatteris cartulary, London, British Library, MS Cotton Julius A. i, was subsidised by the abbess Agnes Ashfield and most probably written in the main between 1428 and 1456 by the vicar Henry Buckworth who donated a new antiphoner, legendary, and processional to the parish church.[15] The survival of a cartulary is suggestive about book culture at Chatteris, but it offers little indication of the community's affection for any given saint.

[12] The Barking litany of *c.* 1450 in Cambridge, Cambridge University Library, MS Dd.12.56, fols 157r–164r, does not include any of the Ely saints, which argues against Add. 2604 being from Barking; see *English Monastic Litanies of the Saints after 1100*, ed. by Morgan, I (2012), 61–62. Morgan demonstrates that Æthelthryth's feast features in almost all of the calendars post 1100, whereas Æthelburh of Barking's cult was far more limited; see *English Monastic Litanies of the Saints after 1100*, ed. by Morgan, III (2018), 118–21.

[13] 'Houses of Benedictine Nuns: The Abbey of Chatteris', *The Victoria History of the County of Cambridgeshire and The Isle of Ely*, ed. by Salzman, II (1948), 220–23 (pp. 221–22).

[14] Of the convents here, cartularies, registers, or otherwise from various dates (mostly in Latin and sometimes rather fragmentary) are extant only from Barking, Blackborough, Campsey Ash, Canterbury, Chatteris, Crabhouse, Denney, London: St Mary Clerkenwell, Marham, Syon, Thanington, and Wix, with untraced items from Bruisyard, Carrow, Davington, Denney, London: Holywell, and Swaffham Bulbeck; and destroyed material from Castle Hedingham and Dartford. These are described in G. R. C. Davis, *Medieval Cartularies of Great Britain and Ireland*, revised by Claire Breay, Julian Harrison, and David M. Smith (London: The British Library, 2010), pp. 5–6, 14, 20, 34, 43–46, 53, 59, 63–65, 121–22, 130–31, 144, 190–91, 193–94, and 216.

[15] *The Cartulary of Chatteris Abbey*, ed. by Claire Breay (Woodbridge: Boydell, 1999), p. 56.

MONASTIC ORDER

Ickleton and Swaffham Bulbeck were less impressive communities, with £71 9s. 10½d. and £40 in valuation in 1535. Little is known about Swaffham Bulbeck or its use of books for none survives. Of particular interest, however, is a 1373 episcopal visitation that documented the nuns' liturgical practice at Swaffham Bulbeck. Where they had traditionally followed the Daily Office 'as observed by the monks of Ely', they 'had introduced antiphons, verses, and collects of various saints into the services'; the bishop directed the nuns to save these observances for 'private devotion' and return to a strict observance.[16] The innovations with which these nuns augmented their choir service are intriguing, as they might well accord with having a collection of saints' lives such as that in Add. 2604. Be that as it may, we can only point to a desire some one hundred years before the production of this manuscript to celebrate favoured saints. The relative poverty of the community, however, might argue against their having a decorated book like Add. 2604. Conversely, Ickleton is more promising. In 1444 Ickleton had eleven nuns and nine by 1490.[17] The one important distinction for Ickleton is a litany from *c.* 1516–36 preserved in Cambridge, St John's College, MS 506 and T.9.1 that features more than half of the twenty-two saints in Add. 2604.[18] This subject overlap provides evidence of devotion to many of the saints. Leaving aside the fact that convent litanies are scarce and so comparative evidence is lacking, it may be that this Benedictine house within the diocese of Ely should be considered as more probable than others.

Regarded as a Norfolk convent albeit on what was earlier deemed to be the Suffolk side of the Norfolk/Suffolk border in a bend in the Little Ouse river, Thetford has several significant points of consideration: the first that Thetford had long been an important site in East Anglian religious history as a seat of early bishops, and when the female community moved from nearby Ling in Norfolk around 1160, it was done at the direction of the abbot of Bury St

---

[16] 'Houses of Benedictine Nuns: The Priory of Swaffham Bulbeck', in *The Victoria History of the County of Cambridgeshire and The Isle of Ely*, ed. by Salzman, II (1948), 226–29 (p. 227).

[17] 'Houses of Benedictine Nuns: The Priory of Ickleton', in *The Victoria History of the County of Cambridgeshire and The Isle of Ely*, ed. by Salzman, II (1948), 223–26 (p. 224).

[18] John the Evangelist, Leonard, Martha, Agatha, Cecilia, Æthelthryth, Wihtburh, Sæxburh, Eormenhild, Eadburh, Æthelburh (Ely or Barking?), Modwenna, and Barbara; *English Monastic Litanies of the Saints after 1100*, ed. by Morgan, II (2013), 142–44. This part manuscript and part early printed book is discussed in O'Mara, 'The Late Medieval English Nun and her Scribal Activity: A Complicated Quest', pp. 86–88.

Edmunds.[19] With a value of only £40 11*s*. 2½*d*. in 1535, Thetford was a relatively poor community and so seems a remote choice for such a polished, decorated book.[20] What recommends it is its close association with the monks of Bury St Edmunds, who gave property in Thetford to support the community, which was founded at the site of a previous Bury cell (associated with the church of St George) abandoned in 1160. Thetford's association with the great abbey is compelling, for scribes at Bury copied part of a work by John of Tynemouth (whose *Sanctilogium* is of such importance for the native lives in Add. 2604). This volume is his *Historia aurea* in Oxford, Bodleian Library, Bodley MS 240, along with extracts from John's *martyrologium* and his *Sanctilogium*. It suggests that Bury had copies of these works in its extensive library or had access to them. The *Historia aurea* itself features some of the lives from the *Sanctilogium*, including in this order: Wihtburh, Eormenhild, Æthelthryth, Seaxburh, Modwenna, Cuthburh, Keyna, Osith, Walburh, Wærburh, Æbbe, Hildelith, Cyneburh, and Mildrith. The presence of Ely saints in a manuscript copied out by Bury monks is particularly persuasive. Further, Bury provided annual provisions for the nuns at Thetford, which lay on the main road between London and Norwich.[21] This association and geographical location positions Thetford well to be considered as a home of Add. 2604. Litanies from Bury provide support: routinely the Ely saints are celebrated in such litanies, and one in particular, London, British Library, MS Harley 5334, dated *c*. 1450 features (alongside John the Baptist, John the Evangelist, Leonard, Agatha, and Cecilia) Æthelthryth, Seaxburh, Wihtburh, and Eormenhild, along with Edith, Modwenna, and an Æthelburh (although it is unclear which saint of that name is intended).[22] Why the monks at Bury or their spiritual daughters, the nuns

---

[19] 'Houses of Benedictine Nuns: The Priory of St George, Thetford', in *The Victoria History of the County of Suffolk*, ed. by Page, ɪɪ (1907), 85–86 (p. 85); the very same entry for Thetford convent occurs in the second volume (1906) of *The Victoria History of the County of Norfolk*, ed. by Doubleday and Page (pp. 354–56). The earlier cell lay within the Saxon town south of the river. By about 1160 when the nuns arrived, this town had been abandoned to be replaced by a new town (Thetford) north of the river; see Bond, 'Medieval Nunneries in England and Wales', p. 54.

[20] 'Houses of Benedictine Nuns: The Priory of St George, Thetford', in *The Victoria History of the County of Suffolk*, ed. by Page, ɪɪ (1907), 85–86 (p. 85).

[21] 'Houses of Benedictine Nuns: The Priory of St George, Thetford', in *The Victoria History of the County of Suffolk*, ed. by Page, ɪɪ (1907), 85–86.

[22] *English Monastic Litanies of the Saints after 1100*, ed. by Morgan, ɪ (2012), 69–72. This is not likely to be Æthelburh of Ely, since Eorcengota is not included in the litany and the two routinely appear together, as they are linked in Bede's original narrative.

MONASTIC ORDER 119

of St George's Thetford, would elect to produce a legendary for use that did not include George or indeed Edmund (their respective dedicatees), is another matter.[23] It may have been because of the basis of their hagiolatry, though one could easily imagine both George and Edmund complementing the narrative of chastity highlighted in the many lives of Add. 2604. It might well also be that the nuns had access to those lives in other books. Another question is why these Benedictines would choose to focus such a collection on the Ely women. One reason may well have been that the Thetford parish church of St Etheldreda or St Audry's (that is, Æthelthryth), which was near the convent on the south side of the river, held a relic of the saint: her smock, which attracted local pilgrimage. In keeping with Æthelthryth's own pain from a goitre on the jaw, the smock was reputed to bring healing from tooth-ache and throat pains.[24] The parish, which had long been in the keeping of the abbots of Ely, and after 1106, the bishops of Ely, was not particularly well financed, but income from pilgrimage kept the church viable until the Dissolution. A papal indulgence for 12 March 1403 in the time of Boniface IX outlined the following:

> Relaxation of two years and two *quadragene* of enjoined penance to penitents who on the principal feasts of the year and those of St. Etheldreda and the dedication, the octaves of certain of them and the six days of Whitsun week; and of a hundred days to those who during the said octaves and days, visit and give alms for the conservation of the parish [church] of St. Etheldreda, Tesford (sic), in the diocese of Norwich, in which is preserved most fairly and devoutly the smock (*camisia*) of the said saint, and in which, through the merits of the same, God shows many notable and wonderful signs.[25]

This relic, preserved in a church dedicated to Æthelthryth, attests to a long-standing local devotion to the saint that had begun before the Norman Conquest.[26]

---

[23] Edmund was associated with their time in Ling and George with the Thetford foundation.

[24] The church and the relic are discussed in Thomas Martin, *The History of the Town of Thetford in the Counties of Norfolk and Suffolk, from the Earliest Accounts to the Present Time* (London: J. Nichols, 1779), pp. 77–81. For further details, see Nichols, *The Early Art of Norfolk*, p. 192. The church was in the centre of Thetford, near St Mary the Less, but no longer exists; see the plan of Thetford's numerous ecclesiastical centres in *An Historical Atlas of Norfolk*, ed. by Trevor Ashwin and Alan Davison, 3rd edn (Chichester: Phillimore, 2005), p. 45, with discussion on p. 44.

[25] *Calendar of Entries in the Papal Registers Relating To Great Britain and Ireland: Papal Letters, V: A. D. 1396–1404*, ed. by W. H. Bliss and J. A. Twemlow (London: Mackie and Co. for His Majesty's Stationery Office, 1904), p. 589.

[26] Blanton, *Signs of Devotion*, p. 306.

III. CONVENT AND GEOGRAPHICAL LOCATION

Proximity alone might have been the reason for interest in Æthelthryth and her sister saints, but it appears that the nuns, on occasion, used the parish church for the installment of a newly elected prioress. On 1 August 1418 Margaret Chykering was presented to the bishop for examination and confirmation in the parish church of St Etheldreda.[27] The nuns also used nearby St Mary's church for the same purpose, suggesting that when the installation of a prioress was conducted, it was a public affair, which brought the nuns out of the convent and into the community to meet the bishop and parishioners. Interest then in the Ely saints is more likely, given that the Bishop of Ely appointed the vicar of St Etheldreda's.

Unlike East Anglia as a whole, there is nothing connected with the two Benedictine foundations in London or Middlesex that would particularly indicate that either of them had a devotion to the specific East Anglian saints in Add. 2604. Apart from liturgical book bequests in a will of 1379, little is known about St Helen's in Bishopgate from a literary perspective.[28] Of Stratford at Bow the main point of interest is that it was fashionable among the aristocracy in the fourteenth-century and provided the model for Geoffrey Chaucer's frivolous 'Madame Eglentyne' in *The Canterbury Tales*.[29]

If we look to the various houses of Austin canonesses in the East Anglian region, it would not be wrong to consider carefully the possibility of Campsey Ash Priory in Suffolk, which was a community that boasted significant patronage by the nobility and is known to have had several books. In its scope, Add. 2604 shares affinities with the collection of vernacular saints' lives preserved in London, British Library, MS Additional 70513, which preserves lives of Æthelthryth and Modwenna.[30] The Campsey manuscript, containing both

---

[27] Francis Blomefield, *An Essay Towards a Topographical History of the County of Norfolk [...]*, 11 vols, 2nd edn (London: Printed for William Miller by W. Bulmer and Co., 1805–10; first published 1739–75), II (1805), 92.

[28] For details see Bell, *What Nuns Read*, p. 148.

[29] *The Religious Houses of London and Middlesex*, ed. by Barron and Davies, p. 244, who suggest that a nun named 'Argentyn' may have been partly the model for Chaucer's satire.

[30] For discussion of the manuscript, see Wogan-Browne, *Saints' Lives and Women's Literary Culture, c. 1150–1300*, pp. 170–76; Delbert Russell, 'The Campsey Collection of Old French Saints' Lives: A Re-examination of its Structure and Provenance', *Scriptorium*, 57 (2003), 51–83 + planches couleur 4–7; and Emma Campbell, *Medieval Saints' Lives: The Gift, Kinship and Community in Old French Hagiography*, Gallica, 12 (Cambridge: Brewer, 2008), pp. 181–204. For a comparison of the lives in Add. 2604 and MS Additional 70513, alongside the collection of Latin lives of native saints in London, British Library, MS Lansdowne 436, see Blanton, 'The Devotional Reading of Nuns'.

MONASTIC ORDER   121

universal and native saints' lives, is written in Anglo-Norman French. It was
produced for the canonesses 'de lire a mangier' ['for reading at mealtimes'] as
noted in an ownership inscription on fol. 265v. The Middle English lives in
Add. 2604 would have provided an apropos complement to these French lives,
which begs the question if a similar vernacular compilation was not produced
for them in the fifteenth century. This community was well supported, and
at the evaluation of the institution in 1535, Campsey Ash's revenues totalled
£182 9s. 5d.[31] They also had an in-house resource for the copying of books.
Founded first by Maud de Ufford (Countess of Ulster) in 1383 and enhanced
by Isabella Beauchamp Ufford in 1390, a chantry with a warden and four chaplains was housed within the monastery precinct.[32] These priests would have
been well-positioned to translate such a collection of saints' lives for use by the
nuns. Further, Campsey Ash held a number of estates in Suffolk, Norfolk, and
Essex, and it is notable for being the only female house within the Liberty of
Etheldreda, a legal franchise in east Suffolk under the governance of the prior
and convent of Ely from the mid-tenth century.[33] Still, there is one obvious
objection to Campsey Ash as a possible home. It is noteworthy that Campsey
Ash books tend to include a pressmark and/or ownership or donor inscription. The range of these pressmarks suggest a considerable library, which would
therefore make Campsey Ash a fitting home for Add. 2604.[34] Yet, this emphasis
on identifying books at Campsey Ash argues against its association with Add.
2604, which has no identifying medieval marks.[35] Further, Campsey's locale is
far removed from what may be the immediate dialect of the manuscript.

There is nothing to draw attention to any of the other East Anglian
Augustinian houses (though we shall return to Flixton later), apart from what
may be some incidental details associated with Crabhouse, the sisters of which

[31] 'Houses of Austin Nuns: The Priory of Campsey', in *The Victoria History of the County of
Suffolk*, ed. by Page, II (1907), 112–15 (p. 114).

[32] Oliva, *The Convent and Community in Late Medieval England*, p. 113.

[33] Bailey, *Medieval Suffolk*, p. 4. West Suffolk in the Liberty of St Edmund was granted to
Bury St Edmunds in the middle of the eleventh century.

[34] Bell, *What Nuns Read*, notes of the potential size of the library: 'Just how large we do not
know, but if there were at least 94 books in one *distinctio* and 141 in another, and if there were
a plurality of *distinctiones*, the library at Campsey might have rivalled that at Christ Church,
Canterbury!' (p. 43).

[35] It is not clear if the contents of Add. 2604 were bound before its post-medieval one; as
noted in I. The Manuscript, the pages have been trimmed for the current binding.

paid twenty-six marks in 1425 for two antiphoners.[36] The convent was dedicated to John the Evangelist, and from 1469 had a prioress named Dame Etheldreda or Audrey Wulmer who would have had Æthelthryth as her name saint. The convent was close to the church of Wiggenhall St Mary the Virgin, which had a number of carved benchends depicting various nuns as well as many saints, including Barbara (possibly), Agatha, Mary Magdalene, Leonard, Æthelthryth, and Margaret, among others.[37] But Crabhouse, like Blackborough, Marham, and Shouldham, was located in the sparsely populated fens and so was rural and poor. Conversely, even if there is no hint of devotion to East Anglian saints in the three London Augustinian houses, Clerkenwell and Holywell were wealthy enough to have encouraged a manuscript like Add. 2604.[38] And not only were Holywell and Kilburn dedicated to John the Baptist, the saint who appears first in Add. 2604, but at the Dissolution Kilburn was said to have owned various legendaries (to which we shall return when considering books in the respective convents).[39] The only other Augustinian house here is that of Canonsleigh in Devon, about which little is known, and only merits inclusion because of its dedication (discussed below).

One would not wish to rule out the remaining houses in this survey purely on order alone. As Jocelyn Wogan-Browne shows in relation to the Campsey Ash manuscript, such rigid demarcations cannot be made:

> From [p. 11] the texts of Benedictine Barking in the twelfth century to the reading of Campsey's late thirteenth-century Augustinan canonesses to the Franciscan additions to the manuscript at the turn of the thirteenth and fourteenth centuries, the Campsey book constitutes an important representation of women's conventual literary culture for the entire period.[40]

Yet no immediate rationale presents itself here for why a Birgittine (Syon), Cistercian (Marham), Dominican (Dartford), Franciscan (Bruisyard, Denney, and London: Aldgate), or Gilbertine (Shouldham) house would have a manuscript collection of universal and Benedictine early East Anglian saints in its

[36] Gilchrist and Oliva, *Religious Women in Medieval East Anglia*, p. 53.

[37] The identifications are derived from Coletti, *Mary Magdalene and the Drama of Saints*, p. 59.

[38] With London: Aldgate and London: Bishopgate amongst others, Clerkenwell, Holywell, and Kilburn were in the next rank after the 'Big Five'; Bell, *What Nuns Read*, p. 10.

[39] Bell, *What Nuns Read*, pp. 143–44.

[40] Wogan-Browne, *Saints' Lives and Women's Literary Culture*, pp. 10–11, with a list of the manuscript's texts and authors in Figure 6 (p. 171).

CONVENT DEDICATIONS

possession. It cannot be totally ruled out, particularly not among the houses that were close to the cult centre of Ely such as Denney or had large numbers of books such as Dartford or Syon. But there is no intrinsic reason on the grounds of order *alone* to argue for any of these convents as the natural home for Add. 2604.

Indeed, of all these houses, apart from Denney (discussed below), the only convent that might have a claim to be the original home of Add. 2604's source is Syon and this has nothing to do with its order as such. As is fully explained in V. Latin Sources and Analogues, Karlsruhe, Badische Landesbibliothek, Cod. Sankt Georgen 12 is the surviving first half of a two-volume *Sanctilogium salvatoris*, containing numerous saints' lives from the *Legenda aurea* and John of Tynemouth's *Sanctilogium* that echo the composition of universal and native lives in Add. 2604. This was produced for the Syon patron, Margaret Holland, Duchess of Clarence (before 1388–1439). It may therefore be that there is some connection between the source material being used in this manuscript and that in Add. 2604. There is indeed much evidence of the influence of Birgittine spirituality on piety in East Anglia. There is also some overlap in the ways in which the Add. 2604 lives are laid out with chapter or section headings and some of the Middle English lives emanating from Syon (as explained in VI. Reading the '*Lyves and Dethes*' below). Yet this does not mean that Syon would be a natural fit for Add. 2604, even if a Syon home might not be ruled out on the basis of dialect. There is no real evidence that Birgittine nuns had a particular devotion to East Anglian saints. Admittedly, the litany in Cambridge, St John's College, MS 11 (fols 38v–39v), a collection of Birgittine legislative documents, includes in its list of female saints the Kentish Mildrith and Milburh, alongside Edith and Æthelthryth who are found in Add. 2604, but this is hardly a pronounced East Anglian concentration (unlike the Ickleton litany), though its inclusion of the rare Domitilla is more striking (fol. 39v). Furthermore, as will be evident in the discussion of books below, Add. 2604 was not the sort of volume regularly found in the nuns' library as the Syon sisters tended to opt for more mystical works.

Convent Dedications

Where religious order might be one way to consider a possible home, dedications provide another avenue. We might expect that a series of saints' lives that could be used for table reading or private devotional reading to include a community's patron saint, as noted with Barking. Virtually all the nunneries listed above were dedicated to the Virgin Mary as was customary, but some had an additional saintly or other dedicatee (with question marks to indicate uncertainty as dedications sometimes changed or are rendered variously by different sources):[41] Barking (Æthelburh); Blackborough (Katherine); Bungay (Holy Cross); Bruisyard (Annunciation); Cambridge: St Radegund (Radegund); Canonsleigh (John the Evangelist and Æthelthryth); Canterbury (Sepulchre); Carrow (John the Evangelist?); Castle Hedingham (James and the Holy Cross); Chatteris (All Saints?); Crabhouse (John the Evangelist); Dartford (Margaret); Davington (Mary Magdalene); Denney (James, Leonard, Clare?); Flixton (Katherine); Ickleton (Mary Magdalene); Kilburn (John the Baptist); London: Aldgate (Francis); London: Bishopgate (Helen); London: Holywell (John the Baptist); Malling (Andrew?); Marham (Barbara and Edmund); Minster-in-Sheppey (Seaxburh); Redlingfield (Andrew); Shouldham (Holy Cross); Stratford at Bow (Leonard); Syon (Saviour and Birgitta); Thanington (James); and Thetford (George).

It may be asked if there is anything intrinsic about this selection of saints' lives *as a whole* that connects it *exclusively* to one convent rather than another. For instance, are we to make a case for Canonsleigh because of its unique dedication to Æthelthryth, for Canonsleigh again plus Crabhouse or possibly Carrow because of a dedication to John the Evangelist, for Denney and Stratford at Bow because of Leonard, for Kilburn and London: Holywell because of John the Baptist, for Marham because of Barbara, or for Minster-in-Sheppey because of Seaxburh? A different answer may be provided for each. Interesting as Canonsleigh's dedication to Æthelthryth is, there is nothing else to link this convent to the other East Anglian saints in the manuscript, and most particularly, its geographical locale shows no connection either with Add. 2604's dialectal provenance or its manuscript decoration. A provenance in Crabhouse for such a relatively nicely produced manuscript is probably unlikely given its poverty and size, though Carrow's revenues at the Dissolution puts it in a better position for a claim. Carrow's geographical position next to Norwich where a number of roodscreens feature Æthelthryth is suggestive, but as noted, there is no evidence of devotion to the saint by Carrow nuns, except for her inclusion in a thirteenth-century litany. Similarly, even with its link to Barbara, there is no obvious reason why our manuscript (with its concentration on early royal saints and its pretty illumination and amusing cadel heads would have been

---

[41] In some cases there is uncertainty about the dedications, with commentators varying; where this occurs, a question mark is provided by the name to signal doubt or disagreement.

CONVENT DEDICATIONS

destined for Marham, one of only two incorporated Cistercian foundations for women in the country.[42]

Much more significant in this respect is the presence of Leonard at Denney or of John the Baptist at Kilburn. Not only was Denney dedicated to Leonard, but it had firm connections with nearby Ely, the cult centre of Æthelthryth and her sororal family that figure so prominently in Add. 2604.[43] There are other connections between Denney and literary patronage. As we note in IV. Hagiographical Context and the Selection of Saints, Osbern Bokenham translated individual lives of female saints at the request of several lay women in Suffolk, and the manuscript was gathered together as a legendary, possibly for the Franciscan nuns at Aldgate outside London or at Denney in Cambridgeshire.[44] Another potentially interesting link between Add. 2604 and Denney is the early French connection between Waterbeach and France that would make the inclusion of French saints such as Columba of Sens and Leonard justified.[45] Yet there is still one stumbling block: it is not clear why such an obviously Benedictine production would have been intended for a Franciscan nunnery; at the very least, had it been meant originally for Denney, one might have expected the legendary to include the Franciscan founder of their order, Clare, whose feast was on 12 August, which does not quite fit neatly into the now-missing quire 11, between 31 August and 12 September. (Her translation feast is 3 October and the finding of her body 23 September).

---

[42] In addition to the two official Cistercian communities, Marham in Norfolk and Tarrant Keynston in Dorset, there were some twenty-five unofficial Cistercian ones; Elizabeth Freeman, 'Cistercian Nuns in Medieval England: The Gendering of Geographic Marginalization', *Medieval Feminist Forum*, 43 (2008), 26–39 (p. 28).

[43] There are, of course, some unusual choices in the saints represented; there is no obvious reason why Domitilla or Columba of Sens should be found in a collection of saints native to or popular in East Anglia. In the cases of Agatha, Barbara, and Cecilia their popularity was evident, especially in Norfolk (from which most evidence exists); see Nichols, *The Early Art of Norfolk*, pp. 160, 167–68, and 175–76. See further n. 111 of IV. Hagiographical Context and the Selection of Saints.

[44] A. I. Doyle suggests the collection may have been intended for the use of minoresses at Denney Abbey or London: Aldgate. See 'Books Connected with the Vere Family and Barking Abbey', *Transactions of the Essex Archaeological Society*, n.s. 25 (1958), 222–43 (p. 235 n. 8).

[45] The foundation at Waterbeach was established with help from four French nuns. The convent (like other English Franciscan houses) lived under the rule devised by Isabelle, the sister of St Louis IX, for the convent at Longchamp founded in 1255; see the 'Houses of Minoresses: Abbey of Waterbeach', in *The Victoria History of the County of Cambridgeshire and The Isle of Ely*, ed. by Salzman, II (1948), 292–95 (p. 292), with the Abbey of Denney on pp. 295–302.

When considering houses with dedications that match the names of saints in Add. 2604, more likely is Minster-in-Sheppey, which is not only dedicated to Seaxburh, one of the Ely saints, but being in Kent provides an interesting base for this novel combination of East Anglian and Kentish royal saints, including Eanswith, who is also featured in Add. 2604. Eanswith's brother, Eorcenberht, married Seaxburh, connecting the Kentish royal family to the East Anglian. Her other brother, Eormenred, married Oslafa and their daughter Æbbe (also called Domne Eafa or Domneva) was the mother of Mildrith of Thanet. This provides a link to Eadburh, the third abbess of Thanet after Mildrith, who is more rarely culted but occurs in Add. 2604. After the killing of her brothers, Æbbe founded Thanet on land given by Seaxburh's son in expiation. This ancient Kentish history illustrates the close connections between the Ely saints and the various Kentish women in Add. 2604. Most tantalisingly, we know that at the Dissolution, Sheppey had 'a boke of Saynts lyfes', a description that suggests a legendary written in English.[46] The community might well have celebrated Seaxburh's origins as a princess of the East Anglian royal house, and in doing so, would have been especially interested in celebrating her two daughters, Eormenhild and Eorcengota, and her granddaughter, Wærburh. Unfortunately, we have no surviving litany from Minster-in-Sheppey that would illustrate that community's hagiographical devotion but we can well imagine what it would have been, given Seaxburh's heritage. What we can assert is that if Add. 2604 were intended for a Kentish monastery, we would expect to find Mildrith of Thanet featured, especially since the lesser-known Eadburh of Thanet was included. Mildrith was highly culted in Kent, and her name appears in thirty-four late-medieval litanies. Yet, she is not included in Add. 2604. One reason may be that her feast day of 13 July would have placed her alongside the Ely women who are celebrated in Add. 2604 in July alongside Seaxburh.[47] As no pages are missing from this portion of the manuscript (after Wihtburh on 8 July and before Edith of Wilton on 16 September), it does not appear that Mildrith was ever included. Further, the Kentish genealogical details in Add. 2604 are downplayed in the translations of the Kentish saints' lives, occlud-

[46] Bell, *What Nuns Read*, p. 155.

[47] Eormenhild (13 February) and her daughter Wærburh (3 February), were moved to 6 July with Eormenhild's mother Seaxburh. Eorcengota and Æthelburh (26 February) were placed on 7 July, and Wihtburh (17 March) on 8 July. This coalesced the feasts of the Ely women so that they were celebrated in the fortnight after the feast of Æthelthryth on 23 June, which suggests that the community that owned Add. 2604 celebrated Æthelthryth's as a major feast.

ing the connections between the Ely women and their Kentish cousins. This downgrading of the Kentish saints in Add. 2604 may therefore indicate that no Kentish convents are to be linked to the volume, even if there were no particular circumstances to rule out some of them such as the scandal-ridden convent of Higham in the early sixteenth century.[48] There is then a limit to how far such name tracing can go. There is no steady association between one convent or another and Add. 2604 so one needs to investigate further.

Visitation Records

There is a great deal that can be learnt about the state of male and female religious houses over time from monastic visitations, albeit with certain limitations. Some houses were either not subject to episcopal visitation but to the provincials of the order or were liable to episcopal visitations that did not take place or have left no record. In sum, as noted by Elizabeth Makowski, mendicant orders were exempt from episcopal visitation; the Franciscan annals hardly mention visitations by their provincials; the pre-Reformation records of the Dominicans are lost, while the London registers make no reference to Syon visitations.[49] Added to this is the problem that episcopal records from medieval England are edited in a haphazard fashion. For the convents being considered here it is therefore not possible to carry out a systematic analysis. But for the eight convents subject to visitation in the diocese of Norwich (that is, excluding Bruisyard, Marham, and Shouldham) there is plenty of information in the accounts of the visitations made by the bishops, their commissaries, or suffragans between 1492 and 1532.[50] In 1492 Bishop James Goldwell visited Carrow and Thetford, plus Norman's Hospital, which consisted at this time of a master and sisters only. In 1493 Campsey Ash, Bungay, and Flixton were visited, but no female convents in 1494. After Goldwell's death on 15 February 1499, there was a vacancy during which time the archbishop of Canterbury, John Morton,

---

[48] Higham was in such a poor way that it was suppressed in 1522 by John Fisher, bishop of Rochester; Maria Dowling, *Fisher of Men: A Life of John Fisher, 1469–1535* (London: Macmillan; New York: St Martin's, 1999), pp. 56–57, with notes on pp. 184–85. Yet even here there were some books as Agnes Swayne left with 'a psalter or hymnal' and 'an English book' (p. 57).

[49] Elizabeth Makowski, *English Nuns and the Law in the Middle Ages: Cloistered Nuns and their Lawyers, 1293–1540*, Studies in the History of Medieval Religion, 39 (Woodbridge: Boydell, 2011), p. 4.

[50] *Visitations of the Diocese of Norwich, A.D. 1492–1532*, ed. by A. Jessopp, Camden Society, n.s. 43 (1888).

initiated a visitation of the Norwich diocese in 1499 that included (in order of their visits) Carrow, Bungay, Flixton, Campsey Ash, and Redlingfield though the details are skeletal.[51] Richard Nykke (or Nix) took over as bishop in 1501 and conducted six-yearly visits from 1514 to 1532 (and possibly before that, though no record survives). In 1514 the order of convents visited was Thetford, Blackborough, Crabhouse, Campsey Ash, Redlingfield, Flixton, Bungay, and Carrow. In 1520 the order was geographically more or less the same: Thetford, Crabhouse, Blackborough, Campsey Ash, Redlingfield, Flixton, Bungay, and Flixton (a continuation of the earlier visit). In 1526 the visitation took in Carrow, Campsey Ash, Redlingfield, Thetford, Bungay, Flixton. Finally, in 1532 the following were visited: Carrow, Campsey Ash, Redlingfield, Thetford, Blackborough, Bungay, and Flixton, in addition to Norman's Hospital.[52]

In all these visits between 1492 and 1532 there were very few that uncovered real abuses and in most cases no need for reform was noted. A few of the visits would appear to have been conducted in a cursory fashion: for instance, in July 1520 all that is noted of Thetford is its poverty and for Crabhouse and Blackborough a single line saying that all was well. Episcopal injunctions for remedial action are only provided after the following visitations: Campsey Ash on 1 August 1514, again on 27 June 1526, with *comperta* disclosed on 25 June 1532; Redlingfield on 7 August 1514; Flixton on 11 August 1514 and on 14/20 August 1520; and Carrow on 14 June 1526 and 10 June 1532.[53] In 1514 in his Campsey Ash injunction the bishop simply asked that the prior-

---

[51] Christopher Harper-Bill, 'A Late Medieval Visitation — The Diocese of Norwich in 1499', *Proceedings of the Suffolk Institute of Archaeology and History*, 34 (1977–80), 35–47. The material is calendared in *The Register of John Morton, Archbishop of Canterbury, 1486–1500*, III: *Norwich sede vacante, 1499*, ed. by Christopher Harper-Bill, The Canterbury and York Society, 89 (2000), pp. 160–68.

[52] Visitations to religious houses are discussed in V. M. O'Mara, 'Preaching to Nuns in Late Medieval England', in *Medieval Monastic Preaching*, ed. by Carolyn Muessig, Brill's Studies in Intellectual History, 90 (Leiden: Brill, 1998), pp. 93–119, and most particularly for present purposes in Veronica O'Mara, 'Preaching to Nuns in the Norwich Diocese on the Eve of the Reformation: The Evidence from Visitation Records', in *Monastic Life in the Medieval British Isles: Essays in Honour of Janet Burton*, ed. by Karen Stöber, Julie Kerr, and Emilia Jamroziak (Cardiff: University of Wales Press, 2018), pp. 189–212, with appendices on pp. 202–12 that provide a full list of all the visitations (male and female).

[53] For the respective visitations and injunctions, see *Visitations of the Diocese of Norwich, A.D. 1492–1532*, ed. by Jessopp, pp. 133–34, 219–20, 290–92, 138–40, 142–44, 185–86, 190–91, 208–10, and 273–75, and the discussion in O'Mara, 'Preaching to Nuns in the Norwich Diocese on the Eve of the Reformation'.

ess should produce and display the inventory; in 1526 the precentrix of the same house, Margaret Harman, said that the liturgical books needed repair to which the bishop acceded. There was a long list of complaints at Campsey Ash in 1532 accusing the prioress, Ela Buttery, of strictness, parsimony, and the provision of very poor food. The nuns at Redlingfield complained about a number of troubles in 1514 ranging from the severity of the subprioress to the lack of curtains in the dormitories and the non-use of the refectory. In Flixton in 1514 the nuns also had various complaints that included the non-observance of discipline and silence, and failure to rise for the religious services. By 1520 the Flixton complaints were somewhat fewer though the prioress, like her predecessors (and many other superiors in medieval English convents), did not render her accounts; and slept alone away from the dormitory. The bishop's representatives ordered the number of dogs to be reduced to one; that the prioress be accompanied by a sister chaplain when she slept outside the dormitory; that accounts be provided; and that Richard Carr be removed from the prioress's service. In Carrow in 1526 there were complaints from the nuns about services being said and sung too quickly, silence not being kept, and certain feasts not being observed. There were complaints about the liability of obedientaries for breakages and the custom of a Christmas game where a junior nun assumed the role of the abbess (a variant of the Boy Bishop ceremony). In 1532 the Carrow nuns reported, amongst other matters, infringements of the habit, the ill behaviour of younger nuns, the lack of a lectern in the church, and failure to observe certain feasts. With the exceptions of Flixton in 1514 and Carrow in 1526 and especially in 1532, most of the faults noted in the episcopal visitations were minor misdemeanours. Despite some of the lurid tales reported about medieval nuns, on the strength of these visitations there is no perceived moral or spiritual inadequacy amongst female religious in the Norwich diocese let alone anything that would necessarily prohibit an interest in the saints found in Add. 2604.[54] But beyond this, we cannot go. While the numbers and names of nuns

---

[54] See, for example, the various dramatic stories in Eileen Power, *Medieval English Nunneries c.1275 to 1535*, Cambridge Studies in Medieval Life and Thought (Cambridge: Cambridge University Press, 1922), especially pp. 436–74. For a more detailed and nuanced view, see the examination of religious houses in the dioceses of Lincoln and Norwich between 1430 and 1530 in Christian D. Knudsen, 'Naughty Nuns and Promiscuous Monks: Monastic Sexual Misconduct in Late Medieval England' (unpublished doctoral dissertation, Centre for Medieval Studies, University of Toronto, 2012). See also F. Donald Logan, *Runaway Religious in Medieval England, c. 1240–1540*, Cambridge Studies in Medieval Life and Thought, Fourth Series (Cambridge: Cambridge University Press, 1996).

are provided — a handy indication of the size of the convents — books are virtually never mentioned, apart from the occasional reference to those for the services. For books we need any information available from book provenance, wills, and occasionally from Dissolution inventories.

Books

Of the thirty-four convents here (including Canonsleigh for the sake of completeness) manuscripts or printed books in actuality (or as references in wills or by other means) are associated with twenty-one (either generally to the convent or to particular individuals): Barking, Bruisyard, Campsey Ash, Canonsleigh, Carrow, Castle Hedingham, Dartford, Denney, Flixton, Higham, Ickleton, Kilburn, London: Aldgate, London: Bishopgate, London: Holywell, Malling, Marham, Minster-in-Sheppey, Redlingfield, Syon, and Thetford.[55] The other houses would no doubt have had at least the required liturgical volumes, but there is no known record of these. In this list there are three of the 'Big Five' — Barking, Dartford, and Syon and so they lead the way in terms of numbers. According to computations by David Bell (excluding most liturgical and administrative documents), the extant books for English convents (which may only be a small fraction of the original number) are as follows. There are forty-eight volumes linked to the Syon nuns, two untraced books, plus twelve that could have belonged to the sisters or the brothers, and other examples from varied evidence. Fifteen manuscripts are recorded for Barking, alongside other potential examples, while Dartford has nine manuscripts. The remaining numbers are less impressive, with Campsey Ash and London: Aldgate with five manuscripts each and a sixth untraced; Carrow had three manuscripts; Bruisyard had two, while Canonsleigh, Castle Hedingham, Flixton, Higham, Ickleton, London: Holywell, Malling, and Thetford had one each. References in other sources (such as wills) exist for Barking, Bruisyard, Campsey Ash, Denney, Flixton, Higham, London: Aldgate, London: Bishopgate, Malling, Marham, Minster-in-Sheppy, Redlingfield, Syon, and Thetford. These overall numbers are supplemented by Mary Erler who attributes five other manuscripts and five printed books to Syon, two manuscripts to Denney, one each

---

[55] Full details are given in Bell, *What Nuns Read*, pp. 107–35,138–39, 142–44, 148–53, 155, 160–61, and 171–212. Bell's original work is supplemented by Erler, *Women, Reading, and Piety in Late Medieval England*, pp. 139–49, to which there is a response in Bell, 'What Nuns Read: The State of the Question' , where Bell also notes another rental associated with Dartford (p. 132).

BOOKS   131

to Barking, Bruisyard, and Malling, a printed book to Dartford, and a manuscript copy of a printed book to London: Aldgate, while a missing printed
book associated with Campsey Ash has been traced to The Morgan Library &
Museum in New York.[56]

A fair number of the extant books comprise liturgical material such as Latin
psalters and the like. Most of the non-liturgical codices are in English, though
some convents demonstrate a particular fondness for French: Barking had a
large French composite devotional book and another manuscript containing
the *Vies des pères* and other texts; Campsey Ash owned the collection of saints'
lives in Anglo-Norman; and Flixton's one book was a volume of a French Bible,
while London: Aldgate and Malling were both bequeathed French books in
wills.[57] With a few exceptions (such as the *Brut* in Dartford or a fragment of
Chaucer's *Parlement of Foules* in Syon), the range of material is what might
be expected in a nunnery, albeit that the presence of Wycliffite material in
Barking and Thetford might come as a surprise to some.[58] Otherwise works by
Walter Hilton were especially popular and Campsey Ash, Dartford, London:
Aldgate, and Syon all had one or more of his volumes; Nicholas Love's *Mirror
of the Blessed Life of Jesus* Christ could be found at Barking and Syon; the
English translation of Heinrich Seuse's *Horologium sapientiae* was available
in Campsey Ash and Dartford; two works of Richard Rolle are extant from
Barking and Dartford; while the local East Anglian writers, John Capgrave
and John Lydgate, could each be found at Campsey Ash, with various other
works by Lydgate also at Dartford and Syon.[59] Finally, Canonsleigh had a

[56] For the newly identified copy of the *Chastysing of goddes chyldern* printed in Westminster
by Wynkyn de Worde in 1493 (STC 5065), see New York, The Morgan Library & Museum,
CHL1799 (Copy 2); as noted in Bell, *What Nuns Read*, it is inscribed by 'Elyzabeth Wyllowby'
who donates the book to 'Dame Catherine Symonde' in the first decades of the sixteenth century endorsing her not to sell it or remove it from Campsey Ash but to give it to one of the
sisters, pp. 125–26 (p. 125). As many as possible of the manuscripts and printed books listed
above have been investigated in the course of this *Study* to see if any of them compared in script
or decoration with Add. 2604 (all listed in the Bibliography). This means that a wide range of
manuscripts and archival material (as listed in Bell, *What Nuns Read*) from Barking, Bruisyard,
Campsey Ash, Chatteris, Chester, Crabhouse, Dartford, Denney, Derby, Edinburgh, Flixton,
Godstow, Goring, Hampole, Higham, Ickleton, Kington St Michael, London: Aldgate, London: Holywell, Marrick, Nun Coton, Nuneaton, Polsloe, Romsey, Shaftesbury, Swine, Syon,
Tarrant Keynston, Thetford, Wherwell, Wilton, and Winchester has been examined.

[57] Bell, *What Nuns Read*, pp. 112–16, 124–25, 138, 151, and 153.

[58] Bell, *What Nuns Read*, pp. 130–31, 195, 109, and 211 respectively.

[59] Bell, *What Nuns Read*, pp. 224–27.

132   III. CONVENT AND GEOGRAPHICAL LOCATION

copy of *Ancrene Riwle*, with three folios at the end with some Latin verses to Æthelthryth.[60]

When it comes to hagiographical texts, in addition to the well-known Campsey Ash saints' lives manuscript already noted, Malling had a Middle English verse life of St Margaret.[61] Other books both hagiographical and otherwise are mentioned in various wills and/or Dissolution inventories. The convent of London: Bishopgate received a portforium and a psalter in a will of 1349. The nuns of Malling were willed a copy of the *Manuel de pechez* in 1368. Isabel (a London: Aldgate nun) was bequeathed seven French books in 1399 by her mother, Eleanor, Duchess of Gloucester, while Matilda, a nun in the same convent received four books in 1415, including the *Pricke of Conscience*, from her brother, Henry Scrope of Masham.[62]

Searches of local wills as a group also reveal numerous bequests to convents; these are normally financial but very occasionally include books. There are routine monetary donations to convents or individual nuns in wills from Bury St Edmunds, for example.[63] Bequests of books to convents only occur once, in the 1463 will of John Baret (considered in II. Language and Dialectal Provenance); he gives to 'Dame Jone Stoonys iii s. iiij d. and myn book of ynglych and latyn with diuerse maters of good exortacions, wretyn in papir and closed [fol. 102b] with parchemyn.'[64] Some local donations are well known such as that of the

---

[60] Bell, *What Nuns Read*, p. 126.

[61] Blackburn, Museum and Art Gallery, 091-21040 is a very fine manuscript that was given by the abbess of Malling, Elizabeth Hull, to her god-daughter, Margaret Neville (b. 26 September 1520); Bell, *What Nuns Read*, pp. 152–53.

[62] Bell, *What Nuns Read*, pp. 148, and 151–53.

[63] Donations to the following convents or to individual nuns in these houses may be noted: Thetford, Bungay, Ickleton, and Castle Hedingham (Agnes Stubbard, 1418); Thetford (John Notingham, 1437); Swaffham Bulbeck (Alica Langham, 1448); Thetford and Campsey Ash (John Baret, 1463); Redlingfield (Baldwin Coksedge, 1467); Redlingfield, Thetford, Bruisyard, and Soham [except that there was no known convent there], Ickleton, and Campsey Ash (John Smith, 1480); Thetford, Shouldham, and Wiggenhall [which was not a convent so presumably Crabhouse was meant]; Blackborough, Cambridge (St Radegund's), Chatteris, Swaffham Bulbeck, Denney, Ickleton, Crabhouse, Bruisyard, Campsey Ash, and Flixton (Margaret Odeham, 1492); Thetford (John Perfay, 1509); *Wills and Inventories from the Registers of the Commissary of Bury St. Edmund's and the Archdeacon of Sudbury*, ed. by Tymms, pp. 2, 6, 12, 35, 44, 55–56, 73, and 109.

[64] *Wills and Inventories from the Registers of the Commissary of Bury St Edmund's and the Archdeacon of Sudbury*, ed. by Tymms, pp. 15–44 (p. 35); Baret also specifies that 'my book with the sege of Thebes in englysh' (p. 35) is to go to his cousin, John Cleye, who is a priest. The

BOOKS   133

Norwich widow Margaret Purdauns (or Spurdaunce) who in 1481 gave money
to eight convents in East Anglia and made a few book bequests including a
copy of the *Doctrine of the Hert* to Bruisyard and a copy of what must have
been the *Revelations* of St Birgitta of Sweden to Thetford.[65] References to other
books exist, but many will be hidden in local records or lost to history.[66]

Equally missing in many cases are the inventories made at the time of the
Dissolution, though some fortunately survive. Of the convents here, Kilburn
may thus be seen in a new light. Although without any surviving manuscripts,
it clearly once possessed a quantity of books. An inventory dated 11 May 1536
lists two English 'bookes of Legenda aurea' and two massbooks both in manuscript and print, four processionals and 'two Legendes' all in parchment or
paper, as well as two chests of 'diverse bookes'.[67] The concentration on saints'
lives and the extent of the library holdings is noteworthy. It is only matched by
the Dissolution list from Minster-in-Sheppey that likewise contained 'a boke
of Saynts lyfes', as seen above. There is an extensive (for a nunnery) unidentified
number of books scattered around the inventory, such as the seven books in
the vestry 'whereof j goodly mase boke of parchement, and dyvers other good
bokes' and 'an olde presse full of old boks of no valew' in the Lady Chapel.[68]
Other Dissolution inventory lists are less helpful; those from Campsey Ash,
Castle Hedingham, Marham, and Redlingfield merely specify that most of
the holdings were liturgical and that the books from Flixton were of 'lytell

---

will of Barbara Mason, the last abbess of Marham, which was drawn up on 4 September 1538
and probated on 14 September 1538 (pp. 133–35), in common with most of the other wills
here makes no mention of books, though she bequeaths goods including 'my beste vayle' (p.
133) and wishes for 'a marbell stonne' with scripture on her grave (p. 134).

[65] Erler, *Women, Reading, and Piety in Late Medieval England*, pp. 75–80 (p. 76).

[66] For book bequests in Norwich wills, see Tanner, *The Church in Late Medieval Norwich
1370–1530*, pp. 193–97. Oliva, *The Convent and Community in Late Medieval England*,
pp. 161–83 and 230–32, examines testamentary and other patronage of convents. In *The Cartulary of Chatteris Abbey*, ed. by Breay, bequests to Chatteris are dealt with on pp. 54–57. Catherine Paxton, 'The Nunneries of London and its Environs in the Later Middle Ages' (unpublished doctoral dissertation, University of Oxford, 1992), pp. 95–113, analyses testamentary
bequests to nuns between 1370 and 1420, though with very few mentions of books (p. 106).

[67] Bell, *What Nuns Read*, pp. 143–44.

[68] Mackenzie E. C. Walcott, 'Inventories of (I.) St. Mary's Hospital or Maison Dieu, Dover;
(II.) The Benedictine Priory of St. Martin New-Work, Dover, for Monks; (III.) The Benedictine
Priory of SS. Mary and Sexburga, in the Island of Sheppey, for Nuns: With Illustrative Notes',
Archæologia Cantiana being Transactions of the Kent Archæological Society, 7 (1868), 272–306
(pp. 287–306). The books alone are conveniently listed in Bell, *What Nuns Read*, p. 155.

worth'.[69] That from Chatteris provides a detailed itemisation of kitchen equipment, but makes do with only noting 'certen old bookes'.[70]

This survey of book holdings (either actual or reported) serves to highlight an interest in devotional reading in convents with some emphasis on the hagiographical, even if overall it does little to confirm an obvious particular home for our manuscript. On the strength of this evidence, much might be made of Add. 2604's potential location in a house with a larger library such as Barking, Dartford, or Syon, but equally smaller and poorer houses like Flixton possessed books. In truth, the results of this analysis may be laid alongside the various others outlined here as another piece in the jigsaw where individual pieces are only of value for their contribution to the composite picture.

Partial Conclusion

Where we have considered religious order, dedications, devotion to individual saints, visitation reports, known library holdings and/or book bequests, and Dissolution inventories, we have excavated several clues that might help isolate possible homes for Add. 2604. While there are cases with no evidence one way or another, there are others where historical circumstances would indicate that a particular convent was never going to be in the running, for example, Higham. All told, the strongest contenders in East Anglia, for the diverse reasons explained above, are probably Campsey Ash, Chatteris, Denney, Ickleton, and Thetford, though many have drawbacks to some extent. If London or Middlesex houses are to be considered (and we think this unlikely), the only real candidate would be Syon on the grounds of a potential source connection or possibly Kilburn if one were to make much of books no longer extant. But none of these houses may be securely connected to Add. 2604 or at this point emerge as an obvious front-runner. We remain stymied by the lack of identifying evidence of medieval ownership or use. Yet if we turn to the post-medieval evidence in Add. 2604, we find some intriguing clues that are very suggestive — hence the following

[69] Francis Haslewood, 'Inventories of Monasteries Suppressed in 1536', *Proceedings of the Suffolk Institute of Archæology and Natural History*, 8 (1894), 83–116; pp. 88–90 (Flixton), pp. 95–98 (Redlingfield), and pp. 113–16 (Campsey Ash); R. C. Fowler, 'Inventories of Essex Monasteries in 1536', *Transactions of the Essex Archaeological Society*, n.s. 9 (1906), 280–92; pp. 289–92 (Castle Headingham); *The Victoria History of the County of Norfolk*, ed. by Doubleday and Page, ɪɪ (1906), 369–70, p. 370 (Marham).

[70] *The Cartulary of Chatteris Abbey*, ed. by Breay, pp. 415–21 (p. 417).

excursus on the earliest known owner of Add. 2604, George Tasburgh (who is also especially addressed alongside later owners in I. The Manuscript) and the Tasburgh Family in Suffolk and Norfolk. He and his recusant forebears, alongside various other interconnected gentry Catholic families, tried to keep Catholicism alive in East Anglia and further afield over several centuries. Evidence about George Tasburgh's wider family highlights one specific convent, and raises the possible significance of another, as well as providing insight into some potential modes for the manuscript's transmission. Like much of the history of Add. 2604, this narrative is complex and involved, but important for understanding the provenance history of Add. 2604 and similar manuscripts.

George Tasburgh in the Eighteenth Century

The Tasburgh family, no doubt originating in the village of this name just south of Norwich, first appear in the records in the fourteenth or fifteenth century before fading out towards the end of the eighteenth century.[71] At different points in history they had two family seats, one in South Elmham St Peter in the extreme north-east of Suffolk (the Flixton Tasburghs) and one in Bodney in the extreme south-west of Norfolk (the Bodney Tasburghs). There were also other members of the family who settled in Middlesex, Dublin, and so forth. We start with the immediate Bodney Tasburghs and work backwards. George was the son of Francis Tasburgh (d. 1747) and Mary D'Ewes, the great-granddaughter of Sir Simonds D'Ewes (d. 1650), the antiquarian from Stowlangtoft in Suffolk.[72] Notwithstanding the strict Puritan

---

[71] The complicated Tasburgh family history has been meticulously traced by the late Nesta Evans and Francis Young; our work has been immeasurably helped by the research of both. See Nesta Evans, 'The Tasburghs of South Elmham: The Rise and Fall of a Suffolk Gentry Family', *Proceedings of the Suffolk Institute of Archaeology and History*, 34 (1980), 269–80, and Francis Young, 'The Tasburghs of Bodney: Catholicism and Politics in South Norfolk', *Norfolk Archaeology: A Journal of Archaeology and Local History*, 46 (2011), 190–98, and Francis Young, 'The Tasburghs of Flixton and Catholicism in North-East Suffolk, 1642–1767', *Proceedings of the Suffolk Institute of Archaeology*, 42 (2012), 455–70. See also Roger Virgoe, 'A Norwich Taxation List of 1451', *Norfolk Archæology: Or Miscellaneous Tracts Relating to the Antiquities of the County of Norfolk*, Norfolk and Norwich Archæological Society, 40 (1989), 145–54 (p. 149, where John Tasburgh is listed for £20).

[72] For the children of the antiquarian from his two wives, Anne Clopton and Elizabeth Wilughby/Willoughby (of whom nine out of twelve died as infants or children), see J. Sears McGee, *An Industrious Mind: The Worlds of Sir Simonds D'Ewes* (Stanford, CA: Stanford

beliefs of their great-grandfather, Mary and all her sisters married Catholics: Merelina's first husband was Richard Elwes and her second Richard Holmes; Delariviere was the spouse of Thomas Gage, and Henrietta the wife of Thomas Havers.[73] George, Mary's youngest child (1729–83), had two sisters Margaret (1714–81) and Mary (1717–93), both of whom became Augustinian nuns in Bruges. Mary (Sister Maria Frances) was professed on 23 April 1741 and Margaret (Sister Margaret) on 8 October 1748.[74] George also had an aunt (his father's sister, Mary), who likewise had been an Augustinian canoness (Sister Mary Bernard); she was professed in Bruges on 12 September 1700 and died on 7 April 1715. At various points in the seventeenth century there were five other nuns in the family as a whole,[75] as well as three Jesuits and one

University Press, 2015), p. 438. Mary, who had died before 28 March 1744, was the daughter of Sir Simonds D'Ewes (d. 1722), the son of Sir Willougby D'Ewes (d. 1685), the only surviving son of the antiquarian. She was the sister of the fourth and final baron, Sir Jermyn D'Ewes (d. 1721), and of Merelina, Delariviere, and Henrietta. To what extent the sisters may have inherited any antiquarian leanings is open to question. Their father, Simonds, appeared to have no such interest as in 1705 he sold off the huge library of his grandfather, Sir Simonds D'Ewes, for £450 to Robert Harley; these manuscripts were subsequently absorbed into the Harley Collection; Andrew G. Watson, *The Library of Sir Simonds D'Ewes*, British Museum Bicentenary Publications (London: The Trustees of the British Museum, 1966), pp. 56–63. This was expressly against the wishes of the antiquarian who drew up a number of wills in Latin and English; he specifically wished his library to be kept intact and accessible to others. In his final will in 1650 he bequeathed his library to his only surviving son, Willoughby; London, The National Archives (hereafter TNA), Prerogative Court of Canterbury and related Probate Jurisdictions: Will Registers, Prob 11/212/835.

[73] Francis Young, *The Gages of Hengrave and Suffolk Catholicism 1640–1767*, Catholic Record Society Publications, Monograph Series, 8 (Woodbridge: Boydell, 2015), p. 100. Recusant Catholics in the interests of dynastic and religious responsiblities made endogamous alliances; see Kate Gibson, 'Marriage Choice and Kinship among the English Catholic Elite, 1680–1730', *Journal of Family History*, 41 (2016), 144–64. These well-connected Catholic marriages provide a potentially useful context for the acquistion of a manuscript like Add. 2604.

[74] For further details, see 'Who were the Nuns?: A Prosopographical Study of the English Convents in Exile 1600–1800' (https://wwtn.history.qmul.ac.uk/search/howto.html) (accessed 1 April 2023).

[75] These were a daughter (Jane), an Augustinian professed in Louvain/Leuven on 31 July 1622/23 (to whom we shall return); Elisabeth, a Benedictine professed in Gent on 26 June 1665; Catherine, a Benedictine professed in Gent on 5 October 1669; Mary, an Augustinian professed in Louvain/Leuven on 10 August 1684; and Anne, a Franciscan professed in Bruges in 28 October 1685; for further details, see the 'Who were the Nuns?' website.

GEORGE TASBURGH IN THE EIGHTEENTH CENTURY 137

Benedictine monk into the eighteenth century.[76] And one of these Jesuits was even regarded as a saint.[77]

On his father's death in Gent in 1747 (by which time his mother was also dead) George was still a minor though set to inherit the estate in due course.[78] George's sisters are mentioned in their father's will dated 14 September 1744 with a codicil on 27 June 1746 and probated on 24 March 1746 [1747]. Mary was already in Bruges and so was granted just £5 annually, while Margaret was bequeathed several large sums, starting with 'Twelve hundred pound capital Stock in old South Sea Annuities'; she was also to be the beneficiary of the estate if George died before twenty-one or without lawful heirs. Other provision was also made 'in case my Said daughter Margaret ingages in a religious State or becomes a Nun'; should this happen (as it did), the sums willed to her should go to George and she should be given £500 on the day of her profession and £5 annually thereafter. His father requests that his executor and trustee, Dr Charles Jerningham, a physician trained in Montpellier from one of the foremost Catholic families in East Anglia (also known as Jernegans), be the guardian of the children and that he have 'a particular regard to the Education of my Son' and that if Margaret remain in England after his death and if Lady Jerningham with whom she now is, cannot have her or dies, that Charles 'will prevail with his own dear spouse to harbour my said daughter till she is other-

---

[76] The Jesuits were Henry (1641–1718), Thomas (1672–1727), and Richard (1693–1735), and the Benedictine was Henry who died in 1769; Young, 'The Tasburghs of Bodney', p. 191, and Young, 'The Tasburghs of Flixton and Catholicism in North-East Suffolk, 1642–1767', p. 456.

[77] Thomas Tasburgh died in Dublin and was buried at St Michan's Church in the city centre. In 1832 it was reported that 'Many miracles were wrought at the tomb of this Father, and his remains were, in consequence, almost carried away by the people [...]'; see Young, 'The Tasburghs of Bodney', pp. 194 and 197 n. 43 for this quotation. Thomas's journal is preserved in Dunedin, New Zealand, The University of Otago, Hocken Collections, Archives and Manuscripts, Misc-MS-1818. It is catalogued as '[Elliot family?]: Diary of an English landlord in Dublin attempting to gain rents owed from the family's "Estate of Congue" (1726–1727)', that is, the Abbey of Cong in County Mayo. It has been transcribed by Brigid Clesham and is available on the pages of the Cumann Seandálaiochta agus Staire na Gallimhe/Galway Archaeological and Historical Society (https://gahs.ie/transcript-of-the-journal-of-thomas-tasburgh-s-j-on-his-visit-to-ireland/) (accessed 1 April 2023).

[78] Francis's wife Mary is not mentioned in his will of 1747 as she had already died (on 28 March 1744) by the time her sister Delariviere made her will; see the relevant wills in n. 94. In a letter to the same sister dated 23 February (with no year) Mary mentions her two daughters whom she calls Fanny and Molly; see Cambridge, Cambridge University Library, MS Hengrave 88/3/90.

wise disposed of'.[79] Given that Margaret was professed as a nun in Bruges on 8 October 1748, she had not troubled the Jerninghams for long after her father's death.[80] In George's case he had been taken by his father to the English College at Douai on 13 March 1744 but returned to England on 23 April 1747, presumably because of the death of Francis in Gent in the same year.[81] George moved to Bodney at some point in 1751, possibly living with the Jerninghams (whose family seat was at Costessey Hall near Norwich) until then.[82]

On 6 March 1755 George married Teresa Gage, the daughter of the M. P., Sir Thomas Gage (d. 1754) of High Meadow in Gloucestershire. The senior branch of the Gage family line based at Firle Place (in Firle, four miles from Lewes, in what is now East Sussex) had officially conformed to the Church of England probably in the mid-1720s. In 1744 on the death of his cousin, Sir William Gage (who had converted to Catholicism), Teresa's father succeeded to the baronetcy and to Firle Place.[83] Teresa predeceased George on

---

[79] All details here are to be found in London, TNA, Prerogative Court of Canterbury and related Probate Jurisdictions: Will Registers, Prob 11/753/353. Lady Jerningham is Margaret Bedingfield (d. 1756), the wife of Charles's brother John, who was one of the Catholic Bedingfields of Oxburgh Hall, near Bodney. Charles's first wife, Elizabeth Roper, died in 1736; see Natalie Walters, 'Illustrations from the Wellcome Library: The Jernegan-Arundell Correspondence', *Medical History*, 53 (2009), 117–26 (p. 119), who also notes that Montpellier was one of the two most eminent medical schools in France at the time (p. 122). The reference to 'his own dear spouse' refers to Charles's second wife, Frances Belasyse.

[80] For this date, see the website 'Who were the Nuns?'.

[81] Young, 'The Tasburghs of Bodney', p. 195.

[82] In 1767 a census of Catholics to be laid before the House of Lords was compiled by the bishops in the twenty-six Anglican dioceses on the instructions of the archbishops of Canterbury and York. Depending on the diocese, these official returns omit or include names, alongside the standard ages, sexes, occupations, and length of residence in the parish; see *Returns of Papists 1767*, ed. by E. S. Worrall, Catholic Record Society, Occasional Publications, 1–2, 2 vols (1980–89), I: *Diocese of Chester* and II: *Dioceses of England and Wales, except Chester*, where the Norwich diocese may be found on pp. 122–29 and Bodney on p. 122 (with names omitted). The names are provided from the original return in Joy Rowe, 'The 1767 Census of Papists in the Diocese of Norwich: The Social Composition of the Roman Catholic Community', in *Religious Dissent in East Anglia*, III: *Proceedings of the Third Symposium*, ed. by David Chadd (Norwich: Centre for East Anglia Studies, University of East Anglia, 1996), pp. 187–234 (p. 233). From this census it is clear that in 1767 George had been sixteen years at Bodney and his wife Teresa, fourteen years; George was aged thirty-eight and Teresa was fifty-five.

[83] The history of the Gage family is complicated, but may be simplified as follows. As noted, the senior branch was that at Firle Place in Sussex; there were also the Gages who lived at Hengrave Hall, about three miles north-west of Bury St Edmunds (into which George's aunt

GEORGE TASBURGH IN THE EIGHTEENTH CENTURY 139

12 August 1773 without offspring. In April 1780 George was married again, this time to Barbara Fitzherbert of Swynnerton in Staffordshire (d. 1808), who was the daughter of Thomas Fitzherbert and his second wife, Mary Teresa Throckmorton of the eminent Catholic family of Coughton Court in Warwickshire; once again there were no children.

George died on 14 September 1783, having made a will on 12 November 1782 that was probated on 8 November 1783.[84] In his will, which takes the form of a strict settlement,[85] there is a stipulation that to modern eyes would seem an unusual one, but was not unexpected in the eighteenth century especially amongst well-born Catholics who died without (legitimate) heirs and

---

Delariviere had married); and there were the Gages of Coldham Hall in Stanningfield, about five miles south-east of Bury St Edmunds. The last Gages were actually the Rookwood Gages by virtue of the marriage of Elizabeth Rookwood (1683–1759) to John Gage (1688–1728). When the male line died out in 1767, the baronetcy passed from the Hengrave Gages to the Rookwood Gages. The Catholic Simpson family of the Suffolk actor, dramatist, and novelist, Elizabeth Inchbald (1753–1821) from Stanningfield (about five miles south-east of Bury St Edmunds), was accustomed to attend the private chapel of the Rookwood Gage family in Coldham Hall. There are a few entries in Elizabeth's diaries about the Gage family and/or the Sunday services; see *The Diaries of Elizabeth Inchbald*, ed. by Ben P. Robertson, The Pickering Masters, 3 vols (London: Pickering and Chatto, 2007), I, 249, 256, 267, 270, 271, 272, 332 n. 1 (all relating to 1781), and III, 249–50 (1820). For full details of the Gages, see Young, *The Gages of Hengrave and Suffolk Catholicism 1640–1767*, which has a map on p. xi and the genealogy on p. xii.

[84] London, TNA, Prerogative Court of Canterbury and related Probate Jurisdictions: Will Registers, Prob 11/1110/108. In an item describing Bodney village and the medieval church of St Mary in the *Norwich Mercury* for Saturday, 22 November 1902, it is noted (p. 3) that there are inscriptions to George and Teresa in this church.

[85] Put simply, strict settlement was the means whereby succession was restricted. It drew on three elements: entail (the descent of an estate mainly through the male line, normally the first-born son), a life tenancy (use of the land for a man's life), and trustees (who kept the estate in trust and preserved the rights of others such as daughters); see Barbara English and John Saville, *Strict Settlement: A Guide for Historians*, University of Hull, Occasional Papers in Economic and Social History, 10 (Hull: University of Hull Press, 1983), especially ch. 1, 'The Model', pp. 11–52. Tasburgh goes into detail about what is to happen to his estate, working his way through the complexities of his wife's marriage settlement and outlining a number of possible scenarios made necessary by his lack of direct heirs; he even applies the stipulation about taking his surname to all potential inheritors in succession. The named executors are his wife and his cousin, Thomas Havers of Thelveton (the son of his aunt Henrietta), perhaps significantly alongside Robert Edward, ninth Baron Petre, the principal representative nationally of the 'old' Catholics.

who wanted to keep their estates intact and free from seizure.[86] George specified that, should his widow and beneficiary Barbara Fitzherbert re-marry, her
future husband should take the name of Tasburgh. When Barbara subsequently
married George Crathorne of Crathorne in Yorkshire a few years later, this was
duly applied for and sanctioned by Act of Parliament.[87] Among various bequests
that included £5 per year to his sister Mary in the convent in Bruges (his other
sister Margaret in the same convent having predeceased him in 1781), he left
the large sum of forty pounds annually to Ann Gage of Brussels in fulfillment of
a bond made to her in September 1773. Herein lies a mystery the circumstances
of which were uncovered by Francis Young.[88] Although fathering no children
within wedlock, George Tasburgh was said to have seduced Ann Gage (the
daughter of Sir Thomas Gage of Bury St Edmunds), when she was on a visit to
Teresa Tasburgh. A child was subsequently born and George 'afterwards went
a Pilgrimage to Jerusalem to atone for his Sin'.[89] The episode was deemed so

[86] Before the various Relief Acts culminating in the Catholic Emancipation Act of 1829
punitive laws existed that prevented Roman Catholics from purchasing land, inheriting property, and holding civil or military offices or seats in Parliament. The Relief Act of 1778 enabled
Catholics to hold land on more advantageous leases, but it was not until the Relief Act of
1791 that permission was given to Catholics to practise their religion without incurring civil
penalties.

[87] On 2 March 1786 in the third session of the sixteenth parliament in the reign of
George III a petition was presented on behalf of George Crathorne, Barbara's new husband.
This referred to George Tasburgh's will and mentioned an Indenture of Settlement from 29
July 1783 that specified that the new spouse should obtain an Act of Parliament to authorise
him and his male heirs to adopt the Tasburgh name. Leave was given to bring in this Bill and
the permission was granted on 20 March 1786; for details see *Journals of the House of Com-
mons from January the 24th, 1786, in the Twenty-Sixth Year of the Reign of King George the
Third, to December the 14th, 1786, in the Twenty-Seventh Year of the Reign of King George the
Third* ([London]: Printed by Order of the House of Commons, n.d.), XLI, 273–74 and 363.
Although the request specifies male heirs, George Crathorne (Tasburgh) and Barbara Fitzherbert had only one child, Maria Augusta Roselia (a name that is referred to in various formats
by commentators), who also adopted the Tasburgh name. Later on her husband, Michael Anne
(of Burghwallis in Yorkshire), took the name of Tasburgh, though later reverting to Crathorne.
For her dramatic escape from France (in around 1809) as a seventeen-year old hidden in a coffin destined for a dead nun, see the memoir by the grand-daughter of Barbara Fitzherbert: *The
Recollections of a Northumbrian Lady, 1815–1866: Being the Memoirs of Barbara Charlton
(née Tasburgh), Wife of William Henry Charlton of Hesleyside, Northumberland*, ed. by L. E.
O. Charlton (London: Jonathan Cape, 1949), pp. 19–20, and 'Who were the Nuns?' website.

[88] Young, 'The Tasburghs of Bodney'. p. 195.

[89] This account, written *c.* 1818 by Thomas Gage (1781–1820), seventh baronet of Hengrave, is found in Cambridge, Cambridge University Library, MS Hengrave 1/4, p. 317.

GEORGE TASBURGH IN THE EIGHTEENTH CENTURY   141

scandalous that it became the subject of an untraced novel called *The Faithless Guardian* written some time before 1818.[90]

Nevertheless, George Tasburgh would seem to have been highly regarded in the neighbourhood as the local newspaper, the *Norfolk Chronicle* for Satruday, 20 September 1783, records his death on the second page: 'On Saturday [Sunday] last died, George Tasburgh, of Bodney, in this county, Esq. He was very much respected by his tenants and neighbours, and truly esteemed by all within the circle of his acquaintance, as as [*sic*] a polite gentleman and good landlord'. After his death, as noted in I. The Manuscript above, Bodney Hall was leased from 1792 to 1811 to a group of Benedictine nuns from the French community of Montargis who had been forced to flee after the French Revolution.[91] This move was facilitated by another Lady Jerningham (Frances Dillon) and possibly through the family connections of George's second wife.[92]

George Tasburgh's ownership of Add. 2604 is evident only from a note by a later owner, George Bird Burrell. There is no known record of a sale catalogue for books after Tasburgh's death, and his will, which is very detailed in some of its bequests, makes no mention of a library or books.[93] Likewise, only two of the other later extant Tasburgh wills refer to books.[94] Frances

---

[90] As shown by Francis Young, in his discussion of *A Simple Story* (1791) by the contemporary Suffolk novelist, 'Elizabeth Inchbald's "Catholic Novel" and its Local Background', *Recusant History*, 31 (2012–13), 573–92, it was not unheard of for authors to take some plot and character leads from the surrounding families and local circumstances. In particular he cites Inchbald's contacts with the Gage family.

[91] Dominic Aidan Bellenger, *The French Exiled Clergy in the British Isles after 1789: An Historical Introduction and Working List* (Bath: Downside Abbey, 1986), pp. 90–93 with notes on pp. 97–98; Mason, 'Nuns of the Jerningham Letters'; Tonya J. Moutray, *Refugee Nuns, The French Revolution, and British Literature and Culture* (London: Routledge, 2016), pp. 78–83 with notes on p. 89. See also nn. 52 and 53 in I. The Manuscript.

[92] One of the nuns was an aunt of Barbara Tasburgh's new husband, George Crathorne (now Tasburgh); Bellenger, *The French Exiled Clergy in the British Isles after 1789*, pp. 91 and 97 (n. 86). Anne Swinburne was also a Bedingfield descendant and was said to have heard about Bodney via her family's former steward; Mason, 'Nuns of the Jerningham Letters' p. 39 and 72 (n. 27). On arrival the nuns were received by the Prince of Wales (later George IV) and Mrs Fitzherbert, who was the former wife of Barbara's brother, Thomas Fitzherbert (her second husband, who had died in 1781).

[93] For instance, he specifies that his Italian manservant is to have various itemised clothes.

[94] All extant Tasburgh wills from the Flixton and Bodney lines as well as other members of the Tasburgh family living elsewhere for which records are available in London, TNA, Prerogative Court of Canterbury and related Probate Jurisdictions: Will Registers have been examined; also included are those of George Tasburgh's aunt Delariviere Gage

Tasburgh (formerly Neville) decreed in 1724 that the library bequeathed by her late aunt Frances Wintour or Winter (the wife of Thomas Neville) should stay at Holt in Leicestershire for the benefit of the Neville family. This library must have included manuscripts as Frances's signature may be found on fol. 1r of what is now Cambridge, Cambridge University Library, MS Additional 6688, a mid-fifteenth-century Sarum missal; inscriptions show that it belonged in Neville Holt but ultimately was associated with Worcestershire.[95] In 1732 Henry Tasburgh stipulated that in the event of his wife's death and his daughter dying unmarried before the age of twenty-one, his pictures and books were to go to his nephew Francis (George's father) at Bodney, and that the same should apply to his estate. Mary Clare Tasburgh, who is interred in St Pancras Church in London, married Sir Thomas Gerard on 2 July 1749 and died on 27 October 1768, leaving three daughters. It therefore has to be assumed that her father's books did not make their way to Bodney. At any rate this shows that as a family the Tasburghs were not unused to dealing with manuscripts and that Bodney Hall was the sort of

and his cousin Henrietta Havers, and Charlotte Norris, a Benedictine at Bodney Hall. All these below can be traced in the family genealogy, apart from Sara Tasburgh (as a member of the Church of England, she was probably from a different family). The relevant items are (with name, date, and probate date in modern form): Prob 11/157/178 (John Tasburgh; 9 September 1626; 10 February 1629 [1630]); Prob 11/218/191 (Sara Tasburgh; 23 February 1650; 29 August 1651); Prob 11/410/407 (John [Jack] Tasburgh; 7 January 1691 [1692]; 15 July 1692); Prob 11/502/207 (Charles Tasburgh; 3 February 1704 [1705]; 21 June 1708); Prob 11/570/233 (John Tasburgh; 1 November 1698; 24 November [?] 1708 [codicil]; 19 September 1719); Prob 11/580/439 (Margaret Tasburgh; 26 November 1720; 12 July 1721); Prob 11/598/344 (Frances Tasburgh; 27 June 1724; 28 June 1724 [codicil]; 20 July 1724); Prob 11/666/143 (Richard Tasburgh; 18 March 1728 [1729]; 17 July 1734); Prob 11/685/342 (Lettice Wybarne; 5 March 1736 [1737]; 28 June 1737 [codicil]; 20 October 1737); Prob 11/687/74 (Henry Tasburgh; 27 September 1732; 10 January 1737 [1738]); 28 June 1737 [codicil]; 20 October 1737); Prob 11/738/379 (Susanna Tasburgh; 5 December 1741; 20 March 1744 [1745]); Prob 11/750/399 (Delariviere Gage; 28 March 1744; 7 November 1746); Prob 11/753/353 (Francis Tasburgh; 14 September 1744; 27 June 1746 [codicil]; 24 March 1746 [1747]); Prob 11/1082/80 (Teresa Tasburgh; 6 May 1770; 10 September 1781); Prob 11/1110/108 (George Tasburgh; 12 November 1782; 8 November 1783); Prob 11/1290/88 (Henrietta Havers; 11 February 1795; 9 May 1797); and Prob 11/1368/84 (Charlotte Norris; 30 October 1801; 9 January 1802). For the only references to books in their wills, see below.

[95] Paul Binski, Patrick Zutshi, and Stella Panayotova, *Western Illuminated Manuscripts: A Catalogue of the Collection in Cambridge University Library* (Cambridge: Cambridge University Press, 2011), item 242 (p. 226) and Plate LXXXI (between pp. 230 and 231).

GEORGE TASBURGH IN THE EIGHTEENTH CENTURY   143

place where books and paintings might naturally belong. Although far from
the grandeur of the extant Hengrave Hall, the available evidence for Bodney
Hall (sold in 1821 and demolished by 1896), would suggest a relatively fine,
if modest, house.[96] Yet it must have been relatively commodious to accommodate later the nuns of Montargis (of which there were said to have been over
thirty) as well as the schoolchildren they housed. In the 1807 description of
the depopulated village of Bodney by Blomefield it is noted that 'The manor-
house stands near the church, and is a large convenient old house built of
clunch, stone, &c. with good gardens and walks adjoining to the river side'.[97]
The house, which must have dated from the sixteenth or seventeenth century, was on the same site as a medieval manor owned by Thetford Priory;
it appears on William Faden's county map of 1797.[98] A drawing from 1812
made by Maria Augusta Roselia (d. 1844), the only child of George's second
wife with her second husband, depicts a two-storey house set in a small park
with a couple of other buildings adjacent. It has a central porch with five windows either side on both levels plus a number of attic windows, a depiction
supported by the details of the house sale.[99]

Books or no books (a matter to which we shall return), we have in George
Tasburgh's family the most promising clues to the earlier provenance of Add.
2604. The potential link between the Tasburghs and one putative medieval
convent takes us back through the generations to the beginning of the family's
history in South Elmham in north-east Suffolk.

[96] The dates are in *The Recollections of a Northumbrian Lady, 1815–1866*, ed. by Charlton,
pp. 31 and 59–60.

[97] Blomefield, *An Essay Towards a Topographical History of the County of Norfolk [...]*, VI
(1807), 17.

[98] The site is described briefly in Tom Williamson, Ivan Ringwood, and Sarah Spooner,
Lost Country Houses of Norfolk: History, Archaeology and Myth (Woodbridge: Boydell, 2015),
pp. 99–100.

[99] Bellenger, *The French Exiled Clergy in the British Isles after 1789*, p. 91. In 1785 the sale
notice for the house carried by various newspapers such as the *Morning Chronicle* for Thursday,
28 April 1785, list a hall, drawing room, dining room, tea-room, study, six master-bedrooms
and so forth 'with other convenient rooms for a gentleman's family', and including coach
houses, stabling for sixteen horses, 'a pleasure garden', and a kitchen garden. As noted in n. 44 of
1. The Manuscript, a furniture sale is recorded for April 1788.

The Tasburghs: A Recusant Family in Suffolk and Norfolk

It is not known precisely when the Tasburghs settled in South Elmham.[100] The most certain records date from the mid-fifteenth century in the time of John Tasburgh and his wife Margery both of whom left wills in 1473 and 1485, the years of their respective deaths. There are mentions of books in both wills but nothing that equates with Add. 2604.[101] More is known of their son, John Tasburgh II (d. 1509), who left an account book with a draft of his will dated 27 March 1507.[102] His son was John Tasburgh III (d. 1552) whose son was John Tasbugh IV (1533–1607) who in turn also had a son named John (1576–1629). There are no books listed in the account book or the inventory of the goods of Jane Tasburgh in Norwich drawn up on 16 December 1613.[103] It was during the time of John III that Flixton Priory was acquired, a convent that had clearly been dear to the family as John II in his draft will had bequeathed 13s and 4d for its repair.[104] Following its surrender on 4 February 1537, Flixton

---

[100] The early detailed history of the family is given in Evans, 'The Tasburghs of South Elmham'; to avoid confusion between the numerous Tasburghs named John, Evans's mode of referencing by number is adopted. The will of the fifteenth-century John Tasburgh is briefly discussed in Colin Richmond, *John Hopton: A Fifteenth Century Suffolk Gentleman* (Cambridge: Cambridge University Press, 1981), pp. 201–04; see also Colin Richmond, 'The Advent of the Tasburghs: A Documentary Study in the Adair Family Collection', *Common Knowledge*, 20. 2 (2014), 296–336.

[101] Norwich, Norfolk Record Office, Norwich Consistory Court Probate Records: Wills, Will Register, Gelour 27 and Will Register, Hubert 72 respectively. Richmond, 'The Advent of the Tasburghs', gives a detailed account of both wills (with some transcription) on pp. 306–08 and 309–11; noted here are bequests by John to Flixton church (St Mary's) of 'a manuel and a processionari [...]'x qwayers of a grayle redy wretyn' (p. 306), and 'my best portewos a grayel A processionari With a primer ' (p. 307), while Margery asks that an antiphoner 'be bought at my coste' (p. 309) for St Peter's Church in South Elmham, and also bequeaths to others her 'masse bookes' (p. 309) and her 'best primer' (p. 310). We have no idea where the Tasburghs might have acquired these books or indeed what influence if any Edward Tasburgh (John and Margery's son) might have had on their acquisition or production. He graduated in Canon Law from Cambridge in 1479, became rector of Barningham in 1481 and vicar of Assington (both in Suffolk) in 1494 which then became vacant by February 1513. These dates would be appropriate for the production of Add. 2604, but there is no evidence otherwise that would link him to the manuscript. For his biography, see A. B. Emden, *A Biographical Register of the University of Cambridge to 1500* (Cambridge: Cambridge University Press, 1963), p. 577.

[102] Suffolk Archives, Ipswich, The Hold, 741/HA12/Unlisted 85.

[103] Suffolk Archives, Ipswich, The Hold, 741/HA12/Unlisted 17.

[104] Suffolk Archives, Ipswich, The Hold, 741/HA12/Unlisted 85.

was leased to the former steward Richard Warton (or Wharton) on 10 July 1537 and then acquired for £988 by John Tasburgh III in 1544.[105] Nesta Evans notes that 'It is not clear when the Tasburghs moved from St Peter's Hall [their original house in South Elmham] to Flixton Abbey, nor how long they lived at the latter before building or enlarging Flixton Hall', but goes on to speculate how the addition 'of the ecclesiastical windows, porch and flushwork panels' to St Peter's Hall must date from building work carried out in 1539 and that these features must have derived from Flixton Priory; these features of the well-preserved St Peter's Hall (Figure 22) include a stained glass window depicting St Katherine (the dedicatee of the Priory).[106] The later Flixton Hall (separate from St Peter's Hall and Flixton Priory), which may have been a rebuilding or enlargement of a pre-existing house, dates either during the time of John Tasburgh IV or his son.[107] (See Figure 23 for St Mary's Church, Flixton, where many of the Tasburghs are interred.)

Probably one of the most important people for the history of the family's fortunes in the post-Dissolution period was the wife of the fifth John, Lettice Cressy, whom he married in 1593/4. Lettice was the daughter of James Cressy, who had married Jane West, the daughter of William West, Lord de la Warr. Jane subsequently married Thomas Tasburgh, the half-brother of her son-in-law, John Tasburgh (Lettice's husband); her first husband was Thomas Wenman and her fourth and final spouse, Ralph Sheldon. John Tasburgh was knighted by James I at the Charterhouse in London in 1603 and built up his fortune

---

[105] 'Houses of Austin Nuns: The Priory of Flixton', in *The Victoria History of the County of Norfolk*, ed. by Doubleday and Page, II (1906), 117 and B. Gordon Blackwood, *Tudor and Stuart Suffolk* (Lancaster: Carnegie Publishing, 2001), p. 316.

[106] Evans, 'The Tasburghs of South Elmham', pp. 270–71, who speculates that the Tasburghs may have acquired these materials from Richard Warton (or Wharton) before they owned the building. All that remains of Flixton Priory is a length of wall and some fabric in Abbey Farm; Gilchrist and Oliva, *Religious Women in Medieval East Anglia*, p. 91. St Peter's Hall is described in E. Farrer, 'St. Peter's Hall, South Elmham', *Proceedings of the Suffolk Institute of Archæology and Natural History*, 20 (1930), 48–72, with illustrations on unnumbered pages adjacent to pp. 48, 56, and 57. St Peter's Hall, with its many ecclesiastical features, is well preserved; it currently functions as a restaurant and special events venue together with St Peter's Brewery. We are very grateful to the former owner of St Peter's Hall, for kindly facilitating a guided tour of the building in September 2018.

[107] Evans, 'The Tasburghs of South Elmham', pp. 274–76, deals with the intricaces of the building of Flixton Hall. Its later grand expansions when it was owned by the Adair family and subsequent demolition in 1952/3 are detailed (with illustrations) in W. M. Roberts, *Lost Country Houses of Suffolk* (Woodbridge: Boydell, 2010), pp. 271–75.

in Suffolk. He and Lettice produced a family of thirteen children.[108] Most importantly for the history of the Tasburghs, Lettice was a Catholic and so was responsible for ultimately bringing the family back to the Catholic faith of their medieval forebears. In the tussle for their children's souls, Sir John's endeavours to keep his family on the straight road to Protestantism failed abysmally. The greatest trial was over the future of a daughter (apparently his first-born girl, Jane). This is recorded both in Sir John's own words in a damaged and an undated letter and in the Chronicle of St Monica's in Louvain/Leuven. In the former some rift is highlighted when Sir John comments that he is not angry at his daughter for her non-attendance at church or with Lady Lettice for persuading her not to attend.[109] In the latter the situation is presented as being akin to the sort of struggle that the virgin martyr Barbara had with her enraged father in Add. 2604. In a lengthy and dramatic section of the Chronicle it is noted how she was Sir John's oldest and most beloved child, how she fell in love with a French Catholic who was then banned from Sir John's house, while he tried to get her to renounce her religion by promising her half his estate — clearly an idle promise as the estate would have been destined for the oldest son.

> But seeing that no fair means prevailed, he was very angry, and determined by severity to make her yield unto his will. Whereupon, one day he called her to him, in the presence of her mother, and was so sharp and wrathful with her that, at last, he said he would cut her tongue out of her head if she spoke one word more in defence of her religion, and would not renounce the same. But for all that she would not yield, whereupon he turned her away, bidding her to depart from him and never to expect one penny from him, as though she were not his child. This happened upon St Agnes's day [21 January], which made her afterwards take the name of Agnes at her profession.[110]

---

[108] Young, 'The Tasburghs of Flixton and Catholicism in North-East Suffolk, 1642–1767', p. 456, but 'Cherleine' should be 'Katherine' as noted in John Tasburgh's will made in 1626 (Prob 11/157/178); Jane is omitted from the will as she had already been professed in Louvain/Leuven. Plate 16 in Andrew Moore and Charlotte Crawley, *Family and Friends: A Regional Survey of British Portraiture* (London: HMSO, 1992), p. 18 (with discussion on p. 83) shows a painting of the British School of *c.* 1615–16 of Lettice with four of her daughters and two sons (Charles and Cressy).

[109] Suffolk Archives, Ipswich, The Hold, 741/HA12/Unlisted 76.

[110] *The Chronicle of the English Augustinian Canonesses Regular of the Lateran, at St Monica's in Louvain (Now at St Augustine's Priory, Newton Abbot, Devon) 1548 to 1625*, ed. by Adam Hamilton (Edinburgh: Sands and Co., 1904), pp. 255–56 (p. 256).

THE TASBURGHS: A RECUSANT FAMILY IN SUFFOLK AND NORFOLK 147

The account goes on to tell how she lived secretly in the house and spent a hard Lent subsisting on the skins or heads of herring until her grandmother (Jane Tasburgh) sent for her (to Norwich), saw that she had a vocation, provided her with resources, and arranged for her to go to Dr (Matthew) Kellison, the President of the English College. The account concludes:

> He provided her place here in our cloister because she would not be at Douay with her cousin, for that she lived then in an open monastery not enclosed. And so she came hither, and after her time of probation made her holy profession at the age of twenty-five years, changing her name to Agnes.[111]

This no doubt embellished account of Sister Agnes's journey to profession as an Augustinian on 31 July 1622/3 is contextualised somewhat by earlier comments on Sir John 'who was a hot Protestant, but her mother [Lettice] was a good Catholic, and daughter to the old Lady Tasburgh [Jane], also a good Catholic'.[112] After a long section on Jane Tasburgh's charity and piety, the matter is returned to again triumphally just before the confrontational scene above:

> Her daughter [Lettice Cressy] also was a good Catholic, but her husband, Sir John, a most perverse heretic, yet he permitted his wife to keep her religion, but would have all his children to be brought up in heresy. Yet Almighty God ordained so well that in time they all came to be Catholic, except only one daughter, who, having been converted as the others, yet by her husband was perverted again.[113]

---

[111] *The Chronicle of the English Augustinian Canonesses Regular of the Lateran*, ed. by Hamilton, p. 256.

[112] *The Chronicle of the English Augustinian Canonesses Regular of the Lateran*, ed. by Hamilton, p. 253. Sister Agnes's time in the convent of St Monica's in Louvain/Leuven also has its tumults. In 1635 during the siege of the city when the seventy-one nuns were split into two, with one party staying in the convent and the other leaving, she was one of the nuns who left to take refuge at Nazareth in Bruges; see Victoria Van Hyning, *Convent Autobiography: Early Modern English Nuns in Exile*, British Academy Monographs (Oxford: Oxford University Press for the British Academy, 2019), pp. 130–32, including Table 1 on pp. 131–32, in which her name is listed (p. 131). It is noteworthy that alongside her were the daughters of some other eminent Catholic families in East Anglia: Augustina Bedingfield, Christina Jerningham, and Grace Bedingfield (p. 131).

[113] *The Chronicle of the English Augustinian Canonesses Regular of the Lateran*, ed. by Hamilton, p. 255.

Later Sir John sent his sons Charles and Cressy to Christ's College Cambridge under the tutelage of the erudite Hebraist and biblical scholar Joseph Mede [Mead] (1586–1638) where they stayed from 1626 to 1628.[114] Yet after his father's death, Charles became a confirmed Catholic and in 1631–32 Lettice sent the next two sons, Peregrine and John [Jack], to be educated at the English College in Douai.

From then on the family continued to uphold the Catholic faith and as a consequence suffered the usual deprivations and investigations that were the lot of Catholic households until liberated fully by the Catholic Emancipation Act of 1829.[115] Overall the Tasburghs managed reasonably well to survive Parliamentarian sequestrations, the Popish Plot of 1678, and the 1688 Revolution. They exercised as much influence in their wider communities as their recusancy would allow as well as establishing the only Benedictine mission in the country in 1657, a mission that is still in existence via the monks of Downside Abbey, the successors of St Gregory's, Douai.[116] But, for the want of male heirs, the Tasburghs did not last until 1829. The Flixton estate passed from generation to generation until the last male heir, George Tasburgh (not our manuscript owner), died in 1736 without living male issue; the estate passed to his sister Leticia Wybarne who died in 1737. The only male heir being a Benedictine monk (her son, Henry Wybarne), Leticia bequeathed the estate to her daughter Charity Wybarne; it was then sold by the latter's executors after her death in 1752/3 — ironically — to the Protestant Adair family from Ballymena in Co. Antrim in Ireland.[117] The second family line in Bodney had been started when Cressy Tasburgh bought the manor from Edward Mostyn from Flintshire in the mid to late 1650s; dying before 1662 without offspring, his brother John [Jack] inherited and so began the Bodney family line. Jack's son, John Beaumont Tasburgh, inherited the estate on the death of his father in 1692; in turn his son Francis took over the estate that was bequeathed to

---

[114] In his account book, Cambridge, Christ's College, Archives, T.11.3, Mead details the boys' expenses, including their reading materials; for references to the Tasburgh sons, see fols 81v–85v and 97r–98v. We are very grateful to Lucy Hughes for help with this reference.

[115] These are fully described in Young, 'The Tasburghs of Flixton and Catholicism in North-East Suffolk', 1642–1767', and Young, 'The Tasburghs of Bodney'.

[116] The complex narrative of this mission is told in Young, 'The Tasburghs of Flixton and Catholicism in North-East Suffolk, 1642–1767', pp. 462–67, who notes that the monks [formerly of Downside Abbey] serve the Catholic churches of Beccles and Bungay (p. 466).

[117] Prob 11/685/342 (Lettice Wybarne; 5 March 1736 [1737]; 28 June 1737 [codicil]; 20 October 1737).

ADD. 2604 AND ITS PROVENANCE

149

George (the owner of Add. 2604) on the death of Francis in 1747.[118] During George's lifetime there is evidence from 1762 of various Jesuit chaplains at Bodney, and after his death, as seen above, Bodney Hall was inhabited by Benedictine nuns.[119] And so we come full circle.

Add. 2604 and its Provenance

It would make sense to assume that when the Tasburghs came into the possession of Flixton Priory in 1544, they also inherited any books associated with the convent in the same way as they appeared to have helped their own building programme from the abbey's physical remains. Choosing Flixton as the home of Add. 2604 is an easy solution to the provenance problem. Yet, looked at objectively in the light of the other evidence above, Flixton is not one of the front runners for the location of Add. 2604. Although it had one known book and was in a relatively good spiritual state at the Dissolution, it was also the poorest convent in East Anglia, with an income of £23 4s. 1½d. in the *Valor Ecclesiasticus* in contrast to the richest, Campsey Ash, at £182 9s. 5d.[120] While poverty in itself is not a barrier to book ownership as volumes may be donated or inherited and many convents acquired their books in this fashion, there are few positive reasons why Flixton, an Augustinian house far away from the cult centre of the saints at Ely, might have been the expected home for Add. 2604. While it is not clear when precisely in the sixteenth century the Tasburghs began to incline towards Protestantism, there is definite evidence of John Tasburgh IV's Puritanism.[121] In view of this, the family might or might not have prized a medieval book of saints' lives from Flixton nunnery had one been found there. Enticing therefore as the possibility of Flixton convent is as the locale of Add. 2604, it is salutary to think of other options in terms of the Tasburgh ownership.

[118] Prob 11/410/407 (John [Jack] Tasburgh; 7 January 1691 [1692]; 15 July 1692); Prob 11/753/353 (Francis Tasburgh; 14 September 1744; 27 June 1746 [codicil]; 24 March 1746 [1747]). In Jack Tasburgh's will Bodney is not mentioned; we do not have the will of John Beaumont Tasburgh.

[119] For the Jesuits, see Young, 'The Tasburghs of Bodney', p. 196 with notes on p. 198.

[120] 'Houses of Austin Nuns: The Priory of Campsey' and 'Houses of Austin Nuns: The Priory of Flixton', in *The Victoria History of the County of Suffolk*, ed. by Page, II (1907), 112–15 (p. 114), and pp. 115–17 (p. 116).

[121] Evans, 'The Tasburghs of South Elmham', pp. 271–72.

Given that there were two branches of the family, one in St Peter South Elmham in Suffolk and one in Bodney in Norfolk, the manuscript could have been acquired originally by either side of the family at any time (with the Catholic Lettice Cressy, the wife of the fifth John, being an obvious potential source). In building the picture it is hard to know what to make of details that may be totally incidental.[122] Even serendipitous discoveries may lead nowhere. For example, in a will that was made on 4 February 1445 by John Tolle of South Elmham (who sold property to the first John Tasburgh that enabled him to establish himself in St Peter South Elmham), there is a bequest to St Peter's Church of a book described as 'unum librum integrum vocat. an hool legende'.[123] The mention of 'integrum' and 'hool' are particularly intriguing given the current imperfect state of Add. 2604, as is the fact that John's daughter Ellen was a nun in Flixton convent. Yet this cannot be our manuscript as the date is too early.

Like the Flixton Tasburghs, the family in Bodney also had an interest in acquiring dissolved monasteries. The first of the Bodney line, Jack Tasburgh, took over the lease of Cong Abbey in County Mayo in Ireland in 1667.[124] This is not to imply that the manuscript came from there, an unsustainable idea given the prevalence of Irish rather than English in that part of the country. But it shows an interest in an earlier Catholic past, even if this were more on the grounds of financial return than piety. And there are other ways by which Add. 2604 may have entered the family. As seen from its history above, the Tasburghs were patrons of missionary activity and they themselves bred sufficient numbers for the religious orders down through the years to have acquired a manuscript like Add. 2604, including George's two sisters who would have lived at Bodney before their mother's death and their guardianship with Lady Jerningham. It was also a family linked to a local network of similar Catholic gentry either through family, marriage, or friendship, as noted above: the Bedingfields in Oxburgh Hall a few miles west of Bodney; the Gages in

---

[122] For example, Jane Tasburgh (the wife of Thomas Tasburgh and mother of Lettice Cressy and also of the poet Richard Wenman from her first marriage) was the dedicatee of a work by William Basse. In Add. 2604 one of the items is *A helpe to discovrse*, another work mistakenly attributed to Basse. This could imply that Jane Tasburgh had been the source of the original print that led to the later manuscript copy in Add. 2604 rather than, in all probability, the later compiler George Bird Burrell; see I. The Manuscript above.

[123] Suffolk Archives, Ipswich, The Hold, 741/HA12/B2/6/1, discussed by Richmond, 'The Advent of the Tasburghs', pp. 301–02 (p. 302).

[124] Young, 'The Tasburghs of Bodney', pp. 192–93.

ADD. 2604 AND ITS PROVENANCE

Hengrave Hall just north of Bury St Edmunds and directly south of Bodney; the Havers in Thelveton near Diss in south Norfolk, just over the Suffolk border; the Jerninghams in Costessey Hall just north-east of Norwich, and later the Throckmortons of Coughton Court in Warwickshire. With the possible exception of the last family (on dialectal grounds), the manuscript could have ended up with the Tasburghs via any of these contacts. The document repository of the Gages was in the evidence room in Hengrave Hall.[125] And the Gage family of Coldham Hall also had an extensive library as seen in the bibliography begun in 1737 by Elizabeth Rookwood (1684–1759).[126] Included was a book of hours probably produced in the 1460s in Bruges that is still extant as Cambridge, Cambridge University Library, MS 10079.[127] This significantly demonstrates that these were the sort of families who held on to medieval manuscripts. They were also the type of people with close family connections to the Tasburghs as both George Tasburgh's aunt, Delariviere D'Ewes, and his first wife's sister, Charlotte Gage, had married into the Gage family of Hengrave Hall. If acquired through any of these means, in theory Add. 2604 could have come from anywhere in the East Anglian region or beyond. In reality, if it came directly into the Tasburgh family of Bodney itself or via the Bedingfields or Gages, it would make more sense for it to have come from somewhere in the local area. And, if this were the case, the nearest convents to Bodney were Marham and Shouldham to the north-west and Thetford to the south-east.

In the analysis above, neither the Cistercian Marham nor the Gilbertine Shouldham stood out. It is hard to see what a relatively ornate manuscript like Add. 2604 would have been doing in Marham, even if it was dedicated to Barbara, and Marham has no surviving manuscripts by which to judge its normal standards. Admittedly, as a double monastery, Shouldham would have had the brothers on hand to translate and/or write out Add. 2604 and it was the second richest convent in the region, with a value of £138 18s. 1d. in the

---

[125] *Rookwood Family Papers, 1606–1761*, ed. by Francis Young, Suffolk Records Society, 59 (Woodbridge, Boydell: 2016), p. xiv, where it is noted that the contents of Hengrave Hall were sold in 1952 and that papers and documents are either held at the Suffolk County Record Office (now Suffolk Archives) or Cambridge University Library.

[126] *Rookwood Family Papers, 1606–1761*, ed. by Young, pp. xlvi–l and 61–93.

[127] Francis Young, 'Early Modern English Catholic Piety in a Fifteenth-Century Book of Hours: Cambridge University Library MS Additional 10079', *Transactions of the Cambridge Bibliographical Society*, 15 (2015), 541–59.

Valor Ecclesiasticus and so could have financed a decorative manuscript.[128] But problems remain: no manuscripts survive from Shouldham so there is no basis on which to judge the nuns' usual reading material and one also wonders why Gilbertine nuns would have owned a manuscript of Benedictine saints.

These problems do not apply to the Benedictine convent of Thetford which, albeit not a wealthy house with a valuation of £40 11*s.* 2½*d.* at the Dissolution, was in a good position both geographically and otherwise to be the home of Add. 2604. Several of its advantages have already been highlighted above: a close association with Bury St Edmunds that could have provided both the scribe for the manuscript and more particularly the source material for the translation of the native saints; its relative proximity to the cult centre at Ely; and the known devotion in the town of Thetford to Æthelthryth (and her smock). In addition, the Cluniac Priory in Thetford was said to have held not only Æthelthryth's coffin but also relics of Barbara and Leonard, both of whom figure in Add. 2604.[129] Oxborough Church, near Bodney and the family seat of the Bedingfields, was dedicated to John the Evangelist and had representations of him, John the Baptist, Wihtburh, and Æthelthryth on its panels.[130] As noted, the Thetford convent figured in a number of Bury wills. It is of interest too that Thetford itself also had Austin Friars, Augustinian Canons, Dominicans, a secular college, a range of hospitals, and numerous parish clergy so there were plenty of religious, in addition to any convent chaplains, Bury monks, or local secular priests, to render spiritual guidance to the nuns or provide written material for them. If the estimation of the language in Add. 2604 is correct, then Thetford would be a perfectly fine locale for a production that is not only in a broadly Suffolk dialect, but one that seems to bear some affinity with the area around Bury St Edmunds (fully discussed in II. Language and Dialectal Provenance).[131] Given what is known of the nuns' surviving books, the saints' lives in Add. 2604 would have been most appropriate for the Thetford nuns. It

---

[128] 'House of Gilbertines: The Priory of Shouldham', in *The Victoria History of the County of Norfolk*, ed. by Doubleday and Page, II (1906), 412–14 (p. 413).

[129] Nichols, *The Early Art of Norfolk,* pp. 167, 192, and 211.

[130] W. W. Williamson, 'Saints on Norfolk Rood-Screens and Pulpits', *Norfolk Archæology: Or Miscellaneous Tracts Relating to the Antiquities of the County of Norfolk*, Norfolk and Norwich Archæological Society, 31 (1957), 299–346 (p. 335).

[131] Although manuscripts can clearly move beyond their dialectal area, they can also remain locally. For instance, as noted previously, two manuscripts owned by nuns in Campsey Ash, London, British Library, MS Arundel 396 and Cambridge, Corpus Christi College, MS 268, are both localised near Campsey Ash in LPs 8380 and 8390; see LALME, III, 486–87.

ADD. 2604 AND ITS PROVENANCE

would have taken its place alongside an English translation of the *Revelations* of St Birgitta of Sweden bequeathed by Margaret Purdauns (or Spurdaunce) in her 1481 will and the Wycliffite New Testament (in Alnwick Castle) owned by Katherina Methwold, who was recorded as a Thetford nun between the visitations of 12 November 1492 and 22 November 1514 (when she was sub-prioress). In these visitations themselves there was no cause for concern apart from the note about their poverty in 1520.[132] Some care was also taken about the repair of books in 1514 and the nuns themselves would appear to have been trying to uphold educational standards according to their own lights.[133]

Thetford was also in the vicinity of wealthy patrons such as Anne Harling (succcessively married to Sir William Chamberlain, Sir Robert Wingfield, and Lord Scrope of Bolton) from East Harling. In her will in 1498 she made various charitable bequests to numerous monastic foundations such as Thetford and other convents, and was a lay sister at many of them, including Syon Abbey.[134] She, in common with other prominent East Anglian patrons like John Clopton of Long Melford (who was also part of the Syon lay confraternity), could have been a conduit for Birgittine spirituality. This might go some way to explaining source connections between Add. 2604 and the Sankt Georgen manuscript mentioned above (and discussed further in V. Latin Sources and Analogues). All told, the production of a manuscript like Add. 2604 for this convent or its presentation to this convent would not be a stretch too far.

Truthfully, there is no proof one way or another for the hypothesis that Add. 2604 may have originated in the Thetford convent and come to Bodney Hall. The house was dissolved in 1537 when it was leased to Sir Richard Fulmerston of Ipswich who obtained it outright in 1540. In his will and codicil of 24

---

[132] *Visitations of the Diocese of Norwich, A.D. 1492–1532*, ed. by Jessopp, p. 155.

[133] *Visitations of the Diocese of Norwich, A.D. 1492–1532*, ed. by Jessopp, pp. 90–91, where Sister Sara Frost noted — and was supported by Elizabeth Hoth (who became prioress later) — 'quod priorissa intendit recipere brevi in moniales indoctas personas et deformes et præsertim Dorotheam Sturges generosam surdam et deformen' (p. 90).

[134] *Testamenta eboracensia: A Selection of Wills from the Registry at York*, ed. by James Raine and John William Clay, Publications of the Surtees Society, 6 vols, 4, 30, 45, 53, 79, and 106 (London: J. B. Nichols and Son; and other publishers and places, 1836–1902), IV (1869), 149–54; Gibson, *The Theater of Devotion*, pp. 96–106 and passim. Various studies exist of Anne Harling's devotional collection, the finely executed London, British Library, MS Harley 4012, dating from *c.* 1460 with its prose lives of Katherine of Alexandria and Margaret, and verse life of Anne; see, for example, Anne M. Dutton, 'Piety, Politics and Persona: MS Harley 4012 and Anne Harling', in *Prestige, Authority and Power in Late Medieval Manuscripts and Texts*, ed. by Felicity Riddy (Woodbridge: York Medieval Press, 2000), pp. 133–46.

January 1566 [1567] probated on 21 November 1567 he left what he called 'my chief mansion howse at Thetforde', which was presumably the church convent (noted below), to his daughter Frances and her husband Edward Clere, a Member of Parliament who subsequently inherited Blickling.[135] Although Fulmerston ordered an inventory of his goods to be made, and gave gold chains to his son-in-law and his daughter, there is no mention of any books. But, as noted, books are rarely listed in wills. The property then descended down through the Clere family.

After the rupture of the Dissolution and the sale or demolition of monastic buildings, books — in common with the religious themselves — were left to chance. As noted by Andrew Watson, 'Given lack of instructions from above, no care was taken of the contents of the libraries [...] the books were left to a variety of fates — occasionally swift removal by some departing religious to elsewhere in the neighbourhood, more often theft, perhaps worst of all total neglect by abandonment in the completely or partly destroyed buildings'.[136] Significantly some of the buildings of Thetford convent were still standing more or less intact in the eighteenth century. In 1805 it is noted in Blomefield's Norfolk history:

> At the Dissolution, this monastery did not suffer so much as the generality of them did; the church was a large one, and when Sir *Rich. Fulmerston* came to dwell here, it was turned into lodgings, and other convenient rooms; Sir *Edward Clere* new regulated the western front of the house, and opened a passage into the road, after which it assumed the present name of the *Place*; but the whole monastery remained till the year 1737, without much alteration [...].[137]

The writer goes on to say that in 1738, though still standing, the church had become a barn, and the monastery demolished with a new farmhouse by the site. More surprisingly still, he notes:

> The chest in which the *nuns* evidences were kept stood lately in the *Long Gallery* or *Ambulatory*, which was a fine room, of a great length, extending through the

---

[135] London, TNA, Prerogative Court of Canterbury and related Probate Jurisdictions: Will Registers, Prob 11/49/348.

[136] Andrew G. Watson, *Medieval Manuscripts in Post-Medieval England*, Variorum Collected Studies Series (Aldershot: Ashgate, 2004), p. xvi.

[137] Blomefield, *An Essay Towards a Topographical History of the County of Norfolk [...]*, II (1805), 93. Martin, *The History of the Town of Thetford*, attaches plates to his chapter (pp. 98–111) depicting grave-stones from the convent and the building in the first half of the eighteenth century (between pp. 110 and 111).

ADD. 2604 AND ITS PROVENANCE

whole building, facing the court on the north side, the west window surveyed the fields, and the east their pleasant grove, fish-ponds, and river: it had two or three chimneys on the south side, and a fine view all the way up the river to *Bernham*; but this was spoiled by the small lodging rooms that were made the whole length of it in Sir *Edward's* time.[138]

It is not always easy to map Blomefield's history exactly on to later archaeological reports, but there is a broad consensus. It appears that Fulmerston converted the church to a house called The Place. This was replaced in *c.* 1610 by another house, and at this point the church became a barn (one its many uses). Later still, at some point in *c.* 1740, another house was built which remains today. As noted in one of the archaeological reports:

> Later structures include the former gateway to the post-Dissolution mansion, now isolated in a field to the west, Nunnery House (probably 18th century, though possibly earlier) and Nunnery Cottages (late 16th century, extended in the mid-19th century).[139]

The important point is that the convent had not disappeared from view in earlier times. Indeed, remnants of it are still in existence today in The Nunnery across Nuns Bridges in Thetford. Here part of the original church, with a nave of *c.* 140 feet/40 metres long running east-west and lacking aisles, is clearly visible (Figure 24) alongside other features of the later dwelling houses.[140]

In the centuries after the Reformation various efforts were made to find, disseminate, and study the literature that was lost. This was aided by the rise of auction houses in the late seventeenth century and in the industry of clerical non-juror book collectors like Thomas Baker (1656–1740), and moneyed men such as James West (d. 1772), quite apart from nobility like Robert Harley

---

[138] Blomefield, *An Essay Towards a Topographical History of the County of Norfolk [...]*, II (1805), 94.

[139] Phil Andrews, 'St George's Nunnery, Thetford', *Norfolk Archaeology: A Journal of Archaeology and Local History*, 41 (1993), 427–40 (p. 427). Alongside seven modern archaeological figures, four plates depicting engravings of parts of the nunnery are reproduced from drawings by Joseph Wilkinson, *The Architectural Remains of the Ancient Town and Borough of Thetford in the Counties of Norfolk and Suffolk* (London: Rodwell and Martin, 1822).

[140] The Nunnery is currently home to the British Trust for Ornithology (BTO) where there is also a wildlife site, Nunnery Lakes Reserve. We are very grateful to the archivist of the BTO, Lesley Hindley, for kindly giving us a guided tour of the buildings in July 2022, and for making available documentary and pictorial material about their history, including the useful leaflet by Chris Mead, and for faciliating the digital image used in Figure 24.

(1661–1724).[141] East Anglia, particularly Norfolk, was singularly blessed in the sort of people who had a vested interest in uncovering the archival past. These included scholars of national importance like Simonds D'Ewes (1602–50), Peter Le Neve (1661–1729), Thomas Tanner (1674–1735), Thomas Martin (1697–1771), Francis Blomefield (1705–52), and John Fenn (1739–94). In addition, there were more local figures such as Charles Parkin (1689–1765), rector of Oxborough, and George Burton (*c.* 1717–91), rector of Elveden and Herringswell near Bodney, who made a list of the lives in Add. 2604 (discussed in I. The Manuscript).[142] Manuscripts moved — sometimes dramatically so — and their history over time could be random, but they might also remain for centuries prized in their own areas. In addition to the factors above, what makes a location in Thetford an attractive proposition is that it would seem to fit into a later pattern. Until its acquistion by the Duke of Sussex in 1826, Add. 2604 had passed from one Thetford owner to another (if Bodney can be considered part of Thetford). While the putative history of the early transmission of Add. 2604 before its acquisition by George Tasburgh or George Tasburgh's family cannot be reconstructed, it may well be that it had stayed in the Thetford area from its inception.[143]

Add. 2604 may have had a home in any of the convents that were seen to have a particular claim, Campsey Ash, Chatteris, Denney, Flixton (acquired by the South Elmham Tasburghs), Ickleton, our favoured Thetford (near the Bodney Tasburghs), or elsewhere. In any case at the end of the fifteenth century some-

---

[141] For a very useful overview of the period, see Nigel Ramsay, 'English Book Collectors and the Salerooms in the Eighteenth Century', in *Under the Hammer: Book Auctions since the Seventeenth Century*, ed. by Robin Myers, Michael Harris, and Giles Mandelbrote (New Castle, DE; London: Oak Knoll Press and The British Library, 2001), pp. 89–110.

[142] The activities of most of these are dealt with in 'The Antiquaries' by Barbara Green in Nichols, *The Early Art of Norfolk*, pp. 286–88.

[143] It may be significant that the last prioress of Thetford, Elizabeth Hoth (the person careful about educational standards in the convent), was still alive in 1553. She is described to the royal commissioners as '*Eliz. Hooth*, of the age of an hundredth years, and now dwelling in the parish of St. *James* in *Norwich*, prioress of the late priory of *Thetford*, liveth continentlie, and hath a pention of 5*l.* paid her yearly, at *Norwich* and *Bury*, at two terms in the year by even portions, and hath nothing to live upon but the same pention, and is reputed a good and catholick woman'; see Blomefield, *An Essay on the Topographical History of Norfolk [...]*, II (1805), 92. In the event that she had taken books from the convent, her longevity and her enduring Catholicism might have helped to ensure their survival. This is something that may also be said for many other East Anglian nuns some of whom lived for several decades after the Dissolution; see Oliva, *The Convent and the Community*, pp. 190–92.

where in East Anglia, certain nuns had at their disposal what today might seem at first sight a somewhat amorphous collection, with Domitilla who rarely features in the hagiographical landscape, given prominence alongside the universally popular Cecilia and the most famous English female saint, Æthelthryth. This manuscript in its use of material going back to Bede in the eighth century and Goscelin de Saint-Bertin in the twelfth century was effectively from an earlier time. Yet in its more 'contemporary' sources such as the thirteenth-century Jacobus de Voragine and the fourteenth-century John of Tynemouth it was equally of its time. By selecting John of Tynemouth as source, this vernacular compiler was preserving the best of early English traditions and, by translating universal collections such as the *Legenda aurea* and its like, he was positioning himself — and in turn his readers — in the European mainstream. By combining the variant traditions, universal and native, early and late, insular and other, he was making a unique contribution to England's saintly literature. How the Add. 2604 translator achieved this in the context of international and national hagiographic developments in Latin and the vernaculars will be the focus of the next part of this discussion.

IV. Hagiographical Context and the Selection of Saints

'Of all Latin literary genres, the saint's *vita* is the one that is most characteristic of the Middle Ages'[1] and myriads of such texts were copied, recopied, translated, abbreviated, expanded, altered, or printed during this period.[2] Meanwhile a burgeoning tradition of vernacular lives in prose and verse developed at different rates and to varying degrees throughout Europe. Our aim here is to show how the lives in Add. 2604, both universal and native, fit into this picture, how they reflect Latin and vernacular trends, and, above all, what can be extrapolated about the lives that are selected for inclusion in the manuscript.

[1] Michael Lapidge, 'Editing Hagiography', in *La critica del testo mediolatino: Atti del Convegno (Firenze 6–8 dicembre 1990)*, ed. by Claudio Leonardi, Biblioteca di medioevo latino, 5 (Spoleto: Centro italiano di studi sull'alto medioevo, 1994), pp. 239–57 (p. 239).

[2] Hagiographical bibliography is obviously too extensive for citation here, apart from noting the following. For texts, see *Acta sanctorum [...]*, ed. by the Société des Bollandistes, 67 volumes (Anvers & Bruxelles, and other places, 1643–1940; 3rd edn (Paris and other places: Victor Palmé, 1863–97), for which see further V. Latin Sources and Analogues, especially n. 33. For listings of individual saints, see *Bibliotheca Hagiographica Latina Antiquae et Mediae Aetatis*, ed. by the Société des Bollandistes, 2 vols (Bruxelles: Société des Bollandistes, 1898–1901) and *Bibliotheca Hagiographica Latina Antiquae et Mediae Aetatis: Novum Supplementum*, ed. by Henricus Fros, Subsidia hagiographica, 70 (Bruxelles: Société des Bollandistes, 1986) (hereafter BHL and BHL *Supplementum*). Much work is available in the volumes of *Analecta Bollandiana* and by individual Bollandists such as Hippolyte Delehaye, *Les Légendes hagiographiques*, Subsidia Hagiographica, 18, 4th edn (Bruxelles: Société des Bollandistes, 1955). See also Guy Philippart, *Les Légendiers Latins et autres manuscrits hagiographiques*, Typologie des sources du moyen âge occidental, Fascicles 24–25 (Turnhout: Brepols, 1977), and the follow-up volume with further references, Guy Philippart, *Les Légendiers Latins et autres manuscrits hagiographiques*, Typologie des sources du moyen âge occidental, Fascicles 24–25 (Turnhout: Brepols, 1985). Extensive bibliographical entries are also available in Jacques Dubois and Jean-Loup Lemaitre, *Sources et méthodes de l'hagiographie médiévale* (Paris: Les Éditions du Cerf, 1993); see in particular chapters 1, 2, and 4 respectively, 'Histoire et méthode', 'Passions, vies et miracles', and 'Les Martyrologes', pp. 1–20, 21–57, and 103–34. Readers are referred specifically to *Hagiographies: Histoire internationale de la littérature hagiographique latine et vernaculaire en Occident des origines à 1550*, ed. by Guy Philippart (I–V), Monique Goullet (VI–VII), and Michèle Gaillard and Monique Goullet (VIII), Corpus Christianorum Texts and Studies, 8 vols (Turnhout: Brepols, 1994–2020) for introductory and bibliographical information about hagiographical traditions in Europe in Latin and the vernacular at various chronological points and in different geographical areas; essays are cited below on the first occurrence by author, title, editor, volume, and date.

Saints' lives, which shared narrative features with sanctorale sermons, were important institutionally, liturgically, and personally. Significant in the promulgation of saints' cults, *vitae* were fundamental in the spread of the Christian faith, the solidifying of group identity, and as signifiers of cultural, geographical, and religious interests. Universal lives by their very nature were always disseminated, so a manuscript containing a full range of the lives of the apostles, early martyrs, virgins, and confessors can have limitations in what it reveals about a specific historical time period. Conversely, selections of such lives or groups of national or local figures can have a more obvious value. Such choices enable contrasts to be made over time and region: for instance, the exceptional interest in bishop saints among Latin hagiographers in Germany or the prevalence of contemporary saints in the Latin tradition of the southern Low Countries.[3] In tracking the fortunes of different saints' lives much may be gleaned about institutional concerns, hierarchical agendas, national histories, gender politics, local interests, and individual choices. With regard to the lives in Add. 2604, which we posit were directed at nuns in an East Anglian convent, the last four issues, particularly the female perspective, are potentially the most revealing.

Saints' lives were an integral part of the private devotional life of women religious and those collected in Add. 2604 may therefore be viewed in the context of the development of Latin and vernacular legendary traditions both on the European mainland and in England. Part of the puzzle of the range of material in Add. 2604 lies in why a compiler has seen fit to combine the likes of John the Evangelist with Columba, Hild with Martha, or Benedicta with Leonard. Ultimately, while compilers of legendaries were driven by varying liturgical calendars together with the dictates of their locales, religious orders, or patrons, the selection of specific lives can sometimes have as much to do with the traditions of the age mitigated by personal predilections as anything else, as noted by Guy Philippart:

> Chaque époque a vu naître une littérature hagiographique originale: les Passions épiques des martyrs au déclin de l'Antiquité, les Vies mérovingiennes, les grandes

---

[3] David J. Collins, 'Latin Hagiography in *Germania* (1450–1550)', in *Hagiographies*, ed. by Philippart, IV (2006), 523–83, notes that 'Between 1470 and 1520 German hagiographers composed and edited more lives of bishop-saints than of any other saint type' (p. 534). Valerie Vermassen, 'Latin Hagiography in the Dutch-Speaking Parts of the Southern Low Countries (1350–1550)', in *Hagiographies*, ed. by Goullet, VII (2017), 565–613, comments on how the 'Founders of religious orders and regional saints are by far the most popular' (p. 572). Both of these essays provide excellent surveys of their areas. See also David J. Collins, *Reforming Saints: Saints' Lives and Their Authors in Germany, 1470–1530*, Oxford Studies in Historical Theology (Oxford: Oxford University Press, 2008).

biographies des XIe et XIIe siècles, les légendes franciscaines, etc. Ces créations définissent en quelque sorte le goût du jour. Pour savoir si les éditeurs suivent la mode ou en favorisent la diffusion, il suffit de voir si les légendes choisies sont ou non de leur époque.[4]

To what extent 'le goût du jour' was operating in the selection of lives in Add. 2604 or indeed how one might regard the choices in this particular case are crucial questions, albeit made more difficult than usual owing to the imperfect nature of the manuscript and source complications. Ascertaining what was or was not common in hagiographical collections invariably leads to some examination — no matter how slight — of how Add. 2604 fits into the medieval hagiographical context. To do this, we shall give a very brief overview of the sort of influential Latin legendaries that developed on the Continent before turning to Latin and vernacular legendaries in England. In the last part of this chapter we shall consider the selection of saints' lives in Add. 2604.

Medieval Latin Legendaries from Continental Europe

Over time saints' lives appeared in different guises for varying purposes: in martyrologies, passionals, legendaries, breviaries, as well as in sanctorale and other compilations. Of these, one of the most influential for later developments was the martyrology, with the most famous being the Hieronymian Martyrology (composed in Italy in the fifth century) alongside the martyrologies associated with Bede (d. 735), Florus de Lyon (d. *c.* 860), Ado (d. *c.* 875), and — the most widely circulated — Usuard (d. *c.* 875).[5] Where martyrologies normally

---

[4] Philippart (1977), *Les Légendiers Latins et autres manuscrits hagiographiques*, p. 105.

[5] For an overview of martyrologies, see Henri Quentin, *Les Martyrologes historiques du moyen âge: Étude sur la formation du Martyrologe Romain*, 2nd edn (Paris: Librairie Victor Lecoffre, 1908); Jacques Dubois, *Les Martyrologes du moyen âge latin*, Typologie des sources du moyen âge occidental, Fascicle 26 (Turnhout: Brepols, 1978) and its follow-up, Jacques Dubois, *Les Martyrologes du moyen âge latin*, Typologie des sources du moyen âge occidental, Fascicle 26 (Turnhout: Brepols, 1985). For editions of a few of the most significant, see *Le Martyrologe d'Usuard: Texte et Commentaire*, ed. by Jacques Dubois, Subsidia Hagiographica, 40 (Bruxelles: Société des Bollandistes, 1965); *Édition pratique des martyrologes de Bède, de l'Anonyme lyonnais et de Florus*, ed. by Jacques Dubois and Geneviève Renaud (Paris: Éditions du Centre national de la recherche scientifique, 1976); and *Le Martyrologe d'Adon, ses deux familles, ses trois recensions: Texte et Commentaire*, ed. by Jacques Dubois and Geneviève Renaud (Paris: Éditions du centre national de la recherche scientifique, 1984). For England we have a vernacular martyrology both for the beginning and the end of the medieval period: *The Old English Martyrology: Edition, Translation and Commentary*, ed. and trans. by Christine

provided only a short description of a saint and the related feast, a legendary (or collection of saints' lives) comprised considerably longer narratives. These stories were often fashioned according to early Church models of asceticism, such as the life of Anthony of Egypt (251–356) by Athanasius of Alexandria (*c.* 296–373), or were influenced by the very popular story of Martin of Tours (*c.* 316–97) by Sulpicius Severus (*c.* 360–*c.* 430). Liturgical requirements necessitated hagiographical composition and writers developed longer narratives from a series of lections about a saint — between three and twelve depending on the solemnity of the feast — used in the office of Matins, as was the case of Seaxburh in England whose cult developed directly out of the liturgy.[6] The earliest legendaries written in Latin usually focused on the luminaries of the Roman calendar, the so-called universal saints, such as the apostles, popes, and virgin martyrs.[7]

Hagiographical narratives were not only incorporated into the liturgy but also used for communal reading at mealtimes and at collations, and as devotional texts for private contemplation. As time went on, more legendaries were produced at various rates both in Latin and the vernaculars throughout Europe. As noted by Alison Knowles Frazier in her study of the production of saints' lives by Italian humanists in the fifteenth century:

> Housed thus in a supple variety of forms, the narration of sanctity moved in all the intermediate spaces hidden by the heuristic oppositions of oral and literate, popular and elite, official and domestic, peripheral and central, Latin and vernacular, local and universal.[8]

Rauer, Anglo-Saxon Texts, 10 (Cambridge: Brewer, 2013) and the work by Richard Whitford of Syon Abbey (STC 17532), *The Martiloge in Englysshe after the Vse of the Chirche of Salisbury and as it is Redde in Syon with Addicyons, Printed by Wynkyn de Worde in 1526,* ed. by F. Procter and E. S. Dewick, Henry Bradshaw Society, 3 (London: Harrison and Sons, 1893).

[6] On the use of lessons in the night office, see Thomas J. Heffernan, 'The Liturgy and the Literature of Saints' Lives', in *The Liturgy of the Medieval Church*, ed. by Thomas J. Heffernan and E. Ann Matter (Kalamazoo, MI: Medieval Institute Publications, 2001), pp. 73–105 (pp. 88–105). For a discussion of the lections of Seaxburh, see Virginia Blanton, 'The Kentish Queen as *Omnium Mater*: Goscelin of Saint-Bertin's Lections and the Emergence of the Cult of Saint Seaxburh', in *Writing Women Saints in Anglo-Saxon England*, ed. by Paul E. Szarmach (Toronto: University of Toronto Press, 2013), pp. 191–213.

[7] The sanctorale — or calendar of saints — of the medieval Roman Catholic Church begins with 30 November, the feast of Andrew; the liturgical year then runs through to the end of the following November, highlighting daily feasts of saints. Occasionally the liturgical year could be divided into a winter cycle and a summer cycle.

[8] Alison Knowles Frazier, *Possible Lives: Authors and Saints in Renaissance Italy* (New York, NY: Columbia University Press, 2005), p. 9.

MEDIEVAL LATIN LEGENDARIES FROM CONTINENTAL EUROPE 163

From the late eleventh century there was a particular upsurge in legendaries, but the most notable period of production was in the thirteenth century. In essence the period up to the thirteenth century was marked by the appearance of physically large and extensive, often multi-volume, legendaries associated with monastic scriptoria, at least one of which had a long and complex history. The *Magnum Legendarium Austriacum*, a collection of over five hundred saints from Antiquity to the second half of the twelfth century, is found in six extant exemplars that are very similar in content but not identical. Transmitted within the monasteries located within the political boundaries of the duchies of Austria and Styria, it is found in twenty-one manuscripts and one fragment extending from *c.* 1200 to 1471.[9] In the second half of the thirteenth century the drive was towards what are known as *legendae novae* or abridged legendaries even if to a modern readership they may seem anything but 'abridged' given their overall extent. One of the most encyclopaedic of the earlier hagiographical collections was the *Speculum historiale* of Vincent de Beauvais (1190–*c.* 1264) that originally appeared in the first half of the thirteenth century with its 900 saints' lives.[10] Some later collections were considerably smaller, averaging between twenty to nearly fifty percent of its impressive size. The abridged legendaries were largely connected with the mendicant orders and so it is no surprise that the Dominicans (or Order of Preachers) were leaders in the field. Five Dominican collections stand out from the mid-thirteenth to the first half of the fourteenth centuries: the *Abbreviatio in gestis et miracvlis sanctorum* by Jean de Mailly (*c.* 1190–*c.* 1254);[11] the *Liber epilogorum in*

[9] See Albert Poncelet, '*De magno legendario Austriaco*', *Analecta Bollandiana*, 17 (1898), 24–96, 123–216, and the magisterial essay by Diarmuid Ó Riain, 'The *Magnum Legendarium Austriacum*: A New Investigation of One of Medieval Europe's Richest Hagiographical Collections', *Analecta Bollandiana*, 133 (2015), 87–165.

[10] In essence, of course, the *Speculum majus* or *Bibliotheca mundi* was intended by Vincent de Beauvais to be a selection or summation of contemporary knowledge gathered from innumerable other works and put into a single volume. Divided into three major parts, *Speculum naturale*, *Speculum doctrinale*, and *Speculum historiale*, with a fourth, *Speculum morale*, added after Vincent's death, the aim of the *Speculum historiale* was as a chronological history from the fall of Adam to the year 1254 (and so in some respects was akin to the abridged legendary tradition). Textually the manuscript and early printed traditions are exceptionally complex; for a full explanation (with bibliography and references to digitised editions), see the Vincent de Beauvais website (www.vincentiusbelvacensis.eu) (accessed 1 April 2023).

[11] Antoine Dondaine, '*Le Dominicain Français Jean de Mailly et la Legende doree*', *Archives d'histoire dominicaine*, 1 (1946), 53–102; Jean de Mailly, *Abbreviatio in gestis et miracvlis sanctorvm, svpplementvm hagiographicvm*, ed. by Giovanni Paolo Maggioni, Millennio medievale, 97, Testi, 21 (Firenze: Sismel-Edizioni del Galluzzo, 2013).

gesta sanctorum by Bartolomeo da Trento (*c.* 1200–71);[12] the *Legenda aurea* by Jacobus de Voragine (*c.* 1228–98);[13] the four-part *Speculum sanctorale* by Bernard Gui (1261–1331);[14] and the very capacious *Legendarium* by Petrus Calo di Clugia (or Pietro Calò di Chioggia) (*c.* 1300–48).[15] Alongside these in the same century is the work of a Benedictine, the *Sanctilogium, seu Speculum legendarum* by Gui de Châtres (d. 1350).[16]

These and other legendaries have been classified according to different typologies by François Dolbeau and further discussed by Silvia Nocentini.[17] Broadly speaking, under this scheme legendaries are divided into two main types: specialised, which may be further subdivided into local saints or catego-

---

[12] Antoine Dondaine, 'L'"Epilogus in gesta sanctorum" de Barthélemy de Trente', in *Studia mediaevalia et mariologica*, ed. by Carolo Balić, Pontificium Athenaeum 'Antonianum' (Roma: Antonianum, 1971), pp. 333–60; Bartolomeo da Trento, *Liber epilogorum in gesta sanctorum*, ed. by Emore Paoli, Edizione nazionale dei testi mediolatini, 2 (Firenze: Sismel-Edizioni del Galluzzo, 2001).

[13] Iacopo da Varazze, *Legenda aurea con le miniature del codice Ambrosiano C 240 inf.*, ed. by Giovanni Paolo Maggioni, Edizione nazionale dei testi mediolatini, 20, 2 vols (Firenze: Sismel & Milano: Biblioteca Ambrosiana, 2007); for further detail and bibliography on the *Legenda aurea*, see V. Latin Sources and Analogues and references therein.

[14] For a discussion of the contents, see 'Bernard Gui, Frère Prêcheur', *Histoire littéraire de la France*, 35 (Paris: Imprimerie nationale, 1921), pp. 139–232 (pp. 165–71) and for its organisation, see Agnès Dubreil-Arcin, 'Bernard Gui, un hagiographe dominicain atypique?', *Hagiographie et culte des saints en France méridionale (XIIIᵉ–XVᵉ siècle)*, Cahiers de Fanjeaux: Collection d'Histoire religieuse du Langedoc au Moyen Âge, 37 (Toulouse: Éditions Privat, 2002), pp. 147–73.

[15] Albert Poncelet, 'Le Légendier de Pierre Calo', *Analecta Bollandiana*, 29 (1910), 5–116.

[16] Henri Omont, 'Le Sanctilogium de Gui de Châtres, abbé de Saint-Denys', *Bibliothèque de l'École des chartes*, 86 (1925), 407–10; Constant J. Mews, 'Re-structuring the *Golden Legend* in the Early Fourteenth Century: The *Sanctilogium* of Guy of Châtres, Abbot of Saint-Denis', *Revue bénédictine*, 120 (2010), 129–44.

[17] François Dolbeau, 'Notes sur l'organisation interne des légendiers latins', in *Hagiographie, cultures et sociétés (IVᵉ–XIIᵉ siècles): Actes du colloque organisé à Nanterre et à Paris (2–5 mai 1979)*, Centre du recherches sur l'Antiquité tardive et le Haut Moyen Âge, Université de Paris X (Paris: Études augustiennes, 1981), pp. 11–31. An overview by Silvia Nocentini of the origin and development of legendaries across Europe, based on Dolbeau's classifications, is available at 'Medieval Collections of Saints' Lives', Collaborative European Digital Archive Infrastructure (CENDARI) Archival Research Guide, http://www.cendari.eu/sites/default/files/ARGMedievalCollections.pdf. (accessed 1 April 2023). See also the useful discussion by Giovanni Paolo Maggioni, 'Thirteenth-Century *Legendae Novae* and the Preaching Orders: A Communication System', in *Hagiography and the History of Latin Christendom, 500–1500*, ed. by Samantha Kahn Herrick, Reading Medieval Sources, 4 (Leiden: Brill, 2020), pp. 98–120.

MEDIEVAL LATIN LEGENDARIES FROM CONTINENTAL EUROPE   165

ries of saints (such as apostles or women) and general, which may comprise an atypical collection (in which there is no distinction between the rank of saint) or a systematic one (that focuses on the hierarchy of the saints where martyrs will outrank confessors, and so on). Internally the legendaries may be organised according to three different orders: no order, liturgical order, or non-liturgical order that may be alphabetical, chronological, or hierarchical (or indeed calendrical). Using this taxonomy, Bartolomeo da Trento's collection is a specialised legendary of local saints in liturgical order, while Bernard Gui's work fits into the general systematic category in liturgical order, with its four parts focusing respectively on Christ, the Virgin, and the heavenly hierarchy; apostles, evangelists, and disciples; martyrs; confessors; and virgins. Such categorisations will be useful when we come to discuss the format of the saints in Add. 2604 below.

However, no categorisation or classification can account for the interconnectedness of legendaries throughout the Middle Ages. It is impossible to explain adequately the degree to which one contemporary collection may have influenced another or conversely been oblivious to another, or how any of them may have set the scene for later legendaries. This interpenetration of sources is perhaps best expressed by Paolo Maggioni who notes:

> The primary method in the compilation of *legendae novae* was the epitome. In other words, the compiler did not simply rewrite the original legend and other related sources, but in general chose and encompassed in the text what he considered to be useful selections (sometimes quite lengthy) from other sources. As a result, entire chapters can be found, sometimes in nearly identical form, in various abbreviated legendaries and in their sources, since it could be that the same passages were held to be useful by several authors, or even that they used one and the same epitome.[18]

Legendary tradition is therefore more of a continuous relay race with various twists and turns rather than a straightforward sprint. And those that win the race may not be the expected winner or considered the most deserving champion either then or later, with the primary case of this perhaps being Jacobus de Voragine.[19]

Apart from the various copyings and re-copyings of the abridged legendaries, there were countless other Latin manuscript collections hidden in plain sight in European libraries or lost to posterity, besides all those translated into the European vernaculars. Towards the end of the fifteenth century the

---

[18] Maggioni, 'Thirteenth-Century *Legendae Novae* and the Preaching Orders', p. 106.

[19] The fortunes of and attitudes to the *Legenda aurea* are perceptively discussed in Sherry L. Reames, *The 'Legenda aurea': A Reexamination of its Paradoxical History* (Madison, WI: The University of Wisconsin Press, 1985).

IV. HAGIOGRAPHICAL CONTEXT AND THE SELECTION OF SAINTS

dissemination of the saint's life was further enhanced by the development of print. Some of these collections already had a long history in manuscript, most notably, the *Legenda aurea* (extant in well over a thousand copies and numerous translations), while other authors had more recently come on the scene. One of these was Petrus de Natalibus, the Italian bishop (d. 1406), whose massive twelve volume *Catalogus sanctorum et gestorum eorum ex diuersis multis voluminbus collectus* (indebted to Calo's *Legendarium*) also appeared repeatedly in print.[20] Yet after the *Legenda aurea* (of which there were endless editions from the early 1470s onwards),[21] the printed collection that made the greatest impact was that commonly known as Mombritius, that is, Bonino Mombrizio's (1424–after 1478) *Sanctuarium*, published around 1477 to 1478.[22] Less known — at least today — was the anonymous *Historie plurimorum sanctorum*. This was first published by Ulrich Zel in 1483 as a supplement to the *Legenda aurea*; it was also reprinted separately by Johannes de Westfalia in 1485.[23] The remit of the *Historie plurimorum sanctorum* was to include those lives not found in the *Legenda aurea*: as noted in the latter full title, *Incipiunt historie plurimorum sanctorum nouiter laboriose collecte et prolongate*. Alongside these were national, regional, and/or gendered Latin collections in manuscript or print. For instance, the German Carthusian from Cologne, Hermann Greven (d. after 5 November 1477 or 5 November 1480), wrote a very concise martyrology and a legendary of about 250 items, with a particular concentration on local saints (German, French, and English) that had, as we shall see in V. Latin Sources and Analogues, links with the

---

[20] The Universal Short Title Catalogue (https://www.ustc.ac.uk/) lists thirteen editions (extant in numerous copies) between 1508 and 1545 under the name of Petrus de Natalibus, and others with the same title but under different names from 1493 onwards.

[21] An early attempt at counting these in Latin and translations is available in Robert Francis Seybolt, 'Fifteenth Century Editions of the *Legenda aurea*', *Speculum*, 21 (1946), 327–42.

[22] For references and further information on Mombritius and the *Sanctuarium*, see V. Latin Sources and Analogues.

[23] The 1483 edition tends to be catalogued simply under the *Legenda aurea* title as in Jacobus de Voragine, *Legenda aurea sanctorum, sive Lombardica historia* (Köln [Ulrich Zel], 1483) (USTC 746132); the 1485 version is available as *Historie plurimorum sanctorum* (Louvain: Johannes de Westfalia, October 1485) (USTC 438400). For Johannes de Westfalia, see Rudolph Juchhoff, 'Johannes de Westfalia als Buchhändler', *Gutenberg Jahrbuch*, 29 (1954), 133–36. A full list of the contents of the 1485 edition in the Bodleian Library (H-128) is available at Bod-Inc Online (incunables.bodleian.ox.ac.uk; accessed 27 March 2023). For further information on the *Historie plurimorum sanctorum*, see V. Latin Sources and Analogues.

Historie plurimorum sanctorum.[24] Notable other examples are by two Dutch Augustinians both at the monastery of Rooklooster or Rouge-Cloître in the Forêt de Soignes, some six miles south-east of the cathedral in Brussels.[25] Johannes Gielemans (1427–87) produced the massive *Sanctilogium* in four volumes, comprising over a thousand universal and local lives; the *Hagiologium Brabantinorum* with Brabantine saints linked to Charlemagne in the first volume and saints geographically associated with the Brabant in the second volume; and the *Novale sanctorum* with its emphasis on contemporary saints.[26] Anton Geens (*c*. 1480–1543) compiled an extensive *Legendarium* in four volumes originally comprising some 288 saints (January–February; March–April, which is now lost; May–August; and September–December). Written in the same hand throughout with blank pages at the end of various sections to accommodate subsequent additions, the three volumes, as well as the attached *tabula* for the lost second volume, demonstrate a particular interest in abbots, bishops, and popes. Crucially with regard to our *Study*, some seventy of these lives are of English saints, including five female saints in Add. 2604, and even more importantly they ultimately share the same source as that used in Add. 2604.[27] Some of these late medieval collections were also

[24] Baudouin de Gaiffier, 'Le Martyrologe et le légendier d'Hermann Greven', *Analecta Bollandiana*, 54 (1936), 316–58. See also Pádraig Ó Riain, 'Feasts of Irish and Scottish Saints in Hermann Greven's Martyrology and *Devotionale*: A Review of the Evidence', *Analecta Bollandiana*, 138 (2020), 368–81, where it is noted that the two manuscripts of the martyrology and the one manuscript of the legendary are in Greven's hand (p. 377 n. 39 and p. 378 n. 43).

[25] Vermassen, 'Latin Hagiography in the Dutch-Speaking Parts of the Southern Low Countries (1350–1550)', pp. 586–91 and 605–06. A third well known hagiographer, amongst the many in this monastery, was Johannes Back who produced a *Passionale sanctorum* in *c*. 1450 (pp. 584–86); see further Appendix 1 below.

[26] Albert Poncelet, 'De codicibus hagiographicis Iohannes Gielemans, canonici regularis in Rubea Valle prope Bruxellas', *Analecta Bollandiana*, 14 (1895), pp. 5–88. Gielemans's *Sanctilogium* includes only the native female saints Edith, Eadburh (but of Winchester rather than of Thanet as in Add. 2604), Hild, Leoba, and Mildrith, and his *Hagiologium Brabantinorum* has only Eadburh and Edith. For further information on Gielemans, see Ria van Loenen, 'Johannes Gielemans (1427–1487) en de heiligen van de Brabanders', in *Gouden Legenden: Heiligenlevens en Heiligenverering in de Nederlanden,* ed. by Anneke B. Mulder-Bakker and Marijke Carasso-Kok (Hilversum: Verloren, 1997), pp. 139–49.

[27] See further Appendix 1 below. The extant contents are listed in J. Van den Gheyn and others, *Catalogue des manuscrits de la Bibliothèque royale de Belgique*, 13 vols (Bruxelles: Henri Lamertin, and other places and publishers, 1901–48), v: Historie-Hagiographies (1905), 229–41; Michael Lapidge, 'The *Legendarium* of Anton Geens: A Supplementary Note', *Analecta Bollandiana*, 126 (2008), 151–54, lists the contents of the missing volume (pp. 153–54).

168 IV. HAGIOGRAPHICAL CONTEXT AND THE SELECTION OF SAINTS

connected with current humanistic debates, for instance, *De plurimis claris sceletisque [sic] mulieribus* by the Augustinian Jacopo Filippo Foresti da Bergamo first published on 29 April 1497.

Throughout the Middle Ages saints' lives also appear in sermon collections, some of which later became part of the most widely disseminated printed texts throughout Europe. A selection of ten of the most widespread of these collections follow. These are given in order according to the number of printed editions between 1450 and 1520 and so during the period of the production of Add. 2604. These are:[28] (1) Johannes Herolt (d. 1468), *Sermones Discipuli de tempore et de sanctis* (USTC 745675); (3) Michael (Mihály) de Hungaria (d. 1480) *Euagatorium [...]* (or *Sermones predicabiles*) (USTC 654238); (4) Johannes Werden, Sermones '*Dormi secure' de tempore et de sanctis* (USTC 746378); (5) Pelbartus de Themeswar (Pelbárt Temesvári) (1430–1504), *Pomerium sermones de sanctis* (USTC 684749); (6) Paratus, *Sermones parati de tempore et de sanctis* (USTC 693741); (10) Leonardus de Utino (*fl.* 1444), *Sermones aurei de sanctis* (USTC 746661); (13) Gabriele Barletta, *Sermones quadragesimales et de sanctis* (USTC 997243); (15) Meffret (whose identity is unknown but was possibly Petrus Meffordis of Leipzig who seems to have flourished between 1445 and 1476), *Hortulus reginae* (USTC 2003867); (17) Vicent Ferrer (1350–1419), *Sermones de tempore et de sanctis* (USTC 744841); and (22) Jacobus de Voragine, *Sermones de sanctis* (USTC 746184). Some of these collections reached a huge readership, with Herolt's work the most outstanding example. It has been estimated that its eighty-four editions between 1450 and 1520 would have amounted to almost 49,000

Lapidge notes (p. 152) that Geens used Wynkyn de Worde's *Nova Legenda Anglie* (1516) to populate his collection with a number of English saints, including an interesting collection of native females that is not exhaustive: Æbbe, Æthelburh (Barking), Æthelflæd, Cuthburh, Eanswith, Edith, Fritheswith, Keyna, Margaret of Scotland, Modwenna, Mildrith, Osith, Seaxburh and Wihtburh (but none of the other Ely women), and Wulfhild. The absence of Æthelthryth of Ely is quite noticeable.

[28] The place order numbers derive from Anne T. Thayer, *Penitence, Preaching and the Coming of the Reformation*, St Andrews Studies in Reformation History (Aldershot: Ashgate, 2002), Table 2.8, pp. 36–37, where she accounts for the popularity of thirty-five collections with ten editions or more between 1450 and 1520 available in the Holy Roman Empire, England, France, Italy, The Netherlands, and the Swiss Confederation. The figures range from eighty-four editions for Herolt to thirteen for Jacobus de Voragine. Apart from Pelbartus's and Barletta's collections, the editions appeared overwhelmingly between 1450 and 1500 rather than between 1501 and 1520. The early editions of these works have been checked in the digitised versions available in USTC (with the individual identifier following in each case) and full details provided in the Bibliography.

MEDIEVAL LATIN LEGENDARIES FROM CONTINENTAL EUROPE   169

copies, but even this number of editions is 'small' in comparison to the tally of 126 editions for Jacobus de Voragine's *Legenda aurea* during the same period, quite apart from its countless manuscripts and translations throughout Europe.[29] ·

What we have then in Europe between the late eleventh century and the early sixteenth (and beyond) is a growing accretion of saints' lives in unquantifiable and often intermingled ways that can traverse regional and national boundaries.[30] This textual fluidity makes source study very difficult particularly for the editor of universal saints' lives like those in Add. 2604.[31] Unrelated collections can seem relevant; likely positive identifications can be elusive; both can hinder progress when searching for analogues. For instance, the *Sanctilogium seu Speculum legendarum* of Gui de Châtres contains all the universal Add. 2604 saints apart from Iphigenia (see Table 3 below); these are given in calendar order in the main body of the text, which is divided into twelve books.[32] This is then followed by two further books. The texts in this collection contain cross-references generally to the Martyrology of Usuard and to the *Legenda aurea* (cited, for instance, in Justina on fol. 208r) and to Vincent de Beauvais's *Speculum historiale* (cited, for example, in Benedicta on fol. 218r). Of importance to Add. 2604, Gui de Châtres's collection illustrates a desire to combine universal and popular native saints, even if the only female English saint included in the list for Book 13 on fols 305r–v is Æthelthryth (who occurs third from the end as chapter 101 on fol. 305v). While being unusually transparent with his references and his borrowings, Gui's work is still a complex matrix of sources.

Connections may also be found in the most improbable of places. For example, the work of Italian humanists would appear to be poles apart from that of English hagiographers but is not necessarily so. The Augustinian Jacopo Filippo Foresti da Bergamo adapts his work and his title from the prose work, *De claris mulieribus* written by Giovanni Boccaccio in the early 1360s, a text that was

---

[29] Thayer, *Penitence, Preaching and the Coming of the Reformation*, p. 21 n. 25 and p. 22. In Giovanni Paolo Maggioni, 'La trasmissione dei leggendari abbreviati del XIII secolo', *Filologia Mediolatina*, 9 (2002), 87–107, it is noted that there are more than 1,210 manuscript copies of the *Legenda aurea* (p. 89).

[30] Post-medieval collections also built on or reacted to earlier hagiographical traditions; see, for instance, the work of Aloisius Lippomanus (1500–59), Georg Witzel (1501–73), Laurentius Surius (1522–78), and Petrus Canisius (1521–97).

[31] An additional complicating factor, discussed in V. Latin Sources and Analogues, is the methodology of the *Acta sanctorum* produced by the Bollandists.

[32] London, British Library, MS Royal 13 D. ix.

itself translated into Middle English in prose and verse.[33] Foresti da Bergamo's *De plurimis claris sceletisque* [*sic*] *mulieribus*, published in folio format in Ferrara on 29 April 1497, has an architectural-type presentation scene on the reverse of the title page that depicts the author presenting his book to Beatrice d'Aragona (1457–1508), queen of Hungary and Bohemia, who is seated on a throne in a garden. The volume is a mixture of stories about biblical, Christian, and classical women, with some contemporary Italian women at the end.[34] The book starts with the Virgin Mary, followed by Eve, and Sara (described as a saint and the wife of Abraham on fol. XIIII verso). Each life has an opening woodcut of the relevant woman, with the same woodcuts occasionally repeated. It is interesting that readers would have seen, for instance, the same image (a figure holding a book, with a palm and crown) being associated with the Roman Domitilla and the biblical Martha. *De plurimis claris sceletisque* [*sic*] *mulieribus* has all the universal female saints in Add. 2604 (plus Iphigenia) apart from Benedicta, which makes it *look* like a promising cache of material.[35] In other words, the net needs to be spread widely when investigating the universal saints in Add. 2604 before being able to narrow down potential sources or analogues. And this is quite apart from their presence in the vernacular and largely unedited compilations throughout Europe that defy any systematic investigation.[36]

[33] For details, see *On Famous Women*, ed. by Cowen, p. xi.

[34] Discussed especially in 'The Containment of Court Women: The *De plurimis claris selectisque mulieribus* (1497 and 1521)', in Stephen Kolsky, *The Ghost of Boccaccio: Writings on Famous Women in Renaissance Italy*, Late Medieval and Early Modern Studies, 7 (Turnhout: Brepols, 2005), pp. 117–37 (with woodcut illustrations on pp. 138–39, 141–44). In his book Kolsky explicates Foresti da Bergamo's interdependent context as part of a group of male writers addressing the *querelle des femmes* in Renaissance Italy. Some of these such as Giovanni Sabadino degli Arienti (c. 1444–1510) — from whom Foresti borrowed — also included saints in their compilations.

[35] The surviving list of copies of Foresti's work is extensive, with many in various English libraries; see the Incunabula Short Title Catalogue, ISTC ij00204000 for details (https://data. cerl.org/istc/_search; accessed 27 March 2023); Kolsky, *The Ghost of Boccaccio*, p. 9 and n. 11, and p. 117 also notes its presence in an anthology of 1521 published in Paris that led to even greater visibility.

[36] Some detailed surveys exist; see in particular, Werner Williams-Krapp, *Die deutschen und niederländischen Legendare des Mittelalters: Studien zu ihrer Überlieferungs-Text-und Wirkungsgeschichte*, Texte und Textgeschichte, Würzburger Forschungen, 20 (Tübingen: Niemeyer, 1986), with its valuable Legendenregister on pp. 385–472.

Add. 2604 and the European Latin Tradition

Therefore to discover to some small degree the extent of the Add. 2604 saints (both universal and a few native ones) in European Latin collections, we have analysed the contents of all the compilations mentioned above and, for comparison sake, have also examined the sermon collections.[37] The purpose of this exercise is twofold: to estimate the popularity of the saints' lives in Add. 2604 and to help in the quest for the sources or analogues for these same texts (see V. Latin Sources and Analogues). While it is not a water-tight statistical assessment, it will help to elucidate where Add. 2604's universal saints (and a few English ones) stand in the wider European legendary landscape.[38] The information is provided in three Tables with abbreviations explained below. The items are all given in alphabetical sequence, irrespective of the liturgical order of the saints or the chronological order of the material. The lists include all the universal saints found in Add. 2604. The lives of John the Baptist and John the Evangelist are separated into their two feasts rather then being combined or partly combined as they are in Add. 2604, that is, the Nativity of John the

---

[37] We are mindful, of course, that saints' lives are not sermons even if they often draw on the same narratives. The sanctorale sermons are simply included on the grounds of helping to track the dissemination of certain saints, while not being concerned with liturgical considerations or homiletic content. For illuminating comment, see Siegfried Wenzel, 'Preaching the Saints in Chaucer's England', in *Earthly Love, Spiritual Love, Love of the Saints*, ed. by Susan J. Ridyard, Sewanee Mediaeval Studies, 8 (Sewanee, TN: University of the South Press, 1999), pp. 45–68, for example, 'This representation [of certain saints] may, to a large extent, be due to the fact that their sermons were preached on certain days or even in certain places dedicated to the memory of a saint [...] The sermons we have were clearly part and parcel of the official liturgy, and we must resist the temptation of seeing in them vehicles of a cult of personality as we moderns would understand the term' (p. 50).

[38] In order to make this extensive task manageable and limited, we have chosen one representative manuscript, manuscript tradition, one printed version, or edited text to investigate in the material listed here. This means that we have had to simplify our searches without the complications of variant traditions. We are therefore aware that the answers provided here about the appearance of certain saints may not be completely accurate in all their essentials, but they will provide some indications. Where reputable secondary literature exists that provide contents' lists, we have used these as our guide, with full references provided in the notes, as necessary. In the case of texts that have been printed, we have made use of the digitised copies available on the Universal Short Title Catalogue website (https://www.ustc.ac.uk/) (accessed 1 April 2023). In some cases it has been easier to check a printed edition of a text that first appeared in manuscript (for instance, Vincent de Beauvais's *Speculum historiale*) even if a printed text is not always exactly the same as the manuscript version; in cases where a printed text is referred to, this is specified with the accompanying USTC number provided for the digitised copy consulted.

Baptist (24 June) and the Decollation (29 August), and John the Evangelist (27 December) and John the Evangelist *Ad portam Latinam* or at the Latin Gate (6 May). It also includes the life of Iphigenia that was apparently originally found in Add. 2604 but is now missing (discussed below). With regard to native or insular saints only Æthelthryth, Edith, Hild, Modwenna, Seaxburh, and Wihtburh are listed as relevant as the other native saints are not found in these legendary collections (and all native saints are excluded in Table 5 as none of these European sermon collection includes any English saints).

The information in Table 3 confirms some of what is known or suspected already: the ubiquity of the apostolic saints John the Baptist and John the Evangelist is hardly surprising in the legendaries and neither is the popularity of virgin martyrs like Agatha and Cecilia or the rarity of native English saints. Significant, however, is the fact that, as far as can be ascertained from content lists, no collection combines the Nativity of John the Baptist with his Decollation as happens in Add. 2604 or partly combines John the Evangelist's two feasts. What is noteworthy too is how the lesser known saints in English circles (such as Benedicta and Columba, and especially Domitilla and Iphigenia) are dealt with, and which native English saints are chosen for inclusion. Table 5 also demonstrates the expected dominance of the two apostles but particularly serves to downplay the importance of female saints as only Agatha, Barbara, Cecilia, and Martha merit any attention at all. Table 4, most significantly perhaps, shows a trend in Europe to include not only its own regional saints but also some English ones.

Above all, these Tables, particularly for the universal lives, pinpoint what is or is not unusual about the choice of material in Add. 2604 when set against important examples of European Latin hagiography. Taken as a whole, the lives in Add. 2604 would seem to be following two different trends. On the one hand, in its inclusion of the more obscure female saints, it emulates the abridged legendaries of the thirteenth century. On the other hand, in its emphasis on local saints, it is right up to date with contemporary fifteenth- and sixteenth-century European fashion in its stress on the regional saint. Perhaps most importantly in the majority of cases the lives are not those regularly found in English contexts either in Latin or the vernaculars. Additionally, the native lives are similarly rather specialised.

As will be elucidated in V. Latin Sources and Analogues, the full analysis of the compilations demonstrates that certain preconceptions are immediately shattered. For instance, seven of the universal saints in Add. 2604 figure in the *Legenda aurea*, namely, Agatha, Cecilia, John the Baptist, John the Evangelist, Justina, Leonard, and Martha, but this does not mean that the Add. 2604

ADD. 2604 AND THE EUROPEAN LATIN TRADITION 173

Table 3. The Add. 2604 Universal Lives in Early Continental Latin Legendaries[39]

Saints	Beauvais	Calo	Châtres	Gui	Mailly	Trento	Voragine
Æthelthryth	No	Yes	Yes	No	No	No	No
Agatha	Yes	Yes	Yes	No	Yes	Yes	Yes
Barbara	Yes	Yes	Yes	No	No	Yes	No
Benedicta	Yes	Yes	Yes	No	No	No	No
Cecilia	Yes	Yes	Yes	No	Yes	Yes	Yes
Columba	Yes	Yes	Yes	No	Yes	Yes	No
Domitilla	Yes	Yes	Yes	No	No	No	No
Iphigenia	Yes	No	No	No	No	No	No
Baptist (Nativity)	Yes	Yes	Yes	No	No	Yes [plus Octave]	Yes
Baptist (Decoll.)	No	Yes	Yes	No	No	Yes	Yes
Evang.	Yes	Yes	Yes	Yes	Yes	Yes	Yes
Evang. (*Ad portam*)	Yes	Yes	Yes	No	No	Yes	Yes
Justina	Yes	Yes	Yes	No	No	Yes [plus with Cyprian]	Yes
Leonard	No	No	Yes	Yes	Yes	No	Yes
Martha	Yes	Yes	Yes	Yes	Yes	Yes	Yes

Key:
Beauvais: Vincent de Beauvais, *Speculum historiale*
Calo: Petrus Calo di Clugia (Pietro Calò di Chioggia), Legendary
Châtres: Gui de Châtres, *Sanctilogium, seu Speculum legendarum*
Gui: Bernard Gui, *Speculum sanctorale*
Mailly: Jean de Mailly, *Abbreviatio in gestis et miracvlis sanctorum*
Trento: Bartolomeo da Trento, *Liber epilogorum in gesta sanctorum*
Voragine: Jacobus de Voragine, *Legenda aurea*

[39] The information in this table is derived from the editions or lists in nn. 11–15, from USTC for Beauvais (USTC 749712, *c.* 1473 edition), from London, British Library, MS Royal 13 D. ix for Gui de Châtres, and from a digitised manuscript (MK-0000.005) from the Moravská zemská knihovna [Moravian State Library] for Bernard Gui. Although not a universal saint, Æthelthryth is listed in a few of the collections, the only native saint found in Add. 2604 included.

Table 4. The Add. 2604 Lives in Late Medieval Continental Latin Legendaries[40]

Saints	Foresti	Geens	Gielemans (HB)	Gielemans (Sanct)	Greven	Hist.	Mom.	Nat.
Æthelthryth	No	No	No	No	Yes	No	No	Yes
Agatha	Yes	No	No	Yes	No	No	Yes	Yes
Barbara	Yes	No	No	Yes	Yes	Yes	Yes	Yes
Benedicta	No	Yes	No	Yes	Yes	Yes	No	Yes
Cecilia	Yes	No	No	Yes	No	No	Yes	Yes
Columba	Yes	No	No	Yes	No	Yes	Yes	Yes
Domitilla	Yes	No	No	Yes	No	No	Yes [plus companions]	Yes
Eanswith	No	Yes	No	No	No	No	No	No
Edith	No	Yes	Yes	Yes	Yes	No	No	Yes
Hild	No	No	Yes	Yes	Yes	Yes	No	No
Iphigenia	No	No	No	No	No	No	No	Yes
Baptist (Nativity)	No	No	No	[has Octave]	No	No	No	Yes
Baptist (Decoll.)	No	No	No	[has Invention]	No	No	[has Invention]	Yes
Evang.	No	No	No	Yes	No	No	Yes	Yes
Evang. (*Ad portam*)	No	No	No	Yes	No	No	No	Yes
Justina	Yes	Yes	No	Yes	No	No	Yes	Yes
Leonard	No	No	No	Yes	No	No	Yes	Yes
Martha	Yes	No	No	Yes	No	No	Yes	Yes
Modwenna	No	Yes	No	No	No	No	No	No
Seaxburh	No	Yes	No	No	No	No	No	No
Wihtburh	No	Yes	No	No	No	No	No	No

Key:
Foresti: Jacopo Filippo Foresti da Bergamo, *De plurimis claris sceletisque* [*sic*] *mulieribus*
Geens: Anton Geens, *Legendarium* (March–April volume now lost)
Gielemans (*HB*): Johannes Gielemans, *Hagiologium Brabantinorum*
Gielemans (*Sanct*): Johannes Gielemans, *Sanctilogium*
Greven: Hermann Greven, *Legendarium*
Hist.: Anonymous, *Historie plurimorum sanctorum*
Mom.: Boninus Mombritius (Bonino Mombrizio), *Sanctuarium seu Vitae Sanctorum*
Nat.: Petrus de Natalibus, *Catalogus sanctorum et gestorum eorum ex diuersis multis voluminbus collectus*

[40] The information in this table for Geens, Gielemans, and Greven is derived from the lists in nn. 24–27; that for the early printed texts in USTC as follows: Foresti (USTC 994089), *Historie plurimorum sanctorum* (USTC 438400, 1485 edition), Mombritius (USTC 992962, volume 2 only is digitised), Petrus de Natalibus (USTC 619721, 1513 edition). Numerous copies of all these texts are listed in USTC. Gielemans's *Novale sanctorum* does not contain any of the saints in Add. 2604 so is omitted.

ADD. 2604 AND THE EUROPEAN LATIN TRADITION

Table 5. The Add. 2604 Universal Saints in a Selection of Early Printed Sermons[41]

Saints	Barletta	Ferrer	Herolt	Meffreth	Mihály	Paratus	Pelbartus	Utino	Vor.	Werden
Agatha	No	Yes	No	Yes	No	No	No	Yes	Yes	No
Barbara	No	No	No	Yes	Yes	No	Yes	No	No	Yes
Benedicta	No	No	No	No	No	No	No	No	No	No
Cecilia	No	Yes	No	No	No	Yes	No	No	Yes	Yes
Columba	No	No	No	No	No	No	No	No	No	No
Domitilla	No	No	No	No	No	No	No	No	No	No
Iphigenia	No	No	No	No	No	No	No	No	No	No
Baptist (Nativity)	Yes	Yes	Yes	Yes	Yes	Yes	Yes	Yes	Yes	Yes
Baptist (Decoll.)	No	Yes	No	Yes	No	Yes	Yes	Yes	Yes	Yes
Evangel.	Yes	Yes	Yes	Yes	Yes	Yes	Yes	Yes	Yes	Yes
Evangel. (*Ad portam*)	No	Yes	No	Yes	No	Yes	No	No	Yes	No
Justina	No	No	No	No	No	No	No	No	No	No
Leonard	No	No	No	No	Yes	No	No	Yes	No	No
Martha	No	Yes	No	No	No	No	Yes	No	No	No

Key:
Barletta: Gabriele Barletta, *Sermones quadragesimales et de sanctis*
Ferrer: Vicent Ferrer, *Sermones de tempore et de sanctis*
Herolt: Johannes Herolt, *Sermones Discipuli de tempore et de sanctis*
Meffreth: Meffreth, *Hortulus reginae*
Mihály: Michael (Mihály) of Hungary, *Euagatorium [...]* (or *Sermones praedicabiles*)
Paratus: Paratus, *Sermones parati de tempore et de sanctis*
Pelbartus: Pelbartus de Themeswar (Pelbárt Temesvári) *Pomerium sermones de sanctis*
Utino: Leonardus de Utino, *Sermones aurei de sanctis*
Vor.: Jacobus de Voragine, *Sermones de sanctis*
Werden: Johannes Werden, Sermones '*Dormi secure*' de tempore et de sanctis.

---

[41] These collections have been checked using the USTC references given above.

source has been discovered. The *Legenda aurea* is important for Add. 2604, but only partially so; significant too are certain lives as represented in Mombritius's *Sanctuarium* and the *Historie plurimorum sanctorum* (behind and alongside which lie various identified and unknown manuscripts from different periods). Other collections, such as those by Gui de Châtres or Foresti da Bergamo, either point in the right direction or are a dead end while others, like that by Anton Geens, prove apposite for the native lives. As will become apparent, the work here has shown, not unexpectedly, that it is better to think in terms of intertextuality rather than source study when considering the possible associations of many universal lives in Add. 2604. With regard to the native lives, most of their source is certain, but what led up to this source and beyond it in the shaping of the Add. 2604 lives is equally complex.

Native Saints: Latin Collections in Medieval England

Various early English saints, including many found in Add. 2604 such as Æthelthryth, Eorcengota, and Hild, make an early appearance in medieval England figuring as they do in the *Historia ecclesiastica* of Bede (*c.* 673–735), besides later references in service books and calendars.[42] The use of Latin legendaries in England has a long trajectory and an involved history that can only be hinted at here as a way of helping to contextualise the collection that is Add. 2604.[43] One of the oldest is the late ninth-century Cotton-Corpus

---

[42] For these saints, see *Bede's Ecclesiastical History of the English People*, ed. and trans. by Bertram Colgrave and R. A. B. Mynors, Oxford Medieval Texts (Oxford: Oxford University Press, 1969; repr. 1992), III.8, pp. 236–41; IV.19, pp. 390–97; and IV.23, pp. 404–15. While documented by Bede, the cults of Eorcengota and Æthelburh were not extensively celebrated in England. It is rare, in fact, for them to be included when the Ely female saints are invoked. An effort to track the popularity of English female saints is provided in Wiesje Nijenhuis, 'In a Class of Their Own: Anglo-Saxon Female Saints', *Mediaevistik*, 14 (2001), 125–48. See also Susan J. Ridyard, *The Royal Saints of Anglo-Saxon England: A Study of West Saxon and East Anglian Cults*, Cambridge Studies in Medieval Life and Thought, Fourth Series (Cambridge: Cambridge University Press, 1988); David Rollason, *Saints and Relics in Anglo-Saxon England* (Oxford: Blackwell, 1989); and Barbara Yorke, *Nunneries and the Anglo-Saxon Royal Houses*, Women, Power and Politics (London: Continuum, 2003).

[43] In the discussion of legendaries below, we start with the relevant highlights of the Latin tradition broadly in chronological order before moving to the vernacular. The aim here is not to provide a full history of hagiographical developments in medieval England but to outline the ways in which Add. 2604 may fit into this tradition with a particular concentration on the native saints. The discussion of Latin legendaries here relies to a large extent on the masterful

NATIVE SAINTS: LATIN COLLECTIONS IN MEDIEVAL ENGLAND   177

Legendary (sections preserved in separate manuscripts of later date, London, British Library, MS Cotton Nero E. i and Cambridge, Corpus Christi College, MS 9), produced in northern France and brought into England, from which Ælfric derived his *Lives of Saints* in Old English.[44] Such Latin collections only rarely included insular saints, but when they were re-copied or translated in England, native saints were necessary additions made to support liturgical celebration. One such collection is the two-volume Latin legendary: London, British Library, MS Cotton Tiberius D. iv. Varying in date from 950 to 1200, the contents are *vitae* and miracles of several native male saints: Æthelwold, Alban, Birin, Dunstan, Oswald, and Swithun among them.[45] By the turn of the tenth century various local centres such as Winchester and Canterbury had active hagiographical traditions and the second half of the eleventh century was particularly important for Anglo-Latin hagiography, with the foremost figure being Goscelin de Saint-Bertin (*c.* 1040–1114). A plethora of saints' lives may be attributed to him among which are Edith,

discussion by Michael Lapidge and Rosalind Love, 'The Latin Hagiography of England and Wales (600–1500)', in *Hagiographies*, ed. by Philippart, III (2001), pp. 203–325; useful too is Lapidge's 'Editing Hagiography' in which he details the development of legendaries in early England. See also Theodor Wolpers, *Die englische Heiligenlegende des Mittelalters: Eine Formgeschichte des Legendenerzählens von der spätantiken lateinischen Tradition bis zur Mitte des 16. Jahrhunderts*, Buchreihe Anglia, 10 (Tübingen: Niemeyer, 1964).

[44] Peter Jackson and Michael Lapidge, 'The Contents of the Cotton-Corpus Legendary', in *Holy Men and Holy Women: Old English Prose Saints' Lives and Their Contexts*, ed. by Paul E. Szarmach, SUNY Series in Medieval Studies (Albany, NY: State University of New York Press, 1996), pp. 131–46. For a discussion of the Cotton-Corpus Legendary as a potential source for Ælfric's collection of saints, see E. G. Whatley, 'Late Old English Hagiography, ca. 950–1150', in *Hagiographies*, ed. by Philippart, II (1996), 429–99. For an overview of insular Latin hagiography, see Lapidge and Love, 'The Latin Hagiography of England and Wales (600–1550)'.

[45] This manuscript may have been produced in northern France but the second part (*s.* xii) has associations with Winchester Old Minster, as it features lives and miracles of some forty-five continental saints like Leonard, alongside local saints and universal saints, both male and female. Whereas the early legendary favours bishops and archbishops, there is one twelfth-century passional that has some native women. London, Gray's Inn Library, MS 3 was originally a four-volume legendary from Chester Abbey, but only the first volume survives. It contains Æthelthryth on 23 June in the surviving volume, and in the missing volumes were Mildrith and an Eadburh ('Eadelredi atque eadalberti milredis et eadburge'), Wærburh ('et sic consequenter de sexburga ermenilda etc'), and Eormenhild alongside Agatha, Cecilia, Columba, and Justina, and John the Evangelist. The contents of all four volumes are described in N. R. Ker and A. J. Piper, *Medieval Manuscripts in British Libraries*, 5 vols (Oxford: Clarendon Press, 1969–2002), I (1969), 52–55 (p. 55).

Wærburh, and Wihtburh, as well as lections he wrote for Eormenhild and Seaxburh (as discussed in V. Latin Sources and Analogues). Goscelin's work, therefore, is fundamental in the production of Add. 2604.

After the Norman Conquest there were various works by notable domestic hagiographers such as Osbern (d. *c.* 1095) and Eadmer (d. *post* 1128) of Christ Church Canterbury, William of Malmesbury (d. *c.* 1142), and Aelred of Rievaulx (d. 1167). In addition, there were the hagiographers of Bury St Edmunds and Ely, whose *Liber Eliensis* (compiled between 1131 and 1174) is of fundamental concern for Add. 2604, consisting as it does of a life of Æthelthryth and short accounts of the other Ely saints. Yet the best known Latin collection in England after the Conquest was Jacobus de Voragine's *Legenda aurea* produced in the thirteenth century. Amongst its lives of the Roman martyrs, confessors, and popes, it had only a handful of insular saints: Brigid, Fursey, Patrick, Thomas Becket, and Ursula. The *Legenda aurea*, the most popular hagiographical text of the later medieval period, was quickly translated into the European vernaculars, and was very influential for medieval English hagiography and sermon studies. Above all it was adapted by the inclusion of regional and national saints to render it of particular use locally.[46] Like their continental peers, English writers adapted the *Legenda aurea* to their own needs, although the integration of native saints into collections of universal saints appears to have been somewhat infrequent. Examples include Cambridge, Pembroke College MS 277 (*s.* xiv[in], once owned by a rector of Conesford near Norwich); London, Westminster Abbey Chapter Library, MS 12 (*s.* xiv; unknown provenance as it was part of the post-medieval rebuilding of the abbey library); and Oxford, Balliol College MS 228 (*s.* xiv/xv; a gift of Bishop William Gray of Ely). Scattered across them are the native saints Æthelthryth, Edith, Fritheswith, Mildrith, and Osith.[47]

One of the main interests of the period is the focus on native saints in other Latin manuscripts. London, British Library, MS Cotton Vespasian A. xiv, written *c.* 1200 at Monmouth Abbey features sixteen lives (some different versions of

---

[46] For details of how the *Legenda aurea* has been expanded or contracted, see Barbara Fleith, *Studien zur Überlieferungsgeschichte der lateinischen 'Legenda Aurea'*, Subsidia hagiographica, 72 (Bruxelles: Société des Bollandistes, 1991). See V. Latin Sources and Analogues for a full discussion.

[47] On this point, see Manfred Görlach, 'Middle English Legends, 1220–1530', in *Hagiographies*, ed. by Philippart, I (1994), 429–85 (p. 446 and p. 447 n. 32).

NATIVE SAINTS: LATIN COLLECTIONS IN MEDIEVAL ENGLAND

the same saint) of Welsh saints, including Gwenfrewi (or Winifred).[48] Another collection in scope like Vespasian A. xiv is Exeter, Cathedral Library, MSS 3504–3505 (*c.* 1366), which was compiled by John Grandisson (1327–69), bishop of Exeter. It includes thirty-seven items, almost entirely of male saints of Wales and England. The female saints included are: Æthelthryth, Cuthburh, Edith, Fritheswith, Gwenfrewi, and Sidwell (or Sativola). Like the Grandisson collection, Gotha, Landesbibliothek, Cod. Membr. I.81 from the second half of the fourteenth century (of unknown English origin) shows an affinity for the west country saints of Cornwall and Devon. Among its lives are translations and miracles of some thirty-three male saints but *vitae* of only twelve females appear: Æthelburh, Cuthburh, Eadburh (of Thanet), Edith, Fritheswith, Helen, Hildelith, Milburh, Mildrith, Sidwell, Wulfhild, and Ursula.[49] (To this, might be added the fifteenth-century *Catalogus sanctorum pausantium in Anglia*, which is not a legendary but an extensive accounting of insular saints, their feasts, and their resting places; it again argues for the continued interest in collections featuring native saints.[50]) The circulation of these Latin legendaries, at times with attached liturgical matter such as antiphons and collects, is a significant indication of how these saints' lives were used in male communities. What is more difficult to assess is the use of legendaries in English female religious communities.

Conventual libraries are complicated to reconstruct due to the nature of losses, but references, if not the manuscripts or printed books themselves, document twenty-two legendaries owned or gifted to women religious: six written in Latin, four in French, and twelve in English.[51] No doubt, far more were in use than survive, but these provide a useful context for the production of Add. 2604. Two manuscripts of Latin lives which have some asso-

---

[48] Lapidge and Love, 'The Latin Hagiography of England and Wales (600–1550)', pp. 277–78.

[49] Lapidge and Love, 'The Latin Hagiography of England and Wales (600–1550)', pp. 281–82.

[50] London, British Library, MS Harley 3776, fols 118r–127r and London, Lambeth Palace Library, MS 99, fols 187r–194r; the contents in the Lambeth manuscript are listed in M. R. James, *A Descriptive Catalogue of the Manuscripts in the Library of Lambeth Palace*, 2 vols (Cambridge: Cambridge University Press, 1930–32), II (1932), 162–66 (pp. 163–65). See also D. W. Rollason, 'Lists of Saints' Resting-Places in Anglo-Saxon England', *Anglo-Saxon England*, 7 (1978), 61–93, and Nicholas Grant, 'John Leland's List of "Places where Saints Rest in England"', *Analecta Bollandiana*, 122 (2004), 373–87.

[51] Blanton, 'The Devotional Reading of Nuns', p. 188 and Table 4 on p. 204.

ciation with nuns are: London, British Library, Lansdowne MS 436 from Romsey, and Cardiff, Public Library, MS I.381 from Barking. Lansdowne MS 436, dating from the first half of the fourteenth century, contains forty-three items about insular saints, with an additional four named in the index that are now missing. Æthelthryth and her sisters Æthelburh, Seaxburh, and Wihtburh are prominently clustered together, and Æthelthryth's great-niece Wærburh and her brothers Ruffin and Wulflad are also adjacent to each other. The fifteen women celebrated also include Fritheswith, Hild, Modwenna, Osith, and Ælflæd, the patron of Romsey, where this manuscript was housed in the fifteenth century. The other Latin legendary, Cardiff, Public Library, MS I.381 (fols 81r–146r), dating from the twelfth century, contains seven lives: Æthelburh, David, Ebrulf, Edith, Edward the Martyr, Hildelith, and Mary of Egypt.[52] It is Æthelburh and Hildelith that suggest a provenance of Barking, though one might argue that the life of Edith, the patron of Wilton, or Edward the Martyr, who was enshrined at Shaftesbury, suggest alternative ownership.

This leaves one important work that is fundamental for the study of Add. 2604. As a stand-alone collection of native saints, which could be used to augment the liturgical calendar, the broadest in scope is also the primary source for the native lives in Add. 2604: John of Tynemouth's *Sanctilogium Angliae Walliae Scotiae et Hiberniae* (*c.* 1350), which features 156 entries about saints from a variety of sources (which will, along with its recensions, be discussed in V. Latin Sources and Analogues).[53] Important resources for the *Sanctilogium* were MS Cotton Vespasian A. xiv and Exeter Cathedral MSS 3504–3505. At some point, the *Sanctilogium*, which circulated in liturgical order by feast day, was reordered alphabetically and augmented with additional lives.[54]

---

[52] Described by Ker and Piper, *Medieval Manuscripts in British Libraries*, II (1977), 348–49.

[53] John of Tynemouth's *Historia aurea* includes brief notices of some of these lives and survives in these manuscripts: Cambridge, Corpus Christi College, MSS 5–6 (copied at St Albans); Cambridge, Cambridge University Library, MS Dd.10.22 (containing only the second half; acquired by St Albans after 1422); the three-volume London, Lambeth Palace Library, MSS 10, 11, and 12 (*s.* xiv; from Durham Priory); and Oxford, Bodleian Library, MS Bodley 240 (*s.* xv; includes only the second half, from Bury St Edmunds). V. H. Galbraith also indicates the *Historia aurea* influenced chronicles in several other manuscripts as well. See V. H. Galbraith, 'The *Historia aurea* of John, Vicar of Tynemouth, and the Sources of the St. Albans Chronicle (1327–1377)', in *Essays in History Presented to Reginald Lane Poole*, ed. by H. W. C. Davis (Oxford: Clarendon Press, 1927), pp. 379–98.

[54] *Nova Legenda Anglie*, ed. by Carl Horstman, 2 vols (Oxford: Clarendon Press, 1901),

NATIVE SAINTS: LATIN COLLECTIONS IN MEDIEVAL ENGLAND   181

Wynkyn de Worde printed this revised version in 1516, which he titled *Nova Legenda Anglie*. In the same year an abbreviated English translation of this appeared called *The Kalendre of the Newe Legende of England*. Both of these, which are discussed below, had a healthy circulation if one may judge from the surviving copies.[55]

Prior to the production of Add. 2604, there is a significant use of John's *Sanctilogium* that illustrates a similar initiative to include native saints alongside universal ones. Just after the royal foundation of the Birgittine Syon Abbey in 1415, Margaret Holland, Duchess of Clarence (before 1388–1439) commissioned a two-volume compendium of saints drawn from the Roman martyrology, the *Legenda aurea*, and the *Sanctilogium*; one of the two manuscripts is extant: Karlsruhe, Landesbibliothek Cod. Sankt Georgen 12 (likely well before Margaret's death in 1439).[56] This legendary was executed for the Birgittines of Syon Abbey whose formal name *Ordo sanctissimi Salvatoris* is invoked in the collection's title: *Sanctilogium salvatoris*. Cod. Sankt Georgen 12 is of particular interest for this *Study* of Add. 2604, as it demonstrates that on at least two occasions in the fifteenth century a compiler integrated universal saints from the *Legenda aurea* and native saints from John's *Sanctilogium* into a volume for the use of vowed religious.

---

pp. xv–xxi. It is worth noting that for a long time this reorganisation was attributed to John Capgrave, yet Peter Lucas definitely shows this supposition to be incorrect in Peter J. Lucas, 'John Capgrave and the *Nova legenda Anglie*: A Survey', *The Library*, 5th ser., 25 (1970), 1–10; reprinted in Peter J. Lucas, *From Author to Audience: John Capgrave and Medieval Publication* (Dublin: University College Dublin Press/Preas Choláiste Ollscoile Bhaile Átha Cliath, 1997), pp. 294–306.

[55] This is particularly the case with the Latin (STC 4601); thirty-six surviving copies are recorded in (http://estc.bl.uk/) (accessed 1 April 2023). The apparent circulation of the English (STC 4602) is lower but the twelve extant copies still testify to a not inconsiderable transmission when viewed in the light of the usual survival for early printed religious texts in England. For bibliography on the latter, see V. Latin Sources and Analogues, n. 129. For the Short Title Catalogue (STC), see A. W. Pollard and G. R. Redgrave, *A Short-Title Catalogue of Books Printed in England, Scotland, and Ireland, and of English Books Printed Abroad*, second edition, revised and enlarged by W. A. Jackson, F. S. Ferguson, and Katherine F. Pantzer, 3 vols (London: The Bibliographical Society, 1976–91); (revised at http://estc.bl.uk/).

[56] It is listed as part of the medieval brothers' library; see *Syon Abbey, with the Libraries of the Carthusians*, ed. by Vincent Gillespie and A. I. Doyle, Corpus of British Medieval Library Catalogues, 9 (London: The British Library in association with the British Academy, 2001), p. 212 (items 734–35).

182   IV. HAGIOGRAPHICAL CONTEXT AND THE SELECTION OF SAINTS

Vernacular Hagiographical Traditions in Medieval England

While John of Tynemouth's *Sanctilogium* looms large in the tradition of Latin legendaries in England, it was part of a broader cultural attention to insular saints that has been traced here in the Latin tradition from the ninth century to the early sixteenth. Yet in England, as in most European regions, vernacular hagiography developed alongside that of Latin, with the difference being that the English tradition was in place from a very early stage. In addition to occasional poetic texts on particular saints, there were extensive instances of Old English saints' lives and sanctorale sermons from the tenth century, alongside entries in the *Old English Martyrology* (beginning on Christmas Day) for Æthelthryth, Cecilia, Columba, Hild, John the Baptist (with feasts for his Conception, Nativity, Death, and the Invention), and John the Evangelist.[57] Additional saints appear in the Vercelli and Blickling homilies, and in collections by Ælfric of Eynsham, besides numerous other anonymous lives.[58] Ælfric's *Catholic Homilies* contains the Nativity and Decollation of John the Baptist, and John the Evangelist, while his *Saints' Lives* include Æthelthryth, Agatha, and Cecilia, alongside other universal and native lives. Elsewhere there was also a non-hagiographic item on John the Baptist and two fragments about Seaxburh.[59]

Add. 2604 shares affinities with other legendaries written in the vernacular (in French and Middle English). Yet it is unique for its precise selection of native and insular saints.[60] The earliest collection of Middle English saints' lives

---

[57] *The Old English Martyrology*, ed. and trans. by Rauer.

[58] J. E. Cross, 'English Vernacular Lives before 1000 A. D', and Whatley, 'Late Old English Hagiography, ca. 950–1150' in *Hagiographies*, ed. by Philippart, II (1996), 413–27 and 429–99 and references therein; see also M. R. Godden, 'Old English Composite Homilies from Winchester', *Anglo-Saxon England*, 4 (1975), 57–65; D. G. Scragg, 'The Corpus of Vernacular Homilies and Prose Saints' Lives before Ælfric', *Anglo-Saxon England*, 8 (1979), 223–77; and *Vercelli Homilies IX–XXIII*, ed. by Paul E. Szarmach, Toronto Old English Series, 5 (Toronto: Toronto University Press, 1981).

[59] For lists of all these saints, see Whatley, 'Late Old English Hagiography, ca. 950–1150', pp. 455–72. For an anonymous fragment of a life of Seaxburh in London, Lambeth Palace Library, MS 427, see 'Saint Seaxburh', in *Anonymous Old English Lives of Saints*, ed. and trans. by Johanna Kramer, Hugh Magennis, and Robin Norris, Dumbarton Oaks Medieval Library, 63 (Cambridge, MA: Harvard University Press, 2020), pp. 582–85.

[60] For discussions of English legendaries, see Wolpers, *Die englische Heiligenlegende des Mittelalters*; Görlach, 'Middle English Legends, 1220–1530'; Manfred Görlach, *Studies in Middle English Saints' Legends*, Anglistische Forschungen, 257 (Heidelberg: Winter, 1998);

VERNACULAR HAGIOGRAPHICAL TRADITIONS IN MEDIEVAL ENGLAND 183

is the Katherine Group (*c.* 1200), which features the universal saints Juliana, Katherine of Alexandria, and Margaret, whose lives are written in prose. Yet the most important legendary in the thirteenth century (and beyond) was composed in verse. The production of the *South English Legendary* (*c.* 1275–85) seems to have developed from a liturgical collection refashioned into a legendary of rhyming verse.[61] The original was not a translation from the *Legenda aurea* but instead predated its introduction into England. The more widely circulating *South English Legendary* tradition indicates a significant interest in vernacular versions of universal saints. Add. 2604 saints usually included in manuscripts of the *South English Legendary* are Agatha, Cecilia, John the Baptist (Nativity), Justina, Leonard, and Martha, with Justina being the least popular by far.[62] In this enormous verse collection some lives of native male saints appear but very few native females.[63] The variation among manuscripts

Edwards, 'Fifteenth-Century English Collections of Female Saints' Lives'; Pickering, 'Saints' Lives'; Mary Beth Long, 'Corpora and Manuscripts, Authors and Audiences', in *A Companion to Middle English Hagiography*, ed. by Sarah Salih (Woodbridge: Brewer, 2006), pp. 47–69; and Courtney E. Rydel, 'Legendary Effects: Women Saints of the *Legenda aurea* in England, 1260–1532' (unpublished doctoral dissertation, University of Pennsylvania, 2012). For bibliography, see John Scahill, with Margaret Rogerson, *Annotated Bibliographies of Old and Middle English*, VIII: *Middle English Saints' Legends* (Cambridge: Brewer, 2005). A comparative table detailing the appearance of eighty-nine saints' lives (that is, those that are most popular in texts emanating from England) across a range of English works mostly associated with the *Legenda aurea* is provided in Görlach, 'Middle English Legends, 1220–1530', pp. 442–43.

[61] For the *South English Legendary* and the *Legenda aurea*, see Görlach, 'Middle English Legends, 1220–1530', pp. 448–57. See also *Rethinking the South English Legendaries*, ed. by Heather Blurton and Jocelyn Wogan-Browne, Manchester Medieval Literature and Culture (Manchester: Manchester University Press, 2011). There is not one *South English Legendary* but multiple ones that vary, which is why recent scholars have adopted the plural form.

[62] See the final (unpaginated) leaves of Manfred Görlach, *The Textual Tradition of the South English Legendary*, Leeds Texts and Monographs, n.s. 6 (Leeds: School of English, 1974) where the contents of twenty-four manuscripts are compared; Justina is found only in six of them; in Görlach, 'Middle English Legends, 1220–1530', it is noted that the limited distribution of Petronilla, Justina, and Jakes Interisus 'makes it clear that they are independent additions, possibly by three different authors' (p. 457).

[63] For the history and development, see Görlach, *The Textual Tradition of the South English Legendary*. For details on the number of native saints, see Virginia Blanton, 'Counting Noses and Assessing the Numbers: Native Saints in the *South English Legendaries*', in *Rethinking the South English Legendaries*, ed. by Blurton and Wogan-Browne, pp. 233–50, and Mami Kanno, 'Constructing Gender and Locality in Late Medieval England: The Lives of Anglo-Saxon and British Female Saints in the *South English Legendaries*' (unpublished doctoral dissertation, University of London, King's College, 2016).

complicates an assessment of devotion to individual native saints, but adopting a rudimentary approach that documents the number of times a native life occurs across all the *South English Legendary* manuscripts demonstrates that twenty-four are about native males and seven about native females although no one manuscript includes all seven women.[64] The only female saint to appear in both the *South English Legendary* and Add. 2604 is Æthelthryth. The *Vernon Golden Legend* with its rare selection of saints and the sanctorale part of the *Northern Homily Collection* (both of which are composed in verse and date to the fourteenth century), have no native lives. In the extensive yet strangely ordered *Scottish Legendary* of the last quarter of the fourteenth century there are only two native lives, Machor and Ninian (if one excludes George). Based on the *Legenda aurea*, it comprises many of the popular universal figures found in Add. 2604: Agatha, Cecilia, John the Baptist, John the Evangelist, Justina, and Martha.[65]

While it has been argued that the *Scottish Legendary* was intended for private reading with a particular though non-exclusive interest for the female reader, the devotional and liturgical use of the legendary in England was usually formed to meet the needs of vowed religious.[66] By and large, such collections tended to be comprised solely of universal saints or of universal saints with a small grouping of native (usually male) saints. Where a native saint might occur because of a regional affiliation in Latin collections, it is an infrequent occurrence, even when the *Legenda aurea* was copied for local communities. When vernacular collections such as the manuscripts of the *South English Legendary* circulated, there may well have been a few additional native lives but universal saints dominate. Yet, there are a few exceptions.

The production of verse saints' lives in Middle English accords with an interest in producing hagiographical narratives in French verse, which had long been used in England for secular narratives. About seventy verse saints' lives

---

[64] Blanton, 'Counting Noses and Assessing the Numbers', pp. 234–35: where Brigid and Ursula were included in the *Legenda aurea*, these native female saints augment the English translation: Æthelthryth (three copies); Eadburh (of Nunnaminster, three copies); Fritheswith (eight copies); Mildrith (four copies); and Gwenfrewi (one copy).

[65] Görlach, 'Middle English Legends, 1220–1530', pp. 458–61.

[66] Eva von Contzen, *The Scottish Legendary: Towards a Poetics of Hagiographic Narration*, Manchester Medieval Literature and Culture (Manchester: Manchester University Press, 2016), p. 5; see also the Appendix, 'The Scottish Legendary: Authorship, Dialect and Arrangement', pp. 219–38.

VERNACULAR HAGIOGRAPHICAL TRADITIONS IN MEDIEVAL ENGLAND 185

are extant.[67] Significantly, these include a life of Catherine d'Alexandrie by the nun Clemence of Barking; an anonymous nun's life of Edouard le confesseur from the twelfth century, a life of Audrée by a certain Marie (possibly Marie de France) who may have been a nun at Chatteris in the thirteenth century;[68] a life of Modwenne produced around 1230 in the Benedictine monastery of Burton on Trent; and at the end of the thirteenth or beginning of the fourteenth century eleven short lives mainly of female saints (including Agatha and Martha) by Nicole de Bozon mostly based on the *Legenda aurea*.[69] Several of Nicole de Bozon lives are included in the collection preserved in London, British Library, Additional MS 70513, a late thirteenth- or early fourteenth-century manuscript, owned by the canonesses of Campsey Ash. This legendary of thirteen saints is unusual in that it features regional saints of northern Europe, including the native English saints: Æthelthryth, Edmund Rich, Edward the Confessor, Modwenna, Osith, Richard of Chichester, and Thomas Becket, alongside universal figures, albeit not those in Add. 2604.[70] The lives, written in octosyllabic rhyming couplets, offer a useful complement to those in Add. 2604, even if their generic form differs: they are written in the vernacular and evenly represent both universal and native saints. Both collections, moreover, would have been apropos reading during mealtimes and at collations, as well as during times of private devotion in female communities in England. (As noted in III. Convent and Geographical Location, an inscription in the Campsey Ash manuscript indicates that the book was used for reading during meals. It provides a direct link to understanding how Add. 2604 may have been used as a text for edification or *lectio divina*.)

[67] *Virgin Lives and Holy Deaths: Two Exemplary Biographies for Anglo-Norman Women*, trans. by Jocelyn Wogan-Browne and Glyn S. Burgess (London: Dent; Rutland, VT: Tuttle, 1996), p. xi.

[68] Jocelyn Wogan-Browne, 'Rerouting the Dower: The Anglo-Norman Life of St. Audrey by Marie (of Chatteris?)', in *Power of the Weak: Studies on Medieval Women*, ed. by Jennifer Carpenter and Sally-Beth MacLean (Carbondale, IL: University of Illinois Press, 1995), pp. 27–56.

[69] For a full discussion, see M. Thiry-Stassin, 'L'hagiographie en Anglo-Normand', in *Hagiographies*, ed. by Philippart, I (1994), 407–28.

[70] Blanton, 'The Devotional Reading of Nuns'. The only other collection in French contains only four lives and is associated with the Benedictine nuns at Derby: London, British Library, MS Egerton 2710. This manuscript contains no native saints; passions in prose of John, Peter and Paul, and Bartholomew are complemented by a verse account of Lawrence; see Bell, *What Nuns Read*, pp. 135–36.

186   IV. HAGIOGRAPHICAL CONTEXT AND THE SELECTION OF SAINTS

A complementary example to the Campsey Ash manuscript is a fifteenth-century collection in Middle English verse containing thirteen lives of universal female saints, including Agatha and Cecilia. The Augustinian friar, Osbern Bokenham (1393–after 1463), translated these lives for pious lay dedicatees in Suffolk.[71] The initial production and intention behind these lives therefore seem more akin to the general circulation of individual fifteenth-century lives, in that it would have been more common to find verse lives of saints such as Dorothy, Katherine of Alexandria, or Margaret in miscellanies alongside prayers and devotional treatises like John Lydgate's *Life of Our Lady*. A. S. G. Edwards indicates that London, British Library MS Harley 5272 (*s.* xv[4]) and London, British Library, MS Arundel 168 (*s.* xv) are indicative of this 'gendered and generically congruent' trend; the miscellany, he suggests, served to meet the devotional needs of pious laypeople, particularly female readers.[72] By contrast, the legendary seems to be a form reserved more for vowed religious, if we are to judge by the next incarnation of Bokenham's translated lives of universal female saints: in 1447 they were copied into one manuscript, London, British Library, MS Arundel 327, at the request of Friar Thomas Burgh of Cambridge for a community of nuns.[73] This manuscript, containing lives that first circulated independently until they were gathered together into a collection for the use of nuns — perhaps the minoresses at Denney Abbey in Cambridgeshire — is of particular interest to the present *Study* of Add. 2604, one we contend was also collected for an audience of nuns.[74]

Bokenham's translation of the *Legenda aurea* in the Abbotsford manuscript to which he has added a number of native lives is a similar attempt to showcase native lives alongside universal saints, if not a fully even distribution.[75] As he explains, Bokenham translated this larger collection for the edification of his friends (a trope he also employs in his *Legendys of Hooly Wummen*):

[71] See Osbern Bokenham, *Legendys of Hooly Wummen*, ed. by Mary S. Serjeantson, EETS, o.s. 206 (London: Oxford University Press, 1938), pp. xx–xxi for the dedicatees.

[72] Edwards, 'Fifteenth-Century English Collections of Female Saints' Lives', p. 135.

[73] Osbern Bokenham, *Legendys of Hooly Wummen*, ed. by Serjeantson, p. 289.

[74] Doyle suggests the collection may have been intended for the use of minoresses in 'Books Connected with the Vere Family and Barking Abbey', p. 236 n. 8.

[75] Simon Horobin, 'A Manuscript Found in Abbotsford House and the Lost Legendary of Osbern Bokenham', *English Manuscript Studies, 1100–1700*, 14 (2007), 130–62; Simon Horobin, 'Politics, Patronage, and Piety in the Work of Osbern Bokenham', *Speculum*, 82 (2007), 932–49. For other studies of Bokenham, see Alice Spencer, *Language, Lineage and Location in the Works of Osbern Bokenham* (Cambridge: Cambridge Scholars, 2013).

VERNACULAR HAGIOGRAPHICAL TRADITIONS IN MEDIEVAL ENGLAND 187

[...] the englische boke the whiche y haue compiled of legenda aurea and of oþer famous legendes at the instaunce of my specialle frendis and for edificacioun and comfort of alle tho þe whiche shuld redene hit or here hit [...].[76]

Bokenham's legendary comprises lives in verse and prose, including Agatha, Barbara, and John the Evangelist alongside the insular saints Æthelthryth, Alban, Aldhelm, Augustine (of Canterbury), Botulf, Cedde, David, Dunstan, Felix, Gwenfrewi, John of Beverley, Oswald, Wilfrid, and Wulfstan.[77] Bokenham's production demonstrates, therefore, a considerable interest in providing native lives in English. When he says he has done so at the instigation of special friends, he suggests that this legendary, like the individual lives he translated, were produced for reading by the laity though given its scope we might also see this as a collection appropriate for use in a monastic setting.[78] Be that as it may, the collection is of particular interest in that it unites luminaries of the *Legenda aurea* and celebrated local saints, as does Add. 2604.[79]

This relationship with and dependence on the *Legenda aurea* is also most noticeable in the other major compilations of saints' lives in prose and in many of the surviving sanctorale sermon cycles or collections. The most important and the most widely circulated in manuscript form amongst the former is the *Gilte Legende*, a translation of the *Legenda aurea* via a French intermediary. Extant to varying degrees of completeness in eight manuscripts (with chapters in sixteen medieval and two later copies), this massive compilation contains 179 texts comprising saints' lives and a few other items. Mostly these correspond to those in the *Legenda aurea*, but there are a few additions, omissions, sub-

[76] This rationale is found in his partial translation of Ranulf Higden's (d. 1364) *Polychronicon*; see *Osbern Bokenham, 'Lives of Saints'*, ed. by Simon Horobin, EETS, o.s. 356 and 359, 2 vols (Oxford: Oxford University Press, 2020–22), I, xvi–xvii (p. xvi).

[77] Further, Bokenham claims his translation includes lives of Edward and Oswald, both of which are not found in the Abbotsford manuscript. In 'A Manuscript Found in Abbotsford House and the Lost Legendary of Bokenham', Horobin indicates that missing leaves in precisely the correct locations in the festal year would account for these lives, pp. 139–40.

[78] Horobin suggests that the collection may have been produced for Cecily of York. We wonder if it were intended for her own use, given the markers of status in the book, or intended as a gift to a religious community, see Horobin, 'A Manuscript Found in Abbotsford House and the Lost Legendary of Osbern Bokenham', pp. 149–51.

[79] For a discussion of Æthelthryth and Gwenfrewi in this collection, see Winstead, *Fifteenth-Century Lives*, pp. 60–73.

stitutions, and re-arrangements.[80] This means that the standard *Gilte Legende* has the following texts that figure in some way in Add. 2604 (in order of their arrangement): John the Evangelist, Agatha, John *Ad portam Latinam*, Nativity of John the Baptist, Cecilia, Justina, Leonard, Cecilia (duplicated). Unlike the *Legenda aurea*, the *Gilte Legende* omits the Decollation of John the Baptist and partially substitutes different versions for the Nativity of John the Baptist, a potentially important point for Add. 2604's John the Baptist. Three of the manuscripts also contain to varying extents what are known as the Additional Legends. Most of these thirty-one lives are of native English saints, though only two are female, Fritheswith and Gwenfrewi.[81] Unlike many such collections, the *Gilte Legende* has the advantage of a secure dating and genesis in that the author notes in the colophon to one of the manuscripts:

> And also here endith the lives of Seintis that is callid in latynne Legenda Aurea. And in Englissh the gilte ligende the which is drawen out of Frensshe into Englisshe the yere of oure lorde a M¹ CCCC and xxxviij bi a synfulle wrecche [...] (Oxford, Bodleian Library, MS Douce 372, fol. 163v col. b).

This mention of a French text, the mid-fourteenth-century *Legende dorée* by Jean de Vignay that provides most of the source, is significant because it helps highlight possible French associations of the lives in Add. 2604 with regard to their analogues.

A similar French connection is also evident in the next major translation into English of the *Legenda aurea*, the *Golden Legend* translated by William Caxton and published in 1483 (and into the first decade of the sixteenth century). Here too the translator is explicit about his procedure in his prologue:

> [...] But for as moche as I had by me a legende in Frensshe, another in Latyn and the thyrd in Englysshe, whiche varyed in many and dyuers places, and also many hystoryes were comprysed in the two other bookes which were not in the Englysshe book; and therfore I haue wryton one oute of the sayd thre bookes, which I haue ordryd otherwyse than the sayd Englysshe legende is [...].[82]

---

[80] *Gilte Legende*, ed. by Richard Hamer, with Vida Russell, EETS, o.s. 327, 328, and 339, 3 vols (Oxford: Oxford University Press, 2006–12).

[81] *Supplementary Lives in Some Manuscripts of the 'Gilte Legende'*, ed. by Richard Hamer and Vida Russell, EETS, o.s. 315 (Oxford: Oxford University Press, 2000).

[82] *Caxton's 'Golden Legend'*, ed. by Mayumi Taguchi, John Scahill, and Satoko Tokunaga, EETS, o.s. 355, 357, 2 vols (Oxford: Oxford University Press, 2020–21), I: *Temporale*, xvii.

In describing the mix-and-match format of his collection in which he has been shown to have used the *Legenda aurea*, a printed version (between 1472 and 1475) of the *Legende dorée* by Jean de Vignay, and a version of the *Gilte Legende*, Caxton provides valuable insight into the sort of technique used by Middle English hagiographers and one that will be apparent in the study of the underlying sources and analogues to Add. 2604.[83] Not unexpectedly, Caxton's lives (in order that they appear) include familiar *Legenda aurea* ones: John the Evangelist, Agatha, John *Ad portam Latinam*, the Nativity of John the Baptist, Martha, the Decollation of John the Baptist, Justina, Leonard, and Cecilia, plus Barbara (who is an addition to the standard *Legenda aurea*). While it does have some native English lives, the only female is the Welsh Gwenfrewi.

Besides these major compilations, small groups of single saints' lives in verse and prose continued to be produced.[84] Such saints include the very popular Dorothy, Katherine of Alexandria, and Margaret. Yet in connection with Add. 2604 the most significant is London, British Library, MS Cotton Faustina B. iii (dated *c.* 1420), which has verse lives of Edith of Wilton (fols 194r–280r) and Æthelthryth (fols 265r–279v) ending imperfectly.[85] Featured in the Wilton Chronicle, which highlights the ancient English kings, this pairing of royal women is especially distinctive and suggests the importance of the East Anglian Æthelthryth to the nuns at Wilton. Foremost among the prose lives are those by John Capgrave (1393–1464) from the Augustinian friary in Lynn in Norfolk, and those with links to the Birgittine Syon Abbey. Capgrave wrote two lives in prose: Augustine of Hippo and Gilbert of Sempringham, and two in verse: Katherine of Alexandria and Norbert, with the second life being specifically at the behest of a woman and the first for the benefit of female religious readers.[86] The collection of lives associated with Syon Abbey includes

[83] See *Caxton's 'Golden Legend'*, ed. by Taguchi, Scahill, and Tokunaga, I: *Temporale*, xvii–xxv, for full details.

[84] In Edwards, 'Fifteenth-Century English Collections of Female Saints' Lives', various examples of saints' lives mainly in verse are listed; the prose lives are discussed in Pickering, 'Saints' Lives' (with full manuscript details in each case).

[85] The life of Æthelthryth in the Wilton Chronicle is found in London, British Library, MS Cotton Faustina B. iii, fols 265r–279v; see *Saints Edith and Æthelthryth: Princesses, Miracle Workers, and their Late Medieval Audience, The Wilton Chronicle and the Wilton Life of St Æthelthryth*, ed. and trans. by Mary Dockray-Miller, Medieval Women: Texts and Contexts, 25 (Turnhout: Brepols, 2009), pp. 336–405.

[86] The precise requests are quoted in Pickering, 'Saints' Lives', pp. 256–57.

190   IV. HAGIOGRAPHICAL CONTEXT AND THE SELECTION OF SAINTS

Jerome, John the Baptist, John the Evangelist, and Katherine of Alexandria.[87] Alongside these are a number of anonymous lives, one of the most interesting and unusual being that in Oxford, Bodleian Library, MS Douce 114 that contains the lives of Caterina da Siena, Christina Mirabilis, Elisabeth de Spalbeek, and Marie d'Oignies.[88] Scattered among various other manuscripts (and sometimes inserted into collections or later printed) are lives of Antony the Hermit, Barbara, Birgitta of Sweden, Dorothy, Edward the Confessor, Katherine of Alexandria, Margaret, Ursula, and Zita, and most relevant of all for present purposes, a fifteenth-century prose life of Æthelthryth in Oxford, Corpus Christi College, MS 120 (fols 1r–14r).[89]

This prose account in Corpus Christi College, MS 120 is distinctly different from the version in Add. 2604 and cannot be considered a source, as the comparison of Middle English versions of the life of Æthelthryth in Appendix 2 illustrates. Bound in a limp vellum binding and copied by a competent hand with large, rudimentary red initials that open each of ten chapters and the prologue, the manuscript is properly a booklet, which the translator indicates is intended to circulate independently. He acknowledges it may eventually be copied alongside other lives of the Ely saints:

> [...] this lytle boke shall shew alonly the gracious lyfe of the thyrde doughter of this honorable kyng Anna and Eryswythe, whois name was callyd Audry otherwyse Etheldrede for to auoyde confusioun and tediousnes to the herers, the whiche myte happyn yf the mattyr schuld be intermyxyd or medled with the holy lyvys of the progenitors or brethyrne or systers of the seyde Audry. All other matyrs sett apart, I purpose be the grace of God and thorowgh the suffragys of this holy virgyn shortly after an humble style to comprehende the trewe vertuous lyfe of the seyde virgyn as nye as I can folowe the olde originall therof, the whiche [ys w]ryten in Latyn in the monastery of Ely (fol. 1r–v).[90]

---

[87] *Virgins and Scholars: A Fifteenth-Century Compilation of the Lives of John the Baptist, John the Evangelist, Jerome, and Katherine of Alexandria*, ed. by Claire M. Waters, Medieval Women: Texts and Contexts, 10 (Turnhout: Brepols, 2008).

[88] For discussions, see Brian C. Vander Veen, 'The *Vitae* of Bodleian Library MS Douce 114' (unpublished doctoral dissertation, University of Nottingham, 2007), and Jennifer N. Brown, *Three Women of Liège: A Critical Edition of and Commentary on the Middle English Lives of Elizabeth of Spalbeck, Christina Mirabilis, and Marie d'Oignies*, Medieval Women: Texts and Contexts, 23 (Turnhout: Brepols, 2009).

[89] An edition is currently being undertaken by Ileana Sasu.

[90] Contractions are silently expanded in this transcription, and punctuation added for clarity. Damage to fol. 1v has occluded the letters inserted in brackets. We are grateful to Kerryn Olsen for sharing a copy of her transcription with us many years ago. Any errors here are our own.

VERNACULAR HAGIOGRAPHICAL TRADITIONS IN MEDIEVAL ENGLAND 191

Of particular interest is the notion that this booklet is to be shared among an audience of 'herers', rather than used in solitary devotion.[91] Where the source text for the Wilton life is from Godstow,[92] the translator of Corpus Christi College, MS 120 indicates that his Latin source is 'the olde originall' at Ely. Clearly related to Æthelthryth's *vita* in the *Liber Eliensis*, there are two elements not found in the monastery's chronicle, including her being married at Thetford in Norfolk (fol. 3r) and a miracle in which Æthelthryth places her gloves on a sunbeam, an astonishing sight that indicates her holiness to her first husband (fol. 3v). In sum, the prose life of Corpus Christi College, MS 120 is an intriguing narrative but quite distinct from the version in Add. 2604.

In the extant prose sermons of medieval England between the late twelfth and the late fifteenth centuries it is a surprisingly easy matter to account for the saints that equate with those found in Add. 2604 as there are so few of them. In sum, Agatha, Cecilia, and Leonard figure in one sermon each. Otherwise the most popular saint is John the Baptist followed by John the Evangelist. There are eight sermons for John the Baptist's Nativity, three for his Decollation, one for his Vigil and one on his Octave, as well as one other devoted to him. For John the Evangelist's feast on 27 December there are seven sermons in total and four for his feast *Ad portam Latinam* (on 6 May).[93] There are, of course, other saints in the cycles and collections, mainly universal but with some native or nominally native English saints mostly with a sermon each: Alkmund, Augustine of Canterbury (two sermons), Edmund (archbishop), Edmund (king, two sermons), George (five sermons), Giles, Neot, Oswald, Thomas of Canterbury (seven sermons), and Wulfstan; the only female saint is Gwenfrewi.[94] (A wider

[91] Distinctive too about this version is the identity of Æthelthryth's mother as 'Eryswythe', obviously a form of 'Hereswith' who is named as her mother in the *Liber Eliensis*, ed. by E. O. Blake, Camden Society, Third Series, 92 (London: Royal Historical Society, 1962), I.2, pp. 12–13. For a translation of this work, see *Liber Eliensis: A History of the Isle of Ely From the Seventh to the Twelfth*, trans. by Janet Fairweather (Woodbridge: Boydell, 2005).

[92] *Saints Edith and Æthelthryth*, ed. and trans. by Dockray-Miller, p. 396, ll. 974–79.

[93] For details, see the index of sermon occasions in Veronica O'Mara and Suzanne Paul, *A Repertorium of Middle English Prose Sermons*, Sermo: Studies on Patristic, Medieval, and Reformation Sermons and Preaching, 1, 4 vols (Turnhout: Brepols, 2007), IV, 2658–72. It should be noted that each sermon is counted only once irrespective of how many manuscripts in which it occurs. This means that the sermons on the two Johns, if counted individually, would have a very widespread dissemination as they are both found as part of the *Festial* and Lollard Sermon collections; conversely the other three universal saints are each only found in one manuscript.

[94] If counted as individual unique occurrences (rather than being mathematically calculated in terms of sermons occurring in more than one collection) there are 1,480 Middle

range of lives, both universal and native, is witnessed by late Latin sermon collections in England.[95]) Of the English manuscripts containing such lives only that of John Mirk's *Festial* was ever printed making the life of Gwenfrewi the sole one that would have circulated widely in the editions published between 1483 and 1532.[96]

There were, of course, various medieval saints' lives in English in similar editions or with different texts printed at the end of the fifteenth century and up to the first decades of the sixteenth century (and sometimes beyond), with prose being more dominant than verse.[97] In the former were the following (ordered here by date of printing): Gwenfrewi (1485, STC 25853); Caterina da Siena (1492?, STC 24766; 1500?, STC 24766.3; 1609, STC 4830); Jerome (1499?, STC 14508); Armele (*c.* 1502, STC 772); Katherine of Alexandria (1505?, STC 4813.6; 1510?, not in STC; 1555?, STC 4813.8); Joseph of Arimathea (1507–08?, STC 14806; 1520, STC 14807); Francis of Assisi (*c.* 1515, STC 3270); Barbara (1518, STC 1375); Barbara (1520, STC 1375.5, a translation of Jean Wackerzeele's text); Thomas of Canterbury (1520, STC 23954); Erasmus (1520, STC 10435); Brendan (1521?, STC 3600); and Nicholas of Tollentino (1525?, STC 18528; 1525? STC 18528.5). Verse lives comprised Margaret (1493, STC 17325; 1530?, STC 17326; 1530–32?, STC

English prose sermons; the bulk of these are for the temporale, making it seem that sanctorale sermons were neglected in England. This issue is complicated and so the extant material may not fully reflect what went on in practice (for example, preachers could have narrated the lives of particular saints without the aid of a written sermon); for further discussion, see V. M. O'Mara, 'Saints' Plays and Preaching: Theory and Practice in Late Middle English Sanctorale Sermons', *Leeds Studies in English: Essays in Honour of Peter Meredith*, n.s. 29 (1998), 257–74.

[95] A list of such lives from the 360 sermons he has studied is given in Siegfried Wenzel, *Latin Sermon Collections from Later Medieval England: Orthodox Preaching in the Age of Wyclif,* Cambridge Studies in Medieval Literature (Cambridge: Cambridge University Press, 2005), pp. 250–51 n. 91.

[96] Veronica O'Mara, 'The Early Printed Sermon in England between 1483 and 1532: A Peculiar Phenomenon', in *Circulating the Word of God in Medieval and Early Modern Europe: Catholic Preaching and Preachers across Manuscript and Print (c. 1450 to c. 1550)*, ed. by Veronica O'Mara and Patricia Stoop, Sermo: Studies on Patristic, Medieval, and Reformation Sermons and Preaching, 17 (Turnhout: Brepols, 2022), pp. 71–102.

[97] The number here is small if compared with those being produced in France with its more developed printing centres; see S. Bledniak, 'L'hagiographie imprimée: œuvres en français', 1476–1550', in *Hagiographies*, ed. by Philippart, I (1994), 359–405, who comments that 'Nous recensons actuellement, pour la période considérée — des débuts de l'imprimerie jusqu'à 1550 — soixante-quinze *vitae* relatives à soixante-cinq saints' (p. 362).

VERNACULAR HAGIOGRAPHICAL TRADITIONS IN MEDIEVAL ENGLAND   193

17327); Ursula ([1507–08?], STC 24541.3); George (1515?, STC 22992.1); Radegund (c. 1525, STC 3507); and Wærburh (1521, STC 3506).[98] Significant for Add. 2604 in this list is the appearance of Barbara and Wærburh. Finally, of course, the most extensive — and for Add. 2604 the most important — collection of lives, is *The Kalendre of the Newe Legende of England* (1516, STC 4602) the abbreviated lives taken from the Latin *Nova Legenda Anglie* that ultimately derive from John of Tynemouth's *Sanctilogium* (1516, STC 4601).[99] With this,

---

[98] There is also a life of Mark the Evangelist in prose from some time in the 1500s in London, British Library, MS Harley 5936; and a verse life of St Gregory's mother (1501?, STC 12351.5; 1515, STC 12352; c. 1532?, STC 12353).

[99] John of Tynemouth organised his collection of lives in feast order, as London, British Library, MS Cotton Tiberius E. i illustrates. At some point, this collection was augmented and circulated in alphabetical order before being printed by Wynkyn de Worde in 1516 as the *Nova Legenda Anglie*, which is the version Carl Horstman used for his 1901 edition. The same year as this Latin edition, Richard Pynson printed abbreviated versions in English as *The Kalendre of the Newe Legende of Englande*, ed. by Manfred Görlach (Heidelberg: Universitätsverlag Winter, 1994). The saints overlapping with those in Add. 2604 who appear in *The Kalendre* are: Æthelthryth, pp. 96–97; Eadburh, p. 81; Eanswith, pp. 79–80; Edith, pp. 81–82; Eormenhild, pp. 92–93; Hild, p. 113; Modwenna, pp. 140–41; Seaxburh, pp. 161–62; Wærburh, pp. 170–71; Wihtburh, p. 178. Similar in content to Pynson's edition is a collection entitled, *The Lives of Women Saints of Our Contrie of England*, ed. by Carl Horstman, EETS, o.s. 86 (London: Trübner, 1886). It features Æthelthryth, pp. 67–71; Eadburh, pp. 49–50; Eanswith, pp. 51–52; Edith, pp. 102–04; Eormenhild, pp. 58–59; Hild, pp. 56–58; Modwenna, pp. 92–97; Seaxburh, pp. 54–55 (with Eorcengota and Æthelburh mentioned briefly at the end); Wærburh, pp. 59–60; and Wihtburh, p. 79 in Horstman's edition. The antiquarian John Leland (c. 1503–52) repurposed brief accounts of native saints in a history of each English county in *Collectanea*, ed. by Thomas Hearne, 6 vols (London, Benjamin White, 1774), including Æthelthryth, II, 589–94; Eadburh, III, 165–66; Edith, III, 168–69; Eormenhild, III, 168 (Wlfad, Ruffin, and Coenred are identified as her sons); Seaxburh, III, 164–65; Wærburh, III, 167–68; and Wihtburh, III, 166–67. Following a tradition of collecting native women saints, Nicholas Roscarrock (d. by 13 April 1634), a Cornish Catholic, compiled a hand-written list of saints with brief accounts preserved in Cambridge, Cambridge University Library, MS Additional 3041, which include: Æthelburh, fol. 174v; Æthelthryth, fols 176r–78r; Eadburh, fols 165r–165v; Eanswith, fol. 169r; Edith, fols 178v–179v; Eorcengota (listed in the index but inadvertently left out); Eormenhild, fol. 206r–v; Hild, fol. 252r–v; Modwenna, fols 317r–320r; Seaxburh, fol. 398r–v; Wærburh (listed in the index but this section of the manuscript is missing); and Wihtburh (listed in the index but this section of the manuscript is lost). Some of the Roscarrock lives are in *Nicholas Roscarrock's Lives of the Saints: Cornwall and Devon*, ed. by Nicholas Orme, Devon and Cornwall Record Society, n.s. 35 (Exeter: BPCC Wheatons Ltd, 1992). Later collections include those by John Wilson (c. 1575–c. 1645?) and Jerome Porter (d. 1632), a Benedictine. Wilson was responsible for the first collection of British saints' lives to be printed in the post-Reformation period, *The English martyrologe* published in 1608 (STC

194   IV. HAGIOGRAPHICAL CONTEXT AND THE SELECTION OF SAINTS

we almost come full circle in a movement from universal to native lives, an emphasis that is also very obvious in the later recusant collections produced for an English readership at home or abroad during the sixteenth and seventeenth centuries.

The hagiographical collections noted here are heavily weighted towards male saints, confessors, martyrs, and clerical figures. Lives of female saints were important but were often overshadowed, especially in England, as no insular woman was canonised in the late medieval period. Female saints culted in England were those figures who participated in the early Christian conversions and the establishment of monastic communities. Thus, Add. 2604 is a relatively unique survival. It is written in prose, as so many saints' lives were, but it features native insular women alongside universal women, both biblical figures and virgin martyrs, an amalgam that could provide a useful counterpoint to the readings in a more standard legendary. In this regard it is not unlike some of the continental vernacular compilations that privileged female saints. For instance, London, British Library, MS Egerton 3130 is a thirteenth- or fourteenth-century miscellany of theological works owned by Rookloster or Rouge-Cloître, which has four female saints: Agnes, Gudula, Katherine of Alexandria, and Mary of Egypt. As another example, the librarian Sister Regula (d. 1478) of the convent of Lichtenthal near Baden-Baden produced *Das Buch von den hl. Mägden und Frauen*, a collection of fifty-seven lives, written in her own hand, as part of her conventual

---

25771), in 1640 (STC 25772), and in 1672, which provided brief accounts of the saints according to their feast day. In 1632 Porter published another collection, *The flowers of the liues of the most renowned saincts of the three kingdoms [...]* (STC 20124); this was meant to have followed calendrical order but only January to June ever appeared in print. This emphasis on native saints was also taken up in the next century in the work of Richard Challoner (1691–1781) and his *Britannica Sancta [...]*, 2 vols (London: Printed for Thomas Meighan, 1745). For overviews of these later collections see J. T. Rhodes, 'English Books of Martyrs and Saints of the Late Sixteenth and Early Seventeenth Centuries', *Recusant History*, 22 (1994), 7–25 and Elizabeth Ferguson, 'Veneration, Translation and Reform: The *Lives* of Saints and the English Catholic Community, *c.* 1600–1642', *Recusant History*, 32 (2014), 37–65. As well as being on EEBO, printed facsimiles are available: John Wilson, *The English Martyrologe, 1608*, ed. by D. M. Rogers, English Recusant Literature, 1558–1640, 232 (Ilkley, West Yorkshire: The Scolar Press, 1975), and Jerome Porter, *The Flowers of the Lives of the Most Renowned Saincts, 1632*, ed. by D. M. Rogers, English Recusant Literature, 1558–1640, 239 (Ilkley, West Yorkshire: The Scolar Press, 1975). Wilson includes the full complement of native saints: Wærburh Eormenhild, Eadburh, Æthelthryth, Modwenna, Seaxburh, Eorcengota, Eanswith plus her Translation, Edith, Hild plus her Translation, Wihtburh, and Eadburh. Porter includes Wærburh, Eormenhild, Eadburh, and Æthelthryth.

VERNACULAR HAGIOGRAPHICAL TRADITIONS IN MEDIEVAL ENGLAND 195

programme to translate for the sisters with limited Latinity.[100] Larger compilations still are the paired fifteenth-century French legendaries in London, British Library, MS Additional 41179 and Oxford, The Queen's College, MS 305, both produced in or near Avignon or Carpentras probably in the 1460s, featuring a hundred and twenty-four universal and other female saints, some of which are also found in Add. 2604: Agatha, Cecilia, Columba, Domitilla, and Martha.[101]

Communities developed their own compilations of saints, and it appears that the legendary copied into Add. 2604 was one such, albeit with its own somewhat idiosyncratic selection criteria. When compared with all other extant saints' lives in Middle English in manuscript or early print, Add. 2604 is the only one to contain the universal lives of Benedicta, Columba, and Domitilla.[102] With regard to the native lives, it uniquely contains Middle English lives of Eadburh, Eanswith, Eorcengota (with her aunt Æthelburh appended), Eormenhild, Hild, Modwenna, Seaxburh, Wihtburh, and it features one of the two lives of Wærburh.[103] How such a specialised selection may have emerged is partially revealed by an analysis of those saints included.

---

[100] For a few other German examples of collections of females saints, see W. Williams-Krapp, 'Deutschsprachige Hagiographie von ca. 1350 bis ca. 1550', in *Hagiographies*, ed. by Philippart, I (1994), 267–88 (p. 275). There are, of course, various examples of Latin collections of female saints, such as the *Passionale de virginibus* written between the twelfth and fourteenth centuries in the Benedictine abbey of Saint Laurent in Liège, a collection by the Brethren of the Common Life in Deventer from the late Middle Ages, and a manuscript from the fifteenth century from the Premonstratensian abbey of Berne (near 's Hertogenbosch), as shown in Vermassen, 'Latin Hagiography in the Dutch-Speaking Parts of the Southern Low Countries (1350–1550)', pp. 572 n. 14, 581 and n. 51, and 597–98. See also Appendix 1 below.

[101] Paul Meyer, 'Notice du MS. 305 de Queen's College, Oxford (légendier français)', *Romania*, 34 (1905), 215–36; see also P[aul] M[eyer], 'Légendes hagiographiques en français, II: Légendes en prose', in *Histoire littéraire de la France*, 33 (Paris: Imprimerie nationale, 1906), pp. 378–458, passim. For a full description of MS Additional 41179 see (https://searcharchives. bl.uk) (accessed 1 April 2023) and for MS 305, see Peter Kidd, *A Descriptive Catalogue of the Medieval Manuscripts of The Queen's College, Oxford*, Oxford Bibliographical Society Publications, Special Series: Manuscript Catalogues, 1 (Oxford: Oxford Bibliographical Society, 2017), pp. 131–42, including a description of its 115 miniatures (pp. 137–40).

[102] Virtually all the other universal saints are ones associated with the *Legenda aurea*, so it is not surprising to see these in other Middle English translations.

[103] The other is the 1521 verse life (STC 3506). Abbreviated versions of these lives are also found in *The Kalendre of the Newe Legende of Englande*, ed. by Görlach, but as will be explained in V. Latin Sources and Analogues, this text is connected with that in Add. 2604.

The Selection of Saints' Lives in Add. 2604

As we have seen, the collection of saints' lives in Add. 2604 is divided between universal saints and native, with eleven of each. Yet this apparent uniformity belies a certain strangeness in selection and sequence. Listing the saints in order provokes immediate questions: John the Baptist, John the Evangelist, Columba, Agatha, Cecilia, Barbara, Æthelthryth of Ely, Seaxburh, Wihtburh, Eormenhild, Eorcengota (including a brief account of Æthelburh and a comment about Sæthryth), Wærburh of Chester, Edith of Wilton, Eanswith of Folkstone, Eadburh of Minster-in-Thanet, Hild of Whitby, Martha, Domitilla, Justina, Benedicta, Modwenna, and Leonard. Not only may we wonder about the presence of these precise saints and in this particular order, but also think back to how they compare (or mainly do not compare) with the earlier or contemporary Latin or vernacular collections. We may also consider which saints may be missing.

Add. 2604, which is in one hand of the second half of the fifteenth century, is consistent linguistically; as shown in I. The Manuscript, it probably dates to some point between about 1480 and 1510 and, as discussed in II. Language and Dialectal Provenance, it tends towards an East Anglian locale (possibly Suffolk, speculatively in the region of Bury St Edmunds); and, as will be elucidated in V. Latin Sources and Analogues, it is translated from a range of Latin material. But, it is also missing many pages and sometimes whole quires. We are dealing with an imperfect production and, unless a single source comes to light (rather than the various sources and analogues pinpointed to date), the answers provided here can only ever be tentative. Part of the difficulty is not knowing how imperfect the manuscript is at present. It may be that only a few quires and several pages are missing, which can mostly be accounted for. Conversely, if far more quires are lacking than currently surmised, it is conceivable that Add. 2604 is the wreck of what was once a substantial collection. As it stands, the saints cross quire boundaries and so any argument about the individual groupings being found in separate booklets is not tenable. The only saints contained within separate quire boundaries are Modwenna and Leonard at the end, so conceivably they could have had a distinct history or possibly have circulated individually.

At first glance it may seem odd that this collection almost entirely of female virgins, martyrs, or nuns, opens with two male saints, John the Baptist and John the Evangelist, and closes with another male saint, Leonard.[104] Yet in medieval

---

[104] The discussion below expands on some ideas first raised in our article, 'Cambridge University Library, Additional MS 2604: Repackaging Female Saints' Lives for the Fifteenth-Century English Nun'.

THE SELECTION OF SAINTS' LIVES IN ADD. 2604   197

tradition the chastity of the Evangelist was emphasised, just as the Baptist's link
to the virgin martyrs was evident.[105] The two St Johns share an early icono-
graphic tradition, and they, together with Leonard, are often found as the
dedicatees of medieval English nunneries, as noted in III. Convent and Geographical Location. And their importance to female religious is clearly not just
an English phenomenon.[106] In the context of Add. 2604 they also represent traditional categories of universal saints: two apostles and one confessor (or hermit) in the case of Leonard. The lives of these three males frame a rather eclectic mixture of females, a grouping that can indicate how the universal female
lives serve as a complement to the exemplarity of the native English women.
Yet there are other genuine oddities in the selection of the universal saints.
While many of them are fairly popular in the Middle Ages (the male saints
plus Agatha and Cecilia in particular), there are others that are not so high
profile in the later medieval period in England (Benedicta, Columba, Justina),
one (Martha) who is normally overshadowed by her more famous sister, and
another (Domitilla), whose selection seems quite exceptional, not least because
the compiler has virtually nothing to say about her. This all begs the question
of what has happened to the collection from when it was first produced to its
present state and what mode of organisation was originally at work.

Focusing on the universal saints first of all, it can be assumed — rightly or
wrongly — that the selection is a mere remnant of what once existed, whether in
the 'original' text(s) or in Add. 2604 itself. We say this because it is exceptional
to have a list of universal female virgins that exclude major saints honoured
throughout the liturgical year like Katherine of Alexandria (25 November),
Lucy (13 December), Agnes (21 January), Juliana (16 February), Margaret (20
July), and the native/universal saint, Ursula (21 October), and yet include very

---

[105] For example, alongside John the Baptist, he is included in a list of virgins in *De virgin-
iate* by Aldhelm (d. 709); see Lapidge and Love, 'The Latin Hagiography of England and Wales
(600–1500)', pp. 209–10 (p. 209). See also John Mirk's reference to John the Evangelist's 'grace
of virgynyte', in *John Mirk's 'Festial'*, ed. by Susan Powell, 2 vols, EETS, o.s. 334–35 (2009–11),
I, 31–35 (p. 31, l. 6). For the Baptist's links with virgin martyrs see Katherine J. Lewis, 'Becoming a Virgin King: Richard II and Edward the Confessor', in *Gender and Holiness: Men, Women
and Saints in Late Medieval Europe*, ed. by Samantha J. E. Riches and Sarah Salih, Routledge
Studies in Medieval Religion and Culture, 1 (London: Routledge, 2002), pp. 86–100. See also
Blanton, *Signs of Devotion*, pp. 277–85.

[106] For instance, Williams-Krapp, 'Deutschsprachige Hagiographie von ca. 1350 bis ca.
1550', notes 'Über die in den Frauenklöstern hoch verehrten Johannes Baptista und Johannes
Evangelista, um die mitunter Konkurrenzkämpfe und Streit bezüglich der kultischen Priorität
entstehen konnten, sind zwei bzw. vier Legenden erhalten' (p. 280 and n. 52).

minor figures such as Domitilla, who does not usually have a separate feast day but is normally incorporated with Nereus, Achilleus, and Pancras (12 May). In Add. 2604 the omission of examples such as the former and the inclusion of the latter may presuppose that, in a way that can no longer be reconstructed, the original Latin compilation from which Add. 2604 is derived was a very full one that must have included minor and major figures alike (unless, and less likely, it was a smaller collection designed to augment a larger collection with the usual major figures). As we shall see below, there is an internal reference in Add. 2604 to another universal life that once existed in the manuscript, that of Iphigenia.[107] Her presence would support the hypothesis above. There is also evidence for one other native saint, as discussed below.

Unfortunately, the native lives in Add. 2604 do not offer any further elucidation about the nature of the translator's exemplar but to say that they are translated from John of Tynemouth's *Sanctilogium Angliae Walliae Scotiae et Hiberniae*. As we detail in V. Latin Sources and Analogues, five manuscripts of the *Sanctilogium* are extant, but there is no clear indication any one of them is the source. What had happened to the original Latin collection of the universal saints or native ones up until the time that Add. 2604 was organised can only be hazarded. In other words, we do not know whether the Add. 2604 compiler was working from an already imperfect work, whether he was working from a full text or whether, imperfect or not, he was working from one volume for the universal lives and another for the native lives. Neither is it certain that the translation in Add. 2604 was the first. On balance we have assumed that the Add. 2604 compiler is responsible for this translation and selection; this is in part because it is unlikely that two such idiosyncratic selections existed, although it is not inconceivable for there to have once been an English compendium from which this selection has been made. While we do not know if this translator/compiler may be identified with the copyist, the linguistic 'purity' of the language devoid of Mischsprachen (as explained in II. Language and Dialectal Provenance) would imply that they are one and the same.

Although it is possible to guess when some of the folios went missing and to calculate how much text has gone from individual saints' lives, the number of quires that have disappeared (and at what point) is impossible to say. There

---

[107] Given the relative obscurity of this Egyptian saint in northern collections, the detail that Domitilla is following in the steps of Iphigenia is a clear indication of an exemplar with both saints included.

THE SELECTION OF SAINTS' LIVES IN ADD. 2604 199

may even be losses at the beginning and the end.[108] Currently quires 5 and 11 have definitely been lost, which leaves a gap between the fourth saint, Agatha (5 February), and the fifth, Cecilia (22 November), and another between the fifteenth saint, Eanswith (31 August or 12 September) and the sixteenth, Hild (17 November). A single quire in both instances would make good the missing text, but it could be that more than one quire is gone, and with them quite a great deal of saints, particularly between Agatha and Cecilia. At some point there was an attempt to make Add. 2604 look as complete as possible because a concerted effort was made to excise catchwords that did not signal the words on the following pages so that the lacunae would not be noticed. There was also an effort to provide the manuscript with a title, 'The lyves and dethes of the martyres', though this was no doubt an eighteenth-century enhancement rather than an earlier idea.[109] Be all this as it may, there is still some definite rationale to the manuscript as it stands.

Although they look anything but a coherent whole, in studying the arrangement of lives and considering the feast days represented, we find that there are at least two ways to consider this collection. If we look solely at feast days, the contents of the legendary comprise three mini-cycles broadly following the order of the liturgical calendar. The first of the three mini-cycles begins with the two biblical Johns and ends with the virgin martyr Barbara, running from 24 June to 16 December (rather than the usual 4 December). Physically in the centre are ten English saints (plus a brief notice of another), whose feasts comprise the second cycle, 23 June to 17 November, beginning with Æthelthryth and finishing with Hild. There is a blip in this cycle in that Eanswith's feast of 31 August or 12 September comes after Eadburh's of 13 December. It is possible that the feast of Edith of Wilton (16 September) was confused with the feast day of her aunt Edith of Polesworth (15 July), who is named in her life; likewise, Eadburh of Thanet (13 December) was often confused with the more popular Eadburh of Winchester (17 July). If Edith and Eadburh are reoriented to these July dates, the mini-cycle works seamlessly, running from 23 June to 17 November. The legendary ends with another universal group, starting with the biblical Martha

---

[108] As we are suggesting here, the total number of quires in the original manuscript remains a mystery. Particularly interesting, however, is the fifteenth-century notation, as discussed in I. The Manuscript, which implies that Add. 2604 had eighteen quires, once the copying was complete. While this figure is not completely accurate, it is near enough.

[109] It is estimated that the obliteration of the catchwords and possibly the addition of the title (in part) are the work of a later owner, most probably George Bird Burrell; see I. The Manuscript for details.

and ending with Leonard, which run from 29 July to 6 November. Modwenna, however, complicates this neat arrangement with a feast of 5 July in a decidedly odd placement. It is possible, however, that if Modwenna were celebrated on her translation feast of 9 September, this would smooth out this problem, even if her translation feast was not well documented.[110]

Yet for complicated textual and codicological reasons it is also evident that the collection must also have had at least two other lives, one native (discussed below) and one universal, and possibly many more. At the end of Domitilla the writer implies that the manuscript once had a life of Iphigenia, 'Seynt Effigenye [...] as it is rehersid afore' (18/8–9). We postulate that this life of Iphigenia (likely taken from the life of Matthew with whom Iphigenia is associated and with whom she shares the feast of 21 September) occurred between Agatha (5 February) and Cecilia (22 November) as part of the now missing quire 5 (fols 33r–40v). Judging from their sources or analogues (as is explained in the Overviews and Commentaries to Agatha and Cecilia in the *Edition*), it is estimated that the text missing from the end of Agatha would have fitted on fols 33r–34r and that what is lacking at the beginning of Cecilia could have been accommodated on part of fol. 40v. This would have left sufficient space for the now missing life of Iphigenia. As noted in the Tables above (and in the Overview and Commentary to Domitilla in the *Edition*), the life of Iphigenia is very rare and, where it does occur, it is quite short. We consider that it could not have taken up all the available space (fols 34v–40r), thus making room for one or more other saints. It is also possible that more than one quire is lost at this point. While it is not feasible to work out which or how many universal saints might have been in the manuscript originally, if there were more than one missing quire at this juncture, there are quite a few from which to choose. The virgin martyrs whose feasts fall between 5 February and 22 November include: Dorothy (6 February), Apollonia (9 February), Juliana (16 February), Petronilla (31 May), Margaret (20 July), Christina (24 July), Iphigenia (21 September), and Ursula (21 October). With the exception of Iphigenia, all these saints had some degree of popularity in East Anglia so one guess as to the missing saint or saints is as good as another.[111]

---

[110] *Geoffrey of Burton, Life and Miracles of St Modwenna*, ed. and trans. by Robert Bartlett, Oxford Medieval Texts (Oxford: Clarendon, 2002), pp. xxx–xxxvi.

[111] As pointed out in Eamon Duffy, *The Stripping of the Altars: Traditional Religion in England, c. 1400–c. 1580* (New Haven, CT: Yale University Press, 1992), p. 171, the following occur on church screens: Belstead has Sitha, Ursula, Margaret, and Mary Magdalene plus a male figure; Litcham has Sitha, Cecilia, Dorothy, Juliana, Agnes, Petronilla, Helena, and

THE SELECTION OF SAINTS' LIVES IN ADD. 2604 201

A second way to think about this collection is to consider it as one organised hierarchically. As noted above, the structure of legendaries is collective or individual, that is, either subject to an overall organisational scheme or subject to a plan based on the individual lives included.[112] If there is no liturgical order, the lives may be arranged chronologically, alphabetically, or hierarchically. Add. 2604 is clearly of the individual type, and one can see the grouping as hierarchical: apostles/biblical saints, virgin martyrs, and local saints. If viewed in this way, Add. 2604 has two complete cycles, beginning with John the Baptist and John the Evangelist, followed by virgin martyrs of the universal Church, complemented by the abbess/nuns of the local Church. The second cycle suggests a strong Francophone origin, as it begins with Martha (who traditionally with her sister Mary Magdalene and brother Lazarus evangelised Provence), followed by an eclectic grouping of virgin martyrs, with Modwenna and Leonard as the representative local saints. Although this hierarchical system re-categorises Martha and Leonard with an emphasis on their French connections rather than their universal status, this arrangement makes some sense in terms of the length of saints' lives. Modwenna and Leonard are incredibly long accounts as compared with others in the manuscript, and they would help offset the first cycle, which occupies more than half of the manuscript. If considered as a collection of readings, the lengthy Modwenna and Leonard, coupled with the very brief lives of Martha *et alia*, would balance the grouping of saints in the first cycle.

Part of the difficulty in coming to a firm consensus are certain oddities in the layout and the current position of the last two lives. Modwenna and Leonard are the only saints in the volume in stand-alone quires. As shown in I. The Manuscript, the decoration of Modwenna differs from the rest of the collection and the presence of Modwenna and Leonard in separate quires suggests that they may have been written or added at a slightly different time (albeit by the same scribe), and so could originally have been intended for separate circulation. If the scribe wrote these at a later date, that might account for the lack of decorative spraywork for Modwenna. It could also be that Leonard, which does feature the same decoration as other lives, was written and decorated near the same time — and Modwenna came a little later in the process. (Conversely they

Ursula; North Elmham has Barbara, Cecilia, Dorothy, Sitha, Juliana, Petronilla, Agnes, and Christina; and Westhall has Æthelthryth, Sitha, Agnes, Bridget, Katherine, Dorothy, Margaret, and Apollonia.

[112] See the work by Dolbeau in n. 17 and above.

could have been produced earlier than the other lives.) It needs to be recalled that Add. 2604 was bound or rebound at some point in the late eighteenth or early nineteenth century so it is conceivable that these last two lives were simply put in the wrong order.

Whatever is the case, when considering the contents of Add. 2604, several aspects of the native figures hint at its underlying principle: foremost, this group of native women is the perfect complement to the saints of the *Legenda aurea* and its like. Their summer feasts allowed the owners to celebrate the lives of royal abbesses and nuns of early monastic communities that later became Benedictine.[113] Second, the collection shows a strong preference for East Anglian and Kentish saints. The Ely saints dominate, and their placement liturgically in unbroken succession (physically and liturgically) is but one illustration of their prominence in the collection: Æthelthryth, Seaxburh, Wihtburh, Eormenhild, Eorcengota and Æthelburh (and a comment about Sæthryth), and Wærburh.[114] Further, the Ely women are located in the middle, even as the other sections provide a narrative frame around the local saints, with the male saints serving as bookends. This arrangement is complemented by particular attention afforded to Ely in the rubrics.

Genealogical details outlining the relationship of the Ely saints are given in the incipits; these are designed to inform and remind a reader of the relationship between the women and to present these lives as chapters in the larger narrative about the monastic centre. For example, the title for Æthelthryth reads very simply: 'The life of Seynt Audry of Hely, virgyn and martyr' (fol. 52v). The incipit for Seaxburh is augmented to stress her relationship to her more famous sister featured in the previous life: 'Here begynnyth the life of Seynt Sexburge, sister to Seynt Awdre, which was the next abbess of Hely aftir hir' (fol. 59v). The incipits for Eormenhild and Wærburh follow this pattern, nam-

[113] Virginia Blanton makes the case for John's *Sanctilogium* being principally focused to serve the Benedictine Order in England, in 'Benedictine Devotion to England's Saints: Thomas de la Mare, John of Tynemouth, and the *Sanctilogium* in Cotton MS Tiberius E. i', *Studies in Medieval and Renaissance History*, Third Series, 17 (2023), 105–18.

[114] The monks at Ely moved a number of Ely feasts, which were originally in February and March, to July, when they celebrated them along with the feast of Seaxburh: Seaxburh's daughter Eormenhild (13 February) and granddaughter Wærburh (3 February) were moved to 6 July, her daughter Eorcengota to 7 July, the feast of Seaxburh's sister Æthelburh; Wihtburh whose feast of 17 March is added to Add. 2604 on her translation feast of 8 July. It is unclear when this practice began of celebrating Seaxburh's daughters' feasts in July; see *Goscelin of Saint-Bertin, The Hagiography of the Female Saints of Ely*, ed. and trans. by Rosalind C. Love, Oxford Medieval Texts (Oxford: Clarendon Press, 2004), pp. xxiii–xxvi.

THE SELECTION OF SAINTS' LIVES IN ADD. 2604   203

ing Eormenhild the first daughter of Seaxburh and Wærburh as the daughter of Eormenhild, but at the life of Eorcengota, reads: 'Here begynnyth a shorte lyfe of Seynt Erkengoode, the secunde doughter of Seynt Sexburgh and the awnte of Seynt Wereburgh, and of Seynt Alburgh þat was sister to Seynt Awdre of Hely' (fol. 65r). The incipit not only shows how Eorcengota is related to Seaxburh; it also indicates how she is related to Wærburh, who is featured in the previous life. The rubrics also highlight the fact that a short narrative about Æthelburh, sister to Æthelthryth and Seaxburh, is appended to the end of Eorcengota's life. The inclusion of Æthelburh in the story of Eorcengota follows its source, Bede, who recounts the story of Eorcengota and Æthelburh, as well as Sæthryth, who all travelled to Gaul and became abbesses at Faremoutiers-en-Brie.[115] In effect, the incipit serves to notify the reader of an epitome embedded within, even as it connects all of these women back to Ely's principal saint, Æthelthryth. The final incipit for Wihtburh returns to a more straightforward identification without the elaborate explanations about kinship, which suggests that her connection to the family may have been better known or was less complex in the telling. That said, all the lives open with details connecting the women and emphasising how fols 52v–69r form a coherent whole. One indication of readers' interest is that the opening of Æthelthryth is very worn, despite the protections offered a text that appears in the middle of the collection.

Complementary to the sororal family at Ely are the luminaries Edith of Wilton, Eanswith of Folkestone, Eadburh of Minster-in-Thanet, Hild of Whitby, and Modwenna of Burton on Trent. Where it may seem that each represents a smattering of monasteries dotted across the English landscape — with a particular Wessex flavour — each has an association with East Anglia or Kent (and sometimes both). Eanswith the daughter of Eadbald, and therefore, granddaughter to King Æthelbert and his wife, the Frankish princess, Bertha, who helped Christianise Kent. Edith's father was Edgar of Wessex and her mother, Wulfthryth of Wilton, so she is generally seen as a west country saint, but Edith was born in Kent. As we have seen, she was also paired with Æthelthryth in the Wilton Chronicle. Eadburh is another Wessex saint with a Kentish connection: linked to Mildrith, she became second abbess of Thanet.

The presence of Hild in Add. 2604 seems to belie a focus on East Anglia and Kent saints, but she may be included for her familial associations as much as her legacy as abbess of Whitby: she was sister to Hereswith, mother of Eadwulf,

---

[115] For this story, see *Bede's Ecclesiastical History of the English People*, ed. and trans. by Colgrave and Mynors, III.8, pp. 236–38.

King of East Anglia. He was probably a nephew of Anna, and therefore a cousin of the Ely women, but as noted above, the *Liber Eliensis* makes Hereswith the mother of Æthelthryth and her sisters, so there is a standing tradition that Hild was their maternal aunt. Further, Hild lived at the East Anglian court for one year among the royal family, with the intention of following her sister to Frankia. Of course, the connections between the Northumbrians and Kent are equally important: Hild was also connected to the Kentish family group through the marriage of her uncle Edwin (with whom she was baptised) to Æthelburh, sister of Eadbald of Kent, Seaxburh's father-in-law.[116] Be that as it may, Hild's connections to Kent and East Anglia are not a prominent part of her narrative in Add. 2604. Still, her status as an important figure in the late-medieval hagiographical imaginary may have been more significant in East Anglia than current liturgical evidence illustrates. As but one example, Hild appears in a missal from Bury St Edmunds, which is quite interesting, given our supposition (as we detail in I. The Manuscript and II. Language and Dialectal Provenance) that Add. 2604 was produced, and perhaps stayed, in that area.[117]

Relatively disappointing is that the background of Add. 2604 saints with Kentish associations is not highlighted. In fact, the opposite is true. Unlike the incipits for the Ely saints, those for the other native women do not signal their familial connections. Within their lives, moreover, the elaborate genealogies of the Kentish saints found in John of Tynemouth's Latin versions are excised. Thus, a saint's Kentish royalty is stressed, but not her extended kin group. One consequence of these omissions is that the connections between the Kentish and the Ely saints are occluded. Eanswith, for example, is Seaxburh's sister-in-law and aunt to Eorcengota, Eormenhild, and Wærburh. These relationships are not made manifest in the lives themselves, nor are they highlighted in the incipits, as we might expect if the Kentish and East Anglian connection were important. Given the emphasis on the genealogical details of the Ely saints in Add. 2604, the lack of information on the Kentish saints is striking and suggests a desire to set the East Anglian sororal family apart from the other native figures.

---

[116] *Bede's Ecclesiastical History of the English People*, ed. and trans. by Colgrave and Mynors, IV.23, pp. 406–07 and II.9, pp. 162–63, respectively.

[117] Christiane Kroebel, 'Remembering St Hilda in the Later Middle Ages', in *Late Medieval Devotion to Saints from the North of England: New Directions*, ed. by Christiania Whitehead, Hazel J. Hunter Blair, and Denis Renevey, Medieval Church Studies, 48 (Turnhout: Brepols, 2022), pp. 321–39 (p. 331).

THE SELECTION OF SAINTS' LIVES IN ADD. 2604   205

Finally, there is Modwenna, an Irish saint who shares no direct connection to the Ely or Kentish saints. Certainly, her life stands out, so one wonders about special devotion to her cult that this legendary might represent. The oddity of having Modwenna placed outside the cycle for the native saints suggests that her life may not have been originally planned to be included. The lack of spraywork to open her life is likewise suggestive.[118] Our suspicion, if Modwenna was part of the original programme, is that she was intentionally separated from the native cycle, for if placed according to her feast of 5 July, her life would have disrupted the grouping of Ely women, separating Æthelthryth on 23 June from her sister saints on 6, 7, and 8 July. Further, the lives of the Ely women cross quire boundaries, so it is quite clear that they were framed as a unit and that Modwenna was not intended to be inserted in the correct liturgical order by feast day. As the longest life in Add. 2604, Modwenna's life comprises three quires of eight (with fol. 126 cut out). As mentioned earlier, the very long life and miracles of Modwenna may originally have been intended as a single stand-alone text, one that would take a number of days to read. As scholars have noted about the Latin and French versions of her life, the account operates as a series of episodes, which were organised by Geoffrey of Burton and as a result lend themselves to reading during collations or meal times.[119] One hypothesis that does not work is that Modwenna may have been included at the end as a type of foreign saint just as Leonard was. Leonard's French associations serve to link him with the saints Benedicta, Columba, and Martha who precede Modwenna, which means this Irish saint would have disrupted a francophone grouping. The sources lying behind the life of Modwenna also testify to her 'Englishness'; evident too in Add. 2604 is Modwenna's solid predilections for England itself, so her presence may well be, as we suggest above, to complete the two hierarchical cycles: her lengthy life in the second offsets the collection of native lives in the first.

Whatever the rationale for this native assembly, it is clear that two attributes are important: royalty and monastic profession. Further, only two of the native saints in Add. 2604 are not distinguished as abbesses, Eanswith and Eormenhild (who according to Ely tradition was an abbess). Any saint(s) missing in quire 11 would therefore almost certainly share these characteristics. They must also derive from John of Tynemouth's *Sanctilogium*. Of the thirty-one entries for female lives in the various manuscripts in the *Sanctilogium*, ten

---

[118] See I. The Manuscript.

[119] *Geoffrey of Burton, Life and Miracles of St Modwenna*, ed. and trans. by Bartlett, pp. xx–xxvi.

were translated into Add. 2604, as well as an eleventh, which comes from a narration following the life of Seaxburh. The remaining figures in John's collection include: Æbbe of Coldingham (25 August); Æthelflæd of Romsey (23 October); Brigid (1 February); Cyneburh, the Mercian princess, and her sister saints Cyneswith and Tibba (6 March) culted at Peterborough; the Barking saints Æthelburh (11 October), Cuthburh (31 August), Hildelith (24 March), and Wulfhild (9 September); Fritheswith of Oxford (19 October); Gwenfrewi (3 November); Helen (18 August) Juthwara (28 November), Keyna of Wales and Cornwall (8 October); Margaret of Scotland (16 November); Maxentia (20 November), Milburh (23 February), Mildrith of Thanet and later of Canterbury (13 July); Osith of Chich (7 October); Osmanna (9 September), and Walburh of Wimborne and later Heidenheim (25 February). We can add here Ursula (21 October) who appears in London, British Library, MS Cotton Tiberius E. i, the copy of John's *Sanctilogium* made at St Albans, but given that her *vita* did not circulate in later recensions, it seems unlikely that she is the missing saint. Moreover, Ursula's presence in the universal calendar, as is true of Brigid, discounts her.[120] If we cull further any saint whose feast does not fit the gap between Eanswith and Hild, we are left with ten possibilities: Æthelflæd, Æthelburh, Cuthburh, Fritheswith, Gwenfrewi, Keyna, Margaret of Scotland, Osith, Osmanna, and Wulfhild.

To determine which of these lives might have been translated for Add. 2604, it makes sense in a volume clearly focused on monastic vocations that the hermits Keyna and Osmanna would not be chosen. Nor does Æthelflæd seem particularly encouraging: while she was an abbess of Romsey, she was not royal. The northern saints Æbbe of Coldingham and Margaret of Scotland do not have strong associations with East Anglia or Kent, despite the fact that Æbbe (her aunt by marriage) supervised Æthelthryth's novitiate at Coldingham. One might fully expect Æthelburh from Barking, one of the most important Benedictine nunneries in southern England, to be featured in Add. 2604. Her Essex cult would be well-known throughout East Anglia, and she was known to the rubricator, who made sure to mention in the explicit that Æthelthryth's sister was not *that* Æthelburh from Barking, should readers be confused.[121] The fact that Æthelthryth and the Barking abbess are not usual companions in col-

---

[120] For a recent discussion of the cult of Ursula in England, see Sanok, *New Legends of England*, pp. 237–73. See also *The Cult of St Ursula and the 11,000 Virgins*, ed. by Jane Cartwright (Cardiff: University of Wales Press, 2016).

[121] For important discussions of Barking, see the essay collection *Barking Abbey and Medieval Literary Culture*, ed. by Brown and Bussell.

THE SELECTION OF SAINTS' LIVES IN ADD. 2604 207

lections of saints' lives or in litanies gives us further pause, as does the uncertainty regarding Æthelburh's royalty. Of the other Barking saints, Cuthburh's Latin *vita* was promulgated until 1500, but it would be odd to have her or the lesser Wulfhild and not the community's founder, Æthelburh.[122]

While one can easily appreciate why many of the females in John's *Sanctilogium* were not presented in Add. 2604, a rationale for not including the highly celebrated Fritheswith, Gwenfrewi, Mildrith, or Osith is not easily understood, especially since their cults were promoted to some degree in vernacular writings. To provide some comparative context, it is instructive that two versions of Fritheswith's life as an abbess, a shorter version for a monastic audience and a longer version for a lay audience, appear in eight manuscripts of the *South English Legendary* — and by consequence in two copies of the *Gilte Legende*, the first English translation in prose.[123] Such a dispersal in manuscripts from the Midlands might indicate that this Oxford saint's life would have circulated widely in Middle English, and yet to our knowledge, the saint does not appear in vernacular collections outside of the *South English Legendary* tradition (which may have been rendered obsolete linguistically by the late fifteenth century when Add. 2604 was compiled).[124] She does not have any connection, moreover, to Ely or Kent. Still, Fritheswith's feast of 19 October would fit well liturgically and was ordered by the Convocation of Canterbury in 1480, at the same time that Æthelthryth's was mandated to be celebrated.[125] Given that we place the production of Add. 2604 between *c.* 1480 and 1510, this decree gives some support to an identification of Fritheswith as the missing native life, even as it offers a rationale for the presentation of Æthelthryth and her sororal family.

---

[122] The only medieval vernacular text of Cuthburh appears to be that included in the late Middle English translation of John's *Sanctilogium*, printed by Richard Pynson in 1516: *The Kalendre of the Newe Legende of Englande*, ed. by Görlach, pp. 74–75 (STC 4602). For a discussion of three Latin versions about Cuthburh, see Rebecca Rushforth, 'The Medieval Hagiography of St Cuthburg', *Analecta Bollandiana*, 118 (2000), 291–324.

[123] *Middle English Legends of Women Saints*, ed. by Sherry L. Reames, with Martha G. Blalock and Wendy L. Larson (Kalamazoo, MI: Medieval Institute Publications, 2003), pp. 23–50 (p. 24). For a discussion of Fritheswith and other native female saints in the *South English Legendary*, see Blanton, 'Counting Noses and Assessing the Numbers'.

[124] Oddly enough, Fritheswith is not included in London, British Library, MS Lansdowne 436, a collection with west country associations.

[125] R. W. Pfaff, *New Liturgical Feasts in Later Medieval England* (Oxford: Clarendon Press, 1970), p. 3.

The abbess Gwenfrewi has a feast of 3 November that fits liturgically, and her cult enjoyed royal favour in the fifteenth century. As we have seen, her life was included in the *Gilte Legende*, Mirk's *Festial*, and Bokenham's lives, and it is also the subject of a Middle English carol by John Audelay.[126] Still, while her relics were claimed by the Benedictine monks of Shrewsbury, Gwenfrewi was a Welsh virgin martyr without a strong connection with the Ely saints or their Kentish cousins.

More probable seems to be Mildrith, first abbess of Thanet and the highly culted great-granddaughter of King Æthelbert of Kent, yet she appears in only four manuscripts of the *South English Legendary* and not in any other late-medieval English accounts.[127] That a second abbess from Thanet, Eadburh, is featured in Add. 2604 is an argument in Mildrith's favour, as she was daughter of the community's founder and its first abbess. The two are prominently celebrated together in *Vita sanctorum Aethelredi et Aethelberti martirum et sanctarum uirginum Miltrudis et Edburgis*, which is preserved in Gotha, Forschung-und Landesbibliothek, Cod. Membr. I.81, fols 185v–188v.[128] The incipit for Eadburh, moreover, stresses their connection: she is the 'abbess of Tenett aftir Seynt Mildrede' (fol. 76r). In addition, Mildrith was a great-niece of Eanswith. Mildrith's feast of 13 July, however, presents difficulties for her candidacy, as it does not fall between 31 August and 17 November. Moreover, Mildrith's life would need to come before Eadburh's on 13 December for the referencing in the incipit to work properly.

Osith was abbess of Chich on the Essex coast, whose feast of 5 October fits the liturgical sequence. As evidence of the circulation of her cult, the life of this martyr is found in Romsey's Latin legendary in London, British Library, MS Lansdowne 436, fols 29r–30r, which has female saints from Dorset, Hampshire, Shropshire, and Worcestershire, as well as elsewhere. Osith also has the distinction of being one of three native female saints (along with Æthelthryth and Modwenna) in the French collection from Campsey Ash: London, British

---

[126] Sanok, *New Legends of England*, pp. 98–132.

[127] Mildrith appears in these *South English Legendary* manuscripts: London, British Library, MS Egerton 1993, fols 176r–178r, Oxford, Bodleian Library, MS. Eng. poet. a. 1, fols 41vb–42rb, Oxford, Bodleian Library, MS Bodley 779, fols 302r–303v; Aberystwyth, Llyfrgell Genedlaethol Cymru/National Library of Wales, MS 5043, fol. 3r.

[128] For a discussion of Mildrith's early cult, see D. W. Rollason, *The Mildrith Legend: A Study in Early Medieval Hagiography in England*, Studies in the Early History of Britain (Leicester: Leicester University Press, 1982).

THE SELECTION OF SAINTS' LIVES IN ADD. 2604   209

Library, MS Additional 70513, fols 134v–147v.[129] Thus, this virgin martyr is featured in two legendaries that have demonstrable associations with female religious houses. Furthermore, Osith ranks as one the most regularly invoked saints in the litanies, and specific to Add. 2604, she has a key role in a miracle of Modwenna's life, which gives additional credence to her case.

A final, if highly speculative, method for determining which of these saints is the most likely is to consider how much may be missing from the Add. 2604 lives of Eanswith and Hild to determine the approximate length of the lost life. If quire 11 had eight folios (or sixteen pages), as the other gatherings do, and was ruled similarly, with an average of about twenty-nine lines per folio (which is typical in this section of the manuscript), we can estimate that the missing quire had about 432 lines, give or take. The scribe usually included about nine words per line, except where champ letters disrupt his work. If we imagine that there are about nine words for each of the 432 lines, we get a figure of about 3,900 words. How does this help? When we look at Horstman's edition of John's *Sanctilogium*, we find that he prints about nine or ten words per line, so we can estimate how many printed lines would fit in the missing quire, minus the lines required to complete the life of Eanswith and begin the life of Hild (provided they were not emended in any way). As noted in the Overviews and Commentaries for these lives in the *Edition*, we imagine we have lost about two and one-half pages of Eanswith's life and about four and one-half pages of Hild's. Working on the assumption that there is but one lost quire, we can estimate that the missing saint's life would have covered about nine pages or about 2,187 words. That would mean we need to find a life that would run about 220 lines in Horstman's printed text, though we would need to subtract space for a champ letter and decoration, as well as two explicits (one for Eanswith and another for the missing saint) and two incipits (one for the missing saint and another for Hild), which reduces our target number to about 200. The number of printed lines for each saint whose feast fits the liturgical spread between 31 August and 17 November, along with that for Mildrith who is named in Eadburh's incipit, are: Æthelflæd, 85; Æthelburh of Barking, 181; Cuthburh, 108; Fritheswith, 155; Gwenfrewi, 247; Keyna, 67; Margaret of Scotland, 253; Mildrith, 194; Osith, 174; Osmanna, 73; and Wulfhild, 138. While it is possible that the two shortest lives could have been inserted together, there is no

---

[129] Blanton has compared the native female saints in Add. 2604 with those featured in London, British Library, MS Lansdowne 436 (a Latin collection associated with Romsey Abbey in Hampshire) and London, British Library, MS Additional 70513 (a French collection associated with Campsey Ash Priory in Suffolk) in 'The Devotional Reading of Nuns'.

good reason for either Keyna or Osmanna, as noted above. Gwenfrewi and Margaret of Scotland's lives are far too long, and Æthelflæd and Cuthburh, too short. The most likely candidates appear to be Æthelburh of Barking (who is mentioned in the explicit for Æthelburh of Ely but is implicitly ruled out by the lack of interest in Barking saints), Mildrith (who is named in the incipit for Eadburh), and Osith (who features in the life of Modwenna). Our supposition is that it was Osith, given her prominence in legendaries and litanies, as well as her cult's proximity to Ely, even as we want it to be Mildrith of Thanet whose feast day does not fit the sequence. Barring the recovery of the lost quire, we shall never know.

Taken as a whole, there is in this unique selection of saints' lives, imperfect as it is, a certain rationale not immediately obvious on first acquaintance. We cannot determine the ultimate organising principle. Yet detailed codicological investigation combined with some liturgical information has uncovered evidence for two possibilities: as three liturgically ordered mini-cycles or as two hierarchical summer cycles of saints' feast days. Whether or not the collection can be fixed in a particular pattern, what is witnessed here is an obvious drive to combine apostles, martyrs, virgins (including abbesses and nuns), confessors, and hermits, with a seemingly balanced emphasis on the universal and the native. If the manuscript were destined for some convent in East Anglia, as it almost certainly was, then the combination of universal saints such as Barbara and Martha, who were popular in the area, with the luminaries of East Anglian sainthood makes perfect sense.[130] As we have demonstrated, Add. 2604 with its attention to local and native saints, a feature that was becoming a growing preoccupation in later continental and English hagiography, is fash-

---

[130] The relative popularity of various saints in different areas may be gauged from the study of artefacts and material goods preserved in churches, dedications, litanies, *vitae*, and wills; see III. Convent and Geographical Location. In 'Holy Maydens, Holy Wyfes', Duffy notes that Barbara figured (alongside Edmund, Dorothy, and Agnes) as the most popular non-apostolic saint on East Anglian rood-screens (Table A, pp. 178–79). Duffy, *The Stripping of the Altars*, p. 178, also comments on the presence of Barbara and Martha in a verse devotion in Cambridge, Fitzwilliam Museum, MS 55, an East Anglian Book of Hours from *c.* 1480, and notes how the same list of nine saints (plus Christina) is found in a set of verse prayers by John Lydgate, monk of Bury St Edmunds. Two magisterial overviews of the more 'official' liturgical recognition of saints in England are available in Richard W. Pfaff, *The Liturgy in Medieval England: A History* (Cambridge: Cambridge University Press, 2009), and Sherry L. Reames, *Saints' Legends in Medieval Sarum Breviaries: Catalogue and Studies*, York Manuscript and Early Print Studies, 2 (Woodbridge: York Medieval Press, 2021), both of which also contain information with regard to East Anglia and the veneration of some of the saints in Add. 2604.

THE SELECTION OF SAINTS' LIVES IN ADD. 2604   211

ioned according to 'le goût du jour'. In many respects it seems to be a decidedly old-fashioned gathering of saints in the continental tradition with its inclusion of figures hardly known in England such as Benedicta or Columba (let alone Domitilla or Iphigenia). Likewise there is a particular francophone bias in its saints, but this is offset by the selection of a local set of East Anglian and Kentish lives. In many respects it is an altogether novel collection characterised by what might be termed 'le goût personnel'. When examined against the Latin and vernacular traditions, it is neither fully one thing nor another. It is set apart by its varied selection of material, its indefinite order, and its idiosyncratic combination of sources and analogues, ranging from the *Legenda aurea* to other hagiographical collections such as Mombritius and the *Historie plurimorum sanctorum* as well as being the only example in Middle English of translations of lives from John of Tynemouth's mid-fourteenth-century *Sanctilogium*. There is a precedent for this combination of universal and native sources in the early fifteenth-century Cod. Sankt Georgen 12, yet, as we shall see in V. Latin Sources and Analogues, how the sources and analogues are handled is unique to the compiler of Add. 2604.

V. Latin Sources and Analogues

What sources and analogues underlie the very diverse though apparently codicologically intentional collection in Add. 2604?[1] Or, put another way, and building on the exploration in IV. Hagiographical Context and the Selection of Saints, to what extent can we trace the genesis of the twenty-two separate lives in Add. 2604 and cast light on the interconnections of the material? Some of the saints such as John the Baptist and Æthelthryth have a sound, if embellished, pedigree be it biblical or historical; others like Domitilla are vague figures with a tenuous link to reality. And the analogous available source material, both editorial and bibliographical, is uneven: for instance, multiple texts exist of the Barbara legend whereas very little in the literature remains on Benedicta.[2] There is therefore a mixture of complications, including the convoluted nature of some of the primary source or analogue material: the *Legenda aurea* by Jacobus de Voragine (*c.* 1228–98) that first emerged in the second half of the thirteenth century, the *Sanctuarium* of Boninus Mombritius printed around 1477 to 1478 and the anonymous *Historie plurimorum sanctorum* printed in 1483 and 1485. Quite apart from all this are the complexities involved in the production of the *Acta sanctorum* begun by the Bollandists in the middle of the seventeenth century and without which no hagiographical source study would be possible.

Not surprisingly, the sources and analogues detected fall into two main groups (in order as they are in Add. 2604): those for the universal saints, John the Baptist (1), John the Evangelist (2), Columba (3), Agatha (4), Cecilia (5), Barbara (6), Martha (17), Domitilla (18), Justina (19), Benedicta (20), and Leonard (22); and those for the native saints, Æthelthryth (7), Seaxburh (8), Eormenhild (9), Wærburh (10), Eorcengota with her aunt Æthelburh (11),

---

[1] It is not the only unique selection of material in England; another notable example is the rather idiosyncratic choice of the seven Middle English verse legends of Paula, Ambrose, A Virgin in Antioch, Theodora, Bernard, Augustine, and Savinian and Savina in the fourteenth-century *Vernon Golden Legend* in *Sammlung altenglischer Legenden*, ed. by Carl Horstmann (Heilbronn: Gebr. Henninger, 1878), pp. 3–97.

[2] The *Bibliotheca Hagiographica Latina* references to Barbara cover five pages (BHL, i, 142–46) with another five pages in the BHL *Supplementum* (pp. 110–14), while Benedicta takes up only half a page (BHL, i, 162–63) and a few lines in the BHL *Supplementum* (p. 129). It should be noted that the BHL does not catalogue lives composed after 1500 which is some disadvantage when studying Add. 2604.

Wihtburh (12), Edith (13), Eadburh (14), Eanswith (15), Hild (16), and Modwenna (21). We shall deal with these two categories separately, beginning with the universal saints (which may be divided into a number of sub-groups depending on their source or analogue) before moving to the native, and then drawing the two strands together by examining a manuscript that features both categories.

The lives in Add. 2604 are incontrovertibly translated from Latin even if the translator never gives any hint of this himself.[3] Apart from the give-away signs from Latinate syntax, there is a recognised definite source for the native lives and various sources or analogues for the universal lives. The narratives in Add. 2604 were translated from a manuscript that already had this selection (plus those now missing from Add. 2604) or from a manuscript that had a more extensive collection, or the translation in Add. 2604 was compiled from multiple different manuscripts.[4] Our overall impression is that the translation and the selection of the texts, from whatever source they derive, is the responsibility of the compiler of Add. 2604, in other words, that he alone, acting as confessor or chaplain (or at the behest of some such) for some convent in East Anglia took it upon himself to produce an appropriate selection of saints for the nuns in his charge. We suppose this mainly on the grounds that it is a *sui generis* compilation and so it is unlikely that two such would have existed in this exact form. There would have been no reason for it to have pre-existed in Latin for the nuns in question (or virtually any other English female religious) considering the limited Latinity of medieval English nuns. This is a point that is re-inforced by the almost wholesale omission of Latin in the texts (discussed in VI. Reading the *'Lyves and Dethes'*). While it is possible that the Add. 2604 compiler was copying from a pre-existing English translation in whole or in part, we think this very improbable given the linguistic uniformity of Add.

---

[3] Few Middle English hagiographical or homiletic authors are truly explicit about their sources. Even if they occasionally explain their methodology, this is rarely transparent; for instance, in the prologue to the Syon life of Katherine of Alexandria the compiler discusses his combination of sources without specifying what these are; see *Virgins and Scholars*, ed. by Waters, p. 276, ll. 3–12. The compiler of Add. 2604 is silent on the topic throughout even avoiding the mention of internal references provided in his sources and analogues; see VI. Reading *'Lyves and Dethes'*.

[4] As described in I. The Manuscript, George Bird Burrell, a later eighteenth-century owner, probably tidied up and added later material to the manuscript contents, but apart from potentially adding the lives of Modwenna and Leonard (which we think unlikely) to be bound with the rest, the current disposition of Add. 2604 is a medieval one. See further IV. Hagiographical Context and the Selection of Saints.

V. LATIN SOURCES AND ANALOGUES   215

2604. Considering its lateness and 'standardising' tendencies, it is difficult to localise the language precisely but there are no obvious traces of a scribe trying to adapt himself to an earlier dialect (discussed in II. Language and Dialectal Provenance). It is also clear from the Add. 2604 lives as a whole that stylistically only one translating hand was involved. Whether the translator was using a single manuscript or multiple manuscripts for his material is unknown. Ease of working would dictate a translational choice of one manuscript source for the universal lives and one manuscript source for the native items in Add. 2604, but common sense does not always prevail in such cases. The native lives are clearly translated from just one collection, John of Tynemouth's *Sanctilogium Angliae Walliae Scotiae et Hiberniae* (*c.* 1350) so a single manuscript source or part thereof may be postulated here.[5] The range of analogues used for the universal saints may imply multiple manuscripts, though not necessarily so. As shown in I. The Manuscript, the hand is a trained one and Add. 2604 is professional looking. On a few occasions the scribe has left gaps in the text clearly to be filled in later.[6] This could indicate that he was copying from someone else's indecipherable notes, but given the evidence from eye-skip and the overall linguistic uniformity, we do not think this is the case.[7] We assume that any gaps or eye-skip are the result of his copying either from his own notes or from his previous copy or part thereof. (Whether the translator and scribe are the same person is another issue; given the lack of contradictory evidence, we assume that they are.)

While the Latin source for the native lives was no doubt a manuscript produced in England, the ultimate manuscript or manuscripts of the universal lives may well have come originally from the Continent. (The universal lives may even have derived from unrecognised printed continental sources, though our suspicion is that the sources or analogues are manuscript ones given the tendency for printed lives to be more abbreviated, as seen below.) In addition, the dating parameters are rather fluid. Add. 2604 may date from the end of the fif-

---

[5] This collection was printed by Wynkyn de Worde in 1516 as the *Nova legenda Anglie* (STC 4601). The modern edition, *Nova Legenda Anglie,* ed. by Horstman, which is based on this first printing, uses London, British Library, MS Cotton Tiberius E. i and Oxford, Bodleian Library, MS Tanner 15 as points of comparison. As will be explained below, and demonstrated in Appendix 2, there is such little textual difference among all the copies, whether manuscript or print, that we have used Horstman's edition for citation and quotation throughout this *Study* and the *Edition.*

[6] See the Textual Apparatus in the *Edition* for gaps in the texts.

[7] See the Textual Apparatus in the *Edition* for examples of eye-skip in the texts.

teenth century or even beginning of the sixteenth. It combines a range of material from biblical figures all the way to Leonard (whose cult does not develop until the eleventh century). The sources and analogues identified cover a range of two centuries from the thirteenth to the fifteenth and some may derive from much earlier sources.[8]

By checking a wide assortment of Latin and English legendary material listed in IV. Hagiographical Context and the Selection of Saints we formed a detailed notion of the popularity or otherwise of the saints in Add. 2604 across Europe. Some of the saints are unsurprisingly standard in every legendary and sanctorale collection (as well as every litany) so that it is hardly possible to find a case where the apostles John the Baptist or John the Evangelist are omitted, while Leonard is relatively popular but not at all in the same league as the aforementioned. Of the female saints in Add. 2604 Cecilia would count as decidedly the most ubiquitous in legendaries and sanctorale cycles, with Agatha being relatively prevalent overall. Barbara is not widespread in some ways (for example, she is not part of the original *Legenda aurea* and does not tend to appear in sermon cycles), yet her cult makes a definite impact nonetheless. As noted by Mathilde van Dijk in her excellent study of Barbara in Dutch tradition, 'The first versions of her life in Latin date from the ninth century, but she did not become truly important until the fourteenth century' and in the fifteenth century the virginal Barbara sequestered in her tower makes an excellent role model as 'a cloistered nun *avant la lettre*'.[9] Barbara is therefore one of the saints with an extremely varied literary tradition with frequent 'one-off' lives. Justina occurs in legendaries (though not in sermons) but normally only in relation to Cyprian, where her part is usually downplayed; her appearances alone are limited. Of the remaining universal lives in Add. 2604, Martha appears occasionally in legendary tradition, with Benedicta less so, followed by Columba less so again, with stand-alone versions of Domitilla's life being exceptionally rare (though she can be presented briefly with Nereus and Achilleus). With

---

[8] There are many instances of much earlier sources being used in hagiographical texts and for earlier saints being marshalled for particular purposes; for instance, the telling example of a ninth-century life of Ida of Herzfeld being skilfully reconfigured by a secular priest employed by the abbey of Werden, Johannes Cincinnius (*c.* 1485–1555) 'as part of the abbey's more general campaign to reinvigorate the cult of the saints in the region'; see Collins, 'Latin Hagiography in *Germania* (1450–1550)', pp. 530–32 (p. 531).

[9] Mathilde van Dijk, *Een rij van spiegels: De Heilige Barbara van Nicomedia als voorbeeld vrouwelijke religieuzen*, Middeleeuwse Studies en Bronnen, 71 (Hilversum: Verloren, 2000), pp. 238 and 241 of the English Summary.

V. LATIN SOURCES AND ANALOGUES   217

regard to the English native saints, Æthelthryth was the most popular both in native and occasionally in non-native traditions; the only other female English saints that rated a mention outside England were Edith, Eadburh, and Hild. When compared with all other extant saints' lives in medieval English either in manuscript or early print, Add. 2604 alone comprises the universal lives of Columba, Domitilla, and Benedicta, and is one of the few to contain Martha, Justina, and Leonard. With regard to the native lives, it uniquely contains these native figures in Middle English: Seaxburh, Eormenhild, Eorcengota with her aunt Æthelburh, Wihtburh, Eadburh, Eanswith, Hild, and Modwenna. Where Æthelthryth was honoured in five Middle English lives (three in verse, two in prose) before 1500, Wærburh and Edith were featured in only two (one each in verse and prose).[10]

The discussions in IV. Hagiographical Context and the Selection of Saints provides some valuable insights into which sources or analogues might be worth pursuing and here we expound upon those ideas. For the universal lives we shall start with the most definite source, the *Legenda aurea*, among many indefinite ones, the early printed *Sanctuarium* of Mombritius, the early printed *Historie plurimorum sanctorum*, alongside a range of unidentified or partially identified manuscripts found in the *Acta sanctorum*. Following this, we are on more certain ground with the identification of the source of the native lives in John of Tynemouth's *Sanctilogium*, even if it is complicated textually. Our discussion will then be completed by an examination of Karlsruhe, Landesbibliothek Cod. Sankt Georgen 12, a Syon manuscript that is the only known collection that extensively combines universal lives with John of Tynemouth's *Sanctilogium*. This deluxe volume *looks* as if it should be the source of the main lives in Add. 2604, but we conclude otherwise.

---

[10] In addition to the prose version in Add. 2604, the Middle English lives of Æthelthryth are: (1) a verse epitome in three copies of the *South English Legendary* (London, British Library, MS Egerton 1993, fol. 163r–v; Oxford, Bodleian Library, MS Bodley Eng. poet. 1. a, fol. 33r–v (the Vernon manuscript); and Oxford, Bodleian Library, MS Bodley 779, fols 279v–280r); (2) a prose life in Oxford, Corpus Christi College, MS 120, fols 1r–16r; (3) Osbern Bokenham's translation in rhyme royal in Edinburgh, Advocates Library, MS Abbotsford, fols 117va–120rb; and (4) a life in quatrains following the verse life of Edith (fols 194r–258r) written in the Wilton Chronicle, preserved in London, British Library, MS Cotton Faustina B. iii, fols 265r–279v. (1) is edited by Tristan Major, 'Saint Etheldreda and the *South English Legendary*', *Anglia*, 128 (2010), 83–101 (pp. 98–99); see also Appendix 2 below. The verse life of Wærburh is Henry Bradshaw's poem in rhyme royal, *The Life of Saint Werburge of Chester*, ed. by Carl Horstmann, EETS, o.s. 88 (London: Trübner, 1887), which also includes a brief account of Æthelthryth (i, ll. 1835–1981) and of Seaxburh (i, ll. 1982–2128).

Sources and Analogues of the Universal Lives in Add. 2604: Background

To track down the precise sources or analogues of the universal lives in Add. 2604 is like searching for the proverbial 'needle in a haystack'. While John the Baptist, John the Evangelist, Cecilia, and Martha are taken (with some adjustments) from the *Legenda aurea*, the sources or analogues of Columba, Agatha, Barbara, Domitilla, Justina, Benedicta, and Leonard are far more complex, connected as many of them are to legendary sources that are visible to a greater or lesser extent in the *Legenda aurea*, the *Sanctuarium*, the *Historie plurimorum sanctorum*, various manuscripts underlying the *Acta sanctorum*, and beyond. Before beginning the investigation, it will be helpful to look briefly at the composition and compilation of the source and analogue texts as a way of demonstrating the complex hagiographical web underlying Add. 2604.

There is probably more written about the *Legenda aurea*, its genesis, and its influence, than any other legendary in the Middle Ages.[11] Extant in considerably over a thousand manuscripts and over a hundred and twenty printed editions up to 1520 alone, it was transmitted throughout Europe like no other collection and so formed the backbone of a myriad of vernacular legendaries both in manuscript and early print.[12] Many of these *Legenda aurea* manuscripts were adapted and augmented in different ways. Barbara Fleith's classification

[11] Besides the exceptionally useful study by Reames, *The 'Legenda aurea': A Reexamination of its Paradoxical History*, a small but important sample from which this *Study* has benefited in particular are the numerous informative essays in the following collections: *'Legenda aurea': sept siècles de diffusion*, Actes du colloque international sur la *'Legende aurea': texte latin et branches vernaculaires à l'Université du Québec à Montréal, 11–12 mai 1983*, ed. by Brenda Dunn-Lardeau (Montréal: Éditions Bellarmin; Paris: Librairie J. Vrin, 1986); *'Legenda aurea' – 'la Légende dorée' (XIII⁰ – XV⁰ S.)*, *Actes de Congrès international de Perpignan (séances 'Nouvelles recherches sur la "Legenda aurea" ')*, ed. by Brenda Dunn-Lardeau, Le moyen français, 32 (Montréal: Éditions CERES, 1993); G. P. Maggioni, *Ricerche sulla composizione e sulla trasmissione della 'Legenda aurea'*, Biblioteca di Medioevo, 8 (Spoleto: Centro Italiano di Studi sull'Alto Medioevo, 1995); Jacques de Voragine, *'La Légende dorée': Edition critique, dans la revision de 1476 par Jean Batallier, d'après la traduction de Jean de Vignay (1333–1348) de la 'Legenda aurea' (c. 1261–1266)*, ed. by Brenda Dunn-Lardeau, Textes de la Renaissance, 19 (Paris: Honoré Champion, 1997); and *De la sainteté a l'hagiographie: Genèse et usage de la 'Légende dorée'*, ed. by Barbara Fleith and Franco Morenzoni, Publications romanes et françaises, 229 (Genève: Librairie Droz S.A., 2001).

[12] Maggioni, 'La trasmissione dei leggendari abbreviati del XIII secolo' (p. 89); Thayer, *Penitence, Preaching and the Coming of the Reformation*, p. 21 n. 5; see also Seybolt, 'Fifteenth Century Editions of the *Legenda aurea*', and Robert Francis Seybolt, 'The *Legenda aurea*, Bible, and *Historia scholastica*', *Speculum*, 21 (1946), 339–42.

of such manuscripts demonstrates how the original 178 saints' lives (or 182 items including some other material), what she terms the 'Normalcorpus', was enhanced to varying degrees to produce the so-called 'Fremlegenden'.[13] Fleith goes to inordinate lengths to classify over 1,042 *Legenda aurea* manuscripts. In tracing the added (and deleted *Legenda aurea* saints) in the individual manuscripts, she provides the saints with their own codes (for example, Benedicta is B24). Working with the various indices, it is possible to ascertain the contents of any *Legenda aurea* manuscript investigated and to see how common a particular saint is across the board. Fleith sometimes made use of library catalogues rather than first-hand investigation so not all the information is complete or entirely accurate.[14] More problematic still, a reference to the presence of B24 in any one manuscript does not reveal whether or not the text in question is the same, only that the relevant manuscripts contain an added Benedicta. As noted below, these lists only serve to point in a particular direction rather than providing immediately what is required for the sort of source study needed for Add. 2604. In essence they are more useful for indicating the popularity of any particular saint and also for noting *Legenda aurea* manuscripts in English and related repositories. Bearing these concerns in mind, we have extrapolated from Fleith to determine that copies of the *Legenda aurea* (either augmented or otherwise) are in various repositories in the following locations (with the number of copies in brackets): Aberdeen (1), Aberystwyth (1), Bristol (1), Cambridge (18), Dublin (2), Durham (1), Edinburgh (2), Glasgow (1), Hereford (2), Leeds (2), London (22), Manchester (1), Oxford (27), Winchester (1), and Worcester (1), eighty-three manuscripts in total. This still provides no true idea of how many manuscripts there were in England as a whole or indeed if the ones listed were part of the medieval holdings. Understandably too there will be many other survivals Fleith did not uncover. As far as we know, there is no cumulative list of *Legenda aurea* manuscripts from medieval England. There is a useful account by Courtney Rydel of a small selection of *Legenda aurea* manuscripts (with a few translations) currently in the British Library and Cambridge University Library (plus one in Lambeth Palace Library); she categorises these thirty-six manuscripts into English provenance, unknown provenance, conti-

---

[13] Both are listed in Fleith, *Studien zur Überlieferungsgeschichte der lateinischen 'Legenda Aurea'*, pp. 432–33 and 435–97 respectively.

[14] See, for instance, O. S. Pickering's review of Fleith's book in the *Journal of Ecclesiastical History*, 44 (1993), 338–39, where he points out confusion in the description of *Legenda aurea* manuscripts in Leeds University Library.

nental provenance, and so forth.[15] Recourse can also be made to certain catalogues that itemise the information, but overall it is impossible to account for what survives today let alone what existed in the Middle Ages.[16] Part of the difficulty in tracing *Legenda aurea* manuscripts also hinges on its varied titles in earlier references, medieval library lists, and wills.[17] Scholars are therefore stymied when it comes to checking *Legenda aurea* manuscripts in England quite apart from *Legenda aurea* manuscripts on the Continent whether augmented or not.[18] This surfeit of material is therefore a very mixed blessing.

By comparison, Mombritius's *Sanctuarium* that was printed only once should be more straightforward but for a work that is now so well known, it has a somewhat vague history.[19] This collection of some 326 saints' lives or 330 items (four of which merely concern feast days, according Frazier), was printed in folio in Milan around 1477 to 1478.[20] It is divided alphabetically into 143 entries in volume 1 and 187 in volume 2, and survives today in at least eighty copies.[21] Containing an eclectic mix of saints ranging from first-century fig-

---

[15] Rydel, 'Literary Effects', pp. 99–100 and n. 253.

[16] See, for instance, Ker and Piper, *Medieval Manuscripts in British Libraries*; *Legenda aurea* manuscripts are listed (under Jacobus de Voragine's works) by I. C. Cunningham and A. G. Watson in v (2002), 66.

[17] See, for example, the various references in the *Corpus of British Medieval Library Catalogues*. Using information from Susan Hagen Cavanaugh's 'A Study of Books Privately Owned in England: 1300–1450' (unpublished doctoral dissertation, The University of Pennsylvania, 1980), Rydel, 'Literary Effects', pp. 110–14 and especially nn. 282–87, makes an extensive attempt to disaggregate *Legenda aurea* manuscripts from others and to list the private owners of the *Legenda aurea* in medieval England.

[18] There are nevertheless some careful studies of these in the different vernaculars; for instance, Williams-Krapp, *Die deutschen und niederländischen Legendare des Mittelalters* deals with 'Die "Elsässische Legenda aurea" ', pp. 35–52 and 'Die "Südmittelniederländische Legenda aurea" ', pp. 53–187.

[19] See the detailed discussion in ch. 3, 'The Last Medieval Legendary', in Frazier, *Possible Lives*, pp. 101–67.

[20] Frazier, 'The Last Medieval Legendary', in *Possible Lives*, provides a careful account (pp. 121–67) of the political and other factors in Milan that would support her rationale for dating, '[...] we can speculate that printing commenced, at the latest, in the spring or summer of 1478' (p. 121); it was definitely printed by mid-September 1478 as a purchase note from 14 September 1478 testifies (p. 120).

[21] Frazier, 'The Last Medieval Legendary' in *Possible Lives*, points out that it is the first alphabetical legendary in print, albeit with some slips (p. 142); she also notes that 'The number and nature of the extant copies are the subject of a census still in progress; the size of the print run cannot be estimated from the survival rate' (p. 102 n. 5).

SOURCES AND ANALOGUES OF THE UNIVERSAL LIVES IN ADD. 2604   221

ures to Caterina da Siena (d. 1380), it shows a heavy bias in favour of third and fourth-century martyrs. It has most of the universal lives found in Add. 2604 (but none of the English saints): Agatha, Barbara, Cecilia, Columba, Domitilla (alongside Euphrosyne and Theodora as well as being part of Nereus and Achilleus), John the Evangelist, Justina (both with Cyprian and singly), Leonard, and Martha; it lacks Benedicta and the Nativity of John the Baptist though it has the Invention (or Discovery of the Head of John the Baptist). The publisher and publication date are not given in the volumes; there is no title page and even the now-familiar title itself is derived from the heading of the *tabula* or index at the beginning of each volume. Most surprisingly of all in a general European context (though not an Italian one), the person responsible for this collection and for getting it into print, perhaps as part of a consortium, was not a cleric but a layman. As outlined by Alison Frazier in her magisterial study of fifteenth-century Italian humanists as hagiographical authors, Mombritius (1424–c. 1480) had multiple roles throughout his life: lawyer, goldsmith, editor, professor of rhetoric, and so on.[22] Yet despite what may be gleaned about his biography, the most important piece of information is missing: no manuscript of his printed text exists and so we are almost completely in the dark about his sources. All there is to go on is a comment by Jean Bolland in the *Acta sanctorum*, 'Boninus Mombritius Mediolanensis duo ingentia volumina edidit, quibus Acta Sanctorum complexus est, ut ea in manuscriptis codicibus reperit, ita fideliter, ut ne menda quidem scriptionis correxerit, quae minus iucundam lectionem reddere solent'.[23] As noted by Frazier, it is not clear whether Bolland's praise for Mombritius (whose work is used extensively in the *Acta sanctorum*) is unalloyed: on the one hand, he is congratulated on his accuracy; on the other hand, a true humanist would have been prepared to correct a faulty text.[24] Significantly there is one mention of a manuscript connected with the *Sanctuarium*. Filippo Argelati (1685–1755) makes reference to having seen a manuscript that may have been Mombritius's autograph or at least produced

[22] Mombritius made his will on 24 December 1478, but the date of his death is uncertain; see Frazier, 'The Last Medieval Legendary', in *Possible Lives*, p. 114 and pp. 109–14 for his various careers.

[23] Quoted by Frazier, 'The Last Medieval Legendary', in *Possible Lives*, p. 101.

[24] Frazier, 'The Last Medieval Legendary', in *Possible Lives*, p. 111, refers to how Mombritius carefully corrected the work of another and she also notes the 'graceful presentation' of the text 'relatively free from market pressures' (p. 119); there is also some evidence that the *Sanctuarium* may have been unfinished or rushed (p. 164) and also for both Mombritius's transcriptional care (with errors included) *and* correctional tendencies (pp. 164–65).

in the fifteenth century in the library of the Augustinian hermits at San Marco in Milan (that is, the older Augustinian convent rather than that of Santa Maria Incoronata): 'Ipsas ego inspexi variis in bibliothecis manuscriptas in pergameno, ab editis diversas, et signanter in Bibliotheca Eremitarum S. Marci huius urbis extat volumen ingens *Vitas Sanctorum* continens, sub nomine Mombriti, ordine diverso dispositas, mutatis pluribus quoque verbis [...].[25] Unfortunately, there is no longer any trace of this manuscript. What relationship it had with the *Sanctuarium* is not known, though further comment by Argelati reveals various differences between this manuscript version — which may have been a precursor to or a copy of the printed text — and the *Sanctuarium*.[26] Frazier speculates on the libraries that Mombritius may have used (if he gathered his own materials) including the Doumo library in Milan and the Bobbio library.[27] She, like Gerhard Eis before her, also identifies the texts in the *Sanctuarium* that derive from the *Legenda aurea* and the *Speculum historiale*.[28] As she says:

> [...] a start might be made at reconstituting the lost fifteenth-century manuscript of Mombrizio's work by subtracting from the *Sanctuarium* the accounts traceable to the *Legenda aurea* and the *Speculum historiale*. The core that remains may indicate

---

[25] Boninus Mombritius, *Sanctuarium seu Vitae Sanctorum*, ed. by Two Monks of Solesmes, 2 vols (Paris: Albertus Fontemoing, 1910), I, xxvi; Frazier, 'The Last Medieval Legendary', in *Possible Lives*, p. 106, and nn. 21 and 22.

[26] Frazier, 'The Last Medieval Legendary', in *Possible Lives*, provides illuminating detail about what is known of the putative manuscript version in comparison to the printed *Sanctuarium*. Various interesting differences are found; for instance, the saints are given in liturgical order rather than the printed alphabetical order (p. 140) and seven saints listed in the manuscript are not found in the *Sanctuarium* (pp. 153–54 and nn. 229–30, and 157–58 and n. 245). Most importantly, George is said to be in the manuscript but is not in the print whereas Katherine of Alexandria occurs in the print but not in the manuscript; see pp. 153–64 where Frazier discusses the importance of the absence of George and the presence of Katherine of Alexandria in the printed text while also comparing the Katherine text with another manuscript version associated with the *Magnum Legendarium Austriacum* tradition as a way of helping to illustrate Mombritius's editorial procedure with its humanistic textual interventions.

[27] Frazier, 'The Last Medieval Legendary', in *Possible Lives*, pp. 140 and 165.

[28] Gerhard Eis, *Die Quellen für das Sanctuarium des Mailänder Humanisten Boninus Mombritius: Eine Untersuchung zur Geschichte der großen Legendensammlungen des Mittelalters*, Germanische Studien, 140 (Berlin: Emil Ebering, 1933) provides a list on pp. 23–24; the only life that has relevance to those in Add. 2604 is Leonard which Eis says derives from the *Legenda aurea* (p. 23). Frazier, 'The Last Medieval Legendary', in *Possible Lives*, usefully sets out the number of borrowings in Table 3.1 (p. 139) in 'Mombrizio's *Sanctuarium* by Month'; see also n. 182 on p. 139.

SOURCES AND ANALOGUES OF THE UNIVERSAL LIVES IN ADD. 2604   223

the editor's desires for the collection, although at some remove that still must be estimated.[29]

As noted by Eis and Frazier (citing the 1910 edition of the *Sanctuarium*), there are seventy-three lives that are more or less from the *Speculum historiale* and twenty-two from the *Legenda aurea*. In like manner the *Legenda aurea* emerged from a matrix of sources so the same may be said for both the *Sanctuarium* and the next text, the *Historie plurimorum sanctorum* (all of which, of course, makes the isolating of sources and analogues for the lives in Add. 2604 immensely complicated).

If the difficulty with the *Legenda aurea* focuses on too many manuscripts, the problem with the *Historie plurimorum sanctorum*, like the *Sanctuarium*, is the very opposite. The *Historie plurimorum sanctorum*, printed in Cologne in 1483 as a supplement to the *Legenda aurea* and reprinted singly in Louvain in 1485, contains Barbara (both Passion and Translation), Benedicta and Columba, as well as Edith and Hild. The 1485 text finishes with an alphabetical list of the saints included but the organisation of the text itself is calendrical, beginning with the sanctorale feasts for December. The fact that it does not contain Agatha, Cecilia, Domitilla, John the Baptist, John the Evangelist, Justina, Leonard, or Martha is not surprising. All except Domitilla were part of the original *Legenda aurea*. The exclusion of Domitilla is not unexpected, given that most treatments of her occur alongside that of Nereus and Achilleus, as happens in the *Legenda aurea*. It is more important that no full source manuscript has been found for the *Historie plurimorum sanctorum* and neither is the identity of the author or compiler known. The printer responsible for the 1485 edition, Johannes de Westfalia who was known for importing books into England, went by a number of names, as explained by Rudolf Juchhoff:

> Was aber hat Johannes de Westfalia mit Johann von Aachen zu tun? Sie sind identisch. Johannes de Westfalia hat sich selbst zwar nie als von Aachen bezeichnet. Er selbst nennt sich in seinen Drucken in der ersten Zeit abwechselnd Johannes de Paderborne in West-[p. 135]falia, Johannes de Westfalia Paderbornensis dioecesis oder kurz Johannes de Westfalia, bis seit 1480 die letztgenannte Form überwiegend gebraucht wird, so daß er in der Druckergeschichte vorzugsweise unter diesem Namen bekannt ist.[30]

---

[29] Frazier, 'The Last Medieval Legendary', in *Possible Lives*, p. 152.

[30] Juchhoff, 'Johannes de Westfalia als Buchhändler', discusses the book importation on pp. 133–34; this is further discussed in Paul Needham, 'Continental Printed Books in Oxford, *c.* 1480–83: Two Trade Records', in *Incunabula: Studies in Fifteenth-Century Printed*

There is one manuscript link with the printed text in the work of Hermann Greven (d. 5 November 1477 or 5 November 1480). As noted in IV. Hagiographical Context and The Selection of Saints, the Carthusian Greven from the diocese of Paderborn compiled a legendary of 250 texts, particularly localised saints of English, French, and German extraction. This abridged legendary is extant in Berlin, Staatsbibliothek, MS Theol. lat. fol. 706. According to De Gaiffier building on Poncelet before him:

> [...] des 250 légendes qui contient le manuscrit de Greven, plus de cent se retrouvent dans l'édition de Cologne, c'est-à-dire environ la moitié de l'imprimé. Il n'est pas douteux que l'auteur anonyme qui a réuni pour l'impression les textes de l'édition incunable, n'ait largement puisé dans l'œuvre du chartreux colonais. La dépendance de l'incunable par rapport au manuscrit se révèle aussi par l'identité de nombreux *incipit* et *desinit*, très caractéristiques et qui ne se retrouvent pas ailleurs [...]
>
> Des 150 textes, qui n'ont pas été repris par l'éditeur de 1483, une centaine environ reproduisent des Vies identifiées et recensées dans la *Bibliotheca Hagiographica Latina*. Pour une cinquantaine, nous n'avons pu decouvrir aucun texte qui leur corresponde exactement; mail il n'est en général pas difficile de retrouver la Vie ou la Passion que leur est apparentée.[31]

In taking over a hundred texts from Greven, making use of a hundred and fifty of the more common lives from elsewhere and combining them with fifty others, the editor of the printed text aptly demonstrates how compilatory methods were the same for print and manuscript culture. And the Paderborn connection between Greven and Johannes de Westfalia is interesting. As noted by Vermassen, the *Historie plurimorum sanctorum* 'completed with saints' lives from the Rhineland, the Meuse area and the Southern Low Countries' was 'meant to be a compilation of *legendae novae* specifically for the Rhine area and the Netherlands'.[32] The versions of the two native saints in the *Historie plurimorum sanctorum*, Hild and Edith, show a similar pattern in that the most recognised (and local) authority is used for both: Bede for Hild (fols Cxcviii verso–Cxcix verso and Goscelin de Saint-Bertin for Edith (fols Cxxx verso b–Cxxxi[i] recto b). Even more interesting from our point of view is that the

---

Books Presented to Lotte Hellinga, ed. by Martin Davies (London: The British Library, 1999), pp. 243–70.

[31] De Gaiffier, 'Le Martyrologe et le légendier d'Hermann Greven', p. 331; see also p. 331 n. 3 for the list of overlapping lives and the description of the manuscript on pp. 333–55.

[32] Vermassen, 'Latin Hagiography in the Dutch-Speaking Parts of the Southern Low Countries (1350–1550)', in *Hagiographies*, ed. by Goullet, vii (2017), p. 603.

SOURCES AND ANALOGUES OF THE UNIVERSAL LIVES IN ADD. 2604 225

edition did not draw on John of Tynemouth's epitomes but from the Bede and Goscelin's accounts directly. Such cases aptly demonstrate the intermingled nature of the sources, something that will be even more obvious in our next example.

Finally, the sources of the *vitae* collected in the *Acta sanctorum* are the most complicated of all those here. This is linked with the ways in which these volumes (covering saints from 1 January to 10 November plus the introduction or Propylaeum to December) were put together. This was done over some four centuries by the Bollandists (the Jesuit editors so named in 1641 after the first editor Jean Bolland (1596–1665),[33] building on the work of Héribert Rosweyde (1569–1629).[34] One of the most concise descriptions of the work is that by François Dolbeau:

> D'abord, les *Acta Sanctorum*, classés selon le calendrier liturgique, sont une entreprise de très longue haleine, qui fut annoncée dès 1607 [p. 106] dans un livre programmatique, relancée selon un plan différent à partir de 1630 et poursuivie jusqu'en 1940. En second lieu, leur publication fut interrompue, entre 1794 et 1845, alors qu'elle était parvenue au milieu d'Octobre, en raison des bouleverse-

---

[33] The situation is further complicated by the different editions of the *Acta sanctorum*. Put simply, there are three editions comprised of a varying number of volumes: the original edition published in Antwerp, Brussels, and other places from 1643, a second printed by Sébastien Coleti and Jean-Baptiste Albrizzi in Venice between 1734 and 1770 that only contains forty-three volumes, and a third published by Victor Palmé of Paris under the direction of J. B. Carnandet between 1863 and 1870. The first edition was reproduced in an 'Impression anastaltique' by the Éditions 'Culture et Civilisation' in Brussels in 1966–71 and again in 1999 in an online edition published by Chadwyck Healey (http://acta.chadwyck.co.uk). For details see 'Un trésor iconographique méconnu: Les Gravures des *Acta Sanctorum*', in *Bollandistes: Saints et Légendes, Quatre siècles de recherche*, ed. by Robert Godding and others (Bruxelles: Société des Bollandistes, 2007), pp. 75–96; see especially pp. 93–95 for the complex layout of the different editions. Throughout this *Study* and *Edition* we cite the Paris edition as the one most readily available to readers, but the 1966–71 reproduction and the online version have also been consulted so as to ensure that the readings quoted from the Paris edition are the same as those in the original edition (which they are). Rather than providing overall volume numbers or years, for greater ease of reference we give the month, the volume for that month, the pages and the paragraph numbers as relevant; for instance, there are three volumes for February and so the relevant text of Agatha (5 February) occurs in the *Acta sanctorum*, Februarii Tomus Primus, pp. 621–24, paragraphs 1–15, where this first volume covers 1 to 6 February.

[34] The Bollandists provide a general introduction to the methodology of the volumes, see *Acta sanctorum*, Januarii Tomus Primus, pp. xiii–lxi, but it is of very limited use with regard to the manuscripts used.

ments provoqués par la Révolution française. Enfin, la collection est restée inachevée et ne couvre pas la période qui va du 11 novembre au 31 décembre.[35]

Dolbeau goes on to stress that the work of the Bollandists must not be held up to current-day critical standards:

> Les mois de janvier à avril et les trois premiers tomes de mai, publiés de 1643 à 1680, sont antérieurs à l'acte de naissance de la paléographie, c'est-à-dire au *De re diplomatica* de Mabillon, paru à Paris en 1681. D'autre part, il serait stupide de faire grief aux anciens Bollandistes d'avoir ignoré l'importance des livrets, des types de collections, des expertises codicologiques, qui sont des concepts entraperçus au XIXe siècle et développés au XXe. Les méthodes [p. 108] philologiques modernes, inspirées de la science allemande, furent appliquées pour la première fois dans le tome XIII d'Octobre, en 1883. Tous les volumes précédents doivent être jugés en fonction de leur époque et selon d'autres critères.[36]

The volumes published by the Bollandists between 1643 and 1794 fall into three periods: (1) the first five volumes for January and February; (2) from the three volumes for March in 1668 to the third volume for June in 1701; and (3) from 1702 to 1794.[37] The production of these volumes was facilitated by consultation of manuscripts in the Low Countries and northern France particularly by early Bollandists such as Héribert Rosweyde, Jean Bolland, Godfried Henschen (known as Henschenius, 1601–81), and Daniel Papebroch (1682–1714).[38] In addition, material was given by friends and benefactors or was bought. The widespread literary expeditions throughout Europe by various Bollandists between 1660 and 1752 are listed by Dolbeau:

---

[35] François Dolbeau, 'Les Sources manuscrites des *Acta sanctorum* et leur collecte (XVIIe–XVIIIe siècles)', in *De Rosweyde aux 'Acta Sanctorum': La Recherche hagiographique des Bollandistes à travers quatre siècles, Actes du Colloque international (Bruxelles, 5 Octobre 2007)*, ed. by Robert Godding and others, Subsidia hagiographica, 88 (Bruxelles: Société des Bollandistes, 2009), pp. 105–47 (pp. 105–06).

[36] Dolbeau, 'Les Sources manuscrites des *Acta sanctorum* et leur collecte (XVIIe–XVIIIe siècles)', pp. 107–08.

[37] Dolbeau, 'Les Sources manuscrites des *Acta sanctorum* et leur collecte (XVIIe–XVIIIe siècles)', pp. 114–15.

[38] Donald Sullivan, 'Jean Bolland (1596–1665) and the Early Bollandists', in *Medieval Scholarship: Biographical Studies on the Formation of a Discipline*, ed. by Helen Damico, Joseph B. Zavidil, and others, Garland Reference Library of the Humanities, 1350, 2071, and 2110, 3 vols (New York, NY: Garland, 1995–2000), I: *History*, 3–14.

SOURCES AND ANALOGUES OF THE UNIVERSAL LIVES IN ADD. 2604   227

Le stock initial de copies (*apographa, ecgrapha*), qui représente encore une part subs-
tantielle des *Collectanea Bollandiana*, fut enrichi ensuite à l'occasion de différents
voyages littéraires: entre 1660 et 1662, d'Anvers à Rome, via l'Allemagne à l'aller et
la France au retour (Henschen et Papebroch); en pays mosan et mosellan, en 1668
(les mêmes); à Florence et à Rome, en 1681 (Janninck); à travers l'Allemagne et
l'Autriche, en 1688 (Janninck et Baert); à Rome, entre 1697 et 1700 (Janninck); à
Vienne, en 1715 (Du Sollier); en Espagne, en 1721 (Pien et Cuypers); en France,
Italie, Allemagne et Hongrie, en 1752 (Stilting et Suyskens). Les voyageurs consul-
taient des manuscrits et repéraient des textes nouveaux qu'ils ramenaient à Anvers
après les avoir transcrits, ou dont ils demandaient des copies effectuées sur place et
expédiées ensuite en Belgique.[39]

Despite the rigour of this collecting activity, by the end of the eighteenth century and turn of the nineteenth the Museum Bollandium in Antwerp was
dispersed following the papal suppression of the Jesuits in 1773 (restored in
1814).[40] Combined with the somewhat haphazard methodology adopted by
earlier hagiographers and their vagueness when referring (if at all) to the sources
from which they were transcribing, this dispersal and subsequent loss of books
from the early Bollandist Library means that it is incredibly difficult — often
impossible — to trace many of the manuscripts used in the *Acta sanctorum*. We
are fortunate to have a listing of the medieval Latin hagiographic manuscripts
held by the Bollandists as well as those manuscripts originally owned by the
Bollandists, now known at the *Collectanea Bollandiana* in the Bibliothèque
royale de Belgique/Koninklijke Bibliotheek van België (hereafter KBR), but

[39] Dolbeau, 'Les Sources manuscrites des *Acta sanctorum* et leur collecte (XVIIᵉ–XVIIIᵉ
siècles)', p. 111. See also 'Les Voyages scientifiques', in *Bollandistes: Saints et Légendes, Quatre
siècles de recherche*, ed. by Robert Godding and others (Bruxelles: Société des Bollandistes,
2009), pp. 105–47.

[40] By 1773 fifty volumes (up to 7 October) had been published. The present Bollandist
Library was established in Brussels in 1837 when work on the *Acta sanctorum* was begun again.
It contains about 500,000 volumes; 1,000 current periodicals; some 25,000 books printed
before 1801; 120 volumes of *Collectanea Bollandiana* (the seventeenth- and eighteenth-century
transcripts of saints' lives gathered for the *Acta sanctorum*); manuscripts from the sixteenth
to the nineteenth century; a thousand manuscripts of which ninety-seven are medieval, plus
one hundred incunabula, as well as various liturgical, Armenian, Georgian, and Slavic material,
and a large collection of items on beatification and canonisation. Following the suppression,
many of the medieval manuscripts were sent to the Bibliothèque royale de Belgique (the KBR),
though some were lost, and the printed books mostly auctioned. The *Collectanea Bollandiana*
that had been gathered for the purposes of the *Acta sanctorum* can be found (only in part) in
the KBR and (again in part) in the current Bollandist Library. See https://www.bollandistes.
org/library for details; accessed 1 April 2023.

this can take us only so far given the plethora of material underlying the *Acta sanctorum*.[41]

In the light of the genesis of the four main sources and analogues above, the universal lives in Add. 2604 may ultimately spring from a Latin manuscript or manuscripts first produced in Italy, the Rhineland, the Low Countries, or France. Given the pronounced French-based nature of many of the non-English saints included in Add. 2604 (Benedicta of Origny, Columba of Sens, Leonard of Nobilac, and the biblical Martha who was associated with the evangelisation of Provence), they probably derived ultimately from France or the southern part of the Low Countries (present-day Belgium). How or when this putative manuscript or manuscripts may have reached England to be used for the translation of the English texts in Add. 2604 remains an imponderable.

Universal Lives in Add. 2604 and their 'Legenda aurea' Source

When searching for the sources of saints' lives in late medieval English literature or indeed in virtually any other European language, one thing is certain: the first port of call is normally the *Legenda aurea*, that vast compilation of material for which the term 'best seller' is hardly adequate. A number of Add. 2604's universal saints figure in that collection proper, namely, Agatha, Cecilia, John the Baptist, John the Evangelist, Justina, Leonard, and Martha. Yet only Cecilia, John the Baptist, John the Evangelist, and Martha are actually taken from the *Legenda aurea*. Other sources or analogues have to be found for Agatha, Barbara, Benedicta, Columba, Domitilla, Justina, and Leonard. Why the Add. 2604 compiler did not translate Agatha, Justina, and Leonard from the *Legenda aurea* is a mystery; it may be that the manuscript he was using had a mixture of source material or that the translator himself wished to explore further afield.

In John the Baptist, John the Evangelist, Cecilia, and Martha there is the first sub-set of universal sources (these lives are given in the order in which they

---

[41] This descriptive list of the hagiographic Latin material amongst the ninety-seven pre-1500 manuscripts is available in H. Moretus, 'Catalogus Codicum hagiographicorum latinorum Bibliothecæ Bollandianæ', *Analecta Bollandiana*, 24 (1905), 425–72. The Bollandist manuscripts in the KBR may be found, *inter alia*, in Van den Gheyn and others, *Catalogue des manuscrits de la Bibliothèque royale de Belgique*, especially I: Écriture sainte et Liturgie (1901) and V: Historie-Hagiographie (1905). In all the references here, as is customary, the numbers (in brackets) allotted in Van den Gheyn's catalogue are included.

UNIVERSAL LIVES IN ADD. 2604 AND THEIR 'LEGENDA AUREA' SOURCE   229

appear in Add. 2604).[42] These are all mainly rather careful translations from the *Legenda aurea*, that is, to the extent that they may be compared with the standard edition.[43] (And, as discussed above, given the multiplicity of *Legenda aurea* manuscripts, both known and unknown, in the absence of any other manuscript leads, an editor gratefully accepts the standard edition as the fixed point in an otherwise shifting textual universe.) Indeed, the only striking difference is the omission of the usual etymologies provided by Jacobus de Voragine at the beginning of his lives. In both the Johns these are excised (presumably this was also the case in the now acephalous Cecilia). The exclusion of such etymologies has a long history in English.[44]

The first example, the life of John the Baptist, draws on two separate *Legenda aurea* lives, that for the feast of the Nativity on 24 June and that on the Decollation or Beheading on 29 August.[45] In its careful blending of the two lives it is unusual from the start as most other Latin or Middle English lives of John the Baptist — hagiographical or homiletical — deal separately with both.[46] These two feasts are combined so seamlessly in Add. 2604 that the join between them cannot be seen in this imaginative re-structuring that

---

[42] All the comparisons below between the lives in Add. 2604 and their sources or analogues are presented in skeletal form as complete details, together with the relevant quotations from Middle English and Latin, are given in the Overview and Commentary to each saint's life in the *Edition*. In the discussion here we simply provide the main reference to the source and/ or analogue text.

[43] Iacopo da Varazze, *Legenda aurea con le miniature del codice Ambrosiano C 240 inf.*, ed. by Maggioni. In this edition the typographical errors from the previous critical edition of 1998 have been corrected and so the 2007 edition has been used here, but with reference to the 1998 edition as appropriate; see Iacopo da Varazze, *Legenda aurea: Edizione critica*, ed. by Giovanni Paolo Maggioni, Millennio medievale 6, Testi 3, 2nd revised edn, 2 vols (Firenze: Sismel-Edizioni del Galluzzo, 1998).

[44] As noted by Görlach, 'Middle English Legends, 1220–1530' (p. 454), those lives in the verse *South English Legendary* dependent on the *Legenda aurea* routinely omitted such etymologies. They are likewise omitted in the *Gilte Legende* and in the Syon lives of the two Johns.

[45] LXXXI, 'De sancto Iohanne Baptista' and CXXI, 'De decollatione sancti Iohannis Baptiste' as found in Iacopo da Varazze, *Legenda aurea con le miniature del codice Ambrosiano C 240 inf.*, ed. by Maggioni, i, 604–14 (versos only), and ii, 970–83 (versos only).

[46] See the relevant Tables in IV. Hagiographical Context and The Selection of Saints' Lives. An exception is the *Gilte Legende* life that draws on the Nativity and the Decollation added to other unsourced material; see *Gilte Legende*, ed. by Hamer, i, 38–39. The Syon life of John the Baptist just uses three exempla from the Decollation in its final chapter; see *Virgins and Scholars*, ed. by Waters, p. 436. Bokenham's John the Baptist in the Abbotsford manuscript makes no mention of the Decollation; see *Osbern Bokenham 'Lives of Saints'*, ed. by Horobin, ii, 157–60.

alternates from one narrative to another. As evident from the *Gilte Legende*, which also draws on the two occasions, the Add. 2604 compiler is not the first to conflate both feasts. The translation is close to the Latin, with only a few minor changes; for instance, the Add. 2604 translator tends to omit the names of patristic authors and does not bother to provide his source references even when these are specified in the original. Most particularly, all lengthy explanatory passages of theological import found in the source are excluded. John the Baptist's miracles are privileged in Add. 2604; at the end of his life, the usual order of certain miracles is even inverted so as to lead neatly on to the life of John the Evangelist. Even though widely separated liturgically, the translator (or more particularly the original Latin compiler) would seem to be going out of his way to signal a connection between the two; this is also stressed by his final note that John the Baptist was born on the day that John the Evangelist died. A version of this comment is found in the *Legenda aurea* but earlier in the text; its relocation demonstrates the compiler's decisive plan for the placement of the two Johns in the manuscript.

The case of John the Evangelist is more streamlined as it relies almost entirely on the life of John as found in the *Legenda aurea* apart from a preamble in Add. 2604. This outlines John's early life that in turn echoes some of the genealogy found in the *Legenda aurea* Nativity of Mary and cites the apocryphal tradition of John's intended marriage at Cana.[47] Some of the information in this opening, which is also found in the first chapter of the Syon life of John the Evangelist, may be traditional rather than traceable to any single source.[48] In the Add. 2604 life overall there is some alternation between *Legenda aurea* feasts, this time between John's main feast on 29 December and the feast of *Ad portam Latinam* (or John at the Latin Gate) on 6 May, but this is much more limited than in the preceding, with only a few sentences taken from the latter.[49] In this life, which is also close to the *Legenda aurea* source, apart from occasional omissions and a few elaborations, the main emphasis is on John the Evangelist's ordeals and miracles.

---

[47] CXXVII, 'De nativitate sancte Marie virginis', in Iacopo da Varazze, *Legenda aurea con le miniature del codice Ambrosiano C 240 inf.*, ed. by Maggioni, II, 1004–23 (versos only).

[48] See *Virgins and Scholars*, ed. by Waters, p. 437, where she points out that details in the first chapter may derive from the *Legenda aurea* Nativity of Mary source, though noting that the *trinubium* theme is commonplace.

[49] IX, 'De sancto Iohanne Evangelista', with a few sentences from LXV, 'De sancto Iohanne ante Portam Latinam', in Iacopo da Varazze, *Legenda aurea con le miniature del codice Ambrosiano C 240 inf.*, ed. by Maggioni, I, 102–13, and I, 526–27 respectively (versos only).

Clearly the life of John the Baptist was taken ultimately from a *Legenda aurea* that had both Nativity and Decollation and that of John the Evangelist originally derived from a copy that had the Nativity of Mary and the account of John at the Latin Gate (as well as Justina, and perhaps Clement and Nereus and Achilleus, as evidence below will show), in other words, possibly a full text. It is open to question whether the Add. 2604 English translator was the person responsible for combining this selection of material from the *Legenda aurea* or whether he was working from another text where these combinations had already been made. Our strong supposition is that he was simply translating from a ready-made version. For example, a precedent already existed from 1438 in the *Gilte Legende* combination of the two John the Baptist feasts; this is reinforced by evidence from Justina below.

The two other lives translated from the *Legenda aurea*, Cecilia and Martha, are even more straightforward. The life of Cecilia, celebrated on 22 November, starts imperfectly owing to a lost quire (fols 33–40) between the end of Agatha and the beginning of Cecilia and it also lacks fol. 44. Calculations of the missing texts support the hypothesis that one quire would have been more than adequate to contain the respective sections in both lives (and another life or lives); it is also estimated that what is missing at the beginning of the life of Cecilia could have fitted on fol. 40v.[50] Albeit for the absent text (presumably not including the etymology normally excised in Add. 2604), it is very close to its *Legenda aurea* source.[51] In Add. 2604 only four sentences from the *Legenda aurea* are omitted, a little reference by Ambrose to the crown of martyrdom. Attempts at expansion are for the purposes of clarification or for the sake of adding interest.

The life of Martha, the third and final biblical saint included in Add. 2604, begins with a paragraph outlining her parentage and sibling relations and a brief mention of her lack of a husband. No direct source or analogue has been found for this section; it is obviously dependent in part on the Bible and in turn driven by an attempt by the translator to prove Martha a pure maid before her exile with Mary Magdalene and Lazarus to the south of France. Otherwise the life is based on the *Legenda aurea* text (and for the feast of 29 July rather than

---

[50] For the calculations of what else may have been missing here, see IV. Hagiographical Context and The Selection of Saints' Lives.

[51] CLXV, 'De sancta Cecilia', in Iacopo da Varazze, *Legenda aurea con le miniature del codice Ambrosiano C 240 inf.*, ed. by Maggioni, II, 1322–31 (versos only).

any of the variant Martha feasts).[52] Overall the translation from the *Legenda aurea* is close, except for a few additions and alterations, and one confused section. Like those of the two Johns (and no doubt Cecilia in its complete state), the life of Martha lacks the fanciful etymology of the saint's name routinely found at the beginning of the *Legenda aurea* chapters (and not in Martha).

Leaving any small changes to one side, the four lives here are clearly translated from the *Legenda aurea* itself rather than from some loose derivative thereof. Yet the way in which the narratives of John the Baptist (in particular) and John the Evangelist have drawn on different lives in the *Legenda aurea* (plus the added preamble at the opening of Martha if it is not the translator's own creation) would indicate that even if textually close to the edited *Legenda aurea*, there is some distance between the original *Legenda aurea* and the Add. 2604 witnesses. There is no way of isolating what this intermediary might be, though there are a few textual hints about the ultimate derivation of some of the readings in Add. 2604's Latin source manuscript/s. The *Legenda aurea* falls into at least two main redactions (LA1 and LA2), with the latter being the basis for the standard edition by Maggioni. Where occasional slight differences occur between Maggioni's edition and Add. 2604, there is some sporadic tendency for the readings found in Add. 2604 to follow what Maggioni terms V(E)/V(E)*, that is, where V is one of the best witnesses of LA1, 'uno dei testimoni più coerenti della prima redazione'; it is cited in a second critical apparatus along with E (stemmatically unrelated to it).[53]

Study of the *Legenda aurea* manuscripts listed by Fleith reveals the presence of some of the non-*Legenda aurea* saints found in Add. 2604, but no manuscript may be identified with Add. 2604, that is, in having the same list of saints, apart from one twelfth- to fourteenth-century manuscript, Bruxelles, KBR 9810–14 (3229) that comes close. In other words, we do not know what the *Legenda aurea* intermediary was but also undiscovered are the manuscript sources that underlie the non-*Legenda aurea* universal saints in Add. 2604. But there are analogues aplenty and in many cases what may be called standard *Acta*

---

[52] CI, 'De sancta Martha', in Iacopo da Varazze, *Legenda aurea con le miniature del codice Ambrosiano C 240 inf.*, ed. by Maggioni, I, 764–69 (versos only).

[53] In Iacopo da Varazze, *Legenda aurea con le miniature del codice Ambrosiano C 240 inf.*, Maggioni describes his procedure in detail, I, xxi–xxix: V stands for Padova, Biblioteca Universitaria, MS 1229 and E is Milano, Biblioteca Ambrosiana, A 17 inf, both from the thirteenth century. For examples of the V(E) and V(E)* readings, see the relevant Overviews and Commentaries in the *Edition*. The variants in Add. 2604 have also been fully checked against these readings.

UNIVERSAL LIVES IN ADD. 2604 AND OTHER SOURCES AND ANALOGUES   233

sanctorum editions of these lives. A consideration of these saints demonstrates the complexity of their sources or analogues.

Universal Lives in Add. 2604 and other Sources and Analogues

Of the remaining universal lives the easiest to account for is Leonard. The life of Leonard for 6 November is found in the *Legenda aurea* but in a much more abbreviated form than in Add. 2604.[54] The *Legenda aurea* life says little about Leonard's early life, unlike the Add. 2604 version, and only three of its six miracles equate with those in Add. 2604, which is packed with miracles. The Add. 2604 life of Leonard is very close to that printed in the *Acta sanctorum* and is in fact a close example of the traditional life as found in manuscripts particularly from France, with its great emphasis on his miraculous powers.[55] The English text is imperfect due to many lost folios but, apart from minor differences, the Add. 2604 version closely resembles the *Acta sanctorum* and so the missing sections can be reconstructed. The editors of the *Acta sanctorum* text note that 'Vitae antiquioris S. Leonardi supersunt exemplaria manu scripta saltem centum et quinquaginta, in plurimis totius Europae bibliothecis dispersa.'[56] For once the Bollandists are explicit about the number of manuscripts consulted: thirty-five (mostly from the eleventh to the thirteenth century) and a critical apparatus is supplied. What is noticeable is that besides some variation in the kind or order of appended miracles, the text of Leonard seems remarkably stable whether in an eleventh- or a sixteenth-century rendering. Consequently therefore, while it is not possible to tie it to one particular source manuscript, in the light of such textual stability this hardly matters.

Justina on 26 September and Benedicta on 8 October also derive from versions printed in the *Acta sanctorum* but with a more uncertain relationship to

---

[54] CLI, 'De sancto Leonardo' in Iacopo da Varazze, *Legenda aurea con le miniature del codice Ambrosiano C 240 inf.*, ed. by Maggioni, II, 1184–89 (versos only).

[55] *Acta sanctorum*, Novembris Tomus Tertius, pp. 149–55, including seven miracles on pp. 155–59. This text is also found in [François] Arbellot, *Vie de Saint Léonard, solitaire en Limousin: Ses miracles et son culte* (Paris: J. Lecoffre, 1863), pp. 277–89; ten miracles edited from various manuscripts follow (pp. 289–301).

[56] *Acta sanctorum*, Novembris Tomus Tertius, p. 148; in *Vie de Saint Léonard, solitaire en Limousin* Arbellot's first manuscript is from the Bibliothèque de Limoges and dates from the early sixteenth century (1522). All the others are from the Bibliothèque nationale in Paris (referred to in the edition as the Bibliothèque Impériale) and are variously dated from the eleventh to the fourteenth century.

the source (or analogue). Of these Justina is the most complicated textually, owing to a very brief section taken from the *Legenda aurea*.[57] As with the life of Leonard, the text in the *Legenda aurea* overall reads more like an abbreviated version. The nearest analogue to Justina is that printed in the *Acta sanctorum*, a text that, with minor differences, is virtually the same as that for Justina and Cyprian in the *Sanctuarium* until near the end where the *Sanctuarium* expands the narrative.[58] The correspondence between the Add. 2604 text and that in the *Acta sanctorum* is very close, albeit not a word-for-word translation. Into the text is knitted some borrowing from the *Legenda aurea*, a total of five lines in all. This occurs during episode after episode of devilish disguises in an attempt to cajole the pious virginal Justina to give way to her potential suitor Agladius. Three devils are sent in turn by Cyprian to sway Justina, the last of which makes use of three disguises, as a maiden, a young man, and Justina herself. This is followed by three further types of disguise: Cyprian in the guise of a woman and a bird, and Agladius (the maligned suitor) in the form of a sparrow. Unlike the fluid movement in John the Baptist between the Nativity and the Decollation, the join between the *Acta sanctorum* and the *Legenda aurea* sections of the narrative is a little jarring. Yet textually the borrowing from the *Legenda aurea* is very important. While the Latin version underpinning the manuscript on which the English translator was drawing is unfortunately unknown, this borrowing helps with the dating. This interpolated Justina patently cannot have been earlier than the composition of the *Legenda aurea* in the thirteenth century, and would also seem to have been carried out at an early stage in its transmission history.[59] It may therefore provide a clue to narrow down the date of the original source manuscript of the translations of the universal lives. It also indicates that the person responsible for first amalgamating the texts that comprise the lives of John the Baptist and John the Evangelist made use of a manuscript that may also have included a life of Justina only tangentially related to the *Legenda aurea*. In terms of transmission history, these three Latin texts are therefore at a more 'advanced' stage, as it were, in *Legenda aurea* developments.

The life of Benedicta begins imperfectly owing to the missing fols 106–107 that also affect the end of Justina. Benedicta equates with an anonymous version

[57] CXXXVIII, 'De sancta Iustina', in Iacopo da Varazze, *Legenda aurea con le miniature del codice Ambrosiano C 240 inf.*, ed. by Maggioni, II, 1088–93 (versos only).

[58] *Acta sanctorum*, Septembris Tomus Septimus, pp. 200–02; Boninus Mombritius, *Sanctuarim seu Vitae Sanctorum*, ed. by Two Monks of Solesmes, II, 70–75.

[59] Personal communication. We are grateful to Paolo Maggioni for this helpful comment.

UNIVERSAL LIVES IN ADD. 2604 AND OTHER SOURCES AND ANALOGUES   235

cited in the *Acta sanctorum* as 'Acta | Fabulosa, | Auctore Anonymo'.[60] As usual the Bollandist compilers are vague about the identification of the manuscript(s) being edited; the text is simply headed, 'Ex codice nostro, primo Vallicellensi, deinde clarissimi viri Balthazaris Moreti, collato cum aliis'.[61] Information on later ownership of the base manuscript by Balthasar I Moretus (1574–1641), who was in sole charge of the Officina Plantiniana in Antwerp from the death of his brother Jan II Moretus (1576–1618) until his own death, and a reference to how it was collated 'cum aliis' is not a great deal of help. Only detailed detective work with regard to Barbara uncovers the fact that the exact manuscript is now Bruxelles, KBR, MS 7460 (for which see further below). Lives of Benedicta are rare; it does occur in the *Historie plurimorum sanctorum* but in an abbreviated fashion. The translator of the text in Add. 2604 uses a manuscript equivalent to that found in the *Acta sanctorum* making it the nearest edited analogue. The Add. 2604 text is quite close in content and sometimes verbally identical to the Latin but overall the precise textual relationship is unclear. Although there are only a few sporadic alterations and one major omission in Add. 2604, the verbal texture is such that it is improbable that the English writer is translating from the particular version found in the *Acta sanctorum*.

With the next life, Agatha, matters become even more vague. Like Leonard, the life of Agatha is more curtailed in the *Legenda aurea* than in Add. 2604.[62] And the English of Add. 2604 goes a little beyond the Latin of its analogue to stress Agatha's vigour against her persecutor. In the *Acta sanctorum* the source of the Agatha life is described as 'ex Bonino Mombritio et xvi Latini MSS'.[63] The three divisions of the text in the *Acta sanctorum* are not replicated in Add. 2604. Because of the closeness of the manuscript and the printed text in the *Acta sanctorum*, it is not possible to say whether the Add. 2604 translator was basing his work on a manuscript or directly on Mombritius's text; as it is a named source, Add. 2604 is compared with the *Sanctuarium*.[64] Overall the text in Add. 2604 is slightly more expansive than the Latin. Although the last few

[60] *Acta sanctorum*, Octobris Tomus Quartus, pp. 219–22 (p. 219).

[61] *Acta sanctorum*, Octobris Tomus Quartus, p. 219.

[62] XXXIX, 'De sancta Agatha', in Iacopo da Varazze, *Legenda aurea con le miniature del codice Ambrosiano C 240 inf.*, ed. by Maggioni, I, 296–301 (versos only).

[63] *Acta sanctorum*, Februarii Tomus Primus, pp. 621–24 (p. 621).

[64] Boninus Mombritius, *Sanctuarium seu Vitae sanctorum*, ed. by Two Monks of Solesmes, I, 37–40. A very careful comparison of the *Acta sanctorum* text with the *Sanctuarium* reveals only very rare minuscule textual variants that are of no consequence; the only real differences occur at the opening and in the conclusion; see the Overview to Agatha in the *Edition*.

paragraphs are lacking in Add. 2604's Agatha due to the missing quire (fols 33–40), it is reckoned that these paragraphs could have been accommodated on fols 33r–34r.[65] Even with missing text we have a firm analogue for Agatha, which is far more than can be said for the next saint, Domitilla.

The legend of Domitilla is confusing (with three women identified as Flavia Domitilla): the Add. 2604 life so short and — by the translator's own admission — so little information is known, that it is impossible to find not only a source but also an analogue. In just over thirteen manuscript lines all the Add. 2604 compiler says is that Domitilla, who lived during the reign of Domitian in the time of John the Evangelist, was consecrated a nun by Pope Clement following in the footsteps of Iphigenia (a life now lost from Add. 2604, if indeed it ever existed in the English manuscript) who was veiled during the time of Matthew. He attributes his information to the life of Clement (23 November). It is true that there is a mention in the *Legenda aurea* life of Clement of his consecrating Domitilla (described as Domitian's niece), but that is as far as it goes.[66] More detail is available in the *Legenda aurea* life of Nereus and Achilleus (12 May).[67] Here she is also described as the niece of Domitian. About to marry Aurelian, she is converted by her eunuchs Nereus and Achilleus, veiled by Clement, and sent into exile. Summoned back by Aurelian, who uses Euphrosyne and Theodora in an attempt to induce her, he prepares the wedding celebrations of all three. Intending to take Domitilla by force, Aurelian exhausts himself through dancing and expires. Domitilla and the two other converted virgins are put to death by fire. As seen in IV. Hagiographical Context and the Selection of Texts, there are so few examples of the life of Domitilla in legendary tradition that source study tends to be a dead end. While she occurs in the imported ninth-century Cotton-Corpus Legendary, she is found nowhere else in Middle English, apart from in Add. 2604. Yet her presence in Vincent de Beauvais's *Speculum historiale* and Foresti da Bergamo's *De plurimis claris sceletisque* [*sic*] *mulieribus* published on 29 April 1497 testify to a wider transmission. It may well be that the Add. 2604 life is simply based on an entry in a martyrology and that no expansion has taken place to make the Domitilla narrative into a proper saint's life. One of

---

[65] For further information, see IV. Hagiographical Context and The Selection of Saints.

[66] CLXVI, 'De sancto Clemente', in Iacopo da Varazze, *Legenda aurea con le miniature del codice Ambrosiano C 240 inf.*, ed. by Maggioni, II, 1332–47 (versos only).

[67] LXX, 'De sanctis Nereo et Achilleo', in Iacopo da Varazze, *Legenda aurea con le miniature del codice Ambrosiano C 240 inf.*, ed. by Maggioni, I, 570–73 (versos only).

the most important and earliest martyrologies, that of Usuard for 7 May notes how Flavia Domitilla, the virginal niece of Flavius Clemens, was consecrated by Clement and exiled by Domitian to the island of Pontia, thereby linking her with Euphrosyne and Theodora who were martyred by fire.[68] Usuard completely omits the lurid details of Aurelian's priapic dancing. It is not clear therefore how to interpret what the Add. 2604 translator is saying; it may be true that he simply got the germ of information about Domitilla from the life of Clement even if is odd to include a saint about which nothing is known. Yet, if he knew Jacobus de Voragine's life of Clement, it is expected that he might also have known the life of Nereus and Achilleus. Either he only knew the information he cites (either from the life of Clement or a martyrology) or he has deliberately censored the details of Domitilla's life as being unsuitable for a congregation of nuns. In other examples in Add. 2604 where a husband wishes to engage in sexual congress with his wife (the lives of Cecilia and Æthelthryth), the husband in question is deflected in a more seemly fashion (in the first case by angelic conversion and in the second by skilful episcopal persuasion). Usuard's version is also used for Domitilla by Gui de Châtres in his *Sanctilogium* so perhaps a similar elision of the details is evident here.[69]

Universal Lives in Add. 2604 and Complex Analogues

Finally, there are the two saints who would have been represented in the *Acta sanctorum* had the volume for December ever been produced: Barbara (16 December) and Columba (31 December). The lack of this volume means that there is no 'official' or 'standard' with which to compare the translations in Add. 2604. The problem of how to contextualise both texts with regard to sources or analogues will therefore be explored here in two ways: (1) an examination of some of the evidence for added lives of Barbara and Columba to *Legenda aurea* collections and in similar compilations and (2) some manuscript detail on the Bollandist gathering activities, particularly for the December volume.[70]

---

[68] *Le Martyrologe d'Usuard: Texte et Commentaire*, ed. by Dubois, pp. 225–26.

[69] London, British Library, MS Royal 13 D. ix.

[70] We are, of course, very aware that the sources and analogues of the saints' lives in Add. 2604 may not have been ones encountered by the Bollandists. But given that the other non-*Legenda aurea* lives in this manuscript, Agatha, Benedicta, Justina, and Leonard, may be traced to versions in the *Acta sanctorum*, it would seem entirely reasonable to concentrate the search mainly on Bollandist material rather than to attempt unfeasible searches in other libraries throughout Europe. We have, however, been kindly informed by the late Richard Hamer that

Full information on the material discussed here and/or underpinning the comments below is in Appendix 1: Universal Latin Saints' Lives: Sources and Analogues. This Appendix incorporates a selection of *Legenda aurea* manuscripts of varied provenance (English, Flemish/Italian, French, German, unknown), some of which, but not all, contain added items. It also includes relevant Latin hagiographical manuscripts in the Bollandist Library in Brussels and a range of material from the *Collectanea Bollandiana* and beyond in the KBR.

Unlike the life of Barbara, which has a plethora of entries, that of Columba is restricted to 1892–96 (plus a few variants) in the BHL and BHL *Supplementum*, categorised according to their brief incipits and explicits.[71] Yet the usual BHL skeletal information where one incipit often looks much like another combined with Fleith's strange glossing of Columba as Columbanus, the Irish male saint (possibly the result of some other mix-up with Columba of Iona) means that it is difficult to trace added lives of Columba to *Legenda aurea* manuscripts. In her list of augmented manuscripts it is to be presumed that a few of Fleith's thirty-five examples of Columba (Columbanus) refers to the female saint Columba (C 56).[72] With the exception of Barbara, this number vastly exceeds any of the other non-*Legenda aurea* saints in Add. 2604. Without a full examination, it is impossible to quantify the female Columba examples or to tell how similar or varied these texts are, as may be seen from a few known *Legenda aurea* or *Legenda aurea*-related manuscripts of varied provenance currently in English repositories.

Eton, Eton College, MS 203 is a mid-fourteenth-century manuscript from the Benedictine Abbey of St Aubin, Angers, containing the original *Legenda aurea* with six additional items, including Columba (fol. 376r–v).[73] Glasgow,

---

in the course of his researches he did not know of any manuscripts that equated precisely with the collection in Add. 2604. This view has also been generously confirmed by Brenda Dunn-Lardeau and Paolo Maggioni.

[71] BHL, pp. 285–86, and BHL *Supplementum*, pp. 218–19.

[72] For instance, Glasgow, University Library, MS Gen. 1111, is listed by Fleith but this contains the female Columba, as discussed below. Fleith lists one example of an added Agatha (A 27), four of Benedicta (B 24), four of Domitilla (D 23), seven of Leonard (L 19), eleven of Justina (J 25), and nearly a hundred and ninety of the life of Barbara (B 5), excluding her translation and miracles that have separate entries (B 6 and B7). These figures are extrapolated from the lists in Fleith, *Studien zur Überlieferungsgeschichte der lateinischen 'Legenda Aurea'*, pp. 450–97.

[73] Ker and Piper, *Medieval Manuscripts in British Libraries*, II (1977), 778–79 (p. 778) and 916–19 (p. 918).

UNIVERSAL LIVES IN ADD. 2604 AND COMPLEX ANALOGUES   239

University Library, MS Gen. 1111 contains an augmented and illustrated *Legenda aurea* (listed in Fleith as *LA* 231). Interwoven between the *Legenda aurea* Advent and the Dedication of the Church (fols 6ra–268va) are seventeen lives not part of the *Legenda aurea*, including Barbara (fols 11vb–13ra). Following on are fifty-one non-*Legenda aurea* lives (fols 268va–374va), including Columba (fols 276va–277rb) and Benedicta (fols 334vb–336vb). An alphabetical table itemises the lives, whether *Legenda aurea* or not (fols. 1r–3v).[74] This manuscript demonstrates an example of the three lives of Barbara, Benedicta, and Columba travelling together. London, British Library, MS Burney 347 is a fifteenth-century manuscript of unknown provenance containing various saints' lives including Columba (fol. 29ra–29va). Although listed as a *Legenda aurea* manuscript by Fleith (*LA* 365), this is not completely true as it is dependent on the *Legenda aurea* and Jean de Mailly's *Abbreviatio in gestis et miracvlis sanctorvm* (as explained in Appendix 1). Another example of an inadequately described manuscript is London, British Library, MS Arundel 330. While listed by Fleith as a *Legenda aurea* manuscript (*LA* 379), its noticeably brief life of Justina immediately calls this into question (see Appendix 1). Yet there are connections between and among different manuscripts. For example, the life of Columba that occurs in Eton, MS 203 and MS Burney 347 is effectively the same text, beginning 'Cum aurelianus imperator senonis' and deriving from de Mailly's collection (cited in Appendix 1), while MS Gen. 1111 has a different opening, 'Crudelis aurelianus imperator de partibus'. What this difference might imply about other augmented *Legenda aurea* manuscripts is anyone's guess; at the very worst it may show that each added saint needs individual investigation.

Moving to the known Latin hagiographical collections in the Bollandist Library, MSS 5, 14, 72, 288, 347, 433, 467, and 506, none of them contains Columba even though they have some versions of the universal saints discussed in this *Study* (see Appendix 1). With regard to the manuscripts with Columba from the *Collectanea Bollandiana* in the KBR one very early and one very late example may be chosen. Bruxelles, KBR, MS 7984 (3191) was previously MS P in the Bollandist Collection. It dates from the tenth century and formerly belonged to the Benedictine monastery of St Peter in Wissembourg in Alsace. It is a very early example of a collection of saints' lives (male and female) that

---

[74] Ker and Piper, *Medieval Manuscripts in British Libraries*, II (1977), 916–19; although earlier referred to as being executed in Flanders, Ker notes a connection with Piacenza, as well as post-medieval Italian memoranda (p. 919).

includes Columba (fols 21r–22v). In the post-medieval period Bruxelles, KBR, MS 8990-91 (3527) is a another manuscript from the *Collectanea Bollandiana* this time showing the collecting activities of the Bollandists. It is a confusing compilation concentrating on saints from the very end of December in multiple seventeenth-century hands. It includes numerous items on Columba on fols 173r–175r, 180r, 181r–182r, 183r–184r, 184r–v, 185r–186r, 187r–188v, 189r–190r, 197r–v, 200r–204r, followed by two printed items before fol. 207, fols 208r–210r. Some of this material would no doubt have helped in providing the planned life of Columba intended for the December *Acta sanctorum*. Various lives of Columba are included, though it is impossible to say which if any of the versions might have been chosen as the 'official' *Acta sanctorum* one. Neither is it known how the Add. 2604 life of Columba might be connected with other hagiographical manuscripts currently in the KBR (or elsewhere) that were once in England; for instance, Bruxelles, KBR, MS II.2559 (3315), a thirteenth-century manuscript of male and female saints lives with Columba on fols 61vb–63rb once belonged to the Phillipps Collection. And examples of manuscripts all over Europe may be multiplied as a result of the information held on card catalogues in the Bollandist Library and in updates in the *Analecta Bollandiana*.[75] Most particularly, the opening of the Add. 2604 Columba cannot be mapped directly on to any of the BHL entries that all stress Aurelianus's agency before mentioning Columba whereas Add. 2604 begins with 'In þe tyme that Seynt Columbe lyved in erth þe emperour Aurelian' (3/3), though this may be just a translational choice given the Add. 2604's writer's penchant for highlighting the female saint rather than her male persecutor.

Comparisons can also usefully be made with the more widely available early printed editions, which of course also encapsulates the manuscript tradition. Columba on occasion makes an appearance in the early printed editions of the *Legenda aurea*; for example, the editions printed in the late 1470s by Conrad Winters de Homborch and Johannes Koelhoff both have an appended Columba as part of thirty-eight extra saints after the *Legenda aurea*. She occurs eighth from the end before the Conception of Mary. This is the same text found in the *Historie plurimorum sanctorum* published in 1483 and 1485

---

[75] In the Bollandist Library there is an extensive alphabetised card catalogue with manuscript updates to the individual entries in the BHL and BHL *Supplementum*, while François Dolbeau regularly provides such updates in the *Analecta Bollandiana* volumes. This material provides some insight into the enormous extent of manuscripts for individual saints. We are grateful to Pietro d'Agostino and François De Vriendt for kindly making this material available to us.

UNIVERSAL LIVES IN ADD. 2604 AND COMPLEX ANALOGUES   241

that begins 'Ingressus est aurelianus ciuitatem senonis' (fol. viiib verso of the
1485 edition). In turn this life is related to that in Mombritius's *Sanctuarium*
but is not the same version; it begins 'Aurelianus imperator de partibus orientis
adueniens.'[76]

The Add. 2604 Columba has a complicated textual relationship with the
Sanctuarium and indeed the *Historie plurimorum sanctorum*/non-Graesse
Legenda aurea.[77] The content of the life in Add. 2604 is the same as that in the
Sanctuarium, the main difference being that it is Mombritius's text that is abbreviated.[78] In the light of general translational procedure, this is somewhat paradoxical. The usual expectation would be for the English to be more abbreviated
than the Latin. Yet the *Sanctuarium* is not alone in its degree of abbreviation
as an even more severely contracted version occurs in the *Historie plurimorum
sanctorum*/non-Graesse *Legenda aurea*. This *Historie* text has basically the same
narrative (and sometimes the same wording), albeit that it retains some of the
plot essentials that have been omitted by Mombritius, but are present in Add.
2604. The printed Latin versions contain the same outline of Columba's life,
that in Add. 2604 is not only more expansive, but in keeping with the translator's usual method is also more expressive. The sense in Add. 2604 is basically
the same as that in the *Sanctuarium*, but not always the exact wording. It would
seem therefore that this English version of the text — whatever its source — is
closer to whichever Latin manuscript was first used as the basis of these printed
versions. The relationship between Columba in Add. 2604 and the printed editions is qualitatively different from that witnessed in the lives dependent on
the 'Normalcorpus' *Legenda aurea*. Whereas they are close — even if at times
re-ordered — translations, in Columba the natural order is reversed, with the
Add. 2604 manuscript preserving a fuller version of the text than its so-called
sources or analogues. One possibility for this fuller version might be a text like

---

[76] Boninus Mombritius, *Sanctuarium seu Vitae Sanctorum*, ed. by Two Monks of Solesmes,
I, 370.

[77] For simplicity sake, a distinction is made here between the different prints of the *Legenda
aurea* (see Barbara below). In order to prevent confusion and to cut down on the references, in
the discussion below only the *Historie plurimorum sanctorum* will be mentioned, but it should
be taken as read that everything that is said about this collection here and in the Overview and
Commentary in the *Edition* also applies to the editions of what we are calling the non-Graesse
Legenda aurea by Conrad Winters de Homborch and Johannes Koelhoff. There may also be
other *Legenda aurea* printed editions that likewise includes this version of Columba.

[78] Boninus Mombritius, *Sanctuarium seu Vitae sanctorum*, ed. by Two Monks of Solesmes,
II, 370–71.

242   V. LATIN SOURCES AND ANALOGUES

those in the post-medieval MS 8990–91 (3527), an example of early Bollandist manuscript transcriptions that concentrates on multiple copies of Columba (as listed in Appendix 1). For instance, the ending of the life on fols 187r–188v is especially like that in the Add. 2604 Columba. It may also be noted that the degree of abbreviation found in the *Sanctuarium* for the life of Columba is not evident for its Agatha; it is questionable therefore whether the ultimate Latin compiler derived both of these texts from the same manuscript (if it were a single manuscript that underpinned the *Sanctuarium*).

It is at this point that an edition (or rather transcription) of the life of Columba from a mid-eighth-century manuscript, Paris, Bibliothèque Nationale, fonds latin, MS 12598 (fols 103v–105v), proves significant. This manuscript, whose provenance is associated with the monastery of Corbie, contains other saints' lives both male and female including Agatha and Cecilia (see Appendix 1). Apart from its opening, which highlights Aurelian rather than Columba, this is essentially a very similar text to that translated in Add. 2604. It opens 'In dieb[us] illis adveniens aurilianus a part[ibus] superiorib[us] et cum gens quædam esset quæ heresim coleret [...]' (fol. 103v).[79] By comparing Add. 2604 to this version as well as to the later ones found in the early printed editions it is possible to isolate what changes the Add. 2604 writer might have made to his translation. However, this is not to say that this manuscript (or the text represented by it) is the actual source manuscript of Add. 2604. While it would be somewhat unusual for a late medieval English writer to translate from such an early codex, it is also true that there are some differences between the text in Add. 2604 and that in MS 12598. Yet, links between MS 12598 and the Benedictine abbey of Corbie in Picardie in northern France, with its renowned library, help to stress the French influence, writ large, on the lives in Add. 2604; in other words, it would not be surprising if the ultimate source manuscript or manuscripts derived from a similar area.

Such complications with Columba are as nothing when compared with the textual history of Barbara. Her legend circulated widely in the Middle Ages, sometimes her life alone and sometimes split into the life and extensive miracles. Her cult was especially widespread in the Low Countries.[80] And such lives could also cross linguistic boundaries and regions; a particularly note-

---

[79] This is found in a volume that is very difficult to access: Guy Chastel, *Sainte Colombe de Sens* (Paris: J. de Gigord, 1939), pp. 325–28 (p. 325). In the quotation above the abbreviations are expanded and put within square brackets.

[80] BHL, pp. 142–46, and BHL *Supplementum*, pp. 110–14. For the circulation, see Van Dijk, *Een rij van spiegels*.

UNIVERSAL LIVES IN ADD. 2604 AND COMPLEX ANALOGUES   243

worthy example of this is the lengthy life by the Flemish Augustinian, Jean de Wackerzeele (d. after 1397), that is found as part of the additional lives in the *Gilte Legende*.[81] Rydel notes that 'Every single printed edition [of the *Legenda aurea*] that I surveyed includes St. Barbara and the Conception of Mary, entries that typically do not appear in the Latin corpus but do so in some vernacular traditions'.[82] Although she is not right about the absence of Barbara in Latin manuscripts in the extended *Legenda aurea* tradition (as shown by Fleith's calculations) her comment about the popularity of Barbara in early printed editions of the *Legenda aurea* is very interesting.[83] Here too there is a vast array of editions, calculated by Seybolt at ninety-seven in Latin alone between 1470 and 1500.[84] To make matters even more confusing, the story of Barbara circulated in three main versions (with variants). These are best described by Van Dijk in her study of Barbara in the Dutch tradition:

> The short life is based on the earliest Latin version [...] The long and the extra-long life are usually presented as part of a larger text, the *Compilatio de Sancta Barbara*. The *Compilatio* was created around 1400 and contains a prologue, the new version of the life, and a story on the translation of her relics and miracles, preceded by a separate prologue [...] In the long and extra-long lives, Saint Barbara is baptised by Saint John the Baptist [...] According to the long and extra-long lives, she learns the tenets of the Christian faith from Origen and an angel of Our Lord, who appears in a vision [...] The extra-long life is a variant on the long life and adds several episodes, for instance of the saint's mystical marriage to Christ.'[85]

It is clear from the outset that Barbara (whose feast in Add. 2604 is cited as 16 December rather than the more traditional 4 December) is an example of a short life as there is no mention of Origen or the angel, and nothing about her miracles. Barbara is baptised by an anonymous priest, but there is a reference to John the Baptist (the baptiser of Barbara in the long and extra-long versions) who acts as a role model: 'And in that same watir she was cristned of a certeyn Cristen preste, in the which place a certen tyme she lyved with honysoklys and wild hony, as Seynt Iohn Baptist did in desert' (6/30–33).

---

[81] *Supplementary Lives in Some Manuscripts of the 'Gilte Legende'*, ed. by Hamer and Russell, pp. 381–470.

[82] Rydel, 'Literary Effects', p. 87.

[83] See n. 72 above.

[84] These are all listed in Seybolt, 'Fifteenth Century Editions of the *Legenda aurea*', pp. 328–32; further information on editions is available on the USTC website.

[85] Van Dijk, *Een rij van spiegels*, p. 239 (English summary).

Barbara's entry in the BHL runs from 912 to 931, with numerous variants (albeit with slight differences in their incipits).[86] Of all the universal stories found in Add. 2604, this is the one where it is least easy to find an obvious close analogue amongst this mass of material, let alone a source manuscript. Appendix 1 lists a few examples among the multitude of *Legenda aurea* manuscripts with an added Barbara. Cambridge, Cambridge University Library, MS Additional 6452 is a fourteenth-century manuscript of German provenance that contains much variation in the order of chapters from the *Legenda aurea*. There is also a lengthy section of added saints on fols 240r–250v, beginning with Barbara (fol. 240ra–va). And, as we have already seen, Glasgow, Glasgow University Library, MS Gen. 1111, includes Barbara in its augmented *Legenda aurea* (beginning on fol. 11vb), but with a different incipit.

Barbara's popularity is also evident from her occurrence in five of the medieval Latin hagiographical manuscripts in the Bollandist Library: MSS 5, 14, 288, 433, and 467. MS 288 has another copy of the long life of Barbara and her miracles by Jean de Wackerzeele (fols 21ra–37ra). MS 467 is a fifteenth-century manuscript of the *Legenda aurea* with various chapters omitted and other short lives intermingled. Its Barbara on fols 152ra–153va, which has the same incipit as in MSS 5 and 433, and in Cambridge, Cambridge University Library, MS Additional 6452, is positioned before Nicholas (6 December), which shows that it was intended for 4 December and not for 16 December as in Add. 2604.[87]

This same variety of text is evident in other manuscripts either from the *Collectanea Bollandiana* in the KBR or elsewhere, for instance, in the work of Johannes Back. Bruxelles, KBR, MS 7917 (3189) is a fifteenth-century collection of female saints' lives, beginning with Katherine of Alexandria and ending with Cecilia (fols 198va–204rb). It also includes de Wackerzeele's Barbara (fols 25ra–48vb), who is followed by Lucy and then Martha (fols 50rb–51va), while Agatha appears later (fols 65va–67vb). There is a seventeenth-century index at the beginning of the manuscript headed 'P MS 17', the original shelf-mark in the Bollandist Collection. Although manuscripts in the KBR with a life of

[86] In the card catalogue held in the Bollandist Library the entries run up to 971, with some of the entries (for example, 915) being attested by numerous manuscripts.

[87] The dating of the feast can be sufficient in itself to show the relationship between the Latin and the English; an example of this is in the eighteenth-century edition where 4 December is given at the end; see Franciscus Antonius Zaccaria, *De Rebus ad historiam atque antiquitates ecclesiæ: Dissertationes Latianæ* (Fulginæ: Pompejus Campana, 1781), i, 137–42. In most respects, apart from the date, this version is quite similar to that in Add. 2604.

Barbara are numerous (as they will be in many other collections throughout Europe), for present purposes it is the manuscripts with a Bollandist connection that are most important.

First, there is the manuscript mentioned above in relation to Benedicta. Bruxelles, KBR, MSS 7460 and 7461 (3176) are among the many manuscripts in the KBR listed under the heading of *Collectanea Bollandiana*, but these two may be traced back directly to the *Acta sanctorum*. This is one of the instances where — after some detective work — a link was found between the actual manuscript being used by the compilers of the *Acta sanctorum* and a traceable current manuscript, on the strength of a reference at the beginning of Benedicta in the *Acta sanctorum*, to 'Ex codice nostro, primo Vallicellensi, deinde clarissimi viri Balthazaris Moreti, collato cum aliis'. These two large thirteenth-century volumes in double columns with elaborate initial capitals and running titles originally belonged to the French Cistercian abbey of Vaucelles. Later they were acquired by Balthasar I Moretus (1574–1641), and later again became MSS P. 159 and P. 160 in the Museum Bollandianum, before being acquired by the KBR in 1807. As noted in the *Acta sanctorum*, the first volume (MS 7460) does indeed contain Benedicta (fols 21vb–24rb), and the second volume (MS 7461) contains Leonard (fols 11va–14ra), Cecilia (fols 67va–70va), and Barbara (fols 194ra–195va). In one of the few instances where manuscripts are cited in the *Acta sanctorum*, this manuscript is also listed in its life of Leonard.[88]

Secondly, as was the case with Columba, there is another typically disordered looking post-medieval manuscript from the *Collectanea Bollandiana* produced by the Bollandists as part of their collecting activities and for the purpose of producing the 'official' life of Barbara in the December *Acta sanctorum* volume that never appeared. Bruxelles, KBR MS 8964 (3516) contains a mass of items in various shapes and sizes and in different hands alongside some interleaved printed items from the seventeenth and eighteenth centuries. The material included focuses on the saints from the beginning of December which means that there are many items on Barbara dispersed throughout (fols 132r–157r, 161r–163v, two printed items before fol. 179, fols 179r–186r, 187r–190r, 191r–193v, 195r, 196r–197r, 200r–203r, 216r–219v, 220r–221v, 228r–233v, 235r–237r, 237r–240v, and 241r–v). What this 'official' life of Barbara would have been is unclear as there were many variants — as here — from which to choose.

---

[88] See the Overview of Leonard in the *Edition*.

The complexities do not end because there were also the numerous added versions of Barbara in early print. These fall into augmented *Legenda aurea* editions, as noted above by Rydel, and other 'new' hagiographical collections. The fact that the *Legenda aurea* in print had an added Barbara has been known since Theodor Graesse published his edition around the second half of the nineteenth century.[89] In his third edition of 1890 no fewer than sixty-one extra lives are included. He is silent about the identity of his base text, though scholars have worked out that it depended on a version printed in the earlier 1470s (1474 or 1475) in Basel.[90] In the beginning of this version Barbara cogitates at length about false gods. She then gets involved in correspondence on the nature of God with the philosopher Origen. The version finishes with two exemplary stories concerning Barbara. Clearly this text that begins 'Erat tempore Maximiani imperatoris vir quidam gentilis in Nicomedia' is related to what Van Dijk calls 'the long version' of the legend.

As with manuscript compilers, the editors of incunabula did not necessarily add the same version of Barbara, as may be seen, for example, by the two editions published in the later 1470s by Conrad Winters de Homborch and Johannes Koelhoff. These are the editions that have an appended Columba as part of thirty-eight extra saints after the *Legenda aurea*. They also include a Barbara as the first text in the list. This begins 'Temporibus imperatoris maximiani erat quidam uir Dyoscorus nomine diues valde sed paganus' and so is different from the text edited by Graesse. But in common with the Columba text, this 'non-Graesse Barbara' *is* the same text found in the printed *Historie plurimorum sanctorum*. In turn this life may be compared with that in Mombritius's *Sanctuarium*, except that the Mombritius version is influenced by the Origen story. Furthermore, when set beside a manuscript version of an added Barbara, such as that in Cambridge, Cambridge University Library, MS Additional 6452, the early printed text in the *Historie plurimorum sanctorum*/non-Graesse *Legenda aurea*, it is the manuscript that is slightly more contracted.

---

[89] *Jacobi a Voragine, Legenda aurea, vulgo Historia lombardica dicta*, ed. by Th. Graesse, 3rd edn (Bratislava: Koebner, 1890), pp. 898–902.

[90] See Reames, *The 'Legenda aurea': A Reexamination of Its Paradoxical History*, pp. 68 and 244 n. 77 (citing Baudouin de Gaffier). Ker and Piper, *Medieval Manuscripts in British Libraries*, II (1977), 916, refer to this edition as that by Michael Wenssler; this is USTC 746111, published not after 1474. This digital copy starts with the same additional saints as edited by Graesse, albeit that it ends with a different life of Arbogastus. It therefore contains only a fraction of the lives in the 1890 edition, and so excludes Barbara.

The Barbara in Add. 2604 is close to that in the *Historie plurimorum sanctorum*/non-Graesse *Legenda aurea*; yet the relationship between the two is not as expected in that the narrative in Add. 2604 acts as a type of source rather than the other way around. Admittedly the Add. 2604 translator had a penchant for elaboration, but whatever Latin version he was using, it would appear to have been a little fuller than that used in the composition of these printed texts. As noted above, while we do not know what this version was, there is evidence that it might well have been a version akin to that in Bruxelles, KBR, MS 7461 (3176), one that the Bollandists may have intended to use for their 'official' version of one of the short lives of Barbara. This text is very like that in the printed versions but it is also slightly more expansive and a few of these expansions (but not all) appear in the English; this Latin Barbara also has the merit of being dated to 16 December (as fully explained in the Commentary and Overview of Barbara in the *Edition*).

Universal Lives in Add. 2604: Overview

In sum, to link the Add. 2604 universal lives to any particular manuscript witnesses is currently an impossibility. The genesis of the primary sources or analogues themselves is too complex, and tracking down the range of manuscript possibilities would necessitate a lifelong trawl through European libraries.[91] Of all the manuscripts surveyed by Fleith in her examination of the expanded *Legenda aurea*, none of them contains all the relevant Add. 2604 saints and only sixteen manuscripts include a couple of these in the same manuscript. Indeed, of the manuscripts surveyed in the course of this *Study*, bar Cod. Sankt Georgen 12 that will be discussed below, only the 'Passionale virginibus' in Bruxelles, KBR, MS 9810-14 (3229) (described in Appendix 1) contains all the virgin martyrs found in Add. 2604. Yet this is not the source manuscript. What may be confirmed is that the four lives based directly on the *Legenda aurea*

---

[91] We are keenly aware that there is always the possibility that such a manuscript or source text for any individual lives is hiding in broad daylight and that we have not searched in the right places despite all our efforts. Every editor agonises over the dilemma of how to search for source manuscripts and over when to decide that enough is enough. Should relevant material be discovered by other scholars, we hope that we would show the same grace demonstrated by Eddie Jones on the discovery of a new manuscript of a work that he had recently edited; E. A. Jones, 'A Mirror for Recluses: A New Manuscript, New Information and some New Hypotheses', The *Library: The Transactions of the Bibliographical Society*, Seventh Series, 15 (2014), 424–31.

probably derived at least in part from manuscript(s) at some remove from the original *Legenda aurea*. Furthermore it is evident that the Francophone bias and Greven-influenced nature of the *Historie plurimorum sanctorum* implies a manuscript tradition from northern France or the Low Countries; and that whatever manuscript(s) formed the basis of the translations it was a fuller text than evident in the early printed analogues. In other words, certain Add. 2604 lives exemplify a precursor to the early printed editions.

The failure to find 'the needle in the haystack' exacerbated by the 'pick and mix' attitude of medieval hagiographers may be frustrating but is hardly surprising. What is important is not merely the tracking down of a particular source manuscript — valuable and all as that may be — but in discovering the illuminating ways in which the compilers of legendaries throughout Europe creatively worked with their material, as we have seen. The translator of Add. 2604 is definitely one such example of someone with an authorial agenda.[92] From what has been traced, it is clear that the compiler's general method with the universal lives is to provide a close translation (to the extent that comparison may be made to substantiate this), with only a few minor stylistic changes, such as the omission of the names of patristic authors and sources, and the addition of questions to explicate material. Longer explanatory or theological material is excluded completely; where necessary, expansions serve the need for clarification. Above all, the translator is interested in the narrative and uses various techniques to emphasise this so that the stories he tells are both dramatic and engaging. This approach carries over into his translations of native saints' lives.[93] In the universal section it is the virgin martyrs who are pre-eminent; in the native section it is the nuns and abbesses who powerfully make their mark as exemplary miracle workers demonstrating God's continued beneficence.

---

[92] He is hardly alone in this. For example, as noted in Collins, 'Latin Hagiography in *Germania* (1450–1550)', 'Bartholomaeus Krafft (d. 1496), the prior of the monastery of Blaubeuren in Württemberg, directed the compilation of the *Passionale decimum*. This legendary consisted of 75 entries describing the lives of almost 100 saints. The *vitae* were collected [p. 563] from numerous sources: abbreviated individual lives taken from regionally produced hagiographical texts and other legendaries such as selections from the *Sanctuarium Mombriti*' (pp. 562–63).

[93] See VI. Reading the *'Lyves and Dethes'* for a full discussion.

Native Saints in Add. 2604 and their Source: John of Tynemouth's 'Sanctilogium'

When we turn to the sources for the eleven native saints, we are on much firmer ground than with the universal lives, as the former are translated, sometimes word for word, from a substantial collection of insular lives known as the *Sanctilogium Angliae Walliae Scotiae et Hiberniae*, which John, the vicar of Tynemouth, organised in the mid-fourteenth century. This legendary is derived from *vitae* found in monastic libraries across England and into Wales, with the exception of a few native saints who figured as important luminaries of the *Legenda aurea*, such as Patrick and Brigid of Ireland and Edward the Confessor of England.[94] As a collector, John rearranged and truncated source material to provide brief narratives that would have been ideal for celebrating insular saints liturgically. His is a sizeable legendary but by no means exhaustive, which means that the selection of saints is instructive, especially when considered in light of the contents of Add. 2604.

Of the 156 entries for saints in the *Sanctilogium*, more than half are English.[95] In general, these are historical figures who shaped the English Church in the early days of conversion, which means that bishops and archbishops, as well as royal figures, constitute the lion's share of the collection. There is also a decidedly gendered slant to the legendary, with only twenty-nine entries about female saints. Of these, all but eight are about English women (including Margaret of Scotland who was of the house of Wessex). The remaining figures are the Irish saints Brigid, Maxentia, Modwenna, and Osmanna, who are complemented by the Welsh saints Gwenfrewi (Winifred) and Keyna and the British Juthwara and Ursula. The attention to female holiness in Add. 2604 — of twenty-two saints, nineteen are female and of these, eleven are native women — shows a notable difference from John's male-centric corpus, but the prominence of Englishness remains. The native women in Add. 2604 are all English with the exception of Modwenna, who was culted in England at Burton upon

---

[94] See the discussion of 'John of Tynemouth and his *Sanctilogium*', which details the range of sources and the places John travelled, in Lapidge and Love, 'The Latin Hagiography of England and Wales (600–1550)', 305–09.

[95] A strict accounting is difficult in a number of cases, as some saints are presented as ancillary to another, as is the case with Eorcengota and Æthelburh, who appear as a narration appended to the life of Seaxburh. Other saints are grouped in one entry, as is the case with Cyneburh, Cyneswith, and Tibba. So while there are more females presented, this accounting lists only the number of entries in John's *Sanctilogium*.

Trent and may have been considered 'English' rather than 'Irish', just as other émigrés, such as Augustine of Canterbury (who was Roman), were adopted into the English assemblage of saints. Of the twenty-nine entries about females in the *Sanctilogium*, ten were selected for Add. 2604, and the translator/compiler divided the narration of Eorcengota and Æthelburh from the life of Seaxburh to form an independent, eleventh life. The eleven lives, as noted in IV. Hagiographical Context and the Selection of Saints, illustrate a deliberate focus on Ely, as six of the eleven are Ely saints.

The Overviews and Commentaries for the native saints in the *Edition* provide more precise details about John's sources, but it is helpful to realise that the priest relied on the major Latin hagiographers of England — Bede (*c.* 673–735), Eadmer (*c.* 1060–*c.* 1128) and Osbern of Canterbury (*c.* 1050–*c.* 90), Goscelin de Saint-Bertin (*c.* 1040–1114), William of Malmesbury (*c.* 1095–*c.* 1143), Aelred of Rievaulx (*c.* 1110–67), Florence of Worcester (d. 1118), Simeon of Durham (died after 1129), Reginald of Durham (died *c.* 1190), and Ranulf Higden (*c.* 1280–1364) — as well as continental hagiographers, including Vincent de Beauvais (*c.* 1190–1264) and Jacobus de Voragine.[96] John's usual methodology, if possible, was to consult a community's most 'authoritative' text about its patron saint as in the case of Geoffrey of Burton's (d. 1150) life of Modwenna and of Goscelin de Saint-Bertin's life of Edith.[97] At Ely, the story is complicated, if only because a larger set of hagiographical sources was available. John used the monastery's twelfth-century chronicle and cartulary, *Liber Eliensis* — a voluminous work in three books, the first of which comprises an expansive *vita* of Æthelthryth and descriptions of the other Ely saints — to compose his redaction of the life of Æthelthryth, which is an enhanced version based on Bede's narrative. From Goscelin, himself an itinerant hagiographer who had worked at Ely for a time, John also developed the lives of Wærburh and Wihtburh, as well as lections for Seaxburh and Eormenhild.[98] Lacking an account of Æthelthryth's niece Eorcengota and sister Æthelburh, John turned

---

[96] Lapidge and Love, 'The Latin Hagiography of England and Wales (600–1550)', p. 306, and *Nova Legenda Anglie*, ed. by Horstman, I, xxxi.

[97] *Geoffrey of Burton, Life and Miracles of St Modwenna*, ed. and trans. by Bartlett, and *Writing the Wilton Women: Goscelin's 'Legend of Edith' and 'Liber confortatorius'*, ed. by Stephanie Hollis and others, Medieval Women: Texts and Contexts, 9 (Turnhout: Brepols, 2004).

[98] This evidence suggests Goscelin may never have composed lives for Seaxburh or Eormenhild, only writing lections to celebrate their feasts. See *Goscelin of Saint-Bertin, The Hagiography of the Female Saints of Ely*, ed. and trans. by Love, pp. lxxviii–lxxx.

to Bede who had written about the women who went to continental convents.[99] John was thorough in his research: where he could simply have used Bede's celebrated account of Æthelthryth, as other redactors had done, he used the *vita* and miracles provided in the *Liber Eliensis* to refine Bede's narrative and reorganise it chronologically.

Understanding John's general methodology in collecting is particularly helpful when considering *vitae* for which sources are no longer available. His life of Hild is derived directly from Bede's prose life but includes miracles from another unidentified source, which, based on differences in narrative, could only have had a passing relation to a Glastonbury life in leonine hexameters that includes them, Cambridge, Trinity College, MS O.9.38 (item xlviii).[100] Likewise, John's account of Eanswith is the only witness of a written tradition, but the compiler's methodology, as well as his repeated use of local sources, with Bede and Goscelin as favoured authors, allows us to suggest he worked from a local account, perhaps one written by Goscelin, who found a permanent home at Christ Church Cathedral in Canterbury where Eanswith's cult was celebrated after her relics were transferred there from Folkestone.[101]

The Manuscripts of John of Tynemouth's 'Sanctilogium'

Having examined the shape of John's collecting and the relevant female saints in his legendary, we must also consider how the legendary became the source for Add. 2604. Whether it was a bespoke production or one that was copied from another manuscript of translated lives remains unclear, as we are unable to identify any one of the five extant manuscripts of the *Sanctilogium* as the source the translator used in rendering his Middle English lives of native saints. The manuscripts themselves are quite enlightening about the circulation of John's compendium, so we offer an overview of each to illustrate the monastic network in which it circulated and its importance for late medieval monastic reading.

---

[99] *Bede's Ecclesiastical History of the English People*, ed. and trans. by Colgrave and Mynors, IV.23, pp. 404–15.

[100] 'A Latin Poem on St. Hilda and Whitby Abbey', ed. by A. G. Rigg, *The Journal of Medieval Latin*, 6 (1996), 12–43.

[101] Virginia Blanton, 'The Lost & (Not) Found: Sources for Female Saints' Legends in John of Tynemouth's *Sanctilogium*', in *The Blackwell Companion to British Literature*, ed. by Robert DeMaria, Jr., Heesok Chang, and Samantha Zacher (Oxford: Blackwell, 2014), I, 65–80.

The earliest of the manuscripts containing the *Sanctilogium* is London, British Library, MS Cotton Tiberius E. i. Now bound in two volumes, it presents the lives in calendar order (January to December) by saint's feast, albeit with four lives out of sequence at the end of the second volume.[102] Also appended to the collection is a life of the local saint Christina of Markyate (1096/98–*c.* 1155), which is copied in a similar hand on fols 145r–167v of the second volume. At least two features of MS Cotton Tiberius E. i suggest that the life of Christina was not an original part of the legendary. A blank folio (144v) separates Christina's *vita* from the rest of the collection, though it does appear that the leaf was washed and may have contained the opening of Christina's life, which is acephalous.[103] Also, the life of Christina at twenty-two leaves is significantly longer than John's usual epitomes, which typically run to only a couple of folios. As a point of comparison, Modwenna's *vita*, which is the longest of the saints in Add. 2604, is found on fols 26vb–31va in the second volume of MS Cotton Tiberius E. i, making it a quarter of the length of Christina's *vita*. Christina was celebrated at St Albans because of her close connection to several of the abbots, but neither her cult nor her *vita* seems to have circulated beyond St Albans.[104] Further, the life of Christina is not included in other copies of John's legendary, providing additional evidence that it was not originally intended and that its appearance in MS Cotton Tiberius E. i was a result of local devotion.

Another distinctive aspect of MS Cotton Tiberius E. i is its liturgical apparatus. Approximately 177 narrations, which would have been used for preaching, follow many of the saints' lives, while antiphons and collects for celebrating individual feasts during Nocturns (part of Matins) were included in the lower margins, with similar decorative initials that indicate they were planned

---

[102] For a description of the current state of the codex, which was damaged in the Cotton Library fire of 1731, see Blanton, 'Benedictine Devotion to England's Saints'.

[103] Horstman indicates that he tried some chemicals on various folios to recover faded or washed inscriptions, and it appears that on fol. 144v a short section of lines was treated. See his remark to this effect on p. xii of the introduction to his edition, *Nova Legenda Anglie*, I.

[104] Christina's life is not included in later recensions of the *Sanctilogium*, and it appears it was added to MS Cotton Tiberius E. i because of an on-going devotion to her cult following her profession at St Albans where her brother was sub-prior. See *The Life of Christina of Markyate: A Twelfth Century Recluse*, ed. and trans. by C. H. Talbot, Medieval Academy Reprints for Teaching (Oxford: Oxford University Press, 1959; repr. Toronto: University of Toronto Press, in association with the Medieval Academy of America, 1998), 1–33 (pp. 8–10, especially).

THE MANUSCRIPTS OF JOHN OF TYNEMOUTH'S 'SANCTILOGIUM'   253

paratextual elements.[105] This liturgical matter is missing from other recensions of the *Sanctilogium*, but some narrations are retained in their original positions or moved to accompany other lives in the collection in later manuscripts.[106]

As mentioned above, the collection is organised by saint's feast in the liturgical calendar, running from 5 January (Edward the Confessor) to 30 December (Egwine). The native saints in Add. 2604 are principally found in volume two, as MS Cotton Tiberius E. i is currently bound: Æthelthryth (fols 19ra–20va); Modwenna (fols 26vb–31va); Seaxburh (fols 31va–32va); Eorcengota and Æthelburh as a narration at the end of Seaxburh (fol. 32ra–32rb); Wihtburh (fols 32va–33rb); Eanswith (fols 60ra–61rb); Edith (fols 66va–68ra); Hild (fols 113va–115rb); and Eadburh (fols 126va–127rb). The remaining two saints are in volume one: Wærburh (fols 34rb–35rb) and Eormenhild (fols 39va–40ra), 3 February and 13 February, respectively. The arrangement of saints in Add. 2604 makes a very interesting comparison: Add. 2604 removes Modwenna (5 July) from the July sequence and inserts Eormenhild and Wærburh on 6 July with Seaxburh and Wihtburh (17 March) on 7 July, so that all of the Ely saints are grouped together after Æthelthryth (23 June). This might be the reason Modwenna's life appears at the end of Add. 2604 before Leonard. It may be that the translator's source had already made this reordering of Ely saints, as the grouping of Wihtburh with Seaxburh in MS Cotton Tiberius E. i suggests that some of the Ely cults were already being celebrated in the octave of Æthelthryth's feast. This evidence also indicates that the source the translator used was in liturgical order by feast, since the Ely saints are far more dispersed in collections organised alphabetically.

While it is the earliest witness of the *Sanctilogium*, MS Cotton Tiberius E. i, is not an autograph. Its provenance, however, provides some clues about its production and possible relationship with an exemplar. According to an *ex dono*, Thomas de la Mare, while abbot of St Albans (1349–96), gave the manuscript to Redbourn Priory (some four miles distant) for daily reading by monks on retreat at this dependency.[107] The manuscript shares stylistic elements in

---

[105] *Nova Legenda Anglie*, ed. by Horstman, I, xii–xv.

[106] Sally Harper, 'Traces of Lost Late Medieval Offices?: The *Sanctilogium Angliae, Walliae, Scotiae, et Hiberniae* of John of Tynemouth (*fl.* 1350)', in *Essays on the History of English Music in Honour of John Caldwell: Sources, Style, Performance, Historiography*, ed. by Emma Hornby and David Maw (Woodbridge: Boydell, 2010), pp. 1–21.

[107] In 2018 using ultra-violet light, Virginia Blanton found the donor inscription, which reads: '(H)unc librum dedit dompnus Thomas de la M(are abbas monasterii S. Albani Anglorum) prothomartiris, deo et ecclesiae beati Amphibali (de Redburn, ut fratres ibidem in cursu

keeping with other books produced at St Albans in the late fourteenth century and can be assigned a date in the 1380s.[108] Genealogies for Oswin, the patron saint of Tynemouth Priory, and Margaret of Scotland, who was also honoured there, are drawn in the margins below their lives. These augmentations might indicate that the manuscript was copied from a Tynemouth exemplar, perhaps even one at the priory, which was a St Albans dependency. St Albans monks were routinely appointed to Tynemouth before being recalled to the abbey. The presence of the genealogies could be an indication that the St Albans scribe had at some point been assigned to Tynemouth and was offering detailed information about its patron saints to readers at St Albans.

The association of MS Cotton Tiberius E. i with Thomas de la Mare is particularly instructive. When one examines Abbot Thomas's career as a reformer, which began during his tenure as Prior of Tynemouth Abbey (1340–49), it becomes evident why the *Sanctilogium* was important for his monks to read. It is at Tynemouth that he would have known John, who was the vicar of the parish.[109] John was not only a collector of saints' lives but also a prolific writer, producing a chronicle titled *Historia aurea* that features English saints as major figures in Christian conversion, as well as a *lectionarium* (now lost), and a *martyrologium* (of which only a portion is extant).[110] The parish of Tynemouth lay within the diocese of Durham (up the coast from Durham Priory) but

ex)istentes per eius lecturam poterint celestibus instrui, (et per Sanctorum exempla virtutibus insigniri).' Letters and words in parens indicate missing text; lost phrasing is inserted by a printed record in William Nicolson, *English Historical Library*, 2 vols (London: Abell Swall, 1696), II, 31. Nicolson's record shows slight differences from what is preserved in the manuscript. For the recovery of this inscription and a multispectral image showing it, see Blanton, 'Benedictine Devotion to England's Saints', p. 108.

[108] James G. Clark, *A Monastic Renaissance at St Albans: Thomas Walsingham and his Circle c. 1350–1440*, Oxford Historical Monographs (Oxford: Clarendon Press, 2004), p. 116.

[109] John Taylor, 'John Tynemouth, (*fl. c.* 1350)', ODNB (https://doi.org/10.1093/ref:odnb/27466; accessed 1 April 2023). For a slightly different biography, see John Block Friedman, *Northern English Books, Owners, and Makers in the Late Middle Ages* (Syracuse, NY: Syracuse University Press, 1995), p. 91.

[110] John's oeuvre is outlined by Lapidge and Love, 'The Hagiography of England and Wales (600–1550)', p. 305. In his *Catalogus Scriptorum Ecclesiæ*, Henry of Kirkstede (the librarian known as Boston of Bury at Bury St Edmunds) also attributed to him a number of commentaries on the Bible, as recorded by John Bale, *Index Britanniae Scriptorum*, ed. by Reginald Lane Poole, with Mary Bateson (Oxford: Clarendon Press, 1902), pp. 176–77. See also *History of Northumberland*, ed. by Edward Bateson and others, 15 vols (Newcastle-Upon-Tyne: Andrew Reid; London: Simpkin, Marshall, Hamilton, Kent, 1893–1940), VIII (1907), 127 n 1.

used the nave of Tynemouth's priory church as its sacred space. The prior of Tynemouth had the right to appoint the parish clergy. This arrangement placed the vicar under the spiritual supervision of the bishop of Durham, and simultaneously under the administrative supervision of the prior of Tynemouth (and ultimately, the abbot of St Albans). These associations would have fostered access to hagiographical material in the important Benedictine libraries at Durham and St Albans, but it is Thomas de la Mare as Tynemouth's prior who may have been the patron of some, if not several, of John's works.[111]

Thomas de la Mare proactively encouraged intellectual activities for his Tynemouth monks, and once he became abbot of St Albans and president of the General Chapter in England (a role he held for thirty years), he was a fervent reformer. As Clark notes, Abbot Thomas 'compiled and issued a series of statutes to reinvigorate monastic study at the universities, making substantial changes to the curriculum and requiring each community to support its students with sufficient funds'.[112] He was also a strong proponent of liturgical correctness in the Divine Office, and a collection of native saints' lives would have been an important resource in this regard.[113] That MS Cotton Tiberius E. i contains liturgical matter (collects and antiphons) illustrates how the lives could have been used in the daily Office and within the Mass. Thomas's insistence on the education of monks, as well as their devotional reading, is but one indication of his support for a project like John's *Sanctilogium*. His political influence, moreover, is further proof of his ability to stress the value of such a collection of native saints among the Benedictines, even as he could promote the Order by stressing Benedictine preference for royal saints of the early English Church. Doing so would have been an astute political move, as the abbot moved in the most elite circles. His prominent associates included Edward III, Edward the Black Prince, Richard II, and John of Gaunt, as well as the archbishops of York and Canterbury.[114] It is in this light that we can see that John's *Sanctilogium* would have been an ideal collection — with its royal and episcopal saints — to support the educational aims of Thomas de la Mare in particular and the spiritual (and political) aims of the Benedictines more

---

[111] See Blanton, 'Benedictine Devotion to England's Saints', pp. 105–18, for a fuller discussion of this suggestion.

[112] James G. Clark, 'Thomas de la Mare', ODNB (https://doi.org/10.1093/ref:odnb/18039) (accessed 1 April 2023).

[113] Clark, 'Thomas de la Mare'.

[114] Clark, 'Thomas de la Mare'.

generally. As head of the General Chapter of the English Benedictines, Thomas was in the position to ensure the distribution and circulation of the legendary among monastic audiences, both male and female. In pressing for liturgical correctness, he was well-positioned to insist that monks and nuns use John's epitomes of native saints in their liturgical and devotional lives.

Some measure of the influence of John's collection is indicated by the four fifteenth-century manuscript copies and one sixteenth-century edition, printed by Wynkyn de Worde as *Nova Legenda Anglie*. The manuscripts themselves differ in arrangement from MS Cotton Tiberius E. i and are further distinguished by their packaging. Three manuscripts present the *Sanctilogium* as a discrete, self-contained collection (albeit with minor differences in the saints included), and the fourth, Karlsruhe, Badische Landesbibliothek, Cod. Sankt Georgen 12 — made for Syon Abbey — integrates the *Sanctilogium* with lives from the *Legenda aurea* and the Roman martyrology to form a magisterial collection of over 800 saints' lives in liturgical order by feast. The Syon manuscript will be discussed below as a distinctive collection of native and universal saints lives akin to Add. 2604, while the other manuscripts described here illustrate the circulation of John's legendary among monastic audiences.

It is not entirely clear when John's collection was reorganised alphabetically by saint name rather than by feast date — a modification that would have made it far easier to locate a given life when needed and one that may indicate an attention to devotional rather than liturgical use — but three manuscripts illustrate this change: York, York Minster Library MS XVI.G.23; London, British Library, MS Cotton Otho D. ix; and Oxford, Bodleian Library MS Tanner 15.[115] Individual lives in each seem to be consistent with a predictable replication of text. In Appendix 2: Latin and Middle English Versions of Æthelthryth, a passage from the life of Æthelthryth shows that each of the fifteenth-century manuscripts, including Syon's Cod. Sankt Georgen 12, plus the printed Latin text, illustrate only the most minute differences (such as transposition of words) or the stylistic differences in scribe (such as 'Ff' as a capital instead of 'F' or the use of 'v' instead of the more usual 'u'). In only one case does a word substitution occur (in MS Tanner 15, the word 'quaquam' is used instead of 'multorum' in 'Predixit quoque obitus multorum [...]'). Tiny markers of dif-

---

[115] When Horstman edited Wynkyn de Worde's 1516 edition, he checked the contents of each life against those in MS Cotton Tiberius E. i and MS Tanner 15, noting minor word changes or errors. He was not aware of Cod. Sankt Georgen 12, and while he did know about the York manuscript, he did not consult it: *Nova Legenda Anglie*, I, xv–xvi. See further n. 5 above.

THE MANUSCRIPTS OF JOHN OF TYNEMOUTH'S 'SANCTILOGIUM'

ference show some affinity between the York and Sankt Georgen manuscripts: for instance, the word 'superne' is not included in the phrase 'Laudetur ergo pietas deitatis superne' and the word 'urbis' is missing in the phrase 'et prope urbis murum sarcophagum', found in the other copies. By and large, however, the lives conform to the presentation found in MS Cotton Tiberius E. i, suggesting that the four manuscripts are ultimately derived from this common exemplar or one nearly identical. This consistency is no doubt related to the fact that three manuscripts are associated with high-status Benedictine male communities and that the circulation of an exemplar or exemplars would have been fairly straightforward as part of Thomas de la Mare's campaign. That the Birgittine community at Syon Abbey had access to a manuscript that replicated the Benedictine tradition is not at all surprising, given the close connections between St Albans and Syon.[116]

York, York Minster, MS XVI.G.23 has two items: both are saints' lives but from distinct collections. They are copied by the same hand yet separated by adjacent indices in the codex's centre at fols 107v–108v. The first item, fols 1r–107v, is an excerpt of Petrus Calo's massive compendium of saints and concludes: 'Explicit secunda pars in tertio volumine legendarum collectarum per fratrem Petrum Calo de Clugia ordinis Fratrum Predicatorum'.[117] John's *Sanctilogium* is the second item on fols 109r–192v and contains 153 of the lives; Hildelith, Tatheus, and Ursula are missing, though Tatheus is listed in the index (the same omission is found in MS Tanner 15).[118] The manuscript itself is beautifully written. Its decorative paratextual elements show a particular attention to facility in reading with alternating blue and red capitals used to distinguish each sentence within a life. To differentiate epitomes in the manuscript, four-line blue initials with red flourishing open each. The two collections are distinguished by large penwork initials at the beginning (fols 1r and 109r). Especially striking is the decoration of the index for the *Sanctilogium*. Where the list of saints that ends the selection from Petrus Calo is undecorated, a large penwork initial 'A' for 'Adrianus' opens the index of John's collection, and alter-

[116] George R. Keiser, 'Patronage and Piety in Fifteenth-Century England: Margaret, Duchess of Clarence, Symon Wynter and Beinecke MS 317', *The Yale University Library Gazette*, 60 (1985), 32–46 (p. 38).

[117] This small portion of the multi-volume *Legendarium* by Petrus Calo, John of Tynemouth's Dominican contemporary, precedes the *Sanctilogium*. For a list of manuscripts and their contents, see Poncelet, 'Le Légendier de Pierre Calo', pp. 44–48.

[118] Ker and Piper make this point in *Medieval Manuscripts in British Libraries*, IV (1992), 705–06 (p. 705).

nating red and blue initials are used for each saint's name (fol. 108r). The scribe was Henry Mere, a peripatetic German who is known to have worked for the prior of Christ Church, Canterbury between 1446 and 1448/9. Mere identifies himself several times in the York manuscript and adds the date 1454 on fol. 192v.[119] It is not known if the manuscript was a York Minster commission or if it was acquired soon after its production. A different hand adds this inscription of ownership, which Ker dates to *s.* xv/xvi: 'Iste liber pertinet ad vestibulum Ecclesie metropolitice Ebor' (fol. 193v). Two similar inscriptions appear on fol. 194r, though the dates of the inscriptions are not from the time the manuscript was copied.[120]

Where the scribe's identity and the ownership of the York manuscript is fairly secure, very little can be discerned about the production, use, or ownership of MS Cotton Otho D. ix, which was severely damaged in the library fire at Ashburnham House in 1731. Some folios are partially legible, but others are reduced to small fragments or were lost entirely. The best preserved show that the book was written in a handsome textualis with a more ornate programme of decoration than the York manuscript. Blue paraphs ornament rubricated running heads that identify the saint(s) included on each folio, and penwork initials mark section divisions within the lives. Each life also begins with a rubricated title and has, depending on the importance of the saint, a two-, three-, four- five-, or seven-line penwork initial to set off the entry. The largest of these initials indicate particular attention to those who served as archbishops of Canterbury, which might indicate a Christ Church provenance. The first folio confirms that the book was made for a high-status community like Christ Church: the collection opens with an illuminated initial ornamented by elaborate spraywork with gold balls. A ribbon border frames the top and left margins. Based on the style of the decoration, the manuscript is dateable to

---

[119] 'A Fifteenth-Century Scribe: Henry Mere', in M. B. Parkes, *Scribes, Scripts and Readers: Studies in the Communication, Presentation, and Dissemination of Medieval Texts* (London: Hambledon, 1991), pp. 249–56 (first published in the *Bodleian Library Record*, 6 (1961), 654–59), and David Rundle, 'English Books and the Continent', in *The Production of Books in England, 1350–1500*, ed. by Alexandra Gillespie and Daniel Wakelin (Cambridge: Cambridge University Press, 2011), pp. 276–91 (p. 282). Linne R. Mooney describes him as a freelance scribe in 'Locating Scribal Activity in Late Medieval London', in *Design and Distribution of Late Medieval Manuscripts in England*, ed. by Margaret Connolly and Linne R. Mooney (York: York Medieval Press, 2008), pp. 183–204 (p. 203). Clark also describes Henry Mere as an exemplary itinerant scribe in *A Monastic Renaissance at St. Albans*, p. 112.

[120] The manuscript is described in Ker and Piper, *Medieval Manuscripts in British Libraries*, IV (1992), 705–06; see p. 706 for the inscription above on fols 193v and 194r.

THE MANUSCRIPTS OF JOHN OF TYNEMOUTH'S 'SANCTILOGIUM' 259

s. xv^med, which is in keeping with Horstman's estimation of its having been written before 1450.[121] In 1696, Thomas Smith printed a contents list of 148 lives before MS Cotton Otho D. ix was damaged by fire, but Horstman suggests that this list is not entirely trustworthy and that the count could be closer to 154, with only Tatheus and Ursula lacking, but it is very difficult to determine based on the loss of various leaves.[122]

Of the three manuscripts in this group, MS Tanner 15 is the only copy of John's *Sanctilogium* with an absolutely secure provenance and date: it contains a colophon (fol. 581r) stating that Prior Thomas Goldstone II of Christ Church, Canterbury commissioned the book, and that it was written by Jacobus Neell, a Norman born in Rouen, who completed it in 1499:

> Perfectum est hoc opus, vvulgariter intitulatum De Sanctis Angliae. ad laudem et honorem omnipotentis dei. ac sanctae Cantuariae ecclesiae. ex Impensis Reverendi in Christo patris domini Thomae Goleston eiusdem ecclesiae Prioris. Ac sacrarum literarum professoris egregii. Per me Iacobum Neell Normannum ac Rothomagi natum. Anno verbi incarnati. 1499. Deo gratias.

A lovely illuminated nine-line initial opens the *Sanctilogium* ornamented with spraywork featuring berries and flowers that extends across the top of the text block and half-way down the left side.[123] Running heads and two-line initials call out the various saints' lives. The manuscript is beautifully penned but is not as luxurious a copy as MS Cotton Otho D. ix. MS Tanner 15 contains 153 lives (and as above, shares the same contents as the York manuscript). It also contains a unique feature: the index includes a brief comment on each saint, perhaps to excite interest or to help readers recall details of the lives.[124] The entry for Eanswith reads: 'Eanswida virgo fontem contra naturam ipsam sequi fecit' (fol. i recto). That for Eormenhild reads: 'Ermenilda regina multos ad fidem allexit' (fol. i verso). Most entries, therefore, are about an aspect of a saint's holy activities and a reference to place is rarely noted, as it is for Æthelthryth: 'Etheldreda regina virgo apud Hely floruit' (fol. i verso). The manuscript also

---

[121] *Nova Legenda Anglie*, ed. by Horstman, I, xv.

[122] Smith does include Edward the Confessor, which Horstman thought he had not. See Thomas Smith, *Catalogus Librorum Manuscriptorium Bibliothecæ Cottonianæ* (Oxford: Sheldon Theatre, 1696), pp. 76–77.

[123] Very similar in appearance is the decoration that adorns the Acts of Thomas Goldstone in the martyrology of Christ Church, Canterbury, which is London, British Library, MS Arundel 68, fol. 65r, dated to 1520.

[124] *Nova Legenda Anglie*, ed. by Horstman, I, xv.

260 V. LATIN SOURCES AND ANALOGUES

contains material, including lections, about the Welsh saint Dubricius, archbishop of Llandaff, followed by a *vita* of the Irish saint, Berach, both of whom also appear in the *Sanctilogium*. Copied at the end of the fifteenth century by a noted scribe, this manuscript demonstrates the value of John's collection in the most prestigious and powerful monastic community in England.

Before turning to Syon Abbey's copy of the *Sanctilogium*, it is worth mentioning that there is evidence of another lost manuscript. Oxford, Bodleian Library, MS Bodley 240 (dated 1377) contains the second part of John of Tynemouth's *Historia aurea* and extracts of his *martyrologium* and *Sanctilogium*. On p. 621 is a reference that indicates Bury had a 'Legenda de sanctis Angliae' — a title very similar to that used in MS Tanner 15 — which may refer to John's collection.[125] Given the stature of Bury's famed library, it would not be at all surprising for the community, which had strong links to the royal court, to have a copy of the *Sanctilogium*, especially as extracts of his other works are found in MS Bodley 240. Another reason to believe it refers to John's legendary is that Bury's librarian, Henry of Kirkstede, identified John as author of the *Historia aurea*, the *Sanctilogium*, and a *martyrologium*. Henry indicated that John was still alive in 1366, a comment that suggests he knew the vicar personally.[126] In any case, the production of three manuscripts of John's *Sanctilogium* in the latter half of the fifteenth century and the association of these recensions with important libraries at York and Christ Church, Canterbury, indicates that the collection circulated among the most important Benedictine monasteries and remained

---

[125] Richard Sharpe, 'Reconstructing the Medieval Library of Bury St Edmunds Abbey: The Lost Catalogue of Henry of Kirkstead', in *Bury St Edmunds: Medieval Art, Architecture, Archaeology and Economy*, ed. by Antonia Gransden, The British Archaeological Association Conference Transactions, 20 (Leeds: British Archaeological Association, 1998), pp. 204–18, at p. 212 (H.55) and p. 215 (S.146). H.55 is identified as MS Bodley 240; S.146 is untraced. If the reference in MS Bodley 240 to a 'Legenda de sanctis Angliae' is a reference to London, British Library, MS Cotton Otho D. ix, it would be necessary to reassess the supposed mid-fifteenth-century date. It is possible, of course, that an earlier copy of John's *Sanctilogium* was in the library at Bury, prior to the destruction of Bury books and documents in the riots of 1327–31, and another replaced it. For this history of Bury, see *Henry of Kirkestede: Catalogus de libris autenticis et apocrifis*, ed. by Richard H. Rouse and Mary A. Rouse, Corpus of British Medieval Library Catalogues, 11 (London: The British Library in association with the British Academy, 2004), pp. xliv and lxxvi.

[126] We might also expect that the other great Benedictine library, Durham, had a copy of the *Sanctilogium*, especially as John, as vicar of Tynemouth, was supervised by the abbot of Durham. It makes sense that Tynemouth Priory would have had one as well, since the parish church was in the nave of the priory church.

THE MANUSCRIPTS OF JOHN OF TYNEMOUTH'S 'SANCTILOGIUM'   261

influential from the 1380s onwards. Continued demand for the collection is evident by the Canterbury copy made in 1499. This may be why Wynkyn de Worde elected to print it in 1516. His edition, arranged in alphabetical order by saint name, was based on a recension like MS XVI.G.23, MS Tanner 15, or MS Otho D. ix, yet it shows considerable changes in content: as Horstman noted in editing the collection, there are fifteen additional lives, including ones for the newly canonised saints John of Bridlington and Osmund; new versions of the lives of Richard and Ursula are substituted for those found in MS Cotton Tiberius E. i; the *Purgatorio* and Tundal narratives that accompany the life of Patrick are omitted, as are the Constitutions of Thomas Becket; and a prologue is introduced.[127] That same year, Richard Pynson printed brief extracts in English in a collection titled *The Kalendre of the New Legende of Englande*. In the prologue, the rationale for the translation is explicit: 'for theym that vnderstande not the Laten tonge, that they atte theyr pleasure may be occupied therwith and be therby þe more apte to lerne the resydue when they shall here the hole Legende'.[128] The scope and title of the collection is further distinguished as

> [...] þe pryncypall intent of this treatyse to be as a kalendre to shewe þe names of þe seyntes of theyr countrey & where they lye as it shal do. When it apperyth so ferre in þe legende as it doth moost comenly, but not in all places, to shewe also some lytell thynge of theyr vertues & myracles with some parte of theyr storyes shortlye towched. [...] euerythynge in this treatyse is shortly touched more lyke to be a kalendre than a legende [...] this lytyll treatyce maye conuenyentlye be callyd the Kalendre of the Newe Legende of Englonde.[129]

---

[127] Horstman indicates that there are some superficial differences in the lives, as compared with MS Cotton Tiberius E. i: *Nova Legenda Anglie*, ed. by Horstman, I, pp. xv–xxi.

[128] *The Kalendre of the Newe Legende of Englande*, ed. by Görlach, p. 42, ll. 3–5.

[129] *The Kalendre of the Newe Legende of Englande*, ed. by Görlach, p. 46, ll. 129–32, 137–38, 142–43. For discussions of *The Kalendre*, see Ann M. Hutchison, 'What the Nuns Read: Literary Evidence from the English Bridgettine House, Syon Abbey', *Mediaeval Studies*, 57 (1995), 205–22; '*The Lyfe of Seynt Birgette*: An Edition of a Swedish Saint's Life for an English Audience', ed. by Ann M. Hutchison, and Veronica O'Mara, in *'Booldly but meekly': Essays on the Theory and Practice of Translation in the Middle Ages in Honour of Roger Ellis*, ed. by Catherine Batt and René Tixier, The Medieval Translator/Traduire au Moyen Âge, 14 (Turnhout: Brepols, 2018), pp. 173–208, which includes a discussion of the extant copies of *The Kalendre*, pp. 174–82; and Mary Erler, 'The Early Sixteenth Century at Syon: Richard Whitford and Elizabeth Gibbs', in *Manuscript Culture and Medieval Devotional Traditions: Essays in Honour of Michael G. Sargent*, ed. by Jennifer N. Brown, and Nicole R. Rice, York Manuscript and Early Print Studies, 1 (Woodbridge: York Medieval Press, 2021), pp. 310–26. Erler suggests that Richard Whitford was responsible for *The Kalendre* (pp. 311–16).

That Pynson, who calls himself the printer to King Henry VIII, has made these native lives available to a larger audience — lay and certainly monastic as well — is some indication of the on-going value of these native lives, 'for there can no thynge be loued & honoured but it be knowen'.[130]

As is indicated above, changes to John's legendary are suggestive about its use in various contexts, which is why the fourth — and likely the earliest — of the fifteenth-century manuscripts containing the *Sanctilogium Angliae Walliae Scotiae et Hiberniae* is so intriguing. Karlsruhe, Badische Landesbibliothek, Cod. Sankt Georgen 12 is the first of an original two-volume collection of lives arranged in calendar order by saint's feast. This volume migrated to the Continent presumably during one of the two peregrinations of the Birgittine Order.[131] In 1642, it appeared in the collection of Father Georgius Abbot of Sankt Georgen (Villingen), as is inscribed on fol. 1r. It is not clear when or how the second volume was lost. The surviving volume finishes imperfectly at the beginning of September but an alphabetical index (fols 1v–4v) and a highly decorated calendar of feasts (fols 5r–7v) at the outset provide a clear indication of the intended contents of both volumes. Universal figures from the *Legenda aurea* and the Roman martyrology, as well as material for Birgitta of Sweden's nativity, canonisation, and translation — as would have been apropos for a Birgittine community — were integrated with the native saints in John's *Sanctilogium*, resulting in a collection of more than 800 lives, titled *Sanctilogium salvatoris*. Like the *Sanctilogium* of Gui de Châtres, the *Sanctilogium salvatoris* is divided into twelve books (one for each month of the Roman calendar), followed by two books of miracles. The index provides the name of each saint, along with the book and chapter in which the feast occurs, such as *Liber* 6, *capitulum* 24 for the feast of John the Baptist on 24 June. As such, the compendium was designed as an exhaustive, yet easily navigable, encyclopedia of sanctity that integrated John's native lives with a universal pantheon of saints. Commissioned by Margaret Holland, Duchess of Clarence (*c.* 1386–1439), Cod. Sankt Georgen 12 was an elaborate gift for Syon Abbey, the first and only Birgittine house in England, founded by Henry V in 1415.[132]

---

[130] *The Kalendre of the Newe Legende of Englande*, ed. by Görlach, p. 46, ll. 134–35.

[131] Christopher de Hamel, *The Library of the Bridgettine Nuns and their Peregrinations after the Reformation: An Essay by Christopher de Hamel, with the Manuscript of Arundel Castle* (Otley: Roxburghe Club, 1991).

[132] These volumes are identified as M. 1 and M. 2 in the early sixteenth-century catalogue of Syon Abbey, and they are nos 734 and 735 in the edition of this catalogue: *Syon Abbey, with the Libraries of the Carthusians*, ed. by Gillespie and Doyle, p. 212.

KARLSRUHE, BADISCHE LANDESBIBLIOTHEK, COD. SANKT GEORGEN 12   263

Margaret was sister-in-law to Henry V by her second marriage to Thomas, Duke of Clarence, c. 1412.[133] The celebrated scribe, Stephen Dodesham (d. c. 1482), copied the manuscript of Latin lives early in his career, likely before he became a Carthusian monk, first at Witham and later at Sheen.[134] It is quite possible that Simon Wynter, who served as the duchess's confessor and who translated for her a life of Jerome, may have suggested the usefulness of such a collection of saints' lives.[135] The manuscript is a deluxe production, beautifully decorated with borders and spraywork, eight historiated initials, one for each of the books in the surviving codex, with the ninth left blank.[136] Important for our study of Add. 2604, the Cod. Sankt Georgen 12 index of saints illustrates what the two volumes would have contained: a combination of our two categories of saint.

Karlsruhe, Badische Landesbibliothek, Cod. Sankt Georgen 12: Universal and Native Lives

Foremost, all of the native saints in Add. 2604 are listed: Æthelthryth, Eanswith, Eadburh, Edith, Eorcengota, Eormenhild, Hild, Modwenna, Seaxburh, Wærburh, and Wihtburh. With the exception of Domitilla and the now missing Iphigenia, all the universal lives are also in the alphabetical index: Agatha, Barbara, Benedicta, Cecilia, Columba, John the Baptist (for the feasts of the Invention, Nativity, Decollation, and Conception respectively on 24 February, 24 June, 29 August, and 24 September), John the Evangelist (at the Latin Gate and the Death on 6 May and 27 December), Justina and Cyprian, Leonard, and Martha.[137] At the beginning of the volume these are all set out again in an elaborately organised calendar of saints in monthly order, feast by feast. Unfortunately, because this manuscript is in an imperfect state and many of the saints featured in Add. 2604 would have occurred in the now-lost second

---

[133] Keiser, 'Patronage and Piety in Fifteenth-Century England', p. 34.

[134] A. I. Doyle, 'Stephen Dodesham of Witham and Sheen', in *Of the Making of Books: Medieval Manuscripts, their Scribes and Readers: Essays Presented to M. B. Parkes*, ed. by P. R. Robinson and Rivkah Zim (Aldershot: Scolar Press, 1997), pp. 94–115 (p. 115).

[135] Keiser, 'Patronage and Piety in Fifteenth-Century England', pp. 37–39.

[136] Ellen J. Beer, *Initial und Miniatur: Buchmalerei aus neun Jahrhunderten in Handschriften der Badischen Landesbibliothek* (Basel: Feuermann-Verlag, 1965), p. 51.

[137] Martha is mistakenly listed as 'Maria domini hospita' on fol. 3v. The simple slip is due to eyeskip as the previous entry is for 'Maria virgo et mater'.

volume, we cannot assess fully the relationship between Cod. Sankt Georgen 12 and Add. 2604. We offer here a consideration of sources for both the universal and the native saints to consider how these two manuscripts align (or not).

Given that Cod. Sankt Georgen 12 finishes with 1 September, full comparison with Add. 2604 can only be made with the universal lives of Agatha (5 February) and John the Baptist (24 June). Although it lacks the main feast of John the Evangelist on 27 December, it does have *Ad portam Latinam*; this life figures in a handful of sentences in the Add. 2604 John the Evangelist and so will allow a little comparison. And the Cod. Sankt Georgen 12 life of Nereus and Achilleus (12 May) may be examined in case it casts any light on Domitilla in Add. 2604. As indicated above, the sources and analogues of the universal lives in Add. 2604 are mixed. Yet considering the complete overlap in the lives between the Cod. Sankt Georgen 12 and Add. 2604, one might expect to find the 'source' or at least a definite 'analogue' in the Syon manuscript. Yet unlike Add. 2604, which does not depend at all on the *Legenda aurea* Agatha but makes use of another version as found in the *Acta sanctorum*, the life of Agatha in Cod. Sankt Georgen 12 (fols 42vb–43rb) is an almost exact rendition of the *Legenda aurea* narrative.[138] The only major difference is the omission of an etymological discussion of Agatha's name. A word-by-word comparison between the Cod. Sankt Georgen 12 manuscript and the edited *Legenda aurea* reveals only a few omitted phrases, plus very sporadic and very minor verbal alterations. The opposite happens with the John the Evangelist *Ad portam Latinam* (fols 89rb–89va); whereas the sentences used in Add. 2604's John the Evangelist derive directly from the *Legenda aurea*, the *Ad portam Latinam* life in Cod. Sankt Georgen 12 is totally unlike Jacobus de Voragine's version.

John the Baptist in Cod. Sankt Georgen 12 (fols 134ra–135va) is more intriguing than the Agatha or the John the Evangelist. Even though both Add. 2604 and Cod. Sankt Georgen share a *Legenda aurea* source in the Nativity of John the Baptist, the text in the Sankt Georgen manuscript is clearly not the source — or an analogue — of that in Add. 2604. Quite apart from the fact that the Add. 2604 narrative is almost equally based on the Decollation (for which the Sankt Georgen manuscript has a separate life as well as a text for John's Conception and the Invention), the Add. 2604 adapts a far more ruthless method of excision overall. Whole swathes of text are left out; for example, the long section about John's father being punished for his lack of faith before

---

[138] XXXIX, 'De sancta Agatha', in Iacopo da Varazze, *Legenda aurea con le miniature del codice Ambrosiano C 240 inf.*, ed. by Maggioni, I, 296–301 (versos only).

KARLSRUHE, BADISCHE LANDESBIBLIOTHEK, COD. SANKT GEORGEN 12   265

John's birth, John's nine privileges, and the five reasons for his being worthy. The only points of overlap are the mutual exclusion of the etymology of John's name and in the section about John's worthiness (where Cod. Sankt Georgen has the greatest efficiency and Add. 2604 omits the section completely). One other point of interest is the tendency for both to omit patristic attributions. In the case of John the Baptist, one patristic quote is left in the Sankt Georgen text, but the *Legenda aurea* reference to the relevant Church Father is excluded. Although the Add. 2604 writer does delete the references wholesale as does the Sankt Georgen compiler, he nevertheless downplays them wherever possible. In the English translation of Add. 2604 this fits in with making the material more appropriate for medieval nuns with indifferent Latin, but why the Sankt Georgen compiler excludes all such references is a mystery considering that the whole manuscript is in Latin and all the original quotations are included. Apart from that, the life of John the Baptist in Cod. Sankt Georgen 12 is a faithful version of the *Legenda aurea* text with only very occasional and minor verbal transpositions or alterations. Yet while the Agatha only has a few inconsequential variants, in the John the Baptist, whole phrases and sentences are eliminated throughout. The most concentrated series of omissions covers sentences 135–54 of the printed *Legenda aurea* text, but with a few sentences from the *Legenda aurea* interwoven between the parts like an intricate piece of darning. The one elaboration concerns the meeting of Mary and Elizabeth and the naming of John by Zachariah, with a reference to John's time in the desert, based on Luke 1. The writer of Add. 2604 also includes this biblical passage, but the text in each case is decidedly different.

The Add. 2604 text of Domitilla is too inconsequential to allow for proper comparison yet a focus on it casts some light on Cod. Sankt Georgen 12. The Sankt Georgen life of Nereus and Achilleus (fols 93rb–93va), which focuses almost exclusively on Domitilla, is not taken from the *Legenda aurea*; instead it is a patchwork from the life of Nereus and Achilleus as found in the *Acta sanctorum*.[139] (Of interest, the next life in Sankt Georgen, that of Pancratius, derives closely from the version in the *Legenda aurea*.) In any case the Add. 2604 writer implies that his information is obtained not from Nereus and Achilleus but from that of Clement, which is now missing from Cod. Sankt Georgen 12. As

---

[139] See the life of Nereus and Achilleus in the *Acta sanctorum*, Maji Tomus Tertius, pp. 7–9. The Cod. Sankt Georgen 12 text equates with the *Acta sanctorum* version as follows: with various sentences omitted the text uses the first chapter from the first paragraph to the beginning of the sixth, then skips to the second chapter and uses parts of paragraphs eight and nine, before moving to the third chapter and using some of the first chapter before going its own way.

noted above, the nearest derivation of Domitilla would appear to be a martyrological one so any connection between it and texts in Sankt Georgen is immaterial. And the same might be said for the missing Iphigenia in Add. 2604; it may also have been a passing martyrological reference like the Domitilla. In any case, the Sankt Georgen life of Matthew (with its mention of Iphigenia) would have been in the second volume that is now missing.

There is in truth no close textual connection between Cod. Sankt Georgen and the universal lives in Add. 2604 (of default a small sample). Although unusually they both combine the important collection from John of Tynemouth with at least part of Jacobus de Voragine (though Cod. Sankt Georgen has many more lives and other sources), they have gone their own way in their use of the *Legenda aurea* and, it is to be assumed, with the other materials no longer extant in the Sankt Georgen volumes. We have seen how the Add. 2604 writer chose to use another version of the Agatha legend rather than depend on that in the *Legenda aurea* which is straightforwardly rendered in Cod. Sankt Georgen 12, whereas the writer of the latter collection was content to use de Voragine for his life of Pancratius but had gone elsewhere for the preceding Nereus and Achilleus. Conversely the placement of the two feasts of Barbara and Martha in the now lost second volume would suggest that these two lives may also differ from those in Add. 2604. Whereas Barbara's feast, which is not found in the regular *Legenda aurea*, is given as 16 December in Add. 2604, in the Syon index and monthly list it is cited under two days, 4 and 16 December, which would more than likely indicate a different text. Martha's feast on 17 December in the Cod. Sankt Georgen 12 index and monthly list would also strongly suggest that it was another Martha legend rather than the *Legenda aurea* text (with its 29 July placement) used in Add. 2604. Whether the Sankt Georgen compiler used the standard Cecilia narrative from the *Legenda aurea* as found in the Add. 2604 manuscript must also remain a mystery. Likewise open to speculation are the Sankt Georgen versions of Justina and Leonard compared with those in Add. 2604; if the Sankt Georgen compiler depended on the traditional *Legenda aurea* versions of these, he would have differed yet again from the Add. 2604 writer where the nearest analogue to the Justina legend is that printed in the *Acta sanctorum* combined in the middle with a section from the *Legenda aurea* and the nearest analogue to the story of Leonard is also that in the *Acta sanctorum*.

Comparison between the universal lives in Add. 2604 and those that are in or would have been in Cod. Sankt Georgen 12 gives rise to more questions than it answers, but it does illustrate that the Syon manuscript was not the source manuscript or in many ways even an analogous manuscript for the universal

KARLSRUHE, BADISCHE LANDESBIBLIOTHEK, COD. SANKT GEORGEN 12   267

saints in Add. 2604. One thing the two manuscripts do share is the tendency to move from the *Legenda aurea* to other sources, be they what is now represented in the *Acta sanctorum* or otherwise. (And there is an extensive number of lives in Cod. Sankt Georgen that cannot be linked to Jacobus de Voragine's *Legenda aurea* or to John of Tynemouth's *Sanctilogium*.)

The results are similarly complicated for the native lives. But they are even more conclusive. First, we must lay out the evidence to see how Cod. Sankt Georgen 12 and Add. 2604 are alike regarding the eleven native lives before determining the concurrences between them. All of the native lives in Add. 2604 are listed in the index for Cod. Sankt Georgen 12. Three native lives, however, are missing with the loss of the second volume: Edith (16 September), Hild (17 November), and Eadburh (13 December). Of those that remain, all are clearly derived from John of Tynemouth's *Sanctilogium*. As we have noted above, the translator of the lives in Add. 2604 remains fairly faithful to the priest's epitomes — with the exception of Wærburh and Wihtburh — so we are on firm ground seeing the two collections as derivatives of a common source text, but a few oddities indicate that they are not as closely linked as we might hope. To illustrate the similarities, we turn first to the life of Seaxburh, which is ultimately drawn from a series of lections by Goscelin de Saint-Bertin that John of Tynemouth copied verbatim, showing minor alterations to the opening and closing, as well as isolated deletions. The Middle English translator in Add. 2604 follows John closely, adding the detail that Seaxburh's daughter Eorcengota 'went to a monastery beyonde the see and ther dyed graciously as a pilgryme and shewith grete miracles ther she lyeth' (8/10–12), a statement drawn from the narration about Eorcengota that follows the account of Seaxburh in John's legendary. The only significant deletions include the omission of Seaxburh's sons, Egbert and Hlothhere. In the Latin life in Cod. Sankt Georgen 12 this version is truncated, as it skips phrases and whole sentences to shorten the narrative considerably. A careful corrector inserted four of those omitted lines in the lower margin of fol. 144r, which has been ruled to accommodate the insertions. These corrections are addressed in the volume's Prologue, where the scribe indicates that some lives were amended after consulting a more authoritative copy of John's *Sanctilogium*, though we do not know which manuscript this may have been.

This points to a particularly significant aspect of Cod. Sankt Georgen 12: some of the native lives demonstrate this kind of contraction of the narrative and these abbreviated lives are often (but not universally) augmented by marginal insertions to re-establish the integrity of John of Tynemouth's texts. As the comparison of manuscripts containing the *Sanctilogium* life of Æthelthryth in Appendix 2 illustrates, the copying is fairly consistent with only an occasional word inversion or substitution. Thus, it is easy to compare how significant the contraction is in Cod. Sankt Georgen 12. Another example occurs in the life of Æthelthryth, Seaxburh's sister and founder of Ely, whose narrative ultimately derives from Bede's *Historia ecclesiastica* by way of the *Liber Eliensis*, as noted above. On fols 133v–134r of Cod. Sankt Georgen 12, all of the omitted sections from John of Tynemouth are inserted in the ruled lower margin, using an innovative series of figures as indicators of where these marginal notes should be inserted as a reader progresses.

Of the Add. 2604 texts, the amount of contraction and marginal re-insertion in Cod. Sankt Georgen 12 varies, with some texts like Eormenhild being exactly the same as it is in John's *Sanctilogium* and others such as Wihtburh showing a very messy and confused use of John's narrative. The life of Wihtburh in Cod. Sankt Georgen 12 on fol. 144v is a truncated use of John's version, with some twelve lengthy sentences omitted. Only two lines missing from MS Cotton Tiberius E. i are re-inserted in the margin. Another reader has interacted with the text, underlining sections in brown ink. Three notes by this later hand are about the two translations of Wihtburh's relics and a miracle at her tomb, along with their dates. These additions are called out by three manicules, also in brown ink. These amplifications recall some of the material in MS Cotton Tiberius E. i, which were not re-inserted in Cod. Sankt Georgen 12, perhaps as an indication of the missing elements. In addition, the Wihtburh in the Sankt Georgen manuscript does not conclude with the usual testing of Wihtburh's incorrupted body but instead inserts details about Saints Killian and Procopius. Where some native lives, such as that for Æthelthryth, show corrections that bring Cod. Sankt Georgen 12 into alignment with MS Cotton Tiberius E. i — and thus into position to be considered an exemplar or a copy of a common exemplar of the lives in Add. 2604 — the evidence from the life of Wihtburh indicates that the first manuscript of the *Sanctilogium* Dodesham used was imperfect or drawn from a derivative version and the corrections do not make up for the discrepancies. What is even more important is that the version of Wihtburh in Cod. Sankt Georgen 12 does not align with the translation in Add. 2604, which suggests that another intermediary may lie between them.

Our study of Cod. Sankt Georgen 12 serves to show that outside Syon or perhaps in conjunction with Syon, a vernacular compiler writing for nuns in East Anglia was part of a later medieval trend for combining the universal with the native, a trend that would grow across Europe once the likes of Mombritius and Johannes Gielemanns started promulgating their huge collections of hagiographical material. To be sure, Add. 2604 is a clear manifestation

CONCLUSION   269

of the extensive Latin network of native lives that were circulating in fifteenth-century England, but it derives from a version more like the St Albans MS Cotton Tiberius E. i than an abbreviated form like those that appear in Cod. Sankt Georgen 12. Further, when compared to Richard Pynson's 1516 printing of *The Kalendre of the New Legende of Englande*, which features incredibly abbreviated translations of the native lives in John's *Sanctilogium*, we find that there is little agreement in the contractions. Unlike the skeletal lives printed in *The Kalendre*, the eleven complete lives of native saints found in Add. 2604 do ample justice to Tynemouth's *Sanctilogium*. The abbreviations do not read at all like the more complete lives in Add. 2604. Thus, Add. 2604 cannot claim to be a direct cousin of the lives in *The Kalendre* (as is obvious from the extract printed in Appendix 1).

Conclusion

So where does this leave us? It is conceivable that there were some links (not now recoverable) between Syon and the compiler of Add. 2604. This would make sense given the pronounced connections between Syon and East Anglian devotional spirituality. It is equally plausible that what we are witnessing here are two independent developments that are part of a European trend to combine universal and native hagiographical material. The second explanation would seem to be more likely considering that the use of similar sources such as the *Legenda aurea* and John of Tynemouth's *Sanctilogium* do not lead to any obvious textual connections. As we have seen, the Add. 2604 translator goes his own way in how he deals with the universal lives be they from the *Legenda aurea* or elsewhere and his use of John of Tynemouth does not match up with that in Cod. Sankt Georgen 12. Taken as a whole, the translation in Add. 2604 is ultimately dependent on, connected with, or parallel to Bede, the *Liber Eliensis*, Goscelin de Saint-Bertin, the *Sanctilogium*, the *Legenda aurea*, the *Sanctuarium*, the *Historie plurimorum sanctorum*, as well as a range of other legendaries and possibly a few martyrologies.

At the beginning of this discussion, the universal and the native lives were rigidly put into two demarcated zones and their sources or analogues traced separately. While it is true that the sources and analogues of the universal saints are far more mixed than those of the native lives, the work carried out in this *Study* has highlighted the fact that the lives in Add. 2604 may ultimately have derived from a Latin manuscript that already contained a combination of the two types of saint, somewhat like Cod. Sankt Georgen above. Or, as noted previously, the Add. 2604 compiler may himself have arranged his collection through translating material from a couple of manuscripts or indeed from a wider range of source texts that suited his own purposes. In a case like this whether the elusive source manuscript can been discovered or not is almost a moot point. What is significant is that a range of analogous material has been unearthed after painstaking sifting. We have in Add. 2604 a unique collection of Middle English saints' lives — the likes of Agatha and Benedicta and so forth — for all of whom, in one way or another, we have been able to discover Latin sources and analogues aplenty. Before the *Nova Legenda Anglie* was printed in 1516, we have also seen that there were various separate manuscript initiatives to bring John of Tynemouth's collection to a learned audience, clearly a monastic one who could engage with the Latin text. Importantly, Add. 2604 provides the only known example of a manuscript that attempts something similar in the vernacular for a different audience, a readership of women religious somewhere in East Anglia whose training in Latin was no doubt limited or non-existent. To all of these lives we shall now turn.

VI. READING THE 'LYVES AND DETHES'

The collection of saints' lives in Add. 2604 provides unique evidence of a production for a house of nuns whose vocations are highlighted in the text. Produced for a female readership, the lives in this manuscript (both the native and the universal), serve not only to put these nuns firmly in touch with their historical past but to provide general models for their contemporary lives.[1] Whatever the ultimate sources he used — and these are disparate, as discussed previously — the translator garnered his materials in such a way as to make them seem a strong collective centered around female monasticism. In this way late fifteenth- or early sixteenth-century nuns in an East Anglian convent were reading, or having read to them, improving and somewhat exotic stories that purported to explain the lives of women like themselves, women who rejected all worldly suitors and so kept themselves chaste for Christ. These lives are not preoccupied with the day-to-day disciplines and rituals of religious life; neither do they serve to hector the nuns nor subject them to theological discussion. And at no point are the nuns 'troubled' with any knowledge about the genesis of such material that is treated throughout as a unitary whole irrespective of how many Latin sources are involved.[2] This audience is presented with a single hagiographical volume without any recognition of the underlying sources or analogues, the chronological disjunctions, or the cultural complexities of the subject matter. We are mindful throughout this discussion and the *Edition* as a whole that we are not dealing with 'original' material in the strict sense of the term. Like much medieval literature, these texts are in large part a reflection of the choices made by earlier source writers. Nevertheless, we want to stress here the subtle changes made by the Middle English translator and to explore the ways in which these lives would have appeared to and been used by their medieval audience or readership.

---

[1] Such material could have been read contemporaneously or later by women (or men) who were not members of religious orders, but given the emphasis on nuns and abbesses throughout, the strongest argument is that the manuscript's original audience was made up of nuns. The lives could have been appreciated by nuns from elsewhere, albeit that an East Anglian provenance is the most obvious; for suggestions as to which convent or convents in East Anglia may have been the home of these original nuns, see III. Convent and Geographical Location.

[2] In other words, there are the lives, with their multiple influences (as interpreted in this *Study*), and the text as given to a late medieval readership.

These contemporary nuns are not called upon to suffer directly for the faith in the fashion of Roman martyrs like Agatha or Cecilia. Yet like their early English forebears wrestling with societal norms and physical deprivations, the truth is that these nuns are part of this same tradition, spouses of Christ who are obliged to confess the religious life faithfully in small matters as well as large. In the engaging lives laid out before them these readers are provided with moral templates for how to behave in this world and — most importantly — on their way to the next.[3]

Format and Use of the Saints' Lives

Besides the variation in length, immediately apparent upon examining the lives copied into Add. 2604 is that they all contain what may loosely be termed 'section summaries' that provide a précis of the action and miracles within each life. We first begin with an overview of similar practices to contextualise the presentation in Add. 2604. Of course a structured format in medieval manuscripts is not that unusual either for liturgical or historic reasons. As Thomas Heffernan explains, the Divine Office required the compilation of legendaries for celebration of saints' feasts, but it was the liturgy of Matins that helped shape the saint's life as a genre.[4] Of importance for us here is that there is a long tradition of saints' lives being developed or divided into short units for reading during Matins, normally containing twelve, three, or one lesson, depending on the significance of the feast and/or time of year. Likewise, as has been so usefully shown by George Keiser, 'From the late fourteenth century onwards the value of an ordered text and finding devices was recognised by many compilers of practical books in the vernacular, and preparing an *ordinatio* became a part of the process of compilation for them'.[5] As Keiser notes in his in-depth study

---

[3] For a list of some of the contributions, stylistic and otherwise, which have helped to inform this chapter, see n. 6 of the Preface above.

[4] Heffernan, 'The Liturgy and The Literature of Saints' Lives', pp. 73–105. Heffernan notes how the lives of the fourteenth-century Aberdeen Breviary 'repeatedly use the first *lectio* to introduce the saint's genealogy [...]; the second *lectio* often briefly depicts early childhood and intellectual prowess; *lectiones* three to eight generally are given over to enumerating deeds from the saint's life [...]; finally, the ninth *lectio* briefly indicates the piety of the saint and concludes with his death and the assurance of his salvation in Christ', p. 97. In a similar way the Hours of St Dunstan found in a fifteenth-century Sarum Breviary 'also shows the characteristic division into discrete lessons, in this case twelve, each approximately thirty to thirty-five lines long', p. 99.

[5] George R. Keiser, 'Serving the Needs of Readers: Textual Division in Some Late-Medieval

FORMAT AND USE OF THE SAINTS' LIVES

of the complex development of chapter divisions in John Lydgate's *Lyf of Our Lady*, '[...] attention to the presentation of texts can lead to a better understanding of what scribes and printers recognized as the needs of contemporary readers and how they attempted to serve them'.[6] Such *ordinatio* could include large initial capitals, rubricated headings, chapter numbers, running titles, marginalia, prologues, tables, lists of sectional divisions, and chapter headings. Among the many specific examples at various levels of sophistication Keiser cites John Trevisa's 1398 translation of Bartholomaeus Anglicus's *De proprietatibus rerum*, the 1408 translation of Vegetius's *De re militari*, William Caxton's 1485 printed edition of Thomas Malory's *Morte Darthur*, and Wynkyn de Worde's printed copy of *Valentine and Orson* from *c.* 1510. But most of the instances mentioned comprise devotional or hagiographical material.[7]

The extent of the *ordinatio* in such works is variable throughout the period. In an early fifteenth-century devotional book with one of the widest circulation in medieval England such headings are an established feature. *The Mirror of the Blessed Life of Jesus Christ*, as well as being divided into the days of the week (as in its source), has chapter summaries throughout as in 'Of þe manere of lyuyng of þe blessede virgine Marie. Capitulum secundum.'[8] Similarly the devotional text, *The Doctrine of the Hert* aimed at a religious sister, has a prologue and a list of detailed chapter contents, which also precede each of the seven chapters of this lengthy work, such as '*Capitulum primum*. How and in what wise a mynche shulde make redy here herte to God be the yifte of drede'.[9]

English Texts', in *New Science out of Old Books: Studies in Manuscripts and Early Printed Books in Honour of A. I. Doyle*, ed. by Richard Beadle and A. J. Piper (Aldershot: Scolar Press, 1995), pp. 207–26 (p. 209). The ordered Latin scholarly text between the twelfth and the fourteenth century is carefully described in Malcolm Beckwith Parkes, 'The Influence of the Concepts of *Ordinatio* and *Compilatio* on the Development of the Book', in *Medieval Learning and Literature: Essays Presented to Richard William Hunt*, ed. by J. J. G. Alexander and M. T. Gibson (Oxford: Clarendon Press, 1976), pp. 115–41. *Inter alia* he notes that features such as running titles and chapter headings before each book are 'an ancient practice', pp. 122 and n. 1 and 123 and n. 1 respectively. He also draws attention to the way in which the Dominican Robert Kilwardby (d. 1249) in his synopses of the works of the patristic Fathers summarises the different sections of each chapter so as 'to bring out the distinctive qualities of each book', p. 125 and n. 2.

[6] Keiser, 'Serving the Needs of Readers', p. 207.

[7] Some of these are noted below, besides other examples most pertinent to this *Study*.

[8] Nicholas Love, *The Mirror of the Blessed Life of Jesus Christ: A Full Critical Edition*, ed. by Michael G. Sargent (Exeter: University of Exeter Press, 2005), p. 19, ll. 30–31.

[9] *The Doctrine of the Hert*, ed. by Whitehead, Renevey, and Mouron, p. 5.

In the *Gilte Legende* (translated in 1438) the hundred and seventy-nine individual lives are given a chapter number only and introduced simply with a combined 'Here ends' and 'Here begins' formula.[10] The thirty-one *Supplementary Lives* virtually all have variants of the combined 'Here ends' and 'begins/next begins/follows/next follows' formula. A few of the texts are provided with a summary, minus chapter numbers, in the midst of the lives, such as 'Of þe laste wordis that Seinte Edwarde spake' in Edward the Confessor.[11] In the *Legendys of Hooly Wummen* by Osbern Bokenham, an Augustinian at Clare Priory in Suffolk, and found in London, British Library, MS Arundel 327 (written for Thomas Burgh, the Cambridge Augustinian friar in 1447), the preliminary matter is restricted to an indication in Latin or English of where there is a prologue, while each life is signalled by '*Vita*' or the 'Here begins [...]' formula, without any chapter or section headings, although there is a list of contents at the end on fol. 193r.[12] The Abbotsford manuscript of Bokenham's lives has the routine 'Here begynnyth [...]' or simply 'The Lyfe of [...]' but only occasional 'Here endith'; champ initials mark new lives. As it is an acephalous text, one cannot tell if there was once a prologue, but there are running heads at the top of the folio with the verso having 'The Life of' and the recto the saint's name. Bokenham's fellow Augustinian, John Capgrave at Lynn in Norfolk, provides chapter headings in his life of Augustine (though not in his life of Gilbert) in the holograph London, British Library, MS Additional 36704. These are quite brief and are not set apart from the main text but embedded (even though underlined in red and preceded by a red paraph mark at the end of the previous prologue or chapter). For instance, on fol. 6r the first chapter is introduced at the end of the prologue with 'Of þe cuntre and þe town where he was bore' (followed by 'capitulum 1' in red).[13] The mid-fifteenth century

---

[10] *Gilte Legende*, ed. by Hamer, with Russell.

[11] *Supplementary Lives in Some Manuscripts of the 'Gilte Legende'*, ed. by Hamer and Russell, pp. 3–38 (p. 26, l. 925). The other texts with full summary headings are Erkenwald, Jerome, and Barbara, with the 'Pardon of all the churches in Rome', 'What the church betokeneth', and Thomas of Canterbury having only simple title headings to sections rather than summaries as such. The life of Jerome is the same text as that written by Simon Wynter, though it lacks the prologue and chapter lists (see n. 14 below). The life of Barbara is translated from a Latin text by the Flemish Augustinian, Jean de Wackerzeele (*fl.* 1370–1400), which is extant in Durham, Durham University Library, MS Cosin V.iv.4 and London, Lambeth Palace Library, MS 72.

[12] Osbern Bokenham, *Legendys of Hooly Wummen*, ed. by Serjeantson.

[13] The life of Augustine is on fols 5r–45r (with a prologue on fols 5r–6r) and that of Gilbert on fols 46r–116r (with a prologue on fols 46r–47r). Augustine comprises forty-five chap-

FORMAT AND USE OF THE SAINTS' LIVES 275

life of Æthelthryth in Oxford, Corpus Christi College, MS 120 is divided into ten chapters but without summaries. From the same period in the lives of John the Baptist, John the Evangelist, Jerome, and Katherine extant in Cambridge, St John's College, MSS N. 16 and N. 17 there are chapter summaries as well as prologues and lists of chapter headings. For instance, after the prologue and contents/chapter list, the first chapter heading in the life of Katherine is 'Of þe progenitours of Seynt Kateryn and how sche was of þe Emperours blood of Rome. Capitulum .j.'[14] Such summarising traditions continue into the next century in early printed verse and prose lives. For instance, in the verse life of Radegund by Henry Bradshaw (d. 1513) printed in *c.* 1525 (which opens with a list of headings though they are not labelled chapters) we have: 'Howe quene Radegunde shewed a great myracle deliueryng prisoners out of captiuite.'[15]

Despite this rich tradition of aids in reading, Add. 2604 has no prologue, contents list, chapter list, or chapter numbers.[16] Neither is there any indication of authorship, scribe, or sources[17] and, as explained in I. The Manuscript, the title that is now pasted on to the lives may not be original or not completely so.[18] The summary headings are variable in length and detail, with some isolat-

---

ters; Gilbert is made up of sixty chapters; the final text in the manuscript, a tract on the Twelve Patriarchs on fols 116r–119r, is not divided into chapters.

[14] *Virgins and Scholars*, ed. by Waters, p. 284, ll. 102–03. For other manuscripts of the lives of Jerome and Katherine, see pp. 1–2, to which may be added another copy of Jerome; see S. J. Ogilvie-Thomson, *The Index of Middle English Prose: Handlist XXIII, The Rawlinson Collection, Bodleian Library, Oxford* (Cambridge: Brewer, 2017), MS Rawlinson D. 112, [1]–[2] (for the prologue and the text), pp. 212–13. These lives have the following chapters: John the Baptist (eighteen chapters); John the Evangelist (eighteen chapters); Jerome (nineteen chapters); and Katherine of Alexandria (twenty-nine chapters). All have prologues (with a single combined prologue functioning for the Baptist and the Evangelist) and chapter lists.

[15] Henry Bradshaw, *Here begynneth the lyfe of saynt Radegunde* (London: Richard Pynson, *c.* 1525), STC 3507, fol. bi verso.

[16] Lacking therefore are the sort of aims and objectives outlined in the Prologue to the *Gilte Legende*: 'Here biginnyth the meroure and the liuynge of holie martres and of seintis that suffriden here in her liuis great peyne and passioune in encresinge her ioie in the blisse of heuen, to excite and stere symple lettrid men and women to encrese in vertue bi the offten redinge and hiringe of this boke. For bi hiringe mannes bileuinge is mooste stablid and istrengthid [...]', *Gilte Legende*, ed. by Hamer, with Russell, 1 (2006), 3, ll. 1–6.

[17] Whether or not Add. 2604 derived from a manuscript with an opening prologue and chapter numbers is open to debate.

[18] This is pasted on in parts probably by an eighteenth-century owner, George Bird Burrell; see I. The Manuscript.

ing a single event while others cover many paragraphs in a modern edition. They cannot be designated as chapter headings as many of the sections are very short. Presumably the summaries were provided in order to highlight what the translator himself deemed to be important twists in the narratives. On the whole such section summaries do not occur in the sources or analogues identified. One of the main sources of the universal lives, the *Legenda aurea*, lacks all such headings, as do the more immediate analogues, Mombritius's *Sanctuarium* and the *Historie plurimorum sanctorum*. Likewise the direct source of the native lives, John of Tynemouth's *Sanctilogium*, does not have such headings and neither does the analogue in the Sankt Georgen 12 manuscript.[19] There is, however, one potential overlap. The *Liber Eliensis*, one of two sources for the life of Æthelthryth and of Wihtburh, opens with a prologue before being divided into three books with chapter headings. Each of the three books begins with a list of chapter headings and a prologue. Similarly, Goscelin de Saint-Bertin's Life of Edith of Wilton, which is found in Oxford, Bodleian Library, MS Rawlinson C. 938, folios 1r–29r (*s.* xiii), includes a prologue and a series of chapter headings.[20] It is therefore not clear if the compiler of Add. 2604 was influenced in his choice of summaries either by earlier or contemporary precedents — and it could have been both.[21]

The fact that Add. 2604 is designed in this way *may* indicate that the reading of the collective lives was to last for an extended period of time (although there are other interpretations). It has already been noted in IV. Hagiographical Context and the Selection of Saints that the contents of Add. 2604 as they currently stand may form three cycles. Each little cycle may last from approximately late June to late November (a period of approximately six months), or to be precise, from John the Baptist on 24 June to Barbara on 16 December; from Æthelthryth on 23 June to Hild on 17 November; and from Martha on 29 July

---

[19] For a full discussion of the relationship of these manuscripts to the lives in Add. 2604, see V. Latin Sources and Analogues.

[20] These chapter headings, such as 'How her royal parents equipped this jewel of the church with learning' are listed in the most recent edition: 'Goscelin's Legend of Edith', trans. by Michael Wright and Kathleen Loncar, in *Writing the Wilton Women: Goscelin's 'Legend of Edith' and 'Liber confortatorius'*, ed. by Stephanie Hollis and others, Medieval Women: Texts and Contexts, 9 (Turnhout: Brepols, 2004), pp. 15–93 (pp. 21–22). The phrasing is notable in that many of the chapter headings begin with 'How' as they do in Add. 2604.

[21] One way or another, given the chapter summaries in the Syon lives and *Supplementary Lives* to the '*Gilte Legende*' (see nn. 11 and 14), the lives in Add. 2604 may be said to be of the moment in terms of presentation.

FORMAT AND USE OF THE SAINTS' LIVES

to Leonard on 6 November.[22] If each cycle were divided into folios (including those now missing or cut out), this would mean that the first cycle would last from fols 1r–52v (fifty-two folios), the second from fols 52v–93r (forty-one folios), and the last one from fol. 93r to fol. 152v (fifty-nine folios). Conversely, as also noted, Add. 2604 may form two hierarchical cycles for summer feasts: from John the Baptist to Hild (24 June to 17 November) and from Martha to Leonard (29 July to 6 November), making two unequal sections of fols 1r–93r (ninety-three folios) and fols 93r–152v (fifty-nine folios). In any case whatever the intended order, leaving aside those lives that are known or suspected to be missing, if the structure of the whole manuscript is examined, we get the following series of sections (with full information in Appendix A: Section Summaries and Appendix B: Miracles that are found in our *Edition*):

1. **John the Baptist** (fols 1r–11v)
   (seven section summaries; fourteen miracles)

2. **John the Evangelist** (fols 11v–21v)
   (seven extant section summaries; twelve miracles)

3. **Columba** (fols 22r–25v)
   (three section summaries; three miracles)

4. **Agatha** (fols 25v–32v; imperfect at the end)
   (six extant section summaries; three miracles plus one missing)

5. **Cecilia** (fols 41r–47v; imperfect at the beginning and in the middle)
   (three extant section summaries; six miracles)

6. **Barbara** (fols 47v–52v) (five section summaries; eight miracles)

7. **Æthelthryth** (fols 52v–59r; imperfect towards the end)
   (nine extant section summaries; twelve miracles)

8. **Seaxburh** (fols 59v–61r) (no section summaries; one miracle)

9. **Eormenhild** (fols 61r–62v) (three section summaries; two miracles)

10. **Wærburh** (fols 62v–65r) (four section summaries; six miracles)

11. **Eorcengota** (and **Æthelburh**) (fols 65r–66v)
    (two section summaries; four miracles)

12. **Wihtburh** (fols 66v–69r) (five section summaries; seven miracles)

---

[22] For the cycles and complexities with regard to some of the feast days, see IV. Hagiographical Context and the Selection of Saints.

13. **Edith** (fols 69v–75v)
    (nine section summaries; fourteen miracles)

14. **Eadburh** (fols 76r–79r) (ten section summaries; nine miracles)

15. **Eanswith** (fols 79r–80v; imperfect at the end) (three extant
    section summaries; three miracles plus potentially one missing)

16. **Hild** (fols 89r–93r; imperfect at the beginning)
    (four extant section summaries; seven miracles)

17. **Martha** (fols 93r–97v) (three section summaries; eight miracles)

18. **Domitilla** (fols 97v–98r) (no section summaries; no miracles)

19. **Justina** (fols 98r–105v; imperfect at the end) (four extant
    section summaries; seven miracles plus probably one missing)

20. **Benedicta** (fols 108r–112v; imperfect at the beginning) (two extant
    section summaries; three miracles plus probably one missing)

21. **Modwenna** (fols 113r–136v; imperfect in the middle)
    (thirty-two extant section summaries; thirty-two miracles)

22. **Leonard** (fols 137r–152v; imperfect throughout) (three extant
    section summaries; six miracles plus probably six missing)

Recalling then the idea of the mini-cycles, if each one of these is calculated, we find that there are thirty-three sections in the first cycle, fifty in the second, and thirty-eight in the third, or, if there are two cycles, eighty-three in the first and thirty-eight in the second. Admittedly, these figures are far from exact given the missing folios, but currently the lives represent a total of one hundred and twenty-one sections. These vary considerably in length but on average are about a folio (although sometimes much less, particularly at the end of lives where there are many miracles). Apart from the very lengthy life of Modwenna that has twenty-five sections and Leonard (where so much is missing that it is difficult to be accurate), the average number of sections veers between one and ten. Such a breakdown in the texts would therefore easily facilitate reading in manageable stints; something particularly necessary given the temporal rigidity of the monastic day.

To get an idea of how the sections work within each life — and how they might have been used for daily or occasional reading — we may examine the section summaries in three complete lives, one biblical, one universal, and one native life in John the Baptist, Barbara, and Eadburh (for the complete list, see Appendix A: Section Summaries in the *Edition*).

FORMAT AND USE OF THE SAINTS' LIVES 279

1. John the Baptist (fols 1r–11v) (7 section summaries)

> **fol. 1r**: Here begynnyth the lyfe of Seynt Iohn Baptist

> **fol. 1r**: Of the holy birth of Seynt Iohn Baptist, howe his modir was warnyd for to bringe forth a childe in hir olde age of the same aungell that our lady was gret with [1]

> **fol. 3r**: Howe this holy childe Iohn at twelue yere olde went into desert for to fle ydell speches and delycates of the worlde [2]

> **fol. 3v**: Howe aftirwarde for he reprovid Herode in as moche as he was weddid to his brothers wyfe and lyued with hir in avowtry he was behedid [3]

> **fol. 5r**: Of the bonys of Seynt Iohn, howe they were gadrid togedir aftir his deth and brennyd, and howe somme of the bonys were founde and brought to Ierusalem vnbrent [4]

> **fol. 6r**: Howe by reuelacion the hed of Seynt Iohn Baptiste was founde [5]

> **fol. 8v**: Of a miracle, howe his holy fynger which shewed and poynted Criste Ihesus was founde whan he sayde *Ecce agnus dei* [6]

> **fol. 9r**: Of the miracles that were shewed in diuerse places to diuerse men of Seynt Iohn Baptist [7]

> **fol. 11v**: Thus endith the lyfe of Seynt Iohn Baptiste.

6. Barbara (fols 47v–52v) (5 section summaries)

> **fol. 47v**: Here begynnyth the life of Seynt Barbara the virgyn and martir

> **fol. 47v**: Howe this holy mayde Seynt Barbara was desired for to be weddid and in what wyse she excused hir to hir fadir [1]

> **fol. 48v**: Howe this holy mayde was blamyd of hir fadir because she made the masons for to make the third wyndowe [2]

> **fol. 49v**: Howe she stode afore the iustice and answerd mightely in defending of Cristen faythe [3]

> **fol. 50v**: Howe our lorde comfortid that holy maid in all hir passions and howe cruelly the iustice cutt of hir brestis of from hir body [4]

> **fol. 51v**: Howe hir fadir at last lad hir to an hille and there, aftir tyme she had made hir prayers to God, he smote of hir hede [5]

> **fol. 52v**: This endith the martirdome of Seynt Barbara.

14. Eadburh (fols 76r–79r) (10 section summaries)

fol. 76r: Here begynnyth the holy life of Seynt Edburgh, abbes of Tenett aftir Seynt Mildrede

fol. 76r: Of the holy begynnyng of Seynt Edburgh and howe [she] founde hir nece Seynt Mildrede lighing all hole in hir tombe [1]

fol. 76v: Howe she continued to the laste ende and what vertues she vsed [2]

fol. 77r: Of a yong man which was dome from his birth, howe by miracle of this holy mayde myght speke [3]

fol. 77r: Of a prest of the monastery of Seynt Edburgh which was necligent of the relikes of Seynt Edburgh what vengeaunce fell to him [4]

fol. 77v: Of a chartour of fundacion of hir monastery, howe it might not brenne in þe fyre [5]

fol. 78r: Of a woman which was longe seke, howe by miracle of ths holy mayde was made all hole [6]

fol. 78r: Of a miracle shewid to a preste which was tormentid of þe Danes [7]

fol. 78r: Of a thefe what vengeaunce fell to him because he wolde not knowlege his trespace truly [8]

fol. 78v: Of a woman that helyd by miracle of Seynt Edburgh which had be many yeris afore seke [9]

fol. 78v: Of diuerse opinions whethir she lyeth shryned at Seynt Austeyns or at Seynt Gregories [10]

fol. 79r: Thus endith þe life of Seynt Edburgh.

The summaries indicate how the lives are structured narratively and how they function to different effects. They serve, like a contents page, to give the reader an overall view of each life. Indeed, they may be said to work almost like book-marks to help the reader find her way through the texts. Reading is further facilitated by the fact that catchwords occur throughout the manuscript and not just at the end of quires; this is a feature common in printed books but also enables a reader to negotiate the text more easily (particularly if being read aloud). Above all, what is very apparent from these summaries (as in all the lives in Add. 2604) is the relative proportioning of a life in terms of biography and/ or miracle working, and the degree to which either or both are privileged. At a glance we can see that John the Baptist has an even balance between the two.

FORMAT AND USE OF THE SAINTS' LIVES

The life begins by tracing the high points of his biblical history in the first three sections: his miraculous birth, his time in the desert, his encounter with Herodias that leads to his beheading. The summary of the narrative combines both an exemplary life and wondrous powers, particularly in the hereafter. There may be fourteen miracles in his life yet only three are deemed important enough for their own summary heading: the burning of his bones, the discovery of his head, and the relic of his finger, with the final section being a catch-all heading for the rest of his postmortem miracles, 'Of the miracles that were shewed in diurse places [...] (fol. 9r). Conversely the emphasis in Barbara's life is not on her eight miracles but on the potency of her life on her way to martyr-dom. The five sections serve to reveal the full plot of Barbara's history (which in turn echoes the life story of every other virgin martyr): her refusal to marry, her devotion to the Trinity, her defence of her Christian faith, her physical punishments, her beheading. By maintaining her virginal state, Barbara proves her sanctity on earth. Eadburh, on the other hand, exerts her sanctity primarily after her physical life has ended. This is clearly obvious in that five of the ten summaries are devoted to miracles of various kinds and a couple to acts of vengeance meted out respectively to a priest (later miraculously rescued by Eadburh) who neglects Eadburh's relics and to a thief whose unrepentance condemns him. Eadburh is therefore grounded in her community in death as well as in life. Clearly the way in which all these lives are composed owes much not only to the sources or analogues underpinning them, but also to how the compiler (or his immediate sources) viewed such works and presented them to the public.

As is shown in Appendix B in the *Edition* where the range of miracles is given in full (and as will be illustrated *inter alia* below), the miracles through-out Add. 2604 tend to fall into different categories: as portents of the saints' present or future sanctity, as illustrative of their overcoming the tortures of their oppressors, or as miraculous works performed by the saints either before and/or after their physical deaths. There are patterns to these miracles in operation throughout the volume as well as some subtle differences. In the universal lives there are more miracles in those of the three male saints, John the Baptist, John the Evangelist, and Leonard (except that they are also correspondingly longer lives). The lives of the female martyrs focus on miracles testifying to their suffering and relief thereof: Columba is defended by a bear from an attempted rape; Agatha's breasts are cut off but later restored; and Cecilia emerges unscathed from three days in a bath of boiling water, and so forth. Apart from an angel miraculously attending Agatha's burial (now missing owing to lacking folios) and Martha's curative powers after her death, many of the universal lives lack postmortem miracles, apart from Leonard where there is an excess of miracles at the end (though many of these are now imperfect owing to missing folios). It is noteworthy that saints such as Barbara often have numerous postmortem miracles attached to their lives, but these do not occur in Add. 2604.[23] Either the compiler did not wish to use these miracles or, alternatively, they were not appended to his Latin sources. That the latter explanation is the more likely is borne out by the fact that the miracles linked to the male lives are all found in their sources or analogues.

In the universal lives the overall focus in the miracles inevitably concerns the smoothing out or the speeding up of the path to heaven. In the native lives the concentration — although with the same ultimate aim — is understandably more on the quotidian. Miracles are particularly ubiquitous in the native lives, where the translator provides multiple instances of a saint's efficacy in the everyday world, although this move is one that his source uses as well. As noted, the life of Eadburh (as with many of the native saints) is really just a long list of miracles with a section summary devoted to each. Native saints are celebrated here for their interventions in the lives of those who petition them for help in sickness, as well as for help against tyrannical behaviour, as in the life of Eormenhild. The miracles show their power over the natural world, including turning water into wine (Modwenna), making water change its course (Eanswith), drawing water into a protective moat (Æthelthryth), and Wærburh, Eanswith, and Hild all have miracles in which the saints command the behaviour of various birds or fowl. The saints' potency over the worldly is also manifest in miracles in which those who abuse their power are defeated: sheriffs lose out (Æthelthryth and Modwenna), a local lord is thwarted (Wihtburh), a bailiff who strikes a gamekeeper is overcome (Wærburh), and a schoolmaster who beats children is punished (Eormenhild). Incorruption of the body is extremely important in the lives of Æthelthryth, Wærburh, Eorcengota, Æthelburh, Wihtburh, and Edith. This is the premier sign of God's beneficence for their exemplary lives as well as a tangible sign of virginity. Aside from the resurrection of the dead (either human or animal), the most common miracles across all of the lives, both universal and native, are those in which the saints deliver petitioners from some type of bondage: Eormenhild releases the Ely schoolmaster from the twisted bondage in which she places him; Martha relieves King Clodeve of France of his kidney or groin problems; and Leonard delivers the Queen of France in

---

[23] This is in contrast, for instance, to Barbara in the *Supplementary Lives* to the *'Gilte Legende'*, where miracle after miracle occurs at the end of the life; *Supplementary Lives in Some Manuscripts of the 'Gilte Legende'*, ed. by Hamer and Russell, pp. 383–470 (pp. 440–70).

FORMAT AND USE OF THE SAINTS' LIVES

childbirth, while the common motif of the delivery of a petitioner from prison is found in the lives of Æthelthryth, Eormenhild, and Leonard.

The fact that the lives are structured in this way, with such an overall emphasis on miracles, may be connected with how these lives were expected to be used. If the manuscript were intended for an East Anglian nunnery, as we argue, then it makes sense for the emphasis to be on miracles that have been carried out locally (or at least in the wider region). But, this does not imply that the native lives are privileged over the universal. As we shall see below in The Narrative, what is most important about this volume is the way in which the compiler cuts across chronological boundaries, tying native and universal narratives together thematically, even as he uses similar structural and stylistic strategies. These lives were to be appreciated as a unit, even if their mode of division allowed them to be read, as need be, in what are sometimes quite small sections.

How they were used can only be surmised, but we know that there were many opportunities for devout reading in medieval convents throughout Europe, even if the surviving evidence is somewhat lop-sided and the English situation has to be largely reconstructed and re-imagined on the basis of information from elsewhere.[24] The relative dearth of manuscripts, the almost wholesale loss or destruction of the physical fabric of medieval English convents, and the lack of concrete information from England means that we rely particularly on evidence from research on Dutch, German, and Swedish convents.[25] Much information is available about the prevalence of refectory or table reading in German and Swedish nunneries where saints' lives could be used for the purpose.[26] In the Swedish Birgittine tradition the usual structure of table reading was quite defined and owed much to what was typical of monastic theology. The Birgittine rule specified two opportunities in the day for table reading:

[24] For the evidence that is available about devout reading among women (both secular and religious) in medieval England, see the relevant references in n. 6 of the Preface.

[25] Such issues are fully discussed in the introductions to and essays in the following collections all edited by Blanton, O'Mara, and Stoop: *Nuns' Literacies in Medieval Europe: The Hull Dialogue*; *Nuns' Literacies in Medieval Europe: The Kansas City Dialogue*; and *Nuns' Literacies in Medieval Europe: The Antwerp Dialogue*.

[26] See, for instance, Cynthia J. Cyrus in *The Scribes for Women's Convents in Late Medieval Germany* (Toronto: University of Toronto Press, 2009), especially pp. 114–17, and Jonas Carlquist, 'The Birgittine Sisters at Vadstena Abbey: Their Learning and Literacy, with Particular Reference to Table Reading', in *Nuns' Literacies in Medieval Europe: The Hull Dialogue*, ed. by Blanton, O'Mara, and Stoop, pp. 239–51. For the English Birgittines see Hutchison, 'What the Nuns Read'.

during meal times between 8am to 9am, and 4pm to 5pm; additionally some of the time from 6pm to 7pm was also set aside for edifying reading.[27] Of course, a book primarily designed for table reading would not preclude its being read by an individual nun with the ability to do so. In the case of Add. 2604 it takes about three minutes to read each folio aloud at a measured pace, making the whole of John the Baptist about thirty minutes long, Barbara fifteen minutes long, and Eadburh ten minutes long. And the pacing is important. Nuns at Barking were given one book per year. This hardly indicates a rapid reading speed, though what was distributed officially may not have comprised a nun's only reading material.[28]

In format Add. 2604 would have made for ideal reading. It is small enough for an individual to hold, and the layout and script are very clear. The opening illuminated initials and obvious titles make finding the individual lives easy while the section summaries also serve to make the lives more user-friendly for the individual reader, whether this be the person in charge of any table reading (if the book was used for this purpose) or the private reader. The summaries enable relatively easy searching for the reader(s) interested particularly in miracle stories as well as allowing discrete sections to be read at different points without necessarily losing the overall plot. In any case this is usually straightforward apart from convoluted cases like Justina or lengthy examples like Modwenna. A reader could easily have found the preferred parts and skipped those least favoured. There are various contemporary medieval precedents for this. Nicholas Love in his *Mirrour of the Blessed Life of Jesus Christ* has no scruples about encouraging his readers to exercise their own judgement in selecting material. While acknowledging that Bonaventure (or rather pseudo-Bonaventure, the supposed author of the *Meditationes Vitae Christi*) divided his work into contemplations for the seven days of the week, in the explicit Love nevertheless argues for a greater freedom for his reader, even if he had maintained the same structure:

---

[27] Carlquist, 'The Birgittine Sisters at Vadstena Abbey', p. 241.

[28] The Barking *Ordinale* specified that this annual distribution should take place on the Monday in the first week of Lent. At that time a nun should return the book given her in the previous year, confess and do penance if she had not read it, and then accept another book for the current year; *The Ordinale and Customary of the Benedictine Nuns of Barking Abbey*, ed. by J. B. L. Tolhurst, Henry Bradshaw Society, 65–66, 2 vols (London: Henry Bradshaw Society, 1927–28), I (1927), 67–68, with notes by Dame Laurentia McLachlan O.S.B. in II (1928), 373–74 where it is pointed out (p. 373) that this distribution is in line with ch. 48 of the Rule of St Benedict.

THE NARRATIVE

[...] þerfore it semeþ not conuenient to folowe þe processe þerof by þe dayes of þe
wike after þe entent of þe forseide Bonauentur, for it were to tediouse as me þinkeþ,
& also it shulde so sone be fulsome & not in confortable deynteþ by cause of þe
freelte of mankynde þat haþ likynge to here & knowe newe þinges & þoo þat bene
seldome herde bene oft in the more deynteþ. Wherefore it semeþ to me beste þat
euery deuout creature þat loueþ to rede or [to] here þis boke take þe partes þerof as
it semeþ most confortable & stirying to his deuocion, sumtyme one & sumtyme an
oþere, & specialy in þe tymes of þe ʒere & þe festes ordeynet in holy chirche, as þe
matires bene perteynent to hem.[29]

Simon Wynter in his prologue to his life of St Jerome in the Syon collection is
equally indulgent of his reader when he says

Thus ys this werke diuided into .xix. chapititris, that ʒe shall not bene ouer wery to
rede hit, whyle ʒe may at yche chapitris ende haue a restynge place, and oon tyme
rede oon, anothir tyme anothir ʒyf ʒe haue leyser to rede no moo at ones.[30]

Being guided throughout, someone reading Add. 2604 may have taken a similarly easy-going approach in their reading. The text is broken down into manageable structural units, and, as we shall see, the narrative style also facilitates
ready understanding and pious enjoyment.

The Narrative

However and wherever the lives were read (either in the refectory or in private),
the reading experience was enhanced by the vibrant and engaging style of the
writer in Add. 2604, which is very much that of the story-teller.[31] In his use of
lively dialogues, colourful descriptions, and emotive speeches, he gives a powerful voice to the devout saint, particularly the female virgin, while at the same
time connecting implicitly with the medieval nun.[32] Reading the lives sequen-

[29] Nicholas Love, *The Mirror of the Blessed Life of Jesus Christ*, ed. by Sargent, p. 220, ll. 25–36.

[30] *Virgins and Scholars*, ed. by Waters, p. 182, ll. 52–54. The life of Jerome was written at
the behest of Margaret Holland, Duchess of Clarence, who commissioned Karlsruhe, Landesbibliothek Cod. Sankt Georgen 12 (discussed in V. Latin Sources and Analogues); it may be
that Wynter was addressing his remarks specifically to Margaret, though they could equally
apply to any reader as Margaret was enjoined in the prologue to have copies made of the work.

[31] In this discussion we shall continue to refer interchangeably to the narrator, translator,
compiler, or writer of Add. 2604, meaning the text as we have it in the manuscript.

[32] The Add. 2604 translator is not, of course, unique either in English or European circles in making efforts to envigorate his narrative; for instance, in Emma Gatland, *Women from*

tially one is struck by their unified tone and coherent focus. In this respect we differ markedly from the interpretation put forward by Cynthia Turner Camp. Stemming from her central thesis that English vernacular lives can be as much history as hagiography (with which we would not disagree), in her concentration on Æthelthryth (with some reference to the other early English saints in Add. 2604), she notes of Martha, Domitilla, Justina, and Benedicta:

> These four early Christian women fit uncomfortably into this affinity. What role, then, do they play in the collection? I suggest these lives function as a contrast class, defining ideal English conventual life by possessing only one possible trait of good abbesses and nuns — the label. These four saints' marginality is crucial, because as margin they establish the conceptual edge of the community, structurally delimiting the bare minimum necessary to be incorporated into this pedigree. As such, they cement this lineage's most significant features: consecration as nun, and to a lesser degree holy female kin. They also highlight by contrast the traits shared by the other nuns: Englishness, ascetic renunciations, the edification of nunneries.[33]

As we hope to have shown throughout this *Study*, this is but a partial view of this complicated collection and the permeable borders between hagiography and history, between native and universal, between this world and the next.

Although much is missing through the imperfect form of the manuscript, what is here reads consistently like the work of one translator or compiler (who is probably the same person), written in one East Anglian dialect for one audience. Stylistically on occasion the Latinate syntax and diction — often the bane of late Middle English translators — militate against total stylistic success.[34]

---

the *'Golden Legend': Female Authority in a Medieval Castilian Sanctoral*, Colección Támesis, Serie A: Monografías, 296 (Woodbridge: Tamesis, 2011), it is pointed out that in a particular manuscript of her edited Castilian text based on the *Legenda aurea* 'The changes might have been intended to produce more accessible texts, and often result in more immediate and vivid hagiographic accounts' (p. 134). Vitz expands on differences between Latin and vernacular hagiography, with particular reference to the *Legenda aurea*; Evelyn Birge Vitz, 'From the Oral to the Written in Medieval and Renaissance Saints' Lives', in *Images of Sainthood in Medieval Europe*, ed. by Renate Blumenfeld-Kosinski and Timea Szell (Ithaca, NY: Cornell University Press, 1991), pp. 97–114. Other ways of rendering a saint's narrative concrete and immediate are explored in Florence Bourgne, 'Translating Saints' Lives into the Vernacular: *Translatio Studii* and *Furta Sacra* (Translation as Theft)', in *The Medieval Translator: Traduire au Moyen Âge*, 5, ed. by Roger Ellis and René Tixier (Turnhout: Brepols, 1996), pp. 50–63.

[33] Camp, *Anglo-Saxon Saints' Lives as History Writing*, p. 97.

[34] The phenomenon of translation and its varied results is usefully dealt with in Samuel K. Workman, *Fifteenth Century Translation as an Influence on English Prose*, Princeton Studies in English, 18 (Princeton, NJ: Princeton University Press, 1940). More up-to-date discus-

THE NARRATIVE   287

These difficulties consist of simple cases of non-English word order, for instance, in the life of Cecilia, 'come in Tyburce' (5/47–48), or being defeated by place-names that the translator invariably renders in a semi-Latinate fashion.[35] Or occasionally they can involve convoluted syntactical muddles, as noted in the various Commentaries in our *Edition*. But overall the Add. 2604 writer manages to translate his varied sources if not always adroitly then very competently. His usual method is to stay close to the source or analogue; this is certainly the case for the native lives dependent on John of Tynemouth's *Sanctilogium*, and for the universal lives of John the Baptist, John the Evangelist, Cecilia, and Martha that are definitely translated from the *Legenda aurea*. In some of the other lives the results are more varied, although this may have as much to do with the non-identification of definite sources as anything else.[36] At no point is there any evidence that this is a writer who involves himself in what has been called John Lydgate's 'saintly poetics' or John Capgrave's 'vernacular humanism', in other words, an engagement with classical authors and the associated discourse of laureation.[37] Indeed, this is a writer who seems immune to the influence of the showy classics or the quest for self-conscious literariness and may be content partly to accept that 'Texts about sanctity are self-sufficient in their authoritative claims; hence it stands to reason that the texts do not need, and even forbid, the authors' creative input'.[38] Yet within what might be regarded as

sions of translation practice are available in *The Oxford History of Literary Translation*, 1: *To 1550*, ed. by Roger Ellis (Oxford: Oxford University Press, 2008); see especially the following essays: Nicholas Watson, 'Theories of Translation', pp. 73–91; A. E. B. Coldiron, 'William Caxton', pp. 160–69; Vincent Gillespie, 'Religious Writing', pp. 234–83; and Alexandra Barratt, 'Women Translators of Religious Texts', pp. 284–95. For the work of medieval translation across the European vernaculars, see the various volumes of *The Medieval Translator/Traduire au Moyen Âge* series edited by Roger Ellis and others by various publishers from 1989 onwards.

[35] Notes on these Latin place-names are given in the Commentaries to the individual saints and in Appendix C: Place-Names in our *Edition*.

[36] See the individual Overviews and Commentaries in our *Edition*.

[37] These are both terms used in the introduction to *Sanctity as Literature in Late Medieval Britain*, ed. by Von Contzen and Bernau, pp. 6–7, and elsewhere in this interesting collection of essays.

[38] *Sanctity as Literature in Late Medieval Britain*, ed. by Von Contzen and Bernau, p. 10. It would seem that in this regard the lives in Add. 2604 have more in common with an earlier tradition of hagiographical writing such as the *Scottish Legendary* (*c.* 1390) in resisting the 'literary turn'; see in particular, Eva von Contzen, 'Narrating Vernacular Sanctity: The Scottish Legendary as a Challenge to the "Literary Turn" in Fifteenth-Century Hagiography', in *Sanctity as Literature in Late Medieval Britain*, ed. by Von Contzen and Bernau, pp. 172–90.

288   VI. READING THE 'LYVES AND DETHES'

such old fashioned parameters, where the immutable plot is key, he makes these lives his own.

As demonstrated by Eva von Contzen, part of the difficulty with 'the analysis of saints' lives as narratives is the fact that hagiography is a very conservative and inflexible genre, which relies heavily on translations and the borrowing of stock elements'.[39] Drawing on a wide range of modern narrative theories, she envisages the solution in the separation of the 'story' level (the content) from the 'discourse' level (how the content is communicated).[40] In this respect crucial too are medieval attitudes to translation, to the extent that these can be extrapolated from the available evidence.[41] In the case of the writer of Add. 2604 we have no sense of what he thought about translation. He himself is anonymous and, unlike some of his contemporaries, he left no prologue, no address to the reader, nor statement of intent. But, in one instance at least, it is possible to show how he deals with a known source in comparison to some fellow hagiographers.[42] The choice of excerpt is the self-contained exemplum in the life of John the Evangelist that tells of the two young men who are taught the difference between worldly and spiritual wealth by John. The source of this is the *Legenda aurea* life of the Evangelist and it is found in his life in Add. 2604, the *Gilte Legende*, Bokenham's Abbotsford legendary, the Syon life, and the *Golden Legend*, alongside Mirk's *Festial* for good measure (though it is missing from the other extensive orthodox sermon collection, the *Speculum sacerdotale*). As may be seen from the six translations quoted below in Appendix 3: Middle English Translations of John the Evangelist, each writer is following

The texts are available in *Legends of the Saints in the Scottish Dialect of the Fourteenth Century*, ed. by W. M. Metcalfe, The Scottish Text Society, 13, 18, 23. 25, 35, 37, 3 vols (Edinburgh: William Blackwood and Sons, 1887–96).

[39] Von Contzen, *The Scottish Legendary*, p. 13.

[40] Von Contzen, *The Scottish Legendary*, p. 14; see ch. 1, 'Towards a Narrative Poetics of Medieval Saints' Lives', pp. 31–52, for a wide-ranging theoretical discussion.

[41] See Watson, 'Theories of Translation', in which he explores what may be gleaned about medieval attitudes. Such ideas are also explored in *The Idea of the Vernacular: An Anthology of Middle English Literary Theory, 1280–1520*, ed. by Jocelyn Wogan-Browne and others, Exeter Medieval Texts and Studies (Exeter: University of Exeter Press, 1999).

[42] There are few universal lives in Add. 2604 that routinely occur in other Middle English prose collections with the main two being John the Baptist and John the Evangelist. The life of the former (being a mixture of the Nativity and the Decollation) is complex; the life of the latter is more straightforward and so an extract from this is chosen for comparison. For the Add. 2604's writer's translational treatment of the Native Saints (a far more complicated case), see Appendix 2 and the discussion in V. Latin Sources and Analogues.

THE NARRATIVE   289

the Latin according to his own lights and also in accordance with whatever manuscript of the *Legenda aurea* was being used in each case. They demonstrate quite a range on the discourse level either adding incidental details or elaborating on the facts. Even such a small sample gives a few hints about textual relationships. For instance, following the Latin 'Duo insuper iuuenes', all the translations refer to 'two young men' apart from Caxton who calls them 'two brethern'. In virtually all cases, including the standard Latin, on their introduction the youths are anonymous. However, Bokenham goes on later to refer to them as 'two brethern' and to name them, 'of whiche oon was clepid Accius and that othir hight Rugius' and the Add. 2604 translator calls them 'Actil and Eugenye'. These names demonstrate that both Bokenham and the Add. 2604 translator were using a *Legenda aurea* manuscript in the VE* tradition. This variant of the standard *Legenda aurea* reads 'honorati: quorum unus Accius, alter Eugenius uocabatur'.[43] Either Bokenham misread 'Eugenius' for 'Rugius' or his source manuscript had this name, while 'Actil' as a variant of 'Accius' is not implausible. Another example sets Mirk and Caxton apart from the other translators. Mirk refers to the youths coming 'into þe cyte of Pargame' as does Caxton with 'into the cyte of Pergania [*Pergama?*]', but, following the standard Latin, none of the other translators names the place. This single shared detail shows that in a way that cannot now be reconstructed both Mirk and Caxton were making use of a particular tradition of the *Legenda aurea*. The final decision to be made by all the writers is whether or not to include John's lengthy sermon after this extract; only Mirk (paradoxically as a preacher himself) and the Syon life choose to exclude it. Yet irrespective of their decisions and variable textual traditions, they all more or less qualify as close translations and so keep the plot or story level intact. In effect they conform with the Latin, but in different ways.

In the context of the life one translation is about as effective as another and the Add. 2604 hagiographer shows himself to be as competent as a known professional like Bokenham. Indeed, taken as a whole, their techniques are not dissimilar, with their emphasis on telling a good story unencumbered by detail or explication. As noted by Simon Horobin in his overview of Bokenham's life of George:

---

[43] ix, 'De sancto Iohanne Evangelista', in Iacopo da Varazze, *Legenda aurea con le miniature del codice Ambrosiano C 240 inf.*, ed. by Maggioni, I, 102–13 (p. 104, critical apparatus for sentence 41).

Bokenham frequently omits additional sources quoted by Jacobus, especially ones that involve learned debate concerning the authenticity of the events described, or that engage in more complex theological matters [...] they reflect Bokenham's overriding concern with narrative, and a desire not to interrupt the story with excessive summary and commentary.[44]

The Add. 2604 translator, as we shall see, is writing very much in the tradition that where the plot may be a given and so not to be tampered with, the rendition of that story should be as dramatic and as interesting as possible. Like the writer of the verse legends in the *Scottish Legendary*, this will involve him in the use of dialogue wherever he can.[45] In addition, he will present and prune his narrative to make the most effective story possible while always keeping within acceptable plot parameters.

In accord with his hagiographical sense, there is no evidence that the Add. 2604 writer went out of his way to add new material, apart from anything needed for the purposes of clarification. For instance, in the explicit to the life of Eorcengota (and Æthelburh) when he declares Æthelburh to be '(not the abbes of Berkyng but the abbes of Brige in Fraunce)' (11/48). Indeed, some of the more graphic or homely images that might seem at first sight to be 'original' are actually found in the sources or analogues, for example, the reference to one of the tempting fiends melting away like wax in the life of Justina or the comparison of Leonard looking after his followers to a hen minding her chicks. More significantly, we witness strategic choices being made by the translator: to slim down extraneous detail, to ignore complexity, to accentuate connections among saints, and to elevate above all the speech acts of confessional or martyred virgins.

Like the best narrators, he makes a decided effort to carry his readership or audience with him. The writer has a tendency to insert questions not found in his sources when he is about to explain something; for instance, in the life of John the Baptist: 'Nowe why was Zakarye aferde of the vision of the aungell?' (1/20); 'But, nowe, why was Seynt Iohn called Helye?' (1/25–26); and 'Why was that?' (1/46). He stresses that events have taken place as ordained or ordered, for fear the point may be missed; in the life of John the Baptist when John's head is to be cut off, we are told crisply, 'It was so' (1/125) or when a poor man is commanded to take the saint's head to Emessa, 'He did so' (1/193). In the

[44] *Osbern Bokenham, 'Lives of Saints'*, ed. by Horobin, I (2020), xxix.

[45] Von Contzen, *The Scottish Legendary*, ch. 3, 'Words and Deeds: Character Depiction and Direct Discourse', pp. 87–124.

THE NARRATIVE   291

sources such confirmations are often taken as read, but the narrator here usually ensures that the little twists and turns of the plot are provided.[46] And he also colludes with his readers or listeners so that they do not lose interest: in the life of John the Baptist he says 'Of this I shall telle you a goode ensample' (1/349) and in the life of Eorcengota (and Æthelburh) 'I passe + ouer tho miracles and will say somwhat of hir passing out of this worlde' (11/16–17). The translator's approach serves to ingratiate him with his audience; in the latter life he admits that he can only 'wryte a litill nowe for I fynde no more of hir than I write here' (11/3). Such self-referential asides are occasionally found among other writers of the period, but are particularly noticeable in Add. 2604.[47] Whether or not some of these comments are carried over from his (mostly unknown) sources for universal lives, they lend an authenticity to the narrative. Of the asides in the native lives, only one is from John of Tynemouth: 'And thankid be God and Seynt Edburgh' (14/109). Otherwise, they are uniquely the translator's in the life of Eorcengota and Æthelburh, in the section summaries, and at the end of a section (11/2–3, 11/16–17, 11/37, 11/46). There is also an aside in Wihtburh (12/66). When in the life of Eorcengota he names Eormenhild as the sister of Eorcengota 'whos [fol. 65v] lyfe is writen afore' (11/2) — which is true in that Eorcengota's life precedes Eormenhild's in Add. 2604 — the modern scholar is consequently more likely to believe that the volume once had a life of Iphigenia that no longer exists. It is referenced in the life of Domitilla, who 'folowed the steppes of Seynt Effigenye þat was in hir dayes, whan Seynt Mathewe [was], veyled and consecrate, as it is [fol. 98r] rehersid afore' (18/7–9).

The writer is at times particularly explicit about his difficulties in ascertaining his facts. An example of this is in the life of John the Baptist when he wonders about whether or not Herodias's daughter was drowned by falling through the ice, which — albeit in the *Legenda aurea* source — is expanded

[46] There are, of course, some exceptions to this: for instance, John of Tynemouth, the source of the life, notes that Wihtburh was first buried in Dereham; by omitting this fact, the Middle English translator creates a logistical problem when the body is eventually translated into Dereham church; see the Commentary to 12/40–47 in our *Edition*.

[47] For instance, in the tract on the Twelve Orders of the Patriarchs on fols 116r–119r in London, British Library, MS Additional 36704 John Capgrave says in his final sentence (with abbreviations expanded and editorial capitalisation and punctuation added), 'This son because he is ȝongest of age is likned on to an ordre whech is not in þe world, as þei sey, but in Northfolk. Foure houses had þei and on of hem is fall onto < þe> kynges hand and he gaue it to Walsingham; þe hous hite Petirston. Oþer informacion of hem haue I not at þis tyme' (fol. 119r).

upon here. He gives the impression that he is taking his readers into his confidence. At the end of the life of Eadburh he acknowledges the multiple claims to her relics and the whereabouts of her resting place, either at St Gregory's or St Augustine's in Canterbury, and then gives up with 'Whos opinions and altercacion I leve to be discussed of wyse men for as I fynde <in> euery eyþer place so I wryte' (14/120–21). And he admits quite openly that he can find no more about Domitilla: 'I suppose, because of grete persecucions that were that tyme in þe begynnyng of the chirch, ther was no more mencion made of hir life [...]' (18/5–6). Likewise, he is keen to be seen to make determined efforts to ascertain the truth of various sources; for instance, when he closes down speculation about John the Evangelist's wedding to Mary Magdalene, he says '(where and whan can nowhere be founde writton)' (2/26–27). In this particular case, of course, he may be using the typical rhetorical ploy of apophasis by drawing attention to the very point that is being glossed over, the well-known myth of the intended marriage of Mary Magdalene and John the Evangelist.[48] Yet the approach here is also very much in keeping with what might be expected for an audience of nuns, who no doubt should not be overly reminded that the virginal role model, John the Evangelist, so favoured as a dedicatee of English convents,[49] was in some medieval quarters associated with the greatest prostitute of the Middle Ages, albeit one who also became the best known penitent sinner and female reforming preacher.[50] While the Add. 2604 translator may just have been taking such cues directly from his source copy, this sense of the writerly presence is one that is bound to intrigue.

Overall the feeling of verisimilitude by an engaged narrator is increased by the lives' characteristic use of a great deal of dialogue (often missing from the sources or analogues). These benign exchanges with the saints or heated con-

---

[48] For a discussion of the apocryphal tradition linking John's virginity, his supposed wedding, and the marriage at Cana, see Annette Volfing, *John the Evangelist in Medieval German Writing: Imitating the Inimitable* (Oxford: Oxford University Press, 2001), 'The Biographical Tradition', pp. 11–59 (pp. 26–33).

[49] For such dedications, see Alison Binns, *Dedications of Monastic Houses in England and Wales, 1066–1216*, Studies in the History of Medieval Religion, 1 (Woodbridge: Boydell, 1989). Leaving aside the Virgin Mary with 235 dedications in monastic churches, John the Evangelist ranks fifth with eighteen dedications, just behind John the Baptist with twenty-one (p. 18).

[50] For Mary Magdalene, see Katherine Ludwig Jansen, *The Making of the Magdalen: Preaching and Popular Devotion in the Later Middle Ages* (Princeton, NJ: Princeton University Press, 2000).

THE NARRATIVE 293

frontations between them and their opponents ensure that the narratives have few *longueurs*. The common use of direct speech, even in cases where there is indirect speech in the source (for instance, in Modwenna 21/123–28) gives the impression of events unfolding within earshot. Immediacy is also evident in the way the writer routinely makes sure to cite the main people by name, a feature not always found in the sources or analogues. For instance, in the life of Cecilia in the translation of sentences 58, 59, 77, 82, and 94 from the *Legenda aurea* the name of the person being addressed is added in each case.[51] Likewise, for example, the importance of Æthelthryth in the life of Seaxburh is emphasised through the mention of her name on six occasions (in the source pronouns are used for five of these). Further, there is an easy familiarity throughout in the way certain participants seek to address their interlocutors at every turn, and the writer can therefore make subtle distinctions in modes of address. Sometimes too he adds a colloquial flair to render the dialogue more realistic; for instance, in the life of Agatha the persecutor's straightforward ultimatum to the virgin is 'Quintianus dixit: Elige tibi unum e duobus [...]', but in the English he sounds more like a ferocious pantomime villain: 'Than in a grete angyr Quyncian seyde to hyr, "Nowe, nowe, chese on of thes ii thinges [...]' (4/80–81). Every effort is made in the translations to render the assailants of the saints as extreme tyrants but often too as ridiculous figures who are never going to gain the upper-hand when it counts: the father and the justice in the life of Barbara are often referred to as being 'wode wroth/e' (6/53, 6/83, 6/138), which makes both sound completely out of control, while in the life of Justina her suitor Agladius, described in the Latin as an 'ignorans infelix', is simply referred to as 'the foole' (19/68). Effectively the medieval female religious reading or listening to these lives are being introduced to the participants through their own words and the nuns' reactions are being moulded by a writer who tries to earn their trust through his imaginative narratorial techniques.

Yet this same writer, who is so punctilious in presenting himself as a diligent investigator, rarely substantiates his statements beyond hearsay. It would seem that he does not want to trouble the reader/listener by providing references or to engage in elaborate — or indeed any — theological controversy or debate, even when both references and exposé are available in his sources. He is satisfied to subsume most authorities under the general title of 'stories'; indeed, in all the lives there is only a handful of cases where the actual patristic or other references are given. One might mention Ambrose, Jerome, Bede, and

---

[51] See the Overview and Commentary to the life of Cecilia in our *Edition* for full information.

John Beleth in John the Baptist (1/46, 1/117, 1/142, and 1/270); Jerome in John the Evangelist (2/248); and Eusebius and Jerome in Martha (17/71 and 17/79). The only memorable specific sources cited are the *Tripartita historia* and Gregory's *Dialogues* in John the Baptist (1/243 and 1/304). In virtually all cases where he uses the generic 'stories', the sources or analogues provide the authority or reference. One can only deduce from these omissions in Add. 2604 that the compiler does not expect his audience to be interested in or knowledgeable about this information or wish to pursue the matter further. Linked to this, and no doubt an indication of the educational level (perceived or otherwise) of his female audience, readers, or listeners, they are virtually always left untroubled by any Latin. In the twenty-two lives there are only eighteen Latin quotations, respectively in the lives of John the Baptist, John the Evangelist, Æthelthryth, Edith, Eadburh, Martha, Justina, Benedicta, Modwenna, and Leonard.[52] Some of these examples are lines from hymns, such as the *Te deum laudamus* in Edith (13/22) or *Gloria in excelsis deo* in Eadburh (14/82), and are not translated. Likewise, passages for liturgical rites are not rendered into English, such as '*In manus tuas domine commendo spiritum meum*' in the life of Martha (17/120–21). Presumably these passages would have been well-known to the audience. Other examples in Latin, such as this line from the psalter in the life of Martha: '*In memoria eterna erit iusta hospita mea ab audicione mala non timebit*' (17/147–48) and readings from the epistle, '*Christus nos redemit de maladicto legis*' (19/284) and gospel, '*Filius meus hic perierat et inventus est*', in Justina (19/286–87), and Old Testament, '*Cultus iustice scilencium*', in Modwenna (21/711) are translated for the reader. This would suggest an audience not entirely comfortable with Latin texts.[53] Similarly, the translator avoids theological explanations. Probably the most obvious example in Add. 2604 is the omission of long sections in the life of

---

[52] Even in comparison with relatively straightforward Middle English sanctorale or other sermons this is a *very* limited range of patristic authorities and biblical references. For these see O'Mara and Paul, *A Repertorium of Middle English Prose Sermons*, I, xlvi and passim.

[53] For all of these Latin examples, see the relevant Commentaries in our *Edition*. Much has been written about the relative Latinity of medieval European nuns; it is unnecessary here to rehearse the multiple and varied arguments put forward in studies such as the three volumes of *Nuns' Literacies in Medieval Europe* and references therein (see the Preface above, n. 6). Taking the overall situation into account, there is limited evidence for Latin knowledge among late medieval English nuns; for instance, one of the repeated complaints in episcopal visitations (albeit not always an impartial source) is that of nuns' failure to understand their own documentary (Latin) material; see further the references in nn. 50–52 of III. Convent and Geographical Location. There are also some specific examples such as Nicholas Rerysby (Resby,

THE NARRATIVE 295

John the Baptist detailing how John's father was punished for his lack of faith before John's birth, the section after his birth about John's nine privileges, and the five reasons for his being worthy. This means that the Add. 2604 compiler never gets bogged down in elaborate divisions or subdivisions. His narratives are consistently hagiographical (bordering on romance in the strict medieval sense of the term) and never homiletic.

In the same way as he omits lengthy explanatory passages that inconveniently interrupt the onward march of the narratives so the writer of Add. 2604 feels free to abbreviate or omit historical details that might slow down the pace or distract from his focus. This is especially obvious with the native saints.[54] Within the lives of the main Ely saints (Æthelthryth, Seaxburh, Æthelburh, and Wihtburh, and their various relatives) there is a deliberate focus on East Anglian genealogy, with details of how each of the women is related to each other. But the writer only takes this so far and truncates genealogical details even when they are given in his source; for example, John of Tynemouth includes Æthelthryth's two brothers, Adulphus and Iurminus, but these go unmentioned in Add. 2604. And sometimes the Add. 2604 writer takes this even further: in the life of Wærburh he abbreviates the opening of John of Tynemouth's narrative by eliminating the genealogical history of the royal family of Kent. Although we cannot be certain in all cases why he omits details in the way he does (and the previous case is a good example of such uncertainty), there are instances where he does so because he wants the focus to be entirely on the female saint under discussion.[55] A good example of this is in the life of

Reysby), Master of the Order of St Gilbert of Sempringham in Lincolnshire, commissioning Capgrave to produce a life of St Gilbert for the 'solitary women' of his order who could not understand Latin, quoted in Pickering, 'Saints' Lives', p. 257.

[54] We would therefore argue that the common rather straightforward separation between martyrs as ahistorical and native saints as historical needs to be tempered somewhat in the case of Add. 2604; for a discussion of such issues see Klaus P. Jankovsky, 'National Characteristics in the Portrayal of English Saints in the *South English Legendary*', in *Images of Sainthood in Medieval Europe*, ed. by Renate Blumenfeld-Kosinski and Timea Szell (Ithaca, NY: Cornell University Press, 1991), pp. 81–93.

[55] In *New Legends of England*, Sanok says that 'A central thesis of this book is that Middle English legends of native saints served as an important narrative forum for exploring competing forms of secular and religious community at local, national, and supernational scales: the monastery, the city, and local devotional groups; the nation and the realm, European Christendom and, at the end of the fifteenth century, a world that was suddenly expanding across the Atlantic' (p. 2). She then proceeds to discuss individual lives to support her thesis, mentioning Add. 2604 only briefly. While it is not possible to be entirely forthright about the translator's

Hild: the translator omits the names of the five bishops (Bosa, Ætla, Oftfor, John, and Wilfrid), which are listed in John of Tynemouth's text and are well-known from John's source (Bede). John of Tynemouth had already excised the long passage outlining their careers, but the translator goes beyond to focus on Hild and her teaching rather than on the bishops. Likewise, he also often ignores the names of minor characters (for example, the deacon who deals with Cyprian's conversion in the life of Justina is named Asterius in the Latin but is anonymous in the English), which again focuses more attention on the saint.[56]

In line with the compression of multiple lines of investigation and the omission of extraneous detail, the translator does not seek to localise or his-toricise in the universal lives. He often omits place-names (or renders them in such a Latinate form that they are virtually incomprehensible) and he skims over interpretative complications (for instance, the differences between the various Herods at the beginning of John the Baptist, all of which are patiently explained in his *Legenda aurea* source). He is content to present historical peri-ods in a broad fashion. In the universal lives he grounds the events in the time of a reigning Roman emperor, which often does little to date the action for the uninitiated. In the other lives he routinely uses the reign of kings for dating purposes, such as Clovis I in the life of Leonard. Sometimes this also allows him to allude to other events such as in the life of Æthelthryth where the mention of Edmund, King of East Anglia (d. 869) is linked to the Danish invasions. But overall his chronological grasp is fairly tenuous and sometimes he does not seem to notice chronological anomalies and dating inconsistencies.[57] For someone so concentrated on the lives and deaths of these saints, even his ability to itemise their feast-days is a bit irregular to say the least. Of the non-atelous lives only John the Baptist, John the Evangelist, Æthelthryth, Seaxburh, Eormenhild, Eadburh, Hild, Columba, Barbara, and Benedicta (where 18 October is given, a mistake for 8 October) are provided with the dates of the feasts.[58]

---

historic purpose in presenting the native lives in Add. 2604, in his intentional naming of uni-versal saints who share feasts with the native women he illustrates how these religious are an integral part of the pantheon of saints in the Roman Catholic church.

[56] At times this policy is not prudent, for example, he omits the name of Justina's father, Edisius, at the beginning but then oddly adds it much later in the text (19/46, 19/50).

[57] In some cases such historical confusion can be part of his narratorial strategy in that it serves to level out or paper over chronological gaps, for instance, the example of Modwenna and Edith of Polesworth below.

[58] It is likely that the date would also have been provided in Leonard had it been complete as it is given in the sources and analogues.

THE NARRATIVE

Yet there is no doubt a sound reason for this ahistorical approach. In some ways the compiler seems wedded to preserving the early English past (mainly in East Anglia), by filling half the volume with native lives, using Old English for place-names when Middle English would have been expected, as in 'Streneshall' for Whitby in the lives of Hild and Modwenna, and even clinging occasionally to outmoded forms of expression.[59] In other respects he seems more intent on collapsing the distinctions between chronological eras. There may be a world of difference between and among biblical times, early Roman Christianity, the Early English period, and France at various points, but the narrator here largely overlooks this. The life of the veiled nun (in the medieval sense) is not what is normally expected in the legends of Roman virgin martyrs and yet the transla-tor almost invariably ensures that their monastic associations are cited even if, as with Justina, the virgin only becomes a nun a few lines from the end, 'Aftir time þat Cipriane was made bisshope, he veyled Iustine and made hir abbes and modir of many holy nonnes' (19/311–12). In addition, Martha is defined as an abbess in the incipit and Benedicta in the explicit, and even Domitilla, whose life-story is minimalist to say the least, is veiled as a nun. In fact, of the virgin martyrs only Columba, Agatha, Barbara, and the married Cecilia are not nuns or abbesses. All the native women are abbesses apart from Eanswith and Eormenhild who are described as nuns. Whatever the circumstances, what-ever the date, what is important is that the women to whom this manuscript is directed should see themselves as part of an ongoing monastic world. Nuns in English convents are being asked to identify with the likes of Justina as if she were one of their own; her unlocalised and unhistorised fiendish visitations in the night could equally be theirs, and like her, they will have the power of the cross to preserve them. Should they be tempted to renounce their virginity, they can remind themselves of the warnings of Eanswith:

'Dere fadir, if it be in your power for to ordeyn for me an husbonde which shall nevir digh, which I shuld love without cessing and fayling, of whom I might bringe forthe frute evirlasting and haue endles gladnes of my childryn, I graunt gladly for to do aftir your counseyle. Ells, fadir, I forsake all weddinges, of the which com nothinge ells but dedly frute and wayling of childryn and corrupcion of virginite' (15/12–17).

[59] 'Streneshall' occurs in Hild at 16/24, 16/26, 16/161, 16/169, and in Modwenna at 21/422, with 'Whitbye' mentioned only once in Hild (16/26). In a traditional Old English way, he routinely uses 'winters' for years when mentioning someone's age and refers to 'sister doughtir' for niece in Domitilla (18/1) and 'syster son' for nephew in Modwenna (21/230–31).

The saints in Add. 2604 are part of a wider interconnected circle of other saints, all ready to help these nuns. Throughout the writer goes to extraordinary lengths to forge links among them. On a local level, he emphasises the complicated familial kinship group of the East Anglian saints, where Eormenhild is the daughter of Seaxburh and niece of Æthelthryth and her sisters Æthelburh and Wihtburh, and where in turn Wærburh is the daughter of Eormenhild and thus granddaughter of Seaxburh and a great-niece of Æthelthryth and her sisters, and so forth. There are also frequent references that connect the native with the native and the native with the universal here and beyond. Even allowing for the customary usage in medieval times of feast days for dating purposes, it is still striking that Æthelthryth's feast of 23 June is cited in relation to the vigil of the Nativity of John the Baptist; Seaxburh dies on the eve of the Translation of Thomas of Canterbury on 8 July; the death of Eormenhild is tied to the feast of Agatha on 5 February; Eadburh expires on the feast of Lucy on 13 December; the death of Hild falls on the feast of Edmund Rich on 17 November. This is the translator's innovation and not a feature of his source, John of Tynemouth. It suggests he wants the native saints to be seen within the pantheon of universal saints. Elsewhere, other connections are made: the two Johns are linked together at the end of the life of John the Baptist through the clever placing of an exemplum about the primacy of both saints, and through the comment that John the Evangelist died on the day that John the Baptist was born, 27 December. In the life of Edith her aunt Edith of Polesworth is mentioned and Edith herself is compared to Martha and Mary; while Barbara is connected to John the Baptist. The compiler invariably prefaces the individual names at each mention throughout Add. 2604 with the honorific 'Seynt' while in the course of the lives a whole heavenly host is invoked. In total (including the examples above), some fifty saints (some more than once) are noted in passing — both more and less well known from St Edmund of East Anglia to St Front (or Fronto) of Périgueux.[60] Saints help to set the scene: Eadburh

---

[60] The number of saints listed as such in Add. 2604 and referred to in various ways is extensive. The list below also includes references to churches or altars named for these saints and a few biblical or source citations, but excludes the multiple internal cross-references to the Ely saints. In order of appearance the saints are as follows: Ambrose, Jerome, Tecla, Martin, Gregory, and John the Evangelist (in John the Baptist); Anna, James the Greater, Peter, Andrew, Jerome, Edward the Confessor, and John the Baptist (in John the Evangelist); Silvester (in Columba); Peter (in Agatha); Urban (in Cecilia); John the Baptist and Lucy (in Barbara); Wilfrid, Æbbe, Augustine of Canterbury, Æthelbert, John the Baptist, Luke, Æthelwold, Edmund of East Anglia, and Benedict (in Æthelthryth); Thomas of Canterbury (in Seaxburh); Agatha (in Eormenhild); Blaise (in Wærburh); Burgondofara [Fara] (in Eorcengota) and Thomas of

THE NARRATIVE 299

becomes abbess of Thanet after her aunt St Mildrith; Martha is the sister of St Mary Magdalene; Domitilla is located with reference to St John the Evangelist and St Clement; Modwenna is introduced in an account of the ministry of St Patrick. Saints ordain events: Saints Dunstan and Æthelwold wish Edith to be abbess of Winchester, Barking, and Wilton (even if Edith refuses and remains at Wilton). Saints help other saints in the making: Agatha's breasts are healed by St Peter; Æthelthryth is aided by St Wilfrid in preserving her virginity even in the face of her second husband's demands, and she is accompanied by Saints Benedict and Seaxburh in releasing a man from prison. Saints are honoured by those who will themselves be decreed saints: Modwenna builds a chapel in honour of St Andrew; Leonard makes an altar in memory of St Remigius. And angels too have their part to play whether it be as attendant at a burial as in the life of Agatha, as a heavenly choir as Eorcengota and also Hild are led to heaven, or communing with Modwenna as she stands in the water of a well reading her psalter.

In this somewhat ahistorical and atemporal world overseen by saintly and angelic figures the motifs of hagiography (and indeed romance literature) recur throughout the lives. Alongside the usual physical torments and spiritual triumphs, there are encounters with the enemy; bargains; battles; dramatic rescues; escapes; heavenly interventions; journeys; predictions, reversals of fortune; saintly visitations; and visions. This world is described for the nuns in a series of dramatic events and spectacular miracles, bound together with similar tropes, and elevated throughout by highly-wrought speeches from the female saints. There are reanimations starting with the resurrection of Drusiana in the life of John the Evangelist (an episode now missing owing to a lacking folio) and later that of the poisoned men. Hild raises a fowl from the dead. Modwenna restores a hog for the king's shepherd and resurrects Osith after

Canterbury (in the Æthelburh section of Eorcengota); Æthelwold and Thomas of Canterbury (in Wihtburh); Æthelwold, Modwenna, Dunstan, Edward the Confessor, Denis, and Alphe (in Edith); Mildrith, Augustine of Canterbury, Lucy, Gregory (in Eadburh); Peter (in Eanswith); Paul and Edmund of Pontigny (in Hild); Maximian, Jerome, Front (or Fronto), Marcelle, and Remigius (in Martha); John the Evangelist, Clement, Peter, Iphigenia, and Matthew (in Domitilla); 'Anthinius' (in Justina); Patrick, Brigid of Kildare, Michael ('at Edinburgh'), Andrew of Scotland (in Modwenna); and Remigius and Martial (in Leonard). In addition to these, Elizabeth is noted in the life of John the Baptist and Mary Magdalene is mentioned in the life of Martha, while Edith of Polesworth occurs in the lives of Edith of Wilton and Modwenna, with the latter also including a mention of Peter and Paul, though none of these is referred to explicitly as a saint. In John the Baptist a St 'Syrape' is invented between Jerome and Tecla owing to a confusion with the Latin. Only Benedicta lacks a reference to any other saint.

drowning; she also raises a pagan girl and a blasphemer. Valerian encounters an angel protecting the virginity of his wife Cecilia while Tonberht sees protective fire around Æthelthryth on their wedding night. Barbara escapes through a rock, and her father is burnt to powder after her beheading. Wærburh's bailiff has his head turned backwards as punishment. The thief and the Danes in the life of Eadburh shed their bowels or bleed anally. Cædmon receives the power of song in the life of Hild. Jesus buries Martha with his own hands. The dead body of Modwenna carried on a bier turns towards England as its preferred place of rest.

The lives — be they based on a biblical or hagiographical narrative, linked to a native or a universal source, concerned with a male martyr or confessor, a female martyr, or a married woman turned nun — understandably have their own particular characteristics. Yet when read sequentially, one sees the resemblances rather than the individual differences that stand out in each life. The nuns who read these lives were introduced to another sphere where the saints have dominion over the animal and the natural world (most obviously in the native lives), and where the powers of the celestial kingdom are always evident. Poisonous and polluting dragons are expelled in the life of John the Baptist. A bear keeps Columba safe from her assailant. The sheep of a shepherd who betrays Barbara are turned into locusts (alias grasshoppers). Wild geese feel shame for desiring crops and are banished by Wærburh. Deer sent by the Virgin Mary provide milk to feed Wihtburh's community. Wild fowl agree to fly away leaving corn untouched in the life of Hild. Venomous serpents are transformed into stones by Hild. In the following narrative people are saved by Martha from slaughter by a monstrous dragon (another relative of the serpent). In the life of Justina the suitor Agladius is changed into a sparrow and back again, thereby stranding himself on a window-ledge. A wolf guards a calf as commanded by Modwenna. Leonard appears in the likeness of a dove to free a man from prison.[61] Trees appear out of nowhere: Æthelthryth's staff pitched in the ground becomes a great oak. Water is re-directed or miraculously produced by saintly command: in the life of Æthelthryth the sea flows around a hill to protect her from the pursuit of her second husband and later her prayer produces water for her nuns; Eanswith provides a well for her oratory as does Leonard for his; while Modwenna is not only capable of filling a cistern with water, but also

[61] For the topic of animals in hagiography, see Dominic Alexander, *Saints and Animals in the Middle Ages* (Woodbridge: Boydell, 2008), especially ch. 5, 'Sainted Princesses and the Resurrection of Geese', pp. 85–112, which discusses Wærburh (though not from Add. 2604) alongside various continental saints.

THE NARRATIVE   301

able to change water into wine and stone into salt. Even the elements show
portents of favour with a star demonstrating Wihtburh's approval for her
translation to Ely. This world and the next are invariably connected through
dreams, prophecies, and visitations. A dream reveals the impending murder of
Edith's half-brother, Edward. Death is prophesied in the lives of Æthelthryth,
Eorcengota, Wærburh, and Modwenna. Glunelach and Modwenna travel to
both heaven and hell. Edith visits Wolfrid (Edith's mother Wulfthryth) and
Dunstan after her death, and she appears at her god-daughter's christening. Her
nuns see Modwenna after her death. Hild's soul is seen to ascend to heaven by
the women of her community. Æthelthryth helps a petitioner, as does her niece
Eormenhild who comes to the aid of schoolboys tormented by a schoolmaster.

The lives are replete with foolish pagan tyrants who try to kill the saint by
dismemberment and/or by self-deluding men who seek to dis-inter, mutilate, or
destroy the sanctified corpses. In the biblical lives saints are decapitated, bones
are burnt, and a head discovered in the life of John the Baptist, while John the
Evangelist endures burning oil and poison; only Martha escapes fairly lightly
by being put to sea in a boat at the beginning of her narrative (itself a trope in
exilic and pilgrimage literature). Martha, of course, is not a martyr like John the
Baptist or the other universal virgins. As a leader of her community, in many
ways she has more in common with strong native saints like Edith, Hild, or
Modwenna. Martha demonstrates a certain God-given authority: she preaches;
she subdues a dragon; she restores a drowned man to life; she stages the scene
of her own death.[62] In the native lives the suffering, when it does occur, is more
'domestic', either symbolic of past worldly extravagances, such as in the swelling
on Æthelthryth's neck that represents her previous habit of adorning her neck
with jewellery or self-imposed deprivations as in the case of Seaxburh. (As a
point of comparison, Appendix 2 below offers the passage about Æthelthryth
as it is presented in different Middle English versions to illustrate the distinc-
tiveness of the Add. 2604 version.) The emphasis in these stories is mainly on
the agency of the nuns in their communities and the legacy of their miracle-
working in their afterlives. There are, in addition, several mentions of attacks
on the relics of the saints or trouble at their tombs that show the saint's efficacy,
such as in the life of Æthelthryth when her tomb is desecrated by a Dane; in

---

[62] See Diane E. Peters, 'The Iconography of St Martha: Some Considerations', *Vox Benedictina*, 9: 1 (1992), 30–65, and Martha M. Dass, 'From Holy Hostess to Dragon Tamer: The
Anomaly of Saint Martha', *Literature and Theology*, 22 (2008), pp. 1–15, for a discussion of
Martha not only as a female St George in her encounter with the dragon but as a powerful
woman in her own right.

Wihtburh, when her tomb is broken but miraculously restored; or in Eadburh, when a priest is negligent with Eadburh's relics. There are several miracles in which someone tries to take a piece of clothing from a saint but is rebuked, as in the life of Edith when a nun tries to steal her headband. In other miracles, property held by the saint's community is improperly taken and the saint effects its return, as in the lives of Æthelthryth who ensures that estates appropriated by the Norman Picot are returned and when Modwenna restores alms stolen from a nun by blinding the thieves.

In the narratives of the virgin martyrs a different sort of agency is at work with the scene typically set up for the confrontation between the righteous woman (whose virginity equates with her Christianity) and her pagan assailant: Quyncian the duke of Sicily (Agatha); Almache the justice (Cecilia); her own father and an anonymous justice (Barbara); the emperor Aurelian (Columba); Agladius the lover and Cyprian the magician (Justina); and Matrocle the justice (Benedicta). Whereas the native women defend their chastity or maintain their virginity by avoiding their husbands or abstaining from marriage, these virgin martyrs have to prove themselves more actively by facing up to their inordinate sufferings and impending slaughters with resolution and bravery.[63] As is usual in such cases, no degree of torture — whether it involves being surrounded by fire (Columba), having one's breasts cut off and being laid on burning coals (Agatha), left to sit in boiling water (Cecilia), stripped naked and scourged throughout the city (Barbara), tormented by demonic visitations (Justina); hanged on a gibbet and flayed with iron rods (Benedicta) — deflects the saint from her firm purpose. Again and again these lives are filled with triumphalist speeches where the women defy their persecutors and their minions at every turn. For instance, Agatha tells the bawds (Affrodosie and her daughters) sent to sway her from the Christian path: ' "Laboure no more aboute me for my soule is fastenyd and groundid in Criste and made stedfaste by him, and therfore all your wordis I lekyn to wynde, your promises and byhestis to rayne, and all your thretinges to flodis [...]" ' (4/33–36). When they stand up to the tyrants, they do so in full knowledge of eventual spiritual success; as Benedicta says to the tyrant Matrocle: ' "I haue God that is in hevyn to my helper to whom I haue avowed my virginite, which hath power of euery creature; him I serue bothe day and nyght and in his seruice I desire to continue dayes of my

---

[63] Æthelthryth maintains her virginity despite having had two husbands (see the Commentary to 7/8–19 and 7/20–74 in our *Edition*). In the case of Eanswith, marriage is avoided by means of a trial that her suitor fails and Christ succeeds in (see the Commentary to 15/26–47 in our *Edition*).

THE NARRATIVE   303

lyf" ' (20/47–50). They know, as Barbara does, when addressed by Christ, that succour and joy are at hand:

> 'Be comfortid in me, Barbara, and truste well that grete ioy shall be amonge Cristen peple in erth of thyn holy passion which thou suffred for my love and yit at laste to the grete plentevous ioy in heyven for thi mede. Drede not therfore the thretinges of the tyraunt, for I am with the and shall delyuer the from all paynes that ben putt to the' (6/92–96).

And when release from suffering finally comes, Christ calls to Barbara from heaven ' "Come, my fayre soule; come and receyve the most ioyfull and swettist endles rest of my fadir for all that thou hast axid it is grauntid to the" ' (6/161–62). It is very noticeable throughout that in the universal and native lives alike there is a resounding use of this same spousal phraseology with its echoes of the Song of Songs, ' "Come, my welbelouyd [...]" ' (John the Evangelist, 2/270); ' "Come, my swete colver [...]" ' (Columba, 3/125); ' "Come, my soule [...]" ' (Eadburh, 14/37); and ' "Come nowe, my dere hostes [...]" ' (Martha, 17/108–09). Such repetitive speeches help to bind the narratives together.

The nuns in an East Anglian convent (or indeed any other medieval readership or audience) are unlikely to be called upon to suffer extremes of torture for their faith. Their struggles may be more those summed up in the life of Modwenna when she appears after her death to one of her nuns and reproves the behaviour in the convent. She notes that silence is not kept and the usual observances overlooked, thus echoing the regular infringements of monastic discipline cited in episcopal visitations:[64]

> Than the thirde day aftir that she was dede, on of hir systers aftir complyn sygh where she knelyd — as she was wont to do — and prayed, holding vp her hondis to do as though she had be alyve, which nonne was somewhat aferde and fylle doun to hir fete and sayde, 'Lady, modir, will ye any thinge? What will ye that I do?' Than she sayde, 'Sey tomorowe to my systers that I, Modewenne theire modir, sendith theym worde that they shuld [fol. 135v] not suppose I am dede, for I lyve verely with oure lorde Ihesu Criste and that I haue herde of somme of hem howe they breke sylens togedir aftir complyn and other tymes whan they shuld not, not

---

[64] With a few exceptions these disciplinary problems are not noticeable amongst East Anglian nuns; see the discussion in III. Convent and Geographical Location about episcopal visitations to East Anglian convents. Further useful information on administrative and legal affairs in convents is available in Valerie G. Spear, *Leadership in Medieval English Nunneries,* Studies in the History of Medieval Religion, 24 (Woodbridge: Boydell, 2005) and Makowski, *English Nuns and the Law in the Middle Ages.*

keping holy sylens as they shuld. Is it nowe out of your mynde what the prophete seyth, *Cultus iustice scilencium*, "The worship of God is scilens". Yit my body is with you onberyed and ye so sone foryete the teching of God and reguler obseruaunces whos boundes ye owght not for to breke. Do not so, my goode doughters. Sett not litill by smale obseruaunces left by negligens; lytill and litill ye offende in gretter which God forbede. And, goode doughter, aftir tyme thou haste tolde hem this, make the redy for aftur these seven dayes thou shalt come to me.' And so it was. (21/701–17).

Although there is varied content — part of the fascination of Add. 2604 — nuns across the ages are connected to each other and to the saints of wider Christendom.[65] Overall there is remarkable consistency in the lives. The same methodology and stylistic approach are used throughout so that readers do not get the sense of varying underlying sources or analogues. Most notably, whether discussing noble Roman martyr virgins, Early English queens-turned-abbesses, or pious male figures, the narrator expects the reader to be carried along by the strength of the narrative.

Devotional reading and historical documentation make a connection between and among these nuns. When Thanet's ancient conventual documents are thrown into the fire by an archbishop of Canterbury, the foundational charter is saved from burning through the implicit auspices of Eadburh, '[...] whan all þe strowes were brennyd into asshis, that wold not brenne' (14/73–74). Nuns in an East Anglian convent are thereby reminded of the importance of their own foundation history and their links with the past, in the same way as the various exemplary stories highlight the need to protect their relics. On a more pragmatic level, this miracle also serves to help ensure that they preserve their charters and documents so as to avoid censure from the ecclesiastical patriarchy. This is especially important given that one of the recurring complaints in English episcopal visitations centred on the failure of female religious to produce (or in many cases to understand) their foundational and documentary materials.[66] When a book is sent to Modwenna and is later rescued from the water, these same nuns are made to recognise the value of preserving the written word. Edith of Polesworth sends Osith (Osye) to Modwenna saying to her, ' "Go to my lady Modewenne and beyre hir this boke [fol. 127v] wherin

---

[65] Leaving aside the fact that Add. 2604 in its current state is imperfect and that other saints may have been included originally, there is still strong evidence to show that the mixed focus original to this manuscript is not something imposed on it by later owners (see further I. The Manuscript).

[66] See the references in n. 52 of III. Convent and Geographical Location.

THE NARRATIVE   305

she may rede and peraventure fynde somethinge of contemplacion which may
lyke hir right well" ' (21/431–34).[67] When Osith falls into the river with the
book, Edith and Modwenna pray for her delivery:

> Than bothe knelyd doun and prayed devouutly. And whan they had done,
> Modewenne rose vp and with a clere voyce clepid thries togedir the childe and
> seyd, 'Osy, Osy, Osy, in the name of the holy trinite, come forth out of this flode þat
> thou art drenchid in and, by the myght of strenght of the trinite, apere afore vs hole
> and sounde.' Modewenne had vnneth seyd the wordis, but þat the childe answered
> and seyde thries togedir with a clere voyce these wordis, 'Here I am; here I am; here
> I am, lady'; and so apperyd afore theyme. Than Modewenne and Edith toke that
> child with gret ioy and thankyd our lorde of his speciall grace and beleft the childe
> to Edith and toke the boke to hirself and went home ayene into Erlonde, takyng
> [fol. 128v] with hir Bryde, and left in Ynglonde Athea and Luge[r] for to gouerne
> tho monasteryes which she had made. (21/456–67)

It is important that both person (in a voice reminiscent of the discovery of the
head of Edmund of East Anglia) and book are rescued and that Modwenna
takes the book on her next journey back to Ireland.[68] Knowledge is literally
being spread abroad. The written word functions geographically and historically across space and time. When Edith of Wilton starts to read the lives of
saints, her favourite narrative concerns this same Edith of Polesworth who is
said to have lived at the time of Modwenna:

> And as she encresid in age, so she encresid in vertues and conyng, oft tymes reding
> seyntes lyves, but amonge all that she radde she lyked best the maydinly and reli-
> gious lyvng of hir awnte Edith in Seynt Modewen is dayes, which was sister to hir
> fadir is brodir and was abbes of Pollisworth in Staffordshire, lyvng there with grete
> vertues lyvng, as this yonge Edith did in Wylton abbey (13/23–28).

It is irrelevant for both the latter narratives above that Edith of Polesworth,
who is here called the sister of the tenth-century king Æthelstan, cannot pos-

---

[67] For the historical inaccuracy here, see below. The Add. 2604 writer also pays no attention to the linguistic situation; in medieval Ireland four languages were operative to greater or
lesser extents at different points: Irish, Latin, Norman French, and English, quite apart from
Old Norse in the earlier period.

[68] In one of the most famous miracles in English (and indeed East Anglian) saints' lives,
the head of the ninth-century Edmund lets its location in the wood be known after Edmund's
beheading by the Vikings, as in Lydgate's life in London, British Library, MS Harley 2278,
when the pious followers of the king seek him, 'The hed answerde thryes: "Her, her, her" ' (fol.
66v); see *The Life of St Edmund King and Martyr*, introduction by Edwards.

sibly have been alive in the days of the sixth-century Modwenna. As nuns they share a continuity of religious and devotional life that cuts across all temporal boundaries. What is important is that Edith of Wilton finds instructive and enjoyable reading in her book of saints' lives, which no doubt contained the lives of various early virgin martyrs as well as that of illustrious English nuns, in other words, a sort of mirror image of Add. 2604 itself.

Written in what has been referred to as 'a golden age of Middle English hagiography', the work of the anonymous Add. 2604 writer may be set beside those of the well known — and frequently discussed (often repetitively so) — East Anglian writers, John Lydgate, Osbern Bokenham, and John Capgrave.[69] Yet this is a writer who does not have (or perhaps keeps hidden) the theological sophistication of the Cambridge-educated Capgrave and eschews the socio-political drive of Lydgate with his concern for good governance both spiritual and temporal. In many ways the work of the Add. 2604 writer bears closest comparison to Bokenham's; they share a decided interest in female saints, a penchant for translating material that expands on the *Legenda aurea*, and a noteworthy ability to engage their readers. They even include a few of the same lives (though in Bokenham's case these can be in verse and/or prose): Æthelthryth, Agatha, Barbara, Cecilia, and John the Evangelist.[70] Yet the Add. 2604 writer is far removed from Bokenham in other respects; unlike the latter, he never intrudes himself into the narrative by discussing his patrons or disclosing his motivations. In some respects this silence is frustrating. While there is extensive biographical and historical detail for the other writers, all we have for the Add. 2604 scribe/translator/compiler/writer are the saints' lives themselves and whatever we have been able to extrapolate in the present *Study* about the Add. 2604 lives and their context, the manuscript, and its history. Yet the great advantage of this is that the manuscript can stand on its own merits as a text purely to be read, something the compiler of Add. 2604 clearly had in mind given the engaged way he approached his task.

[69] Winstead, *Fifteenth-Century Lives*, p. 1. This work particularly focuses on Lydgate (pp. 11–39) and Bokenham (pp. 41–74) in its first two chapters with some passing references to Capgrave in the course of its examination of 'the promotion in fifteenth-century hagiography of an intellectualized, strongly feminized piety' (p. 5). There is an extensive range of study of all three writers; much of this work is listed in Scahill, with Rogerson, *Annotated Bibliographies of Old and Middle English*, VIII: *Middle English Saints' Legends* with chapters 9 and 11 devoted respectively to Bokenham (pp. 109–19) and Capgrave (pp. 143–53), with the work of Lydgate treated at various points.

[70] For further information, see IV. Hagiographical Context and the Selection of Saints.

THE NARRATIVE   307

In the course of Add. 2604 the writer makes use of self-referential reminders
to his readership or audience that he is working from written sources, sometimes in terms of what the sources lack in evidence or detail. Such references
as those above to the books and the reading of saints' lives likewise function as
meta-narratives. In the same way as Edith, a nun in an English convent, reads
the lives of her forebears, so the nuns addressed in Add. 2604 are reading or
listening to the lives of their sister ancestors, including Edith herself.

Conclusion

The legendary in MS Add. 2604 illustrates particular attention to the concerns of English nuns at the end of the Middle Ages. Where the lives demonstrate figures of holiness whose determined action could be imitated, they also offer dialogues and outcomes that illustrate strong-minded leadership in the face of a range of challenges, both temporal and spiritual. These miracle-workers show the efficacy of female godliness, even as the results of their interventions elevated them within the community of God. As our discussion in VI. Reading the '*Lyves and Dethes*' asserts, these narratives could be enjoyed for their performative aspects and ruminated upon for their spiritual uplift. Further, the miracles effected through and by virgins, nuns, and abbesses speak to their spiritual and temporal agency. Amongst wonders, prophecies, and visions, there are also the more quotidian events that focus on nuns who behave improperly but are corrected gently by their abbesses, such as the sister in the life of Modwenna who covets new shoes. These episodes demonstrate an awareness of real human desires that often did not mesh with conventual expectations of humility. These narratives offer not only sober instruction in good living but also delightful moments of engagement with the natural world and ludic moments of the absurd.

Where the audience for this legendary was almost certainly enclosed and separated from worldly concerns, the narratives illustrate a series of dynamic exchanges with secular authorities, tyrants, and lay people. Indeed, the representation of these female figures as active agents in public spaces, authorised by God to resist various kinds of incursions on their authority, their properties, and their spiritual lives, no doubt provided some satisfaction for readers and hearers whose lives were more constrained. This collection would have filled important needs in the lives of English nuns — vocational, spiritual, and imaginative.

As we have demonstrated here, these lives were translated from a wide range of Latin sources and analogues both homegrown and European, but they coalesce into an attractive representation of biblical, Roman, and English exemplarity. Indeed, set against the backdrop of other hagiographical productions in England and Europe, there is much that is unique about this collection of lives, not least the many examples that do not occur elsewhere in Middle English. Supported by the figures of John the Baptist, John the Evangelist, and Leonard, who were often the dedicatees of English convents, the female saints in Add. 2604 provide narratives of passionate engagement. The serialisation of these narratives, divided into various sections outlining key events in the saints' lives, provide on-going forms of spiritual guidance and passionate performance. The foundation of new communities by engaging female leaders like Æthelthryth and Hild remind readers and hearers of the agency of their English forebears, even as the evangelising of women like Martha provide a tangible link from the biblical past to their historical present. The life and death of a virgin martyr may have broadly unfolded according to the typical hagiographical template. Yet in hearing the verbal exchanges between female saints such as Agatha and Justina and their secular or diabolical interlocutors, the audience for Add. 2604 could imagine how they too could maintain their physical integrity and defend their communities — and their own personal faith — from harm. Thus, the nuns could effectively have absorbed meaning from any of the lives in this collection.

In this *Study* we too have attempted to make meaning from Add. 2604, an imperfect manuscript that has no provenance linguistically or geographically before the late eighteenth century. It is devoid of particulars about its translator/scribe and lacks information about a patron, dedicatee, audience, or locale. And it is undated, unmoored from a particular source manuscript, and altogether without a secure context. In effect Add. 2604 appears to be a *tabula rasa*. But much can and has been gleaned here from the physical manuscript itself, from its decoration, its language, its additional material, its plethora of later owners, particularly the recusant George Tasburgh and the antiquarian George Bird Burrell. We have focused in detail on the manuscript and on the texts themselves and their actual or potential sources. In considering the wider hagiographical context and convent histories we have built up a narrative about this manuscript which we argue was destined for East Anglian nuns in the vicinity of Ely. As we have shown, this is a complicated story. It may not be agreed upon in all its essentials and throughout we admit to what is tentative or uncertain. For instance, the standardised language allows for a suggested rather than a secure localisation in Suffolk and there is a range of possibilities for the identity of the convent, most particularly Campsey Ash, Chatteris, Denney, Flixton, Ickleton, and our favoured Thetford. Yet this *Study* should do much to offer a way into understanding these particular saints' lives as well as opening up vistas to other such collections. We trust that others will find this unique survival an important complement to late medieval English saints' lives. We invite them to take up these lives, edited for the first time in our companion volume, *Saints' Lives for Medieval English Nuns, II: An Edition of the 'Lyves and Dethes' in Cambridge University Library, MS Additional 2604*, and enjoy the riches they offer about late medieval English devotion.

Appendix 1

Universal Latin Saints' Lives: Sources and Analogues

(i) Examples of the 'Legenda aurea' in manuscript and print (with or without additional lives)

Manuscripts[1]

Cambridge, Cambridge University Library, MS Additional 618, a fourteenth-century manuscript of Italian provenance, is an example of one of the multiple *Legenda aurea* manuscripts (listed by Fleith as *LA* 136) that contain numerous omissions and re-orderings,[2] though in this case no local additions.[3]

Cambridge, Cambridge University Library, MS Additional 6452, is a fourteenth-century manuscript of German provenance (probably from Württemberg owing to internal evidence) that contains much variation in the order of chapters from the *Legenda aurea* (listed in Fleith as *LA* 136a). In this case there is also a lengthy section of added saints on fols 240r–250v, beginning with Barbara (fol. 240ra–va). The manuscript concludes with a calendar (fols 252r–256v), with November and December lacking owing to missing folios.

---

[1] All the material here has been examined at first hand, apart from the Eton and Paris manuscripts. We are grateful to Carlotta Barranu for kindly providing images of the Eton life of Columba. We have consulted the digitised copy of the Paris manuscript at https://gallica.bnf.fr/ark:/12148/btv1b9066719b.r=1214812598%2012598?rk=64378;0; accessed 18 June 2023); see also n. 16 below.

[2] References to the entry in Fleith, *Studien zur Überlieferungsgeschichte der lateinischen 'Legenda Aurea'* are given when available.

[3] A full description of both the Cambridge Additional manuscripts is available in Ringrose, *Summary Catalogue of the Additional Medieval Manuscripts in Cambridge University Library Aquired before 1940*, pp. 3–4 and 238–39. For all other Cambridge University Library manuscripts, see the relevant entries in *A Catalogue of the Manuscripts Preserved in the Library of the University of Cambridge*, ed. for the Syndics of the University Press, 5 vols (Cambridge: Cambridge University Press, 1856–67).

312 APPENDIX I

Cambridge, Cambridge University Library, MS Ee.6.31, a fifteenth-century compilation of material, opens with the *Legenda aurea* on fols 4ra–135vb (listed in Fleith as *LA* 130). A list of contents, detailing the full *Legenda aurea*, is given on fols 4vb–6ra, but well over half the texts are missing as it finishes during the Resurrection on fol. 135b. On fol. 3v a donor inscription is helpfully provided, 'Liber domus Sancti Edmundi ex dono venerabilis Magistri Ioannis Hanworth'. This refers to the Priory of St Edmund, a study centre in Cambridge for the Gilbertine Canons from the late thirteenth century onwards. Hanworth (or Hamworth) was an Oxford 'Magister' apparently in the first half of the fifteenth century. The second half of the manuscript is in Cambridge, Trinity College, MS 1395, which was also given to the Gilbertines by Hanworth, as well as an imperfect early fourteenth-century copy of the *Sentences* of Peter Lombard (now London, British Library, MS Additional 18899).[4]

Cambridge, Cambridge University Library, MS Ff.2.20 is a fourteenth-century manuscript that has a range of material in the midst of which are twelve lives from the *Legenda aurea* (listed in Fleith as Komp/Käp) on fols 58rb–80va, none of which is found in Add. 2604.

Cambridge, Cambridge University Library, MS Ff.5.31 is a copy of the *Legenda aurea* (listed as *LA* 132 by Fleith) with a clear provenance. On the top of the opening page is written 'Legenda sanctorum I. Frome Ecclesie Christi Canterberiensis'. John Frome was professed a Benedictine monk in 1337; an Oxford scholar thereafter, he was a lector at Christ Church, Canterbury at various points between 1350 and 1365.[5]

Cambridge, Cambridge University Library, MS Oo.7.46, a miscellaneous collection of material, has lives from the *Legenda aurea*, with two additional lives (listed as *LA* 135 by Fleith), beginning imperfectly in the life of Clement, and written on paper in a seventeenth-century hand.

Cambridge, Pembroke College, MS 277, dating from the early fourteenth century, is a good example of an early copy of the *Legenda aurea* of English provenance (listed as *LA* 123 by Fleith). On an opening flyleaf (fol. ii recto) there is a reference to 'Thomas atte Chirche de blofeld nuper rector ecclesie Sancti Michaelis de Conesford in Norwyco [...]'. At the end of the manu-

---

[4] A. B. Emden, *A Biographical Register of the University of Oxford to A.D. 1500*, 3 vols (Oxford: Clarendon Press, 1957–59), II (1958), 285.

[5] Emden, *A Biographical Register of the University of Oxford to A.D. 1500*, II (1958), 730.

UNIVERSAL LATIN SAINTS' LIVES

script (fol. 349v) there are further inscriptions, one of which alludes to 'M. I. Sowthow' or John Southo (d. 1446), a fellow of Pembroke Hall, who is described as the rector of 'fforneset', that is, Forncett (one of three such places in Norfolk). At the end of the list of contents eleven English saints are added, including Æthelthryth.[6]

Eton, Eton College Library, MS 203, a mid-fourteenth-century manuscript from the Benedictine Abbey of St Aubin, Angers, contains the original *Legenda aurea* with six additional items including a life of Columba (fol. 376r–v).[7] This previously unidentified life is the same as that found in Jean de Mailly's collection.[8]

Glasgow, Glasgow University Library, MS Gen. 1111, a manuscript from the second half of the fifteenth century divided into two volumes (fols 1–193 and 194–374) contains an augmented and illustrated *Legenda aurea* (listed in Fleith as *LA* 231). Interwoven between the *Legenda aurea* Advent and the Dedication of the Church (fols 6ra–268va) are seventeen lives not part of the *Legenda aurea*, including Barbara (fols 11vb–13ra). Many of these lives are preceded by an image of the saint. Following on are fifty-one non-*Legenda aurea* lives in random order (fols 268va–374va), including Columba (fols 276va–277rb) and Benedicta (fols 334vb–336vb). An alphabetical table itemises the lives, whether *Legenda aurea* or not (fols. 1r–3v). Unlike the previous example, this Columba is not from Jean de Mailly's collection. Although earlier referred to as being executed in Flanders, Ker notes a connection with Piacenza, as well as post-medieval Italian memoranda.[9]

London, British Library, MS Arundel 330 is a Latin collection of Carthusian provenance of the late fourteenth century comprising various material. Described as a 'passional' in the prologue (fol. 1ra), the first part of the manuscript begins with Advent (fol. 1ra–1va), and finishes with the Dedication of the Church (fols 70va–71vb). It contains John the Evangelist (fols 4vb–5vb), Agatha (fol. 11va–11vb), John the Evangelist at the Latin Gate (fol.

---

[6] For a full description of the manuscript, see R. M. Thomson, *A Descriptive Catalogue of the Medieval Manuscripts of Pembroke College, Cambridge* (Cambridge: Brewer, 2022), p. 155.

[7] Ker and Piper, *Medieval Manuscripts in British Libraries*, II (1997), 778–79 (p. 778).

[8] Jean de Mailly, *Abbreviatio in gestis et miracvlis sanctorvm, svpplementvm hagiographicvm*, ed. by Maggioni, pp. 66–67.

[9] Ker and Piper, *Medieval Manuscripts in British Libraries*, II (1997), 916–19.

20ra–b), the Nativity of John the Baptist (fols 25va–26rb), the Octave of John the Baptist (fol. 29va–29vb), the Decollation of John the Baptist (fols 48va–49ra), Justina (fol. 55va), Martha (fol. 60ra–60va), and Cecilia (fols 66rb–67va). It does not contain lives of Barbara, Benedicta, Columba, Domitilla (though Nereus and Achilleus are found on fol. 21ra–21vb), or Leonard. It is particularly noteworthy for its very short life of Justina that takes up just one column, beginning 'Jvstina uirgo nobilis et speciosa ualde' (fol. 55va). This life is infinitely shorter than that in the *Acta sanctorum*, the *Legenda aurea*, the *Abbreviatio in gestis et miracvlis sanctorvm* or that translated in Add. 2604. This manuscript is listed as a copy of the *Legenda aurea* in Fleith (*LA* 379); this is not the case to judge from its Justina or indeed its John the Evangelist or the Nativity of John the Baptist (and nor do these depend on the *Abbreviatio in gestis et miracvlis sanctorvm*).

London, British Library, MS Burney 347 from the fifteenth century opens with a contents list (fols 1ra–2vb) beginning with Andrew, Nicholas, and Lucy and ending with Gordian, Sixtus, and Peter, followed by spaces for three other lives not filled in. The relevant lives occur as follows: Columba (fol. 29ra–29va), Agatha (fols 48va–50ra), John the Evangelist at the Latin Gate (fol. 120ra–120va), Nativity of John the Baptist (fols 136va–137va), Martha (fols 163va–165ra), the Decollation of John the Baptist (fols 186ra–188va), Justina (fols 206vb–209ra) with a separate life of Cyprian (fol. 202rb), Leonard (fols 223rb–224rb), and Cecilia (fols 242vb–243va). The order as a whole moves to Advent and so forth at the end and the manuscript finishes imperfectly in Quinquagesima. This manuscript is listed in Fleith (*LA* 365) as a copy of the *Legenda aurea*; this is not completely true as it draws on the *Legenda aurea* and the *Abbreviatio in gestis et miracvlis sanctorvm*. For instance, while Martha derives from the *Legenda aurea*, Leonard is a copy by Jean de Mailly.[10] Likewise its Columba is from the latter collection.[11] There are no added lives of Barbara, Benedicta, or Domitilla (though Nereus and Achilleus occur on fols 130vb–131va).

---

[10] Jean de Mailly, *Abbreviatio in gestis et miracvlis sanctorvm, svpplementvm hagiographicvm*, ed. by Maggioni, pp. 431–33.

[11] Jean de Mailly, *Abbreviatio in gestis et miracvlis sanctorvm, svpplementvm hagiographicvm*, ed. by Maggioni, pp. 66–67.

UNIVERSAL LATIN SAINTS' LIVES

Incunabula

In *Jacobi a Voragine, Legenda aurea, vulgo Historia lombardica dicta*, ed. by Th. Graesse, 3rd edn (Bratislava: Koebner, 1890), pp. 898–902, there is a life of Barbara from a printed *Legenda aurea* from the early 1470s that appears alongside sixty other added saints. This life of Barbara is not the same as that in the different editions by Conrad Winters de Homborch and Johannes Koelhoff in the later 1470s.

Some early incunabula editions of the *Legenda aurea* already contained a substantial list of saints added to what Fleith calls the 'Normalcorpus'. Two such instances may be found in the editions printed by Conrad Winters de Homborch and Johannes Koelhoff in the later 1470s.[12] In the first case there is an unpaginated list of contents to the 'Normalcorpus' of the *Legenda aurea* at the beginning of the text (with the foliation written in by hand). At the end of this list there is a reference to 'Aliam tabulam' at the end of the book. The *Legenda aurea*, with its hand-coloured initials and handwritten medieval foliation, then follows. As promised, another list of contents is found at the end, 'Item hystorie sequentes additesunt ad historiam lombardicam' (fol. CCCxxij recto a). There follows a list of thirty-eight saints, beginning with Barbara and ending with Hubert, and with Columba eighth from the end. Barbara (fols CCCxxij recto a–CCCxxiij recto b) precedes the Conception of the Virgin Mary. In this particular copy the volume ends imperfectly in the life before Columba, the Translation of Lebuino, but it would have occupied just over two columns (see USTC 746119).

In the second case, the edition printed by Koelhoff, there is a table of contents at the beginning (sig. a 2 verso a–a 3 verso b), but with no mention of an additional table. The *Legenda aurea* then follows on. After the *Legenda aurea*, the same sort of heading as in the previous edition is found, 'Item hystorie sequentes additesunt ad historiam lombardicam' (sig. rr 1 recto a) followed by the same list of thirty-eight saints, including Barbara (sig. rr 1 recto b–rr 2 recto b) and Columba (sig. yy 1 recto b–yy 1 verso b). At the very end of the volume there is an unpaginated alphabetical list of the saints; this includes the *Legenda aurea* saints but also integrates those that have been added.

---

[12] We have examined the copies of these editions in the Ruusbroec Research Centre in Antwerp; the shelfmark for the Winters copy is L. P. 11 (1099 B 4) and for the Koelhoff copy it is L. P. 14 (1099 B 6).

(ii) Société des Bollandistes: Latin Hagiographical Manuscripts

Of the ninety-seven medieval Latin hagiographical manuscripts still found in the Bollandist Research Institute and Library (that is, Société des Bollandistes), there are eight (from different periods) that contain some of the universal lives found in Add. 2604. These are as follows, with the items given in the order of appearance.[13]

MS 5 is a large vellum twelfth-century manuscript originating from a monastic library in Grimberg that is set out in double columns with finely executed initial large capitals, though it is imperfect at the end with part of the final folio cut out. It opens with the lives of Peter and Paul and then contains the lives of Cyprian and Justina (fols 65va–66va), Cecilia (fols 95va–97va), Barbara (fols 112rb–113ra), Agatha (fols 164rb–165va), and Domitilla, who is included in the title alongside Nereus and Achilleus, Euphrosyne, and Theodora (fols 248vb–250rb).

MS 14 (identified as Q MS 7, 'Ex abbatia Tongerloensi ad nos rediit'), a large vellum manuscript in double columns from the tenth century, contains an extensive collection of short lives including Domitilla, alongside Eufrosyne, Theodora, Sulpicius, and Servilianus (fol. 13rb–vb), the Decollation of John the Baptist (fol. 40ra–va), Cyprian and Justina (fols 94rb–97va), Cecilia (fols 121rb–125rb), Barbara (fols 133va–134va), and John the Evangelist (fols 144va–146vb). Then bound into the same manuscript is another from the thirteenth century on fols 162–237. This is again laid out in double columns with the use of very interesting illuminated capitals. It contains the life of Domitilla, again alongside Eufrosyne, Theodora, Sulpicius, and Servilialus [*sic*] (fols 182rb–183rb) and a tract on John the Evangelist (fols 184rb–217vb). This is a good example of the type of manuscript used by the early Bollandists where material of different dates were combined and more than one copy of the same saint included, as happens here with Domitilla, a saint who is normally very rare.

MS 72, a plain vellum manuscript (apart from very large red initials) from the twelfth century formerly owned by a monastery in Gladbach, contains the life of Agatha (fols 113r–116r), situated before the life of Valentine and so on in liturgical order.

---

[13] Full details are available in Moretus, 'Catalogus codicum hagiographicorum latinorum Bibliothecæ Bollandianæ'.

UNIVERSAL LATIN SAINTS' LIVES

MS 288, a paper manuscript of the fifteenth century in double columns, has lives of Augustine, Amalberga, Gerard, Barbara, and Francis. This Barbara is another copy of the long life of Barbara and her miracles by Jean Wackerzeele (fols 21ra–37ra). The manuscript is signed at three points by the Augustinian Arethurus Reyniers including fol. 37ra where the date of 1464 is provided for the completion of Barbara. It is noteworthy that, as usual in Wackerzeele manuscripts, headings are given before each section of the narrative (a technique common in the Add. 2604 lives).

MS 347, a neat fifteenth-century manuscript, has an extensive collection of lives ranging from apostles to popes to virgins and martyrs, beginning with Lucy and ending with the Purification of the Virgin. Included in this group is a life of Agatha (fols 14va–16va) positioned before Juliana.

MS 433, 'Liber monasterii Heimbergensis [...]', a tightly bound plain quarto vellum manuscript in single columns of the thirteenth century that has been severely trimmed for its early modern binding, contains a mixed collection including Barbara (fols 21v–23v) and Cecilia (fols 100r–107r).

MS 467 is a fifteenth-century paper manuscript of the *Legenda aurea* with various chapters omitted and other short lives intermingled. It is written in double columns by a heavily abbreviated cursive hand that includes a life of Barbara (fols 152ra–153va). This is positioned before the life of Nicholas, which would imply that it was intended for 4 December and not for 16 December as happens in the Add. 2604 life of Barbara.

MS 506 (*olim* MS 48 in the Museum Bollandianum and *olim* 'abbatiae Marchianensis') is a tightly bound vellum manuscript in single columns of the eleventh century combined with some thirteenth-century material containing the life of Cyprian and Justina (fols 128r–134v).

318   APPENDIX I

(iii) Examples of manuscripts that are/were part of the Collectanea Bollandiana/Museum Bollandianum or have saints similar to those in Add. 2604[14]

Bruxelles, KBR, MS 197 (3131) is the second volume of Johannes Back's two-part *Passionale sanctorum* (possibly of three parts) written in the priory of Rookloster in the southern Low Countries.[15] It opens with a calendar of feasts from the Assumption to the end of November. Included here are the Decollation of John the Baptist (fols 39vb–43vb), Cyprian and Justina (fols 102ra–103va), Leonard (fols 171vb–173va), and Cecilia (fols 196ra–203rb).

Bruxelles, KBR, MS 409 (3135) is a very full collection of fifteenth-century saints' lives in liturgical order from the end of November to the end of March. This is the first part of Johannes Back's *Passionale sanctorum* from Rookloster. This nicely presented manuscript includes Barbara (fols 18vb–24vb) and Agatha (fols 131rb–133ra). What is interesting here is that, despite the attribution to Back, there is evidence of considerable dependence on the *Legenda aurea* (not noticed in Fleith). For instance, the life of John the Evangelist (fols 57rb–59vb) is taken from the *Legenda aurea*, with a different ending; the life of Agatha has Voragine's etymology with the life having a different opening but the same ending as in the *Legenda aurea*. At the end of the manuscript the provenance is provided 'Liber monasterii rubeeuallis in zonia iuxta bruxellam scriptus per manus fratris iohannis back [...]'.

Bruxelles, KBR, MSS 7460 and 7461 (3176) are among the many manuscripts in the KBR listed under the heading of *Collectanea Bollandiana*, but these two may be traced back directly to the *Acta sanctorum*. This is one of the rare instances where a link can be found between the actual manuscript being used by the compilers of the *Acta sanctorum* and a traceable current manuscript. In *Acta sanctorum*, Octobris Tomus Quartus, p. 219, the life of

---

[14] In all the references here, as is customary, the numbers (in brackets) allotted in Van den Gheyn's *Catalogue des manuscrits de la Bibliothèque royale de Belgique*, are included. The folio numbers cited are those by Van den Gheyn whether or not other (confusing) systems of foliation or pagination occur in the manuscripts. The *Collectanea Bollandiana* in the KBR refers to manuscripts that were originally part of the Museum Bollandianum (the old Bollandist Library before its dispersal).

[15] Vermassen, 'Latin Hagiography in the Dutch-Speaking Parts of the Southern Low Countries (1350–1550)', usefully discusses MSS 197, 409, 9291 and 9810-14 at various points.

UNIVERSAL LATIN SAINTS' LIVES   319

Benedicta is headed, 'Ex codice nostro, primo Vallicellensi, deinde clarissimi viri Balthazaris Moreti, collato cum aliis'. The manuscript may be identified with Bruxelles, KBR MS 7460 and MS 7461, two large thirteenth-century volumes in double columns with elaborate initial capitals and running titles. Before its acquisition by Balthasar I Moretus (1574–1641), it belonged to the French Cistercian abbey of Vaucelles. Originally MSS P. 159 and P. 160 in the Museum Bollandianum, the volumes were acquired by the KBR in 1807, as clearly stamped at the opening of each. As noted in the *Acta sanctorum*, the first volume (MS 7460) does contain Benedicta (fols 21vb–24rb), and the second volume (MS 7461) contains Leonard (fols 11va–14ra), Cecilia (fols 67va–70va), and Barbara (fols 194ra–195va).

Bruxelles, KBR, MS 7917 (3189), is a fifteenth-century collection of female saints' lives, beginning with Katherine of Alexandria and ending with Cecilia (fols 198va–204rb). It also includes Wackerzeele's Barbara (fols 25ra–48vb), who is followed by Lucy and then Martha (fols 50rb–51va), while Agatha appears later (fols 65va–67vb). On the first page the manuscript is inscribed, 'Pertinet ad librariam domus sancti Ieronomi In traiecto'; there is a seventeenth-century index at the beginning of the manuscript headed 'P MS 17', the shelf-mark in the Museum Bollandianum. This index is followed by another one, nicely laid out by a fifteenth-century hand in alphabetical order.

Bruxelles, KBR, MS 7984 (3191), previously MS P in the Museum Bollandianum, dates from the tenth century and formerly belonged to the Benedictine monastery of St Peter in Wissembourg in Alsace. It is a very early example of a collection of saints' lives (male and female) that includes Columba (fols 21r–22v).

Bruxelles, KBR, MS II.2559 (3315), from the thirteenth century, is another collection of saints' lives (again male and female) that has Columba (fols 61vb–63rb) in liturgical order following Silvester. Before it was acquired by the KBR in 1900, this manuscript was part of the Phillipps Collection (no. 14916) and so would have been in England in earlier times.

Bruxelles, KBR, MS 8964 (3516) is a typically disordered looking post-medieval manuscript from the *Collectanea Bollandiana* produced by the Bollandists as part of their collecting activities. It contains a mass of items in various shapes and sizes and in different hands alongside some interleaved printed items from the seventeenth and eighteenth centuries. The material included focus on the saints from the beginning of December which means

320   APPENDIX I

that there are many items on Barbara dispersed throughout the manuscript
(fols 132r–157r, 161r–163v, two printed items before fol. 179, fols 179r–186r,
187r–190r, 191r–193v, 195r, 196r–197r, 200r–203r, 215r–v, 216r–219v,
220r–221v, 228r–233v, 235r–237r, 237r–240v, and 241r–v). Clearly on the
basis of such material a planned life of Barbara was intended for an *Acta sancto-rum* volume that was never produced.

Bruxelles, KBR, MS 8990-91 (3527) is another manuscript from the
Collectanea Bollandiana showing the collecting activities of the post-medieval
Bollandists. Like Bruxelles, KBR, MS 8964, it is a disordered compilation in
multiple seventeenth-century hands. This manuscript focuses on saints from
the very end of December and so includes a myriad of items on Columba
scattered throughout (fols 173r–175r, 180r, 181r–182r, 183r–184r, 184r–v,
185r–186r, 187r–188v, 189r–190r, 197r–v, 200r–204r, two printed items
before fol. 207, 208r–210r). There is annotation at various points, for example,
on fol. 181r next to the life of Columba, 'Ex ms 5 Audomari vetusissimo'. Some
of this material would have helped in providing the planned life of Columba
intended for the December volume of the *Acta sanctorum* volume that never
appeared.

Bruxelles, KBR, MS 9291 (3224), a manuscript from the Benedictine abbey
of St Laurent de Liège dated on the final folio to 1480, is an example of abbreviated lives from the *Legenda aurea* plus traditional lives, miracles, and so forth.
This begins with the life of Laurence and ends with a sermon to religious. It
is an interesting example of the sort of selections made and the ways in which
items from the *Legenda aurea* may be combined with less usual lives, such as
'Passio sancti Cucufatis martyris' (fols 169r–172r). Hypothetically Add. 2604
may have derived from a manuscript or manuscripts operating in this sort of
tradition.

Bruxelles, KBR, MS 9378 (3327) is a fifteenth-century manuscript originally
from St Laurent de Liège laid out in double columns that has a few items on
Barbara, including miracles (fols 3ra–5ra and fols 164va–169rb), her life (fols
18rb–19va), passion (fols 19va–21vb), and translation (fols 21vb–22vb). It also
includes John the Evangelist (fols 46rb–51vb), Martha with Mary Magdalene
(fols 83ra–86ra), and Agatha (fols 113vb–116ra). At the opening there is a
calendar from December to April.

Bruxelles, KBR, MS 9810-14 (3229), a large rather plain manuscript from
the Benedictine abbey of Saint-Laurent de Liège, is clearly signalled at the

UNIVERSAL LATIN SAINTS' LIVES

opening as a 'Passionale de virginibus'. Although not a source manuscript, this twelfth- to fourteenth-century manuscript contains virtually all of the Add. 2604 universal female saints, apart from Martha who is not a martyr: Benedicta (fols 25r–27v), Justina, albeit with Cyprian as usual (fols 30v–33v), Domitilla, alongside Theodora, Euphrosyne, Sulpicius, and Servilianus (fols 33v–34r), Barbara (fols 34v–35v), Agatha (fols 80r–82v), Columba (fols 107v–108r), and Cecilia (fols 133v–142r).

Bruxelles, KBR, MSS 11986, 982, and 11987 (3234), respectively for January–February, May–August, September–December, are the three surviving manuscripts of Anton Geens's hagiographical collection. Each begins with a list of contents, including a list of those in the missing second volume (March–April) given at the beginning of the first volume. Written by a small neat hand or hands of the early sixteenth century, there is some overlap in content with Add. 2604 (as noted in Table 4 in IV. Hagiographical Context and the Selection of Saints). MS 982 has a life of Justina (fol. 2r–2v), and then four of the native saints: Modwenna (fols 154r–158v), Seaxburh (fols 158v–159r), Wihtburh (fol. 159r–v), and Eanswith (fols 297v–298v). MS 11987 contains Edith (fols 28v–29v) and Benedicta (fols 133r–134v). Although far more capacious than Add. 2604 now is or perhaps ever was, Geens's work provides the same sort of mixture of universal and native saints, including native English saints. These native lives connect with those in Add. 2604, as Geens's lives of the English female saints above derive from John of Tynemouth's *Sanctilogium* or the early printed *Nova Legenda Anglie*.

(iv) Columba

Paris, Bibliothèque Nationale, fonds latin, MS 12598 dates from *c.* 750. Its provenance is associated with the renowned Benedictine abbey of Corbie in Picardie in northern France. It contains the following saints' lives (though not in this order): Agatha, Agnes, Cecilia, Columba, Crispin and Crispinian, Eufemia, Fuscian and Victoricus, Germanus of Auxerre, Juliana, Justus, Lambert, Lucy, Lucian, Martin, Matthew, Medard, Remigius, Servatius, and Vedast. The life of Columba on fols 103v–105v is very close to that in Add. 2604.[16]

---

[16] This life is transcribed in Chastel, *Sainte Colombe de Sens*, pp. 325–28. See the Overview and Commentary to Columba in the *Edition*.

Appendix 2

LATIN AND MIDDLE ENGLISH
VERSIONS OF ÆTHELTHRYTH

This short extract from the life of Æthelthryth, which originates in Bede's *Historia ecclesiastica*, is offered to illustrate the varied ways in which this passage was developed and augmented in the Latin tradition, especially in John of Tynemouth's *Sanctilogium*, and how it has been translated into Middle English in both verse and prose. The Latin transcriptions from various manuscripts of the *Sanctilogium* demonstrate the consistency of the copies over time — and give an idea of the working text the Add. 2604 translator must have used, as discussed in V. Latin Sources and Analogues. The passages below are given in broadly chronological order.[1]

(i) Latin Versions

Bede, 'Life of Etheldreda', *Bede's Ecclesiastical History of the English People*, ed. and trans. by Colgrave and Mynors, IV.19, pp. 394, 396 (*c.* 731)

Cumque post tot annos eleuanda essent ossa de sepulchro, et extento desuper papilione omnis congregatio, hinc fratrum inde sororum, psallens circumstaret, ipsa autem abbatissa intus cum paucis ossa elatura et dilutura intrasset, repente audiuimus abbatissam intus clara uoce proclamare: 'Sit gloria nomini Domini.' Nec multo post clamauerunt me intus, reserato ostio papilionis, uidique eleuatum de tumulo et positum in lectulo corpus sacrae Deo uirginis quasi dormientis simile. Sed et discooperto uultus indumento monstrauerunt mihi etiam uulnus incisurae, quod feceram, curatum, ita ut mirum in modum pro aperto et hiante uulnere, cum quo sepulta erat, tenuissima tunc cicatricis uestigia parerent. Sed et linteamina omnia, quibus inuolutum erat corpus, integra

---

[1] Many of these texts are transcriptions from manuscript witnesses. Original spelling has been retained, but contractions and abbreviations have been silently expanded. Capitalisation, word-division, and punctuation are editorial. Corrections or insertions are marked with < >. Where it has been necessary to excise material for ease of comparison in longer narratives, ellipses have been inserted without summary.

apparuerunt et ita noua, ut ipso die uiderentur castis eius membris esse circum-
data.' Ferunt autem quia, cum praefato tumore ac dolore maxillae siue colli
premeretur, multum delectata sit hoc genere infirmitatis, ac solita dicere: 'Scio
certissime quia merito in collo pondus languoris porto, in quo iuuenculam
me memini superuacua moniliorum pondera portare; et credo quod ideo me
superna pietas dolore colli uoluit grauari, ut sic absoluar reatu superuacuae leuitatis, dum mihi nunc pro auro et margaretis de collo rubor tumoris ardorque
promineat.'

'Life of Etheldreda', *Liber Eliensis*, ed. by Blake, 1.20, 21, 27, pp. 38, 40, 44–45 (1106 x 1169)

Et cum prefato tumore premeretur, fertur quod multum delectata sit hoc infirmitatis genere tota amplectens alacritate, quasi delicias et ornamenta glorie, ac
solita ciere: 'Scio certissime quia merito in collo pondus languoris porto, in quo
iuvenculam me memini supervacua moniliorum pondera portare. Illud enim
mihi etas iuvenilis ingessit, quod collum monilibus perornare consuevi, unde
divine pietati laudes et gratias refero, quod illinc dolor prodeat ubi eram solita
delectabilem ministrare fulgorem. Et credo quod ideo me superna pietas dolore
colli uoluit grauari, ut sic absoluar reatu supervacuae levitatis, dum mihi nunc
pro auro et margaretis de collo rubor tumoris ardorque promineat.' [...][2] Rapta
est ad Dominum virgo Æðeldreða in medio suorum nono Kalendas Iulii post
annos viitem ex quo abbatisse gradum susceperat et eque, ut ipsa iusserat, non
alibi quam in medio suorum iuxta ordinem quo transierat ligneo in locello est
sepulta. [...] Cunque statuto die post tot annos sacre virginis corpus ac sponse
Christi elevanda essent ossa de tumulo et in basilica decentius tumulanda, pars
plurima devote plebis confluxerat ad huius translationis sancta solempnia et,
quoniam res talis confirmari debet testimonio plurimorum, prefatus antistes
sancte memorie Wilfridus [...] atque innumeri qui novere et adfuere id ipsum
testati sunt, sed et inter ceteros ad ampliorem rei certitudinem et veritatis evi-
dentiam medicus Kinefridus, qui sicut morienti illi ita et elevate de tumulo
presentialis affuit, ut in tam mirando et pro raritate pretioso miraculo testis
existerat, memor itaque ille incisure quam quondam fecerat in eius corpore
qui referre erat solitus, quod illa infirmata habuerit tumorem maximum sub
maxilla. Aptato igitur et desuper decenter composito papilionis umbraculo,

---

[2] The *vita* is an extensive one of thirty-four chapters of the fifty that comprise Book I of
the *Liber Eliensis*. As a result, the description of the elevation and translation of Æthelthryth's
incorrupt body is extended over several chapters.

[cum] omnis congregatio, hinc fratrum, illinc sororum, psallens sepulcrum eius circumstaret, aggere deiecto fossa defoditur et theca de pulvere elevatur. Ipsa autem abbatissa sancta Sexburga ab aperto sepulture hostio cum paucis tamquam ossa elatura et dilutura ingreditur et, facto modico intervallo, repente de intus audivimus ipsam voce magna proclamare: 'Sit gloria nomini Domini altissimo'. Et ut ista pateintus, reserato papilionis hostio, vidique elevatum de tumulo et postium in lectulo corpus sacre virginis, quasi dormienti simile.

John of Tynemouth, *Sanctilogium*, London, British Library, MS Cotton Tiberius E. i, fols 19ra–20ra, fol. 19va–b (*c.* 1380s)

Predixit quoque obitus multorum de suo monasterio transeuntium ex hoc mundo. Finem insuper suum, et qua finitura erat, spiritu prophetico pestem predixit. Pressa demum quodam maxille tumore ac colli dolore, delectata fertur plurimum hoc infirmitatis genere, solita suis dicere cum uirtute tolerantie: 'Pondus languoris portans merito in collo afficior: reminiscor me in eo gestasse monilium pondera: quod ultra quam debuit etas iuuenilis facere consueui. Laudetur ergo pietas deitatis superne, si sic absoluar a reatu leuitatis superuacue, dum pro auro et margaritis nunc michi promineat de collo rubor ardorque tumoris.' Hac itaque ingruente morbi molestia, medicus peritus accersitur; qui fiducia artis sue fisus, tumorem illum pungens incidit sub maxilla, ut prurulentus humor effluerent tanti tumoris. Cumque leuius per biduum se habere uideretur, tertia die prioribus aggrauata doloribus, felici commertio dolorem omnem et mortem commutans, completis in abbatisse officio septem annis, nono kalendas julii ad dominum migrauit, et in locello ligneo sepeliri meruit. Cum autem sexdecim annis in terra sepulta iaceret crebrescentibus circa tumulum eius miraculis, et corpus de terra leuari et ad locum decentiorem transferri deberet, famuli aptum lapidem quesituri nauiculam ascendentes, ad urbem Grantcestre desolatam ex insperato deuenerunt: et prope urbis murum sarcophagum mire puchritudinis et marmoris albi reperientes, assumpto secum lapide gaudentes reuersi sunt. Statu^t^o translationis corporis sancte uirginis die, aperto que locello, sine omni corruptela uel diminutione aliqua cum uestibus quibus sepulta fuerat, ita incorrupta et illesa et integra est reperta ac dormienti simillima, ac si eadem die fuisset sepulta. Tumor autem colli eius, sola cicatrice inscisure remanente, sanus reperitur.

APPENDIX 2

John of Tynemouth, *Sanctilogium*, Karlsruhe, Badische Landesbibliothek, Cod. Sankt Georgen 12, fols 133va–134ra, fol. 133vb (before 1439)

Predixit quoque obitus multorum de suo monasterio transeuntium ex hoc mundo. Ffinem insuper suum, et qua finitura erat, spiritu prophetico pestem predixit. Pressa demum quodam maxille tumore ac colli dolore, delectata fertur plurimum hoc infirmitatis genere, solita suis dice cum virtute tolerantie: 'Pondus langoris portans merito in collo afficior reminscor me in eo gestasse monilium pondera: Quod vltra quam debuit etas iuuenilis facere consueui. Laudetur ergo pietas dietatis superne si sic absoluer a reatu leuitatis superuacue dum per auro et margaritis nunc michi promineat de collo rubor ardor que tumoris.' Hac itaque ingruente morbi molestia medicus peritus accersitur; qui fiducia artis sue fisus, tumorem illum pungens incidit sub maxilla, vt prurulentus humor efflueret tanti tumoris. Cumque leuius per biduum se habere videretur, tertia die prioribus aggrauata doloribus, felici commertio dolorem omnem et mortem commutans, completis in abbatisse officio septem annis, . ix. kalendas iulii ad dominum migrauit, et in locello ligneo sepeliri meruit. Cum autem in terra sexdecim annis in tercia sepulta iaceret crebrescentibus circa tumulum eius miraculis, et corpus de terra leuari et ad locum decentiorem transferri deberet, <famuli aptum lapidem quesituri nauiculam ascendentes, ad urbem Grantcestre desolatam ex insperato deuenerunt: et prope urbis murum sarcophagum mire pulchritudinis et marmoris albi reperientes, assumpto secum lapide gaudentes reversi sunt. Statuto translationis corporis sancte virginis die, aperto que locello,>[3] sine omnem corruptela vel diminutione aliqua cum vestibus quibus sepulta fuerat, ita incorrupta et illesa et integra est reperta ac dorminenti simillima, ac si eadem die fuisset sepulta. Tumor autem colli eius sola circatrice incissure remanente, sanus reperitur.

John of Tynemouth, *Sanctilogium*, London, British Library, MS Cotton Otho D. ix (*s. xv*) [visible but illegible]

John of Tynemouth, *Sanctilogium*, York, York Minster Library, MS XVI.G.23, fol. 147ra–va, fol. 147rb (1454)

Predixit quoque obitus multorum de suo monasterio transeuntium ex hoc mundo. Finem insuper suum, et qua finitura erat, spiritu prophetico pestem predixit. Pressa demum quodam maxille tumore ac colli dolore, delectata fertur plurimum hoc infirmitatis genere, solita suis dicere cum virtute tollerantie:

---

[3] This insertion is a correction made by the original scribe in the lower margin.

LATIN AND MIDDLE ENGLISH VERSIONS OF ÆTHELTHRYTH

'Pondus languoris portans merito in collo afficior: reminiscor me in eo gestasse monilium pondera: quod vltra quam debuit etas iuuenilis facere consueui. Laudetur ergo pietas deitatis, si sic absoluar a reatu leuitatis superuacue, dum pro auro et margaritis nunc michi promineat de collo rubor ardorque tumoris.' Hac itaque ingruente morbi molestia, medicus peritus accersitur; qui fiducia artis sue fisus, tumorem illum pungens incidit sub maxilla, vt prurulentus humor effluerent tanti tumoris. Cumque leuius se per biduum habere videretur, tertia die prioribus aggrauata doloribus, felici commertio dolorem omnem et mortem commutans, completis in abbatisse officio septem annis, nono kalendas iulii ad dominum migrauit, et in locello ligneo sepeliri meruit. Cum autem sexdecim annis in terra sepulta iaceret crebrescentibus circa tumulum eius miraculis, et corpus de terra leuari et ad locum decentiorem transferri debuit, famuli aptum lapidem quesituri nauiculam ascendentes, ad vrbem Grancestre desolatam ex insperato deuenerunt: et prope murum sarcophagum mire puchritudinis et marmoris albi reperientes, assumpto secum lapide gaudentes reuersi sunt. Statuto translationis corporis sancte virginis die, aperto que locello, sine omni corruptela vel diminutione aliqua cum vestibus quibus sepulta fuerat, ita incorrupta et illesa et integra est reperta ac dormienti simillima, ac si eadem die fuisset sepulta. Tumor autem colli eius, sola cicatrice inscissure remanente, sanus reperitur.

John of Tynemouth, *Sanctilogium*, Oxford, Bodleian Library, MS Tanner 15, fols 254va–257rb, fol. 255rb (1499)

Predixit multum obitus quoque de suo monasterio transeuncium ex hoc mundo. Finem insuper suum, et qua finitura erat, spiritu prophetico pestem predixit. Precessa demum quodam maxilli tumore ac colli dolore, delectata fertur plurimum hoc infirmitatis genere, solita suis dicere cum virtute tolerancie: 'Pondus languoris portans merito in collo afficior: reminiscor in eo gestasse monilium pondera: quod ultra quam debuit etas iuuenilis facere consueui. Laudetur ergo pietas deitatis, si sic absoluar aream leuitatis supervacuam, dum pro auro et margaritis nunc michi promineat de collo rubor ardor que tumoris.' Hac itaque ingruente morbi molestia, medicus peritus accersitur; qui fiducia artis sue fisus, tumorem illum pungens incidit sub maxilla, vt prurulentus humor efflueret tanti tumoris. Cumque leuius se per biduum habere videretur, tertia die prioribus agrauata doloribus, felici commercio dolorem omnem et mortem commutans, completis in abbatisse officio septem annis, nono kalendas iulii ad dominum migrauit, et in locello ligneo sepeliri meruit. Cum autem sexdecim annis in terra sepulta iaceret crebrescentibus circa tumulum eius miraculis, et corpus de terra leuari et ad locum decenciorem transferri deberet, famuli aptum lapidem quesituri nauiculam ascendentes, ad vrbem Grancestre desolatam ex inspirato deuenerunt: et prope murum sarcophagum mire puchritudinis et marmoris albi reperientes, assumpto secum lapide gaudentes reuersi sunt. Statuto translacionis corporis sancte virginis die, aperto que locello, sine omni corruptela vel diminucione aliqua cum vestibus quibus sepulta fuerat, ita incorrupta et illesa et integra est reperta ac dormienti similia, ac si eadem die fuisset sepulta. Tumor autem colli eius, sola cicatrice inscissure remanente, sanus reperitur.

Wynkyn de Worde, *Nova Legenda Anglie*, ed. by Horstman, I, 426, ll. 19–24 (1516)[4]

Predixit quoque obitus multorum de suo monasterio transeuntium ex hoc mundo. Finem insuper suum, et qua finitura erat, spiritu prophetico pestem predixit. Pressa demum quodam maxille tumore ac colli dolore, delectata fertur plurimum hoc infirmitatis genere, solita suis dicere cum virtute tolerantie: 'Pondus languoris portans merito in collo afficior: reminiscor me in eo gestasse monilium pondera: quod vltra quam debuit etas iuuenilis facere consueui. Laudetur ergo pietas deitatis superne, si sic absoluar a reatu leuitatis superuacue, dum pro auro et margaritis nunc michi promineat de collo rubor ardorque tumoris.' Hac itaque ingruente morbi molestia, medicus peritus accersitur; qui fiducia artis sue fisus, tumorem illum pungens incidit sub maxilla, vt prurulentus humor effluerent tanti tumoris. Cumque leuius per biduum se habere videretur, tertia die prioribus aggrauata doloribus, felici commertio dolorem omnem et mortem commutans, completis in abbatisse officio septem annis, nono kalendas iulii ad dominum migrauit, et in locello ligneo sepeliri meruit. Cum autem sexdecim annis in terra sepulta iaceret crebrescentibus circa tumulum eius miraculis, et corpus de terra leuari et ad locum decentiorem transferri deberet, famuli aptum lapidem quesituri nauiculam ascendentes, ad vrbem Grancestre desolatam ex insperato deuenerunt: et prope vrbis murum sarcophagum mire puchritudinis et marmoris albi reperientes, assumpto secum lapide gaudentes reuersi sunt. Statuto translationis corporis sancte virginis die, apertoque locello, sine omni corruptela vel diminutione aliqua cum vestibus quibus sepulta fuerat, ita incorrupta et illesa et integra est reperta ac dormienti simillima, ac si eadem die fuisset sepulta. Tumor autem colli eius, sola cicatrice incisure remanente, sanus reperitur.

---

[4] Horstman checked his edition against MSS Cotton Tiberius E. i and Tanner 15.

LATIN AND MIDDLE ENGLISH VERSIONS OF ÆTHELTHRYTH

(ii) Middle English

'Life of St Audrey', *South English Legendary*, London, British Library, MS Egerton 1993, fol. 163r–v (fol. 163v), ed. by Major, ll. 30–48, pp. 98–99 (*s.* xiv²/⁴)

Ate laste as God it wolde · toward hire ende heo drow,
Wel longe bifore hire deþ · as hire sostren seiȝe
Heo seide whanne heo scholde henne [·] 7 whiche time deiȝe.
7 whoch of hire sostren scholden · wiþ hire henne wende
7 riȝt as heo hedde iseid · hire life heo brouȝte to ende.
7 wiþ gret honor as riȝt was · an erþe was ibrouȝt
Ur Lord haþ for hire loue · uaire miracle iwrouȝt.
Sixtene ȝer þis holi maide · an erþe lay so
Ar heo were up inome · 7 in schrine ido.
So þat Sexborw [hire] soster · was abbesse mani a day
After hire in þilke house · þer hire bodi lay.
Þo þis bodi sixtene ȝer · an erþe hadde ileiȝe so
Þe abbesse hire soster nom it up · 7 let hit in a schrine do.
Hire bodi heo fond also fair · as heo aliue were
Cler 7 round 7 fair inow · riȝt as heo slepe þere.
Also uareþ þis wiues ȝut · þat maidnes comeþ to deþe
And so longe mid here lordes beþ · a[s] ic wene hi mowe wel eþe.
Þe schete wherin heo was iwounde · as swote was also
7 as white as hi were · þo heo was þeron do.⁵

Wilton Chronicle, London, British Library, MS Cotton Faustina B. iii, fols 194r–274v, in *Saints Edith and Æthelthryth*, ed. by Dockray-Miller, pp. 366, 370, 386, 388, ll. 485–92, 525–31, 826–51

[In an extended narrative in which Æthelthryth's illness and death is recounted, the abbess prophecies her death but asks Cynefrith to lance a tumour under her jaw. After the leech performs the operation, the abbess falls into a slumber in which she dreams that an angel appears to her, saying]

---

⁵ Two later manuscripts of the *South English Legendary* present this life of Æthelthryth with slight variations: Oxford, Bodleian Library, MS Eng. poet. 1. a, fol. 33r–v (*c.* 1390), and Oxford, Bodleian Library, MS Bodley 779, fols 279v–280r (1400 x 1450).

'Hedur now Goddus sone of hevene to ȝow send me,
to tell þe þat þis swellyng, þe whiche is þy nek abouȝt,
For penaunce of synne was now ysend to þe,
For þe synne of þy ȝong age, when þou were wyld and prouȝt.
For when þou wer a child of ȝong age,
Forsothe in þyne hert þou were somdell prouȝt,
Both of þy bewte and of þy worthy lynage,
and ryall colers of gold þou weredust þy nek abouȝt. [...]'
Bot when þis blessude virgyn was þus forth past,
hurre blessude soule up to God in trinite,
and in a trene chest þen was ycast
hurre semelyche body so fayre and so fre.
And þey buryedone hurre in þat same place,
Ryȝt as hurre owne wyll was to,
and sixstene wynter þer inne he was [...]
And when þey knewen and herden þe bellus ryng and knylle,
so schryll wyth ouȝt ony touche of monnes hond,
Seynt Wilfride went anon þe tombe tyll
and Sexburwe went anon and þo doune in to þe grond.
Bot when Seynt Wilfride hadde yseye all this,
in his hert forsothe he was wondre gladde,
and doune in to þe tombe wyth Sexburwe ygon he is.
And tweyn other bysshoppus wyth hym he hadde.
And touchede þe chest þo he dude wyth his hondys
and þerof he toke away þe lede þo after anone,
and hurre blessude body as hole þer lygynng he fond
As ever hit was wyth inne þat chest ydon.
As whyte, as rody, and as freysshe,
hurre fayre body was þer as hit þo lay,
and wyth ouȝt ony corrupcion of hurre fleysshe,
Ryȝt as þaw hit hadde ben leyde wyth in þe chest þat same day.
Hurre lures weron white as ony lely floure,
y meynde wyth rod ryȝt as hit was best,
and hurre body was of þe same coloure
Ryȝt semely and sote and eke full honest.
And þe grete swellyng, þe whiche was her nekke abouȝt,
was vanysshede away, and nothyng senene,
and þe wonde was clene, holl wyth ouȝt ony douȝt,
and all hurre body lay þer bothe streȝt and evene.

LATIN AND MIDDLE ENGLISH VERSIONS OF ÆTHELTHRYTH 331

Hurre body lay þer as semely in everichemonnes sy3t,
Ry3t a lyve as þaw hit 3et were.

'Life of St Audry', Oxford, Corpus Christi College, MS 120, fols 12r–v, 13v (*s. xv*)

She had a grett and paynfull sore vndyr hir ere swellyng downe to hir nekke, the whiche sore a surgyon callyd Kynfryde dyd launce, and aftyr that launcyng to days togethur she was sumwhat relesyd of hir payne. Notwithstondyng her vehement paynys and vexacion that she so feryd by the anguysshe of hir sykknes, yet she [...] shewyd them many tokyns of inwarde penaunce and contricion for hir trespacys done to God long before in hir youthe, confessyng opynly before them all that God sent to hir that stroke full deseruyngly for hir synnys and spirtually in that place of hir nekke, rather than in ony other place for iuste punyshement of hir wanton plesure in her youthe, in that she was wonte than to were abowte hir nekke owchys and chaynys of gold with other precyouse ornamentes as grett estates ar wonte to do. The .iii.de day aftyr she was infectyd her payn began ageyn to encrese in asmoche that she felte tokyns of dethe sone aftyr to folowe, wherfor she sent for all the hole congregacion of hir monastery to whome she gaue many gostly exortacions [...]. She also dissiryd them to bery hir withought pompe or worldly solempnyte, and not in the cherche butt in the churcheyarde amonge hir systers aftyr that ordyr that they ware beryed. Thys done, she full deuoutly receyvyd the sacramentes of the churche and at the laste yeldyd hir holy sowle vpp to the presence of the gloryouse trynite in the 3ere of owre lorde. dc .lxxix. the ix.th kalendes of July. [...] Sexburgh seeyng that so moche peple wer resortyng to the graue of hir syster Audry ensuengly now .xvi. yerys togethur wer releuyd of many aduersyteis bothe of body and of mynde, she thought yt beste bothe to the honour of God and also for the ese of the peple to remoue hir relyquis into the churche. [...] When this joyfull daye was come, all the peple assembled in the churcheyarde to beholde this gracious dede, amonge whome ther was the olde father Kenefryde, su<r>gyon, that cutt hir sore before she dyed. Ther was also the holy Archebisshopp Wylfryde, sumtyme confessor to the gostly Audry and the true wyttnes of hir contynuall chastyte. All thynges duely preparyd, the honorable abbas with hir hole cloyster, bothe of brotherne and systerne, cam to the graue of the forseid noble monyall with joyfull and gostly syngyng and prayers. The brotherne stode on the on syde abought the graue and the systers vpon the othur syde contynueng this heuynly melody whill the abbas with fewe of hir systers enteryd vndyr the tente (that was made ouer the tombe) to take owte secretly the holy bonys of hir syster,

Audry, the whiche she supposyd then only ther had remaynyd. Butt when they lyftyd vpp the coueryng of the cheste wherin the body was beryed .xvi. yerys before, she founde the body as hole as ytt had ben beryd the same day. Of the whiche thyng she meruelously astonyd sodenly cryed with a lowde voyce seyng, 'Honour be to the name of God foreuer.' This confortable voyce the peple stondyng abought heryng gretly reioysyd in ther hartes. She then dissiryng to haue more wytnes in this myracle callyd in to the tente ~~the bysshopp wyfryde~~ <Kynefryde> who also se hir takyn ought of thate tombe all hole bothe in body and vestures the whiche apperyd as newe as they wer that day þat they wer layde in wythe hir. They also, takyng away the coueryng of hir face and nekke, se ther a meruelous syght for the sore vnder hir ~~ere~~ cheke, that was full of corrupcion when she was beryed, was clene wythowte mattyr or fylthenes. And, thoowe yt was opyn vnder a deforme and vgle maner when she was beryed, yett nowe ytt was all closyd and ther aperyd noo thyng of yt but alonly a lytyll skarre wher ytt was cutt and to ther syght she laye as she had ben in a sownde slepe.[6]

Osbern Bokenham, Edinburgh, Advocates Library, MS Abbotsford, fols 119ra–120ra, in *Osbern Bokenham, 'Lives of Saints'*, ed. by Horobin, II, 149–55, ll. 365–85, 413–17, 421–27, 463–66, 514–65 (*s.* xv)

And fynally the spirite of prophecie
She had, by which thurgh Goddis grace
How many persones she tolde shuld die,
And which by pestilence in hir place,
And how hirself amonge hem shuld pace,
Neither first ner last but in such degree,
That myd hem alle hir passage shuld be.

And within short while aftir so it byfelle,
Liche as she had seid, certynly.
For in hir necke a pestilence swelle
Grete grue and rede even vpon hy,
Which whan she felt ful devoutely
Vp to heven-ward liftyng both her eyne,
Al folk hir heryng thus did seyne:

---

[6] But for <g> in 'congregacion' which is spelled 'conqregacion', insertions marked with < > and deletions struck out are scribal corrections.

'Gramercy, lorde, which of thy grete grace
Vouchistsafe mercyfully me to visite
With a pestilence soore, and on such place
Where I was wone me to delite,
In my youthe to beren grete wyte
Of golde and siluer, wherfor now there
Where I than synned, I peyne bere.' [...]

And in that agonye she forth hens went.

That is to seyn she chaungid hir hous
Which corruptible was, mortal and variable,
For anothir which right glorious
And incorruptible is, stedfast and stable [...]

And whan thus from this wrecchid valey,
The nynthe kalend of Iule was went
This noble gemme vnto the place hy
Of heven, aboue the sterrid firmament,
Hir body they buried with humble entent
Myddis hir sustris, in a cophir of tree,
In the ordre she deied, as chargid had she. [...]

And whan the abbesse Sexburgh such habundance
Of myraclis encresyn sawe there dayly,
She hir purposid to translate and enhauncen
Oute of that place, hir sustris body [...]

Aboute fourtenyght aftir Myghelmasse
Vnto hir sustris grave she went,
And did it ovircuren with a tent,
That no man shuld see that blissid body,
Til the boones were wasshen and made redy.

And rounde aboute the tent al the company
Of hi[r] sustris stooden, and prestis also,
Syngyng and preyeng ful devoutely,
While the abbesse with a fewe clepid hir to
Went in and did the grave vndoo.
Which doon, the body truly thei founde
As it was buried, al hole and sounde.

That is to seyn that no corrupcioun
Was therupon, ner feculencie,
From the hede abouen to the foot doun,
As fer as the abbesse coude aspye.
For forhede and cheke, mouth and iye,
And al the face eke, was as fresh to see
As she not ded but aslepe had be.

And not oonly hir body but the clothis also,
In which it wrappid was and wounde,
With al othir thyngis longyng therto,
Withoute putrefaction heyl were and sounde,
As though tho nevir had leyn on grounde.
And therto of odour as redolent, certeyn,
As tho amonge flouris or spices had leyn.

And whan the abbesse perceivid al this thyng,
With a lowde voice she thus gan cry:
'To the name of God, laude and preysyng
Mote be now and evirmore endelesly,
Which vs hath shewid here his mercy.'
And forthwith she the pavillioun dore vnshett,
And to see this wondir othir folk in lett.

Amonge which, of moste auctorite
And right sufficient witnesse forto bere,
Was blissid Wilfrid, which had be
Hi[r] confessour biforn ful many a yere.
Kenefrid the leche was also there,
Which biforn hir deth hir soore did stynge,
And was eke there with hem at hir buryeng.

And oo thyng in special this leche Kenefride,
Evir aftir while he lived did testifye:
That the wounde in hir neck moist and wide,
Which hymself made was curid and drye,
So fair that vnnethe he coude aspeye
Where it was, which afir his faculte,
Semyd impossible evir curid to haue be.

LATIN AND MIDDLE ENGLISH VERSIONS OF ÆTHELTHRYTH 335

Hir clothis had also such vertu
That who hem touchid with ony sikenesse,
Thurgh grace of our lorde Christ Jhesu,
He curid was anoon, were it more or lesse.
And as al there present born wittenesse [...]

'Life of Seynt Audry [...]', Cambridge, Cambridge University Library, MS Additional 2604, ll. 88–109, 112–15, 121–32 (*c.* 1480–*c.* 1510)

She tolde also by spiryte of prophecie of the deth of many of hir monastery what daye and what houre they shuld passe out of this worlde; hir owne day also whan she shuld dye and of what seknes she tolde, for she said that she shulde dye of a swenysye. And so she did, for whan our lorde had touched hir with a swelling in the cheke and a boluyng in the nekke, she wolde say ofte tymes that she had more ioye therof than of any other seknes. For she wolde some tyme say to hir systres that she was glad for [to] haue suche a speciall seknes, for as moche as somtyme she sayde she had gret ioy for to aray hir nek with broches and houches in hir yonge age, 'Therfore, blessid be the yifte of God and God in his yefte that thus hathe [fol. 55v] chaunged worldly ioyes into gostly iewellis, which shuld purge and clense my soule fro the trespas of wanton lightnes that I vsed in my yowthe; therfore nowe, for gold and precious stones shynith in my cheke and in my nek the rednes and the hete of swellinges.' In so myche that seknes encresed day by day that at laste a wyse leche was sent aftir for to do his cure. The leche come and laughed and cut that swelling vndir hir cheke so that the mater went oute and the swelling abatid; and aftir that she was well esyd and lightid to dayes aftir. But the third day it swellid ayen that she chaunged this wrecchid life by temperall deth into euerlasting lyfe, and so passid out of this worlde on Seynt Iohn Baptist even whos holy body was layde in a chest of tre and beried.

Aftir tyme this holy virgyn Seynt Awdre had lay in the grounde sixtene yere, for many miracles that was shewed where that she lay, it was ordenyd by Seynt Sexburge, which was aftir hir abbes, that the holy body shuld be translated and layed in a more solempne place. [...] At the day sett of translacion, which was of Seynt Luke is evyn, the abbes, Sexburge, went first into the grave with certeyn of hir sistern and brethern and sett honde vpon the chest, and in the taking vp they herd a voyce which sayde alowde, *Sit nomini domini gloria*, that is, 'To the name of our God be ioy and glorye.' Than thei openyd the chest and founde the body vncorrupte, swete smelling and lyghing as she had that same day first be layde therin, more like as she had be aslepe than ded. The seknes also that she had in her nek apperid all hole withoute any wounde, saue a litill marke in maner of a seme ther she was cutte. Of the which bare wittenes the same leche that lawnced it which was ther present amonge all other peple and seyd that he himselfe lawnced it.

The Kalendre of the Newe Legende of Englande, ed. by Görlach, pp. 96–97, ll. 22–31 (1516)

& before her deth she had a great swellynge in her throte & in her cheke, wherin she moche delytyd, & sayde it was a great goodnes of our Lorde if that peyne myghte put away the peyne þat she was worthye to haue for her pryde and offencys in werynge golde & precyous stonys aboute her necke when she was yonge. And when a surgeon had cutte the sore place and that easyd her for a tyme, the thyrde day after the peyne came agayne. And she yeldyd her soule to our Lorde the .ix. kalendas of Iuly after she had ben abbesse .vii.yere. & when she had had lyen .xvi. yerys her body & all her clothys were founde vncorrupte, and her necke was hoole & a tokyn apperyd of the cuttynge.

Appendix 3

MIDDLE ENGLISH TRANSLATIONS OF JOHN THE EVANGELIST

This short extract from the life of John the Evangelist that derives from the *Legenda aurea* is given below to illustrate the varied ways in which this passage can be translated into Middle English as discussed in VI. Reading the *'Lyves and Dethes'*. It also highlights the difficulty of isolating particular *Legenda aurea* manuscripts for the life in Add. 2604 (or elsewhere), an issue that is discussed in V. Latin Sources and Analogues. The English passages below are given in broadly chronological order.[1]

Jacobus de Voragine, 'De sancto Iohanne evangelista', in Iacopo da Varazze, *Legenda aurea*, ed. by Maggioni, I, 102–12, p. 104 (late thirteenth century)

[41]Duo insuper iuuenes honorati horum exemplo uenditis omnibus et pauperibus erogatis apostolum sunt secuti. [42]Quadam autem die uidentes seruos suos pretiosis indumentis fulgentes et in uno pallio se egentes contristari ceperunt. [43]Quod cum sanctus Iohannes aduertisset eo quod facie tristes essent, uirgas et lapides minutos a litore maris deferri fecit et eos in aurum et gemmas conuertit. [44]Qui issu apostoli uniuersos aurifices et gemmarios per septem dies querentes reuersi sunt dicentes quod illi nunquam tam purum aurum et tam pretiosas gemmas se uidisse testati sunt. [45]Dixitque eis: [46]'Ite et redimite uobis terras quas uendidistis quia celorum premia perdidistis, estote floridi ut marcescatis, estote diuites temporaliter ut in perpetuum mendicetis.' [47]Tunc apostolus contra diuitias cepit diutius disputare ostendens quod sex sunt que nos ab immoderato diuitiarum appetitu debent retrahere. [...] [*John's sermon follows.*]

---

[1] Capitalisation, word-division, and punctuation are those of the relevant editors.

John Mirk, 'De sancto Iohanne euangelista', in *John Mirk's Festial*, ed. by Powell, I (2009), 31–35, p. 33, ll. 74–87 (late 1380s)

Anoþur day too yong men and rych by prechyng of Ion þey soldon alle hure good and sewedon Ion. Þenne on a day, as þey comyn into þe cyte of Pargame, when þey seyon þyke þat weren hure seruandes byfore gon in rych aray and heo hemself in pore wede, by temptacyon of þe fynd þey forþoghton here purpos and weren sory þat þey hadden lafte soo hure good. Þenne anon by reuelacyon of þe priuete of God Ion kn[e]w here þoght and sayde to ham: 'Y see how þe deuyl tempteth ʒow and maketh ʒow to forþynk ʒoure purpos þat ʒe were in. Wherfore goth to þe wode and bryngeth eyþur of ʒow hys burþon of ʒerdes, and aftur goth to þe see and bryngeth eyþur of ʒow hys burþon of smale stones', and þey dudon soo. Þen at þe prayere of Ion þe ʒerdus turned into gold and þe stones into precyous ieweles, and þen Ion seyde to hem: 'Now taketh þys gold and þese precyous stones and beth also rych as ʒe were byfore, and knoweth wel þat ʒe han l[os]t þe kyndam of heuen.' [*John's sermon does not follow.*]

'Saint Iohn Euangelist', *in Virgins and Scholars*, ed. by Waters, 124–76, p. 152, l. 398–p. 154, l. 420 (*c.* 1428–39)

How Sainte Iohn conuerted two ʒonge men, and arered from deeth the thrydde yonge man. Capitulum .xiij.

Amongst this puple that see this dede were othir two ʒonge men that by example of this myracle and by techynge of Saint Iohn went and soolde al that thay hadde and ʒaaf hit to pore folke and come and [34r] folewed this holy apostle Saynt Iohn in pouerte and in mekenes. Afterward on a day, as thay come wyth Sainte Iohn in the cyte and see hem that were her seruauntes cladde in precious clothes and in greet plente of werldly riches, þay bygan to waxe sory and heuy, seynge her seruauntes so weel and rychely arayed and hemself so febly arayed and so pore. And whan Saint Iohn see hem so heuy and perceyued the cause, he sent hem and bad hem fet hym roddes of trees, and smale stones from the see syde. And whan thay had doon soo, than Saint Iohn torned tho roddes into goold, and tho stones into most precious gemmes, and bad bere hem to goldsmythes and to hem that medled wyth precious stones to assay whethir thay were good goold and good gemmes or noo. And aftur þay had goo and assayed seuen dayes togydir, thay come aʒeyn and sayde that by preef of alle men thay see neuer noon so good <goold> ne so precious gemmes so thay were. Than sayde Saint Iohn vnto thoo two ʒonge [p. 154 *sic*] men, 'Gooth and byeth aʒeyn therwyth tho londes and rentes that ʒe haue soolde, and take ʒoure ioye

MIDDLE ENGLISH TRANSLATIONS OF JOHN THE EVANGELIST

339

therof in erthe, for the medes of heuen ȝe haue lost. Beth ryche aftur the worlde and beggers wythouten ende'.

Than Saynt Iohn bygan to <dispute> and to preche aȝeynst the loue of worldly ryches, and therof he made a longe sermoun. [*John's sermon does not follow.*]

'Here endithe [...] and nexst beginnithe the blessed lyff of Seint Iohn the Ewangelist. Capitulum .viij.ᵐ', in the *Gilte Legende*, ed. by Hamer and Russell, I (2006), 50–57, p. 51, l. 49–p. 52, l. 63 (*c.* 1438)

And .ii. other yong men bi the ensaumple of hem solde all that thei hadde and gave it to pore men and folued the apostell. And on a day as thei seen her owne servuantes shine in precious clothes and they were in pore mantellis thei begonne to shewe hevi chere. Seint Iohn that perceyued this made bryng to hym yerdes and smalle stones of the riuere and conuerted hem into golde and into precious stones. Bi the comaundement of the apostell thei went to [the] goldesmithes to wete [p. 52] if thei were verray true, the whiche said truly that they hadde neuer sene beter golde ne finer stones. And thanne the apostell saide to hem: 'Gothe and beyethe youre lond ayein that ye haue solde, for ye haue lost the guerdon of heuene, and therfore flourithe here that ye mowe fade, and bethe ryche in temporall rychesse that ye may be beggers witheoute ende.' And thanne the apostell beganne to dispute a gret while ayeinst rychesse, shewyng that there bene .vj. thinges that shulde withedrawe oure thought fro disatempre richesse. [...] [*John's sermon follows.*]

'Here begynneth the life of Seynt Iohan the evangeliste', in *Osbern Boken-ham, 'Lives of Saints'*, ed. by Horobin, I (2020), 97–104, p. 98, l. 107–p. 99, l. 132 (*c.* 1449)

Two yung men also honourable and worthy in that citee thrugh thexample of these two brethern, of whiche oon was clepid Accius and that othir hight Rugius, soolden a[l] that thei hadden and youen the price to pore men and folowed the blissid apostle Iohan, and by vertue of God wroughten many mira-cles. And vpon a day as thei seyen theym, which some tyme biforn weren her seruauntis, araied in clothis of golde and silke and shynyng in faire glorious gar-nementis, and hemself wrappid but in symple and pore mantels, thei begonne to waxen hevy therof and sory [p. 99] in her hertis. And whan Iohan, by her countenaunce and her chere the inwarde hevynesse of her hertis had perceived, he sent anoon to the wode for smale hasel yerdis and to the see banke for smale rounde stoones, which he turned into precious [*sic*] and the yerdis into golde, and delyuerid hem to these two yung men and sent hem aboute the cytee to al the goldsmythes and iuellers to make a preef whethir the golde and the precious stoones were gode and sufficient or nought. And aftir vij daies thei came ageyn to thappostle [fol. 192va] and seid that the decree of hem alle was concordely that thei nevir seyn more fyne golde ne more precious stoonys. 'Goth than', quoth thappostle to hem bothe, 'and with this golde and with thise precious stoones byeth ageyn the londes and the posssesions which ye solden. For the rewarde that ye shuld han had therfore, that is to seyn the blisse of heven, ye han loste. 'Goth and florisshith', quoth he, 'in this worlde, for ye shul w[e]lken in the tothir worlde. Goth and be riche temperally, that ye mow beggen eternally.' And anoon thappostle bigan to prechen a gode while ageyns richesse and couetise, and shewid and declarid sixe thyngis which shuld restreyne mennys affeccions from the inordinate appetite of richesse and of worldly havure'. [...] [*John's sermon follows.*]

'Here begynnyth the life of Seynt Iohn Euangeliste', Cambridge, Cambridge University Library, MS Additional 2604, ll. 79–98 (*c.* 1480–1510)

Than othir twayne yonge men ther were which sigh this grete miracle, that were callid Actil and Eugenye, solde all her possessions of temperall goodis and yaf the money therof to pore peple and folowed Seynt Iohn as his disciples. Than on a day, as they seigh theyr owne seruauntes go well arayed [fol. 15v, p. 28] and they porely, they were right sory and hevy. Whan Seynt Iohn perceyved this that they were sory for suche a cause, he anone toke smale yerdis and grauell stones of the see and turned hem into golde and siluer and toke that golde and syluer to the two yonge men and bad hem go shewe it to goldsmythes and preve whethir they were trewe golde and siluer or not. They did so and come ayene to him and seyde that thise goldsmythes seyn they sigh nevir purer golde ne syluer ne bettir.

Than seyde Seynt Iohn to theym, 'Go', he seyde, 'and take the same golde and syluer and bye your londe and rent ayen that ye haue solde, for the kyngedome of heven ye haue loste. Gothe nowe an[d] levith florysshingly in the worlde that ye mowe wex lene of heuenly ioye; lyveth nowe in ricches temperally that ye mow be beggars endlesly.' And so the ii yonge men went from hym. Than Seynt Iohn myghtely prechid ayenst ricches of the worlde and sayde that seven thinges ther ben that shuld withdrawe a man or woman <from the> vnmesurably appetide and desyre of worldely ricches. [...] [*John's sermon follows, but with the six things changed to seven.*]

William Caxton, 'And next foloweth of Saynt Iohan theuangeliste', in the *Golden Legend,* 1483 edition, STC 24873, C recto column a–C iij recto colunn b, Cj recto column a

Than the two brethern moche riche and honoured in the cyte of Ephesim anon they sold al their patrymony and gaf it for the loue of God. But after whan they cam into the cyte of Pergania [*Pergama?*] and sawe them that had ben theyr seruauntes clothed in silke and in grete honour of the world and themself hauyng but a poure mantel or perauenture a pore cote, anon they repented them that they had gyuen away their goodes in almes to poure people. Thys apperceyued Saynt Iohn and saide to them, 'I see that ye ben heuy and sorouful of thys that after the doctryne of Ihesu Criste ye haue gyuen your goode for Goddes sake wherfore yf ye wyl haue agayn the valewe of youre goodes, brynge to me roddes of the trees and stones of the ryuage of the see.' And so they dyde. And whan Saynt Iohan had them, anon by hys prayer, he chaunged the roddes into fyn gold and the comyn stones into precious stones. And Saynt Iohan bad them to take them and shewe to the maistres that had knowleche in suche iewellis yf the roddes were gold and the comyn stones precyous stones. After they cam agayn and said to Saynt Iohan, 'Syre, the maistres saye that they sawe neuer so fyne gold ne so precious stones.' Seynt Iohan thenne said to them, 'Goo ye and bye ye agayn your londes that ye haue solde for ye haue lost the reward of heuen. Be ye riche temporelly for to be beggers perpetuelly.' Thenne began he to preche in despytyng the rychesses and to shewe vi causes why we ought to restrayne vs for to loue rychesses. [...] [*John's sermon follows.*

BIBLIOGRAPHY

Archives Cited

Beverley, East Riding of Yorkshire Record Office, DDCC/135/63
Cambridge, Christ's College, Archives, T.11.3
Gloucester, Gloucestershire Archives, D23/F18
London, The National Archives (TNA), Prerogative Court of Canterbury and related
Probate Jurisdictions: Will Registers:
Prob 11/49/348
Prob 11/157/178
Prob 11/212/835
Prob 11/218/191
Prob 11/410/407
Prob 11/502/207
Prob 11/570/233
Prob 11/580/439
Prob 11/598/344
Prob 11/666/143
Prob 11/685/342
Prob 11/687/74
Prob 11/738/379
Prob 11/750/399
Prob 11/753/353
Prob 11/1082/80
Prob 11/1110/108
Prob 11/1290/88
Prob 11/1368/84
Norwich, Norfolk Record Office, Archdeaconry of Norwich: Marriage Licence Bonds
and Affidavits, ANW 24/78/25
Norwich, Norfolk Record Office, Archdeaconry of Norwich Probate Records: Wills,
ANW, Will Register, 1772–1773 (1773), fo. 156, no. 92
Norwich, Norfolk Record Office, Archdeaconry of Norwich Probate Records: Wills,
ANW, Will Register, 1823–1825 (1823), fo. 123, no. 87
Norwich, Norfolk Record Office, Bradfer-Lawrence Collection, Miscellanea, BL/MC 39
Norwich, Norfolk Record Office, The Colman Manuscript Collection, Society of United
Friars, Communications and related Papers, COL 9/110
Norwich, Norfolk Record Office, Norfolk and Norwich Archaeological Society Collec-
tion, NNAS G6/10 (formerly G2)
Norwich, Norfolk Record Office, Norwich Consistory Court Probate Records: Wills,
Will Register, Gelour 27

344 BIBLIOGRAPHY

Norwich, Norfolk Record Office, Norwich Consistory Court Probate Records: Wills, Will Register, Hubert 72

Sheffield, Sheffield City Archives, Arundel Castle Manuscripts, ACM/DD/153(19)

Suffolk Archives, Ipswich, The Hold, 741/HA12/B2/6/1

Suffolk Archives, Ipswich, The Hold, 741/HA12/Unlisted 17

Suffolk Archives, Ipswich, The Hold, 741/HA12/Unlisted 76

Suffolk Archives, Ipswich, The Hold, 741/HA12/Unlisted 85

Manuscripts Cited

Aberystwyth, Llyfrgell Genedlaethol Cymru/National Library of Wales, MS 5043

Aberystwyth, Llyfrgell Genedlaethol Cymru/National Library of Wales, MS 20541 E

Baltimore, Walters Art Gallery, W. 721

Berlin, Staatsbibliothek, Cod. theol. lat. fol. 706

Blackburn, Museum and Art Gallery, MS 091-21040

Bruxelles, Bibliothèque royale de Belgique/Koninklijke Bibliotheek van België (KBR), MS 197

Bruxelles, KBR, MS 409

Bruxelles, KBR, MS 982

Bruxelles, KBR, MS 7460

Bruxelles, KBR, MS 7461

Bruxelles, KBR, MS 7917

Bruxelles, KBR, MS 7984

Bruxelles, KBR, MS 8964

Bruxelles, KBR, MS 8990–91

Bruxelles, KBR, MS 9291

Bruxelles, KBR, MS 9378

Bruxelles, KBR, MS 9810–14

Bruxelles, KBR, MS 11986

Bruxelles, KBR, MS 11987

Bruxelles, KBR, MS II.2559

Bruxelles, Société des Bollandistes, MS 5

Bruxelles, Société des Bollandistes, MS 14

Bruxelles, Société des Bollandistes, MS 72

Bruxelles, Société des Bollandistes, MS 288

Bruxelles, Société des Bollandistes, MS 347

Bruxelles, Société des Bollandistes, MS 433

Bruxelles, Société des Bollandistes, MS 467

Bruxelles, Société des Bollandistes, MS 506

Camarillo, CA, St John's Seminary, Edward L. Doheny Memorial Library, MS 3970 (*olim*)

Cambridge, Cambridge University Library, MS Additional 618

Cambridge, Cambridge University Library, MS Additional 2604

BIBLIOGRAPHY

Cambridge, Cambridge University Library, MS Additional 3041
Cambridge, Cambridge University Library, MS Additional 5906
Cambridge, Cambridge University Library, MS Additional 6452
Cambridge, Cambridge University Library, MS Additional 6688
Cambridge, Cambridge University Library, MS Additional 10079
Cambridge, Cambridge University Library, MS Dd.10.22
Cambridge, Cambridge University Library, MS Dd.12.56
Cambridge, Cambridge University Library, MS Ee.6.31
Cambridge, Cambridge University Library, MS Ff.2.20
Cambridge, Cambridge University Library, MS Ff.5.31
Cambridge, Cambridge University Library, MS Gg.4.12
Cambridge, Cambridge University Library, MS Mm.3.13
Cambridge, Cambridge University Library, MS Oo.7.46
Cambridge, Cambridge University Library, MS Hengrave 1/4
Cambridge, Cambridge University Library, MS Hengrave 88/3/90
Cambridge, Corpus Christi College, MSS 5–6
Cambridge, Corpus Christi College, MS 9
Cambridge, Corpus Christi College, MS 268
Cambridge, Fitzwilliam Museum, MS 55
Cambridge, Pembroke College, MS 277
Cambridge, St John's College, MS N. 16
Cambridge, St John's College, MS N. 17
Cambridge, St John's College, MS 75
Cambridge, St John's College, MS 506 and T.9.1
Cambridge, Trinity College, MS 1395
Cambridge, Trinity College, MS O.2.1
Cambridge, Trinity College, MS O.9.38
Cambridge, Trinity College, MS R.3.19
Cambridge, Trinity College, MS R.3.21
Cambridge, MA, Harvard University Library, Houghton Library, Widener MS 2
Cardiff, Public Library, MS I.381
Città del Vaticano, Biblioteca Apostolica Vaticana, MS Rossiana 275
Dublin, Trinity College Dublin, MS 428
Dunedin, New Zealand, The University of Otago, Hocken Collections, Archives and
    Manuscripts, Misc-MS-1818
Durham, Durham University Library, MS Cosin V.iii.24
Durham, Durham University Library, MS Cosin V.iv.4
Edinburgh, Advocates Library, MS Abbotsford
Eton, Eton College, MS 203
Exeter, Cathedral Library, MSS 3504–3505
Glasgow, University Library, MS Gen. 1111
Gotha, Forschungs- und Landesbibliothek, Cod. Membr. I.81
Karlsruhe, Badische Landesbibliothek, Cod. Sankt Georgen 12

London, British Library, MS Additional 7096
London, British Library, MS Additional 10304
London, British Library, MS Additional 11565
London, British Library, MS Additional 14848
London, British Library, MS Additional 18899
London, British Library, MS Additional 22567
London, British Library, MS Additional 33736
London, British Library, MS Additional 35298
London, British Library, MS Additional 36704
London, British Library, MS Additional 39177
London, British Library, MS Additional 41179
London, British Library, MS Additional 70513
London, British Library, MS Arundel 68
London, British Library, MS Arundel 71
London, British Library, MS Arundel 168
London, British Library, MS Arundel 327
London, British Library, MS Arundel 330
London, British Library, MS Arundel 396
London, British Library, MS Burney 347
London, British Library, MS Cotton Faustina B. iii
London, British Library, MS Cotton Julius A. i
London, British Library, MS Cotton Nero E. i
London, British Library, MS Cotton Otho D. ix
London, British Library, MS Cotton Tiberius D. iv
London, British Library, MS Cotton Tiberius E. i
London, British Library, MS Cotton Vespasian A. xiv
London, British Library, MS Cotton Vespasian B. i
London, British Library, MS Egerton 876
London, British Library, MS Egerton 1993
London, British Library, MS Egerton 2710
London, British Library, MS Egerton 3130
London, British Library, MS Harley 630
London, British Library, MS Harley 1211
London, British Library, MS Harley 2278
London, British Library, MS Harley 3776
London, British Library, MS Harley 4012
London, British Library; MS Harley 4775
London, British Library, MS Harley 5272
London, British Library, MS Harley 5334
London, British Library, MS Harley 5936
London, British Library, MS Lansdowne 436
London, British Library, MS Royal 13 D. ix
London, British Library, MS Yates Thompson 47

BIBLIOGRAPHY   347

London, Gray's Inn Library, MS 3
London, Lambeth Palace Library, MSS 10, 11, and 12
London, Lambeth Palace Library, MS 72
London, Lambeth Palace Library, MS 99
London, Lambeth Palace Library, MS 427
London, Westminster Abbey Chapter Library, MS 12
Los Angeles, J. Paul Getty Museum, 83.ML.103 (MS Ludwig IX.7)
Madrid, Biblioteca Nacional de España, MS 6422
Manchester, The John Rylands University Library, MS Eng. 1
Milano, Biblioteca Ambrosiana, A 17 inf
New Haven, Yale University Library, Beinecke Rare Book and Manuscript Library, MS 365
New York, Public Library, Spencer MS 3
Oxford, Balliol College, MS 228
Oxford, Bodleian Library, MS Arch. Selden B. 10
Oxford, Bodleian Library, MS Bodley 108
Oxford, Bodleian Library, MS Bodley 240
Oxford, Bodleian Library, MS Bodley 779
Oxford, Bodleian Library, MS Digby 34
Oxford, Bodleian Library, MS Douce 114
Oxford, Bodleian Library, MS Douce 322
Oxford, Bodleian Library, MS Douce 372
Oxford, Bodleian Library, MS Eng. e. 18
Oxford, Bodleian Library, MS Eng. poet. a. 1
Oxford, Bodleian Library, MS e Musaeo 42
Oxford, Bodleian Library, MS Rawlinson C. 894
Oxford, Bodleian Library, MS Rawlinson C. 938
Oxford, Bodleian Library, MS Rawlinson D. 112
Oxford, Bodleian Library, MS Rawlinson Poet. 14
Oxford, Bodleian Library, MS Tanner 15
Oxford, Corpus Christi College, MS 120
Oxford, The Queen's College, MS 305
Oxford, University College, MS C. 188
Padova, Biblioteca Universitaria, MS 1229
Paris, Bibliothèque Nationale, fonds latin, MS 12598
San Marino, Huntington Library, MS EL 34 B7
Thetford, Thetford Library, MS L 352
York, York Minster Library, MS XVI.G.23

BIBLIOGRAPHY

Convent Archives, Manuscripts, and Early Printed Books Consulted

BARKING

London, British Library, MS Additional 10596
London, British Library, MS Cotton Julius D. viii
London, Lambeth Palace, 1495.4 (print)
Oxford, Bodleian Library, MS Bodley 923
Oxford, University College, MS 169

BRUISYARD

London, British Library, MS Sloane 2400
Oxford, Bodleian Library, Tanner 191 (print)

CAMPSEY ASH

Cambridge, Cambridge University Library, MS Additional 7220
Cambridge, Corpus Christi College, MS 268 (also Cited)
London, British Library, MS Additional 40675
London, British Library, MS Additional 70513 (also Cited)
London, British Library, MS Arundel 396 (also Cited)

CHATTERIS

London, British Library, Cotton Julius MS A. i (cartulary) (also Cited)

CHESTER

San Marino, Huntington, MS EL 34 B.7 (also Cited)

CRABHOUSE

London, British Library, MS Additional 4733 (cartulary)

DARTFORD

Dublin, Trinity College, MS 490
London, British Library, MS Arundel 61
London, British Library, MS Harley 2254
London, Society of Antiquaries, MS 717
Oxford, Bodleian Library, MS Bodley 255
Oxford, Bodleian Library, MS Douce 322 (also Cited)
Oxford, Bodleian Library, MS Rawlinson G.59
Stratton-on-the-Fosse, Downside Abbey, MS 26542 (*olim*)

BIBLIOGRAPHY

DENNEY
Cambridge, Cambridge University Library, MS Additional 8335
Oxford, Bodleian Library, MS Hatton 18

DERBY
London, British Library, MS Egerton 2710 (also Cited)

EDINBURGH
Edinburgh, Edinburgh University Library, MS 150
Edinburgh, National Library of Scotland, H8.f.17, 1552 (print)

FLIXTON
Cambridge, Cambridge University Library, MS Ee.3.52
London, British Library, Stowe 1083 (deeds)

GODSTOW
Oxford, Bodleian Library, MS Rawlinson B.408

GORING
Cambridge, Trinity College, MS 244

HAMPOLE
San Marino, Huntington, MS EL 9 H.17

HIGHAM
Cambridge, St John's College, MS 271

ICKLETON
Cambridge, St John's College, 506 and T.9.1 (manuscript and print) (also Cited)

KINGTON ST MICHAEL
Cambridge, Cambridge University Library, MS Dd.8.2

LONDON: Aldgate
Cambridge, Trinity College, MS B.14.15
London, British Library, MS Harley 2397

LONDON: Holywell

Oxford, Bodleian Library, MS Douce 372 (also Cited)

MARRICK

Hull, History Centre, U DDCA/2/29/112 (rental)
New York, Public Library, Spencer Collection, MS 19

NUN COTON (see SWINE)

London, British Library, MS Harley 2409

NUNEATON

Cambridge, Fitzwilliam Museum, McClean, MS 123

POLSLOE

Oxford, Bodleian Library, Douce, BB 200 (print)

ROMSEY

London, British Library, MS Lansdowne 436 (also Cited)

SHAFTESBURY

Cambridge, Fitzwilliam Museum, MS 2–1957
Cambridge, Cambridge University Library, MS, Ii.6.40
London, Lambeth Palace Library, MS 3285

SWINE (see NUN COTON)

London, British Library, MS Harley 2409

SYON

Alnwick, The Archives of the Duke of Northumberland at Alnwick Castle,
    DNP: MS 505A
Cambridge, Cambridge University Library, MS Additional 8885
Cambridge, Magdalene College, MS Pepys 13
Cambridge, Sidney Sussex, Bb2.14 (print)
Cambridge, St John's College, MS 139
Dublin, Marsh's Library, MS Z.4.4.3
Durham, Durham University Library, MS Cosin V.iii.16
Durham, Durham University Library, MS Cosin V.v.12
Edinburgh, Edinburgh University Library, MS 59

Exeter, Exeter University Library, Syon Abbey MS 1
Exeter, Exeter University Library, Syon Abbey MS 2
Exeter, Exeter University Library, Syon Abbey MS 6
Exeter, Exeter University Library, Syon Abbey MS 262/1
London, British Library, MS Additional 22285
London, British Library, MS Arundel 146
London, British Library, MS Cotton App. xiv
London, British Library, MS Harley 487
London, British Library, MS Harley 993
London, British Library, MS Harley 2387
London, Lambeth Palace Library, MS 535
London, Lambeth Palace Library, MS 546
London, Lambeth Palace Library, MS 3600
New York, Public Library, Spencer Collection, Eng. 1519 (print)
Oxford, Bodleian Library, MS Auct. D. 47
Oxford, Bodleian Library, MS Bodley 62
Oxford, Bodleian Library, MS Laud Miscellaneous 416
Oxford, Bodleian Library, MS Rawlinson C. 941
Oxford, St John's College, MS 167
Oxford, University College, MS 25 (manuscript and print)

TARRANT KEYNSTON

Dublin, Trinity College, MS 209

THETFORD

Alnwick, The Archives of the Duke of Northumberland at Alnwick Castle, DNP: MS 449

WHERWELL

London, British Library, MS Additional 27866

WILTON

London, British Library, MS Cotton Faustina B. iii (also Cited)

WINCHESTER

Cambridge, Cambridge University Library, MS Mm.iii.13 (also Cited)

Other Manuscripts Consulted

Manuscripts

Cambridge, Cambridge University Library, MS Additional 3042
Cambridge, Cambridge University Library, MS Additional 4122
Cambridge, Cambridge University Library, MS Dd.1.20
Cambridge, Cambridge University Library, MS Dd.4.26
Cambridge, Cambridge University Library, MS Ee.4.32
Cambridge, Cambridge University Library, MS Hh.1.11
Cambridge, Cambridge University Library, MS Ii.4.9
Cambridge, Cambridge University Library, MS Ii.4.20
Cambridge, Cambridge University Library, MS Kk.5.45
Cambridge, Cambridge University Library, MS Ll.5.18
Cambridge, Pembroke College, 240
Cambridge, Sidney Sussex College, MS 37
Dublin, Trinity College, MS 319
Liverpool, Liverpool Cathedral, MS Radcliffe 6
London, British Library, MS Additional 5140
London, British Library, MS Additional 11814
London, British Library, MS Additional 17275
London, British Library, MS Additional 33381
London, British Library, MS Additional 36983
London, British Library, MS Cotton Titus A. xxvi
London, British Library, MS Egerton 645
London, British Library, MS Harley 2977
London, British Library, MS Harley 2382
London, British Library, MS Harley 4011
London, British Library, MS Harley 4260
London, British Library, MS Royal 2 A. xviii
London, British Library, MS Royal 19 B. xvii
London, British Library, MS Royal 17 C. xvii
London, British Library, MS Royal 20 D. vi
London, British Library, MSS Stowe 50 and 51
London, British Library, MS Stowe 53
London, British Library, MS Stowe 949
London, Lambeth Palace Library, MS 51
London, Lambeth Palace Library, MS 200
London, Lambeth Palace Library, MS 432
London, Lambeth Palace Library, MS 536
Oxford, Bodleian Library, MS Bodley 952
Oxford, Bodleian Library, MS Add. A. 42
Oxford, Bodleian Library, MS Gough Suffolk 3
Oxford, Bodleian Library, MS Holkham Miscellaneous 41

BIBLIOGRAPHY   353

Early Printed Books Cited

The titles below are those in ESTC/STC or USTC (with proper names uniformly capitalised) with the reference following. Where attributed, authors are cited; otherwise the works are anonymous.

A helpe to discourse: or, more merriment mixt with serious matters [...], 13th edn (London: Printed by M[oses]. B[ell]. for I. B., 1648)

A helpe to discovrse: or, more merriment mixt with serious matters [...], 11th edn (London: I[ohn]. B[eale] Printed for *Nicolas Vavasour*, 1635) (STC 1552) (USTC 3018267)

Boninus Mombritius, *Sanctuarium sive Vitae Sanctorum* ([Milano: Printer for Boninus Mombritius, *c.* 1477) (USTC 992962)

Chastysing of goddes chyldern (Westminster: Wynkyn de Worde, 1493) (STC 5065)

Gabriele Barletta, *Sermones quadragesimales et de sanctis* (Brescia: Jacobus Britannicus, 1497–98) (USTC 997243)

Henry Bradshaw, *Here begynneth the holy lyfe and history of saynt Werburge, very frutefull for all christen people to rede* (London: Richard Pynson, 1521) (STC 3506)

Henry Bradshaw, *Here begynneth the lyfe of saynt Radegunde* (London: Richard Pynson, *c.* 1525) (STC 3507)

[H]ere after foloweth a treatyse take[n] out of a boke whiche somtyme Theodosius the Emperour founde in Iherusalem in the pretorye of Pylate of Ioseph of Armathy (London: Wynkyn de Worde: [1507–08?]) (STC 14806)

Here after foloweth the lyfe of saynt Gregoryes mother (London: John Mychell, *c.* 1532?) (STC 12353)

Here begynneth of seint Margarete the blissid lif that is so swete [...] (London: Richard Pynson, 1493) (STC 17325)

Here begynneth the kalendre of the newe legende of Englande (London: Richard Pynson [1516]) (STC 4602)

Here begynneth the lyf of saint Katherin of Senis the blessid virgin, a translation of Raymond of Capua's Latin text (Westminster: Wynkyn de Worde, 1492?) (STC 24766)

Here begynneth the lyf of saint Katherin of Senis the blessid virgin, a translation of Raymond of Capua's Latin text (Westminster: Wynkyn de Worde, 1500?) (STC 24766.3)

Here begynneth the lyf of the holy & blessid vyrgyn saynt Wenefryde, a translation by William Caxton of the text of Robert, Prior of Shrewsbury ([Westminster: William Caxton, 1485]) (STC 25853)

Here begynneth the lyfe of Ioseph of Armathia (London: Richard Pynson, 1520) (STC 14807)

Here begynneth the lyfe of saynt Brandon (London: Wynkyn de Worde, 1521?) (STC 3600)

Here begynneth the lyfe of saynte Margaret (London: Robert Redman, 1530?) (STC 17326)

Here begynneth the lyfe of the blessed martyr Saynte Thomas ([London?]: Richard Pynson, [1520]) (STC 23954)

Here begynneth the lyfe of the gloryous confessoure of oure lorde Ihesu criste seynt Francis (London: Richard Pynson, *c.* 1515) (STC 3270)

Here begynneth the lyfe of the gloryous vyrgyn and marter saynt Barbara (London: Julian Notary, 1518) (STC 1375)

Here begyn[n]eth ye lyf of Saynt Ursula after ye cronycles of Englo[n]de (London: Wynkyn de Worde, [1507–08?]) (STC 24541.3)

Here begynnyth the lyfe of the gloryous martyr saynt George, patrone of the royalme of Englonde [...] (London: Richard Pynson, 1515?) (STC 22992.1)

Historie plurimorum sanctorum (Louvain: Johannes de Westfalia, October 1485) (USTC 438400)

Jacobus de Voragine, *Legenda aurea sanctorum, sive Lombardica historia* (Köln: Conrad Winters, 20 August 1478) (USTC 746119

Jacobus de Voragine, *Legenda aurea sanctorum, sive Lombardica historia* (Köln: Johann I Koelhoff, 1479) (USTC 746122)

Jacobus de Voragine, *Legenda aurea sanctorum, sive Lombardica historia* [and] *Incipiu[n]t historie pl[ur]imor[um] s[an]c[t]or[um] novit[er] addite laboriose collecte [et] p[ro]lo[n]gate* (Köln: [Ulrich Zel], 1483) (USTC 746132)

Jacobus de Voragine, *Sermones de sanctis* (Köln: Conrad Winters, *c.* 1478) (USTC 746184)

Jacopo Filippo Foresti da Bergamo, *De plurimis claris sceletisque [sic] mulieribus* (Ferrara: Laurentius de Rubeis, 29 April 1497) (USTC 994089)

Jerome Porter, *The flowers of the liues of the most renowned saincts of the three kingdoms England Scotland, and Ireland written and collected out of the best authours and manuscripts of our nation, and distributed according to their feasts in the calendar [...]* (Douai: n. p., 1632), I (STC 20124)

Jerome Porter, *The Flowers of the Lives of the Most Renowned Saincts, 1632,* ed. by D. M. Rogers, English Recusant Literature, 1558–1640, 239 (Ilkley, West Yorkshire: Scolar Press, 1975)

Johannes Herolt, *Sermones Discipuli de tempore et de sanctis* (Köln: [Ulrich Zel], 1483) (USTC 745675)

Johannes Werden, *Sermones 'Dormi secure' de tempore et de sanctis* (Strasbourg: [Printer of the 1483 Jordanus de Quedlinburg [= Georg Husner] and Johann Prüss], 1489) (USTC 746378)

John Wilson, The *English Martyrologe, 1608*, ed. by D. M. Rogers, English Recusant Literature, 1558–1640, 232 (Ilkley, West Yorkshire: Scolar Press, 1975)

John Wilson, *The English martyrologe containing a summary of the most renowned and illustrious saints of the three kingdoms England, Scotland, and Ireland [...]* ([St Omer: Thomas Gerbels], 1672)

John Wilson, *The English martyrologe conteyning a summary of the liues of the glorious and renowned saintes of the three kingdomes, England, Scotland, and Ireland [...]* ([St Omer: Printed at the English College Press], 1608) (STC 25771)

John Wilson, *The English martyrologe conteyning a summary of the most renowned and illustrious saints of the three kingdomes England, Ireland, & Scotland [...]* ([St Omer: Printed at the English College Press], 1640) (STC 25772)

BIBLIOGRAPHY 355

Laurentius Surius, *De probatis sanctorum historiis [...]*, 6 vols (Köln: Gervinius Calenius et hæredes Quentelios, 1570–75) (USTC 631108 *et alia*)

Leonardus de Utino, *Sermones de sanctis* ([Köln: Ulrich Zell, 1473]) (USTC 746661)

The lif of Saincte Katheryne (London: Richard Pynson, 1505?) (STC 4813.6)

[*The lif of Saincte Katheryne*] (London: Richard Pynson, 1510?) (not in STC)

[*Life of St Gregory's mother*] (London: Richard Pynson, 1501?) (STC 12351.5)

The life of the blessed virgin, Sainct Catharine of Siena. Drawne out of all them that had written it from the beginning [...], a translation by John Fenn of an Italian translation of the Latin version by Raymond of Capua ([Douai: C. Boscard], 1609) (STC 4830)

The life of the glorious and blessed virgin and martyr Saincte Katheryne (London: John Whaley, 1555?) (STC 4813.8)

The lyfe of saynt Erasmus (London: Julian Notary, 1520) (STC 10435)

[*Lyfe of saynt Gregories mo[ther]*] (London: [Wynkyn de Worde], 1515) (STC 12352)

[*The lyfe of saynte Margaret*] (London: John Mychell, 1530–32?) (STC 17327)

The lyfe of seynt Barbara, a translation of Jean Wackerzeele's text (London: Richard Pynson?, *c.* 1520) (STC 1375.5)

The lyfe of the Euangelist Saint Marke, set foorth by the famous doctour S. Hierome (England?: s. n. 15--?) (not in STC)

[*The lyfe of the moost holy hieremyte & glorious confessoure saynt Armele*] (London: R. Pynson, *c.* 1502) (STC 772)

Meffret, *Sermones de tempore et de sanctis, sive Hortulus reginae* ([Basel: Nicolaus Kesler, not after 1483] (USTC 747148)

Michael (Mihály) de Hungaria, *Euagatorium [...]* [or *Sermones predicabiles*] (Köln: Martin von Werden, 1505) (USTC 654238)

Nova legenda Anglie (London: Wynkyn de Worde, 1516) (STC 4601)

[Paratus], *Sermones parati de tempore et de sanctis* ([Nürnberg: Anton Koberger (I) 1502]) (USTC 693741)

Pelbartus de Themeswar (Pelbárt Temesvári), *Pomerium sermones de sanctis [...]* (Hagenau: Heinrich Gran; Augsburg: Johann Rynmann, 1504) (USTC 684749)

Petrus de Natalibus, *Catalogus sanctorum et gestorum eorum [...]*, 12 vols (Strasbourg: impressum per Martin Flach, 1513) (USTC 619721)

[*Saynt Nycholas of Toll-e[n]tyne*] (London: Wynkyn de Worde, [1525?]) (STC 18528)

[*Saynt Nycholas of Toll-e[n]tyne*] ([S.l.: Wynkyn de Worde, 1525?]) (STC 18528.5)

Simon Wynter, *The fyrst chapitre is the lyf of saint Ierom as it is take of legenda aurea [...]* Westminster: Wynkyn de Worde, 1499?) (STC 14508)

Vicent Ferrer, *Sermones de tempore et de sanctis* (Köln: [Heinrich Quentell], 1485) (USTC 744841)

Vincent de Beauvais, *Speculum historiale* (Strasbourg: The 'R' Printer (= Arnold Rusch), *c.* 1473) (USTC 749712)

William Basse, *Three pastoral elegies; of Anander, Anetor, and Muridella* ([London]: Printed by V[alentine] S[immes] for I. B.[arnes], 1602) (STC 1556)

356 BIBLIOGRAPHY

William Caxton, *Thus endeth the legende named in latyn legenda aurea, that is to saye in englysshe the golden legende [...]* ([Westminster: William Caxton, 20 November 1483]) (STC 24873)

William Lyndwood, *Prouinciale seu Constitutiones Anglie: Cum summariis atq[ue] justis annotationibus: honestis characteribus; summaq[ue] accuratione rursum impresse*, ed. by Josse Badius (Paris: André Bocard, 1501) (STC 17107)

William Warner, *Albion's England* (London: *Edm[und] Bollifant* for *George Potter*, 1602)

Primary Sources

Acta sanctorum [...], ed. by the Société des Bollandistes, 67 vols (Anvers & Bruxelles, and other places: Société des Bollandistes, 1643–1940); reproduced in an 'Impression anastaltique' by the Éditions 'Culture et Civilisation' (Bruxelles, 1966–71) and online in 1999 by Chadwyck Healey (http://acta.chadwyck.co.uk); 3rd edn (Paris and other places: Victor Palmé, 1863–71)

Anonymous Old English Lives of Saints, ed. and trans. by Johanna Kramer, Hugh Magennis, and Robin Norris, Dumbarton Oaks Medieval Library, 63 (Cambridge, MA: Harvard University Press, 2020)

Arbellot, [François], *Vie de Saint Léonard, solitaire en Limousin: Ses miracles et son culte* (Paris: J. Lecoffre, 1863)

Bartolomeo da Trento, *Liber epilogorum in gesta sanctorum*, ed. by Emore Paoli, Edizione nazionale dei testi mediolatini, 2 (Firenze: Sismel-Edizioni del Galluzzo, 2001)

Bede's Ecclesiastical History of the English People, ed. and trans. by Bertram Colgrave and R. A. B. Mynors, Oxford Medieval Texts (Oxford: Oxford University Press, 1969; repr. 1992)

Blake, N. F., *Caxton's Own Prose* (London: Deutsch, 1973)

Boninus Mombritius, *Sanctuarium seu Vitae Sanctorum*, ed. by Two Monks of Solesmes, 2 vols (Paris: Albertus Fontemoing, 1910)

Breviarium ad usum insignis ecclesiae Sarum, ed. by Francis Procter and Christopher Wordsworth, 3 vols (Cambridge: Cambridge University Press, 1879–86)

Bury and Norwich Post, Wednesday, 16 April 1788

The Cartulary of Chatteris Abbey, ed. by Claire Breay (Woodbridge: Boydell, 1999)

Caxton's 'Golden Legend', ed. by Mayumi Taguchi, John Scahill, and Satoko Tokunaga, EETS, o.s. 355, 357, 2 vols (Oxford: Oxford University Press, 2020–21)

Challoner, Richard, *Britannia Sancta: or, the lives of the most celebrated British, English, Scottish, and Irish saints: Who have flourished in these Islands, from the earliest times of Christianity, down to the change of religion in the sixteenth century. Faithfully collected from their ancient acts, and other records of British History*, 2 vols (London: Printed for Thomas Meighan, 1745)

The Chronicle of the English Augustinian Canonesses Regular of the Lateran, at St Monica's in Louvain (Now at St Augustine's Priory, Newton Abbot, Devon) 1548 to 1625, ed. by Adam Hamilton (Edinburgh: Sands and Co., 1904)

BIBLIOGRAPHY

A deuout treatyse called the tree & xii. frutes of the holy goost, ed. by J. J. Vaissier (Groningen: J. B. Wolters, 1960)

The Diaries of Elizabeth Inchbald, ed. by Ben P. Robertson, The Pickering Masters, 3 vols (London: Pickering and Chatto, 2007)

The Doctrine of the Hert: A Critical Edition with Introduction and Commentary, ed. by Christiania Whitehead, Denis Renevey, and Anne Mouron, Exeter Medieval Texts and Studies (Exeter: University of Exeter Press, 2010)

Édition pratique des martyrologes de Bède, de l'Anonyme lyonnais et de Florus, ed. by Jacques Dubois and Geneviève Renaud (Paris: Éditions du Centre national de la recherche scientifique, 1976)

Encyclopaedia Britannica [...], ed. by William Smellie, 1st edn, 3 vols (Edinburgh: Printed for [...], 1771)

Encyclopaedia Britannica [...], ed. by James Tytler, 2nd edn, 10 vols (Edinburgh: Printed for [...], 1778–83)

English Monastic Litanies of the Saints after 1100, ed. by Nigel J. Morgan, Henry Bradshaw Society, 119, 120, 123, 3 vols (Woodbridge: Boydell, 2012–18)

Geoffrey of Burton, Life and Miracles of St Modwenna, ed. and trans. by Robert Bartlett, Oxford Medieval Texts (Oxford: Clarendon Press, 2002)

Gilte Legende, ed. by Richard Hamer, with Vida Russell, EETS, o.s. 327, 328, and 339, 3 vols (Oxford: Oxford University Press, 2006–12)

Goscelin of Saint-Bertin, The Hagiography of the Female Saints of Ely, ed. and trans. by Rosalind C. Love, Oxford Medieval Texts (Oxford: Clarendon Press, 2004)

'Goscelin's Legend of Edith', ed. and trans. by Michael Wright and Kathleen Loncar, in *Writing the Wilton Women: Goscelin's 'Legend of Edith' and 'Liber confortatorius'*, ed. by Stephanie Hollis and others, Medieval Women: Texts and Contexts, 9 (Turnhout: Brepols, 2004), pp. 15–93

Henry Bradshaw, *The Life of Saint Werburge of Chester*, ed. by Carl Horstmann, EETS, o.s. 88 (London: Trübner, 1887)

Iacopo da Varazze, *Legenda aurea con le miniature del codice Ambrosiano C 240 inf.*, ed. by Giovanni Paolo Maggioni, Edizione nazionale dei testi mediolatini, 20, 2 vols (Firenze: Sismel & Milano: Biblioteca Ambrosiana, 2007)

Iacopo da Varazze, *Legenda aurea: Edizione critica*, ed. by Giovanni Paolo Maggioni, Millennio medievale 6, Testi 3, 2nd revised edn, 2 vols (Firenze: Sismel-Edizioni del Galluzzo, 1998)

Jacobi a Voragine, Legenda aurea, vulgo Historia lombardica dicta, ed. by Th. Graesse, 3rd edn (Bratislava: Koebner, 1890)

Jacques de Voragine, *'La Légende dorée': Edition critique, dans la revision de 1476 par Jean Batallier, d'après la traduction de Jean de Vignay (1333–1348) de la 'Legenda aurea' (c. 1261–1266)*, ed. by Brenda Dunn-Lardeau, Textes de la Renaissance, 19 (Paris: Honoré Champion, 1997)

Jean de Mailly, *Abbreviatio in gestis et miracvlis sanctorvm, svpplementvm hagiographicvm*, ed. by Giovanni Paolo Maggioni, Millennio medievale, 97, Testi, 21 (Firenze: Sismel-Edizioni del Galluzzo, 2013)

John Bale, *Index Britanniae Scriptorum*, ed. by Reginald Lane Poole, with Mary Bateson (Oxford: Clarendon Press, 1902)

John Leland, *Collectanea*, ed. by Thomas Hearne, 6 vols (London, Benjamin White, 1774)

John Mirk's 'Festial', ed. by Susan Powell, 2 vols, EETS, o.s. 334–35 (Oxford: Oxford University Press, 2009–11)

Journals of the House of Commons from January the 24th, 1786, in the Twenty-Sixth Year of the Reign of King George the Third, to December the 14th, 1786, in the Twenty-Seventh Year of the Reign of King George the Third ([London]: Printed by Order of the House of Commons, n. d), XLI

The Kalendre of the Newe Legende of Englande, ed. by Manfred Görlach, Middle English Texts, 27 (Heidelberg: Universitätsverlag Winter, 1994)

The Laity's Directory; For the Church Service on Sundays and Holy Days, for the Year of our Lord M DCC XCV [...] (London: J. P. Coughlan, 1794)

'A Latin Poem on St Hilda and Whitby Abbey', ed. by A. G. Rigg, *The Journal of Medieval Latin*, 6 (1996), 12–43

Legends of the Saints in the Scottish Dialect of the Fourteenth Century, ed. by W. M. Metcalfe, The Scottish Text Society, 13, 18, 23. 25, 35, 37, 3 vols (Edinburgh: William Blackwood and Sons, 1887–96)

Liber Eliensis, ed. by E. O. Blake, Camden Society, Third Series, 92 (London: Royal Historical Society, 1962)

Liber Eliensis: A History of the Isle of Ely From the Seventh to the Twelfth, trans. by Janet Fairweather (Woodbridge: Boydell, 2005)

The Life of Christina of Markyate: A Twelfth Century Recluse, ed. and trans. by C. H. Talbot, Medieval Academy Reprints for Teaching (Oxford: Oxford University Press, 1959; repr. Toronto: University of Toronto Press, in association with the Medieval Academy of America, 1998)

The Life of St Edmund King and Martyr: John Lydgate's Illustrated Verse Life Presented to Henry VI, a Facsimile of British Library MS Harley 2278, introduced by A. S. G. Edwards (London: The British Library, 2004)

The Lives of Women Saints of Our Contrie of England, ed. by Carl Horstman, EETS, o.s. 86 (London: Trübner, 1886)

'*The Lyfe of Seynt Birgette*: An Edition of a Swedish Saint's Life for an English Audience', ed. by Ann M. Hutchison, and Veronica O'Mara, in *'Booldly but meekly': Essays on the Theory and Practice of Translation in the Middle Ages in Honour of Roger Ellis*, ed. by Catherine Batt and René Tixier, The Medieval Translator/Traduire au Moyen Âge, 14 (Turnhout: Brepols, 2018), pp. 173–208

Le Martyrologe d'Adon, ses deux familles, ses trois recensions: Texte et Commentaire, ed. by Jacques Dubois and Geneviève Renaud (Paris: Éditions du centre national de la recherche scientifique, 1984)

Le Martyrologe d'Usuard: Texte et Commentaire, ed. by Jacques Dubois, Subsidia Hagiographica, 40 (Bruxelles: Société des Bollandistes, 1965)

Middle English Legends of Women Saints, ed. by Sherry L. Reames, with Martha G. Blalock and Wendy L. Larson (Kalamazoo, MI: Medieval Institute Publications, 2003)

The Middle English 'Liber Aureus' and 'Gospel of Nicodemus', ed. by William Marx, Middle English Texts, 48 (Heidelberg: Winter, 2013)

Morning Chronicle, Thursday, 28 April 1785

A Newe Booke of Copies, 1574: A Facsimile of a Unique Elizabethan Writing Book in the Bodleian Library, Oxford, ed. by Berthold Wolpe (London: Oxford University Press, 1962)

Nicholas Love, *The Mirror of the Blessed Life of Jesus Christ: A Full Critical Edition*, ed. by Michael G. Sargent (Exeter: University of Exeter Press, 2005)

Nicholas Roscarrock's Lives of the Saints: Cornwall and Devon, ed. by Nicholas Orme, Devon and Cornwall Record Society, n.s. 35 (Exeter: BPCC Wheatons Ltd, 1992)

Norfolk Chronicle, Saturday, 20 September 1783

Norfolk Chronicle, Saturday, 28 June 1823

Norwich Mercury, Saturday, 22 November 1902

Nova Legenda Anglie, ed. by Carl Horstman, 2 vols (Oxford: Clarendon Press, 1901)

The Old English Martyrology: Edition, Translation and Commentary, ed. and trans. by Christine Rauer, Anglo-Saxon Texts, 10 (Cambridge: Brewer, 2013)

On Famous Women: The Middle English Translation of Boccaccio's 'De Mulieribus Claris', ed. by Janet Cowen, Middle English Texts, 52 (Heidelberg: Winter, 2015)

The Ordinale and Customary of the Benedictine Nuns of Barking Abbey, ed. by J. B. L. Tolhurst, Henry Bradshaw Society, 65–66, 2 vols (London: Henry Bradshaw Society, 1927–28)

Osbern Bokenham, *Legendys of Hooly Wummen*, ed. by Mary S. Serjeantson, EETS, o.s. 206 (London: Oxford University Press, 1938)

Osbern Bokenham, 'Lives of Saints', ed. by Simon Horobin, EETS, o.s. 356 and 359, 2 vols (Oxford: Oxford University Press, 2020–22)

Paston Letters and Papers of the Fifteenth Century, ed. by Norman Davis, Richard Beadle, and Colin Richmond, EETS, s.s. 20, 21, 22, 3 parts (Oxford: Oxford University Press, 2004–05)

The Recollections of a Northumbrian Lady, 1815–1866: Being the Memoirs of Barbara Charlton (née Tasburgh), Wife of William Henry Charlton of Hesleyside, Northumberland, ed. by L. E. O. Charlton (London: Jonathan Cape, 1949)

The Register of John Morton, Archbishop of Canterbury, 1486–1500, III: *Norwich sede vacante, 1499*, ed. by Christopher Harper-Bill, The Canterbury and York Society, 89 (2000)

Returns of Papists 1767, ed. by E. S. Worrall, Catholic Record Society, Occasional Publications, 1–2, 2 vols (1980–89)

Richard Whitford, *The Martiloge in Englysshe after the Vse of the Chirche of Salisbury and as it is Redde in Syon with Addicyons, Printed by Wynkyn de Worde in 1526*, ed. by F. Procter and E. S. Dewick, Henry Bradshaw Society, 3 (London: Harrison and Sons, 1893)

Rookwood Family Papers, 1606–1761, ed. by Francis Young, Suffolk Records Society, 59 (Woodbridge, Boydell: 2016)

Saints Edith and Æthelthryth: Princesses, Miracle Workers, and their Late Medieval Audience, The Wilton Chronicle and the Wilton Life of St Æthelthryth, ed. and trans. by Mary Dockray-Miller, Medieval Women: Texts and Contexts, 25 (Turnhout: Brepols, 2009)

Saints' Lives for Medieval English Nuns, II: An Edition of the 'Lyves and Dethes' in Cambridge University Library, MS Additional 2604, ed. by Veronica O'Mara and Virginia Blanton, Medieval Women: Texts and Contexts, 32 (Turnhout: Brepols, 2024)

Sammlung altenglischer Legenden, ed. by Carl Horstman (Heilbronn: Gebr. Henninger, 1878)

Speculum sacerdotale, ed. by Edward H. Weatherly, EETS, o.s. 200 (London: Oxford University Press, 1936)

Supplementary Lives in Some Manuscripts of the 'Gilte Legende', ed. by Richard Hamer and Vida Russell, EETS, o.s. 315 (Oxford: Oxford University Press, 2000)

Testamenta eboracensia: A Selection of Wills from the Registry at York, ed. by James Raine and John William Clay, Publications of the Surtees Society, 6 vols, 4, 30, 45, 53, 79, and 106 (London: J. B. Nichols and Son; and other publishers and places, 1836–1902)

Vercelli Homilies IX–XXIII, ed. by Paul E. Szarmach, Toronto Old English Series, 5 (Toronto: Toronto University Press, 1981)

Virgin Lives and Holy Deaths: Two Exemplary Biographies for Anglo-Norman Women, trans. by Jocelyn Wogan-Browne and Glyn S. Burgess (London: Dent; Rutland, VT: Tuttle, 1996)

Virgins and Scholars: A Fifteenth-Century Compilation of the Lives of John the Baptist, John the Evangelist, Jerome, and Katherine of Alexandria, ed. by Claire M. Waters, Medieval Women: Texts and Contexts, 10 (Turnhout: Brepols, 2008)

Visitations of the Diocese of Norwich, A.D. 1492–1532, ed. by A. Jessopp, Camden Society, n.s. 43 (1888)

Wills and Inventories from the Registers of the Commissary of Bury St Edmund's and the Archdeacon of Sudbury, ed. by Samuel Tymms, Camden Society, 49 (London: J. B. Nichols and Son, 1850)

Writing the Wilton Women: Goscelin's 'Legend of Edith' and 'Liber confortatorius', ed. by Stephanie Hollis and others, Medieval Women: Texts and Contexts, 9 (Turnhout: Brepols, 2004)

Zaccaria, Franciscus Antonius, *De Rebus ad historiam atque antiquitates ecclesiæ: Dissertationes Latianæ* (Fulginæ: Pompejus Campana, 1781), I

BIBLIOGRAPHY   361

Secondary Studies

Alexander, Dominic, *Saints and Animals in* the *Middle Ages* (Woodbridge: Boydell, 2008)

Allen, Cynthia L., 'The Separated Genitive in English', in *Genitives in Early English: Typology and Evidence* (Oxford: Oxford University Press, 2008), pp. 223–73

Andrews, Phil, 'St George's Nunnery, Thetford', *Norfolk Archaeology: A Journal of Archaeology and Local History*, 41 (1993), 427–40

Ashwin, Trevor, and Alan Davison, eds, *An Historical Atlas of Norfolk*, 3rd edn (Chichester: Phillimore, 2005)

Backhouse, Janet, *The Illuminated Page: Ten Centuries of Manuscript Painting in the British Library* (Toronto: University of Toronto Press, 1997)

Bailey, Mark, *Medieval Suffolk: An Economic and Social History, 1200–1500*, The History of Suffolk, 1 (Woodbridge: Boydell, 2007)

Balston, J. N., *The Elder James Whatman, England's Greatest Paper Maker (1702–59): A Study of Eighteenth Century Paper Making Technology and its Effect on a Critical Phase in the History of English White Paper Manufacture*, 2 vols (West Farleigh, Kent: J. N. Balston, 1992),

Balston, Thomas, *William Balston: Paper Maker, 1759–1849*, A Garland Series, Nineteenth-Century Book Arts & Printing History, ed. by John Bidwell (London: Methuen, 1954; repr. New York, NY: Garland, 1979)

Barnwell, P. S., L. A. S. Butler, and C. J. Dunn, 'The Confusion of Conversion: Streanæshalch, Strensall and Whitby and the Northumbrian Church', in *The Cross Goes North: Processes of Conversion in Northern Europe, AD 300–1300*, ed. by Martin Carver (Woodbridge: Boydell and Brewer, 2006), pp. 311–26

Barratt, Alexandra, 'Women Translators of Religious Texts', in *The Oxford History of Literary Translation*, I: *To 1550*, ed. by Roger Ellis (Oxford: Oxford University Press, 2008), pp. 284–95

Barron, Caroline M., and Matthew Davies, eds, *The Religious Houses of London and Middlesex* (London: Institute of Historical Research, School of Advanced Study, University of London, 2007)

Bateson, Edward, and others, eds, *History of Northumberland*, 15 vols (Newcastle-Upon-Tyne: Andrew Reid; London: Simpkin, Marshall, Hamilton, Kent, 1893–1940)

Beadle, Hilton Richard Leslie, 'The Medieval Drama of East Anglia: Studies in Dialect, Documentary Records and Stagecraft' (unpublished doctoral dissertation, University of York, 1977)

Beadle, Richard, 'Prolegomena to a Literary Geography of Later Medieval Norfolk', in *Regionalism in Late Medieval Manuscripts and Texts: Essays Celebrating the Publication of 'A Linguistic Atlas of Late Mediaeval English'*, York Manuscripts Conferences: Proceedings Series, 2 (Cambridge: Brewer, 1991), pp. 89–108

Beer, Ellen J., *Initial und Miniatur: Buchmalerei aus neun Jahrhunderten in Handschriften der Badischen Landesbibliothek* (Basel: Feuermann-Verlag, 1965)

Bell, David N., *What Nuns Read: Books and Libraries in Medieval English Nunneries*, Cistercian Studies Series, 158 (Kalamazoo, MI: Cistercian Publications, 1995)

Bell, David N., 'What Nuns Read: The State of the Question', in *The Culture of Medieval English Monasticism*, ed. by James G. Clark (Woodbridge: Boydell, 2007), pp. 113–33

Bellenger, Dominic Aidan, *The French Exiled Clergy in the British Isles after 1789: An Historical Introduction and Working List* (Bath: Downside Abbey, 1986)

Bennett, Stuart, *Trade Bookbinding in the British Isles, 1660–1800* (New Castle, DE: Oak Knoll Press; London: The British Library, 2004)

Benskin, Michael, 'In Reply to Dr Burton', *Leeds Studies in English*, n.s. 22 (1991), 209–62

Benskin, Michael, 'The Letters <þ> and <y> in Later Middle English and Some Related Matters', *Journal of the Society of Archivists*, 7 (1982), 13–30

Benskin, Michael, and Margaret Laing, 'Translations and *Mischsprachen* in Middle English Manuscripts', in *So meny people, longages and tonges: Philological Essays in Scots and Mediaeval English Presented to Angus McIntosh*, ed. by Michael Benskin and M. L. Samuels (Edinburgh: Middle English Dialect Project, 1981), pp. 55–106

Benskin, M., M. Laing, V. Karaiskos, and K. Williamson, 'An Electronic Version of A Linguistic Atlas of Late Mediaeval English', http://www.lel.ed.ac.uk/ihd/elalme/elalme.html (Edinburgh: © 2013- The Authors and The University of Edinburgh)

Benskin, Michael, and M. L. Samuels, eds, *So meny people, longages and tonges: Philological Essays in Scots and Mediaeval English Presented to Angus McIntosh* (Edinburgh: Middle English Dialect Project, 1981)

'Bernard Gui, Frère Prêcheur', *Histoire littéraire de la France*, 35 (Paris: Imprimerie nationale, 1921), pp. 139–232

Bibliotheca Sussexiana: The Extensive and Valuable Library of His Royal Highness The Late Duke of Sussex, K.G., &c. &c. [...] Which will be sold by Auction by Messrs. Evans, No. 93, Pall Mall on Monday, 1st July and twenty-three days following. (Sunday excepted) (London: Evans, 1844)

Binns, Alison, *Dedications of Monastic Houses in England and Wales, 1066–1216*, Studies in the History of Medieval Religion, 1 (Woodbridge: Boydell, 1989)

Binski, Paul, Patrick Zutshi, and Stella Panayotova, *Western Illuminated Manuscripts: A Catalogue of the Collection in Cambridge University Library* (Cambridge: Cambridge University Press, 2011)

Blackwood, B. Gordon, *Tudor and Stuart Suffolk* (Lancaster: Carnegie Publishing, 2001)

Blair, John, 'A Hand-list of Anglo-Saxon Saints', in *Local Saints and Local Churches*, ed. by Richard Sharpe and Alan Thacker (Oxford: Oxford University Press, 2002), pp. 527–28

Blanton, Virginia, 'Benedictine Devotion to England's Saints: Thomas de la Mare, John of Tynemouth, and the *Sanctilogium* in Cotton MS Tiberius E. i', *Studies in Medieval and Renaissance History*, Third Series, 17 (2023), 105–18

Blanton, Virginia, 'Counting Noses and Assessing the Numbers: Native Saints in the *South English Legendaries*', in *Rethinking the South English Legendaries*, ed. by Heather Blurton and Jocelyn Wogan-Browne, Manchester Medieval Literature and Culture (Manchester: Manchester University Press, 2011), pp. 233–50

Blanton, Virginia, 'The Devotional Reading of Nuns: Three Legendaries of Native Saints in Late Medieval England', in *Nuns' Literacies in Medieval Europe: The Hull Dialogue*, ed. by Virginia Blanton, Veronica O'Mara, and Patricia Stoop, Medieval Women: Texts and Contexts, 26 (Turnhout: Brepols, 2013), pp. 185–206

Blanton, Virginia, 'The Kentish Queen as *Omnium Mater*: Goscelin of Saint-Bertin's Lections and the Emergence of the Cult of Saint Seaxburh', in *Writing Women Saints in Anglo-Saxon England*, ed. by Paul E. Szarmach (Toronto: University of Toronto Press, 2013), pp. 191–213

Blanton, Virginia, 'The Lost & (Not) Found: Sources for Female Saints' Legends in John of Tynemouth's *Sanctilogium*', in *The Blackwell Companion to British Literature*, ed. by Robert DeMaria, Jr., Heesok Chang, and Samantha Zacher (Oxford: Blackwell, 2014), i, 65–80

Blanton, Virginia, *Signs of Devotion: The Cult of St. Æthelthryth in Medieval England, 695–1615* (University Park, PA: The Pennsylvania State University Press, 2007)

Blanton, Virginia, Veronica O'Mara, and Patricia Stoop, eds, *Nuns' Literacies in Medieval Europe: The Antwerp Dialogue*, Medieval Women Texts and Contexts, 28 (Turnhout: Brepols, 2017)

Blanton, Virginia, Veronica O'Mara, and Patricia Stoop, eds, *Nuns' Literacies in Medieval Europe: The Hull Dialogue*, Medieval Women: Texts and Contexts, 26 (Turnhout: Brepols, 2013)

Blanton, Virginia, Veronica O'Mara, and Patricia Stoop, eds, *Nuns' Literacies in Medieval Europe: The Kansas City Dialogue*, Medieval Women Texts and Contexts, 27 (Turnhout: Brepols, 2015)

Bledniak, S., 'L'hagiographie imprimée: œuvres en français', 1476-1550', in *Hagiographies: Histoire internationale de la littérature hagiographique latine et vernaculaire en Occident des origines à 1550*, ed. by Guy Philippart (i–v), Monique Goullet (vi–vii), and Michèle Gaillard and Monique Goullet (viii), Corpus Christianorum Texts and Studies, 8 vols (Turnhout: Brepols, 1994–2020), i (1994), 359–405

Bliss, W. H., and J. A. Twemlow, eds, *Calendar of Entries in the Papal Registers Relating To Great Britain and Ireland: Papal Letters*, v: *A. D. 1396–1404* (London: Mackie and Co. for His Majesty's Stationery Office, 1904)

Blomefield, Francis, *An Essay Towards a Topographical History of the County of Norfolk [...]*, 11 vols, 2nd edn (London: Printed for William Miller by W. Bulmer and Co., 1805–10, first published 1739–75)

Blurton, Heather, and Jocelyn Wogan-Browne, eds, *Rethinking the South English Legendaries*, Manchester Medieval Literature and Culture (Manchester: Manchester University Press, 2011)

Bond, James, 'Medieval Nunneries in England and Wales: Buildings, Precincts, and Estates', in *Women and Religion in Medieval England*, ed. by Diana Wood (Oxford: Oxbow Books, 2003), pp. 46–90

Bourgne, Florence, 'Translating Saints' Lives into the Vernacular: *Translatio Studii* and *Furta Sacra* (Translation as Theft)', in *The Medieval Translator: Traduire au Moyen Âge*, 5, ed. by Roger Ellis and René Tixier (Turnhout: Brepols, 1996), pp. 50–63

Bowden, Caroline, 'Who were the Nuns?: A Prosopographical Study of the English Convents in Exile 1600–1800', https://wwtn.history.qmul.ac.uk/search/howto.html

Brantley, Jessica, *Reading in the Wilderness: Private Devotion and Public Performance in Late Medieval England* (Chicago, IL: University of Chicago Press, 2007)

British History Online: www.british-history.ac.uk

Brown, Jennifer N., *Three Women of Liège: A Critical Edition of and Commentary on the Middle English Lives of Elizabeth of Spalbeck, Christina Mirabilis, and Marie d'Oignies*, Medieval Women: Texts and Contexts, 23 (Turnhout: Brepols, 2009)

Brown, Jennifer N., and Donna Alfano Bussell, eds, *Barking Abbey and Medieval Literary Culture: Authorship and Authority in a Female Community* (Woodbridge: York Medieval Press, 2012)

Brown, Jennifer N., and Nicole R. Rice, eds., *Manuscript Culture and Medieval Devotional Traditions: Essays in Honour of Michael G. Sargent*, York Manuscript and Early Print Studies, 1 (Woodbridge: York Medieval Press, 2021)

Brown, Jessica C., 'The Birthplace of Saint Wulfthryth: An Unexamined Reference in Cambridge University Library Additional 2604', *Quidditas*, 42 (2021), 220–25

Bugyis, Katie Ann-Marie, *The Care of Nuns: The Ministries of Benedictine Women in England During the Central Middle Ages* (Oxford: Oxford University Press, 2019)

Burrell, Jun., George, *An Account of the Gifts and Legacies that have been Given and Bequeathed to Charitable and Public Uses in the Borough of Thetford, with their Present State and Management; Also, a Chronological Account of the Most Remarkable Events which have Occurred in Thetford, from the Earliest Period to the Present Time* (Thetford: Samuel Mills, 1809)

Burton, T. L., 'On the Current State of Middle English Dialectology', *Leeds Studies in English*, n.s. 22 (1991), 167–208

Camp, Cynthia Turner, *Anglo-Saxon Saints' Lives as History Writing in Late Medieval England* (Cambridge: Brewer, 2015)

Campbell, Emma, *Medieval Saints' Lives: The Gift, Kinship and Community in Old French Hagiography*, Gallica, 12 (Cambridge: Brewer, 2008)

'Cantus: A Database for Latin Ecclesiastical Chant — Inventories of Chant Sources' (https://cantus.uwaterloo.ca)

Carlquist, Jonas, 'The Birgittine Sisters at Vadstena Abbey: Their Learning and Literacy, with Particular Reference to Table Reading', in *Nuns' Literacies in Medieval Europe: The Hull Dialogue*, ed. by Virginia Blanton, Veronica O'Mara, and Patricia Stoop, Medieval Women: Texts and Contexts, 26 (Turnhout: Brepols, 2013), pp. 239–51

Cartwright, Jane, ed., *The Cult of St Ursula and the 11,000 Virgins* (Cardiff: University of Wales Press, 2016)

A Catalogue of the Manuscripts Preserved in the Library of the University of Cambridge, ed. for the Syndics of the University Press, 5 vols (Cambridge: Cambridge University Press, 1856–67

Cavanaugh, Susan Hagen, 'A Study of Books Privately Owned in England: 1300–1450' (unpublished doctoral dissertation, University of Pennsylvania, 1980)

Chastel, Guy, *Sainte Colombe de Sens* (Paris: J. de Gigord, 1939)

BIBLIOGRAPHY   365

Churchill, W. A., *Watermarks in Paper in Holland, England, France, etc. in the XVII and XVIII Centuries and their Interconnection* (Amsterdam: Menno Herzberger & Co., 1935)

Clark, James G., *A Monastic Renaissance at St. Albans: Thomas Walsingham and his Circle, c. 1350–1440* (Oxford: Clarendon Press, 2004)

Clark, James G., 'Thomas de la Mare', ODNB, https://doi.org/10.1093/ref:odnb/18039

Clesham, Brigid, Cumann Seandálaiochta agus Staire na Gallimhe/Galway Archaeological and Historical Society, https://gahs.ie/transcript-of-the-journal-of-thomas-tasburgh-s-j-on-his-visit-to-ireland/

Coldiron, A. E. B., 'William Caxton', in *The Oxford History of Literary Translation*, I: *To 1550*, ed. by Roger Ellis (Oxford: Oxford University Press, 2008), pp. 160–69

Coletti, Theresa, *Mary Magdalene and the Drama of Saints: Theater, Gender, and Religion in Late Medieval England*, The Middle Ages Series (Philadelphia, PA: University of Pennsylvania Press, 2004)

Collins, David J., 'Latin Hagiography in *Germania* (1450–1550)', in *Hagiographies: Histoire internationale de la littérature hagiographique latine et vernaculaire en Occident des origines à 1550*, ed. by Guy Philippart (I–V), Monique Goullet (VI–VII), and Michèle Gaillard and Monique Goullet (VIII), Corpus Christianorum Texts and Studies, 8 vols (Turnhout: Brepols, 1994–2020), IV (2006), 523–83

Collins, David J., *Reforming Saints: Saints' Lives and Their Authors in Germany, 1470–1530*, Oxford Studies in Historical Theology (Oxford: Oxford University Press, 2008)

Contzen, Eva von, 'Narrating Vernacular Sanctity: The Scottish Legendary as a Challenge to the "Literary Turn" in Fifteenth-Century Hagiography', in *Sanctity as Literature in Late Medieval Britain*, ed. by Eva von Contzen and Anke Bernau (Manchester: Manchester University Press, 2015), pp. 172–90

Contzen, Eva von, *The Scottish Legendary: Towards a Poetics of Hagiographic Narration*, Manchester Medieval Literature and Culture (Manchester: Manchester University Press, 2016)

Contzen, Eva von, and Anke Bernau, eds, *Sanctity as Literature in Late Medieval Britain* (Manchester: Manchester University Press, 2015)

Cooper, Thompson, revised by Emma Major, 'George Burton', ODNB, https://doi.org/10.1093/ref:odnb/4128.

Craik, Katherine A., 'William Warner', ODNB, https://doi.org/10.1093/ref:odnb/28770

Cross, F. L., and E. A. Livingstone, eds, *The Oxford Dictionary of the Christian Church*, 3rd edn (Oxford: Oxford University Press, 1997)

Cross, J. E., 'English Vernacular Lives before 1000 A. D', in *Hagiographies: Histoire internationale de la littérature hagiographique latine et vernaculaire en Occident des origines à 1550*, ed. by Guy Philippart (I–V), Monique Goullet (VI–VII), and Michèle Gaillard and Monique Goullet (VIII), Corpus Christianorum Texts and Studies, 8 vols (Turnhout: Brepols, 1994–2020), II (1996), 413–27

Cullum, Patricia, and Jeremy Goldberg, 'How Margaret Blackburn Taught Her Daughters: Reading Devotional Instruction in a Book of Hours', in *Medieval Women: Texts and Contexts in Late Medieval Britain, Essays for Felicity Riddy*, ed. by Jocelyn Wogan-

Browne, and others, Medieval Women: Texts and Contexts, 3 (Turnhout: Brepols, 2000), pp. 217–36

Cyrus, Cynthia J., *The Scribes for Women's Convents in Late Medieval Germany* (Toronto: University of Toronto Press, 2009)

Daas, Martha M., 'From Holy Hostess to Dragon Tamer: The Anomaly of Saint Martha', *Literature and Theology*, 22 (2008), pp. 1–15

Davis, G. R. C., *Medieval Cartularies of Great Britain and Ireland*, revised by Claire Breay, Julian Harrison, and David M. Smith (London, The British Library, 2010)

Davis, Norman, 'A Paston Hand', *The Review of English Studies*, n.s. 3 (1952), 209–21

Davis, Norman, 'Scribal Variation in Late Fifteenth Century English', in *Mélanges de linguistique et de philologie: Fernand Mossé in memoriam*, ed. by Fernand Mossé (Paris: Didier, 1959), pp. 95–103

Delehaye, Hippolyte, *Les Légendes hagiographiques*, Subsidia Hagiographica, 18, 4th edn (Bruxelles: Société des Bollandistes, 1955)

Derolez, Albert, *The Palaeography of Gothic Manuscript Books from the Twelfth to the Early Sixteenth Century* (Cambridge: Cambridge University Press, 2003)

Dijk, Mathilde van, *Een rij van spiegels: De Heilige Barbara van Nicomedia als voorbeeld vrouwelijke religieuzen*, Middeleeuwse Studies en Bronnen, 71 (Hilversum: Verloren, 2000)

Dolbeau, François, 'Notes sur l'organisation interne des légendiers latins', in *Hagiographie, cultures et sociétés (IVe–XIIe siècles): Actes du colloque organisé à Nanterre et à Paris (2–5 mai 1979)*, Centre du recherches sur l'Antiquité tardive et le Haut Moyen Âge, Université de Paris X (Paris: Études augustiennes, 1981), pp. 11–31

Dolbeau, François, 'Les Sources manuscrites des *Acta sanctorum* et leur collecte (xviie–xviiie siècles)', in *De Rosweyde aux 'Acta Sanctorum': La Recherche hagiographique des Bollandistes à travers quatre siècles, Actes du Colloque international (Bruxelles, 5 Octobre 2007)*, ed. by Robert Godding and others, Subsidia hagiographica, 88 (Bruxelles: Société des Bollandistes, 2009), pp. 105–47

Dondaine, Antoine, '*Le Dominicain Français Jean de Mailly et la Legende doree*', *Archives d'histoire dominicaine*, 1 (1946), 53–102

Dondaine, Antoine, 'L"Epilogus in gesta sanctorum" de Barthélemy de Trente', in *Studia mediaevalia et mariologica*, ed. by Carolo Balić, Pontificium Athenaeum 'Antonianum' (Roma: Antonianum, 1971), pp. 333–60

Doubleday, H. Arthur, and William Page, eds, *The Victoria History of the County of Norfolk*, 2 vols (London: Archibald Constable and Co. Ltd, 1901–06)

Doubleday, H. Arthur, William Page, and others, eds, *The Victoria History of the County of Essex*, 10 vols, bibliography, and two bibliographical supplements (London: The St Catherine Press and other publishers, 1903–2000)

Dowling, Maria, *Fisher of Men: A Life of John Fisher, 1469–1535* (London: Macmillan; New York, NY: St Martin's, 1999)

Doyle, A. I., 'Books Connected with the Vere Family and Barking Abbey', *Transactions of the Essex Archaeological Society*, n.s. 25 (1958), 222–43

BIBLIOGRAPHY   367

Doyle, A. I., 'Stephen Dodesham of Witham and Sheen', in *Of the Making of Books: Medieval Manuscripts, their Scribes and Readers: Essays Presented to M. B. Parkes*, ed. by P. R. Robinson and Rivkah Zim (Aldershot: Scolar Press, 1997), pp. 94–115

Dubois, Jacques, ed., *Les Martyrologes du moyen âge latin*, Typologie des sources du moyen âge occidental, Fascicle 26 (Turnhout: Brepols, 1978)

Dubois, Jacques, ed., *Les Martyrologes du moyen âge latin*, Typologie des sources du moyen âge occidental, Fascicle 26 (Turnhout: Brepols, 1985)

Dubois, Jacques, and Jean-Loup Lemaitre, *Sources et méthodes de l'hagiographie médiévale* (Paris: Les Éditions du Cerf, 1993)

Dubreil-Arcin, Agnès, 'Bernard Gui, un hagiographe dominicain atypique?', *Hagiographie et culte des saints en France méridionale (xiiie–xv^esiècle)*, Cahiers de Fanjeaux: Collection d'Histoire religieuse du Langedoc au Moyen Âge, 37 (Toulouse: Éditions Privat, 2002), pp. 147–73

Duffy, Eamon, 'Holy Maydens, Holy Wyfes: The Cult of Women Saints in Fifteenth- and Sixteenth-Century England', *Studies in Church History*, 27 (1990), 175–96

Duffy, Eamon, *The Stripping of the Altars: Traditional Religion in England, c. 1400–c. 1580* (New Haven, CT: Yale University Press, 1992)

Dunn-Lardeau, Brenda, ed., *'Legenda aurea' – 'la Légende dorée' (xiiie–xve s.)*, Actes de Congrès international de Perpignan (séances 'Nouvelles recherches sur la "Legenda aurea" ')*, Le moyen français, 32 (Montréal: Éditions CERES, 1993)

Dunn-Lardeau, Brenda, ed., *'Legenda aurea': sept siècles de diffusion*, Actes du colloque international sur la 'Legende aurea': texte latin et branches vernaculaires à l'Université du Québec à Montréal, 11–12 mai 1983 (Montréal: Éditions Bellarmin, and Paris: Librairie J. Vrin, 1986)

Dutton, Anne M., 'Piety, Politics and Persona: MS Harley 4012 and Anne Harling', in *Prestige, Authority and Power in Late Medieval Manuscripts and Texts*, ed. by Felicity Riddy (Woodbridge: York Medieval Press, 2000), pp. 133–46

Edwards, A. S. G., 'Fifteenth-Century English Collections of Female Saints' Lives', *The Yearbook of English Studies*, 33 (2003), 131–41

Eis, Gerhard, *Die Quellen für das 'Sanctuarium' des Mailänder Humanisten Boninus Mombritius: Eine Untersuchung zur Geschichte der großen Legendensammlungen des Mittelalters*, Germanische Studien, 140 (Berlin: Emil Ebering, 1933)

Ekwall, Ellert, *The Concise Oxford Dictionary of English Place-Names* (Oxford, Clarendon Press, 1936)

e-LALME: A Linguistic Atlas of Late Mediaeval English, www.amc.lel.ed.ac.uk

Ellis, Roger, ed., *The Medieval Translator/Traduire au Moyen Âge* (1989–)

Ellis, Roger, ed., *The Oxford History of Literary Translation, 1: To 1550* (Oxford: Oxford University Press, 2008)

Emden, A. B., *A Biographical Register of the University of Cambridge to 1500* (Cambridge: Cambridge University Press, 1963)

Emden, A. B., *A Biographical Register of the University of Oxford to A. D. 1500*, 3 vols (Oxford: Clarendon Press, 1957–59)

English, Barbara, and John Saville, *Strict Settlement: A Guide for Historians*, University of Hull, Occasional Papers in Economic and Social History, 10 (Hull: University of Hull Press, 1983)

Erler, Mary, 'Devotional Literature' in *The Cambridge History of the Book in Britain*, III: *1400–1557*, ed. by Lotte Hellinga and J. B. Trapp (Cambridge: Cambridge University Press, 1999), pp. 495–525

Erler, Mary C., 'The Early Sixteenth Century at Syon: Richard Whitford and Elizabeth Gibbs', in *Manuscript Culture and Medieval Devotional Traditions: Essays in Honour of Michael G. Sargent*, ed. by Jennifer N. Brown, and Nicole R. Rice, York Manuscript and Early Print Studies, 1 (Woodbridge: York Medieval Press, 2021), pp. 310–26

Erler, Mary, 'Private Reading in the Fifteenth- and Sixteenth-Century English Nunnery', in *The Culture of Medieval English Monasticism*, ed. by James G. Clark (Woodbridge: Boydell, 2007), pp. 134–46

Erler, Mary C., *Reading and Writing During the Dissolution: Monks, Friars, and Nuns 1530–1558* (Cambridge: Cambridge University Press, 2013)

Erler, Mary C., *Women, Reading, and Piety in Late Medieval England*, Cambridge Studies in Medieval Literature (New York: Cambridge University Press, 2002)

Evans, Nesta, 'The Tasburghs of South Elmham: The Rise and Fall of a Suffolk Gentry Family', *Proceedings of the Suffolk Institute of Archaeology and History*, 34 (1980), 269–80

Farrer, E., 'St. Peter's Hall, South Elmham', *Proceedings of the Suffolk Institute of Archæology and Natural History*, 20 (1930), 48–72

Ferguson, Elizabeth, 'Veneration, Translation and Reform: The *Lives* of Saints and the English Catholic Community, *c.* 1600–1642', *Recusant History*, 32 (2014), 37–65

Fisher, John H., *The Emergence of Standard English* (Lexington, KY: The University Press of Kentucky, 1996)

Fleith, Barbara, *Studien zur Überlieferungsgeschichte der lateinischen 'Legenda Aurea'*, Subsidia hagiographica, 72 (Bruxelles: Société des Bollandistes, 1991)

Fleith, Barbara, and Franco Morenzoni, eds, *De la sainteté a l'hagiographie: Genèse et usage de la 'Légende dorée'*, Publications romanes et françaises, 229 (Genève: Librairie Droz S.A., 2001)

Fowler, R. C., 'Inventories of Essex Monasteries in 1536', *Transactions of the Essex Archaeological Society*, n.s. 9 (1906), 280–92

Frazier, Alison Knowles, *Possible Lives: Authors and Saints in Renaissance Italy* (New York, NY: Columbia University Press, 2005)

Freeman, Elizabeth, 'Cistercian Nuns in Medieval England: The Gendering of Geographic Marginalization', *Medieval Feminist Forum*, 43 (2008), 26–39

Friedman, John Block, *Northern English Books, Owners, and Makers in the Late Middle Ages* (Syracuse, NY: Syracuse University Press, 1995)

Fros, Henricus, ed., *Bibliotheca Hagiographica Latina Antiquae et Mediae Aetatis: Novum Supplementum*, Subsidia hagiographica, 70 (Bruxelles: Société des Bollandistes, 1986)

Gaffier, Baudouin de, 'Le Martyrologe et le légendier d'Hermann Greven', *Analecta Bollandiana*, 54 (1936), 316–58

Galbraith, V. H., 'The *Historia aurea* of John, Vicar of Tynemouth, and the Sources of the St. Albans Chronicle (1327–1377)', *Essays in History Presented to Reginald Lane Poole*, ed. by H. W. C. Davis (Oxford: Clarendon Press, 1927), pp. 379–98

Gatland, Emma, *Women from the 'Golden Legend': Female Authority in a Medieval Castilian Sanctoral*, Colección Támesis, Serie A: Monografías, 296 (Woodbridge: Tamesis, 2011)

Gibson, Gail McMurray, *The Theater of Devotion: East Anglian Drama and Society in the Late Middle Ages* (Chicago, IL: University of Chicago Press, 1989)

Gibson, Kate, 'Marriage Choice and Kinship among the English Catholic Elite, 1680–1730', *Journal of Family History*, 41 (2016), 144–64

Gilchrist, Roberta, *Gender and Material Culture: The Archaeology of Religious Women* (London: Routledge, 1994)

Gilchrist, Roberta, and Marilyn Oliva, *Religious Women in Medieval East Anglia: History and Archaeology c. 1100 to 1540*, Studies in East Anglian History, 1 (Norwich: Centre of East Anglian Studies, University of East Anglia, 1993)

Gillespie, Vincent, 'Religious Writing', in *The Oxford History of Literary Translation, I: To 1550*, ed. by Roger Ellis (Oxford: Oxford University Press, 2008), pp. 234–83

Gillespie, Vincent, and A. I. Doyle, eds, *Syon Abbey, with the Libraries of the Carthusians*, Corpus of British Medieval Library Catalogues, 9 (London: The British Library in association with the British Academy, 2001)

Godden, M. R., 'Old English Composite Homilies from Winchester', *Anglo-Saxon England*, 4 (1975), 57–65

Godding, Robert, and others, eds, 'Un trésor iconographique méconnu: Les Gravures des *Acta Sanctorum*', in *Bollandistes: Saints et Légendes, Quatre siècles de recherche* (Bruxelles: Société des Bollandistes, 2007), pp. 75–96

Godding, Robert, and others, eds, 'Les Voyages scientifiques', in *Bollandistes: Saints et Légendes, Quatre siècles de recherche* (Bruxelles: Société des Bollandistes, 2009), pp. 105–47

Gómez Soliño, José Secundino, 'Variación y estandarización en el Inglés moderno temprano: 1470–1540' (unpublished doctoral dissertation, Universidad de Oviedo, 1984)

Görlach, Manfred, 'Middle English Legends, 1220–1530', in *Hagiographies: Histoire internationale de la littérature hagiographique latine et vernaculaire en Occident des origines à 1550*, ed. by Guy Philippart (I–V), Monique Goullet (VI–VII), and Michèle Gaillard and Monique Goullet (VIII), Corpus Christianorum Texts and Studies, 8 vols (Turnhout: Brepols, 1994–2020), I (1994), 429–85

Görlach, Manfred, *Studies in Middle English Saints' Legends*, Anglistische Forschungen, 257 (Heidelberg: Winter, 1998)

Görlach, Manfred, *The Textual Tradition of the South English Legendary*, Leeds Texts and Monographs, n.s. 6 (Leeds: School of English, 1974)

Grant, Nicholas, 'John Leland's List of "Places where Saints Rest in England" ', *Analecta Bollandiana*, 122 (2004), 373–87

Green, Barbara, 'The Antiquaries', in Ann Eljenholm Nichols, *The Early Art of Norfolk: A Subject List of Extant and Lost Art including Items relevant to Early Drama*, Early

Drama, Art, and Music Reference Series, 7 (Kalamazoo, MI: Medieval Institute Publications, 2002), pp. 286–88

Hamel, Christopher de, *The Library of the Bridgettine Nuns and their Peregrinations after the Reformation: An Essay by Christopher de Hamel, with the Manuscript of Arundel Castle* (Otley: Roxburghe Club, 1991)

Harper, Sally, 'Traces of Lost Late Medieval Offices?: The *Sanctilogium Angliae, Walliae, Scotiae, et Hiberniae* of John of Tynemouth (*fl.* 1350)', in *Essays on the History of English Music in Honour of John Caldwell: Sources, Style, Performance, Historiography*, ed. by Emma Hornby and David Maw (Woodbridge: Boydell, 2010), pp. 1–21

Harper-Bill, Christopher, 'A Late Medieval Visitation — The Diocese of Norwich in 1499', *Proceedings of the Suffolk Institute of Archaeology and History*, 34 (1977–80), 35–47

Haslewood, Francis, 'Inventories of Monasteries Suppressed in 1536', *Proceedings of the Suffolk Institute of Archæology and Natural History*, 8 (1894), 83–116

Heawood, Edward, *Watermarks: Addenda and Corrigenda*, Monumenta Chartæ Papyraceæ Historiam Illustrantia, 1 (Hilversum: The Paper Publications Society, 1970)

Heawood, Edward, *Watermarks: Mainly of the 17th and 18th Centuries*, Monumenta Chartæ Papyraceæ Historiam Illustrantia, 1 (Hilversum: The Paper Publications Society, 1950)

Heffernan, Thomas J., 'The Liturgy and the Literature of Saints' Lives', in *The Liturgy of the Medieval Church*, ed. by Thomas J. Heffernan and E. Ann Matter (Kalamazoo, MI: Medieval Institute Publications, 2001), pp. 73–105

Henderson, T. F., revised by John Van der Kiste, 'Prince Augustus Frederick', ODNB, https://doi.org/10.1093/ref:odnb/900

Hill, Carole, *Women and Religion in Late Medieval Norwich*, Royal Historical Society Studies in History (Woodbridge: Boydell, 2010)

Hollis, Stephanie, *Anglo-Saxon Women and the Church: Sharing a Common Fate* (Woodbridge: Boydell and Brewer, 1992)

Horobin, Simon, *The Language of the Chaucer Tradition*, Chaucer Studies, 32 (Cambridge: Brewer, 2003)

Horobin, Simon, 'A Manuscript Found in Abbotsford House and the Lost Legendary of Osbern Bokenham', *English Manuscript Studies, 1100–1700*, 14 (2007), 130–62

Horobin, Simon, 'Politics, Patronage, and Piety in the Work of Osbern Bokenham', *Speculum*, 82 (2007), 932–49

Hutchison, Ann M., 'What the Nuns Read: Literary Evidence from the English Bridgettine House, Syon Abbey', *Mediaeval Studies*, 57 (1995), 205–22

Jackson, Peter, and Michael Lapidge, 'The Contents of the Cotton-Corpus Legendary', in *Holy Men and Holy Women: Old English Prose Saints' Lives and Their Contexts*, ed. by Paul E. Szarmach, SUNY Series in Medieval Studies (Albany, NY: State University of New York Press, 1996), pp. 131–46

James, M. R., *A Descriptive Catalogue of the Manuscripts in the Library of Lambeth Palace*, 2 vols (Cambridge: Cambridge University Press, 1930–32)

James-Maddocks, Holly, 'Scribes and Booklets: The 'Trinity Anthologies' Reconsidered', in *Scribal Cultures in Late Medieval England: Essays in Honour of Linne R. Mooney*, ed. by Margaret Connolly, Holly James-Maddocks, and Derek Pearsall, York Manuscripts and Early Print Studies, 3 (Woodbridge: York Medieval Press, 2022), pp. 146–79

Jankovsky, Klaus P., 'National Characteristics in the Portrayal of English Saints in the *South English Legendary*', in *Images of Sainthood in Medieval Europe*, ed. by Renate Blumenfeld-Kosinski and Timea Szell (Ithaca, NY: Cornell University Press, 1991), pp. 81–93

Jansen, Katherine Ludwig, *The Making of the Magdalen: Preaching and Popular Devotion in the Later Middle Ages* (Princeton, NJ: Princeton University Press, 2000)

Jones, E. A., 'A Mirror for Recluses: A New Manuscript, New Information and some New Hypotheses', The *Library: The Transactions of the Bibliographical Society*, Seventh Series, 15 (2014), 424–31

Juchhoff, Rudolph, 'Johannes de Westfalia als Buchhändler', *Gutenberg Jahrbuch*, 29 (1954), 133–36

Kanno, Mami, 'Constructing Gender and Locality in Late Medieval England: The Lives of Anglo-Saxon and British Female Saints in the *South English Legendaries*' (unpublished doctoral dissertation, University of London, King's College, 2016)

Kathman, David, 'William Basse', ODNB, https://doi.org/10.1093/ref:odnb/1633

Keiser, George R., 'Patronage and Piety in Fifteenth-Century England: Margaret, Duchess of Clarence, Symon Wynter and Beinecke MS 317', *The Yale University Library Gazette*, 60 (1985), 32–46

Keiser, George R., 'Serving the Needs of Readers: Textual Division in Some Late-Medieval English Texts', in *New Science out of Old Books: Studies in Manuscripts and Early Printed Books in Honour of A. I. Doyle*, ed. by Richard Beadle and A. J. Piper (Aldershot: Scolar Press, 1995), pp. 207–26

Ker, N. R., and A. J. Piper, *Medieval Manuscripts in British Libraries*, 5 vols (Oxford: Clarendon Press, 1969–2002)

Kidd, Peter, *A Descriptive Catalogue of the Medieval Manuscripts of The Queen's College, Oxford*, Oxford Bibliographical Society Publications, Special Series: Manuscript Catalogues, 1 (Oxford: Oxford Bibliographical Society, 2017)

Kirby, D. P., *The Earliest English Kings* (London: Routledge, 2000)

Klein, Lawrence E., 'Politeness for Plebes: Consumption and Social Identity in Early Eighteenth-Century England', in *The Consumption of Culture 1600–1800: Image, Object, Text*, ed. by Ann Bermingham and John Brewer (London: Routledge, 1995), pp. 362–82

Knowles, David, and R. Neville Hadcock, *Medieval Religious Houses: England and Wales* (London: Longman, 1971, first published 1953)

Knudsen, Christian D., 'Naughty Nuns and Promiscuous Monks: Monastic Sexual Misconduct in Late Medieval England' (unpublished doctoral dissertation, Centre for Medieval Studies, University of Toronto, 2012)

Kolsky, Stephen, *The Ghost of Boccaccio: Writings on Famous Women in Renaissance Italy*, Late Medieval and Early Modern Studies, 7 (Turnhout: Brepols, 2005)

Kroebel, Christiane, 'Remembering St Hilda in the Later Middle Ages', in *Late Medieval Devotion to Saints from the North of England: New Directions*, ed. by Christiania Whitehead, Hazel J. Hunter Blair, and Denis Renevey, Medieval Church Studies, 48 (Turnhout: Brepols, 2022), pp. 321–39

Krug, Rebecca, *Reading Families: Women's Literate Practice in Late Medieval England* (Ithaca, NY: Cornell University Press, 2002)

Kurath, Hans, Sherman M. Kuhn, and Robert E. Lewis, eds, *Middle English Dictionary*, 115 fascicles (Michigan, MI: University of Michigan Press, 1952–2001), https://quod.lib.umich.edu/m/middle-english-dictionary/dictionary

Laing, Margaret, and Keith Williamson, eds, *Speaking in our Tongues: Proceedings of a Colloquium on Medieval Dialectology and Related Disciplines* (Cambridge: Brewer, 1994)

Lapidge, Michael, 'Editing Hagiography', in *La critica del testo mediolatino: Atti del Convegno (Firenze 6–8 dicembre 1990)*, ed. by Claudio Leonardi, Biblioteca di medioevo latino, 5 (Spoleto: Centro italiano di studi sull'alto medioevo, 1994), pp. 239–57

Lapidge, Michael, 'The *Legendarium* of Anton Geens: A Supplementary Note', *Analecta Bollandiana*, 126 (2008), 151–54

Lapidge, Michael, and Rosalind Love, 'The Latin Hagiography of England and Wales (600–1500)', in *Hagiographies: Histoire internationale de la littérature hagiographique latine et vernaculaire en Occident des origines à 1550*, ed. by Guy Philippart (i–v), Monique Goullet (vi–vii), and Michèle Gaillard and Monique Goullet (viii), Corpus Christianorum Texts and Studies, 8 vols (Turnhout: Brepols, 1994–2020), iii (2001), 203–325

Lee, Brian North, *British Royal Bookplates and Ex-Libris of Related Families* (Aldershot: Scolar Press, 1992)

Lewis, Katherine J., 'Becoming a Virgin King: Richard II and Edward the Confessor', in *Gender and Holiness: Men, Women and Saints in Late Medieval Europe*, ed. by Samantha J. E. Riches and Sarah Salih, Routledge Studies in Medieval Religion and Culture, 1 (London: Routledge, 2002), pp. 86–100

Loenen, Ria van, 'Johannes Gielemans (1427–1487) en de heiligen van de Brabanders', in *Gouden Legenden: Heiligenlevens en Heiligenverering in de Nederlanden,* ed. by Anneke B. Mulder-Bakker and Marijke Carasso-Kok (Hilversum: Verloren, 1997), pp. 139–49

Logan, F. Donald, *Runaway Religious in Medieval England, c. 1240–1540*, Cambridge Studies in Medieval Life and Thought, Fourth Series (Cambridge: Cambridge University Press, 1996)

Long, Mary Beth, 'Corpora and Manuscripts, Authors and Audiences', in *A Companion to Middle English Hagiography*, ed. by Sarah Salih (Woodbridge: Brewer, 2006), pp. 47–69

Lucas, Peter J., 'Consistency and Correctness in the Orthographic Usage of John Capgrave's *Chronicle*', *Studia Neophilologica*, 45 (1973), 323–55; reprinted in Peter J. Lucas, *From Author to Audience: John Capgrave and Medieval Publication* (Dublin: University College Dublin Press/Preas Choláiste Ollscoile Bhaile Átha Cliath, 1997), pp. 203–35

BIBLIOGRAPHY

Lucas, Peter J., 'John Capgrave and the *Nova Legenda Anglie: A Survey*', *The Library: Transactions of the Bibliographical Society,* Fifth Series, 25 (1970), 1–10; reprinted in Peter J. Lucas, *From Author to Audience: John Capgrave and Medieval Publication* (Dublin: University College Dublin Press/Preas Choláiste Ollscoile Bhaile Átha Cliath, 1997), pp. 294–306

Maggioni, Giovanni Paolo, 'Thirteenth-Century *Legendae Novae* and the Preaching Orders: A Communication System', in *Hagiography and the History of Latin Christendom, 500–1500,* ed. by Samantha Kahn Herrick, Reading Medieval Sources, 4 (Leiden: Brill, 2020), pp. 98–120

Maggioni, Giovanni Paolo, 'La trasmissione dei leggendari abbreviati del XIII secolo', *Filologia Mediolatina,* 9 (2002), 87–107

Maggioni, G. P., *Ricerche sulla composizione e sulla trasmissione della 'Legenda aurea',* Biblioteca di Medioevo, 8 (Spoleto: Centro Italiano di Studi sull'Alto Medioevo, 1995)

Major, Tristan, 'Saint Etheldreda and the *South English Legendary*', *Anglia,* 128 (2010), 83–101

Makowski, Elizabeth, *English Nuns and the Law in the Middle Ages: Cloistered Nuns and their Lawyers, 1293–1540,* Studies in the History of Medieval Religion, 39 (Woodbridge: Boydell, 2011)

Martin, Thomas, *The History of the Town of Thetford in the Counties of Norfolk and Suffolk, from the Earliest Accounts to the Present Time* (London: J. Nichols, 1779)

Mason, Margaret J., 'Nuns of the Jerningham Letters: The Hon. Catherine Dillon (1752–1797) and Anne Nevill (1754–1824), Benedictines at Bodney Hall', *Recusant History,* 23 (1996), 34–78

McGee, J. Sears, *An Industrious Mind: The Worlds of Sir Simonds D'Ewes* (Stanford: Stanford University Press, 2015)

McIntosh, Angus, M. L. Samuels, and Michael Benskin, *A Linguistic Atlas of Late Mediaeval English,* 4 vols (Aberdeen: Aberdeen University Press, 1986)

McIntosh, Angus, M. L. Samuels, and Margaret Laing, *Middle English Dialectology: Essays on Some Principles and Problems,* ed. by Margaret Laing (Aberdeen: Aberdeen University Press, 1989)

McKendrick, Scot, *Flemish Illuminated Manuscripts, 1400–1550* (London: The British Library, 2003)

Meale, Carol M., and Julia Boffey, 'Gentlewomen's Reading', in *The Cambridge History of the Book in Britain,* III: *1400–1557,* ed. by Lotte Hellinga and J. B. Trapp (Cambridge: Cambridge University Press, 1999), pp. 526–40

Messent, Claude J. W., *The Monastic Remains of Norfolk & Suffolk* (Norwich: H. W. Hunt, 1934)

Metzger, Bruce M., and Michael David Coogan, eds, *The Oxford Companion to the Bible,* Oxford Companions (New York, NY: Oxford University Press, 1993)

Mews, Constant J., 'Re-structuring the *Golden Legend* in the Early Fourteenth Century: The *Sanctilogium* of Guy of Châtres, Abbot of Saint-Denis', *Revue bénédictine,* 120 (2010), 129–44

M[eyer], P[aul], 'Légendes hagiographiques en français, II: Légendes en prose', in *Histoire littéraire de la France*, 33 (Paris: Imprimerie nationale, 1906), pp. 378–458

Meyer, Paul, 'Notice du MS. 305 de Queen's College, Oxford (légendier français)', *Romania*, 34 (1905), 215–36

Miles, Laura Saetveit, *The Virgin Mary's Book at the Annunciation: Reading, Interpretation, and Devotion in Medieval England* (Cambridge: Brewer, 2020)

Mooney, Linne R., *The Index of Middle English Prose: Handlist XI, Manuscripts in the Library of Trinity College, Cambridge* (Cambridge: Brewer, 1995)

Mooney, Linne R., 'Locating Scribal Activity in Late Medieval London', in *Design and Distribution of Late Medieval Manuscripts in England*, ed. by Margaret Connolly and Linne R. Mooney (York: York Medieval Press, 2008), pp. 183–204

Mooney, Linne R. 'Scribes and Booklets of Trinity College, Cambridge, Manuscripts R.3.19 and R.3.21', in *Middle English Poetry: Texts and Traditions, Essays in Honour of Derek Pearsall*, ed. by A. J. Minnis, York Manuscripts Conferences Proceedings Series, 5 (Woodbridge: York Medieval Press, 2001), pp. 241–66

Mooney, Linne, and Simon Horobin, 'Late Medieval English Scribes', https://www.medievalscribes.com/index.php?page=about&nav=off

Moore, Andrew, and Charlotte Crawley, *Family and Friends: A Regional Survey of British Portraiture* (London: HMSO, 1992)

Moore, Samuel, Sanford Brown B. Meech, and Harold Whitehall, 'Middle English Dialect Characteristics and Dialect Boundaries: Preliminary Report of an Investigation Based exclusively on Localized Texts and Documents', in *Essays and Studies in English and Comparative Literature,* University of Michigan Publications in Language and Literature, 13 (Ann Arbor, MI: University of Michigan Press, 1935), 1–60

Moretus, H., 'Catalogus Codicum hagiographicorum latinorum Bibliothecæ Bollandianæ', *Analecta Bollandiana*, 24 (1905), 425–72

Moshenska, Gabriel, ' "The Finest Theological Library in the World": The Rise and Fall of the *Bibliotheca Sussexiana*', in *Book Collecting in Ireland and Britain, 1650–1850*, ed. by Elizabethanne Boran (Dublin: Four Courts Press, 2018), pp. 168–87

Moutray, Tonya J., *Refugee Nuns, The French Revolution, and British Literature and Culture* (Routledge: London, 2016)

Mustanoja, Tauno F., *A Middle English Syntax: Part I, Parts of Speech*, Mémoires de la Société Néophilologique de Helsinki, 23 (Helsinki: Société Néophilologique, 1960)

Needham, Paul, 'Continental Printed Books in Oxford, *c.* 1480–83: Two Trade Records', in *Incunabula: Studies in Fifteenth-Century Printed Books Presented to Lotte Hellinga*, ed. by Martin Davies (London: The British Library, 1999), pp. 243–70

Nichols, Ann Eljenholm, *The Early Art of Norfolk: A Subject List of Extant and Lost Art including Items relevant to Early Drama*, Early Drama, Art, and Music Reference Series, 7 (Kalamazoo, MI: Medieval Institute Publications, 2002)

Nicolson, William, *English Historical Library*, 2 vols (London: Abell Swall, 1696)

Nijenhuis, Wiesje, 'In a Class of Their Own: Anglo-Saxon Female Saints', *Mediaevistik*, 14 (2001), 125–48

Nocentini, Silvia, 'Medieval Collections of Saints' Lives', Collaborative European Digital Archive Infrastructure (CENDARI) Archival Research Guide, http://www.cendari.eu/sites/default/files/ARGMedievalCollections.pdf

Oakden, J. P., *Alliterative Poetry in Middle English: The Dialectal and Metrical Survey* (Manchester: Manchester University Press, 1930–35; reprinted by Archon Books, 1968)

Ogilvie-Thomson, S. J., *The Index of Middle English Prose: Handlist XXIII, The Rawlinson Collection, Bodleian Library, Oxford* (Cambridge: Brewer, 2017)

Oliva, Marilyn, *The Convent and the Community in Late Medieval England: Female Monasteries in the Diocese of Norwich, 1350–1540*, Studies in the History of Medieval Religion, 12 (Woodbridge: Boydell, 1998)

O'Mara, Veronica, 'The Early Printed Sermon in England between 1483 and 1532: A Peculiar Phenomenon', in *Circulating the Word of God in Medieval and Early Modern Europe: Catholic Preaching and Preachers across Manuscript and Print (c. 1450 to c. 1550)*, ed. by Veronica O'Mara and Patricia Stoop, Sermo: Studies on Patristic, Medieval, and Reformation Sermons and Preaching, 17 (Turnhout: Brepols, 2022), pp. 71–102

O'Mara, Veronica, 'The Late Medieval English Nun and her Scribal Activity: A Complicated Quest', in *Nuns' Literacies in Medieval Europe: The Hull Dialogue*, ed. by Virginia Blanton, Veronica O'Mara, and Patricia Stoop, Medieval Women: Texts and Contexts, 26 (Turnhout: Brepols, 2013), pp. 69–93

O'Mara, Veronica, 'Nuns and Writing in Late Medieval England: The Quest Continues', in *Nuns' Literacies in Medieval Europe: The Kansas City Dialogue*, ed. by Virginia Blanton, Veronica O'Mara, and Patricia Stoop, Medieval Women: Texts and Contexts, 27 (Turnhout: Brepols, 2015), pp. 123–47

O'Mara, V. M., 'Preaching to Nuns in Late Medieval England', in *Medieval Monastic Preaching*, ed. by Carolyn Muessig, Brill's Studies in Intellectual History, 90 (Leiden: Brill, 1998), pp. 93–119

O'Mara, Veronica, 'Preaching to Nuns in the Norwich Diocese on the Eve of the Reformation: The Evidence from Visitation Records', in *Monastic Life in the Medieval British Isles: Essays in Honour of Janet Burton*, ed. by Karen Stöber, Julie Kerr, and Emilia Jamroziak (Cardiff: University of Wales Press, 2018), pp. 189–212

O'Mara, V. M., 'Saints' Plays and Preaching: Theory and Practice in Late Middle English Sanctorale Sermons', *Leeds Studies in English: Essays in Honour of Peter Meredith*, n.s. 29 (1998), 257–74

O'Mara, Veronica, 'Scribal Engagement and the Late Medieval English Nun: The Quest Concludes?', in *Nuns' Literacies in Medieval Europe: The Antwerp Dialogue*, ed. by Virginia Blanton, Veronica O'Mara, and Patricia Stoop, Medieval Women: Texts and Contexts, 28 (Turnhout: Brepols, 2017), pp. 187–208

O'Mara, Veronica, 'A Syon Scribe Revealed by Her Signature: Mary Nevel and Her Manuscripts', in *Continuity and Change: Papers from the Birgitta Conference at Dartington 2015*, ed. by Elin Andersson and others, Kungliga Vitterhets Historie och Antikvitets Akademien, Konferenser, 93 (Stockholm: Kungliga Vitterhets Historie och Antikvitets Akademien, 2017), pp. 283–308

O'Mara, Veronica, and Virginia Blanton, 'Cambridge University Library, Additional MS 2604: Repackaging Female Saints' Lives for the Fifteenth-Century English Nun', *Journal of the Early Book Society*, 13 (2010), 237–47

O'Mara, Veronica, and Suzanne Paul, *A Repertorium of Middle English Prose Sermons*, Sermo: Studies on Patristic, Medieval, and Reformation Sermons and Preaching, 1, 4 vols (Turnhout: Brepols, 2007)

Omont, Henri, 'Le Sanctilogium de Gui de Châtres, abbé de Saint-Denys', *Bibliothèque de l'École des chartes*, 86 (1925), 407–10

Ó Riain, Diarmuid, 'The *Magnum Legendarium Austriacum*: A New Investigation of One of Medieval Europe's Richest Hagiographical Collections', *Analecta Bollandiana*, 133 (2015), 87–165

Ó Riain, Pádraig, 'Feasts of Irish and Scottish Saints in Hermann Greven's Martyrology and *Devotionale*: A Review of the Evidence', *Analecta Bollandiana*, 138 (2020), 368–81

Orme, Nicholas, 'Alexander Barclay', ODNB, https://doi.org/10.1093/ref:odnb/1337

Page, William, ed., *The Victoria History of the County of Kent*, 3 vols (London: Archibald Constable and Co., and other publishers, 1908–32; with the 1908 vol. reprinted in 1974)

Page, William, ed., *The Victoria History of the County of Suffolk*, 2 vols (London: Archibald Constable and Co. Ltd, 1907–11)

Parkes, M. B., *English Cursive Book Hands, 1250–1500* (Oxford: Oxford University Press, 1969)

Parkes, M. B., 'A Fifteenth-Century Scribe: Henry Mere', in *Scribes, Scripts and Readers: Studies in the Communication, Presentation, and Dissemination of Medieval Texts* (London: Hambledon, 1991), pp. 249–56 (first published in the *Bodleian Library Record*, 6 (1961), 654–59)

Parkes, Malcolm Beckwith, 'The Influence of the Concepts of *Ordinatio* and *Compilatio* on the Development of the Book', in *Medieval Learning and Literature: Essays Presented to Richard William Hunt*, ed. by J. J. G. Alexander and M. T. Gibson (Oxford: Clarendon Press, 1976), pp. 115–41

Paxton, Catherine, 'The Nunneries of London and its Environs in the Later Middle Ages' (unpublished doctoral dissertation, University of Oxford, 1992)

Pearsall, Derek, *John Lydgate*, Poets of the Later Middle Ages (London: Routledge and Kegan Paul, 1970)

Peters, Diane E., 'The Iconography of St Martha: Some Considerations', *Vox Benedictina*, 9. 1 (1992), 30–65

Petti, Anthony G., *English Literary Hands from Chaucer to Dryden* (London: Arnold, 1977)

Pettigrew, Thomas Joseph, *Bibliotheca Sussexiana: A Descriptive Catalogue, Accompanied by Historical and Biographical Notices, of the Manuscripts and Printed Books Contained in The Library of His Royal Highness The Duke of Sussex, K.G., D.C.L., &c &c &c &c in Kensington Palace*, 2 vols in eight parts (London: Printed for Longman and Co., Paternoster Row; Payne and Foss, Pall Mall; Harding and Co., Pall Mall East; H. Bohn, Henrietta Street; and Smith and Son, Glasgow, 1827; Longman and Co., 1839)

Pfaff, Richard W., *The Liturgy in Medieval England: A History* (Cambridge: Cambridge University Press, 2009)

Pfaff, R. W., *New Liturgical Feasts in Later Medieval England* (Oxford: Clarendon Press, 1970)

Philippart, Guy, *Les Légendiers Latins et autres manuscrits hagiographiques*, Typologie des sources du moyen âge occidental, Fascicles 24–25 (Turnhout: Brepols, 1977)

Philippart, Guy, *Les Légendiers Latins et autres manuscrits hagiographiques*, Typologie des sources du moyen âge occidental, Fascicles 24–25 (Turnhout: Brepols, 1985)

Philippart, Guy, and others, eds, *Hagiographies: Histoire internationale de la littérature hagiographique latine et vernaculaire en Occident des origines à 1550*, ed. by Guy Philippart (I–V), Monique Goullet (VI–VII), and Michèle Gaillard and Monique Goullet (VIII), Corpus Christianorum Texts and Studies, 8 vols (Turnhout: Brepols, 1994–2020)

Pickering, O. S., 'Review of Barbara Fleith, *Studien zur Überlieferungsgeschichte der lateinischen 'Legenda Aurea'*, Subsidia hagiographica, 72 (Bruxelles: Société des Bollandistes, 1991)', *Journal of Ecclesiastical History*, 44 (1993), 338–39

Pickering, Oliver. 'Saints' Lives', in *A Companion to Middle English Prose*, ed. by A. S. G. Edwards (Cambridge: Brewer, 2004), pp. 249–70

Pollard, A. W., and G. R. Redgrave, *A Short-Title Catalogue of Books Printed in England, Scotland, and Ireland, and of English Books Printed Abroad*, second edition, revised and enlarged by W. A. Jackson, F. S. Ferguson, and Katherine F. Pantzer, 3 vols (London: The Bibliographical Society, 1976–91) (revised at http://estc.bl.uk/)

Poncelet, Albert, 'De codicibus hagiographicis Iohannes Gielemans, canonici regularis in Rubea Valle prope Bruxellas', *Analecta Bollandiana*, 14 (1895), pp. 5–88

Poncelet, Albert, 'De magno legendario Austriaco', *Analecta Bollandiana*, 17 (1898), 24–96, 123–216

Poncelet, Albert, 'Le Légendier de Pierre Calo', *Analecta Bollandiana*, 29 (1910), 5–116

Poska, Allyson M., *Women and Authority in Early Modern Spain: The Peasants of Galicia* (Oxford: Oxford University Press, 2005)

Powell, Susan, ed., *Saints and Cults in Medieval England: Proceedings of the 2015 Harlaxton Symposium*, Harlaxton Medieval Studies, 27 (Donington: Shaun Tyas, 2017)

Power, Eileen, *Medieval English Nunneries c.1275 to 1535*, Cambridge Studies in Medieval Life and Thought (Cambridge: Cambridge University Press, 1922)

Pugh, R. B., Elizabeth Crittall, and others, eds, *The Victoria History of the County of Wiltshire*, 18 vols (London and other places: Oxford University Press, 1957–2011)

Quentin, Henri, *Les Martyrologes historiques du moyen âge: Étude sur la formation du Martyrologe Romain*, 2nd edn (Paris: Librairie Victor Lecoffre, 1908)

Ramsay, Nigel, 'English Book Collectors and the Salerooms in the Eighteenth Century', in *Under the Hammer: Book Auctions since the Seventeenth Century*, ed. by Robin Myers, Michael Harris, and Giles Mandelbrote (New Castle, DE: Oak Knoll Press; London: The British Library, 2001), pp. 89–110

Reames, Sherry L., *The 'Legenda aurea': A Reexamination of its Paradoxical History* (Madison, WI: The University of Wisconsin Press, 1985)

Reames, Sherry L., *Saints' Legends in Medieval Sarum Breviaries: Catalogue and Studies*, York Manuscript and Early Print Studies, 2 (Woodbridge: York Medieval Press, 2021)

Rhodes, J. T., 'English Books of Martyrs and Saints of the Late Sixteenth and Early Seventeenth Centuries', *Recusant History*, 22 (1994), 7–25

Rice, Nicole R., *Lay Piety and Religious Discipline in Middle English Literature*, Cambridge Studies in Medieval Literature (Cambridge: Cambridge University Press, 2008)

Richmond, Colin, 'The Advent of the Tasburghs: A Documentary Study in the Adair Family Collection', *Common Knowledge*, 20. 2 (2014), 296–336

Richmond, Colin, *John Hopton: A Fifteenth Century Suffolk Gentleman* (Cambridge: Cambridge University Press, 1981)

Riddy, Felicity, ed., *Regionalism in Late Medieval Manuscripts and Texts: Essays Celebrating the Publication of 'A Linguistic Atlas of Late Mediaeval English'*, York Manuscripts Conferences: Proceedings Series, 2 (Cambridge: Brewer, 1991)

Ridyard, Susan J., *The Royal Saints of Anglo-Saxon England: A Study of West Saxon and East Anglian Cults*, Cambridge Studies in Medieval Life and Thought, Fourth Series (Cambridge: Cambridge University Press, 1988)

Ringrose, Jayne. *Summary Catalogue of the Additional Medieval Manuscripts in Cambridge University Library Acquired before 1940* (Woodbridge: Boydell, 2009)

Roberts, W. M., *Lost Country Houses of Suffolk* (Woodbridge: Boydell, 2010)

Rollason, D. W., 'Lists of Saints' Resting-Places in Anglo-Saxon England', *Anglo-Saxon England*, 7 (1978), 61–93

Rollason, D. W., *The Mildrith Legend: A Study in Early Medieval Hagiography in England*, Studies in the Early History of Britain (Leicester: Leicester University Press, 1982)

Rollason, David, *Saints and Relics in Anglo-Saxon England* (Oxford: Blackwell, 1989)

Rouse, Richard H., and Mary A. Rouse, eds, *Henry of Kirkestede*: *Catalogus de libris autenticis et apocrifis*, Corpus of British Medieval Library Catalogues, 11 (London: The British Library in association with the British Academy, 2004)

Rowe, Joy, 'The 1767 Census of Papists in the Diocese of Norwich: The Social Composition of the Roman Catholic Community', in *Religious Dissent in East Anglia*, III: *Proceedings of the Third Symposium*, ed. by David Chadd (Norwich: Centre for East Anglia Studies, University of East Anglia, 1996), pp. 187–234

Rundle, David, 'English Books and the Continent', in *The Production of Books in England, 1350–1500*, ed. by Alexandra Gillespie and Daniel Wakelin (Cambridge: Cambridge University Press, 2011), pp. 276–91

Rushforth, Rebecca, 'The Medieval Hagiography of St Cuthburg', *Analecta Bollandiana*, 118 (2000), 291–324

Russell, Delbert, 'The Campsey Collection of Old French Saints' Lives: A Re-examination of its Structure and Provenance', *Scriptorium*, 57 (2003), 51–83 + planches couleur 4–7

Rydel, Courtney E., 'Legendary Effects: Women Saints of the *Legenda aurea* in England, 1260–1532' (unpublished doctoral dissertation, University of Pennsylvania, 2012)

Salih, Sarah, ed. *A Companion to Middle English Hagiography* (Cambridge: Brewer, 2006)

BIBLIOGRAPHY

Salzman, L. F., and others, eds, *The Victoria History of the County of Cambridgeshire and The Isle of Ely*, 10 vols plus an index to I–IV (London: Oxford University Press, 1938–2002)

Samuels, M. L., 'Some Applications of Middle English Dialectology', *English Studies*, 44 (1963), 81–94; reprinted in Angus McIntosh, M. L. Samuels, and Margaret Laing, *Middle English Dialectology: Essays on Some Principles and Problems*, ed. by Margaret Laing (Aberdeen: Aberdeen University Press, 1989), pp. 64–80

Samuels, M. L., 'Spelling and Dialect in the Late and Post-Middle English Periods', in *So meny people, longages and tonges: Philological Essays in Scots and Mediaeval English Presented to Angus McIntosh*, ed. by Michael Benskin and M. L. Samuels (Edinburgh: Middle English Dialect Project, 1981), pp. 43–54

Sanok, Catherine. *Her Life Historical: Exemplarity and Female Saints' Lives in Late Medieval England*, The Middle Ages Series (Philadelphia: University of Pennsylvania Press, 2007)

Sanok, Catherine. *New Legends of England: Forms of Community in Late Medieval Saints' Lives* (Philadelphia, PA: University of Pennsylvania Press, 2018)

Scahill, John, with Margaret Rogerson, *Annotated Bibliographies of Old and Middle English*, VIII: *Middle English Saints' Legends* (Cambridge: Brewer, 2005)

Scott, Kathleen L., *Dated and Datable English Manuscript Borders c. 1395–1499* (London: The Bibliographical Society and The British Library, 2002)

Scott, Kathleen L., 'Instructions to a Limner in Beinecke MS 223', *The Yale University Library Gazette*, 72 (1997), 13–16

Scott, Kathleen L., *Later Gothic Manuscripts, 1390–1490*, A Survey of Manuscripts Illuminated in the British Isles, ed. by J. J. G. Alexander, 2 vols (London: Harvey Miller, 1996)

Scott, Kathleen L., 'Limning and Book-Producing Terms and Signs *in situ* in Late-Medieval English Manuscripts: A First Listing', in *New Science out of Old Books: Studies in Manuscripts and Early Printed Books in Honour of A. I. Doyle*, ed. by Richard Beadle and A. J. Piper (Aldershot: Scolar Press, 1995), pp. 142–88

Scragg, D. G., 'The Corpus of Vernacular Homilies and Prose Saints' Lives before Ælfric', *Anglo-Saxon England*, 8 (1979), 223–77

Seybolt, Robert Francis, 'Fifteenth Century Editions of the *Legenda aurea*', *Speculum*, 21 (1946), 327–42

Seybolt, Robert Francis, 'The *Legenda aurea*, Bible, and *Historia scholastica*', *Speculum*, 21 (1946), 339–42

Sharpe, Richard, *Medieval Irish Saints' Lives: An Introduction to Vitae Sanctorum Hiberniae* (Oxford: Clarendon Press, 1991)

Sharpe, Richard, 'Reconstructing the Medieval Library of Bury St Edmunds Abbey: The Lost Catalogue of Henry of Kirkstead', in *Bury St Edmunds: Medieval Art, Architecture, Archaeology and Economy*, ed. by Antonia Gransden, The British Archaeological Association Conference Transactions, 20 (Leeds: British Archaeological Association, 1998), pp. 204–18

Sharpe, R., and others, eds, *English Benedictine Libraries: The Shorter Catalogues*, Corpus of British Medieval Library Catalogues, 4 (London: The British Library in association with the British Academy, 1996)

Smeyers, Maurits, *Flemish Miniatures from the 8th to the mid-16th Century: The Medieval World of Parchment* (Turnhout: Brepols, 1999), first published as *Vlaamse miniaturen van de 8ste tot het midden van de 16de eeuw. De middeleeuwse wereld op perkament* (Louvain: Davidsfonds, 1998)

Smith, David M., *Guide to Bishops' Registers of England and Wales: A Survey from the Middle Ages to the Abolition of the Episcopacy in 1646* (London: Royal Historical Society, 1981)

Smith, Jeremy, 'On "Standard" Written English in the Later Middle Ages', in 'Communities of Practice: New Methodological Approaches to Adam Pinkhurst and Chaucer's Earliest Scribes', *Speculum* (forthcoming)

Smith, Thomas, *Catalogus Librorum Manuscriptorium Bibliothecæ Cottonianæ* (Oxford: Sheldon Theatre, 1696)

Société de Bollandistes, eds, *Bibliotheca Hagiographica Latina Antiquae et Mediae Aetatis*, 2 vols (Bruxelles: Société des Bollandistes, 1898–1901)

Spear, Valerie G., *Leadership in Medieval English Nunneries,* Studies in the History of Medieval Religion, 24 (Woodbridge: Boydell, 2005)

Spencer, Alice, *Language, Lineage and Location in the Works of Osbern Bokenham* (Cambridge: Cambridge Scholars, 2013)

Stray, Christopher, 'Edmund Henry Barker', ODNB, https://doi.org/10.1093/ref:odnb/1393

Stubbs, Estelle, 'Clare Priory: The London Austin Friars and Manuscripts of Chaucer's *Canterbury Tales*', in *Middle English Poetry: Texts and Traditions, Essays in Honour of Derek Pearsall*, ed. by A. J. Minnis, York Manuscripts Conferences Proceedings Series, 5 (Woodbridge: York Medieval Press, 2001), pp. 17–26

Styler, Ian David, 'The Story of an English Saint's Cult: An Analysis of the Influence of St Æthelthryth of Ely, c. 670–c. 1540 (unpublished doctoral dissertation, University of Birmingham, 2019)

Sullivan, Donald, 'Jean Bolland (1596–1665) and the Early Bollandists', in *Medieval Scholarship: Biographical Studies on the Formation of a Discipline*, ed. by Helen Damico, Joseph B. Zavidil, and others, Garland Reference Library of the Humanities, 1350, 2071, and 2110, 3 vols (New York, NY: Garland, 1995–2000), I: *History*, 3–14

Takeda, Reiko, 'The Question of the "Standardisation" of Written English in the Fifteenth Century' (unpublished doctoral dissertation, University of Leeds, 2001)

Tanner, Norman P., *The Church in Late Medieval Norwich 1370–1530*, Studies and Texts, 66 (Toronto: Pontifical Institute of Mediaeval Studies, 1984)

Taylor, John, 'John Tynemouth (*fl. c.* 1350)', ODNB https://doi.org/10.1093/ref:odnb/27466

Thayer, Anne T., *Penitence, Preaching and the Coming of the Reformation*, St Andrews Studies in Reformation History (Aldershot: Ashgate, 2002)

Thiry-Stassin, M., 'L'hagiographie en Anglo-Normand', in *Hagiographies: Histoire internationale de la littérature hagiographique latine et vernaculaire en Occident des origines à 1550*, ed. by Guy Philippart (I–V), Monique Goullet (VI–VII), and Michèle Gaillard and Monique Goullet (VIII), Corpus Christianorum Texts and Studies, 8 vols (Turnhout: Brepols, 1994–2020), I (1994), 407–28

Thompson, Sally, *Women Religious: The Founding of English Nunneries after the Norman Conquest* (Oxford: Clarendon Press, 1991)

Thomson, R. M., *A Descriptive Catalogue of the Medieval Manuscripts of Pembroke College, Cambridge* (Cambridge: Brewer, 2022)

Van den Gheyn, J., and others, *Catalogue des manuscrits de la Bibliothèque royale de Belgique*, 13 vols (Bruxelles: Henri Lamertin, and other places and publishers, 1901–48)

Van Hyning, Victoria, *Convent Autobiography: Early Modern English Nuns in Exile*, British Academy Monographs (Oxford: Oxford University Press for the British Academy, 2019)

Veen, Brian C. Vander, 'The *Vitae* of Bodleian Library MS Douce 114' (unpublished doctoral dissertation, University of Nottingham, 2007)

Vermassen, Valerie, 'Latin Hagiography in the Dutch-Speaking Parts of the Southern Low Countries (1350–1550)', in *Hagiographies: Histoire internationale de la littérature hagiographique latine et vernaculaire en Occident des origines à 1550*, ed. by Guy Philippart (I–V), Monique Goullet (VI–VII), and Michèle Gaillard and Monique Goullet (VIII), Corpus Christianorum Texts and Studies, 8 vols (Turnhout: Brepols, 1994–2020), VII (2017), 565–613

Vincent de Beauvais: www.vincentiusbelvacensis.eu

Virgoe, Roger, 'A Norwich Taxation List of 1451', *Norfolk Archæology: Or Miscellaneous Tracts Relating to the Antiquities of the County of Norfolk*, Norfolk and Norwich Archæological Society, 40 (1989), 145–54

Vitz, Evelyn Birge, 'From the Oral to the Written in Medieval and Renaissance Saints' Lives', in *Images of Sainthood in Medieval Europe*, ed. by Renate Blumenfeld-Kosinski and Timea Szell (Ithaca, NY: Cornell University Press, 1991), pp. 97–114

Volfing, Annette, *John the Evangelist in Medieval German Writing: Imitating the Inimitable* (Oxford: Oxford University Press, 2001)

Vulić, Kathryn, Susan Uselmann, and C. Annette Grisé, eds, *Devotional Literature and Practice in Medieval England: Readers, Reading, and Reception*, Disputatio, 29 (Turnhout: Brepols, 2017)

Walcott, Mackenzie E. C., 'Inventories of (I.) St. Mary's Hospital or Maison Dieu, Dover; (II.) The Benedictine Priory of St. Martin New-Work, Dover, for Monks; (III.) The Benedictine Priory of SS. Mary and Sexburga, in the Island of Sheppey, for Nuns: With Illustrative Notes', *Archæologia Cantiana being Transactions of the Kent Archæological Society*, 7 (1868), 272–306

Walters, Natalie, 'Illustrations from the Wellcome Library: The Jernegan-Arundell Correspondence', *Medical History*, 53 (2009), 117–26

Warren, Nancy Bradley. *Spiritual Economies: Female Monasticism in Later Medieval England* (Philadelphia, PA: University of Pennsylvania Press, 2001)

Watson, Andrew G., *The Library of Sir Simonds D'Ewes*, British Museum Bicentenary Publications (London: The Trustees of the British Museum, 1966)

Watson, Andrew G., *Medieval Manuscripts in Post-Medieval England*, Variorum Collected Studies Series (Aldershot: Ashgate, 2004)

Watson, Nicholas, 'Theories of Translation', in *The Oxford History of Literary Translation*, I: *To 1550*, ed. by Roger Ellis (Oxford: Oxford University Press, 2008), pp. 73–91

Wenzel, Siegfried, *Latin Sermon Collections from Later Medieval England: Orthodox Preaching in the Age of Wyclif*, Cambridge Studies in Medieval Literature (Cambridge: Cambridge University Press, 2005)

Wenzel, Siegfried, 'Preaching the Saints in Chaucer's England', in *Earthly Love, Spiritual Love, Love of the Saints*, ed. by Susan J. Ridyard, Sewanee Mediaeval Studies, 8 (Sewanee, TN: University of the South Press, 1999), pp. 45–68

Whatley, E. G., 'Late Old English Hagiography, ca. 950–1150', in *Hagiographies: Histoire internationale de la littérature hagiographique latine et vernaculaire en Occident des origines à 1550*, ed. by Guy Philippart (I–V), Monique Goullet (VI–VII), and Michèle Gaillard and Monique Goullet (VIII), Corpus Christianorum Texts and Studies, 8 vols (Turnhout: Brepols, 1994–2020), II (1996), 429–99

Whitehead, Christiania, Hazel J. Hunter Blair, and Denis Renevey, eds, *Late Medieval Devotion to Saints from the North of England: New Directions*, Medieval Church Studies, 48 (Turnhout: Brepols, 2022)

Wilkinson, Joseph, *The Architectural Remains of the Ancient Town and Borough of Thetford in the Counties of Norfolk and Suffolk* (London: Rodwell and Martin, 1822)

Williams-Krapp, Werner, *Die deutschen und niederländischen Legendare des Mittelalters: Studien zu ihrer Überlieferungs-Text- und Wirkungsgeschichte*, Texte und Textgeschichte, Würzburger Forschungen, 20 (Tübingen: Niemeyer, 1986)

Williams-Krapp, W., 'Deutschsprachige Hagiographie von ca. 1350 bis ca. 1550', in *Hagiographies: Histoire internationale de la littérature hagiographique latine et vernaculaire en Occident des origines à 1550*, ed. by Guy Philippart (I–V), Monique Goullet (VI–VII), and Michèle Gaillard and Monique Goullet (VIII), Corpus Christianorum Texts and Studies, 8 vols (Turnhout: Brepols, 1994–2020), I (1994), 267–88

Williamson, Tom, Ivan Ringwood, and Sarah Spooner, *Lost Country Houses of Norfolk: History, Archaeology and Myth* (Woodbridge: Boydell, 2015)

Williamson, W. W., 'Saints on Norfolk Rood-Screens and Pulpits', *Norfolk Archæology: Or Miscellaneous Tracts Relating to the Antiquities of the County of Norfolk*, Norfolk and Norwich Archæological Society, 31 (1957), 299–346

Winstead, Karen A., *Fifteenth-Century Lives: Writing Sainthood in England*, ReFormations: Medieval and Early Modern (Notre Dame, IN: Notre Dame University Press, 2020)

Winstead, Karen A., *Virgin Martyrs: Legends of Sainthood in Late Medieval England* (Ithaca, NY: Cornell University Press, 1997)

Wogan-Browne, Jocelyn, 'Chaste Bodies: Frames and Experiences', in *Framing Medieval Bodies*, ed. by Sarah Kay and Miri Rubin (Manchester: Manchester University Press, 1994), pp. 24–42

BIBLIOGRAPHY

Wogan-Browne, Jocelyn, 'Outdoing the Daughters of Syon?: Edith of Wilton and the Representations of Female Community in Fifteenth-Century England', in *Medieval Women: Texts and Contexts in Late Medieval Britain, Essays for Felicity Riddy*, ed. by Jocelyn Wogan-Browne, and others, Medieval Women: Texts and Contexts, 3 (Turnhout: Brepols, 2000), pp. 393–409

Wogan-Browne, Jocelyn, 'Rerouting the Dower: The Anglo- Norman Life of St. Audrey by Marie (of Chatteris?)', in *Power of the Weak: Studies on Medieval Women*, ed. by Jennifer Carpenter and Sally-Beth MacLean (Carbondale, IL: University of Illinois Press, 1995), pp. 27–56

Wogan-Browne, Jocelyn, 'Saints' Lives and the Female Reader', *Forum for Modern Language Studies*, 27 (1991), 314–32

Wogan-Browne, Jocelyn, *Saints' Lives and Women's Literary Culture, c. 1150–1300: Virginity and its Authorizations* (Oxford: Oxford University Press, 2001)

Wogan-Browne, Jocelyn, 'The Virgin's Tale', in *Feminist Readings in Middle English Literature: The Wife of Bath and All Her Sect*, ed. by Ruth Evans and Lesley Johnson (London: Routledge, 1994), pp. 165–94

Wogan-Browne, Jocelyn, and others, eds, *The Idea of the Vernacular: An Anthology of Middle English Literary Theory, 1280–1520*, Exeter Medieval Texts and Studies (Exeter: University of Exeter Press, 1999)

Wolpers, Theodor, *Die englische Heiligenlegende des Mittelalters: Eine Formgeschichte des Legendenerzählens von der spätantiken lateinischen Tradition bis zur Mitte des 16. Jahrhunderts*, Buchreihe Anglia, 10 (Tübingen: Niemeyer, 1964)

Workman, Samuel K., *Fifteenth Century Translation as an Influence on English Prose*, Princeton Studies in English, 18 (Princeton, NJ: Princeton University Press, 1940)

Yamamoto-Wilson, John R., 'The Protestant Reception of Catholic Devotional Literature in England to 1700', *Recusant History*, 32 (2014), 67–89

Yardley, Anne Bagnall, and Jesse D. Mann, 'Facing the Music: The Whimsical Cadels in a Late Medieval English Book of Hours', *Peregrinations: Journal of Medieval Art and Architecture*, 7. 2 (2020), 52–85

Yorke, Barbara, *Nunneries and the Anglo-Saxon Royal Houses*, Women, Power and Politics (London: Continuum, 2003)

Young, Francis, 'Early Modern English Catholic Piety in a Fifteenth-Century Book of Hours: Cambridge University Library MS Additional 10079', *Transactions of the Cambridge Bibliographical Society*, 15 (2015), 541–59

Young, Francis, 'Elizabeth Inchbald's "Catholic Novel" and its Local Background', *Recusant History*, 31 (2012–13), 573–92

Young, Francis, *The Gages of Hengrave and Suffolk Catholicism 1640–1767*, Catholic Record Society Publications, Monograph Series, 8 (Woodbridge: Boydell, 2015)

Young, Francis, 'The Tasburghs of Bodney: Catholicism and Politics in South Norfolk', *Norfolk Archaeology: A Journal of Archaeology and Local History*, 46 (2011), 190–98

Young, Francis, 'The Tasburghs of Flixton and Catholicism in North-East Suffolk, 1642–1767', *Proceedings of the Suffolk Institute of Archaeology*, 42 (2012), 455–70

INDEX

The purpose of this Index is to enable readers to locate relevant material in this *Study* and to help users of the companion *Edition* to cross-refer to items of interest. To avoid an unnecessarily inflated Index, we include only those people/places/topics/works that are of special significance in this *Study*. The saints in Add. 2604 are individually indexed, with Iphigenia, whose life seems to be missing from the manuscript, given in square brackets; this list also takes account of versions of these lives and references to these particular saints beyond those in Add. 2604. The many other saints mentioned in the *Study* are not indexed, apart from Osith of Chich and Mildrith of Minster-in-Thanet (also within square brackets); a life of either of them, but more likely the former, may have been part of Add. 2604 originally. Medieval persons are entered under their first names; post-medieval people may be found under their surnames.

Acta sanctorum
    See Bollandist/s
Add. 2604, Description of
    Annotation
        Additional Contents: 33–34
        Saints' Lives: 20–22
    Binding: 45
    Catchwords: 4–6
    Collation
        Additional Contents: 31
        Saints' Lives: 4
    Compilation: 38–45
    Contents
        Additional Contents: 23–31
        See also Antiphoner, in Add. 2604; Cut-outs, of letters, in Add. 2604; Handwriting, note on, in Add. 2604; List of Lives, in Add. 2504; Notes, in Add. 2604; Proverbial Sayings, in Add. 2604; St Benedict and the Benedictines, notes, in Add. 2604; St Christopher, a prose extract, in Add. 2604; St Christopher, a verse extract, in Add. 2604
        Saints' Lives: 2–3
        See also Add. 2604, Saints in, and elsewhere
    Date
        Additional Contents: 23
        Saints' Lives: 7–12, 19–20
    Decoration, Calligraphic: 18–19
    Decoration, Illuminated: 12–17

Description, Physical
    Additional Contents: 22–23
    Saints' Lives: 1–2
Hands
    Additional Contents: 23–31
    Saints' Lives: 7–12
Ownership: 34–38
    See also Add. 2604, Provenance of, Ownership
Watermarks: 32
Wear and Repair: 6–7

Add. 2604, Hagiographical Context of, and Selection of Saints in
Legendaries
    Latin
        Comparison: 171–76
        Continental: 161–70
        England, in: 176–81
    Vernacular
        England, in: 182–95
Missing Saints: 196–211 *passim*
Saints' Lives
    English Printed: 192–93
Sanctorale Sermons
    English: 191–92
    Latin: 168–69, 175 Table 5
Selection of Saints:196–211

Add. 2604, Language and Dialect of
Diagnostic Features: 84–87
Dialectal and Lexical Features: 92–96
Dialects
    Norfolk and Suffolk: 88–92
LALME Questionnaire: 72–84
Linguistic Analysis: 70–71
Linguistic Provenance
    East Anglia: 69–106 *passim*
Localisation
    Bury St Edmunds: 103–06
    See also Bury St Edmunds below; Religious Houses, male/dual, Bury St Edmunds;
        John Baret
    Suffolk: 96–102
Standard/Standardisation: 69, 69 n. 1, 86, 86 n. 13, 87, 95, 96, 215, 310

Add. 2604, Literary Discussion of
Devotional Reading: 276–81
Format and Use: 272–85
Miracles: 281–83
Narrative Style: 285–307
Section Summaries: 277–81
Translational Technique: 288–90, 323–36 Appendix 2, 337–41 Appendix 3

INDEX 387

Add. 2604, Native and Universal Saints, Sources and Analogues of
Native Saints
Appendix 2: 323–36
John of Tynemouth: 249–51
Historia aurea: 118, 180 n. 53, 254, 260
Lectionarium: 254
Martyrologium: 118, 254, 260
Sanctilogium Angliae Walliae Scotiae et Hiberniae, Manuscripts of: 251–69
Karlsruhe, Badische Landesbibliothek, Cod. Sankt Georgen 12: 123, 153, 181, 211, 217, 247, 256, 256 n. 115, 257, 262, 263, 264, 265, 265 n. 139, 266, 267, 268, 269, 276, 285 n. 30, 326 Appendix 2
London, British Library, MS Cotton Otho D. ix: 256, 258, 259, 260 n. 125, 261, 326 Appendix 2
London, British Library, MS Cotton Tiberius E. i: 193 n. 99, 206, 215 n. 5, 252, 252 n. 104, 253, 254, 255, 256, 256 n. 115, 257, 261, 261 n. 127, 268, 269, 325 Appendix 2, 328 n. 4
Oxford, Bodleian Library, MS Tanner 15: 215 n. 5, 256, 256 n. 115, 257, 259, 260, 261, 327 Appendix 2, 328 n. 4
York, York Minster Library, MS XVI.G.23: 256, 257, 261, 326 Appendix 2
See also John of Tynemouth and 'Sanctilogium Angliae Walliae Scotiae et Hiberniae' below
Printed Texts
See *'Nova Legenda Anglie'; 'The Kalendre of the Newe Legende of Englande'*
Universal Saints
Appendix 1: 311–21
Appendix 3: 337–41
Background: 218–28
Complex Analogues: 237–47
Barbara, St: 342–47
Columba, St: 338–42
Legenda aurea: 228–33
See also Add. 2604, Native and Universal Saints [...], Karlsruhe, Badische Landesbibliothek, Cod. Sankt Georgen 12: 263–69; Jacobus de Voragine/Iacopo da Varazze, 'Legenda aurea'
Other Sources: 233–37
See also Bollandists, 'Acta sanctorum'; Boninus Mombritius/Bonino Mombrizio, 'Sanctuarium sive Vitae Sanctorum'; 'Historie plurimorum sanctorum'
Add. 2604, Provenance of
Convents
Books: 130–34
See also Nuns, as book owners
Dedications: 123–27
East Anglian and Beyond: 109–13
See also Convents, female, in East Anglia and Beyond
Orders: 114–23
See also Convents, East Anglian and Beyond, Orders of
Visitations: 127–30

Ownership

Tasburgh, George: 135–43

Tasburgh, George, family: 144–49

See also Add. 2604, Description of, Ownership; Convents, female, in East Anglia and Beyond, Flixton; Convents, female, in East Anglia and Beyond, Thetford; Fulmerston, Richard; Tasburgh, George; Tasburgh, George, family of, and selected relatives; Tasburgh George, other family members; Warton/Wharton, Richard

Provenance: 149–57

Add. 2604, Saints in, and elsewhere

Æthelburh of Faremoutiers-en-Brie: xxvi, xxvi n. 3, 3 Table 1, 27, 28, 108, 112 Table 2, 115, 117 n. 18, 118, 118 n. 22, 126 n. 47, 176 n. 42, 179, 180, 193 n. 99, 195, 196, 202, 202 n. 114, 203, 210, 213, 217, 249 n. 95, 250, 253, 277, 282, 290, 291, 295, 298, 299 n. 60

Æthelthryth of Ely: xix Plate 3, xxvi, xxvi n. 3, 3 Table 1, 6, 28, 33, 71, 104, 108, 112, 112 Table 2, 114, 114 n. 9, 115, 116 n. 12, 117 n. 18, 118, 119, 120, 122, 123, 124, 125, 126 n. 47, 132, 152, 157, 168, 169, 172, 173 Table 3, 173 n. 39, 174 Table 4, 176, 177 n. 45, 178, 179, 180, 182, 184, 184 n. 64, 185, 187, 187 n. 79, 189, 189 n. 85, 190, 191, 191 n. 91, 193 n. 99, 194 n. 99, 196, 199, 201 n. 111, 202, 203, 204, 206, 207, 208, 213, 217, 217 n. 10, 237, 250, 251, 253, 256, 259, 263, 267, 268, 275, 276, 277, 282, 283, 286, 289, 293, 294, 295, 296, 298, 298 n. 60, 299, 300, 301, 302, 302 n. 63, 306, 310, 313, 323 Appendix 2

Agatha: xxv, 3 Table 1, 48 Figure 3, 97, 117 n. 18, 118, 122, 125 n. 43, 172, 173 Table 3, 174 Table 4, 175 Table 5, 177 n. 45, 182, 183, 184, 185, 186, 187, 188, 189, 191, 195, 196, 197, 199, 200, 213, 216, 218, 221, 223, 225 n. 33, 228, 231, 235, 235 n. 64, 236, 237 n. 70, 238 n. 72, 242, 244, 263, 264, 265, 266, 270, 272, 277, 281, 293, 297, 298, 298 n. 60, 299, 302, 306, 310, 313 Appendix 1, 314 Appendix 1, 316 Appendix 1, 317 Appendix 1, 318 Appendix 1, 319 Appendix 1, 320 Appendix 1, 321 Appendix 1

Barbara: xviii Plate 2, xix Plate 3, xxv, 3 Table 3, 6, 19, 33, 71, 113 Table 2, 117 n. 18, 122, 124, 125 n. 43, 146, 151, 152, 172, 173 Table 3, 174 Table 4, 175 Table 5, 187, 189, 190, 192, 193, 196, 199, 201 n. 111, 210, 210 n. 130, 213, 213 n. 2, 216, 218, 221, 223, 228, 235, 237, 238, 238 n. 72, 239, 241 n. 77, 242, 243, 244, 245, 246, 246 n. 90, 247, 263, 266, 274 n. 11, 276, 277, 278, 279, 281, 282, 282 n. 23, 284, 293, 296, 297, 298, 298 n. 60, 300, 302, 303, 308, 311 Appendix 1, 313 Appendix 1, 314 Appendix 1, 315 Appendix 1, 316 Appendix 1, 317 Appendix 1, 318 Appendix 1, 319 Appendix 1, 320 Appendix 1, 321 Appendix 1

Benedicta: xxvi, 3 Table 1, 13, 16, 16 n. 26, 160, 169, 170, 172, 173 Table 3, 174 Table 4, 175 Table 5, 195, 196, 197, 205, 211, 213, 213 n. 2, 216, 217, 218, 219, 221, 223, 228, 233, 234, 235, 237 n. 70, 238 n. 72, 239, 245, 263, 270, 278, 286, 294, 296, 297, 299 n. 60, 302, 313 Appendix 1, 314 Appendix 1, 319 Appendix 1, 321 Appendix 1

Cecilia: xviii Plate 2, xxv, xxvi n. 3, 3 Table 1, 13, 16, 35 n. 42, 117 n. 18, 125 n. 43, 157, 172, 173 Table 3, 174 Table 4, 175 Table 5, 177 n. 45, 182, 183, 184, 186, 188, 189, 191, 195, 196, 197, 199, 200, 200 n. 111, 201 n. 111, 213, 216, 218, 221, 223, 228, 229, 231, 232, 237, 242, 244, 245, 263, 266, 272, 277, 281, 287, 293, 293 n. 51, 297, 298 n. 60, 300, 302, 306, 314 Appendix 1, 316 Appendix 1, 317 Appendix 1, 318 Appendix 1, 319 Appendix 1, 321 Appendix 1

INDEX 389

Columba: xxv, 3 Table 1, 4, 16, 27, 47 Figure 2, 48 Figure 3, 125, 125 n. 43, 160, 172, 173 Table 3, 174 Table 4, 175 Table, 177 n. 45, 182, 195, 196, 197, 205, 211, 213, 216, 217, 218, 221, 223, 228, 237, 238, 238 n. 72, 239, 240, 241, 241 n. 77, 242, 245, 246, 263, 277, 281, 296, 297, 298 n. 60, 300, 302, 303, 311 n. 1 Appendix 1, 313 Appendix 1, 314 Appendix 1, 315 Appendix 1, 319 Appendix 1, 320 Appendix 1, 321 Appendix 1, 321 n. 16 Appendix 1

Domitilla: xxiii Plate 7, xxvi, 3 Table 1, 35 n. 43, 52 Figure 7, 93, 123, 125 n. 43, 157, 170, 172, 173 Table 3, 174 Table 4, 175 Table 5, 195, 196, 197, 198, 198 n. 107, 200, 211, 213, 216, 217, 218, 221, 223, 228, 236, 237, 238 n. 72, 263, 264, 265, 266, 278, 286, 291, 292, 297, 297 n. 59, 299, 299 n. 60, 314 Appendix 1, 316 Appendix 1, 321 Appendix 1

Eadburh of Minster-in-Thanet: xxvi, 3 Table 1, 4, 28, 50 Figure 5, 51 Figure 6, 117, 126, 177 n. 45, 179, 193 n. 99, 195, 196, 199, 203, 208, 210, 214, 217, 253, 263, 267, 278, 280, 281, 282, 284, 291, 292, 294, 296, 298, 299 n. 60, 300, 302, 303, 304

Eanswith of Folkestone: xxvi, xxvi n. 3, 3 Table 1, 28, 33, 34, 51 Figure 6, 115, 126, 168 n. 27, 174 Table 4, 193 n. 99, 195, 196, 199, 203, 204, 205, 206, 208, 209, 214, 217, 251, 253, 259, 263, 278, 282, 297, 299 n. 60, 300, 302 n. 63, 321

Edith of Wilton: xxvi, xxvi n. 3, 2, 3 Table 1, 18, 28, 118, 123, 126, 167 n. 26, 168 n. 27, 172, 174 Table 4, 177, 178, 179, 180, 189, 193 n. 99, 196, 199, 203, 214, 217, 217 n. 10, 223, 224, 250, 253, 263, 267, 276, 278, 282, 294, 298, 299, 299 n. 60, 301, 302, 305, 306, 307, 321

Eorcengota of Faremoutiers-en-Brie: xxvi, 3 Table 1, 27, 28, 49 Figure 4, 108, 115, 118 n. 22, 126, 126 n. 47, 176, 176 n. 42, 193 n. 99, 195, 196, 202, 202 n. 114, 203, 204, 213, 217, 249 n. 95, 250, 253, 263, 277, 282, 290, 291, 298 n. 60, 299, 299 n. 60, 301

Eormenhild of Ely: xx Plate 4, xxvi, xxvi n. 3, 3 Table 1, 28, 108, 117 n. 18, 118, 126, 126 n. 47, 177 n. 45, 177 n. 45, 178, 193 n. 99, 194 n. 99, 195, 196, 202, 202 n. 114, 203, 204, 205, 213, 217, 250, 250 n. 98, 253, 259, 263, 268, 277, 282, 283, 291, 296, 297, 298, 298 n. 60, 301

Hild of Whitby: xxvi, 3 Table 1, 13, 16, 28, 71, 93 n. 26, 115, 160, 167 n. 26, 172, 174 Table 4, 176, 180, 182, 193 n. 99, 194 n. 99, 195, 196, 199, 203, 204, 206, 209, 214, 217, 223, 224, 251, 253, 263, 267, 276, 277, 278, 282, 296, 297, 298, 299, 299 n. 60, 300, 301, 310

[Iphigenia]: 169, 170, 172, 173 Table 3, 174 Table 4, 175 Table 5, 198, 198 n. 107, 200, 211, 236, 263, 266, 291, 299 n. 60

John the Baptist: xvii Plate 1, xxv, xxvi n. 2, xxvi n. 3, 3 Table 1, 71, 93, 113 Table 2, 118, 122, 124, 125, 152, 171, 171–72, 172, 173 Table 3, 174 Table 4, 175 Table 5, 182, 183, 184, 188, 189, 190, 191, 196, 197, 197 n. 105, 201, 213, 216, 218, 221, 223, 228, 229, 229 n. 46, 230, 231, 232, 234, 243, 262, 263, 264, 265, 275, 275 n. 14, 276, 277, 278, 279, 280, 281, 284, 287, 288 n. 42, 290, 291, 292 n. 49, 294, 295, 296, 298, 298–99 n. 60, 300, 301, 309, 314 Appendix 1, 316 Appendix 1, 318 Appendix 1

John the Evangelist: xxv, 3 Table 1, 27, 46 Figure 1, 93 n. 26, 112, 112 Table 2, 113 Table 2, 117 n. 18, 118, 122, 124, 152, 160, 165, 171, 172, 173 Table 3, 174 Table 4, 175 Table 5, 177 n. 45, 182, 184, 187, 188, 189, 190, 191, 196, 197, 197 n. 105, 201, 213, 216, 218, 221, 223, 228, 230, 231, 232, 234, 236, 263, 264, 275, 275 n. 14, 277, 281, 287, 288, 288 n. 42, 292, 292 n. 49, 294, 296, 298, 298 n. 60, 299, 299 n. 60, 301, 303, 306, 309, 313 Appendix 1, 314 Appendix 1, 316 Appendix 1, 318 Appendix 1, 320 Appendix 1, 337 Appendix 3

Justina: xxvi, 3 Table 1, 52 Figure 7, 169, 172, 173 Table 3, 174 Table 4, 175 Table 5,

177 n. 45, 183, 183 n. 62, 184, 188, 189, 196, 197, 213, 216, 217, 218, 221, 223, 228, 231, 233, 234, 237 n. 70, 238 n. 72, 239, 263, 266, 278, 284, 286, 290, 293, 294, 296, 296 n. 56, 297, 299 n. 60, 300, 302, 310, 314 Appendix 1, 316 Appendix 1, 317 Appendix 1, 318 Appendix 1, 321 Appendix 1

Leonard: xxiv Plate 8, xxv, xxvi, xxvi n. 3, 3 Table 1, 4, 9, 10, 18, 21, 56 Figure 10, 71, 112 Table 2, 113 Table 2, 117 n. 18, 118, 122, 124, 125, 152, 160, 172, 173 Table 3, 174 Table 4, 175 Table 5, 177 n. 45, 183, 188, 189, 191, 196, 197, 200, 201, 205, 213, 214 n. 4, 216, 217, 218, 221, 222 n. 28, 223, 228, 233, 234, 235, 237 n. 70, 238 n. 72, 245, 245 n. 88, 253, 263, 266, 277, 278, 281, 282, 283, 290, 294, 296, 296 n. 58, 299, 299 n. 60, 300, 309, 314 Appendix 1, 318 Appendix 1, 319 Appendix 1

Martha: xxii Plate 6, xxiii Plate 7, xxvi, 3 Table 1, 27, 52 Figure 7, 71, 92, 117 n. 19, 160, 170, 172, 173 Table 3, 174 Table 4, 175 Table 5, 183, 184, 185, 189, 195, 196, 197, 199, 201, 205, 210, 210 n. 130, 213, 216, 217, 218, 221, 223, 228, 229, 231, 232, 244, 263, 263 n. 137, 266, 276, 277, 278, 281, 282, 286, 287, 294, 297, 298, 299, 299 n. 60, 300, 301, 301 n. 62, 303, 310, 314 Appendix 1, 319 Appendix 1, 320 Appendix 1, 321 Appendix 1

[Mildrith of Minster-in-Thanet]: 28, 34, 118, 123, 126, 167 n. 26, 168 n. 27, 177 n. 45, 178, 179, 184 n. 64, 203, 206, 207, 208, 208 n. 127, 208, 208 n. 128, 209, 210, 280, 299, 299 n. 60

Modwenna of Burton-on-Trent: xxvi, 2, 3 Table 1, 4, 6, 9, 10, 13, 16, 17, 18, 19, 28, 54 Figure 8, 55 Figure 9, 71, 93, 97, 98 n. 39, 117 n. 18, 118, 120, 168 n. 27, 172, 174 Table 4, 180, 185, 193 n. 99, 194 n. 99, 195, 196, 200, 201, 203, 205, 208, 210, 214, 214 n. 4, 217, 249, 250, 253, 263, 278, 282, 284, 293, 294, 296 n. 57, 297, 297 n. 59, 299, 299 n. 60, 300, 301, 302, 303, 304, 305, 306, 309, 321

[Osith of Chich]: xxvi n. 3, 118, 168 n. 27, 178, 180, 185, 206, 207, 208, 209, 210, 299, 304, 305

Sæthryth of Faremoutiers-en-Brie: xxvi, 3 Table 1, 196, 202, 203

Seaxburh of Ely: xxvi, xxvi n. 3, 3 Table 1, 28, 108, 112 Table 2, 118, 124, 126, 126 n. 47, 162, 162 n. 6, 168 n. 27, 172, 174 Table 4, 177 n. 45, 178, 180, 182, 182 n. 59, 193 n. 99, 194 n. 99, 195, 196, 202, 202 n. 114, 203, 206, 213, 217, 217 n. 10, 249 n. 95, 250, 250 n. 98, 253, 263, 267, 277, 293, 295, 296, 298, 298 n. 60, 299, 301, 321

Wærburh of Chester: xx Plate 4, xxvi, 3 Table 1, 28, 35 n. 42, 49 Figure 4, 93, 108, 118, 126, 126 n. 47, 177 n. 45, 178, 180, 193 n. 99, 194 n. 99, 195, 196, 202, 202 n. 114, 203, 204, 213, 217, 217 n. 10, 250, 253, 263, 267, 277, 282, 295, 298, 298 n. 60, 300, 300 n. 61, 301

Wihtburh of Ely: xxi Plate 5, xxvi, xxvi n. 3, 3 Table 1, 18, 28, 71, 89, 108, 114 n. 9, 117 n. 18, 118, 126, 126 n. 47, 152, 168 n. 27, 172, 174 Table 4, 178, 180, 193 n. 99, 194 n. 99, 195, 196, 202, 202 n. 114, 203, 214, 217, 250, 253, 263, 267, 268, 276, 277, 282, 291, 291 n. 46, 295, 298, 299 n. 60, 302, 321

Antiphoner, in Add. 2604: 24–26, 59 Figure 13, 107 n. 2

Anton Geens: 167, 167 n. 27, 174 Table 4, 174 n. 40, 176, 321 Appendix 1

Legendarium: 167, 174 Table 4

Augustus Frederick, the Duke of Sussex, Prince: 34, 37, 37 n. 47

See also Add. 2604, Description of, Ownership

INDEX 391

Barker, Edmund Henry: 37, 37 n. 49, 38, 42, 42 n. 60
    See also Add. 2604, Description of, Ownership
Bartolomeo da Trento: 164, 165, 173 Table 3
    Liber epilogorum in gesta sanctorum: 163–64, 173 Table 3
Bede: 118 n. 22, 157, 161, 176, 176 n. 42, 203, 224, 225, 250, 251, 268, 269, 296, 323
    Appendix 2
    Historia ecclesiastica: 176, 268, 323 Appendix 2
Bernard Gui: 164, 165, 173 Table 3, 173 n. 39
    Speculum sanctorale: 164, 173 Table 3
Bodney, Norfolk
    Bodney Hall: 35, 38, 39, 39 n. 51, 40, 40 n. 53, 43, 135, 138, 138 n. 79, 138 n. 82, 141,
        141 n. 92, 141 n. 94, 142, 142 n. 94, 143
    Bodney Village: 139 n. 84, 143, 148, 149
Bollandist/s: 159 n. 2, 169 n. 31, 213, 225, 225 n. 34, 226, 227, 227 n. 40, 228 n. 41, 233,
    235, 237, 237 n. 70, 238, 239, 240, 240 n. 75, 242, 244, 244 n. 86, 245, 247, 316
    Appendix 1, 318 n. 14, Appendix 1, 319 Appendix 1, 320 Appendix 1
    Acta sanctorum: 169 n. 31, 213, 217, 218, 221, 225, 225 n. 33, 227, 227 n. 40, 228, 233,
        234, 235, 235 n. 64, 237, 237 n. 70, 240, 245, 264, 265, 265 n. 139, 266, 267, 314
        Appendix 1, 318 Appendix 1, 319 Appendix 1, 320 Appendix 1
    See also Add. 2604, Native and Universal Saints, Sources and Analogues of, Universal
        Saints
Boninus Mombritius/Bonino Mombrizio: 166, 166 n. 22, 174 Table 4, 174 n. 40, 176, 211,
    213, 217, 220, 221, 221 n. 22, 221 n. 24, 222, 222 n. 26, 235, 241, 246, 268, 276
    Sanctuarium sive Vitae Sanctorum: 166, 166 n. 22, 174 Table 4, 176, 213, 217, 218, 220,
        221, 221 n. 24, 222, 222 n. 26, 223, 234, 235, 235 n. 64, 241, 242, 246, 269, 276
    See also Add. 2604, Native and Universal Saints, Sources and Analogues of, Universal
        Saints 228–33
Books
    See Add. 2604, Provenance of, Convents, Books; Nuns, as book owners
Bull (Alfred) and Auvache (John): 36
    See also Add. 2604, Description of, Ownership
Burrell, George Bird: 23, 33, 35, 36, 37, 38, 40, 41, 41 n. 56, 41 n. 57, 41 n. 58, 42, 42 n. 59,
    42 n. 60, 43, 43 n. 61, 44, 44 n. 62, 45, 45 n. 64, 64 Figure 19, 65 Figure 20, 141,
    150 n. 122, 199 n. 109, 214 n. 4, 275 n. 18, 310
    Will: 44 n. 62
    See also Add. 2604, Description of, Ownership
Burrell, George Bird, family and relatives of:
    Burrell, Elisabeth (Elisabeth Esther Snare): 44, 44 n. 62
    Burrell, George (relative): 45 n. 64
    Burrell, George (son): 44
    Burrell, John: 44
    Burrell, Thomas: 44, 45 n. 64
Burton, George: 40, 40 nn. 54–55, 41, 44, 60 Figure 15, 61 Figure 16, 156
    See also Handwriting, note on, in Add. 2604 and List of Lives, in Add. 2604
Bury St Edmunds/Bury: 61 Figure 16, 20, 40, 102, 103, 104, 105, 106, 106 n. 60, 109, 111,
    138–39 n. 83, 140, 151, 152, 196
    See Add. 2604, Language and Dialect of, Localisation; Religious Houses, male/dual

392   INDEX

Convents, East Anglian and Beyond, Orders of
    Augustinian/Austin: 110, 111, 112, 112 Table 2, 113 Table 2, 114, 120, 121, 122, 149
    Benedictine: 110, 111, 112 Table 2, 113 Table 2, 114, 116, 117, 119, 120, 152, 206
    Birgittine: 112, 113 Table 2, 114, 122, 123, 153, 181, 189, 257, 262, 283, 283 n. 26
    Cistercian: 110, 113 Table 2, 114, 122, 125, 125 n. 42, 151
    Dominican: 110, 112 Table 2, 114, 122, 127
    Franciscan: 110, 112, 112 Table 2, 113 Table 2, 114, 122, 125, 125 n. 45, 127
    Gilbertine: 110, 113 Table 2, 114, 122, 151, 152
Convents, female, in East Anglia and Beyond
    Barking, Essex: 107 n. 1, 110, 111, 112 Table 2, 114, 115, 116, 116 n. 12, 116 n. 14,
        117 n. 18, 123, 124, 130, 131, 131 n. 56, 134, 168 n. 27, 180, 185, 206, 206 n. 121,
        207, 209, 210, 284, 284 n. 28, 299
    Blackborough, Norfolk: 110, 111, 113 Table 2, 116 n. 14, 122, 124, 128, 132 n. 63
    Bruisyard, Suffolk: 110, 111, 113 Table 2, 116 n. 14, 122, 124, 127, 130, 131, 131 n. 56,
        132 n. 63, 133
    Bungay, Suffolk: 110, 111, 113 Table 2, 124, 127, 128, 132 n. 63
    Cambridge, St Radegund, Cambridgeshire: 107 n. 1, 110, 111, 112 Table 2, 124,
        132 n. 63
    Campsey Ash, Suffolk: 106 n. 62, 107 n. 1, 110, 111, 113 Table 2, 116 n. 14, 120,
        121, 122, 127, 128, 129, 130, 131, 131 n. 56, 132, 132 n. 63, 134, 134 n. 69, 149,
        152 n. 131, 156, 185, 186, 208, 209 n. 129, 310
    Canonsleigh, Devon: 112, 112 Table 2, 122, 124, 130, 131
    Canterbury, St Sepulchre, Kent: 110, 112 Table 2, 124
    Carrow, Norfolk: 110, 111, 113 Table 2, 114, 115, 116 n. 14, 124, 127, 128, 129, 130
    Castle Hedingham, Essex: 110, 111, 112 Table 2, 116 n. 14, 124, 130, 132 n. 63, 133
    Chatteris, Cambridgeshire: 110, 111, 112 Table 2, 116, 116 n. 14, 124, 131 n. 56,
        132 n. 63, 133 n. 66, 134, 156, 185, 185 n. 68, 310
    Crabhouse, Norfolk: 110, 111, 113 Table 2, 116 n. 14, 121, 122, 124, 128, 131 n. 56,
        132 n. 63
    Dartford, Kent: 110, 111, 112 Table 2, 116 n. 14, 122, 123, 124, 130, 130 n. 55, 131,
        131 n. 56, 134
    Davington, Kent: 110, 111, 112 Table 2, 116 n. 14, 124
    Denney, Cambridgeshire: 107 n. 1, 110, 111, 112 Table 2, 116 n. 14, 122, 123, 124, 125,
        125 125 n. 44, 125 n. 45, 130, 131 n. 56, 132 n. 63, 134, 156, 186, 186 n. 74, 310
    Flixton, Suffolk: 110, 111, 113 Table 2, 121, 124, 127, 128, 129, 130, 131, 131 n. 56,
        132 n. 63, 133, 134, 134 n. 69, 144, 145, 145 n. 106, 150, 156, 310
        See Tasburgh, George; Tasburgh, George, family of, and selected relatives;
            Tasburgh George, other family members; Warton/Wharton, Richard
    Higham, Kent: 110, 111, 112 Table 2, 127, 127 n. 48, 130, 131 n. 56, 134
    Ickleton, Cambridgeshire: 107 n. 1, 110, 111, 112 Table 2, 116, 117, 123, 124, 130,
        131 n. 56, 132 n. 63, 134, 156, 310
    London: Aldgate, London/Middlesex: 111, 112, 113 Table 2, 122, 122 n. 38, 124, 125,
        125 n. 44, 130, 131, 131 n. 56, 132
    London: Bishopsgate, London/Middlesex: 111, 113 Table 2, 120, 122 n. 38, 124, 130, 132
    London: Clerkenwell, London/Middlesex: 111, 113 Table 2, 116 n. 14, 122, 122 n. 38
    London: Holywell, London/Middlesex: 111, 113 Table 2, 116 n. 14, 122, 122 n. 38, 124,
        130, 131 n. 56
    London: Kilburn, London/Middlesex: 111, 113 Table 2, 122, 122 n. 38, 124, 125, 130,
        133, 134

INDEX   393

Malling, Kent: 110, 111, 112 Table 2, 124, 130, 131, 132, 132 n. 61
Marham, Norfolk: 110, 111, 113 Table 2, 116 n. 14, 122, 124, 125, 125 n. 42, 127, 130,
    133, 133 n. 64, 134 n. 69, 151
Minster-in-Sheppey, Kent: xvi n. 4, 110, 111, 112 Table 2, 124, 126, 130, 133
Minster-in-Thanet/Thanet, Kent: xvi, 110, 126, 167 n. 26, 179, 196, 199, 203, 206, 208,
    210, 299, 304
Newington, Kent: 110
Redlingfield, Suffolk: 110, 111, 113 Table 2, 124, 128, 129, 130, 132 n. 63, 133,
    134 n. 69
Shouldham, Norfolk: 110, 111, 113 Table 2, 122, 124, 127, 132 n. 63, 151, 152
Stratford at Bow, London/Middlesex: 111, 113 Table 2, 120, 124
Swaffham Bulbeck, Cambridgeshire: 110, 111, 112 Table 2, 116, 116 n. 14, 117,
    132 n. 63
Syon, London/Middlesex: 110, 111, 112, 113 Table 2, 115, 116 n. 14, 122, 123, 124,
    127, 130, 131, 131 n. 56, 134, 153, 162 n. 5, 181, 189, 214 n. 3, 217, 229 n. 44,
    229 n. 46, 230, 256, 257, 260, 262, 262 n. 132, 264, 266, 268, 269, 276 n. 21, 285,
    288, 289
Thanington, Kent: 110, 111, 112 Table 2, 116 n. 14, 124
Thetford, Norfolk [Suffolk]: 68 Figure 24, 110, 111, 113 Table 2, 116, 117, 118,
    118 n. 19, 119, 119 n. 23, 124, 127, 128, 130, 131, 131 n. 56, 132 n. 63, 133, 134,
    152, 153, 154, 156, 156 n. 143, 310
    *See also Fulmerston, Richard; Tasburgh, George; Tasburgh, George, family of, and
        selected relatives; Tasburgh George, other family members; Thetford, Norfolk below*
Waterbeach, Cambridgeshire: 110, 111, 125, 125 n. 45
Wix, Essex: 110, 111, 112 Table 2, 116 n. 14
Cut-outs, of letters from William Lyndwood's *Prouinciale seu Consitutiones Anglie*, in
    Add. 2604: 23

Egan, John: 36, 38
    See also Add. 2604, Description of, Ownership

Fulmerston, Richard: 153, 154, 155
    Will: 154 n. 135
    See also Convents, female, in East Anglia and Beyond, Thetford

Geoffrey of Burton: 205, 250
Gilte Legende: 11 n. 9, 187, 188, 189, 207, 208, 229 n. 44, 229 n. 46, 230, 231, 274,
    275 n. 16, 276 n. 21, 282 n. 23, 288, 339 Appendix 3
    Gilte Legende, Additional Lives: 188, 243, 274, 276 n. 21, 282 n. 23
Goscelin de Saint-Bertin: 157, 177, 178, 224, 225, 250, 250 n. 98, 251, 267, 269, 276
Gui de Châtres: 164, 169, 173 Table 3, 173 n. 39, 176, 237, 262
    Sanctilogium, seu Speculum legendarum: 164, 173 Table 3

Handwriting, note on, in Add. 2604: 61 Figure 16
Henry Mere: 258, 258 n. 19
Hermann Greven: 166, 167 n. 24, 174 Table 4, 174 n. 40, 224, 248
   Legendarium: 167 n. 24, 174 Table 4
Historie plurimorum sanctorum: 166, 166 n. 23, 167, 174 Table 4, 174 n. 40, 176, 211, 213,
   217, 218, 223, 224, 235, 240, 241, 241 n. 77, 246, 247, 248, 269, 276
   *See also Add. 2604, Native and Universal Saints, Sources and Analogues of, Universal
      Saints*
Hussey, Richard Charles: 36, 38
   See also Add. 2604, Description of, Ownership

Jacobus Bergamensis/Jacopo Filippo Foresti da Bergamo: 168, 169, 170, 170 n. 34, 174 Table
   4, 176, 236
   De plurimis claris sceletisque [sic] mulieribus: 168, 170, 174 Table 4, 236
Jacobus de Voragine/Iacopo da Varazze: xxv, 157, 164, 165, 168, 168 n. 28, 169, 169 n. 29,
   173 Table 3, 175 Table 5, 178, 213, 220 n. 16, 229, 237, 250, 264, 266, 267, 318
   Appendix 1, 337 Appendix 3
   Legenda aurea: 123, 157, 164, 164 n. 13, 165 n. 19, 166, 166 n. 23, 169, 172, 173 Table
      3, 176, 178, 178 n. 46, 181, 183, 183 n. 60, 183 n. 61, 184, 184 n. 63, 185, 186, 187,
      188, 189, 195 n. 102, 202, 211, 213, 216, 217, 218, 219, 219 n. 14, 220, 220 n. 16,
      220 n. 17, 222, 222 n. 28, 223, 228, 229, 229 n. 44, 230, 230 n. 48, 231, 232, 233,
      234, 235, 236, 237, 237 n. 70, 238, 239, 240, 241, 241 n. 77, 243, 244, 246, 247,
      248, 249, 256, 262, 264, 265, 266, 267, 269, 276, 286 n. 32, 287, 288, 289, 291, 293,
      296, 306, 311 Appendix 1, 312 Appendix 1, 313 Appendix 1, 314 Appendix 1, 315
      Appendix 1, 317 Appendix 1, 318 Appendix 1, 320 Appendix 1, 337 Appendix 3
   See also Add. 2604, Native and Universal Saints, Sources and Analogues, Universal Saints
      228–33
Jacobus Neell: 259
Jean de Mailly: 163, 173 Table 3, 239, 313 Appendix 1, 314 Appendix 1
   Abbreviatio in gestis et miracvlis sanctorum: 163, 173 Table 3, 239, 314 Appendix 1
Johannes Gielemans: 167, 174 Table 4, 174 n. 40
   Hagiologium Brabantinorum: 167, 167 n. 26, 174 Table 4
   Novale sanctorum: 167, 174 n. 40
   Sanctilogium: 167, 167 n. 26, 174 Table 4
John Baret: 99, 103, 103–04 n. 51, 132, 132 n. 63
   Will: 99, 103, 103–04 n. 51, 132, 132 n. 63
John Capgrave: 94, 94 n. 29, 97, 98, 98 n. 39, 98 n. 41, 105, 131, 181 n. 54, 189, 274, 287,
   295 n. 53, 306, 306 n. 69
John Lydgate: 11, 12 n. 12, 15, 20 n. 29, 98, 101, 103, 104, 104 n. 53, 105, 131, 186,
   210 n. 130, 273, 287, 305 n. 68, 306, 306 n. 69, 422 n. 5
John Mirk: 97, 192, 195 n. 105, 208, 288, 289, 338 Appendix 3
   Festial: 97, 191 n. 93, 192, 208, 288, 338 Appendix 3

INDEX   395

John of Tynemouth: xxv, xxvi, 105, 118, 123, 157, 180, 180 n. 53, 182, 193, 193 n. 99, 198, 204, 205, 211, 215, 217, 225, 249, 251, 254, 257 n. 117, 260, 260 n. 126, 266, 267, 268, 269, 270, 276, 287, 291, 291 n. 46, 295, 296, 298, 321 Appendix 1, 323 Appendix 2, 325–27 Appendix 2
    Sanctilogium Angliae Walliae Scotiae et Hiberniae/Sanctilogium: 118, 123, 180, 181, 182, 193, 198, 202 n. 113, 205, 206, 207, 207 n. 122, 209, 211, 215, 217, 249, 249 n. 95, 250, 251, 252, 252 n. 104, 253, 254, 255, 256, 257, 257 n. 117, 258, 259, 260, 260 n. 125, 260 n. 126, 262, 267, 268, 269, 276, 287, 321 Appendix 1, 323 Appendix 2, 325–27 Appendix 2
    See also Add. 2604, Native and Universal Saints, Sources and Analogues of, Native Saints, John of Tynemouth's 'Sanctilogium Anglie Wallie Scotiae et Hiberniae': 249–51; *'The Kalendre of the Newe Legende of Englande'. 'Nova Legenda Anglie'*

Legenda aurea
    See Jacobus de Voragine/Iacopo da Varazze
Liber Eliensis: 178, 191, 204, 250, 251, 268, 269, 276, 324–25 Table 2, 324 n. 2
List of Lives, in Add. 2604: 27–28, 60 Figure 15

Margaret Holland: 123, 262, 285 n. 30, 181

Notes, in Add. 2604: 27
Nova Legenda Anglie: 167 n. 27, 181, 193, 193 n. 99, 215 n. 5, 256, 270, 321 Appendix 1, 328 Appendix 2
    See also Add. 2604, Native and Universal Saints, Sources and Analogues of, Native Saints
Nuns, as book owners: 123, 125, 125 n. 44, 126, 130, 130 n. 55, 131, 131 n. 56, 132, 132 n. 64, 133, 133 n. 66, 133 n. 68, 134, 153, 156 n. 143, 180, 185, 186, 186 n. 74, 208, 209, 209 n. 129, 262, 284, 284 n. 28, 352–55
    See also Add. 2604, Provenance of, Convents, Books

Osbern Bokenham: 104 n. 52, 105, 106 n. 62, 125, 186, 186 n. 75, 187, 187 n. 77, 208, 217 n. 10, 229 n. 46, 274, 288, 289, 306, 306 n. 69, 332–35 Appendix 2, 339 Appendix 3
    Abbotsford MS/*Lives of Saints*: 187 n. 77, 217 n. 10, 229 n. 46, 274, 288, 332–35 Appendix 2
    Legendys of Hooly Wummen: 104 n. 2, 106 n. 62, 274

Petrus Calo/Pietro Calò di Chioggia: pp. 164, 166, 173 Table 3, 257, 257 n. 117
    Legendarium: pp. 164, 166
Petrus de Natalibus: 166, 166 n. 20, 174 Table 4, 174 n. 40
    Catalogus sanctorum et gestorum eorum ex diuersis multis voluminbus collectus: 166, 174 Table 4
Proverbial sayings in prose, from *A Newe Booke of Copies*, in Add. 2604: 26–27, 60 Figure 14

396 INDEX

Religious Houses, male/dual
 Bury St Edmunds, Suffolk: 20, 104, 105, 105 n. 57, 118, 118 n. 19, 121 n. 33, 152, 178, 180 n. 53, 204, 210 n. 130, 254 n. 110, 260, 260 n. 125
 See also Add. 2604, Language and Dialect of, Localisation, Bury St Edmunds; Bury St Edmunds above
 Christ Church, Canterbury, Kent: 105, 110, 121 n. 34, 178, 251, 258, 259, 259 n. 123, 260, 312
 Durham, Durham: 99, 103 n. 50, 180 n. 53, 219, 254, 255, 260 n. 126, 274 n. 11
 Ely, Isle of Ely: xxvi, xxvi n. 4, 85, 104, 136 n. 61, 108, 109, 111, 112, 115, 116, 116 n. 12, 117, 117 n. 18, 118, 118 n. 22, 119, 120, 121, 123, 125, 126, 126 n. 47, 127, 149, 152, 168 n. 27, 176 n. 42, 178, 190, 191, 196, 202, 202 n. 114, 203, 204, 205, 207, 208, 210, 250, 253, 268, 282, 295, 298 n. 60, 301, 310
 St Albans, Hertfordshire: 180 n. 53, 206, 252, 252 n. 104, 253, 254, 255, 257, 269
 St Augustine's, Canterbury, Kent: 105, 292
 Stoke by Clare, Suffolk: 14 n. 14, 104 n. 52, 105, 274
 Tynemouth, Tyne and Wear (Northumbria): 249, 254, 255, 260 n. 126
 Whitby, North Yorkshire (Northumbria): xxvi, xxvi n. 3, 196, 203, 297
 York, North Yorkshire (Yorkshire): 33, 138 n. 82, 255, 256, 256 n. 115, 257, 258, 259, 260

Saints' Lives
 Native Saints: xxv, xxvi, xxvi n. 3, xxvii, 3 Table 1, 33, 43, 71, 85, 104, 105, 109, 114, 115, 118, 120 n. 30, 121, 123, 152, 157, 159, 167 n. 26, 168 n. 27, 169, 171, 172, 173 n. 39, 176, 176 n. 43, 177, 177 n. 45, 178, 179, 180, 181, 182, 183, 183 n. 63, 184, 184 n. 64, 185, 185 n. 70, 186, 187, 188, 189, 191, 192, 193–94 n. 99, 194, 195, 196, 197, 198, 200, 202, 204, 205, 207, 207 n. 123, 208, 209 n. 129, 210, 211, 213, 215, 214, 217, 224, 248, 249, 250, 251, 253, 255, 256, 262, 263, 264, 267, 268, 269, 271, 276, 278, 282, 283, 286, 287, 288 n. 42, 291, 295, 295 n. 54, 296 n. 55, 297, 298, 300, 301, 302, 303, 321 Appendix 1
 Universal Saints: xxv, xxvi, xxvi n. 3, xxvii, 3 Table 1, 70–71, 121, 122, 123, 157, 159, 160, 162, 167, 169, 170, 171, 172, 173 Table 3, 173 n. 39, 176, 177 n. 45, 178, 181, 182, 183, 184, 185, 186, 191, 191 n. 93, 192, 194, 195, 195 n. 102, 196, 197, 198, 199, 200, 201, 206, 210, 211, 213, 214, 215, 216, 217, 218, 221, 228, 232, 233, 234, 239, 244, 247, 248, 249, 256, 262, 263, 264, 266, 268, 269, 271, 276, 278, 281, 282, 283, 286, 287, 288 n. 42, 291, 296, 296 n. 55, 298, 300, 301, 303, 316 Appendix 1, 321 Appendix 1
Saints, Cults of
 Barking, Essex: 115, 116 n. 12, 117 n. 18, 123, 124, 168, 180, 206, 207, 209, 210
 Bury St Edmunds, Suffolk: 210 n. 130, 298, 298 n. 60, 305
 East Anglia: xxvi, 33, 107, 108, 109, 125 n. 43, 133, 157, 200, 203, 204, 206, 210, 210 n. 130, 214, 296, 297, 298, 298 n. 60, 305
 France: xxvi n 3, 125, 168 n. 28, 177, 177 n. 45, 192 n. 97, 226, 277, 228, 231, 233, 242, 248, 297, 321
 Kent: xxvi, 33, 109, 123, 126, 127, 202, 203, 204, 205, 206, 207, 208, 295
 Thetford, Norfolk: 119, 119 n. 23, 124, 133, 152
Sanctilogium Angliae Wallie Scotiae et Hiberniae/Sanctilogium
 See Add. 2604, Native Saints and Universal Saints, Native Saints; John of Tynemouth

INDEX 397

Sanctilogium salvatoris
   See Add. 2604, Native Saints and Universal Saints [...], Karlsruhe, Badische Landesbibliothek, Cod. Sankt Georgen 12
Sanctuarium sive Vitae Sanctorum
   See Boninus Mombritius/Bonino Mombrizio
Simon Wynter: 263, 274 n. 11, 285, 285 n. 30
South English Legendary: 183, 183 n. 61, 184, 207, 207 n. 123, 208, 208 n. 127, 217 n. 10, 229 n. 44, 329 Appendix 2, 329 n. 5
St Æthelthryth, prose life of: 190, 191, 217 n. 10, 275, 331 Appendix 2
St Benedict and the Benedictines, notes in prose from *Encyclopaedia Britannica*, in Add. 2604: 30–31, 63 Figure 18
St Christopher, a prose extract from *A helpe to discovrse* attributed to William Basse, in Add. 2604: 29–30, 41, 43 n. 61
St Christopher, a verse extract from William Warner's *Albion's England*, in Add. 2604: 28–29, 41, 62 Figure 17
St George, Nunnery, *see* Convents, Thetford
St Peter South Elmham, Suffolk: 39 n. 50, 43, 67 Figure 22, 135, 143, 144, 144 n. 101, 145, 150, 156
   St Peter's Hall: 67 Figure 22, 145, 145 n. 106
Stephen Dodesham: 263, 268
Syon lives: 190, 214 n. 3, 229 n. 44, 229 n. 46, 230, 230 n. 48, 263, 274 n. 11, 275, 275 n. 14, 276 n. 21, 285, 285 n. 30, 288, 289, 338 Appendix 3

Tasburgh, George: 38, 39, 39 n. 51, 40, 41, 41 n. 57, 45, 64 Figure 19, 107, 108, 135, 139 n. 85, 140, 140 n. 87, 141, 141 n. 94, 142 n. 94, 143, 151, 156, 310
   Will: 40 n. 87, 139 n. 84, 142 n. 94
   See also George Tasburgh in the Eighteenth Century: 135–43
Tasburgh, George, family of, and selected relatives:
   Crathorne alias Tasburgh, George: 140, 140 n. 87, 141 n. 92
   Cressy (later Tasburgh), Lettice: 43 n. 61, 145, 146, 146 n. 108, 148, 150, 150 n. 122
   D'Ewes (later Tasburgh), Mary: 39, 39 n. 50, 135, 136, 136 n. 72
   D'Ewes, Simonds (senior): 135, 136 n. 72, 156
      Will: 136 n. 72
   Gage (later Tasburgh), Teresa: 39, 39 n. 51, 138, 138 n. 82, 139 n. 84, 140, 142 n. 94
   Fitzherbert (later Tasburgh), Barbara: 39, 39 n. 51, 139, 140, 140 n. 87, 141 n. 92
   Tasburgh, Francis: 135, 142 n. 94, 149 n. 118
      Will: 137 n. 78, 138 n. 79
   Tasburgh, Jack: 142 n. 94, 148, 149 n. 118, 150
   Tasburgh, Jane: 43 n. 61, 144, 147, 150 n. 122
   Tasburgh, Jane (Sister Agnes): 146, 147, 147 n. 112
   Tasburgh, John (fifth John): 142 n. 84, 144, 145, 146, 146 n. 108, 147
   Tasburgh, Maria Augusta Roselia: 140 n. 87, 143
   Tasburgh, other family members: 38, 39, 43, 43 n. 61, 45, 67 Figure 22, 67 Figure 23, 135, 135 n. 71, 136, 137 n. 77, 140 n. 87, 141, 141–42, 142, 143, 144, 144 n. 100, 144 n. 101, 145, 145 n. 106, 146, 148, 148 n. 114, 149, 150, 151, 156
      Wills: 141–42 n. 94, 144 n. 101
      See also The Tasburgh Family: A Recusant Family in Suffolk and Norfolk: 144–49

Thanet: *See Convents, female, in East Anglia and Beyond, Minster-in-Thanet*
The Kalendre of the Newe Legende of Englande: 181, 193, 193 n. 99, 261, 261 n. 169, 269, 336 Appendix 2
Thetford, Norfolk: 27, 37, 41, 41 n. 58, 42 n. 60, 111, 117, 118, 118 n. 19, 119, 119 n. 24, 143, 151, 152, 155, 156, 191
    See also Convents, female, in East Anglia and Beyond, Thetford
Thomas de la Mare: 253, 254, 255, 257
Thomas Goldstone II: 259, 259 n. 123

Usuard: 161, 169, 237
    Martyrology: 161, 169, 237

Vincent de Beauvais: 163, 163 n. 10, 169, 171, 173 Table 3, 173 n. 39, 236, 250
    Speculum historiale: 163, 163 n. 10, 169, 171, 173 Table 3, 222, 223, 236

Warton/Wharton, Richard: 105, 105 n. 106
    See also Convents, female, in East Anglia and Beyond, Flixton
Whatman, James (elder), and the Whatman firm: 32, 32 n. 40, 66 Figure 21
    See also Add. 2604, Description of, Watermarks
William Caxton: 23, 24, 95, 95 n. 32, 188, 189, 273, 289, 341 Appendix 3
    Golden Legend: 188, 288, 341 Appendix 3
Wilton Chronicle: 189, 189 n. 95, 203, 217 n. 10, 329 Appendix 2

MEDIEVAL WOMEN: TEXTS AND CONTEXTS

All volumes in this series are evaluated by an Editorial Board, strictly on academic grounds, based on reports prepared by referees who have been commissioned by virtue of their specialism in the appropriate field. The Board ensures that the screening is done independently and without conflicts of interest. The definitive texts supplied by authors are also subject to review by the Board before being approved for publication. Further, the volumes are copyedited to conform to the publisher's stylebook and to the best international academic standards in the field.

Titles in Series

Jutta and Hildegard: the Biographical Sources, trans. and introduced by Anna Silvas (1999)

New Trends in Feminine Spirituality: The Holy Women of Liège and their Impact, ed. by Juliette D'Or, Lesley Johnson, and Jocelyn Wogan-Browne (1999)

Medieval Women—Texts and Contexts in Late Medieval Britain: Essays in Honour of Felicity Riddy, ed. by Jocelyn Wogan-Browne, Rosalynn Voaden, Arlyn Diamond, Ann Hutchinson, Carol M. Meale, and Lesley Johnson (2000)

The Knowing of Woman's Kind in Childing: A Middle English Version of Material Derived from the Trotula and other Sources, ed. by Alexandra Barratt (2002)

St Katherine of Alexandria: Texts and Contexts in Western Medieval Europe, ed. by Jacqueline Jenkins and Katherine J. Lewis (2003)

Send Me God: The Lives of Ida the Compassionate of Nivelles, Nun of La Ramée, Arnulf, Lay Brother of Villers, and Abundus, Monk of Villers, by Goswin of Bossut, trans. by and with an introduction by Martinus Cawley OCSO and with a preface by Barbara Newman (2003)

Seeing and Knowing: Women and Learning in Medieval Europe, 1200–1550, ed. by Anneke B. Mulder-Bakker (2004)

Writing the Wilton Women: Goscelin's Legend of Edith and Liber confortatorius, ed. by Stephanie Hollis with W. R. Barnes, Rebecca Hayward, Kathleen Loncar, and Michael Wright (2004)

Household, Women, and Christianities in Late Antiquity and the Middle Ages, ed. by Anneke B. Mulder-Bakker and Jocelyn Wogan-Browne (2006)

The Writings of Julian of Norwich: 'A Vision Showed to a Devout Woman' and 'A Revelation of Love', ed. by Nicholas Watson and Jacqueline Jenkins (2006)

Les Cantiques Salemon: The Song of Songs in MS Paris BNF fr. 14966, ed. by Tony Hunt (2006)

Carolyn P. Collette, *Performing Polity: Women and Agency in the Anglo-French Tradition, 1385–1620* (2006)

Mary of Oignies: Mother of Salvation, ed. by Anneke B. Mulder-Bakker (2007)

Anna M. Silvas, *Macrina the Younger: Philosopher of God* (2008)

Thomas of Cantimpré: The Collected Saints' Lives: Abbot John of Cantimpré, Christina the Astonishing, Margaret of Ypres, and Lutgard of Aywières, ed. by Barbara Newman, trans. by Margot H. King and Barbara Newman (2008)

Claire M. Waters, *Virgins and Scholars: A Fifteenth-Century Compilation of the Lives of John the Baptist, John the Evangelist, Jerome, and Katherine of Alexandria* (2008)

Jennifer N. Brown, *Three Women of Liège: A Critical Edition of and Commentary on the Middle English Lives of Elizabeth of Spalbeek, Christina Mirabilis, and Marie d'Oignies* (2009)

Suzanne Kocher, *Allegories of Love in Marguerite Porete's 'Mirror of Simple Souls'* (2009)

Beverly Mayne Kienzle, *Hildegard of Bingen and her Gospel Homilies: Speaking New Mysteries* (2009)

Mary Dockray-Miller, *Saints Edith and Æthelthryth: Princesses, Miracle Workers, and their Late Medieval Audience: The Wilton Chronicle and the Wilton Life of St Æthelthryth* (2009)

Living Saints of the Thirteenth Century: The Lives of Yvette, Anchoress of Huy; Juliana of Cornillon, Author of the Corpus Christi Feast; and Margaret the Lame, Anchoress of Magdeburg, ed. by Anneke B. Mulder-Bakker, trans. by Jo Ann McNamara, Barbara Newman, and Gertrude Jaron Lewis and Tilman Lewis (2012)

Nuns' Literacies in Medieval Europe: The Hull Dialogue, ed. by Virginia Blanton, Veronica O'Mara, and Patricia Stoop (2013)

June L. Mecham, *Sacred Communities, Shared Devotions: Gender, Material Culture, and Monasticism in Late Medieval Germany*, ed. by Alison I. Beach, Constance Berman, and Lisa Bitel (2014)

Partners in Spirit: Women, Men, and Religious Life in Germany, 1100–1500, ed. by Fiona J. Griffiths and Julie Hotchin (2014)

The Manere of Good Lyvyng: A Middle English Translation of Pseudo-Bernard's Liber de modo bene vivendi ad sororem, ed. by Anne E. Mouron (2014)

Nuns' Literacies in Medieval Europe: The Kansas City Dialogue, ed. by Virginia Blanton, Veronica O'Mara, and Patricia Stoop (2015)

Nuns' Literacies in Medieval Europe: The Antwerp Dialogue, ed. by Virginia Blanton, Veronica O'Mara, and Patricia Stoop (2017)

Janice Pinder, *The Abbaye du Saint Esprit: Spiritual Instruction for Laywomen, 1250–1500* (2020)

Mystics, Goddesses, Lovers, and Teachers: Medieval Visions and their Legacies. Studies in Honour of Barbara Newman, ed. by Steven Rozenski, Joshua Byron Smith and Claire M. Waters (2023)

In Preparation

Saints' Lives for Medieval English Nuns, II: An Edition of the 'Lyves and Dethes' in Cambridge University Library, MS Additional 2604, ed. by Veronica O'Mara and Virginia Blanton (2024)